traces the nature of the conflict between
More and Luther, giving particular em-
phasis to the shades of development in
Luther's thought. Historical, biblical,
classical, and patristic allusions in the
text are explicated and analyzed. The
Responsio should no longer, in view of
this volume, occupy the position which
it has held for so long—the most neglected
of More's major works.

The Yale Edition of the Complete Works of St. Thomas More

VOLUME 5

RESPONSIO AD LUTHERUM

PART I

TEXT AND TRANSLATION

*Published by the St. Thomas More Project, Yale University,
under the auspices of Gerard L. Carroll and Joseph B. Murray,
Trustees of the Michael P. Grace, II, Trust*

SANCTISSIMO DOMINO NOSTRO
domino Leoni.X.pont.max. Henricus dei gra=
tia rex Angliæ, et Franciæ, ac domi=
nus Hyberniæ perpetu=
am felicita=
tem.

VVM PARTIM BEL=
licis, partim alijs longe diuer=
sis studijs, rei publicæ causa,
adolescentiam nostram insu=
euerimus, miraturum te bea=
tissime pater non dubitamus,
ꝙ eius nunc hominis partes
nobis sumpserim⁹, qui omnē
potius ætatem consumpsisset in literis, ut grauem sci=
licet hæresim pullulantem cōprimamus. Sed desinet
(opinor) tua sanctitudo mirari postꝗ causas expen=
derit, quæ nos subegerunt, ut hoc scribendi onus(ꝗꝗ
nō ignari ꝗ sumus impares)subierimus. Vidimus si=
quidem in messem domini iacta zizaniæ semina, pul=
lulare sectas, hæreses in fide succrescere, et tātam per
orbem totum christianum seminatam discordiæ ma=
teriam, ut nemo qui syncæra mēte christianus sit, hęc
tanta mala tam late serpētia, ferre diutius possit, quin
et studium cogatur, et uires qualescunꝗ possit, oppo=
nere. Mirum igitur uideri non debet, si nos quoꝗ, ta=
metsi potestate non maximi, fide tamen ac uolūtate
nemini secundi, in opus tam pium, tam utile, tam ne=
cessarium

First Page of the Presentation Copy of Henry VIII's *Assertio septem
sacramentorum* (reduced)

The Complete Works of
ST. THOMAS MORE

VOLUME 5

Part I

Edited by

JOHN M. HEADLEY

English Translation by
Sister Scholastica Mandeville

Yale University Press, New Haven and London, 1969

EDITORIAL COMMITTEE

Louis L. Martz, *Chairman* · Richard S. Sylvester, *Executive Editor*

Franklin L. Baumer · Gerard L. Carroll · Rev. E. J. Klein
David R. Watkins · William K. Wimsatt, Jr.
Joseph B. Murray (deceased, 1961)

ADVISORY COMMITTEE

Uxori Meae

ACKNOWLEDGMENTS

Any enterprise of this nature represents the collective efforts and generous aid of a number of scholars. The present editor is acutely aware of the debt he owes in this respect. Behind the editor's name stand several persons whose helpful criticism and unstinting assistance can never be fully acknowledged. It is quite fitting that the name of Professor Richard S. Sylvester, the Executive Editor, should be mentioned first: over a period of eight years he has inspired and conspired, agreed and disagreed, cajoled, insinuated, and criticized in a way which makes his continual attention the fulcrum of this work. I wish to acknowledge the collaboration of Sister Scholastica Mandeville, Ad. P.P.S., who translated the text and helped me with many of the classical references. Likewise I am indebted to M. l'Abbé Germain Marc'hadour, who at an early stage in my work provided me with the bulk of More's biblical quotations and allusions. I am grateful to Dr. A. I. Doyle, Keeper of Rare Books, University of Durham, for his early interest in and helpful advice concerning the edition. He has made the unique Durham copy of the Baravellus edition available to the Thomas More Project and his continuing aid in the technical matters of bibliography has proved invaluable for the completion of this work. I wish also to thank Lewis Spitz, R. J. Schoeck, Louis Martz, Roland Bainton, and Father Marc'hadour for their willingness to read the Introduction, and in some cases the Commentary, and for their helpful suggestions. Similarly I am grateful to The Rev. Marcus A. Haworth, S.J., Clarence Miller, and Bernard O'Kelly for criticizing the texts and parts of the Commentary. Mrs. Linda Kaufman, research assistant for the Thomas More Project, deserves special acknowledgment for her sensitive, perceptive comments on both the English and the Latin texts and her careful checking of them through many stages. I also hasten to acknowledge the devoted labors of several assistants who impaired their eyesight in typing, checking, and proofreading: Eva Zornow, Virginia Fortino, Donna Sitterson, Mical Heyman, John Tomaro, and particularly Mary Ludlam, who also did the index. Any errors and misjudgments that may still lurk in these pages are very much my own.

For their kind cooperation I am obligated to the libraries and personnel of the British Museum, the Yale University Library, the Library of the University of North Carolina, the Houghton Library, the Folger Shakespeare Library, and the Pierpont Morgan Library. I also wish to

acknowledge a grant from the Thomas More Project and a paid leave of absence as well as a grant-in-aid from the University of North Carolina.

Finally I wish to express my gratitude for the friendly interest and attention of the Rev. Edward Surtz, S.J. and Dr. Hubertus Schulte-Herbrüggen. And to my wife, who read and criticized the Introduction, my lasting thanks.

J.M.H.

Chapel Hill, North Carolina
December 1968

CONTENTS

LIST OF ILLUSTRATIONS

ERVDITISSIMI VIRI Guilielmi Rossei opus
elegans, doctum, festiuum, pium, quo pulcherrime
retegit, ac refellit insanas Lutheri calumnias:
quibus inuictissimum Angliae Galliaeque regem
HENRICVM eius nominis octauum, Fidei defensorem, haud literis minus quam regno clarum,
scurra turpissimus insectatur: excusum denuo
diligentissime, digestumque in capita, adiunctis
indicibus opera uiri doctissimi Ioannis Carcellij.

Londini. Anno dom.
M. D. XXIII.

The choice, learned, witty, pious work of the most
learned William Ross in which he very admirably
exposes and refutes the frantic calumnies with which
that most foul buffoon, Luther, attacks the invincible
king of England and France, Henry the eighth of that
name, the defender of the faith, renowned no less for his
learning than for his royal power. Printed again with the
utmost care and divided into chapters, with indices added
through the work of the very learned John Carcellius.

London, a.d.,
1523

IOANNES CARCELLIVS
CANDIDO LECTORI.
S. P. D.

QVVM SVPERIORIBVS HISce diebus ad typographi uenissem
5   officinam, conueniendi hominis ac colloquendi gratia: habito
aliquamdiu ultro citroque inter nos sermone, cum alijs de rebus, tum
de libris et literis, tandem quaerenti, ecquid noui haberet in manibus,
ostendit mihi libellum quendam, ab Hispanijs ad se allatum, authore
Ferdinando Barauello, uiro in re theologica perquam eximio. Quo
10   libro ad insanos Martini Lutheri furores, quibus adeo impotenter
impudenterque, imo adeo scurriliter in regem, omnibus summi
principis ornamentis illustrissimum, fuerat debacchatus, respondit:
partim adductus pietate, quod Christi cerneret ecclesiam et religionem, sceleratorum haereticorum factionibus seditionibusque, pas-
15   sim labefactari: partim aegre ferens, impurissimum hominem
praetextu sanctitatis abuti, et Christianae religionis nomine, re uera
stulta arrogantia ac gloriae auiditate inductum ad maledicendum
quibuslibet, nullius ordinis habita ratione.
Hunc igitur libellum cum se in animo habere dixit typographus,
20   emolumenti sui causa, typis rursus excudere: quod emolumentum
non exiguum capturum se ex eo sperabat: quando quidem apud nos
id exemplar haberetur unicum: opusque tale esset, uti non dubitaret
ab omnibus emptum [A₂] iri cupide: ego meam quoque in eo
negocio operam, si quid commodare possem, ei pollicitus: orabam
25   libri ad unum et alterum diem copiam: id quod ipse non inuitus
concessit mihi, orans insuper, si quid nouae commendationis adhibere
possem, operam sibi commodarem meam, qua liber ex eius officina in
manus hominum gratior exiret. Postquam ergo bonam eius partem
diligentius perlegissem, placuissetque: uisus sum egomet mihi non abs
30   re facturus: si, quoniam author continuata oratione totum opus
scripserat: in capita distinguerem, additis titulis cuique, ac indicem
adiungerem: quo facilius lectori singula occurrerent. Simul ut si

Title: For full title in L see n.   1 Guilielmi Rossei] Ferdinandi Barauelli B   8 diligent-
issime] B, diligentisisime R   10 Londini. Anno dom.] An. dom. B
1 Carcellius' letter and the following letter from Barauellus to Lucellus appear only in the B text

2

JOHN CARCELLIUS
TO THE HONORABLE READER,
GREETINGS.

The other day I went to a printer's shop to visit and converse with
the man. After we had chatted together for some time on a variety of
topics and especially on books and writing, I finally asked him
whether he was engaged in any new work. He showed me one little
book brought to him from Spain, written by Ferdinand Baravellus, a
man very outstanding in theology. In this book he answers the insane
ravings with which Martin Luther had so violently and shamelessly,
indeed, so scurrilously raged against a king most distinguished by all
the noble qualities of a most exalted prince. The writer was led to do
this partly from motives of religion, since he perceived that the
Church and religion of Christ were everywhere being weakened by
the factions and dissensions of wicked heretics; partly from vexation
that a most vile man was falsely using the pretext of holiness and the
name of Christian religion, while in fact being led on by foolish
conceit and a greedy desire for renown to slander whomever he
pleased, with no regard for the rank of anyone.

The printer said that he was planning to reprint this work for the
handsome profit which he hoped to gain from it since that copy was
the only one in the country, and it was the kind of work he was sure
everyone would be eager to buy. I promised my help also in the project, in case there were any service I could render. I asked to borrow
the book for a few days; he willingly granted me this, asking moreover
that if I could add to the value of the work in any way, I should
render him that service so that the book might be more favorably
received when it was published from his shop. Therefore, after I had
read through a good part of the work very carefully and found it to
my liking, I thought it would not be useless, since the author had written the whole work straight through without interruption, to divide
the work into chapters with a title added to each chapter, and to add
an index so that single items might be found more readily by the
reader. This would likewise be useful in case further copies were
imported later, which was likely to happen, seeing that printers do not

3

postea plura exemplaria importarentur, quod usu uenturum erat
uerisimile: quando quidem nec uni regioni libros emittunt chalcotypi:
et ea etiam res erat huiusmodi: ut nullius maior expectatio unquam
apud omnes gentes esse uideretur, propter et negocij magnitudinem,
5 et eorum uirorum authoritatem, qui in eo certant: quae enim grauior
causa tractari potest, quam in qua dei optimi maximi agitur religio?
aut quae honoreficentiori patrocinio defendi, atque ea, quam summi
principes, proprijs depositis studijs, pro concione totius orbis susci-
piunt: siquidem, ut alios omnes omnium ordinum homines omittam,
10 Henricus octauus rex Angliae, Fidei non immerito defensor appellatus, neutiquam recusauit, pro Christi causa, cum uili et sordido fraterculo certamine committi: cui quum pro salubribus monitis, sanoque
consilio, nil nisi scommata scurrilia, insanaque conuitia retulisset.
Nec rex magnanimus secundo responso impurum circulatorem digna-
15 retur: hic uir, quem dico, Bara[A₂v]uellus Hispanus natione, ac omni
literaturae genere insigniter doctus, indignatus despicatum nebulonem, impune non solum hominibus, sed etiam diuis ipsis insultare?
ita eum toti descripsit orbi ac denudauit: ut ex nullo speculo liquidius
cerni corporis possit imago, quam ex hoc libello Lutheri detestandus
20 animus intelligi. Cuius, ut dixi, si plura importarentur exempla: haec
tamen nostra hac ratione commendata, typographo: cui plurimum
fauebam, redderentur uendibiliora. Quod quia facere non potui, nisi
mutatis nonnullis, ac alicubi e nostris adiectis, tu mihi candide lector
exorandus es: ut si quid altera parte laboris mei tibi gratificatus sum,
25 id quod certe studui: alteri parti ueniam des: qui tam audacter
alienis scriptis manus admolitus sim. Porro de ipso libro non est, quod
a me multa expectes praedicanda: ipse enim de se, qualis sit, subinde
praebebit indicium. Illud certe profiteor, si perlegeris, fore: uti te nec
operae poeniteat, nec temporis collocati: si modo aut religionis
30 affectu, aut eruditionis desiderio mouearis, aut ingenij amoenitate,
orationis ue festiuitate delecteris. [A₃]

publish books for just one region. Moreover, the contents of the book were such that it seemed to be just what all the people were looking for, both because of the significance of the controversy and because of the reputation of the men who engage in it. What more serious cause can be handled than that in which the religion of God all good and great is concerned? Or what cause can be defended under more honorable patronage than that which the greatest princes, laying aside their proper pursuits, take up before the eyes of all the world? Not to mention all the other men of every rank, Henry VIII, king of England, justly called the Defender of the Faith, did not at all shrink from joining battle in the cause of Christ with a mean and base little friar. When the latter had repaid the king's wholesome admonitions and sound counsel with nothing but scurrilous jeers and violent abuse, and the high-minded king did not honor the vile charlatan with a second response, this man of whom I speak, Baravellus, a Spaniard remarkably learned in every branch of learning, considering it shameful that a despised wretch should with impunity insult not only men but even the saints themselves, represented and exposed the wretch before all the world in such a way that no mirror can give a clearer image of the body than this work enables one to perceive the execrable soul of Luther.

As I said, if further copies of the work should be imported, still the copies which would be enhanced by my plan would assure a better sale to the printer whom I most favored. Since I was not able to do this without making some changes and without occasionally adding some comments of my own, I must beg of you, honorable reader, if I have given you any satisfaction by the one part of my labor, as I have certainly sought to do, to forgive me for the other part in that I have boldly laid hands on the writing of another person. Moreover, as for the book itself, you need not look to me to praise it highly, for it will immediately provide evidence concerning its own worth. This I certainly do promise, that if you read it through, you will regret neither the effort nor the time so spent, provided you are inspired by a love of religion or by desire for learning, or delight in a charming disposition or a witty style.

FERDINANDVS BARAVELLVS ANTI-
QVAE NOBILITATIS ORNATIS-
SIMO VIRO FRANCISCO
LVCELLO. S. P. D.

*Quibus rebus adductus author
hoc opus scripserit*

AVDISTIN VNQVAM VIR EXImie: quibus artibus homo clarissimus, et patriae splendor, patruus tuus me circumuenerit: ut ad hoc opus perscribendum perpellerer? Nam ego profecto quum ab omni litium genere natura semper abhorream: ab illo certe genere abhorreo maxime: sicubi cum eo dimican-

*Abhorrere se ait a certando cum
conuitiatoribus. cuiusmodi est
Lutherus*

dum sit: qui se ratione uictum sentiens, totus uertitur in conuitia. Verum ex Academia dum reuertor domum: ex itinere diuerto in arcem patrui tui: ut cui plus propemodum debebam, quam toti genti meae: eum prius quam meorum quenquam inuiserem. Is igitur, quum uarijs de rebus oriretur sermo: iniecit de industria, sed uelut obiter, mentionem de Luthero: sciscitans, quid de libris eius uiri, sentiret Academia nostra. Respondi, id quod res erat: initio uarie affectos homines, alios nouitate captos, alios nouis rebus insensos. Multis uisum, quaedam neque male scribere, nec prorsus inscite tractare: caeterum quo spiritu moueretur, id demum librorum eius auctu tempus ostensurum. Nec ea quicquam coniectura fefellit. Nam quum assidue alius super alium prodiret liber, et

*Lutherus sui semper uictor
malitia extitit*

postremus quisque deterrimus: tandem prodijt Babylon, uere turris illa Babel: quae in caelum erecta est: unde uir scelestus aggressus est, caelestia Christi sacramenta diuellere. Simul igitur ac perlectum [A₃v] est et uulgatum opus illud: nemo tam excors inuentus est: qui non sentiret, quo spiritu spiraret insanus. Multi itaque meditabantur iam aduersus eius impietates scribere: quum ecce, breui superuenit illustrissimi regis Angliae liber eruditissi-

*Quo spiritu regatur Lutherus ex
eius Babylone apparet*

mus, opus profecto tale: ut, quod ad eam rem attinebat, scribendi causam cunctis eriperet. Sic enim Babylonem illam scele-

20 insensos] infensos *B*

6

FERDINAND BARAVELLUS
OF THE ANCIENT NOBILITY
SENDS GREETINGS TO THE
MOST ILLUSTRIOUS FRANCIS LUCELLUS.

Have you ever heard, distinguished Sir, with what artifice I was
tricked into writing this work by that most honorable man and the
glory of his country, your uncle? Indeed,
though by nature I always shrink from *How the author was prevailed on*
to write this work
every kind of contention, I particularly
shrink from that kind where I have to contend with a person who,
sensing that he has been overcome by
reason, turns wholly to wrangling. Well, as *He says that he shrinks from*
I was returning home from the university, I *contending with wranglers. Such*
is Luther
stopped off from my journey at the castle of
your uncle so that, before any of my own family, I might visit the
man to whom I owed almost more than to my whole family. As
various topics came up in the conversation, then, he deliberately, but
as it were incidentally, threw in a mention of Luther, inquiring what
our university thought about the books of this man. I told him the
facts: that in the beginning there were various reactions, some men
captivated by novelty, others unaware of the new ideas; many
thought that some things were not badly written and were handled
with some skill, but that time alone, with the growing output of his
books, would show what spirit inspired the man. Nor was that
surmise wrong. For when one book after another appeared uninterruptedly, each one worse than the last, there finally appeared the
Babylon, truly that tower of Babel which
was built up against heaven, from which *Luther always appeared to surpass*
himself in malice
the impious fellow undertook to destroy the
heavenly sacraments of Christ. As soon as that work was read
through and circulated among the people, no one was found so
senseless as not to realize what spirit inspired the madman. As a
result, many men were already intending to write against his
blasphemies, when behold there shortly appeared that most
learned book of the most noble king of
England, such a work indeed that, so far as *The spirit that governs Luther is*
evident from his Babylon
that problem was concerned, it deprived

ratarum arcem haeresum, adortus est, expugnauit, euertit: ut operae precium nullum facturus uideretur: si quis arma rursus, aduersus arcem dirutam diuulsamque funditus, intenderet. Hic patruus tuus nactus, quod captabat, locum uidelicet capiendi me: Ferunt, inquit,

5 Lutherum respondisse regi. Respondisse inquam, certe quamquam est impudens, haud committet tamen: ut id conando, reddat manifestius: quam impiam ac stolidam causam foueat: quae nullam defensionis facultatem habeat. At quid si fors accidat, inquit, ut loco defensionis utatur impudentia: et quum nihil dicat, non taceat tamen:

10 potero ne abs te impetrare tunc: ut tuo calamo retegas, atque retundas hominis impudentis amentiam? Ego, nihil minus suspicans, quam id unquam usu uenturum, polliceor inquam, et perlubenter. Nam in

Lutherus pygmaeus pygmaeum sufficit grus: certe si Lutherus fortior esset Hercule: causa reddit im-

15 becilliorem mortuo. Tum ille paulisper auersus in fenestram, prolato libello, En, inquit, Ferdinande librum, et iucunde subridens, uide iam, quod pepigisti facile: perficias, inquit, gnauiter. Tum ego, quod tu mihi pactum, inquam, memoras? quasi ratum habeat pactum lex: quod dolus malus elicuit. Sit, inquit, si uelis dolus: at malus esse qui

20 potest: quo non aliud agi[A₄]tur: quam ut bene facias, et prosis bonis omnibus? Quid multa, rursus recepi me facturum serio? Deductus igitur in cubiculum (nam illa nocte me non est passus abscedere) coepi quam primum Lutheri librum reuoluere: ita eram auidus uidendi: si quid inuenisset ille: quo probabile redderet eorum quic-

25 quam: quae mihi princeps uisus ante fuerat, tam aperte, tam potenter et scripturis et ratione conuincere. Quum coepi legere, deus bone quod nugarum pelagus, quanta furoris abyssus obtulit sese. Caeterum

everyone else of a reason for writing. For he attacked, stormed, over-
threw that Babylon, the stronghold of impious heresies, so thoroughly
that it did not seem worth while for anyone to take up arms again
against a fortress that was overthrown and destroyed from its very
foundation.   5

At this point your uncle lit on what he had been looking for, that is,
a place for catching me. "They say," he remarked, "that Luther has
answered the king."

"Answered?" I replied. "Shameless as he is, surely he will not, by
trying that, act in such a way as to make more clear what a godless   10
and stupid cause he is supporting, one which has no means of
defense."

"But what if it should perchance happen," he said, "that instead of
a defense he employs insolence, and though saying nothing is still not
quiet; will I then be able to persuade you to expose and restrain with   15
your pen the madness of the shameless fellow?"

I, not at all suspecting that this would ever happen, said: "I promise, and very willingly. For a crane suffices against a dwarf. If
Luther were stronger than Hercules, his
cause certainly renders him more feeble   *Luther a pygmy*   20
than a dead man."

Then, turning around for a few moments into the window-recess,
he brought out a book. "Here is the book, Ferdinand," he said. And,
smiling pleasantly, he added, "Now see to it that you carry out diligently what you have pledged easily."   25

Then I said, "What sort of pledge are you talking about? As
if the law held valid a pledge drawn out of me by an evil deception."

He answered, "Let it be deception, if you will; but how can it be
evil when it proposes nothing else but that you benefit and profit all   30
good men?"

Why say more? I again promised, this time seriously, that I would
do it. So I was escorted to my chamber, for he would not hear of my
departing that night. As soon as possible I began to read Luther's
book, so eager was I to see whether he had found any means of   35
rendering probable any of those arguments which I felt that the king
had already refuted quite clearly, quite forcefully both from scripture
and from reason. When I began to read—good God, what an ocean of
nonsense, what a bottomless pit of madness presented itself! But on

de re raro legi quicquam: quod non memoria tenerem, pulchre
soluisse principem: nisi quod uno Lutherus loco uidebatur aut altero,
non prorsus inscite scurrari: cuius rei demirabar mecum, nec ansas
ante perpendisse me et ab rege prudentissimo simul atque eruditis-
5   simo tantum relictum locum. Mitto itaque puerum ad patruum
tuum: si libellus regis esset apud eum: ut dignaretur impertiri mihi.
Librum protinus affert puer: inspicio loca. Sed ibi mirum, quam
statim coepit frigere iocus totus: utpote natus non ex uerbis principis,
sed ex eo, quod Lutherus illa deprauate recensuerat: ut fuco facto,
10 lectori posset apparere festiuus. Igitur postridie iam digrediens, rursus
excuso me: nam de re nihil omissum principi, ab Luthero nihil
adiectum noui: si secus haberet res, non tam ignauum esse me, ut
detractarem, uel eius hortatu, uel publicae utilitatis causa, tam uinci-
bile certamen suscipere. Nunc uero qui meus pudor est haud facile
15 ferre posse: ut qui nihil argumenti, nihil omnino rationis affert: ei ego
ad mera iurgia, mera conuitia, mera deliramenta respondeam: tanquam, ut est apud Horatium: Cum Sarmento committeretur [A₄v]
Messius. Apage, inquit ille, excusationes istas, Ego non respondere
tantum te, sed etiam prolixe respondere uolo, prolatis utrinque uerbis
20 utriusque, subiunctis etiam tuis, quibus id, quod ais, nulli non fiat
perspicuum: quin et naturam istam tuam nimis pudibundam uolo
paulisper expugnes: donec ipsa quoque conuitia regeras, atque
retalies: non tam ut audiat nebulo: quae meritus est: quam ut quae
sola delectant plerosque in illo, eadem delectare consuescant contra,
25 *Cur liberius nonnunquam iocetur*   dum leguntur de illo. Nam si fortasse
author in hoc opere   metuis: ne petulantiae labem tibi res
aspergat: si liberius paulo cum isto nebu-
lone litiges: ego longe profecto contra mi Ferdinande sentio. Nam
qui nullo modo sibi temperare potuit: quin in episcopos, principes,
30 in uicarium Christi, in sanctorum patrum gregem totum, in totam
prorsus ecclesiam tam assidue, tam insana conuitia fraterculus

the actual subject I seldom read any argument which I did not
remember the king to have neatly solved; except that in a few
passages Luther seemed not altogether to miss the mark with his
taunts. I was wondering to myself why I had not earlier carefully
pondered the possibility of such an interpretation and why so im-   5
portant a passage had been left unnoticed by the king, who is as
shrewd as he is learned. So I sent a servant to your uncle to ask that if
he had the book of the king in his possession he would please let me
have it. The servant immediately brought the book and I examined
the passages. But then, strange to say, the joke immediately began to   10
fall completely flat, seeing that it sprang not from the words of the
prince but from the fact that Luther had twisted them in the telling,
so that through fraud he could appear to the reader as witty. On the
following day, therefore, as I was on the point of departing, I again
excused myself, saying that nothing of significance had been omitted   15
by the king and nothing new added by Luther; that if the matter
were otherwise, I was not so cowardly as to refuse to engage in such an
easy struggle, either at his urging or for the sake of the common good;
but that now my sense of honor could hardly bear that I should respond to the sheer brawling, the sheer wrangling, the sheer raving of   20
this man who presents no argument, no reasoning at all. It would be as
though, to quote Horace, Messius were to join battle with Sarmentus.

"Away with those excuses," he said. "I want you not only to
answer him, but even to answer at length, presenting from both sides
the words of each one and subjoining your own comments in which   25
this observation of yours will become obvious to everyone. Indeed, I
want you for a short time to do violence to your excessively modest
nature until you also throw back at him and return in kind that abuse
itself, not so much that the scoundrel may hear what he has deserved
as that what many find their sole pleasure in him may come to   30
delight them on the other hand when it is
read about him. Should you perhaps be   *Why the author at times jokes*
afraid that the encounter will cast the stain   *rather freely in this work*
of wantonness on you if you should contend a little less restrainedly
with this scoundrel, I indeed think far otherwise, my dear Ferdinand.   35
Since this frenzied friarlet could not at all restrain himself from
vomiting out such continuous, such senseless abuse against the
bishops, the princes, against the vicar of Christ, against the whole
company of holy fathers, against the entire church, what reader will

furiosus euomeret: quis tam iniquus erit lector: qui petulantem
putarit eum, imo qui non probet ac collaudet eum: qui nebulonem
Lutheri petulantia   talem uerbis attingat meritis: praesertim
quum ad eum respondeat librum: qui nihil
5   aliud habet quam stultissima iurgia: quibus amentissimus scurra
bacchatur in illustrissimum et corporis et animae decoramentis
omnibus ornatissimum regem. Quid uis amplius: quum nulla esset
recusatio: ualefaciens ac digrediens promisi me scripturum. Itaque
scripsi sic, ut uides. At quoniam patruum tuum nobis ademit deus:
10   et senio confectum corpus auferens, animae uirtutes immortalitate
donauit: nihil mihi facturus uidebar in rem commodius: quam si
quod patruo promisissem: nepoti persoluerem: praesertim tali,
qui, ut absque liberis descedenti, suc[B₁]cedit in fortunas: sic
eruditionem eius eximiam et aegregias uirtutes uideri potest, uelut
15   haereditario iure consecutus. Accipies igitur uir clarissime opus hoc,
et accipies cum schedis omnibus, ne sis nescius quemadmodum,
quod scripsi quicquam patruo debet imputari tuo: ita si quoquam
prodeat istud, uni imputandum tibi. Vale uir ornatissime, et
Barauellum plus quam totum tuum solito fauore complectere. Ex
20   Academia nostra tertio Idus Februar. [B₁v]

be so unjust as to consider that man wanton, indeed as not to approve
and extol that man who attacks such a wretch with words he
deserves, especially when the man answers
that book which contains nothing else but   *Luther's petulance*
the most foolish wranglings with which the completely mad buffoon 5
raves wildly against the most illustrious king who is fully adorned
with all noble qualities of body and mind."

What would you have me say more? Since there was no refusing,
I promised, as I was bidding him farewell and departing, that I
would write the book. And so I wrote it as you see it. But because God 10
took your uncle away from us and while removing his body worn out
with the feebleness of age rewarded with immortality the virtues of
his soul, I felt that I could do nothing more fitting than to pay to the
nephew what I had promised to the uncle, especially to such a
nephew who, while he succeeds to the material possessions of his 15
uncle on the latter's dying childless, can likewise be thought to have
acquired as though by hereditary right his uncle's remarkable learning and outstanding virtues. May you then, most noble Sir, accept
this work, and accept it with all its leaves, lest you be unaware that,
as whatever I have written ought to be credited to your uncle, so any 20
profit that comes from it ought to be credited to you alone. Farewell,
most honored Sir, and embrace with your usual favor Baravellus who
is more than wholly yours. From our university. February 11.

GVILIELMVS ROSSEVS IOANNI
CARCELLIO SVO.
S. D. P.

SI TV MI IOANNES BENE uales, bene est: ego quidem ualeo. At
5 uereor ut satis ualiturus fuerim: ni propere me ex urbe proruissem
rus. Coeperat enim non oriri modo pestis Romae, uerum etiam
grauiter inualescere: quum ego uix adhuc bene collocatus ibi, rursum
trepidus ac sollicitus, huc me cogor subducere, ad lapidem plus minus
uicessimum, exceptus atque inuitatus, ab hospite omnium humanis-
10 simo, et seorsum in Anglorum gentem omnem, in quam paternum
genus refert animo, quantum uix quisquam credat benigno. Hic dum
uersor, hospes quodam die, en inquit, Rossee librum quendam ex urbe
recens missum mihi: quem te opinor ualde uidere uelle: ut quo
Lutherus uestro repondeat regi. Ain uero, inquam, nihil profecto
15 legerim libentius. Nam principis libellum, iam ante annum legi ac
relegi Venetijs: qui non uni mihi talis uisus est: ut opinionem con-
ceperim, nunquam tam stolidum fore Lutherum: ut respondendo
redderet manifestum: quam improbam atque absurdam causam
tueretur: quae nullum defensionis colorem, qui quidem probabilis
20 uideretur, omnino posset admittere: simul haec dicens, auide
corripio ac resigno librum ubi legere incipio, proh deus bone, quantum furoris ba[A₂v]rathrum, quantam furiarum uoraginem reperio.
Dispeream, si inter densas ac perpetuas phreneseos Lutheranae
tenebras, ullum inuenire quiui sanioris animi interuallum. Nugatur,
25 rixatur, scurratur, ac ridet: sed ridet plane sardonium, conscius
nimirum, non in libello regis inuenire se, sed in capitello suo quod
rideat. Nam interim deprehendi eum, quaedam, in quae salsus uideri
posset, affingere. Hospes igitur, ubi me legentem auscultasset diu, non
sine crebra interim atque aperta significatione stomachi (erat enim
30 neque alienus a literis, et animi cum ciuiliter honesti tum in primis
pij) quid tu inquit mi Rossee nebulonem istum blasphemias istas
patieris inultas ferre? qui non modo regem tuum stultis incessit
conuicijs, sed in Caesarem quoque ac pontificem in principes omnes

1 *Rosseus' letter and Carcellius' reply do not occur in the B text*   12 en inquit] en, inquit *L*
20 uideretur] uideretur *L*, uideretnr *R*   31 tu inquit] tu, inquit, *L*; blasphemias] *L*,
blaphemias *R*

WILLIAM ROSS
TO HIS FRIEND JOHN CARCELLIUS,
GREETINGS

My dear John, I hope that you are well, as I am. But I am afraid that
I would not have been feeling quite so well had I not hurriedly rushed 5
out of the city to the country. For the plague had not only begun to
break out at Rome, but also to grow in virulence, when I, who had as
yet hardly settled down there, was forced to withdraw in fresh alarm
and anxiety to this place about twenty miles distant. I was welcomed
and entertained here by a most gracious host. Toward the whole 10
English race in particular, to which he traces his paternal ancestry,
he shows a friendliness that is almost beyond belief. While I was
staying here, my host one day said, "Here, my dear Ross, is a book
recently sent to me from the city, which I think you will very much
wish to see, since it is that in which Luther answers your king." 15

"Really?" I said. "Indeed, there is nothing I would rather read.
The prince's book I read and reread already a year ago at Venice.
Several of us thought it so thorough that I concluded Luther would
never be so stupid as to render evident by answering it how wicked
and ridiculous a cause he was defending, one that could not at all 20
admit of any sort of defense which would be thought creditable."
With this remark I eagerly seized and opened the book. When I
began to read—good God, what a pit of raving madness, what an
abyss of violent passion I discovered! I'll be hanged if among the
dense and uninterrupted darkness of Lutheran madness I could dis- 25
cover any interval of lucidity. He talks nonsense, he wrangles, he
plays the buffoon, he laughs; but laughs like a Sardonian, aware of
course that not in the book of the king but in his own pin-head does
he find anything to laugh at. For at times I caught him falsely adding
certain points so that in attacking them he could appear witty. 30

My host listened to me reading for a long time, meanwhile frequently and openly displaying his disgust, for he was no stranger to
learning and had a fine sense of propriety and above all of reverence
for religion. Then he said: "My dear Ross, why do you allow that
worthless fellow to express those blasphemies with impunity? He not 35
only assails your king with his foolish abuse. Against the emperor also
and the pope, against all the princes of Germany, against all good and

germaniae, in bonos atque eruditos uiros omnes, in omnes denique
diuos impius furcifer obscaenissimis obprobrijs inuehitur. Hunc
tu scurram talia patieris inulta ferre? Inulta ne inquam quo pacto,
qui omnium uicem ulciscitur ipse sese? Nam quae grauior ultio
5 possit optari: quam quum eo dementiae sit adactus: ut impie
conscientiae furijs agitatus, mentis inops, et ad insaniam dissimulan-
dam impotens, ita sibi ui abreptus sit: ut sua manu per omnes paginas
atque omnes propemodum parietes perscribat, insanissimum nebulonem atque impudentissimum scurram esse Lutherum. Nam princeps
10 meus, in quem precipue nebulo scurratur insanus, augustioris est
animi et altioris consilij: quam ut dementissimi scurrae deliramentis
quicquam moueatur. Neque dubito, si Lutheri liber haberet aliquid
quod sit re[A₃]sponso dignum: quin rex illustrissimus pro egregia illa
eruditione, quae illi ad reliqua regiae magestatis ornamenta uelut
15 precipuum quoddam lumen ac decus accessit, facile sit ita responsurus homini: ut mortales omnes intelligant, seruata dignitatis suae
reuerentia, et causam piam strenue, et impium nebulonem lepide,
ab optimo atque eruditissimo principe esse tractatum. Quam
rem Lutherus, quum ex eo libro quem scripsit in eum rex, magno
20 bonorum omnium plausu, magno malorum dolore, didicisset: de industria sic adornauit istum libellum suum, ut sperare posset neminem
fore mortalium, nedum principem: qui nenias tam insanas esset ulla
rescriptione dignaturus. Atque ita ultimus pugnae restaret ipse:
nimirum uelut uictor ac triumphator esse uideretur. At ego, inquit
25 hospes, illum sua spe falsum uelim. Quorsum istud inquam? Quid
faciet qui rescribet? aliud ne, quam explicabit orbi, Lutherum esse
scurram sycophanticum? At istud iamdudum conclamauit ipse. Nam
quid aliud aduersus Catharinum? Quid aliud aduersus doctos alios,
aduersus scholas publicas? Quid aliud aduersus germaniae principes?
30 Aduersus Caesarem, regem, pontificem? Quid aliud e turre sua
babilonica, uelut ex altissimo suggestu proclamauit in totum orbem:
quam esse sese deuotum inferis, inuisum superis, humano generi
nebulonem noxium, ac denique mortalium omnium petulantissi-
mum, et pestilentissimum scurram? Itaque, mihi mire placet

---

4 uicem] vice *L*   21 adornauit] *L*, adorauit *R*   23 restaret] *corr. err. L*, restarat *R*
24–25 ego, inquit hospes,] ego, inquit, hospes *L*   31 altissimo] *corr. err. L*, altistimo *R*

learned men, and finally against all the saints this impious hangdog
inveighs with his disgusting taunts. Will you allow this buffoon to say
such things with impunity?"

"How with impunity," I answered, "since he takes everyone else's
place in avenging himself? What harsher vengeance can be desired 5
than that he has been driven so mad that, impiously aroused by his
raging sense of guilt, out of his mind, and powerless to conceal his
madness, he is so violently carried away that with his own hand he
writes on every page and almost every wall that the most insane
scoundrel and the most shameless buffoon is Luther. My prince, 10
against whom especially this mad scoundrel plays the buffoon, is of
too majestic a spirit and too considered a judgment to be at all disturbed by the nonsense of a raving buffoon. If the book of Luther
would have in it anything worthy of an answer, I have no doubt that
the king, who is most illustrious for the remarkable learning which is 15
added to the other distinctions of his royal majesty like a kind of
special splendor and grace, would easily answer the man in such a
way that everyone would understand that, saving the reverence due
his dignity, this excellent and very learned king had handled a pious
cause vigorously and an impious scoundrel wittily. When Luther 20
recognized this fact from the book which the king wrote against him
to the great applause of all good men, to the great vexation of wicked
men, he deliberately prepared his own book in such a manner that no
mortal, still less the prince, would honor such crazy nonsense with
any written answer. Thus he would be taking the last stand in the 25
fight, doubtless appearing as the victor and conqueror."

"But," said my host, "I would like to see him deceived in that
hope of his."

"What is the point?" I asked. "What will the one who answers
him do but display to the world that Luther is a crafty buffoon? But 30
this he himself has long ago proclaimed. What else has he proclaimed
in his work against Catharinus? What else against other learned men,
against well-known schools? What else against the princes of
Germany? Against the emperor, the king, the pope? What else has he
proclaimed to the whole world from his Babylonian tower as from the 35
loftiest height but that he is dedicated to hell, hateful to heaven, a
noxious wretch to the human race, and finally of all mortals the most
insolent and the most pestilential buffoon? For this reason I am
wholly in agreement with the very sound counsel of that very shrewd

prudentissimi cardinalis illius, sanissimum consilium: qui pontifici huic uere omnium sanctissimo suasit, uti Leonis decessoris sui sen[A₃v]tentiam, de supprimendis Lutheri libris, ita moderaretur: ut eorum lectionem librorum, qui sanctitatis et modestiae fuco latenter
5 insertas haereses, bonis ac simplicibus uiris commendant, ecclesiae penitus interdiceret. Babilonicam uero, et qui sunt eiusdem furfuris: qui nihil habent aliud: quam uere scurrilia iurgia, et bonorum omnium auribus abhominandas haereses, prostare passim legique permitteret. Neque enim periculi quicquam fore, ne bonus quisquam
10 libello corrumpatur eiusmodi: qui sine ratione rixetur, et numeret magis quam probet improbissima quaeque et orbis christiani consensu damnatissima dogmata. Illud uero prouenturum commodi: quod pessimus quisque, quem a legendis haereticorum scriptis, nullum potest edictum cohibere, desinet incautis imponere: quibus nunc
15 persuadent callide, quicquid sentiunt bonis odio esse, id uel non scripsisse, uel non ita sensisse Lutherum: sed hominem innocentem, per emulorum inuidiam, falsam subire calumniam. Nam quaeso te, quisquis hunc ipsum leget libellum, quo regi respondet nebulo, quum nihil in eo reperiet rationis: quum omnia principis argumenta con-
20 stare uidebit: quum istum cernet deprauare multa: mentiri multa: dissimulare fortissima: scurriliter tractare omnia: quid illum putas esse sensurum? An adhuc disideraturum esse responsi quicquam: quod uerberonis ostendat amentiam, tanquam lucernam accendi postulet: cuius ope conspiciat solem? Accedo inquit mi Rossee tibi, rem non
25 egere responso, si quis in utranque partem intendat oculos. Sed quotum quenque futurum putas: qui quum Lutheri librum perlegat, ea sit futurus dili[A₄]gentia: ut inspecto contra libello principis, collatis utrinque uerbis ipsis, eruat Lutheri sycophantiam, ac non potius ex alterius opere, de utriusque ferat sentensiam: persuasus
30 neminem esse tam impudentem scurram: ut (quod isti perpetuum est) aduersarij uerba de industria deprauet. Nam eo minus istud suspicamur: quod ea res et facile possit coargui: et semel deprehensa probrum summum atque indelebile dedecus inurat authori. Proin tu, si me audies, non respondebis modo: uerum etiam respondebis

cardinal who persuaded the present pontiff, truly the holiest of men, that he should amend the decree of his predecessor Leo concerning the suppression of Luther's books in such a way as to forbid to the church completely the reading of those books which under the guise of holiness and moderation commend to good and simple men secretly implanted heresies. But the *Babylon* and books of that scurf, which contain nothing else but truly scurrilous railing and heresies abhorrent to the ears of all good men, the pope should permit to be sold and read everywhere. There is no danger whatever that any good man will be misled by a book of this sort which wrangles without reason and which lists rather than proves all the most impious doctrines and those most condemned by the common agreement of the Christian world. Indeed, this advantage would result, that all the worst men, whom no edict can restrain from reading the works of heretics, will stop imposing on the unwary, whom at present they cleverly persuade—whenever they perceive that some point is offensive to good men—that Luther either did not write it or did not really mean it, but that he is an innocent man subject to false calumny by the ill will of envious men. I ask you: What will be the reaction of anyone on reading that work in which the scoundrel replies to the king, when he finds in it nothing rational, when he sees that all the arguments of the prince stand firm, when he observes that the fellow distorts many arguments, falsely concocts many, conceals the strongest ones, treats all of them jeeringly? Do you think that he will still desire any response to show the madness of the rascal; as though he should demand that a lamp be lighted to help him gaze at the sun?"

"I grant you, my dear Ross," he said, "that the work does not require an answer if one considers both sides of the question. But how many persons do you think will be so diligent in reading the work of Luther that they will detect his trickery by examining the book of the prince as well and comparing the actual words of each writer? Will they not rather from the work of one man pass judgment on the work of both, being persuaded that no one would be such a shameless buffoon that he would deliberately distort the words of his opponent as this fellow continually does? We suspect this so much the less because such a trick can be easily exposed and because, once detected, it brands its author with the deepest disgrace and indelible dishonor. Accordingly, if you will listen to me, you will not only reply but reply

ampliter. Citabisque, et conferes utriusque uerba fideliter: deinde reddes oratione tua uirtutes Lutheri conspicuas: ut locus nullus non sit illustris, in quo uel errat imprudens, uel studio calumniatur, uel dissimulat stolide, uel scurratur nebulonice, uel bacchatur scurriliter,
5 uel mentitur impudenter, uel rixatur improbe, uel blasphemat impie, uel ridet phrenetice, uel dolore ringitur, uel ira disrumpitur, uel madidus indormit, uel ebrius altum stertit, uel sobrius ac uigil insanit. Nec istud mi Rossee, quicquam est quod metuas ne dum stercorea Lutheri scripta, uelut Augei stabulum exhauris, et sua in eum stercora
10 regeris, tuum simul nomen impures: atque in periculum uenias, ne non satis habuisse uidearis honestatis et modestiae rationem. Etenim tam immodestum nebulonem, qui nec aduersus homines, nec aduersus superos temperare sibi potest a scurrilibus conuicijs, si quis non contra tractet ex merito: sed modice modesteque respondeat: nullus
15 erit mihi crede lector aequus, et pius, cui non ista uidebitur et nimis ambitiosa, et prorsus immodesta modestia. Nam istud scio te floccifacere: [A₄v] si calamum nebulo conuertat in te. Sane uero inquam, neque enim adeo desipio: ut magis mihi censeam laudi fore, si lauder a laudato uiro, quam si in me bacchetur illaudatus, atque
20 eodem rictu latret, in me: quo rabidus latrat in superos. Quin tu ergo inquit, rem deo fretus aggredere: facies quod malos urat, oblectet bonos: nec officium tantum declarabis in tuum principem: cuius ingenium, eloquentiam, eruditionem, prudentiam, corporis incomparandas dotes, animi uirtutes excelsas Christianus orbis uelut
25 absolutum regiae sublimitatis exemplar admiratur ac suspicit. Verum etiam apud seruatorem Christum, magnam inibis gratiam: cuius iste scurra nomen, fidemque sub assertionis hypochrisi, penitus molitur extinguere. Quid uis amplius, mi Ioannes? non desijt impellere, donec perpulit. Itaque promisi me facturum: feci, ostendi. Supra meritum
30 modumque laudauit. Orauit me, ut uni atque alteri ex eruditis amicis suis: sibi liceret ostendere. Concessi, modo ne sine permissu meo

fully. You will faithfully quote and compare the words of each writer;
then in your own comments you will render the virtues of Luther
conspicuous so that every passage will stand out in which he either
errs unconsciously, or slanders deliberately, or dissimulates stupidly,
or plays the buffoon basely, or raves scurrilously, or lies shamelessly, or   5
wrangles violently, or blasphemes impiously, or laughs frenziedly,
or snarls in vexation, or bursts with rage, or sottishly sleeps, or when
drunk snores deeply, or when sober and wakeful acts the madman.
Nor do you have any reason to fear, my dear Ross, that, while you
clean out the dungy writings of Luther like the Augean stable and cast   10
his own filth back on him, you will at the same time defile your own
name and fall into the danger of appearing to have had too little
sense of honor and principle of moderation. For in the case of such an
intemperate scoundrel who cannot restrain himself from scurrilous
ranting either against men or against the saints, if anyone, instead of   15
treating him in turn as he deserves should answer him with moderation and restraint, every just and God-fearing reader, believe me, will
consider such moderation exceedingly ostentatious and completely
immoderate. I know that you do not care a straw if the scoundrel
should turn his pen against you."   20

"That is true," I replied, "for I am not so foolish as to think it
would be more praiseworthy for me to be praised by a praiseworthy
man than for a man unworthy of praise to rave against me and bark
at me with the same gaping jaws with which he rabidly barks at the
saints."   25

"Why not, then," he said, "attack the work, relying on God. You
will be doing something to gall wicked men, delight good men. You
will not only manifest your sense of duty toward your prince, whose
character, eloquence, learning, prudence, incomparable gifts of body
and lofty powers of mind the Christian world regards with admiration   30
and looks up to as the absolute model of royal distinction; but you
will also gain great favor with Christ the Savior, whose name and
faith this buffoon strives to destroy utterly under the pious pretense of
defending them."

What would you have more, my dear John? He did not leave off   35
urging me until he prevailed upon me. And so I promised I would
do it; I did it; I showed it to him. He praised it beyond its deserved
measure. He begged my permission to show it to several of his learned
friends. I agreed, provided that no one would hurry it into publication

quisquam properaret edere. Nam decreuisse me, rem seruare mihi
menses aliquot integram: quum ut exactius tractarem quaedam, quod
opus ruri subito sine librorum auxilio confeceram: tum quod interea
superuenerat exemplum epistolae: quam rex ad Saxoniae duces
5 scripserat: ex qua subuereri cepi, ut laturus esset princeps: si quis ex
Anglis amplius, cum isto nebulone contenderet. Rem recepit meae
futuram potestatis. Aufert, ostendit, reddit, hortatur ne cuncter edere.
Viros, quibus ostendisset eruditissimos instetisse uehementer apud se
ut me uel ignaro, uel inuito maturaretur editio. Sed fidem [A₅] suam
10 liberasse se: caeterum suadere, monere, rogare ne doctorum uirorum
uota suspenderem: neue nebulonem paterer diutius simplicium
hominum ignoratione atque inscitia abuti. Si qui forte forent quibus
quae absurde scripsit, aliquid esse uiderentur: ego me pollicitus istud
curaturum, statui protinus librum ad te mittere: ut cuius consilium
15 multis in rebus alijs, mihi sensissem utile, eius prudentia in hoc etiam
opere, uel edendo uel premendo fruerer. Itaque librum Hermano
Pragensi tradidi iuueni olim studioso tui quum istic inseruiret
magistro. Nam is, quod Angliam uiderat, non sterilem fuisse praeceptori suo: quum nec honestum uideretur nec utile, subinde solum
20 uertere, certus atque obfirmans animo istic sedem figere, instituit in
Britanniam remigrare. Aliquot ergo menses ab eius discessu, pende-
bam animi: expectans indies de mea re responsum tuum. At ubi ex
literis, quas .x. Calendas Iunias, huc misisti, librum sensi non esse
perlatum, nec istuc delatum gerulum: metuens aliquid accidisse
25 iuueni (nam de fide eius ne adhuc quidem dubito) parabam rursum
exemplar: quod, ubi primum liceret commode, istuc mitteretur ad
te: quum ecce interim affertur huc, prostare iam librum meum: et
(quod miror) inuentum esse: qui libellum tam illepidum agnorit,
atque adornarit pro suo. Quae res eo fortasse facta est confidentius:
30 quod ego, quoniam ad te mittebam, notus ad notum, nomen meum
operi non praescripseram. Eoque factum arbitror: ut uelut ignorati

---

3 confeceram] *L,* coufeceram *R*   16 fruerer] *L,* frueret *R,* fruatur *corr. err.*

without my permission. I had determined not to take decisive steps on the matter for several months, so that I might investigate certain points more precisely, since I had completed the work in the country hastily without the assistance of books. Besides there had meanwhile appeared a copy of a letter written by the king to the dukes 5 of Saxony from which I had begun to fear that the prince would not put up with it if any other Englishman should try his strength with that scoundrel. My host assured me that the work would remain in my control. He borrowed it, showed it to his friends, returned it to me, exhorted me not to delay publishing it. He said that the men to whom 10 he had shown it, very learned men, had insisted forcefully to him that an edition should be hurried out without my knowledge or consent, but that he had kept his word. Still he urged, advised, begged me not to delay yielding to the entreaties of the learned men nor to allow the scoundrel any longer to abuse the ignorance and inexperience of 15 simple men. On the supposition that there might perhaps be some men who would think the nonsense that he wrote to be of some worth, I promised to attend to it. I determined to send the book to you at once so that on the question of publishing or suppressing this work I might have the benefit of your judgment, since I had found 20 your advice helpful on many other occasions. Accordingly, I turned the book over to Herman of Prague, a young man once very much attached to you when he was studying in England. He had seen that England had been a profitable place for his teacher. So, although it did not seem either proper or useful to leave his own country immedi- 25 ately, he decided to return to Britain, being determined and resolved to establish residence there. For several months after his departure, therefore, I was in suspense, waiting from day to day for your reply about my work. But when I realized from the letter which you sent here on May 23 that the book had not been delivered and that its 30 bearer had not reached England, fearing that something had happened to the young man—for of his trustworthiness I have no doubt even yet—I was preparing another copy so that I might send it to you there at the first opportunity, when, behold, in the meantime it was reported here that my book was already out for sale and—what 35 amazes me—that someone has been found who has acknowledged the work unpolished as it was and produced it as his own. This business was perhaps carried out the more boldly since I, in sending the work to you as from one acquaintance to another, had not affixed my name

patris expositum puerum, homo misericors exceperit atque educarit
pro suo. Verum nunc te quaeso mi Ioannes: effice [A₅v] ut puer
cognoscatur istic, non pater: quoad interim diligenter obseruaris,
quam de se spem parenti praebeat. Nam si aut parum probetur bonis,
5 aut princeps aequo animo non ferat, ab Anglia quenquam amplius,
cum isto scurra committi: sine fruatur qui sustulit. Sin ita ut optamus
doctis probisque placeat, et regem olfacias non indignaturum: a nobis
quoque bene uerberatum uerberonem: tum te mi Ioannes obsecro:
ut gnatum meum non expositum unquam, sed nescio qua fortuna in
10 aliquod ignotum littus eiectum, tu mihi denuo, absque ulla eius, qui
uelut orbum excepit contumelia, uindices ac restituas patri. Vale ex
urbe, nam heri, huc rerum mearum ordinandarum causa remigraui.
Iterum Vale et salue. III. Nonas Augusti. [A₆]

to the work. This is how I think it happened that a compassionate
man received it as a child cast off by an unknown father and brought
it out as his own. But now I beg you, my dear John: see to it that the
child is recognized there, but not the father until you have carefully
observed in the meantime what hope it offers its parent concerning   5
itself. If good men disapprove of it, or if the prince is vexed that anyone else from England engages in combat with that buffoon, let him
who acknowledged the work enjoy that effect. But if, as we hope,
learned and good men are pleased with it, and you sense that the
king will not be vexed that we too have thoroughly flogged the   10
scoundrel, then, my dear John, I beg of you that, without any reproach for him who as it were received the orphan, you lay claim to
and restore again to me, its father, my offspring which was never
exposed by me but by some fortune or other was shipwrecked on some
unknown shore. Farewell from the city; for I returned here yesterday   15
to set my affairs in order. Again farewell and God bless you. August 3.

IOANNES CARCELLIVS GVILIELMO
ROSSEO SVO.
S. D. P.

AD IIII. IDVS SEPTEMbreis, redditae sunt nobis a te literae: quas
5 ego et libentissimus accepi: et diligenter etiam atque etiam perlegi.
Quae quidem tuae literae, nunquam non gratae ad me perueniunt.
Verum hoc tempore, quantum mearum rerum status ferebat, etiam
iucundae fuerunt. Tum quia significarent ea, quibus mihi nihil
optatius potuit accidere: id est, te mortalium omnium mihi charissi-
10 mum saluum esse et incolumem, tametsi non nullo metu perturbatum,
grassantis istic et ardescentis passim morbi pestilentis: atque iam in
Italia quoque reperisse, qui istas tuas uirtutes perspiciant, et admi-
rentur, ac merito fauore prosequantur. Tum quia longo desyderio
cognoscendi quid rerum gereres ipse, quo ante torquebar, iam ueluti
15 diuturna siti, expleto, his perlectis literis paulum animo acquieui.
Male enim timueram, nequid aliter ac uellem tibi contigisset:
propterea quod abs te tot mensium spacio, nihil quicquam accepe-
ram. Siquidem annus paulo minus agitur, ex quo tempore, illam
recepi abs te epistolam: qua me tui Romam itineris certiorem fecisti.
20 Atque ab illo tempore, nunc primum ubi sis, quid agas, ac quid ualeas
audio. Quae res, sane tam mihi molesta fuit quam pro mutua nostra
charitate esse debuit. Eoque magis eram sollicitus de [A₆v] te, quod
neque ab istis publicis internuncijs, aliquid discere licebat: quum
tamen alios nostrates propemodum omnes, narrare mihi possent: quo
25 quisque loco ageret. Quin, neque Hermanus cui te scribis literas et
librum ad me dedisse, huc uenit, nec quid de eo sit factum audiui
unquam, post eius a nobis discessum, qui fuit statim ab obitu
praeceptoris sui: cum tamen saepe de illo quaesierim ex ijs, qui cum eo
una ministrabant (adest enim hic unus et alter Londini). Etenim
30 amabam prorsus iuuenem, ob egregios mores, eruditionem non
spernendam, ac uel in primis, ob singularem et spectatam fidem.
Propter quam praeceptori fuit charissimus. Inueneramque ei
(si aut remansisset hic, aut redisset) conditionem aliquam, non
poenitendam. Vereorque iam, ne quid grauius fuerit in causa,
35 cur fidem non praestiterit, quam quod nollet, iuuenis quantiuis

34 causa] corr. err. L, casu R

26

JOHN CARCELLIUS
SENDS BEST GREETINGS
TO HIS FRIEND WILLIAM ROSS

On the tenth of September, your letter was delivered to me. I was very pleased to receive it and read it through carefully again and again. Your letters, indeed, never fail to please me, but this time it was even a delight, in so far as one can feel delight in my situation. First of all it provided me with the news I most longed to hear; that is, that you who are dearer to me than anyone are safe and well, even though somewhat disturbed by fear of the plague which is raging there and growing more virulent everywhere, and that you have found in Italy also persons who recognize your virtues, and admire them, and honor them with the favor they deserve. Secondly, having satisfied by the reading of your letter my long-felt desire of knowing what you were doing, with which I was tortured before as with a prolonged thirst, my mind was somewhat at ease. For I was terribly afraid that some misfortune had befallen you, since for so many months I had received no word from you. Indeed it is almost a year since I received from you the letter in which you informed me of your trip to Rome. And now for the first time since then I hear where you are, what you are doing, and how you are feeling. This fact was quite distressing to me, as it should have been, considering our mutual affection. And I was the more worried about you because I could not learn anything from the public couriers from your area, although when it came to all our other countrymen they could tell me where each one was staying. You write that you gave Herman a letter and a book for me. Indeed, he has not come here, and I have never heard what has happened to him since his departure from us, which was immediately after the death of his teacher, although I have often inquired about him from those who studied together with him—there are several of them here at London. And indeed I was certainly fond of the young man on account of his unusually fine character, his considerable learning, and above all his singular and proven loyalty, which made him very dear to his teacher. If he had remained or returned here I would have found him some satisfactory position. Now I am afraid that some more serious reason than his own unwillingness has kept such a worthy young man from keeping his promise. Nonetheless, your

27

precij. Caeterum tandem perlatus est liber tuus (utinam prius) qui magno stupore ut uere dicam, animum uerberauit meum: quod iam alienum nomen omnium opinionibus, quotquot opus uiderant, nedum meae insederat. Qui, etiam cum schedas tuas in manibus
5 tenerem, uix demum potui Rosseum meum in illis agnoscere. Ac quemadmodum, qui ingenti aliqua rei, seu bonae seu malae, ac inopina nouitate, repente sunt perculsi, diu pendent in dubio: nec cito possunt animis suis persuadere, id quod aut aegrius est, quam ut uerum uelint, aut iucundius, quam ut sperare possint: ita huius
10 pulcherrimi facti nomen, tam praeter expectationem meam, tam subito in nouum haeredem transcriptum, idque in eum quem ut maxime optabam, [A₇] tam praeclari facti auctorem existere, cum patriae communiter, tum priuatim nostrae amicitiae causa, ita minime expectabam: magnae mihi admirationi, ac pene res incredi-
15 bilis est uisa: non quin te longe etiam maioribus parem, adeoque superiorem et ego norim et alij existimarint: sed ut dixi, quod alter tam astute in hanc se possessionem, ueluti derelictam, insinuarat: ut iure optimo eius esse uideretur. Iam quod ad ipsum spectat opus, tale profecto est omnium doctorum atque proborum sententia, quibus
20 ostendi compluribus, ut summo omnium studio sit apud nos excusum denuo. Mihi uero ita perplacuit (si quid meo tribuis iudicio) ut, quoniam erat continua oratione conscriptum, in capita diuiserim: titulis adiunctis cuique, scholiaque in spacio marginali ascripserim, indicemque apposuerim: quo facilius singula lecturis occurrerent.
25 Proinde, ista te libero cura, quae sit doctorum de eo sententia futura. Quippe qui non minus sedulo me ad eius emissionem sunt hortati hic, quam, ex tuis literis intelligo, te istic incitatum. Non nulli etiam ultro pollicentes pecunias in sumptum eius, quoniam typographi grauatim quicquam aggrediuntur, nisi si quis eos uolet indemnes praestare.
30 Porro de rege, nihil est, quod uereamur: qui ut est eruditione singu-lari, limatissimoque iudicio: ita non dubito, quin idem sit de libro tuo sensurus, quod caeteri praestantes eruditione uiri. Quanquam, cum primum huc allatus esset, Lutheri aduersus se libellus, eique com-monstratus, nihil ille quidem aliud quam irrisit, stulta uerberonis ac
35 scurrilia conuicia. Cumque rogaretur, quid de illo non solum impio,

7 inopina] inopinata *L*

book was finally delivered; I wish it had arrived earlier! To tell the
truth I was astounded by it, because the name of another author had
already fixed itself in the belief of everyone who had seen the work, to
say nothing of myself. Even when I held your sheets in my hands I
could still hardly recognize my dear Ross in them. I was like men who   5
are suddenly thrown into consternation by the great and unexpected
novelty of some incident, whether good or bad. They hang in doubt
for a long time and cannot quickly convince themselves of a fact
which is either more disagreeable than they would wish or more
delightful than they could hope. In the same way it seemed to me   10
amazing and almost unbelievable that the claim to this most
excellent work had been transferred so unexpectedly, so suddenly to
a new owner, and that to a person whom I was least expecting,
though I was particularly desirous that he be the author of such an
illustrious work, both for the sake of our common fatherland and for   15
the sake of our personal friendship. Of course I knew and others
judged that you are quite equal to and even superior to your elders,
but as I have said, another person had so shrewdly insinuated himself
into this possession as though it had been abandoned that it seemed
with perfect justice to be his.   20

Now, as for the work itself, the many learned and good men to
whom I showed it judged it to be of such value that, with the greatest
interest on the part of everyone, it has been printed again in this
country. I personally liked it so much—if my judgment is of any
value to you—that, since it was written straight through without   25
interruption, I divided it into chapters, adding titles to each, wrote
marginal glosses, and added an index so that single details might be
found more easily by the readers. Thus I relieve you of your worry as
to what the judgment of the learned would be about the work. Indeed,
they urged me no less earnestly to publish here than, as I understand   30
from your letter, you were persuaded to do there. Some, of their
own accord, even promised to subsidize its publication, since the
printers are reluctant to undertake a project if there is no one to
underwrite the expense of it for them. As for the king, we have
nothing to fear. Since he is a man of remarkable learning and most   35
refined judgment, I do not doubt that he will have the same opinion
of your book as other men of learning have had. When Luther's book
was first brought here and shown to him, he did nothing but laugh at
the scoundrel's foolish and scurrilous abuse. When asked what he

sed etiam, tum furente [A₇v] sentiret: respondit sibi quidem uideri
dignum Lutherum: qui pro petulentia ac nequitia sua, precium
ferret: quique in omnibus conuiuijs produceretur: ut conuiuas
oblectaret morio. De respondendo autem ad eius meretricia iurgia, se
5 nec ita foedaturum personam suam: ut conuicijs cum eo uelitaret:
nec ita ineptijs operam et oleum perditurum: ut cum eo rationibus
modeste ageret: qui omni rationi et modestiae bellum indixisset. Sed
nec cuiquam authorem fore, ut cum ipso manum amplius con-
sereret: si quis tamen uellet eius insaniam retaliare, infrenique linguae
10 frenum inijcere, non prohibiturum se. Itaque curaui librum tuo
nomine edendum, et compositori suo tanquam post liminio asseren-
dum. Tum exemplari eo, quod abs te accepi, diligenter cum alteris
collato, ubi quid aut mutatum aut insuper additum per te comperi-
mus quod in exemplis nostris non habebatur adijciendum curauimus.
15 Iam quae ipse, in eo elaboraueram de ijs nihil mutaui: ne aut typographo aut mihi tantae perirent impense. Nec mutabo post hac, si
tibi meum hoc factum probatum fuerit. Sin aliter tibi uidebitur: ego
quicquid tu statueris confirmabo. Praeterea quam ad me epistolam
dedisti: quaque, mihi librum donas (qui tuus est amor erga me)
20 praefationis uice anteposui: eique nostram hanc adiunxi: ut posteri
quoque intelligant: quantum tibi debeam. Vale: et communes istic
familiares nostros ex me saluta. Iterum bene vale. Londini. XV. Cal.
Octobreis. [B₁]

16 impense] impensae *L*; post hac] posthac *L*

thought of that fellow who was not only impious but raving mad as well, he answered that he indeed thought Luther deserved to pay the price for his wantonness and wickedness, and to be brought out at every banquet so that the arrant fool might entertain the banqueters. As for answering the fellow's whorish railing, however, he would not 5 so defile his own person as to engage the fellow in a contest of abuse nor would he so waste his time and trouble on trifles as to deal moderately and reasonably with one who had declared war on all reason and moderation. But neither would he urge anyone to engage in further personal combat with the man. Still, if anyone wished to refute his 10 madness and to bridle his unbridled tongue, the prince would not forbid it.

And so I have taken care of publishing the book in your name, and of claiming it for its own author as if by right of recovery. Moreover, I carefully compared the copy I received from you with other 15 copies, and where I found something either changed or further added by you which was not contained in our copies, I arranged to have it added. Of those details which I myself had already carefully worked out I changed nothing, lest dropping them would involve a great expense to me and the printer. Nor will I change them after this if you 20 approve what I have done. If you think otherwise, however, I will confirm whatever you decide. In addition, I have set at the beginning, in place of a preface, the letter which you sent to me and in which you present the book to me; such is your love for me. To it I have added this letter of mine, so that later readers also may understand 25 how much I owe to you. Good-bye. Greet for me our common friends there. Again, good-bye. September 17.

PRAEFATIO LVTHERI, SCRIPTA AD

quendam nobilem Bohemum: qua suam ipse inuidiam ac liuorem, tum in Pontificem, tum in
ipsum Caesarem, ac Germaniae principes
5   uiros uniuersos, prodit: quos omnes
improbissimis conuicijs et
contumelijs improbus
incessit.

GENEROSO ET NOBILI VIRO DOMINO

10   Sebastiano Schlik comiti in Passun Domino
in Elbogen et .c. suo in Christo maiori
Martinus Luther Ecclesiastes
VVittembergensis.

GRATIA ET PAX IN CHRISTO. TERtius et amplius annus agitur
15 (generose comes) quod furiosus, papistarum populus me insimulat
fugae ad Bohemiam, idque mirum in modum sitit audire, scilicet
homines belli, hac sola fama triumphaturi, gloriaturi, et clamaturi:

Verissime dictum   Vicimus, haereticus fugit ad haereticos.
Sic enim uecors illa et indoctissima papis-
20 tici corporis belua, postquam uidet sese eruditione et ueritate uictam,
nec posse stare totam colluuiem suorum asinorum aduersus unum
Lutherum, torquetur et uritur, unicum hoc respiraculum suspirans, ut
fugiam in Bohemiam, ut saltem opprobrio alieni nominis sese solentur,
et terribiles Emim sese fingant, qui prae sua inscitia et mala con-
25 scientia, nullubi audent comparere. Apparui ego iam tertio, coram
eis, denique VVormatiam ingressus sum,

Caesari notam perfidiae impingit   etiam cum scirem mi[B₁v]hi uiolatam esse
nebulo perfidiosissimus.
Principes Germaniae   a Caesare fidem publicam (Nam didi-
fidem contemnere   cerunt principes Germaniae, olim de fide
30   laudatissimae gentis, nunc, in obsequium
idoli Romani, nihil magis quam fidem contemnere, in perpetuam
nationis ignominiam) Sic ausus est fugitiuus et meticulosus Lutherus
in gyrum dentium Behemoth insilire. At illi tremendi Gygantes quid?

11 Elbogen] *L,* Elbogeñ *BR*   14 *B adds gloss* Apostolica scilicet salutatio. *See n.*
19 indoctissima] *BL,* indoctossima *R*   26 *gloss* perfidiae] perfidei *B*   30 obsequium]
obsepuium *B*

32

The preface written by Luther
to a certain Bohemian noble,
in which he betrays his malice and spite toward the pope,
as well as toward the emperor
and all the princes of Germany,   5
all of whom the shameless fellow
assails with the most shameless
railing and reviling.

To the Eminent and Noble
Lord Sebastian Schlick,   10
Count of Bassano, Lord of Elbogen, etc.
and his elder in Christ, Martin Luther,
the Ecclesiastes of Wittenberg.

Grace and peace in Christ. For more than three years, noble count,
the raging rabble of papists have been accusing me of a flight to   15
Bohemia. They have a surprising thirst to hear this charge, being of
course pretty fellows, and are ready at this sole rumor to triumph, to
boast, to proclaim: "We have conquered,
the heretic has fled to the heretics." That   *Spoken most truly*
brainless and illiterate beast in papist form is thus tormented and   20
galled to see itself conquered by learning and truth and the whole
filthy pack of its asses unable to stand against Luther alone. Gasping
out with every breath that I flee into Bohemia, they try to solace
themselves at least with the opprobrium of another's name, and they
make themselves out to be frightful Emims, though because of their   25
stupidity and bad conscience they dare not appear anywhere. I have
appeared before them for the third time now; in fact, I entered
Worms even though I knew that the safe-conduct promised me had
been violated by the emperor. For the
princes of Germany, once a race most   *The most perfidious scoundrel*   30
highly praised for its fidelity, have now   *fixes on the emperor the brand*
learned nothing more in subservience to   *of perfidy. That the princes*
                                           of Germany contemn fidelity
the Roman idol than to contemn fidelity,
to the lasting ignominy of the nation. Thus Luther dared, though
exiled and fearful, to leap into the circle of the Behemoth's teeth. But   35
what did those dreaded giants do?

33

Toto hoc triennio, non est inuentus unus, qui ad nos VVittembergam
concederet, et coram nobis etiam staret, cum et certissimi sint de fide
et tutela (nempe sub Caesaris sui praesidio acturi omnia) adhuc
audent homines effoeminati et excordes sperare triumphum mea
5 fuga, foedissimam suam ignominiam honestaturi, qua toto orbe
celebrantur, sese prae ruditate et pauore animi, non audere in
conspectum unius Lutheri prodire. Quid putas hae fragiles bullae
facerent, si et ipsi cogerentur coram aduersario Caesare et hostibus
praeualentibus sistere? Scilicet, in mille diuerticula fugerent miseri,
10 qui nunc in cuniculis suis sicut sorices mussitant, Lutherus meditatur
fugam. Sic et rex Angliae, hoc libro multa saliua blaterat de fuga mea
in Bohemiam, homo sapiens scilicet qui credit ideo, suum librum
esse uictoriosum et digne scriptum, si ad Bohemos Lutherus fugerit,
tam uecors et muliebris est stolidi regis inuidia. Ego uero, quamuis
15 *Lutheri fauor in Bohemos* ardeat animus uidere Bohemiam, et
religionem papisticis monstris tam odio-
sam, tamen hactenus abstinui et abstinebo, non quod opprobrium
nominis metuam, quod celeberrimae nationi, uilissima hominum fex,
papistae cum summa perfidia et iniuria inusserunt. Nam iustissima
20 *Omnes haereseos insimulat* caussa, Bohemi homicidas istos, et Anti-
praeter se & Hussum christos papistas deseruerunt, postquam
haereticos insignissimos innocentem uirum Ioannem Hussum, ipsi
septies haeretici exusserunt, et utramque
speciem a Christo institutam sacrilege damnauerunt. Hae enim
25 caussae odij papistici in hanc gentem, nec aliquando purpuratae
istius meretricis spurij, agnoscunt ferale suum homicidium, et
damnati euangelij sacrilegium, quin pergunt furorem suum tueri, et
opprobrium, quo ipsi coram deo insignes sunt, alienae et innocenti
nationi imponere. Non ergo opprobrium Bohemici nominis metuo,
30 quae glo[B₂]ria est coram deo, sed quod Christus me hic posuit: ut
torqueam papistica monstra, dum nihil inuenire in me possunt, quod
iactare uellent, in suae incredibilis inuidiae respiraculum. Cruciari
eos uult Christus sua ipsorum inuidia, et dirumpi propria malitia.

---

22 *gloss* Hussum] Husum *B*; Hussum] Husum *B*   32–33 respiraculum. Cruciari eos
uult Christus] respiraculum, Cruciari Christus *L*

During this whole period of three years, there has not been found one man who would come to us at Wittenberg and stand before us also, although they are most assured of security and defense. They would of course be doing everything under the protection of their emperor. Even yet these effeminate and senseless men dare to hope for triumph from my flight, intending to credit their own most shameful ignominy, which proclaims throughout the world that because of their ignorance and fearfulness of spirit they dare not present themselves before Luther alone. What do you think these fragile bubbles would do if they themselves were forced to take a stand before a hostile emperor and overpowering enemies? These wretched fellows would undoubtedly flee into a thousand alleys, who now like shrew-mice chatter in their holes: "Luther plans flight."

So also the king of England in this book gibbers a lot of drivel about my flight into Bohemia; a wise man, indeed, who believes that his book is victorious and fitly written, if Luther has fled to the Bohemians. So silly and womanish is the spite of the doltish king. But however much my soul longs to see Bohemia and the religion so hateful to the papist monsters, *Luther's partiality to the Bohemians* nevertheless I have till now refrained and I will refrain from doing so. It is not that I fear the opprobrium of the name which the vilest dregs of men, the papists, have branded with supreme perfidy and injustice on a most honored nation.

With very just reason did the Bohemians desert these murderers and Antichrist papists when the latter, themselves sevenfold heretics, burned the *He accuses everyone of heresy except himself and Hus, the most notorious heretics* innocent John Hus and sacrilegiously condemned the communion under both kinds instituted by Christ. Such are the causes of the papist hatred for this nation, nor do the bastards of that purple harlot ever admit their cruel murder and the sacrilege of condemning the gospel; rather, they proceed to defend their madness and to impose on another and innocent people the opprobrium with which they themselves are marked before God.

I do not, therefore, fear the opprobrium of the Bohemian name, which is a glory before God; rather, Christ has placed me here to torment the papist monsters, while they can find nothing against me such as they would like to flaunt in breathing out their unbelievable spite. Christ wishes them to be tortured by their own spite and to

Expecto igitur eos hic, et expectabo impotentissimam eorum inuidiam, egregrie irritaturus et torturus donec uixero. Si autem me
occiderint multo maxime cruciaturus. Sic

Cacadaemonem se fore
comminatur

enim datus sum illis in portentum a
5   domino meo Christo, ut siue me uiuificent,
siue occidant nihil gratiae, nihil pacis, nihil solatij, habitura sit
furialis eorum conscientia, ut duplici contritione conterantur, et
praesentis inuidiae cruce, aeternam mereantur gehennae torturam.
Instat enim mors papatus abominabilis, urget eum ineluctabile suum
10   fatum. et (ut Daniel ait) ad finem sui uenit et nemo auxiliabitur ei.
ita concurrimus utrinque, illi extremo

Contemptorem et audacem profitetur
se homo pius scilicet

furore, ego summo contemptu, et uincet
audacia mea in Christo nouissimam
illorum, et iam pallentem furiam. Aliam uero fugam in Bohemiam
15   meditor, ne nihil ueri uaticinentur sibi papistici Pythones, sed de qua
maiorem compunctionis spiritum sint passuri. Haec est, iuxta illud
Mosi: Prouocabo eos in non gente, et in gente stulta irritabo illos.
Nam tantum meis libellis breui (propitio Christo) efficiam, ut
Bohemi a suo opprobio liberi, soli autem

Quam prudenter laudat dum
studet adulari

20   papistae sint nomen abominationis in orbe
terrarum, ut maledictum et anathema sit,
esse papistam. Non quod omnia Bohemorum probem, cum eorum res
ignorem, et sectas esse inter eos audiam, sed quod papistica turba illis
comparata, foetor et nausea futura sit in toto mundo, qui nihil nisi
25   sectae sunt ipsi, adeo ut soli franciscani inter sese ferme sex sectis
scissi sint. Haec autem ad te scribo heros generose, ut mihi initium
huius fugae captem apud te, qui regnas in Bohemiae initio confinis
Germaniae, ut per te tuamque ditionem procedam in totam Bohemiam. Rex laicus scripsit ad sacerrimum suum pontificem. Ego quon-

---

1 impotentissimam] impotentismam *B*; eorum] *BL*, aeorum *R*   3 maxime] *RL*,
muxime *R*   8 gehennae] geennae *B*   10 fatum] factum *B*   15 meditor] non
meditor *BRL*. *See n.*

burst with their own malice. Therefore, I look out for them here, and I will look out for their most violent hatred; I intend to exasperate them thoroughly and torment them as long as I live. But if they slay me, I will torture them so much the more. For I have been given to them as a sign by my Lord Christ, so that whether they let me live or whether they *He threatens to be a cacodaemon* 5 slay me, their raging conscience will have no grace, no peace, no comfort. Thus they will be consumed by a twofold grief, and through the torture of their present spite they will merit the eternal torment of gehenna. The death of the abominable papacy is imminent; its in- 10 eluctable fate besets it. As Daniel said, "It has come to its end and no one will help it." Thus, we rush to the battle from both sides, they with extreme madness, I with supreme contempt, and my boldness shall conquer *This so-called devout man* in Christ their final madness, even now *professes himself contemptuous* *and bold* 15 pale with death.

As a matter of fact, I am contemplating a different kind of flight into Bohemia, so that the prophecy of the papist pythons may not be completely false; but from this flight they will suffer a greater spirit of remorse, in accordance with Moses' words: "I will arouse them to 20 anger among a people not a nation, and I will incite them to envy among a foolish people." Through the mercy of Christ I shall shortly accomplish so much by my books that, with the Bohemians free from their disgrace, the papists alone will be a name of abomination in the world, so that *How shrewdly he praises when* *he is eager to flatter* 25 it will be a curse and anathema to be a papist. Not that I approve the Bohemians in every respect, since I am unacquainted with their teachings and I hear that there are sects among them; but that compared to them the papist rabble will be a stinking nausea in the whole world. These latter are nothing but 30 sects, so much so that the Franciscans alone are divided among themselves into about six sects.

I write these things to you, noble sir, in order to secure the beginning of my flight with you who govern on the borders of Bohemia next to Germany, so that through you and your authority I 35 may advance into all Bohemia. The king, a layman, wrote to his most

Alienissimus quisque ab ecclesia
Luthero christianissimus

dam miseratione papae clericus scribere debui ad christianissimum laicum. Audio enim te incredibili stu[B₂v]dio feruere in puram Euangelii ueritatem, et abominationes et scandala Romanae
5 pestilentiae, undique e tuo dominio profligare. Macte uirtute clarissime heros, sic abolebitur opprobrium Bohemici nominis, et redibit meretrici in sinum suum, sentina illa mendaciorum et fornicationum suarum, ut reuelentur pudenda eius orbi terrarum ad sempiternam ignominiam. Hoc sit initium fugae meae. haec spes
10 optimi exempli, quod imitentur reliqui Bohemi heroes et magistratus. Sic non modo in Bohemiam fugero, sed et habitauero in ea, etiam si hic me exusserit illaudatae meretricis furor. Inuidiam tamen eius simul et succendero et uicero in Christo. Nihil erit illi amplius prosperum. Christus sic statuit, Amen. Gratia domini nostri Iesu
15 Christi seruet et augeat te optime heros in aeternum. Amen. VVittembergae. V. Iulij. [B₃]

---

7 mendaciorum] *B corr. err. L*, mendaciocum *R*

holy pontiff; it was fitting that I, once a *All the men most alienated from*
cleric by the favor of the pope, should write *the church are most Christian*
to Luther
to a most Christian layman. I hear that
you are inflamed with extraordinary zeal for the pure truth of the
gospel and that everywhere in your domain you are utterly destroying 5
the abominations and scandals of the Roman pestilence. Continue
courageously, noble sir; in this way the disgrace of the Bohemian
name will be abolished, and the sludge of the harlot's lies and whor-
ings shall return into her bosom, so that her infamy shall be revealed
to the world, to her everlasting shame. Let this be the beginning of 10
my flight, this hope of an excellent model for the rest of the Bohemian
lords and magistrates to imitate. Thus, I will not only have fled into
Bohemia, but I shall have dwelt there, even if the rage of the ignoble
harlot shall have burned me here. Her spite, nevertheless, I shall at
the same time kindle and conquer in Christ. She shall no longer 15
prosper. Christ has so decreed. Amen. The grace of our Lord Jesus
Christ forever preserve and bless you, most noble sir. Amen.
Wittenberg, July 5, 1522.

RESPONDETVR AD EPISTOLAM LVTHERI INITIO LIBRI SCRIPTAM.
CAP. PRIMVM.

TOTA ISTA SPIRAT EPISTOLA, Thrasonicam Lutheri gloriam:
5 et, in dignitatem Romanae sedis, liuidam nebulonis inuidiam. Qua
nunc intabescens, Bohemis quorum damnatas haereses nuper
execratus est: nunc execrabilis uicissim, et suo ipsius iudicio damnatus, applaudit, et fingit se haereses eorum ignorare, homo aut tam
iniquus, ut eorum res ignoratas ante reprehenderit, aut tam infirmae
10 memoriae, ut quae tam nuper tam acerbe redarguit: eorum omnium
subito iam sit oblitus. Et tamen quum illis maxime conetur adulari:
post laudes aliquot homo sapiens promittit tandem, bone deus
honorem qualem, Sodomae scilicet et Gomorrae gloriam. Nam ut
illorum mores iustificati sunt comparatione

Cuiusmodi laudem Bohemis
15 *tribuat Lutherus*
Hierusalem: ita Bohemorum haereses
iustificabit Lutherus, collata cum illis
nimirum fide Christi. Quam, quo licentius inuadat, atque blasphemet, appellat ubique papisticam: substituens pro fide Christi
perfidiam suam. Nam quum reijciat iudaicam, rideat gentilium, nutet
20 in Bohemica, uix admittat Turcicam, damnet omnino catholicam:
quid reliqui fecit tandem: quod esset ratum ac stabile, praeter
infidelitatem suam? In qua tam superbus exultat, atque insultat
omnibus: ut dubitari non possit: quam totus ex inferis illius spiritum
spirat in terras: quem similis ad inferos superbia deiecit e caelo. Sed
25 illius epistolae precium operae fuerit [B₃v] magnificas ampullas
expendere. Protinus ab initio conuiciatur

Iactantia Lutheri
Caesari et Germaniae principibus: glori-
atur de sua fortitudine, qui sit ausus ire VVormatiam, gnarus sibi
uiolatam esse fidem publicam, uidelicet homo animi destinati
30 martyrio, propter infidelitatem sine charitate, sine qua, nec pro uera
fide, Paulo teste, ualuisset martyrium. Insultat magnifice omnibus,
contra suam sententiam sentientibus: hoc est bonis omnibus: quod

---

6 Bohemis] Bohemos *B*   11 tamen] *BL*, tamem *R*   13 Gomorrae] *BL*, Gomarrae *R*
14 illorum] illoum *B*   17–18 blasphemet] *B*, blaphemet *R*, blasmet *L*   20 Turcicam]
Turchicam *B*   26 conuiciatur] conuitiatur *BL*

40

AN ANSWER IS MADE TO LUTHER'S EPISTLE WRITTEN AT THE BEGINNING OF THE WORK. CHAPTER 1

This whole epistle breathes Luther's Thrasonic vainglory and the scoundrel's malicious spite toward the authority of the Roman See. Not long ago he execrated the condemned heresies of the Bohemians. Now, consumed by spite, himself subject to execration, and condemned by his own judgment of himself, he applauds the Bohemians and pretends to be ignorant of their heresies; a man either so unfair that he censures their teachings before knowing them, or of such a weak memory that he has now suddenly forgotten all those teachings which he so recently condemned with such severity. And yet, since his main purpose is to flatter them, this wise man, after some words of praise, finally promises them—good God, what an honor!—the glory of Sodom and Gomorrha. For as the conduct of these cities was justified by com- *What sort of praise Luther*
parison with that of Jerusalem, so Luther *gives the Bohemians*
will justify the heresies of the Bohemians by comparing them, indeed, with the faith of Christ. That he may the more freely attack and blaspheme this faith, he everywhere refers to it as "papist," substituting for the faith of Christ his own lack of faith. For since he scorns the Jewish faith, mocks that of the pagans, vacillates on that of the Bohemians, hardly allows that of the Turks, and condemns altogether the Catholic faith, what has he finally left fixed and unwavering but his own faithlessness? He so proudly exults in this and insults everyone that no one can doubt how completely he breathes out upon earth the hellish spirit of him whom a similar pride cast down from heaven to hell.

But it will be worth while to consider the boastful bombast of that epistle. From the very beginning he rails at the emperor and the German princes; he boasts of his own *Luther's boasting*
courage in daring to go to Worms, know-
ing that his safe-conduct had been violated; clearly a man with spirit set on martyrdom for the sake of his faithlessness without charity, without which, as Paul testifies, not even for the true faith would martyrdom have had value. He pompously taunts all whose judgment does not coincide with his own; that is, all good men, saying that no

41

homines non audeant ire VVittembergam, et coram ipsius sese
maiestate sistere: uidelicet quum certissimi sint de fide et tutela,
nempe Caesaris praesidio (ut ait) facturi omnia: quasi nihil esset
latronum in uia: qui fere soli sunt Lutheri satellitium: qui eodem
5   animo in suae factionis gratiam non dubitent, disputaturos amoliri
per insidias contra fidem publicam: quo animo spoliant ac trucidant
uiatores, lucri sui gratia contra legem publicam. Ille quum ueniret
VVormatiam, non habebat, quod metueret. Venerat enim, quod
fatetur, fide publica: quam si, ut mentitur nebulo, uiolasset Caesar:
10 quo tandem praesidio fraterculus, omni supplicio dignissimus, aduer-
sante Caesare, prodentibus, ut queritur, Germaniae principibus, tot
millium iter emensus, in curru, uia publica, palam, interdiu, sic
euasisset incolumis? Nimirum de se scriptum uideri uult illud:
Angelis suis deus mandauit de te: ne forte offendas ad lapidem pedem
15 tuum. Imo mali malo fauebant: et boni fidem uiolare nolebant. At
aduersus illum uenturis, mali dumtaxat et perfidi metuendi sunt: qui
nullo fidei uinculo cohibentur a scelere: nullo disposito praesidio, tam
longo itinere satis caueri possunt.[B₄] Quae quum ita sint: mirum
est profecto, Luthero uenire auso nullo suo periculo VVormatiam, in
20 conspectum principum: ut furoris obstinati, triumphum tuto reportaret domum ad compotores suos: neminem audere contra, cum uitae
suae periculo, uenire VVittembergam, tanto praesertim fructu:
nempe ut cum nebulone certet in eius ipsius theatro, dispositis
nebulonum cuneis, qui haeresiarchae suo,

25 *Quam nihil fructus habeat cum*   scripturae uerba in adulterinum sensum
Luthero coram disputaret   torquenti, doctorum omnium antiquorum
authoritatem irridenti, publicam tot aetatum fidem exsibilanti, atque
omnia execranti sacra, ad singulas blasphemias applaudant, atque
ingeminent euge. Ei uero, qui disputaturus uenerit: ad quodque
30   uerbum, uoce, uultu, pede, manu obstre-
Quantum adeat periculi   pant, explodant, exsibilent. Contra quae,
disputaturus cum Luthero   si durabit omnia: et clamores ratione

---

3 Caesaris] *B corr. err. L*, Caesari *R*   24 nebulonum] *B corr. err. L*, nebulonnm *R*
25 *gloss* disputaret] disputare *BL*   28 blasphemias] *BL*, blaphemias *R*   31 exsibilent]
exsibilant *B*

one dares go to Wittenberg to stand before his majesty, although of
course they are most assured of security and defense, for, as he says,
they would be doing everything under the protection of the emperor.
As if there were no robbers on the way, almost the only bodyguard
which Luther has, who would not hesitate for the sake of their faction 5
to destroy through ambush in defiance of public protection those
who would come to dispute with Luther, doing this in the same spirit
with which for the sake of their own gain they rob and cut down
travellers in defiance of public law.

When he came to Worms, he had nothing to fear. He had come, as 10
he admits, under safe-conduct. If, as the scoundrel pretends, the
emperor had violated this safe-conduct, by what protection would the
friarlet most deserving of every punishment, with the emperor hostile
to him, with the German princes, as he complains, betraying him,
after journeying so many miles by carriage along a public highway, 15
openly, in broad daylight, have thus escaped unharmed? No doubt
he wishes us to think that it was of him the text was written: "God has
given His angels charge over you, lest perhaps you dash your foot
against a stone." On the contrary, the wicked were protecting the
wicked, and the good were unwilling to violate the safe-conduct. On 20
the other hand, those who would come to oppose Luther need fear
only the wicked and treacherous men whom no obligation of a safe-
conduct restrains from crime, against whom no provision for a bodyguard can afford sufficient protection on such a long journey. Since
this is so, it is surely strange that, although Luther dared at no danger 25
to himself to come to Worms into the presence of the princes, so that
he might safely report home to his pot-fellows the triumph of his
obstinate madness, yet no one, on the other hand, dares to come at
the peril of his life to Wittenberg, especially since he can expect such
great results. He will contend with the scoundrel in his own theater, 30
where the seats have been packed with scoundrels who, as their
heresiarch twists the words of scripture to
an adulterated meaning, as he jeers at the   *How fruitless it is to dispute
authority of all the learned men of anti-   with Luther personally*
quity, as he hisses at the public faith of so many ages, and as he curses 35
all that is holy, at each blasphemy will applaud and repeat, "Bravo!"
But at each word of the one who would
come to dispute with Luther, with shouting,   *How much danger he undertakes
grimacing, stomping, pounding, they will   who would dispute with Luther*

uicerit: digressum denique perimant. Neque enim nunc eadem rerum
est conditio, atque olim fuit: quum disputabat Eccius. Tum enim re
adhuc in eo statu, ut ualde suae sectae fauerent: nec dum plane
scirent: quam malam causam fouerent: eo quietius et cupidius audie-
5   bant: quod se audituros sperabant: quae ualde audire cupiebant.
Sed ea disputatio quum non undequaque responderit ipsorum spei:
quum tamen essent quaedam in speciem non prorsus improba: et
nunc eum cernant post per furorem adiecisse talia: quae nullo possit
colore defendere: desperata rationis uictoria, triumphum collocant in
10 amentia: non audituri quicquam aequis auribus, quod aduersetur
iniquis animis. Neque tamen nego, in eadem urbe, in qua sibi delegit
latibulum: multos esse uiros honestissimos: multas mulieres bonas ac
pias: sed in re seditio[B₄v]sa, magis eminet insana tumultuantium
turba, quam numerus, etiam maior bonorum et sedatorum ciuium.

15   Lutherus igitur quum doleat libellis aedi-
Cur Lutherus prouocet, ut   tis, ita uictas ac reuictas suas insanas
disputetur coram   haereses, ut nunquam apud suos se uictorem audiat, quin interim excarnificetur intus obprobrij sui conscientia, gnarus omnibus undique gentibus, ex libellis utrinque inter
20 se collatis, clarissima luce patere, quam turpiter euersus, ac prostratus iaceat: pertesus tandem ac perhorrescens iudicium publicum,
pugnaturus, uelut gallus prouocat in suum sterquilinium: ubi coram
gallinis suis cantitet. Verum neminem
Cur scripto potius quam   opinor esse tam insanum: ut in locum
coram sit disputandum
25   ueniat: quo eum hostis uocat ad pugnam:
quum non possit aequior esse planicies, in qua dimicetur, aut minus
insidijs exposita, quam libellis aeditis conflictatio, in qua neutra pars
causari potest, aut perperam quicquam exceptum a notarijs, aut post
corruptum a falsarijs, aut sibi quicquam non prouisum calore subi-
30 tariae disputationis excidisse. Sed quod, ex causae meritis per ocium

---

2 re] res *L*   3 in eo statu] in eo fuit statu *L*   9 defendere] *BL*, defcndere *R*
13 seditiosa, magis] *L*, seditiosa magis *BR*   16 suas] ipsius *B*

interrupt him, hoot at him, hiss him off the stage. If he will persist in the face of all this and overcome their shouts with reason, they will finally kill him on his departure.

Things are not what they were once, when Eck was disputing. For then, because the movement was still at the stage when men strongly 5 favored their own sect and did not yet clearly realize what a bad cause they were fostering, they used to listen more quietly and eagerly because they were hoping to hear what they were very eager to hear. But that disputation in no way answered their hopes, although nevertheless there were certain points apparently not altogether un- 10 acceptable. Now that they see he has later in his madness added such points as he can in no way defend, they despair of a victory of reason and place their triumph in unreason, unwilling to listen with unprejudiced ears to anything which contradicts their prejudiced minds. And yet, I do not deny that in the very city in which he has chosen his 15 hiding place there are many very honorable men, many good and pious women; but in times of unrest the mad rabble of troublemakers stands out more than the even greater number of good and peace-loving citizens. Luther laments that, despite the books he has published, his mad *Why Luther challenges men to* 20 *dispute with him in person* heresies have been so overwhelmed and refuted that he never hears himself acclaimed as victor among his own followers without at the same time being inwardly rent by the consciousness of his own disgrace. He knows that all peoples everywhere, by comparing the books from either side, perceive with utter 25 clarity how shamefully overthrown and prostrate he lies. Wearied at last, and shrinking from a public trial, yet intending to fight, he challenges his foes cock-like to his own dung hill, where he may crow before his hens.

But I think no one is so senseless as to enter the place to which his 30 enemy summons him for a fight, since there cannot be a more level plain for the *Why the disputation should be carried on in writing rather* struggle, or one less exposed to ambush, *than in person* than a controversy carried on by means of published books, in which neither side can pretend, either that any 35 point was falsely kept from the record by the secretaries, or later corrupted by forgers, or that anything had escaped him unforeseen in the heat of a hurried disputation. Rather, what he will have brought forward in the most ordered fashion—whatever he is able to bring

quicquid potest, instructissimum protulerit: id syncaera fide prodibit
in publicum. Ex quibus et nunc clarissime patet: et indies magis
magisque patebit: quam sordido caeno prostratus iaceat, oblitus luto,
atque obuolutus stercore, gloriosus uictor ac triumphator Lutherus.
5 Quae res quum regio libello tam aegregie facta sit: ut nunquam
quicquam aeque Lutherum adegerit in furorem: efficiam hoc libello:
ut omnes Lutherani sentiant: quam stolidum habeant haeresiarcham:
qui sua sapientia nihil effecit aliud: quam infixum ab aduersario
telum, suis ipse manibus infixit altius. Sed priusquam aggrediar
10 librum: libet paulisper cum Luthero rur[C₁]sus redire vvormatiam.
Cuius magnifica commemoratione quiddam mihi redegit in memoriam: ex quo uno totus potest orbis iudicare uanissimi nebulonis et
ingenium stolidum, et mentem gloriae cupiditate dementem.

Detegitur Lutheri stulta ambitio ex
15   honorificentissimis de se, sub alieno nomine,
praedicationibus. Cap. II.

EXTAT libellus excusus hoc titulo: Acta et res gestae Domini
Martini Lutheri Augustiniani in comitijs principum vvormatiae. Is
libellus quo loco sit excusus, non dicit, quo authore compositus
20 tantundem. Sed liquet plane ex ipsa narrationis serie, fuisse aliquem
illius ualde studiosum. Verum non ab ipso tamen factum Luthero,
certissima sunt argumenta scilicet. Nam quum Caesar nominetur
ubique simpliciter Carolus: nunquam nominatur Lutherus, nisi
reuerenter DOMINVS MARTINVS literis maiusculis, uidelicet
25 magnus heros. Interdum sic: HOMO DEI LVTHERVS. Et quum
ij, qui contra loquuntur: prorumpere dicuntur in uerba uirulenta: de
ipso ita scribitur DOMINVS uero MARTINVS pro incredibili
                       humanitate et bonitate sua, benigne res-
        Vide illud
                       pondit. Et sic: Pater clementissimus
30 modestissime respondit. Et tanquam gloria patri totum illius psalmi
librum claudit haec coronis. Deus igitur hominem pientissimum,

8 aduersario] *B corr. err. L*, aduerso *R*

forward at his leisure in accordance with the merits of the case—that will with honest fidelity appear in public. From these considerations, it is now most clearly evident, and from day to day will become more evident, how the glorious conqueror and victor, Luther, lies prostrate in foul filth, smeared with mud, coated with dung. Although the king's book has accomplished this result so thoroughly that nothing has ever goaded Luther to an equal frenzy, I will make all Lutherans understand from the present book how doltish a heresiarch they have, who has accomplished nothing else by his wisdom than to fix more deeply with his own hands the weapon thrust into him by his oppo- nent. Before I take up the book, however, I should like for a short time to return with Luther to Worms. By his boastful mention of this city he has recalled a certain incident to my memory, from which one instance the whole world can judge the doltish character and the ambition-crazed mind of this most conceited scoundrel.

Luther's foolish vanity is exposed from his exaggerated praise of himself under an assumed name.
Chapter 2

There has been published a booklet entitled: *The Acts and Proceedings of the Honored Martin Luther, Augustinian, at the Diet of the Princes at Worms.* This booklet does not indicate where it was printed nor by whom it was compiled. But it is quite clear from the very course of the narra- tion that the author was someone very devoted to Luther. That it was not compiled by Luther himself, however, there are very certain indications. For example, whereas the emperor is everywhere desig- nated simply as "Charles," Luther is never named except in a rever- ent manner as "THE HONORED MARTIN" in capital letters, clearly indicating a great hero. At times he is referred to as, "Luther, the man of God." And whereas those who address him are said to break out into virulent words, Luther himself is described as follows: "But the honored Martin in his extraordinary gentleness and good- ness answered mildly." And in this way: *Note this* "The most forbearing father answered very modestly." And like a *gloria patri* the whole book of that psalm is closed with this flourish: "Therefore may God for a very long time preserve

tuendo et docendo euangelio natum, diutissime seruet ecclesiae suae,
una cum suo uerbo, Amen. Quis ita suspicax unquam natus est: ut
sus[C₁v]picari possit: qui talia de Luthero scripsit: ipsum fuisse
Lutherum? Quis enim Thraso tam glorio-

Thrasonica Lutheri gloria

5　　sus fuit: quem non puderet eiusmodi uel
cogitare de semet? At nunc, obsecro, lector uide: quam penitus
homini memoriam, ac mentem, inanis gloriae titillatio excusserit.
Quum totus liber ita sit tractatus: ut uideri possit ab alio quouis esse
compositus, subito suo sorex indicio prodit

Lutherus sui immemor

10　　se. Oblitus enim sui, quodam in loco sic
ait:

His dictis, orator imperii, increpabundo similis, dixit me non ad rem
respondisse: nec debere in dubium uocari, quae olim in consiliis
essent damnata et definita: ideo a me peti simplex, non cornutum
15　　responsum, an uelim reuocare, uel non? Hic ego. Quando ergo
Caesaris maiestas &c.

Hic uides lector ex rebus vvormatiae gestis, incredibilem illam
clementissimi patris modestiam: qui sub

Modestia Lutheri

alieni tubicinis larua, suas ipse laudes tam
20　　modeste buccinet. Vides admirandam prudentiam: qui non potuit
cauere sibi in tam exiguo libello: ne tam stultum institutum proderet:
cuius puderet etiam morionem.

Verba Lutheri　　　　Ea caecitate et amentia percussit dominus
noster Iesus Christus, uniuersum istud
25　　regnum abhominationis papisticae: ut iam totum triennium, cum
uno Luthero ipsi infiniti uulgi Cyclopes belligerantes, nec dum
intelligere possunt, pro qua re mihi cum ipsis bellum sit.

---

19 larua] *corr. err. L*, lerua *BR*　　　24 istud] *L*, idstud *BR*　　　27 mihi] *corr. err. L*, nihil *BR*

for His church together with His word this most pious man born to defend and teach the gospel. Amen."

What man has ever been born so suspicious as to be able to suspect that the man who wrote such words about Luther was himself Luther? What Thraso was ever so vainglor- *Luther's Thrasonic vainglory* 5
ious that he would not be ashamed even to think in such a manner about himself? But please observe, reader, how completely the titillation of vainglory has driven out the man's memory and mind. When the whole work has been so handled that one can consider it the work of some other person, suddenly the 10 shrewmouse betrays itself by its squeak. *Luther forgets himself*
For forgetting himself, he says in a certain passage:

> At these words, the speaker for the emperor, as though rebuking me, said that I had not answered to the point and that things should not 15 be called into doubt which had once been condemned and defined in councils; therefore I was asked to give a simple, not a sophistical, answer to the question whether I was willing to retract or not. To this I replied: Since the emperor's majesty etc.

Here you see, reader, from the proceedings at Worms, that extra- 20 ordinary modesty of the most gentle father, who under the mask of another trumpeter so modestly trumpets *Luther's modesty*
his own praise. You see the admirable shrewdness of the man who in so slight a book could not avoid betraying a design so foolish that even a fool would be ashamed of it. 25

> With such blindness and madness has our *Luther's words*
> Lord Jesus Christ stricken that whole realm of papist abomination that for three whole years now these innumerable crowds of Cyclopes fighting with Luther alone cannot yet understand why I am at war with them. 30

Aperitur Lutheri insanum institutum et consilium. Cap. tertium.

AIT OMNES, qui cognoscunt pontificem: hoc est omnes Italos, Hispanos, Gallos, Germanos, et quicquid est usquam populi Christi-
5 ani: quos omnes appellat Cy[C₂]clopas, tam diu belligerantes cum uno Luthero, Vlisse uidelicet omnium
Lutherus uidelicet prudentissimo, ita perterebratis esse oculis,
alter Vlisses tanquam Polyphemum: ut quamquam libris ab illo tam multis aeditis, adhuc non possint cernere: quorsum
10 ille tendat. O rem difficilem, et quae non exoculatum Cyclopa, sed Argum aliquem oculatissimum requirat, ac lynceum: qui Lutheri uias uestiget. Esset fortasse res difficilis colubri uiam uestigare super terram: nisi odore pestilentissimo, quaqua uersus serperet, erum- pente, ac terras lue teterrima inficiente, ipse se nimium proderet.
15 Neque enim nunc horum Cyclopum quisquam est adeo caecus: ut non artes eius, et astutias deprehenderit: quam inani commento fugam paret ex Aethna: ut ex hac Cyclopum, ut uocat, elapsus insula, recte tendat ad inferos. Sed unde nullus
Quo tendat Lutherus eum reducat Tyresias.

20   *Verba Lutheri*   Non intelligunt, inquit, frustra tot libellis a me aeditis et palam testantibus, hoc solum a me quaeri, ut diuinae literae solae regnent, sicut dignum et iustum est, humanae uero inuentiones et traditiones e medio tollantur, ceu nocentissima scandala, aut execto ueneno, et
25 euulso aculeo, id est ui cogendi et imperandi, et conscientias illa- queandi erepta, libere et indifferentes tolerentur, ceu quaelibet alia pestis aut infelicitas mundi. Nam ipsi perpetua insania perciti, contra me nihil mouent, nisi statuta hominum, glossas patrum, et facta seu ritus seculorum, ea ipsa scilicet, quae nego et impugno, quae et
30 ipsimet confitentur infida esse. Ego de iure disputo, et ipsi de facto mihi respondent. Ego causam quaero, ipsi opus exhibent. Ego interrogo, in qua potestate hoc facitis, ipsi dicunt, quia sic facimus, et

---

25 ui] *corr. err.*, vi *L*, in *BR*   25–26 illaqueandi erepta,] *L*, illaqueandi, erepta *BR*

Luther's mad intention and design are revealed. Chapter 3.

He says of all those who acknowledge the pope, that is, all the Italians, Spaniards, French, Germans, and all Christian people everywhere, all of whom he calls Cyclopes, that although they have been fighting 5 so long with Luther alone, a Ulysses indeed of consummate shrewdness, they have their eyes gouged out like Polyphemus so that, *Luther is indeed another Ulysses* despite the many books he has published, they still cannot determine where he is heading. What a difficult matter! It would 10 require, not an eyeless Cyclops, but some many-eyed Argos and Lynceus to trace Luther's paths. It would perhaps be a difficult matter to trace the path of a snake over the ground, except that by its offensive odor breaking out wherever it turns and creeps along and by its loathsome corruption infecting the earth it betrays itself only too 15 well. Neither, then, is any one of these Cyclopes so blind that he cannot detect the tricks and shifts of this fellow, with what a worthless subterfuge he prepares himself for flight from Aetna so that, having escaped from this island of the Cyclopes, as he calls them, he heads straight for hell. But from there no Tiresias may lead him back. *Where Luther is heading* 20

They do not understand, he says. In vain have I published so many books plainly *Luther's words* testifying that I seek only that the divine scriptures should have sole rule, as is meet and just, but that human inventions and traditions 25 should be abolished as most pernicious scandals, or with their poison cut out and their sting removed, that is, with their power of forcing and commanding and ensnaring consciences taken away, they should be tolerated freely as things neither good nor bad, just as with any other plague or misfortune of the world. These people, violently 30 agitated by incessant madness, advance no argument against me but the decrees of men, the glosses of the fathers, and the practices or customs of the ages; in other words, those very things which I reject and impugn, which even they themselves admit are untrustworthy. I argue *de jure*; they answer me *de facto*. I seek a reason; they show me a 35 work. I ask: "By what power do you do this?" They answer: "Because this is the way we are doing it, and this is the way we have done it."

sic fecimus. Sit pro ratione uoluntas, pro authoritate, ritus, pro iure, consuetudo, idque in rebus dei. Est apud eos ipsos in scholis suis uiciosissimum genus disputandi, quod uocant, petitionem principij. Hoc discunt et docent usque ad canos, usque ad sepulchrum, [C₂v]
5   tot sudoribus, tot sumptibus miserrimi homines.

Et de rege paulo post.

Hic uero deus noua sua diuinitate mirum in modum insolescens, ac certus quicquid dixerit fieri oportere, aut factum esse, id ex professo etiam testatur, uelle sese dimittere capitale fundamentum meum, et
10   alijs relinquere expugnandum, ac solum aedificium labefactare, id est, stipula et foeno contra rupem uerbi dei pugnare, ut nescias, an ipsa mania sic insanire possit, aut ipsa stoliditas tam stolida sit, quam est caput hoc Henrici nostri, forte ut uerum faciat prouerbium, Aut regem aut fatuum nasci oportuit. Quis morio enim sic diceret, Ego asseram
15   septem sacramenta, sed intactum relinquam principale robur aduersarii? Crederes ab insigni hoste regis, hunc librum aeditum in regis perpetuam ignominiam.

Proponuntur in summa, quae sunt tractanda
in toto opere. Cap. quartum.

20   HAEC IPSA Lutheri uerba lector, in quibus tam impense sibi Lutherus placet: efficiam paulo post, quum ad illius responsum, ut ille uocat generale, perueniam: ut facile quiuis intelligat, ex regis libello sumptis probationibus, non solum esse falsissima: uerum etiam uix tot habere uerba, quot uitia. Praeterea nebulonem istum, non
25   hominum tantum traditiones omnes tollere, etiam eas quibus deberet obedire: sed etiam tollere traditiones dei. Nec eo tamen contentum, illas ipsas dei scripturas, pro quarum regno se pugnare simulat: quibus potest machinis oppugnare. Quo in loco faciam perspicuum: quam insulse rideat eum disputandi morem: ut contra unius authori-
30   tatem scurrae, regia maiestas opponat authoritatem tot [C₃] sanctorum patrum, tot seculorum consuetudinem, et publicam fidem

> Let will take the place of reason, observance the place of authority, custom the place of law, and that in matters pertaining to God. These men have in their schools a most corrupt manner of disputing, which they call "begging the question." This the wretched men learn and teach even to gray hairs, even to the grave, with extreme effort and 5 expense.

And of the king shortly after:

> But this god, growing shockingly arrogant in his new divinity and certain that whatever he has said ought to happen or has happened, goes further and explicitly testifies that he wishes to dismiss my funda- 10 mental principle, leaving it for others to attack, and to overthrow only the superstructure; that is, to fight with straw and hay against the rock of God's word. You would not know whether madness itself could be so mad or dullness itself so dull as is our blockhead Henry. Perhaps this is to verify the proverb: "Kings and fools are born—not 15 made." What fool would say: "I declare that there are seven sacraments, but I shall leave untouched the principal argument of my opponent"? You would think this book were published by a noted enemy of the king to the king's lasting disgrace.

A summary of the matter to be treated in the 20 whole work. Chapter 4.

These very words of Luther, reader, on which he so excessively plumes himself, not only are absolutely false but contain almost as many errors as there are words. A little later when I come to what he calls his general response I will demonstrate this fact according to proofs 25 taken from the king's book, so that anyone may readily perceive it. Besides this, I will show not only that the scoundrel does away with all the traditions of men, even those which he ought to obey, but also that he does away with the traditions of God. And nevertheless not content with this, he attacks by means of every possible stratagem 30 those very scriptures of God for the sovereign authority of which he pretends to fight. In that passage I will make clear how foolishly he ridicules the royal majesty's method of disputing, which consists of opposing to the authority of a single buffoon the authority of so many holy fathers, the custom of so many centuries and the public faith of 35

totius ecclesiae. Simul et illud constare faciam, uitiosum illud disputandi genus in petendo principio, quod tanta cum insultatione
deriuat in alios, solam ipsi atque unicam fere disputandi formam esse.
Idque ipsum illi accidere in his ipsis locis maxime, in quibus illud
5　maxime obijcit atque improperat alijs. Tunc ista uerba, quibus extra
locum se iactat, ut legentibus offundat tenebras: nos loco ad id idoneo
uentilabimus: et paleas istas, quas pro

Paleis comparat Lutheri dogmata　tritico laborat uendere: uento sparsas
dissipabimus. Nam quod homo lepidus uidelicet ac facetus irridet
10　regem: quod asserturus sacramenta testatur ex professo se capitale
fundamentum Lutheri alijs expugnandum relinquere, ac solum quod
superstruxit aedificium labefactare, tangetur eo loco, in quo solo
conuenit: ubi Lutherus idem rursus simili semper conditum sale
repetit. Nempe ubi tractabitur: quod missa bonum opus, oblatio, aut
15　sacrificium Luthero non potest esse: propterea quod sit (ut ait)
testamentum. Ibi uidebis lector, hominis tam festiue dicacis infacetas
facetias, in solum Lutherum ludere. Atque haec quae nunc promitto
tibi, ideo distincte posui: ut eorum quodque, suis a me locis possis
exigere. Quorum ita me debitorem constituo: ut nisi in hoc libello
20　persoluam omnia: nihil omnino uidear persoluisse: contentus, ut
Lutherus in me decantet illud Horatij: Quid dignum tanto feret hic
promissor hiatu.

Respondetur ad id, quod Lutherus fingit se non
credere librum regis ab ipso esse rege compositum et
25　[C₃v] simul ostenditur, quos et quam praeclaros
authores habeat liber Lutheri. Cap. quintum.

INTEREA paulisper ea illa percurram: quibus obiter obiectis ei, sic
homo se sapiens explicat: ut id conando magis ac magis implicet
atque inuoluat. Sed prius mirifice se putauit scilicet irritaturum

the whole Church. At the same time I will also make clear that the
faulty method of disputing by begging the question, which he attributes to others with so much insolence, is his own sole and almost
only form of disputing. Moreover, I will show that he falls into this
practice especially in the very passages in which he most fiercely   5
reproaches and upbraids others for it. Then, at the point suited to the
purpose, we shall winnow those words in which he boasts of himself
so inordinately that he overwhelms his readers with darkness, and we
shall scatter with the winnowing wind this
chaff that he labors to sell for grain. This   *He compares Luther's doctrines*   10
obviously witty and facetious fellow jeers at   *to chaff*
the king for explicitly testifying, when about to defend the
sacraments, that he will leave Luther's chief foundation for others to
attack and that he himself will tear down only the superstructure
built on that foundation. This will be touched on in the only passage   15
which suits it, where Luther keeps repeating the same argument
seasoned always with a similar salt; that is, where we will treat the
argument that for Luther the mass cannot be a good work, an oblation, or a sacrifice, because it is, as he says, a testament. There you will
see, reader, that the witless witticisms of this man of such merry humor   20
make sport of Luther alone. I set down as separate points these things
that I now promise to do for you, so that you can require each of
them from me in its own place. I put myself in your debt for them, so
that if I do not discharge in this booklet all that I have promised I
may be thought to have discharged nothing at all, content to have   25
Luther chant over and over at me these words of Horace: "What will
this braggart produce worthy of such pompous language?"

He answers Luther's pretense of not believing that the
king's book was written by the king himself, and at the
same time he shows what distinguished authors the book   30
of Luther has. Chapter 5.

Meanwhile I shall briefly run through those incidental objections to
Luther from which the wise man makes such efforts to extricate himself that in doing so he more and more implicates and involves himself. But first, the following.   35

regem, si se simularet non credere librum a rege aeditum, ipsius esse
regis: sed Lei uidelicet, aut alicuius (ut ille uocat) pituitosi sophistae:
quasi quisquam Luthere tam pituitosus esset: cuius pituitam non
praeoptet: quisquis non plane furit: quam furiosam bilem tuam.
5 Male torquet nebulonem istum: quod notior est, et non in sola
Britannia celebratior, eruditio eximia regiae maiestatis, cum in alijs
plerisque disciplinis omnibus, tum praecipue in re theologica: quam
ut cuiquam possit persuadere stolidus, alieno libro uoluisse uenari
gloriam regem sapientissimum, ex furioso fraterculo, cum quo magis
10 duxit, opinor, inglorium contendere, quam gloriosum uincere:
praesertim in tali re, quae cum per se clara nunquam non esset: eam
tamen factam sciret aduersarij stultitia clariorem. Nec scripsisset,

Summa principis bonitas   opinor, omnino quicquam aduersus talem
scurram princeps: nisi pro Christi honore
15 nihil sibi duxisset inhonorum: sed ueluti pro Christi nomine pugnam
detrectare nollet, aduersus infidelium (si fors ita ferret) uilissimum: sic
pro Christi fide, calamo certare dignatus est, aduersus haereticorum
stultissimum. Verum uideo: quid Lutherus uelit: optat id quemque credere de libello regis: quod ipse sibi conscius est: et nemo
20 factum nescit in suo. Nam quis ig[C₄]norat, illius responsionem non
unius cuiusquam labores esse? Quod enim unum caput potuisset
unquam tantum stulticiarum parere? Ipsa mediusfidius frenesis
assiduo tot neniarum partu fuisset effaeta. Sed multae (quod plane
compertum est) insanissimorum nebulonum libidines Lutheri foetum
25 hunc informem ac monstrosum genuere. Et sicut in compotationem
solent, suum quisque symbolum conferre: sic in libellum istum
stulticiarum farraginem, communi consilio suum stultorum quisque
nugatorum stulte dictum contulit.

NAM QVVM Lutherus regis accepisset librum, atque aliquid eius
30 delibasset: uitiato gustui coepit salutaris cibus amarescere. Quem
quum deuorare non potuit: iam potando cupiens amariciem eius

Senatus combibonum   eluere, conuocauit compotorum suorum
senatum. Ibi quamquam opus illud malu-
isset perpetuis tenebris abditum: tamen quoniam celari non potuit:

4 furit] *corr. err. L*, fuerit *BR*   30 coepit] cẹpit *BR*, caepit *L*

He thought he would doubtless exasperate the king exceedingly if
he pretended not to believe that the book published by the king was
the king's own, but clearly Lee's, or some phlegmatic sophist's, as he
calls him. As if anyone were so phlegmatic, Luther, as not to prefer the
phlegm of any person whatever who is not completely raving to your   5
raving bile.

This scoundrel is painfully tormented by the fact that the royal
majesty's learning in almost all disciplines and especially in theology
is too well known and, in other lands besides Britain, too celebrated
for the dolt to be able to persuade anyone that the most wise king   10
wished to seek renown through another man's book at the expense of
a frenzied friarlet. I think the king would rather consider it inglorious
to contend with him than glorious to conquer him, especially in such
a contest as, while it would always be intrinsically noteworthy, he yet
knew would be rendered notorious by the folly of his opponent. Nor,   15
I think, would the prince have written anything at all against such a
buffoon except that for the honor of Christ
he considered nothing a dishonor to him-   *The supreme goodness of the*
self; but just as for the honor of Christ's   *king*
name he would not decline to fight against the basest of infidels, if   20
that were his fortune, so for the faith of Christ he deigned to fight with
his pen against the most foolish of heretics.

But I see what Luther wants: he wishes everyone to believe about
the king's book what he is aware of with regard to his own, and what
everyone knows was done in his own book. For who does not know   25
that this fellow's response was not the labor of any one man? What
single head could ever have begotten such a great mass of follies? By
heaven, frenzy itself would have been exhausted from giving birth
incessantly to so much crazy nonsense. But, as is quite well known,
the lusts of many madly raving scoundrels have engendered this   30
shapeless and monstrous offspring of Luther. As at their drinking bouts
each one is accustomed to pay his scot, so into this book, a farrago of
follies, each of the foolish triflers by common design contributed his
own foolish expression. When Luther had received the king's book
and had tasted some of it, the wholesome food began to grow bitter to   35
his perverted taste. Since he was not able to gulp it down, wishing
then to get rid of its bitterness by tippling,   *An assembly of pot-fellows*
he convoked an assembly of his fellow-
tipplers. There, although he would have preferred the work to be

quum calicibus epotis bene firmasset animum: grauatim profert
librum. Legi ceptus, asininas auriculas coepit mordaci radere uero.
Claudunt igitur, ac mox resignant rursus: et iam carptim uertunt: si
quid forte reperiant: quod ratione possint carpere. Nihil occurrit
5   commodum calumniae. Iam ut in rebus difficilibus exquiruntur
sententiae. Nam et mestus esse senatus coepit, et Luthero res ad
                                   restem uergere: nisi quidam eum dextre
      Bicias potator primo aeneidos
                                   sic esset consolatus Bicias. Quid ipsorum
referret: quid scripsisset rex Angliae: aut quid omnino de fide
10 sentiendum esset: qui nihil proposuissent sibi, nisi per tumultum facta
                                   seditione, ipsi tanquam capita factionis
      Prositum Lutheranorum
                                   inclarescere? Vt et ex seductis simplicibus
pecuniam, et ex irritatis eruditioribus caperent uolupta[C₄v]tem.
Qua in re quid nocuerit: quam uera scribat rex: aut ipsorum haereses
15 quam acute refellat. Rescribat tantum Lutherus: et solita sibi insistat
uia: strenue conuitietur ac rideat. Quotus enim quisque futurus sit e
                                   uulgo simplici, quibus imponere, apud
      Biciae consilium strenuum
                                   quos regnare fuerit satis: qui rem totam ab
initio aut uelit repetere: aut repetitam, possit expendere. Proinde ne
20 deficiat animo: neu sic desipiat tamen: ut decernat ratione certan-
dum: probra tantum et conuitia per omnes paginas, hyberna niue
densius, ingerenda: quorum inexhaustus fluuius, Luthero scaturiret e
pectore. His armis tutum Lutherum fore, quibus et ferire possit: et
referiri non possit. Nam generosum regis animum indignaturum, talia
25 in sese dici a talibus: honestorum omnium animis indoliturum,
tantum impune licere nebulonibus. Si rescribat quisquam grauiter et
seuere: contemnet uulgus: quae res Luthero fuerit satis. Sin instituat
quispiam Luthero digna regerere: ridicule fecerit: frigebit enim
dictum: quod in illum dicitur: cuius foedior omni crimine persona
30 est. Sed nec parem quenquam Luthero fore, qui satis fuerit unus,
aduersus decem loquacissimas, et iurgiosissimas meretrices. Et tamen

11 *gloss* Prositum] Propositum *L*   25 honestorum] honest orum *B*

hidden in everlasting darkness, yet, because it could not be concealed, he reluctantly brought out the book, after strongly fortifying his spirit by draining his cups. Once the reading started, it began to grate on their asinine ears with biting truth. They therefore close the book, and then soon reopen it. Now they leaf through it to see if they may per- 5 haps discover something which they can reasonably carp at. Nothing occurs convenient to cavil. Now, as in situations of crisis, opinions are sought. The assembly began to be dejected, and things began to look desperate for Luther, except that some Bitias skillfully consoled him, saying: What difference did it make to them what the *Bitias, a toper in the first book of the Aeneid* 10 king of England had written, or why did they have to consider honesty at all, since they had no purpose but to agitate a noisy rebellion and become famous as the ringleaders of a faction? Thus they would exact money from the seduction of the simple and pleasure from the provoca- *The purpose of the Lutherans* 15 tion of the more learned. Therefore, what did it hurt how truly the king writes or how shrewdly he refutes their heresies? Let Luther just reply and pursue his usual way: let him be quick to rail and mock. It would be enough for them to impose on and dominate the simple folk. How few of *The prompt advice of Bitias* 20 these would either wish to reconsider the whole matter from the beginning or would be able to evaluate it, once reconsidered? So let him not be disheartened nor at any rate so foolish as to decide that the battle must be waged by reason; all that needed to be employed were 25 reproaches and insults on every page, thicker than winter snow, of which an inexhaustible stream would gush forth from Luther's breast. With these weapons Luther would be safe; with them he could both strike and keep himself from being struck in return. The generous soul of the king would be indignant that such things were 30 said against himself by such men; it would grieve the souls of all honorable men that the scoundrels were allowed to get away with so much unpunished. If anyone should write a stern and severe answer, the common people would contemn it, which would be enough for Luther. If, on the contrary, someone should determine to make a 35 retort that fit Luther, he would act ridiculously; for, spoken against a man whose person is fouler than every kind of reproach, his words will have no effect. But neither would anyone be equal to Luther, who could take on single-handed ten of the most garrulous and brawling

ipsos pro sua quenque uirili, non defuturos: atque ita facile uictoriam
ipsius fore. Isto consilio dato, Lutherus animum reuocare coepit: qui
iam fere per posticum fugerat. Verum, quoniam supra solitum sibi
morem opus uidit esse iurgijs: quandoquidem in disputationem nihil
5 habebat aliud: quod prorsus posset afferri: hortatur eos: ut eo quisque
properet pergere: ubi stolidorum iurgiorum et scurrilium scommatum, quam plurimam [D₁] uenari materiam quirent: quarum
rerum, ut quisque collegisset sarcinam: protinus ad se conueherent:
ex illis enim refarsurum se responsionis suae farraginem. Cum his
10 mandatis dimittit consilium. Illi igitur abeunt, alius alio, quo quemque tulit animus: et se per omnia plaustra, uehicula, cymbas, ther-
mas, ganea, tonstrinas, tabernas, lustra, pistrina, latrinas, lupanaria
diffundunt: illic obseruant sedulo, atque in tabellas referunt, quicquid aut auriga sordide, aut seruus uerniliter, aut portitor improbe,
15 aut parasitus scurriliter, aut meretrix petulanter, aut leno turpiter,
aut balneator spurce, aut cacator obscoene loquutus sit. Atque haec
quum aliquot fecissent menses: tum demum quicquid undecunque
collegissent, conuitiorum, iurgiorum, et scurrilium scommatum,
petulantiae, spurciciae, sordium, luti, caeni, stercorum, omnem hanc
20 colluuiem in foedissimam cloacam Lutheri pectus infartiunt. Quam
ille totam, in libellum istum suum conuitiatorium, per os illud
impurum uelut comesam merdam reuomuit. Inde tibi lector aceruus
ille spurcissimorum latratuum, quibus solis stultissimus libellus
impletur. Nam quum de re conatur aliquid, detrahe tantum ornatis-
25 sima illa scurrilitatis emblemmata: statim uidebis lector, e tanto
uerborum cumulo, quam exiguus rerum restet manipulus, et ille
tamen ipse corruptus. Quod, ut tibi magis fiat perspicuum: age,
excutiamus (ut facturus eram) ea uitia: quae paucis obiter obiecta,
multis uerbis contendit reijcere. Etenim facilius erit conijcere, qualem
30 se prebeat in oppugnando altero, qui tam belle defendit sese. [D₁v]

---

7 plurimam uenari] venari plurimam *L*

whores. And yet his pot-fellows themselves, each according to his ability, would not fail to help him, and thus the victory would easily be his.

On being given this advice, Luther began to recover his spirit, which had already almost escaped through the rear. But because he saw that he needed more than his usual brawling, since indeed he had not a single other weapon to employ in the disputation, he urged them each to hurry to the place where they could hunt out the greatest possible matter of stupid brawls and scurrilous scoffs. When each had collected a bagful of these, he should bring it immediately to Luther, for from them he would stuff full his own farrago of a response. With this charge he dismisses the assembly.

They then go off in different directions, each to the place that his spirit suggests, and they scatter among all the carts, carriages, boats, baths, brothels, barber shops, taverns, whorehouses, mills, privies, and stews. There they diligently observe and set down in their notebooks whatever a coachman spoke ribaldly, or a servant insolently, or a porter lewdly, or a parasite jeeringly, or a whore wantonly, or a pimp indecently, or a bath-keeper filthily, or a shitter obscenely. After hunting for several months, then, finally, all that they had collected from any place whatever, railings, brawlings, scurrilous scoffs, wantonness, obscenities, dirt, filth, muck, shit, all this sewage they stuff into the most foul sewer of Luther's breast. All this he vomited up through that foul mouth into that railers' book of his, like devoured dung. From there, reader, you receive that accumulated mass of indecent brawlings, with which alone the utterly foolish book is filled. When he tries to say anything to the point, just remove that very ornate mosaic of scurrility; immediately you will see, reader, how slight a handful of substance remains from such a great heap of words, and yet even that is corrupted. That this may become clearer to you, come, let us examine, as I was about to do, those errors, briefly objected to in passing, which he volubly strives to disclaim. It will be fairly easy to infer how he behaves in attacking another since he so prettily defends himself.

Reuincit impudentem uanitatem Lutheri: qui falso
scribit regem nullam eius repugnantiam proferre,
sed uerbo dumtaxat asserere, illum sibi esse
contrarium. Cap. sextum.

5   *Verba Lutheri*   PRIVSQVAM, inquit, ad rem ipsam
              ueniamus, primum diluam duo crimina,
quae mihi rex Thomisticus, prae impotentia sua muliebri imponit.
Quorum alterum est, esse uidelicet me mihi ipsi contrarium.

HOC igitur crimen ut diluat, tanquam magna innocentiae con-
10 scientia magnifice recenset, aeditorum ab se librorum catalogum: ne
quis eorum uenenorum nesciat nomina: quibus ueneficus, conatus est
Christianum uulgus inficere. Quos ipsos libros quisquis diligenter
inspexerit: tam multas tam apertas tam absurdas, inueniet repugnantias: ut ei nihil aliud hac librorum recensione Lutherus fecisse uidea-
15   *Apposita comparatio* tur: quam si hominem iugulasset inspect-
              ante populo, deinde uocatus in iudicium,
eos ipsos omnes innocentiae suae testes produceret: qui sceleris
fuerant spectatores. Sed hic opinor, aliqua iubebit a me proferri,
illarum contrarietatum exempla: et ex illo mari aliquam afferri
20 lagenam, quasi aut opus sit ostendere: quod nemo non uidet: aut non
    Ambrosius Catharinus olim ei multas ostenderit uir doctissimus
              Ambrosius Catharinus: et ostendantur in
ipso regis libello nonnullae. Quarum si multas hoc loco (ut possum)
producerem, Lutherum (quae est hominis uerecundia) non puderet
25 iterum dissimulare productas: et rursus ut producerentur aliqua
flagitare. Nam cum eius generis multas protulerit uir, ut dixi,
doctissimus, Ambrosius Catharinus: iam Lutherus in morem simiae,
[D₂] per cachinnos ad unum respondet aut alterum: reliqua uero tam
    Impudens calliditas Lutheri aperta, ut nec e scurrilium scommatum
30   diuitijs suis inuenerit ullum: quod posset
opponere: per dissimulationem prorsus reliquit intacta: et ad id se
conuertit: in quo solo ualet: ut uirulentissimis conuitijs, et insanissi-

He refutes the shameless deception of Luther, who falsely
writes that the king cites no instance of his contradiction
but only declares in a word that Luther is inconsistent.
Chapter 6.

Before we come to the point at issue, he
says, I will first exonerate myself of two   *Luther's words*   5
charges which the Thomistic king in his womanish fury lays against
me. Of these, the first is that I am inconsistent.

In order to exonerate himself of this charge, therefore, as though with
a profound awareness of his innocence, he pompously reviews the   10
catalogue of his published books, lest anyone be ignorant of the names
of those poisons with which the poison-maker has tried to infect the
Christian people. Anyone who carefully examines these same books
will find so many, such evident, such absurd contradictions that he
will think Luther has done nothing else by this review of his books   15
than if he had slit the throat of a man in the
sight of the people, and then, when sum-   *An appropriate comparison*
moned to trial, produced as witnesses of his innocence all those
people who had been the spectators of his crime.

But here, I suppose, he will demand that I present some examples   20
of those inconsistencies, that I draw a flask from this sea; as though it
were necessary to point out what everyone sees; or as though
Ambrose Catharinus, a most learned man,
did not long ago point out to him many   *Ambrose Catharinus*
instances; and as though some were not pointed out in the king's book 25
itself. If I did produce many of them at this point, as I can, Luther
would not be ashamed—such is the fellow's horror of evil—to pretend
once more that none had been produced and to demand once again
that some examples be produced. Although, as I have said, the most
learned Ambrose Catharinus presented many instances of that kind,   30
Luther then, like an ape, answered several instances with derisive
laughter. The rest, however, were so obvious that not even from his
wealth of scurrilous scoffs was he able to
find any argument against them. These   *Luther's shameless cunning*
through dissimulation he left completely untouched and turned to the   35
only method in which he is effective, attacking the Roman See by an

mis iurgijs, impeteret sedem Romanam: morionum more, qui, cum
ab alio percutiantur: protinus percutiunt alium. An non simili
dissimulatione utitur: cum nunc ait regem in suo libello, ne unum
quidem locum proferre, saltem exempli gratia: quo Lutheri incon-
5 stantiam conuincat?

        Verba Lutheri   SOLVM rhetoricatur, inquit, gloriosus
                                 rex, hoc modo. Lutherus sibi pugnat:
quis ei credat? Sic dixisse satis fuit defensori nouo ecclesiae et numini
recens in Anglia nato. Caeterum ostendisse exemplum non fuit opus,
10   *En scurrilitas nebulonis*   ne daretur Luthero occasio sese purgandi,
                                   et stultum regem pro dignitate thomis-
tica tractandi.

AN NON ista uerba nebulonis impudentissimi, quisquis audierit:
si neque Lutherum nosset: neque regis librum legisset: protinus
15 persuaderet sibi, regem nullam Lutheri contrarietatem usquam
protulisse: sed de industria celasse: ut ea posset licentius dicere: quae
Luthero negaretur facultas defendendi? At idem si Lutheri legisset
opuscula: is regem nihil peccasse fateretur: si rei nemini non com-
                              pertae probationem nullam proferret.
    Vanitatis omnis antistes   Idem si Lutheri nosset uanitatem: non
20   *Lutherus*   dubitaret, a rege factum: quicquid Lutherus a rege factum esse negarit. Quod si librum regium etiam legisset:
cum ibi tam multa uideret eorum: quorum ne unum quidem ibi esse
scribit Lutherus: quot quantisque modis damnet necesse est, im-
25 probissimi nebulonis mendacissimam sycophantiam. Quam rem uel
is unus locus habunde [D₂v] probauerit: quem primum in medium
proferam. Vel ob id, quod post ista, quae cauillando conatur eludere:
in quibus se non dissentire dicit sibi: sed mutare sententiam omnium
primus existat.
30 NAM QVVM Lutherus in captiuitate babylonica dixisset, omnibus
esse praeceptum: ut eucharistiam sub utraque specie reciperent: et
non ita multo post, in eadem pagina diceret: neutram omnino
speciem cadere sub praecepto: regia magiestas his uerbis, quae
sequuntur: attingit insignem hominis ita secum pugnantis, amentiam.

excess of virulent railing and mad brawling, in the manner of fools who when struck by one person immediately strike another. Does he not employ a similar dissimulation when he says now that the king has not presented in his book even one passage, at least for the sake of example, by which he may convict Luther of inconsistency?   5

> The pompous king, he says, merely *Luther's words*
> spouts rhetoric in this way: "Luther
> contradicts himself; who may believe him?" This simple statement was sufficient for the new defender of the church, the divinity recently born in England. But it was unnecessary for him to have shown an   10
> example, lest Luther be given the opportunity of clearing himself and of dealing with the stupid king according *See the scoundrel's buffoonery*
> to his Thomistic dignity.

Would not anyone who heard these words of the most shameless scoundrel, if he did not know Luther and had not read the book of the   15
king, immediately be convinced that the king had never presented any instances of Luther's inconsistency but had deliberately concealed them so that he could more irresponsibly make statements against which Luther would be denied the opportunity of defending himself? But if this same person had read the trifling work of Luther, he would   20
admit that the king would not have erred in the least by not presenting proof of a matter detected by everyone. Had the same person known Luther's deceitfulness, he would not *Luther high priest of every deceit*
doubt that the king had done whatever
Luther said that the king had not done. But if this person had also   25
read the book of the king, since he would see there so many instances of those contradictions of which Luther writes that not even one is there, how thoroughly and completely would he necessarily condemn the utterly dishonest craftiness of the most wicked scoundrel.

This fact will be abundantly proved by even the one passage which   30
I shall call to your attention first, especially because of the fact that after he tries by cavilling to make light of these passages in which he says that he does not disagree with himself, he is the first to change his opinion on everything.

Now, since Luther had said in the *Babylonian Captivity* that everyone   35
was commanded to receive the eucharist under both kinds, and not much later on the same page said that neither kind at all was a matter of precept, his royal majesty in the words which follow touches on the signal madness of a man so at odds with himself.

Verba regis   "AT VIDE QVAESO, quam uacillet, ac sibi repugnet Lutherus: uno loco dicit, Christum in coena omnibus omnino fidelibus, non permittendo, sed praecipiendo, dixisse: Bibite ex eo omnes. Postea uero, timens ne

5 laicos, quibus in sacerdotum odium adulatur: offenderet: haec uerba subiungit. Non quod peccent in Christum: qui una specie utuntur: quum non praeceperit ulla uti: sed arbitrio cuiuslibet reliquerit: dicens: Quotiescunque haec feceritis: in mei memoriam facietis. sed quod illi peccant: qui hoc arbitrio uolentibus uti, prohibent utramque

10 dari. Culpa non est in laicis, sed in sacerdotibus. Videtis aperte, quod primo dixit esse praeceptum: hic dicit non praeceptum esse, sed cuiuslibet arbitrio relictum. Quid opus est ergo, nos illi contradicere: qui sibi toties contradicit ipse?"

Quaeso te per tuas furias, quid habes hic amice Luthere: quod

15   dicas? Contendes hic te tibi non esse
Lutherus Conuincitur sibi   contrarium: et tam impudens eris aut
contrarius esse   stolidus: ut idem esse defendas: et utramque speciem omnibus esse praeceptam, et neutram esse [D₃] praeceptam cuiquam? Quod si aut tu tam impudens esses: ut peteres: aut

20 quisquam tam insanus, ut ista petenti concederet: tamen nihilo magis posses, ex uanissimae sycophantiae tuae laqueis effugere. Nam quum scribis, ideo regem nullam contrarietatum tuarum exempli causa proferre:ne tibi purgandi tui, detur occasio:perspicuum est desyderare te, non omnino talem, quae purgari non possit: sed uel talem saltem,

25 quam aduersarius uocaret repugnantiam: in qua tibi facultas esset eius uitij notam: si qua posses arte purgare. Ecce prolatus est a rege locus unus: qui legenti librum mihi primus e multis occurrerat: in quo tibi tu tam aperte pugnare conuinceris: ut (quamquam turpiter impudens es) qui locum uulgo notum, stulto silentio dissimules, et

30 improbe mendax: qui, quod alij legunt omnes: et ipse tanto cum dolore legisti: ut ita lectum obliuisci non possis: id nusquam scriptum esse contenderes: adhuc tamen perfricando frontem non potuisti

"But please observe how Luther wavers
and contradicts himself: in one place he *The king's words*
says that at the supper Christ said to each and every one of the
faithful, not by way of permission but by way of command: 'All of
you drink of this.' But afterwards, fearing to offend the laity, whom he 5
flatters into hating the priests, he adds these words: 'Not that they
who use one kind sin against Christ, since He did not command the
use of any kind but left it to the choice of each individual, saying: "As
often as you do these things you do them in remembrance of me." But
they sin who forbid both kinds to be given to persons who desire to 10
exercise this choice. The fault is not in the laity but in the priests.'
You see clearly that first he said it was commanded, then he says it
was not commanded but left to the choice of each individual. What
need is there, then, for us to contradict him who so often contradicts
himself?"   15

By your raving madness I ask you, "What do you have to say here,
friend Luther?" Will you argue here that
you are not inconsistent, and will you be so *Luther is convicted of inconsistency*
shameless or stupid as to defend as one and the same thing the
statement that both kinds were commanded to all and the statement 20
that neither kind was commanded to anyone? But if you were so
shameless as to seek this, or if anyone were so senseless as to grant
what you seek, yet you could not any the better escape from the snares
of your own most deceitful trickery. When you write that the king
produces none of your inconsistencies by way of example, lest you be 25
given the opportunity of clearing yourself, it is plain that what you
desire is not at all the kind of example which cannot be explained
away, but that kind which your opponent at any rate terms a contradiction, in which case you would have the opportunity of clearing
yourself of the reproach of that fault by some trick, if you could. 30

Behold one passage produced by the king; it was the first which
occurred to me from among many as I read the book; in it you are so
clearly convicted of contradicting yourself that, shameless as you are,
you, who conceal by a foolish silence a passage commonly known;
you, wicked liar, who in the case of this passage which everyone is 35
reading and which you yourself have read with such torment that
you cannot forget it thus read, contended that this passage had never
been written; you have yet not been able, by putting on a bold
front, to summon up enough audacity to defend the passage as not

efficere: ut auderes pro loco non pugnante defendere. Quod si
maxime posses: quamquam sic effugeres: ne teneri posses ex eo uno

Id quidem crebrum est Luthero   loco tibi esse contrarius: tamen nihilo
                                   magis uitares: quo minus uincereris im-
5 probissimi planeque digni uero nebulone mendatij, qui tanto cum
fastu iactasti: ne unum quidem locum a rege prolatum esse: uel
exempli certe causa, ne tibi daretur occasio purgandi tui. Quamobrem candide lector (ut ad te misso nebulone reuertar) sufficit hic
unus locus: ad reuincendum (ut dixi) Lutherum impudentissimi
10 mendatij: qui negat a rege locum esse prolatum ullum repugnantiae
suae: ne sibi daretur occasio purgandi sui. Sed quo magis adhuc
uanitas ho[D₃v]minis elucescat, accipe lector et alium.

    SCRIPSIT Lutherus in Babylonica sua, sacramentum ordinis esse

Conuincitur Lutherus sibi   quiddam nouum, et ecclesiae Christi
15   *contrarius*   ignotum: recenter autem inuentum ab
                                   ecclesia papae: et tamen idem fatetur, esse
apud diuum Dionysium: quem non negat esse antiquissimum.
Stolidissimam istam hominis repugnantiam non praeterijt princeps.

Verba regis   Sed ijs uerbis acutissime perstrinxit. "Si
20   solus ex antiquis patribus Dionysius ordinem esse scriberet sacramentum: uel hoc satis esset ad euertendum
Lutherum: qui uideri uult inuentionem eius sacramenti nouam esse.
Repugnat enim esse nouum: quod ab illo fatetur scriptis comprehensum: quem fatetur antiquum." ⁑ Ecce lector, quid non audebit iste
25 mentiri: quem non pudet fingere, nullum locum protulisse principem:
quo dicat eum sibi fuisse contrarium: quando hic unus locus talis est
repugnantia: ut ea prolata, tribus fere uersibus princeps totum
fundamentum nebulonis euerterit. Neminem usquam puto tam
addictum esse Luthero, quin sit fassurus, utrumlibet horum locorum
30 sufficere, ad coarguendam eius impudentiam: quem non puduit tanta
magnificentia iactare, nullum, ne exempli quidem causa, locum a
rege prolatum esse: quo Lutherum diceret, dicere sibi ipsi contraria.

contradictory. But if you could do precisely this, although you would thus escape being considered inconsistent on the grounds of that one passage, still you would not any the more avoid being convicted of the basest dis- *This indeed Luther frequently does* honesty clearly fitting a real scoundrel, since you have boasted with so much arrogance that the king had not produced even one passage, even for the sake of example, lest an opportunity be given you of clearing yourself.

Therefore, honest reader—to return to you after disposing of the scoundrel—this one passage suffices to convict Luther, as I said, of the most shameless dishonesty, since he says that the king has produced no example of his inconsistency lest he be given the opportunity of clearing himself. But in order that the fellow's deceitfulness may come to light still more clearly, listen, reader, to yet another passage.

Luther wrote in his *Babylon* that the sacrament of orders was something new, and unknown to the church of Christ; that it has been recently invented by the church of the pope; and yet he admits that this same sacrament is mentioned by Saint Dionysius, who he does not deny is *Luther is convicted of inconsistency* very ancient. The prince did not pass over this most stupid contradiction on the fellow's part, but he censured it very sharply in the following words: "If Dionysius were the only ancient father who wrote that orders is a sacrament, even this would be enough to *The king's words* overthrow Luther, who would have us think that the invention of that sacrament is something new. For its being new contradicts his admission that it is included in the writings of a man he admits is ancient."

See what lies this fellow will dare to tell, reader; he is not ashamed to pretend that the prince has produced no passage in which he may say that Luther contradicts himself, whereas this single passage is such a contradiction that by producing it the prince has overthrown the rascal's whole foundation in almost three lines. I think no one is so given over to Luther as not to admit that either of these passages will suffice to expose the shamelessness of the man who was not ashamed to boast with such great pomposity that the king had produced no passage, even for the sake of example, in which he might say that Luther contradicted himself. Nevertheless, so that on this point there may be a superfluity rather than the slightest lack, we will add still a

Nos tamen, ut hac in parte supersint potius
Quid? cum eum non puduit in re multa: quam quicquam desit: adijciemus
manifesta sic mentiri adhuc locum tertium: adiecturi supra
decimum: nisi nos puderet in re manifesta sic immorari. QVVM
5 Lutherus urgeri se cerneret apertissimis uerbis ex epistola Iacobi, non
solum in sacramento unctionis extremae, sed etiam in eo: quod eius
[D₄] maledicam linguam, et uirulentum pectus pulchre depinxit
apostolus: ut princeps prudentissimus et sagacissime deprehendit: et
elegantissime tetigit: aestuare coepit insania: et cupiens ulcisci se,
10 primum contempsit epistolam: deinde floccifecit apostolum. Posterius istud leges, ubi uoles, in ipso regis libello. Caeterum illud prius
de epistola tangetur a nobis: quam ita contempsit: ut diceret,
probabile esse, eam non esse apostoli:
Num hanc doctrinam e caelo propterea quod nihil haberet apostolico
habes Luthere?
15 spiritu dignum. Ea in re ipsa regis uerba
subscribam: ut uidere possis: an rex nullum prorsus attulerit locum:
in quo diceret, sibi repugnare Lutherum. Regis ergo uerba sunt haec.
"CERTE SI rationes attulisset Lutherus:
Verba regis quare epistola non esset Iacobi, sed
20 tamen alterius cuiuspiam, qui eodem loqueretur spiritu: potuisset
utcunque ferri. Nunc uero dicit esse probabile: quod sit indigna
spiritu apostolico. Qua in re non alium
Obiicitur Luthero Lutherus obijciam Luthero, quam Lutherum ipsum:
neque enim Luthero quisquam aut saepius ferme, contradicit, aut
25 ualidius, quam Lutherus. Is igitur in sacramento ordinis ait ecclesiam,
hoc habere datum: ut possit discernere uerba dei a uerbis hominum.
Quomodo ergo nunc dicit, epistolam apostolico spiritu indignam
esse: quam ecclesia, cuius iudicium (ut ait) in hac re falli non potest:
apostolico spiritu iudicauit plenam? Quamobrem nunc ita se sua
30 sapientia constrinxit undique: ut aut
Extrica te Luthere necessario comprobet epistolam esse apostoli (cuius contrarium dixit esse probabile) aut dicat ecclesiam, in
scriptura sacra posse diiudicando falli: quod eam posse negauerat."
[D₄v]

13 *gloss* doctrinam e caelo] doctrina me caelo *BR*, doctrinam coelo *L*

third passage. We are ready to add more
than ten, except that we would be ashamed   *Why, when he was not ashamed,*
to dwell so long in this way on an evident   *thus to lie in an evident*
matter.   *matter?*

Since Luther perceived himself to be hard pressed by the perfectly 5
clear words from the epistle of James, not only in the matter of the
sacrament of extreme unction, but also in that the apostle portrayed
precisely the fellow's abusive tongue and poisonous heart, when the
most wise prince caught this point very shrewdly and touched on it
very skillfully, Luther began to boil with fury, and, desiring to avenge 10
himself, he first contemned the epistle, then treated the apostle as not
worth a straw. You will read about this later, when you wish, in the
king's book itself. But first we will touch on his remark about the
epistle, which he contemned so much that he said it was probably not
an apostle's because it contained nothing   15
worthy of the apostolic spirit. I will set   *Surely you do not have this*
down the very words of the king on this   *doctrine from heaven, Luther!*
matter so that you can see whether the king has brought forward no
passage at all in which he might say that Luther contradicts himself. These, then, are the words of the king.   20
"Surely, if Luther had brought forward reasons why the epistle was
not James', but still that of someone else
who spoke in the same spirit, it could have   *The king's words*
been endured somehow. But now he says that it is probably not,
because it is unworthy of the apostolic spirit. In which case I bring no 25
other objection against Luther than Luther himself, for hardly anyone
contradicts Luther more often or more
forcefully than Luther. He, then, in speak-   *Luther is set against Luther*
ing of the sacrament of orders, says that the church has the power of
distinguishing the words of God from the words of man. How then 30
does he now say that an epistle is unworthy of the apostolic spirit
which the church, whose judgment as he says cannot err in this
matter, has judged to be full of the apostolic spirit? Consequently, he
has now so hemmed himself in on all sides by his own wisdom that he
must either necessarily acknowledge that   35
the epistle is the apostle's, and he has said   *Get yourself out of this,*
that the contrary is probable; or he must   *Luther*
say that the church can be deceived in determining the sacred scriptures; this possibility he has denied."

QVID HOC loco lector apertius? Quam frontem habet nebulo:
quem tam aperta negare non pudet? Quid eum necesse est ab his
audire: qui locis istis cum illius impudenti mendacio collatis, uanissimi scurrae scurrilia uerba consyderent: quando scurratur hoc
5   pacto.

Lutheri uerba   QVANDO ergo laruam, uerbis lar-
                             uatis sine exemplo ludere libuit in re tam
Num sic Paulus mordere   seria et sacra. Ego sine larua sed aperte
solebat Luthere?   dico regem Angliae Henricum istum,
10   plane mentiri et scurram leuissimum
mendacijs suis magis referre quam regem. Hoc crimine ego
Lutherus, Thomistam hunc uirulentum palam accuso, et testibus tum
libellis tum lectoribus meis per orbem conuinco. Facessat mihi in hac
re maiestas regia et mea humilitas, cum mendace scurra loquor,
15   regijs titulis uelato de rebus diuinis, quarum iniuriam aduersus
mendacia tueri, pertinet ad quemlibet christianum. Si stultus rex sic
regiae maiestatis obliuiscitur, ut mendacijs apertis in publicum audeat
prodire, idque dum sacra tractat, cur mihi non pulchrum sit,
An ex te nebulo mendacissime   mendacia eius rursus in os eius regerere.
20   ut si quam uoluptatem concepit aduersus
diuinam maiestatem mentiendo, eam amittat, ueritatem aduersus
suam maiestatem audiendo.

EXPENDE quaeso lector aequissimas causas: ex quibus hic uenera-
                             bilis pater fas esse censet, in regem, ueluti
Aegre fert Lutherus uel leuiter   suo iure scurrari. Quoniam rex ausus est
25   *sibi contradici*   dicere, Lutherum sibi ipsi esse contrarium:
id dictum regis Lutherus in duo partitur crimina, eademque ualde
capitalia. Alterum, quod rex hoc dixerit, nullo, ne exempli quidem
causa, prolato loco: ne ipsi locus esset defendendi sui. Qua in re quam
30   uanus et impudens sit uenerandus pater: tertio saltem iam prolato loco
uides. Alterum, quod rex eo dicto mentitur aduersus diuinam maiestatem. At quum nihil dixit aliud rex: nisi quod saepe iam probauit, deli-
rare, et assidue cum se ipso pugnare [E₁] Lutherum: necesse uides esse

---

3 impudenti] impudendi *L*

What is clearer than this passage, reader? What impudence the scoundrel has who is not ashamed to deny such clear evidence! What does he need to hear from these men who, after comparing these passages with the fellow's shameless lying, may consider the buffoon-ish words of the most deceitful buffoon when he plays the buffoon as   5 follows?

Seeing that he was pleased to play behind a mask with masked words in a matter so serious and sacred, a thing without precedent, I say, without a mask and openly, that this King Henry of   10 England is clearly lying and that by his lies he resembles a most frivolous buffoon more than a king. I, Luther, publicly accuse this virulent Thomist of this crime and, with my books as well as my readers as witnesses, convict him throughout the world. In this contest, let me be done   15 with the distinction between his royal majesty and my lowly estate; I am speaking with a lying buffoon veiled by kingly titles concerning divine matters which it is the duty of every Christian to defend against the injury of lies. If the foolish king so forgets his royal majesty that he dares to come out in public with manifest lies, and that while discuss-   20 ing sacred matters, why is it not fair for me to cast his lies back into his mouth, so that, if he has derived any pleasure from lying against the divine majesty, he may lose it by hearing the truth against his own majesty.   25

Luther's words

Did Paul use to be so biting, Luther?

Or from you, you lying scoundrel

Please consider carefully, reader, the very just causes for which this venerable father judges it lawful for him, as if in his own right, to play the buffoon against the king. Because the king has dared to say that Luther contra-dicts himself, Luther divides this statement   30 into two charges, both very capital. The one charge is that the king made this statement without producing any passage, not even for the sake of example, lest Luther have an opportunity of defending him-self. How deceitful and shameless the venerable father is in this matter you see at least from the third passage just presented.   35

It vexes Luther to be even slightly contradicted

The other charge is that by his statement the king lies against the divine majesty. But since the king has said nothing else but what he has already proved many times; namely, that Luther is stark mad and that he constantly contradicts himself, you necessarily see, reader,

lector: ut si hac in parte mentiatur princeps, aduersus maiestatem
dei: maiestas illa dei sit maiestas Lutheri. Neque enim de alio deo
loquutus est rex: itaque manifeste uides: ut hic reuerendus pater
aperte nobis renunciatur deus: et ipsius ore sua buccinatur apotheosis.

5   Imposterum ergo cauendum est: ne hunc nouum inferorum deum,
tam irritabilem irritemus: sed in os cerbereum coniectis offis, cone-

      Palinodia canenda regi   mur placare placentulis: et Stesichori more
                                     palinodiam canendo mitiget rex hoc pacto.

Diuus Lutherus non est sibi contrarius, non inconstans, non mendax,
10   non improbus, non uirulentus, non blasphemus in deum, non insanus,

      Iam arrige aures asine   non nebulo, non haereticus: sed ipsa fide
                                       fidelior, ipso honore honoratior, ipsa pru-

dentia prudentior, dei uero diuis ipsis reuerentior, ipso candore candi-
dior, ipsa probitate probior, ipso pudore pudentior, ipsa constantia
15   constantior, et ipsa ueritate ueracior. Cuius rei uel hoc satis documenti
prebet: quod tantis ampullis ausus est iactare, nullum locum suae repugnantiae protulisse regem, ne exempli quidem causa: ne ipsi daretur
occasio defendendi sui. Quum ipse non nesciat omnibus aperte clarere
regem protulisse loca multa: quorum nullum potens defendere,
20   coactus est, impudentissime dissimulare omnia, et negare producta.
Qua stolidissima negatione uictus est multo turpius: quam ulla unquam uinci confessione potuisset. Quemadmodum ergo Lutherus pro
se petebat lector: ut ex eo regis in se tractando fidem aestimares: quod
rex nullum proferat contrarietatis eius exemplum: ita nunc ego te
25   uicissim precor: ut Lutheri uanissi[E₁v]mam fidem, ex hoc tam

      Aequa postulatio   improbo meṅdatio, tam conuicta uanitate,
                               ex impudentia tam pudenda iudices:

certissimus quamcunque partem hominis excusseris: qualem hac una
in re perspexisti, talem in omnibus esse reperturum.

---

8 palinodiam] *corr. err. L*, palinodia *BR*

that if the prince is lying against the majesty of God in this matter, then that majesty of God is the majesty of Luther. The king has not spoken of any other god; and so you see clearly how this reverend father is openly proclaimed to us as a god, and with his own mouth trumpets his apotheosis.

In the future, therefore, we must avoid arousing this easily aroused new god of the underworld, but by casting honeyed cakes into his Cerberean mouth let us try to pacify him with pastries, and by singing a palinode in the Stesichorean manner let the king soothe him as follows: "The *Palinode to be sung by the king* divine Luther is not contradictory, not inconsistent, not a liar, not wicked, not virulent, not a blasphemer against God, not a raving madman, not a scoundrel, not a heretic; but he is more faithful than faith itself, *Ears erect now, ass* more honorable than honor itself, more prudent than prudence itself, more reverent toward God than the saints themselves, more sincere than sincerity itself, more upright than uprightness itself, more modest than modesty itself, more constant than constancy itself, and more truthful than truth itself." Sufficient proof of which is given even by the fact that he has dared to boast with such bombast that the king did not produce any contradictory passage of his, not even for the sake of example, lest he be given the opportunity of defending himself. Since he knows it is clearly evident to everyone that the king has produced many passages, he is forced, being powerless to defend any of them, to dissemble all of them most shamelessly and to deny that they have been produced. By this most stupid denial he is refuted much more shamefully than he could ever have been refuted by any confession. Therefore, reader, as Luther for his part seeks to have you appraise the trustworthiness of the king in dealing with him from the fact that the king supposedly produces no example of Luther's inconsistency, so now I beg of you in turn that you judge the utterly worthless *A fair demand* trustworthiness of Luther from such wicked dishonesty, such proven deceitfulness, such shameful shamelessness. I am utterly convinced that no matter what aspect of the man you examine, you will find him in every respect as you have perceived him to be in this one respect.

Probat Lutherum parum probe refellere notam
leuis inconstantiae, et crimen stolidae
maledicentiae. Cap. VII.

NAM OPERAE precium est uidere: quam pulchre illa ipsa defendat:
5 in quibus uideri uult, sibi ipsi non fuisse contrarius. Quum obiectum
esset ei: quod olim moderatius errasset, et de indulgentijs, et de
Romani pontificis potestate: postea uero, correptus ira atque inuidia,
sententiam mutasset in peius: homo suauis tuetur se Pauli exemplo
atque Augustini: ut cum illis nemo uitio uertat: quod a malo uertant
10   in bonum: stupidus plane fuerit: qui
  Sic Lutherus Paulum et Luthero non ducat laudi: quod ab sceler-
   Augustinum imitatur ato mutauit in sceleratius. Praesertim cum
constet omnibus, afflante Christo, charitatem illos, et pium erga deum
studium habuisse in consilio: Lutherum nemo nesciat, insufflante
15 diabolo, superbiam immanissimam, odium crudelissimum, inuidiam
         uirulentissimam, consiliarios omnium per-
   Lutheri consiliarii niciosissimos, adsciuisse sibi. Iis suasoribus
homo constanter inconstans (ut nemo repente fit deterrimus) a malo
primum in peius. post gradatim, iam a peiore profecit in pessimum.
20 Et tamen tanquam uia uersa, peruenisset ad optimum, in arduam
illam uirtutis arcem subuectus: inde scilicet sibi plaudit uni: et [E₂]
subiectum terrarum orbem despectans, miseris insultat mortalibus:
ac musto tantae felicitatis ebrius, tam procul e sublimi non sentit:
quantos in se risus e terris excitet eius furiosa stultitia. Quis enim non
25 rideat nebulonem miserrimum, tam furiosas efflantem glorias: quasi
sederet in Christi pectore: cum clausus iaceat in culo diaboli? Inde
crepat ac buccinat magnificas ipse de se uictorias. Inde sese iactat
          uicisse papam, episcopos, monachos, mon-
 Cursim perstringit impia quaedam iales, missas: ac sese probasse, nihil aliud
   ac stolida uerba Lutheri
30   illa esse omnia, quam mera portenta,

---

13 constet] *corr. err. L*, constat *BR* 19 peius.] peius, *BL*

He proves that Luther does not satisfactorily clear
himself of the reproach of capricious inconsistency
and the charge of stupid abuse. Chapter 7.

It is worth considering how skillfully he defends those very passages
in which he would have it appear that he has not been inconsistent. 5
Since it had been objected to him that his errors concerning indulgences and the power of the Roman pontiff had formerly not been so
extreme, but that later, swept along by anger and spite, he had
changed his opinion for the worse, the pleasant fellow defends himself
by the example of Paul and Augustine; since no one deems it a fault 10
in them that they turned from evil to good, one would be clearly
stupid not to consider it a matter of praise
for Luther that he has changed from *This is the way Luther imitates*
Paul and Augustine
vicious to more vicious. Especially since
everyone knows very well that the former, with Christ inspiring 15
them, had charity and pious zeal toward God as their purpose,
whereas no one does not know that Luther, with the devil inflating
him, has taken on the most monstrous pride, the most cruel hatred,
the most virulent spite, and the most
pernicious counsellors possible. Since no *Luther's counsellors* 20
one becomes worst all of a sudden, this constantly inconstant fellow
has advanced with the help of these advisers, first from bad to worse,
then, step by step, from worse to worst. And yet, as though he had
proceeded in the opposite direction and arrived at perfection, having
been carried aloft to that high peak of virtue, from that height he 25
naturally applauds himself alone; looking down on the world
lying below him, he scoffs at miserable mortals, and, drunk with the
new wine of such great felicity, he does not perceive from his distant
height how much laughter he evokes from the earth against himself
by his frenzied folly. 30
Who would not laugh at the most wretched scoundrel blasting out
such frenzied boasts, as though he reclined on the bosom of Christ,
whereas he lies confined within the arse-hole of the devil? Thence he
farts and trumpets his splendid victories. Thence he brags that he has
conquered the pope, bishops, monks, nuns, *He reproves in short order certain* 35
masses; and that he has proved all these *impious and doltish words of*
Luther
things to be nothing but sheer monstrosities,

idola, laruas, mendatia, et ipsissimam abominationem stantem in loco sancto: et quod furor sit sacrilegi populi, uelle per opera coram deo agere, et non sola fide. Inde se gloriatur ecclesiam totam calcare pedibus pediculosus fraterculus, et se futurum ursam in uia, et
5   leaenam in semita, atque hostem tam implacabilem: ut hostilem animum, exustus quoque (nam eum uitae finem ex haereseos conscientia sibi praesagit instare) sit conduplicaturus: et cineribus in mille maria proiectis, persecuturus et fatigaturus ecclesiam. Eodem
nimirum modo, quo sodales eius alij
Lutheri sodales
10   cacodaemones. Obsecro lector, quis uel ex his furiosi uerbis non uideat, furias omnes inferas, excusso homini cerebro, in uacuo sedem sibi fecisse capite? quae adeo dementant eum: ut sentire non sinant: quam ridiculum ac miserabilem toti orbi se Thrasonem prebeat. et quod ex eodem furoris fonte, unde ista
15   conuitia, iurgia, maledicta, blasphemiaeque promanant: effluit illa quoque Stygiae paludis unda: qua sibi uidetur homo demens, maledicentiae crimen eluere, luto nouae maledicentiae. Nam id erat alterum: quod obiectum [E₂v] sibi conatur hoc pacto propellere.

AD ALTERVM, inquit, uitium, nempe
Verba Lutheri
20   mordacitatis, quo me sugillat rex, respondeo. Primum ei probandum fuisse iniquam meam mordacitatem, et papatum innocentem esse. Alioqui cur Christus ipse, Mat.
xxiij. tanta uehementia scribas et phar-
Quam belle probat se non inique iseos mordet et hypocritas, caecos,
ecclesiae maledicere
25   stultos, plenos immunditia, hypocrisi, homicidas criminatur? Et Paulus, quoties uehemens est in concisiones (ut uocat ipse) suas et pseudapostolos, quos adulterantes et cauponantes uerbum dei, canes, dolosos operarios, apostolos Satanae, filios diaboli, plenos dolo et malitia, deceptores, uaniloquos, fascinatores
30   et circulatores uocat? An et hos Thomista
Horum tu Lutherus laruatus mecum accusabit inuidiae et superbiae?

---

28 dolosos operarios,] *L*, dolosos, operarios, *BR*   30 *gloss* Horum] *L*, horum *BR*

idols, phantoms, lies, and the very abomination itself standing in
the holy place; and that it is the madness of a sacrilegious people to
want to act in the sight of God by works and not by faith alone.
Thence this lousy friarlet boasts that he is trampling the whole
church under his feet, and that he will be a bear on the road and a 5
lioness in the path, and an enemy so implacable that even though
burned—for from his consciousness of heresy he has a presentiment
that such an end threatens his life—he will double his hostile soul,
and though his ashes are cast into a thousand seas, he will persecute
and harass the church. In the same way,   *Luther's cronies*   10
doubtless, as his cronies, the other caco-
daemons, have done.

Tell me, reader, who does not see, even from these words of the
madman, that all the infernal furies, after knocking out the fellow's
brains, have taken up residence in his empty noggin? These furies 15
drive him so mad that they do not allow him to perceive what a
ridiculous and wretched Thraso he makes of himself before the
whole world. This is because from that same font of frenzy which
pours out these railings, revilings, abusive language and blasphemies
there also flows forth that surge of the Stygian swamp with which 20
the crazy fellow thinks that he cleanses himself from the taint of
abusive language by the filth of further abusive language. For
this was the other objection brought up against him, which he tries to
throw off as follows.

To the other charge, he says, with which   *Luther's words*   25
the king beats me black and blue, namely,
that of biting language, I answer: first, that he should have proved
my biting language is unfair and the papacy innocent. Otherwise, why
did Christ Himself, in Matthew 23, use
such fiercely biting language against the   *How skillfully he proves that* 30
scribes and pharisees and accuse them as   *he does not unfairly abuse*
hypocrites, blind men, fools, men full   *the church*
of the uncleanness of hypocrisy, murderers? And Paul, how many
times he is vehement against what he calls mutilations, and
against false apostles whom he calls adulterators and hucksters of the 35
word of God, dogs, deceitful workers, apostles of Satan, sons of the
devil, men full of deceit and malice, *You belong to these men, Luther*
deceivers, vain babblers, bewitchers,
charlatans. Will the masked Thomist accuse these persons along with
me of spite and pride?   40

Et paulo post.

Rex uero tanquam obtinuisset papatum sanctum esse, plaustris uirulentiae et maledicentiae suae debacchatur in meam mordacitatem. Stolidum scilicet caput, quod abunde cognouit, papatum apud me
5   pro Antichristi regno haberi.

Quam aequa Lutherus exigat uide

VIDE amice lector, in quas angustias hic coniecit regem: cui priusquam Lutherum argueret maledicentiae, probandum uidelicet fuerit, papatum innocentem esse: nec debuit reuerendus
10   pater, quum uellet blasphemare papatum: probare prius papatum esse nocentem. Hanc ciuilem prudentiam, longo nimirum usu didicit, ex more et consuetudine iudiciorum. Vbi quisquis accusatur, aliquod patrasse facinus: illico probare iubetur non fecisse se. nec tam amens unquam quisquam fuit: ut ab illo, qui reum in ius protraxit: facti
15   probationes exegerit. Verum putat fortasse se reuerendus pater, accusatoris partibus aegregie fecisse satis: quod aliquot iam iurgiosis uoluminibus, probris, et conuitijs perfudit Romanae sedis antistites. quos omnes, nisi rex [E₃] uicissim doceat, fuisse prorsus impeccabiles: iniurius fuerit in reuerendum patrem: nisi permittat eum, citra ullam
20   maledicentiae culpam, non papis aliquot malis, sed ipsi papatui maledicere. Et tam aequus est ac peritus accusator, ebrius iste calumniator: ut quia papas aliquot accusauit: ideo petat a iudicibus: ut in eius gratiam dignentur, non illos, quos accusauit, papas, sed ipsum damnare papatum. tanquam si quis probet, aliquos esse malos
25   consules: obiurget consulatum: aut propter aliquos senatores improbos, senatum omnem postulet, ex omni prorsus urbe depelli: aut si quis denique propter aliquot Lutheri similes fraterculos, fratrum prorsus omnium totos condemnet ordines. Non potest quantumuis impudens Lutherus negare, bonos et sanctos fuisse romanos aliquot
30   pontifices: nec est propheta tantus: ut certo possit praedicere, bonos nunquam futuros: quando nec in praesentis antistitis, aut electionem sanctam, aut inculpatam uitam quicquam queat obijcere: et tamen ex aliquot, quos ipsi libet uocare malos papas: ipsum damnat

---

2 plaustris] *corr. err. L*, palustris *BR*   14 quisquam] *om. L*   21 Et tam] Etiam *L*

And shortly after.

> But the king, as though he had demonstrated that the papacy is holy,
> raves with cartloads of his own virulent abuse against my biting
> language; a blockhead, indeed, who knew full well that in my mind
> the papacy is regarded as the kingdom of Antichrist.   5

See, dear reader, into what straits this fellow has cast the king: before he accused Luther of abusive language, he should of *Note the justice of Luther's demands* course have proved that the papacy is innocent; but the reverend father was not required, when he wished to blaspheme the papacy, to prove 10 first that the papacy is wicked. This legal shrewdness he has undoubtedly learned, by long experience, from the practice and custom of the courts. There, whoever is accused of having committed some crime is ordered to prove on the spot that he did not do it. Nor has anyone ever been so senseless as to demand proof of the deed from the 15 person who brought the criminal to trial. But perhaps the reverend father thinks that he has carried out the role of accuser remarkably well since he has already in several brawling volumes doused the bishops of the Roman See with a flood of reproaches and revilings. Unless the king will in turn show that these bishops have all been utterly sinless, 20 he would be unjust toward the reverend father not to allow him, free of the charge of abusive language, to abuse, not several wicked popes, but the papacy itself.

This drunken pettifogger is so fair and experienced an accuser that because he has accused several popes, he asks the judges to please 25 condemn for his sake, not those popes whom he has accused, but the papacy itself. This is as though a man who should prove that some consuls are wicked would reproach the consulship as such; or because of some dishonest senators would demand that every senate should be driven out of every single city; or, finally, as if someone should, 30 because of several friarlets like Luther, condemn in their entirety all orders of friars.

Luther, however shameless, cannot deny that there have been some good and holy Roman pontiffs, nor is he such a great prophet that he can predict with certainty that there will never be any good pontiffs, 35 since he can bring no objection at all either against the holy election or the blameless life of the present pope; and yet because of several popes whom he chooses to call wicked he condemns the papacy itself.

papatum. Sic igitur arguit nobis reuerendus pater, frater, Martinus
Luther. Aliqui papae fuerunt mali: ergo papatus est malus. Quid, si
quis contra sic argumentetur a simili? Fratres aliquot Augustinenses
sunt haeretici, sediciosi, schismatici: ergo tota fraternitas Augustinen-
5 sium est haeretica, seditiosa, schismatica. Deinde subsumat sic: sed
reuerendus frater, pater, potator Lutherus, est frater augustinensis, et
suppositum fraternitatis illius: ergo frater, pater, potator Lutherus,
est schismaticus, et sediciosus haereticus. Quo pacto posset uestra
[E₃v] paternitas ex ista consequentia, quae tenet per regulam uestrae
10 paternitatis: effugere? Certe non habetis, nisi unum effugium: quod
ante hoc argumentum nobis factum, paternitas uestra uestro fugit ex
ordine. Verum tam argutas argutias, non intelligit, hebes uidelicet
Thomista rex: sed facile perpendit acutus Satanista Lutherus: quum
Christus, et Paulus, tam uehementer arguerint, alter scribas, et
15 phariseos, alter pseudapostolos: in quos potestatem habuerunt: ideo
sibi licere scilicet, pediculoso fraterculo, in reges, principes, pontifices,
et eorum praetextu, quos ipsi uocare libet pseudapostolos, in
apostolatum uerum, pro animi sui furiosa libidine quam libet
impotenter inuehi. Nec illum quicquam illa Christi uerba com-
20 mouent: quae furialem istam eius petulantiam coercere debuerant:
quibus populum iubet Christus: ut scribis ac phariseis quamquam
malis tamen propter Mosi cathedram obtemperarent: nec sedem
sanctam spernerent propter sessores indignos. Quin et Paulus ipse per
iniuriam percussus a pontifice, quum respondisset: Percutiet te deus
25 paries dealbate: admonitus esse pontificem, excusauit se: quod pro
malefacto regesserat maledictum. Et iste nebulo se gloriatur apostolis
Christi, atque ipsi propemodum Christo, parem: dum propter
hominum paucorum uulgo iactatum uitium, in sanctum debacchatur
officium: et Romani pontificis uere paternam charitatem, furiosis
30 iurgijs et conuitijs retaliat. Vides ergo lector candide, quam praeclare
se Lutherus hac in parte gesserit: qui sic ab se maledicentiae crimen,
et inconstantiae, depulit: ut non illa tantum duo sibi retinuerit: sed
impuden[E₄]tis etiam stultitiae ac furoris adiecerit: quae nunquam

---

3 simili] *corr. err. L,* simimili *BR*   11 nobis] *corr. err.,* nobis [*sic*] *BR,* vobis *L*
27 parem: dum] *corr. err.,* parem, dum *L,* parem. Dum *BR*   32 inconstantiae] *corr. err.*
L, constantiae *BR*

This is the way, then, in which the reverend father, Friar Martin Luther, argues with us: Some popes have been wicked; therefore, the papacy is wicked. What if someone in turn should thus argue from your example: Some Augustinian friars are heretical, seditious, schismatic; therefore, the whole Augustinian brotherhood is heretical, seditious, schismatic. Then let him subsume thus: But reverend friar, father, toper Luther is an Augustinian friar, and a counterfeit of that brotherhood; therefore, friar, father, toper Luther is a schismatic and seditious heretic. How could your paternity escape from this conclusion, which is valid according to the rule of your paternity? Surely you have but one escape: that before we make this argument, your paternity escape from the order.

Such subtle subtleties, however, the dimwitted Thomistic king naturally does not understand; but the diabolically clever Luther easily considers that since Christ and Paul so vehemently accused, the one the scribes and pharisees, the other the false apostles, over whom they had power, surely therefore it is permitted to him, a lousy friarlet, to inveigh as intemperately as he pleases against kings, princes, pontiffs, and, under the pretext of attacking those whom he pleases to call false apostles, against the true apostleship, according to the frenzied fancy of his mind. Nor do Christ's words, which should have restrained his frenzied insolence, make any impression on him—the words in which Christ orders the people to obey the scribes and pharisees, however evil, because of the chair of Moses, and not to scorn the holy chair because of its unworthy occupants. Indeed, even Paul himself, although when unjustly struck by the high priest he answered, "May God strike you down, you whitewashed wall," yet on being warned that it was the high priest, alleged as his excuse that he had retorted with abusive speech to an abusive deed. And this scoundrel boasts that he is equal to the apostles of Christ, and almost to Christ Himself, when because of a few men's faults noised about by the crowd he rages madly against the holy office and responds to the truly paternal charity of the Roman pontiff with frenzied railing and reviling.

You see, then, honest reader, how honorably Luther has conducted himself in this matter; he has thrown off from himself the reproach of abusive language and of inconsistency in such a way that he has not only retained those two reproaches for himself but has added also those of shameless folly and madness. From these reproaches he will

ita poterit eluere: quin gloriosum Lutheri nomen, infamatura
perpetuo, corporis ut ipse uaticinatur, exusti cineribus, et in mille
maria proiectis, inhaereant.

Refellit Lutheri generale responsum: quo contendit
5   nihil certo credendum esse: quod probari non
              possit euidente scriptura.
                        Cap. VIII.

HIS IGITVR criminibus sic ab eo depulsis, ut uentus caecias a se
depellit nubes: tandem, ueniamus autem nunc, inquit, ad ipsam rem.
10   Videlicet postquam ex octo et uiginti pagellis, paginas septem tam
                         exigui uoluminis, in tanta re partem
         Perittologia Lutheri
                         quartam ex confesso consumpsisset extra
rem. Tandem incipit iacere fundamentum: quod haberi uult aduersus
omnia: quae regius aduersus eum liber continet: generale responsum.
15   SED HIC uide lector, hominis de sua causa male conscij uane
uafrum consilium: quod et prodit diffidentiam: et inani succurrit
astutia. Audiuit noctem esse pro infirmis copijs: eoque pugnaturus
ipse, statim fugit in tenebras. Responsionem comminiscitur, omissis
                         omnibus, ad quae respondeat: tanquam ad
         Lutheri sciomachia
20   ea singulatim responsurus, in ea parte, qua
se respondere simulat particulariter. Et tamen quum eo uentum est:
uix uerbum ullum inuenias, cum fide recitatum: Firmissimum uero
quodque mira dissimulatione praeteritum. Sed in generali isto
responso praecipue, nulla prorsus re proposita, quam rex obiecerat:
25   conatur animum le[E₄v]ctoris dumtaxat in se conuertere: tanquam
futuro nemine, qui tam stolidam eius solertiam unquam deprehenderet. Nos ergo lector diuersa gradiemur uia. Nam serpentem istum
caecum, e tetris ac tenebrosis latibulis inuitum protrahemus in lucem:
                         et e libello principis excerpta quaedam
         Trade haec memoriae lector
30   isti responsioni praescribemus. Deinde

1-2 nomen, infamatura perpetuo, corporis] *corr. err.*, nomen infamatura, perpetuo corporis,
BR, nomen infamatura perpetuo corporis, *L*   12 consumpsisset] *corr. err. L*, consump-
sissit *BR*

never be able so to clear himself that they will not brand with lasting infamy the glorious name of Luther and cling to the ashes of his body when it has been burned, as he himself prophesies, even though these ashes be scattered into a thousand seas.

He refutes Luther's general response, in which the 5
latter argues that nothing is to be believed with
certainty which cannot be proved by clear
scripture. Chapter 8.

Having driven off these charges from himself as the northeast wind drives off clouds from itself, he finally says: "Let us now come to the 10 point at issue." That is, after he had by his own admission wasted on irrelevancies seven out of twenty-eight pages, or one fourth of so slight a work on *Luther's prolixity* such an important topic, he finally begins to lay the foundation, which he would have us consider the general response to all the arguments 15 contained in the king's book against him.

But here, reader, note the fruitlessly cunning counsel of a man with a bad conscience about his own case—a counsel that both betrays his uneasiness and tries to assist it with worthless craft. He has heard that night is for weak forces, and so, when about to fight, he immediately 20 escapes into darkness. He devises a response in which he leaves out all the objections that deserve a response, as though he were going to respond to them *Luther's sham battle* individually in that section of the work in which he pretends to respond to particular objections. And yet, when you come to that section, 25 you will find hardly any word quoted faithfully; all the strongest arguments, indeed, are passed over with shocking dissimulation. But in this general response especially, not a single objection of the king is brought forward; he tries to turn the mind of the reader only toward himself, as though no one would ever detect 30 such doltish adroitness. We shall therefore proceed by a different way, reader. We shall drag out this blind serpent, despite his resistance, from his disgusting and darksome hiding places into the light; and we shall preface this response of his *Keep this in mind, reader* with certain excerpts from the prince's 35

responsionem ipsam subiungemus. ut quum utrumque simul sub oculis habeas: facilius iudicare possis: hac speciosa responsione, quam uelut omnium responsionum summam posuit: aduersus illas obiectiones principis, ad quas respondere debuit: quam nihil omnino responderit.

5   PRIMVM in sacramento Eucharistiae.
Verba regis
              "Praeterea quod in canone missae quaedam uerba uelut a Christo prolata, recensent: quae nusquam in scriptura sacra leguntur. Et tamen non dubitatur, quin dixerit. Multa enim dicta sunt et facta per Christum: quae nullus
10 Euangelistarum complectitur. Sed quaedam recente memoria, eorum qui interfuerunt, uelut per manus deinceps tradita, ab ipso apostolorum tempore, ad nos usque peruenerunt. Lutherus non dubitat, Christum in coena dixisse: Haec quotiescunque feceritis: in mei memoriam facietis. atque haec usque adeo pro comperto habet,
15 Christi uerba fuisse: ut inde sumat argumentum, neminem cogi ad recipiendum sacramentum, sed rem cuiusque relictam arbitrio, tantum ad hoc astringi: ut quoties facimus: faciamus in memoriam
              Christi. Haec ergo uerba non legit apud
Eo solo Lutherum niti
quod damnat
              Euangelistas, in coena domini. Nam illic
20   nihil aliud legitur, quam, Hoc facite in mei commemorationem. Vbi ergo legit illa uerba: Haec quotiescunque feceritis: an [F₁] non in missa? Opinor certe non alibi. Nam apud apostolum alia sunt. Igitur qui tantum fidit: et utitur illis uerbis: quia reperit in canone: cur non pari fide suscipit eiusdem
25 uerba canonis: quibus missa oblatio dicitur et sacrificium."
     Et alibi de sacramento confirmationis.
"At quum loca quaedam Lutherus ipse commemorat: e quibus (quamquam id Lutherus irridet) habere non absurde potuerit sacramentum confirmationis, initium: cur tam maligne de tota iudicat
30 ecclesia: quasi temere sacramentum suscipiat: propterea quod in illis locis nullum legit uerbum promissionis? quasi nihil omnino promiserit, dixerit, fecerit Christus: quod non complectantur euangelistae. Hac ratione, si tantum Ioannis extaret euangelium: negaret institutionem

---

4 quas] *corr. err. L*, quae *BR*   5 Eucharistiae.] *L*, Eucharistiae, *BR*   6 Praeterea] *corr. err. L*, praeterea *BR*; *Pynson's quotation marks in B and R actually begin with* PRIMVM *in line 5*   25 sacrificium.] sacrificium? *L*   29 confirmationis, initium] confirmationis initium, *L*

book. Then we shall subjoin the response itself, so that when you have both together under your eyes you can more easily judge, by means of this specious response which he has set forth as the perfection of all responses against those objections of the prince to which he was obligated to respond, how he has responded nothing at all.   5

First, on the sacrament of the eucharist.

"Moreover, in the canon of the mass [the priests] repeat certain words as though *The king's words* spoken by Christ which are nowhere read in sacred scripture. And yet, there is no doubt that Christ did speak them. For many things   10 were said and done by Christ which none of the evangelists record. But certain details fresh in the memory of those who were present, having been handed on thereafter as it were from hand to hand since the very time of the apostles, have come down even to us. Luther does not doubt that Christ said at the last supper: 'As often as you do these   15 things you do them in remembrance of me.' He is so certain that these were Christ's words that from them he takes his argument that no one is compelled to receive the sacrament, but that the practice, having been left to the free choice of each individual, is circumscribed only by the condition that as often as we do it we   20 should do it in memory of Christ. He does *Luther relies solely on a procedure* not, therefore, read these words in the *which he condemns* evangelists' accounts of the supper of the Lord. There we read nothing else than: 'Do this in remembrance of me.' Where then does he read the words, 'As often as you do these things,' if not in the mass? I   25 certainly think not elsewhere. In the apostle's account the words are different. Therefore, since he trusts those words so much and uses them because he finds them in the canon, why does he not with equal trust accept the words of the same canon in which the mass is called an oblation and a sacrifice?"   30

And elsewhere concerning the sacrament of confirmation:

"But since Luther himself mentions certain passages out of which the sacrament of confirmation could not unreasonably take its origin (although he jeers at this), why does he, because he does not read in those passages any word of promise, so perversely judge the   35 whole church as if she were rashly accepting a sacrament? As if Christ promised, said, did nothing at all which the evangelists do not include. According to this reasoning, if only the gospel of John were extant, Luther would deny the institution of the sacrament of the

sacramenti in coena domini: de qua institutione nihil omnino praecipit
Ioannes: qui eodem dei consilio non tetigit istud: quo multa alia
praeterierunt omnes: quae fecit Iesus: quae (ut inquit Euangelista)
non sunt scripta in libro hoc: et quae totus mundus non posset capere.
5 Ex quibus nonnulla, per apostolorum ora fidelibus patefacta sunt, et
perpetua deinceps ecclesiae catholicae fide conseruata. Cui, quare

Vter uestrum hic triumphat
Luthere?

non debeas de quibusdam credere (quamquam non legantur in Euangelijs) quum
(ut Augustinus ait) nisi tradente ecclesia
10 scire non posses: quae sint euangelia? Quorum si nullum unquam
scriptum esset: maneret tamen euangelium scriptum in cordibus
fidelium: quod antiquius fuit omnium euangelistarum codicibus:
manerent sacramenta: quae et ipsa non dubito, euangelistarum libris
esse omnibus antiquiora: ne putet Lutherus efficax argumen[F₁v]tum
15 esse, frustra suscepti sacramenti: si non reperiat institutum in
euangelijs. Alioqui si nihil omnino recipiat: quod non tam aperte
legat in euangelio: ut tergeuersandi non sit locus: quomodo credit (si
modo credit: qui fere nihil credit) perpetuam Mariae uirginitatem?
De qua, adeo nihil inuenit in scripturis: ut Heluidius non aliunde
20 quam ex scripturarum uerbis, arripuerit ansam decernendi contrarium. Nec aliud opponitur illi, quam totius ecclesiae fides: quae
nusquam maior est aut fortior, quam in sacramentis. Ego certe
neminem esse puto: qui scintillam ullam habeat fidei: cui persuaderi
possit: quod Christus, qui pro Petro orauit: ne fides eius deficeret: qui
25 ecclesiam suam, supra firmam petram collocauit: pateretur eam, tot

Argumentum a probabili

seculis uniuersam corporalium rerum signis inanibus, erronea fiducia, uelut diuinis
sacramentis obstringi. Si nusquam inde quicquam legeretur: illi
tamen, uerbo mentem domini poterant enarrasse: qui praesentes
30 uersati sunt cum eo: de quibus sic ait: Vos testes estis: qui mecum ab
initio fuistis. Docere poterat, quid debebat fieri, paracletus ipse: de
quo dixit Christus: Quum autem uenerit paracletus, quem ego
mittam uobis, spiritus ueritatis: qui a patre procedit: ille testimonium

---

1 praecipit] *corr. err.*, praescribit *BRL*   14 putet] *corr. err. L*, putat *BR*

Lord's supper, about which institution John writes nothing at all; he
omitted to mention this by the same design of God by which all the
evangelists passed over many other things which Jesus did, which, as
the evangelist says, are not written in this book and which the whole
world could not contain. Of these events, some have been disclosed to   5
the faithful through the mouths of the apostles, and have been
preserved thereafter by the abiding faith of the catholic church. Why
should you not believe her regarding some truths although they are
not read in the gospels, since, as Augustine
says, you could not know which are the   *Which of you triumphs here,*   10
gospels except by the tradition of the   *Luther?*
church? If none of the gospels had ever been written, there would still
remain written in the hearts of the faithful the gospel which is more
ancient than the books of all the evangelists; there would remain the
sacraments which themselves are undoubtedly more ancient than all   15
the books of the evangelists, so that Luther may not think it an
effectual proof of the erroneous affirmation of a sacrament that he
does not discover its institution in the gospels.

"Otherwise, if he admits nothing at all but what he reads in the
gospel so clearly that there is no room for evasion, how is it that he   20
believes—if only he does believe it, since he believes scarcely anything—
the perpetual virginity of Mary? He will find nothing on this point
in the scriptures; so true is this that Helvidius seized the occasion of
decreeing the contrary from no other source than the words of the
scriptures. Nor is any other proof opposed to him than the faith of   25
the whole church, which is nowhere greater or stronger than in the
sacraments. I certainly think that no one who has the slightest spark of
faith can be persuaded that Christ, who prayed for Peter that his faith
would not fail, who established His church upon a firm rock, would
allow her to be universally bound for so   30
many ages by the empty signs of corporal   *Argument from probability*
things through an erroneous trust in them as though they were divine
sacraments. If nothing were read about them anywhere, nevertheless
those men who associated with the Lord personally could have
verbally conveyed His intention; of these men He said: 'You are the   35
witnesses who have been with me from the beginning.' The Paraclete
Himself could have taught what was to be done; of Him Christ said:
'But when the Paraclete shall have come, whom I shall send you, the
spirit of truth who proceeds from the Father, He will bear witness

perhibebit de me. Et rursus. Quum uenerit ille: qui est spiritus
ueritatis: uos ducet in omnem ueritatem. Non enim loquetur a semet
ipso: sed quaecumque audierit, loquetur: et quae futura sunt:
annunciabit uobis. Ecclesia ergo, quum tot et tales habuerit praecep-
5 tores, tot uiuos euangelistas, et spiritum illum: qui ueritatem inspirat: credetur temere instituisse sacramentum, et spem in signo
collocare nihili? Non credetur potius ab [F₂] apostolis: non credetur
potius a spiritu sancto didicisse?"
     Et paulo post de sacramento MATRIMONII.
10 "Negat usquam promissam esse gratiam. Negat usquam institutum
                       esse pro signo. Vnde haec nouit? Quia non
    Fortissimum argumentum Lutheri legitur inquit. O rationem fortem, et
multarum haeresum parentem. Ex hoc fonte uenenum hausit
Heluidius. Nullum sacramentum admittis: cuius institutionem non
15 legis in libro? Quem librum unquam scripsit ille: qui instituit omnia?
De quibusdam, inquis, credo euangelistis Christi. Cur ergo de quibusdam, Christi non credis ecclesiae? quam Christus omnibus praeponit
euangelistis: qui non nisi membra quaedam fuerunt ecclesiae.
                       Quamobrem si fidis uni: cur diffidis
    Talis est Lutherana dialectica
20   uniuersis? Si membro tribuis tantum: cur
toti nihil tribuis corpori? Ecclesia credit esse sacramentum: ecclesia
credit a deo institutum, a Christo traditum, traditum ab apostolis,
traditum a sanctis patribus, per manus deinceps, pro sacramento
traditum, ad nos peruenisse, pro sacramento, per nos tradendum
25 posteris, ad finem usque seculi, pro sacramento uenerandum. Hoc
ecclesia credit: et quod credit, dicit. Hoc inquam, tibi dicit eadem
ecclesia: quae tibi dicit euangelistas scripsisse euangelium. Nam
nisi ecclesia diceret euangelium Ioannis, Ioannis esse: nescires esse
Ioannis. Non enim adsedisti scribenti. Cur ergo non credis ecclesiae:
30 quum dicit, haec Christum fecisse, haec sacramenta instituisse, haec
apostolos tradidisse: quemadmodum credis ei: quum dicit haec
Euangelistam scripsisse?"
     AVDISTI lector unum aut alterum locum e multis: quae scripsit

concerning me.' And again: 'When He shall have come, who is the
spirit of truth, He will lead you into all truth. For He will not speak of
Himself, but whatever things He shall hear, He shall speak, and the
things which are to come He will reveal to you.' Since the church,
then, has had so many and such great teachers, so many living   5
evangelists, and that Spirit who inspires truth, shall we believe that
she has rashly instituted a sacrament and placed her hope in a
meaningless sign? Shall we not rather believe that she has learned
from the apostles; shall we not rather believe that she has learned
from the Holy Spirit?"   10
   And shortly after, concerning the sacrament of matrimony:
   "He denies that grace was anywhere promised. He denies that the
sacrament was anywhere instituted as a sign of grace. How does he
know this? 'Because,' he says, 'we do not
read of it.' O bold reason, and mother of *Luther's strongest argument*   15
many heresies. From this font Helvidius drew his venom. You admit
no sacrament unless you read of its institution in a book? What book
did He ever write who instituted all the sacraments? 'Concerning
some things,' you say, 'I believe Christ's evangelists.' Why then do
you not, concerning some things, believe Christ's church? Christ   20
placed her over all the evangelists, who were only certain members of
the church. Therefore, if you trust an in-
dividual member, why do you not trust *Such is the Lutheran dialectic*
the members taken as a whole? If you grant so much to a member,
why do you grant nothing to the whole body? The church believes   25
this is a sacrament; the church believes that, instituted by God,
passed on by Christ, passed on by the apostles, passed on by the holy
fathers, passed on thereafter from hand to hand as a sacrament, it has
reached us, to be passed on by us to later generations as a sacrament,
to be venerated until the end of the world as a sacrament. This the   30
church believes, and what she believes she declares. The same church
tells you this, I say, as tells you that the evangelists wrote the gospels.
If the church did not say that the gospel of John is John's, you would
not know that it is John's. For you were not sitting by him as he wrote
it. Why, then, do you not believe the church when she affirms that   35
Christ has done these things, that He has instituted these sacraments,
that the apostles have passed them on, just as you believe her when
she says that the evangelist wrote this gospel?"
   You have heard, reader, several passages from among many which

rex: in quibus ostendit multa dicta, facta, tra[F₂v]dita esse per
Christum: quae nullus Euangelistarum complectitur: quae nullis
apostolorum scriptis continentur: nulla scriptura commemorantur:
sed eorum recente memoria, qui interfuerunt: uelut per manus
5 deinceps tradita ab apostolorum tempore, ad nos usque peruenerunt:
et ecclesiam catholicam, in sacramentis et articulis fidei, a spiritu
sancto et doceri et gubernari. Atque ista probat, non ex eo solum,
quod alioqui absurdissima quaedam sequerentur: sed ex apertis
Euangelistarum uerbis, euidentibus etiam sacrarum literarum
10 testimonijs, et ipsius praeterea Christi. Quid ad haec Lutherus
obsecro? Semoue paulisper lector iurgia, cachinnos, risus, et conuitia:
Summa libelli Lutheri   nihil inuenies aliud, quam duas proposi-
                                 tiones has. Nihil uerum ac certum esse
praeter euidentes scripturas: caetera omnia traditiones esse hominum,
15 et cuiusque arbitrio relicta. Sed interim ad rationes, quas affert rex:
ad authoritatem euangelistarum, atque ipsius Christi, quibus probat
praeter ea, quae scripto comprehensa sunt, facta, tradita, praecepta
fuisse alia, quibus omnino responsum esse oportuit: nihil omnino
respondet. Quamobrem qui sic respondet: ut ea, quibus respondere
20 debuerat: omnia relinquat intacta: quid aliud facit: quam plane
fatetur se nihil habere, quod dicat. Quae res, quamquam per se
manifesta est: tamen quo fiat magis adhuc dilucida: Lutheri uerba
recensebimus: et nubes ac nebulas, quibus inuoluit se nebulo:
discutiemus.

25 *Lutheri uerba*   VENIAMVS autem nunc, inquit, ad
                                ipsam rem, et more Aristotelis, qui
Thomistarum deus est, Primo generaliter, deinde specialiter, de causis
istis disputemus. Summum generale et unicum robur Henricianae
sapientiae, in tam regio libello est, [F₃] nulla scripturae authoritas,
30   nulla ratio urgens, sed Thomistica illa
Imo tuum magis qui rationem   disputandi forma, Mihi sic uidetur, Ego
omnem refugias   sic sentio, Ego sic credo. Et ut hic mei
Amsdorfij recorder, sic disputat stolidus rex, sicut ille recitare solet,

the king has written, in which he points out that many things were said and done and taught by Christ which are not recorded by any of the evangelists, which are not contained in any writings of the apostles, not related in any scriptural text. Since his associates held these details fresh in their memory, however, they have been passed on successively, as though from hand to hand, since the time of the apostles and have come all the way down to us. He also shows that the catholic church, in its sacraments and articles of faith, is taught and governed by the Holy Spirit. Moreover, he proves these statements, not only from the argument that otherwise the most absurd results would follow, but from the clear words of the evangelists, as well as the evident testimony of sacred writings, in addition to that of Christ Himself. And what do you think Luther replies to these proofs? Set aside for a while, reader, the railing, the jeers, the mockery and the abuse; you will find nothing else but these *The sum of Luther's book* two propositions: that nothing is true and certain apart from evident scriptures; that all other traditions are the work of men and are left to the free choice of each individual. But in the meantime, to the reasons which the king presents; to the authority of the evangelists and of Christ Himself by which the king proves that other things were done, taught, and commanded besides those which were set down in writing; to these arguments which certainly should have received some answer, Luther answers nothing at all. Therefore, when he answers in such a way as to leave untouched the arguments which he should have answered, what else is he doing but admitting clearly that he has nothing to say?

Although this fact is clear in itself, still, that it may become yet clearer, we will review the words of Luther and disperse the clouds and fogs in which this fogbrain shrouds himself.

Let us come now, he says, to the point at *Luther's words* issue, and in the manner of Aristotle, who is the god of the Thomists, let us first generally, then specifically, dispute about these points. The foremost, general and sole strength of the Henrician wisdom in so regal a book is not any scriptural authority, not any compelling reason, but that *On the contrary, this applies* Thomistic mode of disputing: "It seems *more to you, since you* thus to me; I think thus; I believe thus." *flee all reason* If I may recall here my friend Amsdorf, the doltish king carries on his disputation just as the theologians

disputasse Lipsenses theologistas. Vbi quum respondens negasset assumptum opponenti, probabat idem opponens hoc modo. Oportet sic esse. Illo iterum negante, Denuo et ille, Et quomodo potest aliter esse? Oportet sic esse, pulcherrime, et Thomisticissime, quin et
5   Lipsicissime et Henricissime. Sic cum ego in meo libello hoc Thomisticum generale principium maxime impetijssem, et diuinas scripturas aduersus ritum, usum, consuetudinem, authoritatem hominum
    Noli mentiri bone uir   statuissem, Dominus noster rex nihilominus, pro sua Thomistica sapientia,
10   aliud nihil reddit, quam oportet sic esse, Vsus sic habet, Haec est longa consuetudo, Ego sic credo, Patres sic scripserunt, Ecclesia sic ordinauit. &c. Quod si iterum scripsero mille libros, et probauero per scripturas, usum et authoritatem hominum in rebus fidei nihil esse, facile erit et regi Thomistico, mille libris respondere, et omissis scrip-
15   turis a me inductis, semper iterare, Oportet sic esse, Vsus sic habet, Authoritas hominum sic dicit, atque aliud nihil. Si autem dixero,
    Certe improbior es unus   Vnde probas, usum et authoritatem
    omnibus   humanam ualere? respondet, Oportet
                                  sic esse, Mihi sic uidetur, Sic credo,
20   Nunquid tu doctior es unus omnibus.

QVIS NON rideat, hominis stolidissimi furiosum, et in ipsius ridiculum caput recidentem risum? quando regem nugatur nihil aliud afferre, quam Oportet sic esse: Vsus sic habet: Haec est longa consuetudo: Ego sic credo: Patres sic scripserunt: Ecclesia sic ordi-
25   nauit. Quum nemo nesciat, ipsum Lutherum scire, regem illorum omnium fere nihil dicere: sed ista dicere: Hoc probat ratio: hoc tradidit deus: hoc docuit spiritus sanctus: hoc dicit Euangelista: hoc dicit apostolus: hoc ipse dicit Christus. Ad quae omnia, [F₃v] nihil omnino dicit Lutherus.
30
    Verba Lutheri. Istud non   Intelligis ergo lector, stipites istos intrac-
    tacebit Parmeno   tabiles, hoc tantum quaerere, ut sibi solis
                                  credatur. Ego postulo, non mihi, sed
    apertis dei uerbis credi, illi postulant praerancidis et ueternosis sui cerebri uisionibus credi, contemptis uerbis dei. Neque enim ego uel

at Leipzig did theirs, according to the way Amsdorf likes to recount it.
There, when the respondent had denied the premise of his opponent,
the opponent proved the same premise by saying: "It should be so."
On the respondent's denying the premise a second time, the opponent
replied a second time: "and how can it be otherwise? It should be so." 5
Very neat, and very Thomistic; indeed, very Leipzigian and very
Henrician. In the same way, although I had in my book especially
attacked this Thomistic general principle and had set up the divine
scriptures against the observance, usage, custom and authority of
men, nevertheless our lord the king in his Thomistic wisdom replies 10
nothing but: "It should be so; usage has
it thus; the custom has long been thus; I   *Do not lie, my good man*
believe thus; the fathers have written thus; the Church has thus
ordained, etc." But if I would write another thousand books and
prove through the scriptures that the usage and authority of men are 15
of no validity in matters of faith, it will still be easy for this Thomistic
king to answer with a thousand books and, leaving out the scriptures
adduced by me, to keep repeating: "It should be so; usage has it thus;
the authority of men speaks thus," and not one other word. But if I
would say: "How do you prove that   20
usage and the authority of men have   *You, a single individual, are*
validity?" he answers: "It should be so;   *certainly more wicked than*
it seems thus to me; I believe thus. Are   *everyone*
you, a single individual, more learned than everyone?"

Who will not ridicule this archdolt's raving ridicule that recoils 25
back on his own ridiculous head? He talks nonsense, saying that the
king alleges no other argument but: "It should be so; usage has it
thus; the custom has long been thus; I believe thus; the fathers have
written thus; the Church has thus ordained." Everyone knows, however, that Luther himself knows that the king makes hardly any of 30
these statements, but that he does say: "Reason proves this; God has
revealed this; the Holy Spirit has taught this; the evangelist says this;
the apostle says this; Christ Himself says this." To all these arguments,
Luther says nothing at all.

You understand then, reader, that these   35
stubborn blockheads seek only to have   *Luther's words. Parmeno will*
themselves alone believed. I demand cre-   *not let this pass in silence*
dence not for myself but for the manifest words of God; they demand
credence for the hackneyed and insipid fantasies of their own brain,
while contemning the words of God. I have not denied the usage or 40

usum, uel authoritatem hominum in totum negaui, sed libera esse
uolo, et indifferentia, quaecunque extra scripturas sanctas scripta
sunt, tanquam articulos fidei necessarios fieri recuso ex hominum
uerbis. Tolerari uolo, quae bene dicuntur, et geruntur citra scripturae
5   testimonium. Tolerari autem libere. At trunci isti, nobis articulos fidei
faciunt, ex omni uerbo patrum, quod tantum abest, ut sancti
uoluerint suis scriptis tribui, ut nulla maiore blasphemia offendi
possint, quam dum per lethargicos Thomistas, eorum libera uerba, et
facta, in necessarios articulos, hoc est laqueos mendaces, in perniciem
10   animarum uertuntur.

ECCE lector, quam dilucide proponit Lutherus: quid postulemus
nos: quid ipse uicissim postulet. Nos uidelicet stipites intractabiles
postulamus: ut solis credatur nobis, hoc est solis Italis, Hispanis,
Anglis, Gallis, et denique solis omnibus: quaecunque Christi ecclesia,
15   aut hodie sit, aut usquam gentium, ullo unquam tempore, a Christo
passo fuerit. At Lutherus uir aequissimus, nihil postulat aliud
scilicet: quam ut credatur apertis scripturis: quarum apertissimas
passim trahit in dubium: et aperte torquet in haereses: et quum
urgetur, audet contemnere: quae paulo post faciemus ipsa luce
20   clariora. Sed interea uentilemus illud: quod ait, libera esse et indifferentia, quaecunque extra scripturas sanctas scripta sunt: et
tantum libere tolerari uult: quaecunque bene dicuntur aut geruntur,
citra scripturae testimonium. Istud Luthere si uerum est: cur ad illa
nihil respon[F₄]des omnia: quae tibi obiecit rex? e quibus nos plura
25   suis locis allaturi, pauca protulimus interim: quae quum supra
legerit: qui tuum generale responsum istud leget postea: neque
tactum tibi quicquam illorum uiderit: sed uelut surdo dicta, sic

Redactae in angustiam   praeterita, et dissimulata silentio, non
Lutheri copiae   poterit ignorare: quanta responsionis ido-
30   neae diffidentia, et uerae defensionis
inopia praeterieris. Sed nos quoniam te libenter ista fugere uidemus:
eadem, atque alia itidem talia, quae dolenter aspicis: iterum tibi
atque iterum ob oculos ingeremus. Igitur ut coepi dicere: si libere

26 leget postea:] *corr. err.*, leget postea, *L*, leget: postea *BR*   31 inopia praeterieris] *corr.*
err. L, inopia *om. BR*

the authority of men completely; I simply wish whatever has been
written outside the holy scriptures to be free and indifferent, as I refuse
to have necessary articles of faith fashioned from the words of men. I
wish praiseworthy words and deeds outside the testimony of scripture
to be tolerated, yet tolerated freely. But these lunkheads make articles   5
of faith for us out of every word of the fathers, a thing so far from what
the holy men wished to be attributed to their writings that no blasphemy could be more offensive to them than to have their free words
and deeds turned by the sluggish Thomists into necessary articles of
faith; that is, into lying snares for the destruction of souls.   10

Behold, reader, how clearly Luther presents what we demand and
what he for his part demands. We stubborn blockheads of course
demand that we alone be believed; that is, that only the Italians,
Spaniards, English, French, and finally all men alone should be
believed, wherever the church of Christ exists today or has ever   15
existed anywhere in the world since the death of Christ. But Luther,
an exceedingly just man, demands nothing else of course than that the
evident scriptures be believed, the most evident of which he everywhere drags into doubt and openly twists into heresies; and when
he finds them constricting, he dares to contemn them, as we will   20
later show clearer than day.

Meanwhile, however, let us winnow his statement that whatever is
written outside holy scripture is free and indifferent and that he simply
wishes whatever praiseworthy words and deeds have occurred apart
from the testimony of scripture to be tolerated freely. If this statement   25
is true, Luther, why do you answer nothing to all the objections
which the king brings up against you? We will present many of these
objections in their proper places. Meanwhile, we have cited a few
above. If anyone, after reading them, then reads this general response
of yours and sees that you have not touched on any one of these   30
objections but have passed them over and
concealed them by silence as though they   *Luther's resources reduced to*
were words spoken to a deaf man, he will   *straits*
not be able to ignore how great a fear of being unable to make a fitting
response and how complete a lack of a true defense lead you to pass over   35
these objections. Now since we see that you are glad to evade these passages, we shall again and again set them before you, together with
others like them which it pains you to see.

As I began to say, then, if everything must be held freely and

omnia habenda sint: et nihil certo credendum: quod non sit euidente
scriptura comprehensum (sic enim tu non uno loco confirmas) quid
sibi uult illud apostoli? State, et tenete traditiones: quas didicistis:
siue per sermonem, siue per epistolam nostram. Apostolus, ex aequo
5 seruari iubebat ea, quae per sermonem tradiderat, atque ea quae per
epistolas. Aliquid igitur traditum est non tanquam liberum, sed quod
Friget iam citra scripturam obligaret ecclesiam. Quid
ad hoc dicis Luthere? Quid ais ad illud
euangelistae? Multa facta sunt: quae non sunt scripta in libro hoc.
10 Quae quo minus ab alijs euangelistis dicas esse perscripta: negat ea
totum posse mundum comprehendere. Quid ergo dices, illa omnia
dumtaxat fuisse miracula? quorum etiam multa nesciri poterant
absque periculo fidei? Caeterum sacramenta, in quibus ecclesia non
posset absque peccato superstitionis errare: eorum nihil euangelistas
15 potuisse praetermittere? Istud ne possis praetendere: uides id: quod
etiam tibi rex opposuit, Euangelistam Ioannem non tradidisse
sacramentum eucharistiae. Quod si contendas, [F₄v] ideo non
tradidisse, quia alij Euangelistae comprehenderant: ea ratione potius
omisisset alia, minoris momenti: quae licet ab illis scripta, tamen ille
20 rursus commemorat. Quamobrem negari non poterit, etiam necessarios articulos inter ea fuisse: quae scripta non sunt: sed absque
scripto tradita sunt. Iam Paulus, quum Corinthijs eodem de sacramento scriberet: Ego, inquit, sicut accepi
Confutatur Lutherus euidenti a domino: sic et tradidi uobis. An non sine
scriptura
25 scripto, sicut accepit sine scripto: tradidit?
Imo, adeo nihil omnino tradidisset scripto, neque Corinthijs, neque
Romanis, neque alij cuiquam populo: si quo tempore scripsit:
licuisset alloqui coram. Quae res, si fors accidisset, istis omnibus
derogasses fidem: quae nunc in Paulinis leguntur epistolis. Cuius, ut
30 caeterorum quoque apostolorum, pleraeque desiderantur: et quae
supersunt, quaedam uertuntur perperam: quaedam uertuntur
ambigue: nec in gemina lingua usquequaque concordant exemplaria:

---

13 fidei?] *corr. err. L*, fidei. *BR*   20 Quamobrem] *L*, Qamobrem *BR*   31 supersunt,
quaedam uertuntur] *corr. err. L*, supersunt quaedam: uertuntur *BR*

nothing must be believed for certain that is not evidently included in scripture, for you assert this in several places, then what does the apostle mean when he says: "Stand firm and hold the traditions that you have learned whether by word or by letter of ours"? The apostle was commanding that what he had taught by word of mouth should 5
be preserved equally with what he had taught in writing. Something, then, was taught, not as though it were a matter of free choice, but as a matter which bound the church beyond scripture. What do you say to this, Luther? What do you say to the   *Now his wit droops*
following words of the evangelist: "Many   10
things were done which are not written in this book"? And to prevent you from saying that such incidents were written down by other evangelists, he says that the whole world could not contain them. Why then will you acknowledge as miracles only all those incidents of which many could have been unknown to us without peril to our 15
faith, but will not acknowledge that the apostles could have omitted to mention any of the sacraments, on which the church could not be in error without the sin of superstition? You see that the king, to prevent your pretending this, has also brought up the objection that the evangelist John did not record the sacrament of the eucharist. If 20
you should argue that he did not record it because the other evangelists had included it, then, according to that reasoning, he would rather have omitted other details of less importance which he again relates even though these evangelists had written them. Accordingly, it cannot be denied that even necessary articles of faith were among 25
those teachings which were not written down but were transmitted without writing.

Now Paul, in writing to the Corinthians   *Luther is refuted by a clear*
about this same sacrament, said: "I myself   *scriptural text*
have received from the Lord what I also   30
delivered to you." Did he not deliver this truth without writing as he received it without writing? In fact, he would have delivered nothing at all in writing, either to the Corinthians, or to the Romans, or to any other people, had he been able at the time that he wrote to speak to them personally. Had this perchance happened, you would have with- 35
drawn your faith from all those teachings which are now read in the Pauline epistles. Very many of his epistles, as of the other apostles also, are lost, and of those which are extant, some are translated incorrectly, some are translated ambiguously, the copies in the two

et de sensu certatur incessanter. Ita, quod solum agis: nunquam
deerit ansa negandi, quod uelit: asserendi, quod libet, illi, qui nihil
admiserit praeter euidentes scripturas. Quid illud quaeso, quam uim
habet, quod Christus dixit? Spiritus paracletus, quum uenerit: ille
5 ducet uos in omnem ueritatem. Non dixit, scribet uobis: aut foris ad
aurem loquetur uobis: sed ducet uos: hoc est, intus inclinabit uos: ac
flatu suo, corda uestra diriget in omnem ueritatem. At quos quaeso,
ducet spiritus sanctus in omnem ueritatem? an dumtaxat apostolos,
quibus tunc ore loquebatur Christus? Apostolis ergo dumtaxat et
10 illud dixit: Ego uobiscum sum usque ad consummationem seculi.
Quis ergo dubitat, illud [G_1] Christum dixisse de ecclesia: quod
spiritus sanctus eam ducturus esset in omnem ueritatem? Quid illi,
quibus dictum est: Ite, praedicate euangelium omni creaturae?
Euangelium praedicabant ex scripto? et nouam legem Christus sic
15 referri iussit in tabulas: aut in aes inscribi: ut si quid ibi non legeretur:
id protinus omne reijceretur pro nihilo? Ita ne dei uerbum, ab
apostolo quoque commemoratum, nihil mouet Lutherum: Ego dabo
leges meas in cordibus eorum: et in mentibus eorum superscribam
eas? Non dicit in lapide: non dicit in lignis: sed ut legem ueterem
20 scripsit in lapide primum, post in ligno, sed semper foris: sic nouam
intus dei digito scribet in libro cordis: ut quod minimo tempore
durauit in duriore materia: perpetuo durare faciat in mollissima. Sic
deo placuit ostendere potentiam suam. Saxeae tabulae protinus
fractae sunt: ligneae durauere diu: In corde uero quod scripsit:
25 durabit indelibile. In corde igitur, in
Euangelium in cordibus hominum ecclesia Christi, manet inscriptum uerum
certissime inscriptam euangelium Christi: quod ibi scriptum est
ante libros euangelistarum omnium. Ibi fidem suam sic inscripsit
deus: ut nulla possint haereticorum praestigia delere: quantumuis
30 afferant ex libris euangelij scripturas, in speciem uerae fidei contrarias. Hinc stetit Christi fides, aduersus hostem Christi matris,

---

20 primum, post in ligno, sed semper] *om. L*   23–24 Saxeae . . . diu] Priores saxeae
tabulae protinus fractae sunt: posteriores quidem diu durauere *L*

languages do not agree at all points, and there is incessant controversy about their meaning. Consequently, as to your sole argument, the man who admits nothing but the evident scriptures will never lack pretext for denying what he wishes and for asserting what he pleases.

Tell me, what is the significance of Christ's words: "When the 5
Spirit, the Paraclete, comes He will lead you into all truth"? He did not say, "He will write to you," or, "He will speak to you audibly," but, "He will lead you"; that is, He will incline you inwardly and by His inspiration direct your hearts into all truth. But tell me, whom will the Holy Spirit lead into all truth? Is it the apostles only, to whom 10
Christ was then speaking personally? Then it was to the apostles only that He also said: "I am with you even unto the consummation of the world." Who then will doubt that it was of the church that Christ said that the Holy Spirit would lead her into all truth?

What about the men to whom He said: "Go, preach the gospel to 15
every creature"? Were they accustomed to preach the gospel from a written text? Did Christ command the new law to be recorded on tablets or inscribed on bronze, so that whatever was not read there would be immediately and totally rejected as worthless? Is not Luther moved at all by the words of God, mentioned also by the 20
apostle: "I will put my laws upon their hearts and upon their minds I will write them"? He does not say, "on stone"; He does not say, "on tablets of wood"; but whereas He wrote the old law first on stone, later on wood, yet always externally, He will write the new law inwardly by the finger of God on the book of the heart. Thus what lasted 25
a very short time on harder material, He will cause to last forever on the most pliant material. It has pleased God in this way to manifest His power. The tablets made of rock were broken immediately; those of wood lasted a long time; but what He has written on the heart will last indelibly. 30

On the heart, therefore, in the church of Christ, there remains inscribed the true gospel of Christ which was written there before the books of all the evangelists.

The gospel is written with the greatest certainty in the hearts of men

There God has inscribed His faith so indelibly that no deceptions of 35
heretics can erase it, no matter how many scriptural texts they produce from the books of the gospel that are apparently contrary to the true faith. From this source the faith of Christ stood firm against Helvidius, the enemy of Christ's mother. From this source it stood

Heluidius. Arrius

Heluidium. Hinc stetit, aduersus hostem ipsius Christi, Arrium. Hinc stetit inuicta, aduersus plurimos haereticorum cuneos: qui eam eodem ariete oppugnabant: quo nunc Lutherus oppugnat: dum negarent publi-

5 cam ecclesiae fidem e scriptura probari: aut scripturas esse dicerent fidei contrarias. Sed ecclesia Christi non dubitauit: [G₁v] quicquid spiritus sanctus inspirauit ecclesiae, id esse procul dubio uerum: siue comprehensum id scriptura sit: siue nulla scriptura comprehensum. Imo si qua scriptura produceretur, in speciem contraria: eam fides in

10 corde praescripta docebat, non satis intellectam esse his: quibus ita uideretur: quum esset certissimum, neque Christum ecclesiae suae in articulis fidei deesse, neque spiritum dei ueracem sibi esse contrarium. Quod si adhuc stolide persistas in eo: ut contendas, nihil esse factum, ac traditum, praeter scripturas: nec te ab ea stultitia deducant ea

15 scripturarum testimonia: quae ex ipso regis libello memoraui: quibus tu nihil omnino respondisti: uellem saltem hoc expedias, quod in tota scriptura sacra, pater nusquam uocatur ingenitus, filius nusquam

Expedi si potes hunc nodum Luthere

homusios: nusquam satis aperte legitur, spiritus sanctus a patre filioque procedere:

20 Imo uero sancti spiritus deitatem ipsam, adeo contenderunt haeretici non satis elucere scripturis: ut eum quod testatur beatus Gregorius Nazanzenus, appellarint theon agrapton:

Theos agraptos

hoc est deum: de quo non scribitur: An tu idcirco uetabis, horum quicquam certo

25 credi: et liberum cuique statues: ut citra salutis suae dispendium, patrem neget ingenitum: filium neget homusion: spiritum sanctum neget ab utroque procedere? Quid responderes ad illud: quod de perpetua uirginitate Mariae, adeo nihil omnino reperitur in scriptura: ut magno labore probarit Hieronymus, scripturas non habere

30 contrarium. Quod, quamquam probauit aegregie: non tamen tam euidentibus probauit scripturis: ut sustulerit aduersario omnem facultatem disputandi. Sed totus articulus plane pendet ex ecclesiae fide: cui an in hoc [G₂] articulo pareas: uelim aperte respondeas. Ego

---

9 contraria] *L*, conrraria *BR*   16 saltem hoc expedias,] *corr. err. L*, hoc expedias *om. BR*
18 homusios] *corr. err. L*, homusion *BR*   21 contenderunt] *corr. err. L*, conteuderunt *BR*
22 Nazanzenus] Nazianzenus *L*

firm against Arius, the enemy of Christ Himself. From this source it stood invincible
against the massed troops of heretics who stormed it with the same
battering ram with which Luther is now storming it, when they
denied that the public faith of the church is proved from scripture, or   5
when they said that the scriptures were contrary to the faith. But the
church of Christ did not doubt that whatever the Holy Spirit inspired
in the church was undoubtedly true, whether it was contained in
scripture or not. Indeed, if any apparently contradictory scriptural
text was alleged, the faith written in her heart taught that this text   10
was insufficiently understood by those to whom it seemed so contradictory, since it was a matter of absolute certainty that Christ does not
fail His church on articles of faith, nor does the truthful Spirit of God
contradict Himself.

Helvidius. Arius

If you still stupidly persist, however, in arguing that nothing was   15
done or taught apart from the scriptures, and if you are not drawn
from this folly by those testimonies of the scriptures which I have recalled from the book of the king and to which you have answered
nothing at all, then I wish you would at least grant that in the whole
of sacred scripture the Father is nowhere called "unbegotten," the   20
Son is nowhere called "consubstantial,"
the Holy Spirit is nowhere very clearly
read to proceed from the Father and the
Son. In fact, the heretics argued so insistently that the divinity of
the Holy Spirit is not sufficiently clear from the scriptures that, as   25
Saint Gregory Nazianzen testifies, they
called Him *theos agraptos*; that is, "the God
of whom nothing is written." Will you on this account forbid that any
of these truths be believed for certain, and will you constitute them as
free to each individual, so that at the cost of his salvation a man may   30
deny that the Father is unbegotten, he may deny that the Son is
consubstantial, he may deny that the Holy Spirit proceeds from both?

*Untie this knot if you can,
Luther*

Theos agraptos

What would you answer to the fact that nothing at all is found in
scripture about the perpetual virginity of Mary, so that Jerome had
great difficulty in proving that the scriptures did not contradict this   35
truth? Although he did prove it conclusively, nevertheless he did not
prove it by means of such clear scriptural texts as to deprive his
opponent of every means of disputing it. The whole article clearly
depends on the faith of the church. I wish you would answer frankly

te interim credo, quamquam sis impius, tamen hac sane parte parere:
cui certe si esse putas parendum: aliquid admittis praeter scripturas,
contra fundamentum tuum. Quod si tam impius sis: ut deiparae
uirginis integritatem in dubium uocare non dubites: non eris tamen,
5 opinor, tam impudens: ut eucharistiae sacramentum, quod unum
fere nobis reliquisti: nec tamen a sceleratis digitis tuis impollutum:
nunc rursus neges esse sacramentum. Nec

Quin et Christum esse deum si   illud opinor, recantabis: Nullum sacra-
libeat, negabit   mentum esse, cuius nulla promissio gratiae,
10 nulla peccatorum remissio legitur in scriptura sacra: quod unicum
delegisti tibi, ad omnia sacramenta subuertenda fundamentum. Age
ergo Luthere: hac saltem parte consiste tecum: turpe tibi fuerit, hoc
principali fundamento depelli. Sceleratum negare esse sacramentum
eucharistiae.
15 At ex his duobus, rex effecit: ut alterum tibi fuerit, uelis nolis,
relinquendum. Recognosce nunc nebulo uerba illa principis: quorum
cauterio, meretriciae fronti tuae, eam stultitiae notam, atque impietatis inussit: quam nulla dissimulatione possis obtegere.

Verba regis   "NVNC quoniam ex ipsius Lutheri
20   fundamento probauimus, sacramenta,
quae credit Ecclesia, non aliunde quam a deo potuisse constitui:
etiam si nihil inde prorsus in scriptura legeretur: Videamus, an
scriptura tam nullam omnino mentionem faciat huius sacramenti.
Omnes una uoce fatentur, apostolos in coena domini ordinatos in
25 sacerdotes. Solus istud Lutherus negat: quum plane constet illic,
datam potestatem conficiendi corporis Christi: quod so[G₂v]lus
conficere sacerdos potest. At non est, inquit ille, sacramentum: quia
non fuit illis ulla promissa gratia. Vnde id nouit Lutherus? quia non
legitur, inquit. familiaris est ista Luthero consequentia: Non est in
30 euangelio scriptum: ergo non est a Christo factum: quam colligendi
formam, infirmat Euangelista: quum dicit: Multa facta sunt: quae
non sunt scripta in libro hoc. Sed tangemus tamen Lutherum ali-

Obserua Luthere   quanto propius. Eucharistiam concedit
                     esse sacramentum: quod nisi fateretur:

---

8 *gloss* libeat, negabit] *L*, libeat. negabit, *BR*   17 cauterio] *L*, cautererio *BR*
19 quoniam] *L*, quomiam *BR*   25 istud] *corr. err. L*, iste *BR*

whether you obey her in regard to this article. Although you may be impious, yet I believe that you surely do obey on this point. If you do think she must be obeyed, you are certainly admitting something besides the scriptures, and this is contrary to your fundamental principle. But if you should be so impious that you would not hesitate to cast doubt on the integrity of the Virgin Mother of God, I still do not think you will be so shameless as to deny again that the eucharist is a sacrament.
He will even deny that Christ is God, if he pleases
It is almost the only one you have left us, yet even it is not free from the defilement of your foul fingers. I do not suppose that you will retract your assertion that there is no sacrament where sacred scripture mentions no promise of grace and no remission of sins: this is the single fundamental principle which you have chosen for your work of destroying the sacraments. Come then, Luther, on this point at least be consistent. It will be disgraceful for you to be beaten back by means of this fundamental principle of yours; it will be impious to deny that the eucharist is a sacrament.

And yet the king has forced you, whether you wish it or not, to abandon one of these two alternatives. Recall now, you rascal, the words of the prince; with them as with a burning iron he has branded on your whorish face such a mark of stupidity and impiety that you cannot conceal it with any disguise.

"Now that we have proved according to Luther's own fundamental principle that
The king's words
the sacraments which the church believes could not have been instituted except by God, even though nothing at all were read about them in scripture, let us see whether scripture really does make no mention at all of this sacrament. All men unanimously admit that the apostles were ordained priests at the Lord's supper. Luther alone denies it, although it is quite evident from that passage that they were given the power of changing the bread into the Body of Christ, a thing which only a priest can effect. But it is not a sacrament, he says, because no grace was promised to them. How does Luther know this? Because we do not read it, he says. This line of reasoning is habitual with Luther: It is not written in the gospel; therefore it was not done by Christ. The evangelist invalidates this form of deduction when he says: 'Many things were done which are not written in this book.' But we will touch
Note this, Luther
Luther a little closer still. He grants that the eucharist is a sacrament.

insaniret. At ubi reperit in scriptura, promissam in illo sacramento gratiam? Nam ille nihil recipit nisi scripturas, et easdem claras.

Nusquam hoc sacramentum legitur esse signum gratiae suscipienti

Legatur locus de coena dominica: non reperiet apud ullum euangelistarum, in susceptione sacramenti promissam gratiam. Legitur a Christo dictum: Hic est sanguis meus noui testamenti: qui pro multis effundetur in remissionem peccatorum. Quibus uerbis significauit, semet in cruce per passionem redempturum genus humanum. Sed quum dixit ante: Hoc facite in meam commemorationem: nullam hoc facienti, id est sacerdoti consecranti, aut eucharistiam recipienti, gratiam ibi promittit: nullam peccatorum remissionem. At nec apostolus, in epistola ad Corinthios, quum interminetur male manducantibus iudicium, ullam mentionem facit de gratia bene manducantium. Quod si quid ex capite sexto Ioannis, gratiam promittat suscipienti sacramentum, carnis et sanguinis domini: ne id quidem iuuare Lutherum potest: quippe qui totum illud caput negat, ad eucharistiam quicquam pertinere. Videtis ergo, ut istam promissionem gratiae, quam pro totius sacramenti fundamen[G₃]to magnifice nobis in toto promisit opere: non potest in eo tueri sacramento: quod fere solum reliquit: nisi (quod necesse habet) praeter scripturae uerba recurrit ad ecclesiae fidem."

Imo malitia praepeditus nequit

AVDISTIN haec Luthere prius? an potando lethargum concepisti tantum: ut ista tibi ad aures inclamata, non audias? Cur ad haec obticuisti: quum tam magnifice te respondere iactites? Hoccine tibi dissimulandum fuit: quod unum tibi totum illud fundamentum destruit: quo uno, tu uideri uis, sacramenta destruxisse omnia? Nam quum hoc unum Babylonis tuae fundamentum ieceris, nullum sacramentum esse: cuius promissio gratiae non legeretur apertis scripturae testimonijs: ac nunc idem fundamentum iacias auctius, nihil omnino credendum pro certo: quod non aperte legatur in scriptura sacra, eo te compellit princeps: ut aut eucharistiae tibi sacramentum sit negandum: quod ante fere solum concessisti: aut si uelis in eo

---

4 *gloss* Nusquam hoc sacramentum] *corr. err.*, Nullum sacramentum *BR*, Nusquam sacramentum *L*   11 eucharistiam] *L*, euharistiam *BR*   21 solum] *L*, folum *BR* 32 sacra, eo] *corr. err.*, sacra. Eo *BR*, sacra: Eo *L*

If he did not admit this he would be mad. But where does he find in scripture that grace was promised in that sacrament? He accepts nothing but the scriptures, and evident ones at that. Let him read the passage about the Lord's supper; he will not find in any of the evangelists that grace is promised in the reception of the sacrament. The words of Christ read: 'This is my blood of the new covenant, which is being shed for many unto the forgiveness of sins.' By these words He signified that He would redeem the human race through His suffering on the cross. But when He said earlier: 'Do this in remembrance of me,' He did not in those words promise to the one who does it, that is, to the priest who consecrates or to the one who receives the eucharist, any grace, any remission of sins. But neither does the apostle, in the letter to the Corinthians when he threatens judgment to those who eat unworthily, make any mention of grace for those who eat worthily. And if anything from the sixth chapter of John promises grace to him who receives the sacrament of the Lord's flesh and blood, not even that can help Luther, since he says that that whole chapter has nothing at all to do with the eucharist. You see, then, how this promise of grace which he grandly proposed to us throughout his work as the sole basis of a sacrament cannot be maintained in the case of that sacrament which is almost the only one he has left us, unless, as is necessary, he has recourse beyond the words of scripture to the faith of the church."

Nowhere do we read that this sacrament is a sign of grace to the one who receives it

Have you heard these words before, Luther? Or have you become so drowsy from drinking that you do not hear them shouted into your ears? Why did you fall silent at them, though you boast that you answer so grandly? Did you have to conceal the fact that he completely destroyed the one fundamental principle by which you would seem to have destroyed all the sacraments? Since you laid down, as the one foundation for your *Babylon*, the assertion that there is no sacrament unless we read of a promise of grace in the evident testimony of scripture, and since you now enlarge that foundation by the assertion that nothing at all must be believed for certain which is not clearly read in holy scripture, the prince forces you to the point where you must either deny the sacrament of the eucharist, which before was the only one you admitted; or, if you

Rather, his spite obstructs his hearing

persistere: necesse tibi sit, ab hoc praeclaro fundamento desistere: et praeter scripturae sacrae uerba, confugere ad publicam fidem ecclesiae (ut ipse uocas) papisticae.

Refellit illud, quod si quid praeter scripturam uerum
5   sit, certum tamen esse non possit: et periculum
fore, ne uana pro ueris ueniant in articulos
fidei, et traditiones hominum pro
traditionibus dei. Cap. IX.

QVID RESPONDET frater, pater, potator, ad haec? ebrius dormit:
10   sepultus est in scypho: non [G₃v] audit. An postquam illud uillum edormierit: tum e crapula surgens istud nobis eructabit? Quod quanquam uera sunt aliqua, nullis adhuc scripturis comprehensa: certa tamen esse, et comperta non possunt? Nam quum plurima liceat confingere: dicet uidelicet, quod uera illa ab ijs, quae fingerentur:
15   nulla possemus nota distinguere. Ex quo secuturum, dicet illud absurdum: ut omnes humanas traditiones amplectamur pro traditionibus dei. Si istud uerum est: homo cautus Lutherus est: sed parum cautus Euangelista: parum cautus apostolus: qui quum quaedam (ut ostendimus) non complecterentur scripto: quae necesse fuit ab
20   ecclesia seruari: non uiderunt, aut illa posse aliquando excidere e memoria, aut eorum praetextu, etiam alia, quae ab humana uanitate proficiscerentur, authoritatem sibi posse comparare: quasi simili modo traderentur a deo. Et tamen ita sibi fortis uidetur hac in parte Lutherus: ut centies illud exclamet nobis: nihil esse pro certo et
25   indubitato tenendum: quod non ex scripturis eluceat, et eisdem etiam manifestis, atque euidentibus. Alioqui censet necessario consequi: ut per errorem obliget ecclesia sese,
Num formidolosus es mi homo
ad uana signa, pro ueris sacramentis: dum traditiones hominum putet esse traditiones dei: Aut ex ambiguo
30   scripturae textu, aduersus ueritatem falso adhaereat sensui. Nam hunc errorem censet Lutherus inuincibilem. Hoc loco opponere

---

6 articulos] *corr. err. L*, articulis *BR*   11–12 Quod quanquam] *corr. err. L*, Quanquam *BR*
14 dicet] *corr. err. L*, dicit *BR*   15 secuturum] *corr. err. L*, sequiturum *BR*; dicet] *corr. err. L*, dicit *BR*   22 authoritatem] *L*, authoriratem *BR*

choose to persist in that belief, withdraw by necessity from this infamous foundation and flee for refuge beyond the words of holy scripture to the public faith of the church which you call papist.

He refutes the assertion that although something may be true apart from scripture yet it cannot be certain, and there will be the danger that false teachings will pass as truths into articles of faith and that traditions of men will pass for the traditions of God. Chapter 9.

What does the friar, father, toper answer to these arguments? The sot is asleep; he is buried in his cups; he does not hear. When he has slept off that mouthful, will he then, rising from his drunken stupor, belch at us this objection: that although some things are true which still are not contained in any scriptures, yet they cannot be known for certain? Since man is free to fashion very many traditions, he will doubtless say that we have no sign by which to distinguish the things that are true from those that are of our own fashioning. From this, he says, will follow the absurd conclusion that we will embrace all human traditions as the traditions of God. If this objection is true, Luther is a cautious fellow, but the evangelist was not cautious enough, the apostle was not cautious enough, for they did not see that since certain truths which the church needed to preserve were not recorded in writing, as we have shown, either those truths could eventually slip from memory, or under their guise other teachings proceeding from human falsehood could arrogate authority to themselves as though they were likewise handed down by God. And yet Luther thinks himself so strong on this point that he shouts to us a hundred times: "Nothing must be held as certain and undoubted which does not appear in the scriptures, and clear and evident scriptures at that." Otherwise he considers it a necessary con-sequence that the church will erroneously *Are you fearful, my dear fellow?* bind herself to empty signs in place of true sacraments until she thinks that the traditions of men are the traditions of God, or, in the case of an ambiguous scriptural text, she adheres to the false as against the true interpretation. Luther considers this error to be inescapable.

aduersus utrunque possemus, non unum quempiam ex antiquis
patribus, aut unum locum e scriptura sacra: nisi potius uisum esset

Nihil est hoc uero uerius
obijcere Luthero, unum illum, quem unum
omnibus praefert patribus, omnibus prae-
5 fert Euangelistis, Lu[G₄]therum. Quem ipsum non tam obijciemus
nos: quam prolato loco, lectorem commonebimus, a rege iam olim

Ita solet uincere Luther
obiectum. Et quoniam refelli non potuit
a Luthero, per dissimulationem praeter-
missum silentio. Sic igitur habet rex in sacramento ordinis.

10
Verba regis. Quibus confutat
Lutherum ex uerbis ipsius Lutheri
"SED VELVT ineuitabile telum pro-
mit: quod hoc sacramentum, nullam
habet promissionem gratiae ullibi (ut
inquit) positam: cuius sacramenti, uel uerbo meminisse negat totum
nouum testamentum: et ridiculum (ait) asserere pro sacramento dei:
15 quod a deo institutum nusquam potest monstrari. Nec licet (inquit)
astruere aliquod diuinitus ordinatum: quod diuinitus ordinatum non
est: sed conandum est: ut omnia nobis claris (inquit) scripturis sint
firmata. Vtrum in nouo testamento nulla prorsus fiat huius sacramenti mentio: post excutiemus. Interim sic agam cum illo: tanquam
20 nulla prorsus mentio fieret. Nam eodem telo se sperat omnia ferme
sacramenta perfodere. Aduersus quod telum, ego in scutum mihi
idipsum ferrum conijciam: quod Lutherus ipse fatetur impenitrabile.
Sic enim se habent ipsius uerba.

25
Verba Lutheri in captiuitate
Babylonica ex quibus manifeste
reuincitur
Hoc sane habet ecclesia, quod potest
discernere uerbum dei a uerbis hominum,
sicut Augustinus confitetur se euangelio
credidisse, motum authoritate ecclesiae,
quae hoc esse euangelium praedicabat.

Igitur quum istud habet (ut Lutherus fatetur) ecclesia: quod uer-
30 bum dei discernere potest a uerbis hominum: certum est istud non
aliunde habere, quam a deo. Nec ob aliam causam, quam ne in his
erraret Ecclesia: in quibus non erratum esse oporteat. Sequitur igitur

---

4 praefert] *corr. err. L*, prfertae *BR*   9 ordinis.] Ordinis. *L*, ordinis, *BR*   11 *gloss* regis.]
Regis. *L*, regis *BR*   17 scripturis] *L*, scripcuris *BR*   23 habent] *corr. err. L*, hobent *BR*
28 euangelium] Euangelium *L*, euaugelium *BR*   29 ecclesia] *corr. err.*, Ecclesia *BRL*
29–30 uerbum dei] *corr. err.*, verbum Dei *L*, dei *om. BR*

At this point we could have countered either of these suggestions by quoting several of the ancient fathers or several passages from sacred scripture, except that it seemed better to set against Luther the one and only person whom he esteems more highly than all the fathers, whom he esteems more than all the evangelists; namely, Luther. Rather than cite him directly by way of objection, we shall quote a passage reminding the reader of an objection already raised by the king, which, since Luther could not refute it, he deceitfully passed over in silence. This, then, is what the king says on the sacrament of orders.

Nothing is truer than this truth 5

This is the way Luther usually conquers 10

"But he advances as an inescapable weapon the argument that nowhere is a promise of grace recorded for this sacrament. He says that the whole New Testament makes not one mention of this sacrament. And it is ridiculous, he says, to allege as a sacrament of God what can nowhere be shown to have been instituted by God. We are not permitted, he says, to ascribe to divine ordinance anything which has not been divinely ordained, but he says we must try to confirm everything by clear scriptural texts. Later we will investigate whether the New Testament makes no mention at all of this sacrament. Meanwhile, I shall deal with him as though no mention at all were made, since it is with this same weapon that he hopes to spear almost all the sacraments. Against this weapon I shall take up as my shield the very arms which Luther himself admits are impenetrable. For these are his words:

The king's words, by which he refutes Luther from Luther's own words 15

20

25

The church undoubtedly has the power to distinguish the word of God from the words of men, as Saint Augustine confesses in saying that he believed in the gospel moved by the authority of the church which proclaimed that this was the gospel.

Luther's words in the Babylonian Captivity, from which he is clearly refuted 30

"Since the church, then, as Luther admits, has the power to distinguish the word of God from the words of men, it is certain that she has this power from no other source but God, and for no other cause than that the church may not err in those matters in which errors should not be made. Therefore it follows from this foundation which

35

ex hoc fundamento: quod nobis substrauit Lutherus: ut ecclesia
[G₄v] habeat a deo, non id solum, quod concedit Lutherus: dis-
cretionem uerborum dei, a uerbis hominum: sed etiam discernendi
facultatem, qua in scripturis diuinis, diuinum sensum ab humano
5 discriminet. Alioqui enim, quid profuerit: si Ecclesia (deo docente)
scripturam ueram discernat a falsa: et in scriptura uera, falsum
sensum non discernat a uero? Denique eadem ratione, et istud
sequitur: ut et in his quae non scribuntur: ecclesiam suam doceat
deus: ne per errorem possit, falsa pro ueris amplecti: quum ex ea re
10 non minus impendeat periculi: quam si uel scripturas hominum
teneat pro uerbis dei: uel e ueris dei uerbis, falsum eliciat sensum:
praesertim si falsa suscipiat sacramenta pro ueris, et traditiones
hominum pro traditionibus dei, imo non traditiones hominum, sed
figmenta diaboli: si suam spem in fictis ac uanis corporalium rerum
15 signis (quemadmodum magi faciunt) ecclesia Christi, uelut in
Christi sacramentis collocet. Liquet ergo
Lutherus suo telo misere   manifeste ex eo, quod fatetur Lutherus,
confossus   ecclesiam hoc habere: ut uerba dei discernat a uerbis hominum: Hoc quoque non minus habere, ut tradi-
20 tiones dei discernat a traditionibus hominum: quum alioqui, utrobique possit ex aequo uitandus error exoriri: nec id agat Christus: ne
ecclesia sua hoc aut illo erret modo: sed ne erret ullo. Errare uero
maiore cum iniuria Christi non possit: quam si fiduciam in illo
ponendam solo, ponat in signis nulla prorsus fultis gratia, sed omni
25 bono fidei uacuis atque inanibus. Non igitur errare potest ecclesia, in
suscipiendis sacramentis fidei: non magis inquam quam errare potest
in suscipiendis (qua in re ecclesiam errare non posse fatetur Lu[H₁]-
therus ipse) scripturis. Quae res, si se haberet aliter: multa sequerentur absurda. Sed hoc in primis, quo nihil potest esse absurdius: quod
30 plaeraque omnia fidei christianae dogmata, tot stabilita seculis, ad
succrescentium haereticorum libidinem, denuo reuocarentur in
dubium. Nam si nihil haberi pro certo debet: nisi quod scripturis et
ijsdem (ut Lutherus ait) claris, firmatum est: non solum non assere-
mus diuae Mariae uirginitatem perpetuam: sed et inexhausta

---

14 corporalium rerum] *corr. err. L*, rerum *om. BR*   15 in] *corr. err. L*, ia *BR*   16 *gloss*
suo] *L*, fuo *BR*   28 scripturis] *BL*, scipturis *R*   29 potest] *BL*, poetst *R*   30 plaera-
que] pleraque *BL*   33–34 asseremus] *B corr. err. L*, asseramus *R*

Luther has laid for us that the church has from God not only that power which Luther grants, the distinguishing of the word of God from the words of men, but also the ability to distinguish the divine from the human meaning in the divine scriptures. For otherwise, of what use would it be for the church, with God teaching her, to distinguish the true from the false scripture, if in the true scripture she should not distinguish the false from the true meaning? Then, by the same reasoning, it also follows that even in those matters which are not written down, God teaches His church so that she cannot erroneously embrace the false for the true, since such a possibility would threaten no less danger than if she either considered the writings of men as the words of God or derived a false meaning from the true words of God. This would be the case especially if she should accept false sacraments as true and the traditions of men as the traditions of God; rather, not the traditions of men, but the fabrications of the devil, if the church of Christ should, as magicians do, place her hope in fictitious and worthless signs of bodily things as though they were the sacraments of Christ.

"It is manifestly clear, then, from Luther's admitting that the church has the power to distinguish the words of God from the words of men, that she has no less the power also to distinguish the traditions of God from the traditions of men, since otherwise one or the other error could arise, either of which is equally to be avoided, and since Christ's concern is not that the church should not err in one or the other manner, but that she should not err in any manner. No error could be more offensive to Christ, however, than if the faith which the church should place in Him alone should be placed by her in signs supported by no grace at all but void and empty of all the blessing of faith. The church cannot err, therefore, in accepting the sacraments of faith; no more, I say, than she can err in accepting the scriptures, in which matter even Luther confesses that the church cannot err. If the opposite were true, many absurd consequences would follow, but above all this one, than which nothing can be more absurd, that all the teachings of the Christian faith, established throughout so many ages, would be called into doubt again at the whim of the growing number of heretics. If nothing should be held as certain except what is confirmed by the scriptures, and evident ones at that, as Luther says, not only will we not defend the perpetual

Luther miserably run through by his own weapon

suggeretur fidei oppugnandae materia: si cui unquam libeat aut
nouas excitare sectas, aut resuscitare sepultas. Nam paucissimi fuerunt
haeretici: qui non receperint scripturas: sed omnes fere ex eo, sua
statuebant dogmata: quod aut ea contenderent esse firmata scrip-
5 turis: aut quum illis uiderentur rationi consentanea, contrarium non
definiri scripturis. Quoniam ea, quae proponebantur aduersus suam
sectam, aliter contendebant intelligi: quam orthodoxa intelligebat
ecclesia: et ne clara dici possent, aut alio excogitato sensu, aut prolatis aliunde ex eadem scriptura locis, in speciem ualde contrarijs,
10 omnia sic turbarunt: ut uiderentur ambigua. Ita aduersus Arrium
nisi publica stetisset fides ecclesiae: haud scio: an defuisset unquam
de scripturis disputandi materia."

NON dubito lector: quin, dum legis haec: et admireris et detes-
teris istam nebulonis improbam atque impudentem dissimulationem:
15 qui tanquam surdus eum cantum praetereat: quem nemo non sentit
auriculas eius asininas tanto cum doloris sensu penetrasse: ut nec
ebrius quidem sensum possit eius doloris excutere. Quod enim telum
cadere potuit in Lutherum uiolentius: quam quo factum est: ut suis
ipsius [H₁v] uerbis uulneratus et confossus iaceat. Raro uerum dicit:
20   et tamen id ipsum, quod dicit uerum,
Hic succurrite combiboni uestro   falsitates, quas astruit ipse, conuincit. Quid
Lutheri sodalicium
hic Luthere comminisceris effugij? qua
stolida stropha laborabis elabi? Conuoca nebulonum, potatorum,
scortatorum, sicariorum senatum: explicent te ab hoc labyrintho:
25 suadeant, ut quod saepe fecisti, facias denuo reuoces atque recantes:
si quam unquam syllabam dixisti bene. Clama poenitere te: quod hoc
fassus es: ecclesiae datum, ut scripturas dei discernat a scriptis
hominum. Quod si feceris, id quod plane facies aliquando: simul
concedas oportet, incertum atque inualidum esse illud ipsum: quod
30 ore tantum clamas, corde nihil credis, euangelium. Sin non illud

---

4 firmata] *B*, firma *RL*   21 astruit ipse, conuincit] astruit, ipse conuincit *B*
25 quod . . . denuo] *corr. err.*, quod . . . denuo, *L*, (quod . . . denuo) *BR*

virginity of holy Mary, but also anyone who ever chooses either to bring to life new sects or to revive those that have been buried will be presented with inexhaustible material for attacking the faith. There have been very few heretics who have not accepted the scriptures, but almost all of them established their teachings on the argument either that their doctrines were confirmed by the scriptures, or, when their doctrines seemed conformable to reason, that the contrary was not defined by the scriptures, since they argued that the passages which were brought forward in opposition to their sect were being interpreted otherwise than the orthodox church was accustomed to interpret them. Moreover, to prevent these passages from being called evident, they either contrived another meaning, or they produced from another part of the same scripture passages which were apparently very contrary to the first, and thus kept confusing the whole matter so that it would appear ambiguous. Thus, if the public faith of the church had not stood firm against Arius, I do not know whether he would ever have lacked matter for disputing about the scriptures."

I have no doubt, reader, that as you read these words you experience both astonishment and abhorrence for the wicked and shameless dissimulation of this scoundrel, who like a deaf man ignores that warning which everyone realizes has penetrated his ass-ears so painfully that not even a drunken person could shake off that feeling of pain. For what weapon could have struck Luther more forcibly than that which caused him to lie wounded and transfixed by his own words? He rarely speaks the truth; yet the very thing which he does say truly refutes the *Here, brotherhood of Luther, run to help your pot-brother* falsehoods which he has added to it. What escape will you contrive here, Luther? With what doltish device will you labor to escape? Summon your assembly of scoundrels, topers, whore-masters, assassins; let them lead you out of this labyrinth; let them persuade you to do once more what you have so often done: revoke and recall any syllable which you have ever spoken well. Shout that you regret having admitted that the church has been given the power to distinguish the scriptures of God from the writings of men. But if you do this, and it is clear that you will eventually come round to it, you should at the same time grant that the gospel itself is uncertain and of no authority; the gospel about which you shout so loudly with your mouth, but which you do not at all believe in your heart. Should you not retract, however, but concede that the church

reuoces: sed ecclesiam concedas, hoc habere datum a deo: ut non
possit errare, in discernendis dei uerbis a uerbis hominum: nec eius
aliam possis assignare causam, quam
Quid hic habes, quod obgannias
Luthere?
peculiarem dei curam: qua sic gubernat
5   ecclesiam: ut in rebus tam magni momenti
eam nolit errare, necesse est, illud concedas etiam: quod deus
ecclesiae non deerit in scripturis intelligendis, aut dinoscendis traditionibus, sicubi tale urgeat periculum ex ignorantia: quale fuerit: si
permittatur errare in necessarijs articulis fidei, uel sacramentis: in
10 quibus errare, nihil est aliud, quam fidem subtractam deo, non in
homine ponere, sed in signis inanibus collocare: quod prope deterius
est, quam uitulum adorare conflatilem. Qua in re, quantum absit:
ut Christus desit ecclesiae: ipse testatur, dicens: Ego uobiscum sum
usque ad finem seculi.

15   Ostendit Lutherum tergiuersari stolide, conantem [H₂]
controuersum facere, quae sit ecclesia catholica: et
simul respondetur ad inanes eius logos: quibus
nugatur in Ambrosium Catharinum de
eadem ecclesia. Cap. X.

20 SED HIC fortassis, ut est impudens: quaestionem faciet (id quod
saepe facit) de ecclesia: et totam ecclesiam, quam appellat papisticam: negabit esse ecclesiam illam Christi. Qua in re, ne quid deesset:
nebulonem istum et uere et acute prudentissimus princeps attingit.
Nam in sacramento ordinis, quum recitas-
Verba Lutheri
25   set haec uerba Lutheri, ex captiuitate
Babylonica: Hoc sacramentum ordinis ecclesia Christi ignorat,
inuentumque est ab ecclesia papae: subiungit princeps.
"HAEC pauca uerba, non paruum
Verba regis
habent et falsitatis et absurditatis aceruum.
30 Nam et ecclesiam papae discernit ab ecclesia Christi: quum papa sit
eiusdem ecclesiae pontifex, cuius et
Redarguitur Lutherus mendatii
Christus. Ait ecclesiam inuenisse: quod

6 quod] *B corr. err. L, om. R*   7 dinoscendis] dignoscendis *B*   16–19 et simul respondetur ad inanes eius logos: quibus nugatur in Ambrosium Catharinum de eadem ecclesia]
om. B   31 *gloss* mendatii] mendacij *L*, mendatij *B*

has been given by God the power of inerrancy in distinguishing the words of God from the words of men, and if you cannot assign any other source of this power than the partic-
ular care with which God so governs the *What do you have to snarl here, Luther?* church that He does not consent to her 5 erring in matters of such great importance, then it is necessary for you to concede also that God will never fail His church in interpreting the scriptures or in distinguishing traditions, wherever such a danger besets her from her lack of knowledge as would exist if she were permitted to err on necessary articles of faith or on the sacraments. To 10 err on these matters is nothing else than to withdraw one's faith from God and to place it, not in man, but in empty signs. This is almost worse than to worship the molten calf. In this matter Christ Himself testifies how far He is from failing His church when He says: "I am with you even unto the end of the world." 15

He shows that Luther stupidly boggles in trying to make the identity of the church a matter of dispute, and at the same time he answers the empty prattle of Luther's nonsense against Ambrose Catharinus on the question of the same church. Chapter 10. 20

Impudent as he is, however, he will perhaps at this point raise a question about the church, as he often does, and will say that the whole church which he calls papist is not the church of Christ. In order not to neglect any argument, the prince very shrewdly attacks the rascal on this matter accurately and keenly. In speaking of the 25 sacrament of orders, after recalling Luther's words from the *Babylonian Captivity*, "This sacrament of orders
is unknown to the church of Christ, and it *Luther's words* was invented by the church of the pope," the prince adds:
"These few words contain a great heap 30 of falsehood and nonsense. He distinguishes *The king's words* the church of the pope from the church of Christ, whereas the pope is head of the same church of which Christ is. He says that the church has invented what she did not
invent but received as instituted. He says *Luther is convicted of lying* 35

non inuenit: sed accepit institutum. Ait ecclesiam Christi, hoc
ignorare sacramentum: quum satis constet, nullam fere mundi
plagam esse: quae rite profitetur fidem Christi: quin ordinem
habeat pro sacramento. Nam si posset obscurum aliquem angulum
5 reperire (quod, opinor, non potest) in quo nesciatur sacramentum
ordinis: tamen angulus ille non esset cum reliqua comparandus
ecclesia: quae non Christo solum subest: sed et propter Christum,
unico Christi uicario, papae Romano et ordinem credit esse
sacramentum. Alioqui si perstet in eo Lutherus: ut ecclesiam
10 papae discernat ab ecclesia Christi: et apud alteram dicat ordinem

Eam fortasse uidit in Vtopia

haberi [H₂v] pro sacramento, non haberi
apud alteram: proferat illam ecclesiam
Christi: quae contra fidem papalis (ut uocat) ecclesiae, ignorat
sacramentum ordinis. Interim certe perspicuum est: quum dicat, hoc
15 sacramentum ignorari ab ecclesia Christi, et de Christi ecclesia, dicat
eos, quibus praesidet papa, non esse: utraque ratione ab ecclesia
Christi eum segregare non Romam tantum, sed Italiam totam,
Germaniam, Hispanias, Gallias, Britanniam, reliquasque gentes
omnes, quaecunque Romano pontifici parent: aut ordinem pro
20 sacramento recipiunt. Quos populos omnes quum de Christi tollat
ecclesia: necesse est: ut aut ecclesiam Christi fateatur esse nusquam:
aut more Donatistarum, ecclesiam Christi catholicam, ad duos aut
tres haereticos redigat, de Christo susurrantes in angulo."

VIDES lector, eo rem redegisse regem: ut si ecclesia, quam uocat
25 Lutherus papisticam: non sit ecclesia Christi: necesse sit, aut nusquam esse ecclesiam Christi, aut illic esse tantum, ubicunque sint duo
uel tres haeretici, de Christo susurrantes in angulo.

QVID ad haec respondet Lutherus? tacet: satis laudat: agnoscit
sic intelligere se, Christi uerba, dicentis: Vbicunque sunt duo uel tres
30 congregati in nomine meo: ibi et ego sum in medio eorum. Neque

Cuiusmodi sunt Lutherani

meminit, quicunque seperantur ab ecclesia: eos, etiam si congregentur, ac loquan-
tur de Christo, conciliabulum esse diaboli. Vna est ecclesia Christi:
extra quam, nulla est ecclesia, nisi malignantium. Atqui, nihil miror,

1 ecclesiam] *B*, eclesiam *R*, Ecclesiam *L*   15 ab ecclesia] *B*, ab Ecclesia *L*, ab ecciesia *R*
20 Christi] *BL*, Cristi *R*   22 aut more] *BL*, ant more *R*   23 in angulo] *BL*, inan-
gulo *R*   33 conciliabulum] conciliabilium *RL*, conciliabilum *B*   34 malignantium.]
malignantium. Alioqui si ecclesia catholica non sit Christi: sed conuentus aliquot qui et
ab hac ecclesia *B. See n.*   34 *B omits everything from* Atqui *here to* reliqua *on p. 202, l. 32*

that this sacrament is unknown to the church of Christ, whereas it is
quite certain that almost every region of the earth which truly
professes the faith of Christ also considers orders as a sacrament.
If he could find some obscure corner, and I do not think he can,
in which the sacrament of orders is unknown, nevertheless that 5
corner should not be compared with the rest of the church, which is
subject not only to Christ but also for the sake of Christ to the sole
vicar of Christ, the Roman pope, and which believes that orders is a
sacrament.

"Otherwise, if Luther persists in distinguishing the church of the 10
pope from the church of Christ and says that in the one church orders
is considered a sacrament but is not considered such in the other, let
him bring forward that church of Christ
which, contrary to the faith of the papal   *Perhaps he has seen it in Utopia*
church, as he calls it, is ignorant of the sacrament of orders. Mean- 15
while, when he says that this sacrament is unknown to the church of
Christ and that those whom the pope governs do not belong to the
church of Christ, it is certainly clear that according to both these
reasons he separates from the church of Christ not only Rome, but all
Italy, Germany, Spain, France, Britain, and all the rest of the nations 20
that obey the Roman pontiff or receive orders as a sacrament. When
he takes all these peoples away from the church of Christ, it necessarily follows either that he say the church of Christ is nowhere, or
that, like the Donatists, he reduce the catholic church of Christ to
two or three heretics buzzing in a corner about Christ." 25

You see, reader, that the king has reduced the matter to this point:
if the church which Luther calls papist is not the church of Christ, it
necessarily follows either that the church of Christ is nowhere or that
it is only in whatever place there are two or three heretics buzzing in
a corner about Christ. 30

What does Luther answer to this? He is silent; sufficient praise. He
thus acknowledges that he understands the words of Christ, who says:
"Wherever two or three are gathered together in my name, there am
I also in the midst of them." He does not remember that whoever are
separated from the church, even if they are   35
gathered together and speak about Christ,   *Such are the Lutherans*
are the council of the devil. There is one church of Christ, outside of
which there is no church except that of the wicked.

And yet it does not surprise me at all that Luther answered nothing

Lutherum nihil ad ista respondisse regi. Nam is perpetuus homini
mos est: assidue inculcare [H₃] sua: sed interim semper omnia
transire: quae obijcit aduersarius: quemadmodum in hac ipsa
quaestione fecit: dum responderet Ambrosio Catharino: quem
5 quantumuis irrideat is: qui in eo libro Theseus Luthero fuit in ex-
hauriendis infacetis facetijs: tamen is quoque non dubito quin uideat.
Catharino, plus esse et ingenij et eruditionis in digito: quam habeat
Lutherus in cerebro. Cui quum responderet iste de potestate ponti-

10 *Lutherum nihil respondere, ad*   ficis et ecclesiae: nihil omnino respondit ad
    obiecta sibi a Catharino   ea quae: Catharinus obiecerat. Quae quis-
                                quis aequus et incorruptus legerit, et cum
Lutheri scriptis contulerit: pronunciabit Lutherum egregium esse
nugonem: qui, tacitis omnibus quae dicit is, cui respondet, nihil
respondet aliud: quam nego omnia quae dicis. Nolo distinctiones.
15 Nihil credo praeter scripturas. De scripturae sensu, non credo sanctis
patribus: nam errauerunt omnes. Nolo allegationem inconuenientis.
Allegatio inconuenientis non soluit argumentum: et mille nugas
eiusmodi.

NAM, quum Catharinus, id quod necesse est, ecclesiam istam
20 militantem distinguat a triumphante: quod in altera promiscue
uiuant mali cum bonis, in altera dumtaxat sancti, non uult distinctiones Lutherus: non distincturus, ut uideo, inter electionem, de qua
Christus ait, Multi sunt uocati pauci uero electi, et electionem illam
de qua dicit idem, Nonne duodecim elegi uos, et unus ex uobis
25 diabolus est? At, ne manifeste se nugari fateatur, iubet distinctiones
ex scriptura probari: uelut tum demum crediturus, et tamen idem
nihilominus irridet distinctionem: qua fides charitate formata
distinguitur ab informi. [H₃v]

30   *Verba Lutheri*   Vos finxistis commentum omnium
                         nequissimum illud, informis fidei: quo
facilius et tutius sacrilegia uestra, in scripturas dei seu latrones Moab
mitteretis. Nobis autem Paulus dicit. Quae societas lucis et tene-
brarum? Quae conuentio Christi et Belial.

VIDES ut hanc distinctionem, uelut ex authoritate Pauli, pronun-
35 ciet esse non solum fictam, sed etiam nequissime fictam. Sed interim,

---

6 uideat.] videat, *L*   21–22 distinctiones] *L*, distrinctiones *R*, distinctione *corr. err.*
22 electionem] *L*, electionenm *R*

to these words of the king. This is the man's constant practice: to hammer away at his own ideas incessantly but at the same time always to pass over every objection raised by his opponent. He did the same thing in replying to Ambrose Catharinus on this very question. The fellow who was a Theseus to Luther in dredging up the witless witticisms in that book may deride Catharinus as much as he pleases, yet he also undoubtedly sees that Catharinus has more native ability and learning in his finger than Luther has in his brain. When Catharinus answered him on the power of the pope and of the church, Luther answered nothing at all to Cathar- *That Luther answers nothing* inus' objections. Anyone who reads these *to Catharinus' objections* objections fairly and without bias and compares them with Luther's writings will declare that Luther is a flagrant trifler who, ignoring everything his opponent says, answers only, "I deny everything that you say. I want no distinctions. I believe nothing apart from the scriptures. As for the meaning of the scriptures, I do not believe the holy fathers, for they have all erred. I want no charge of inconsistency. The charge of inconsistency does not solve the argument." And a thousand like trifles.

Catharinus, as is necessary, distinguishes the Church militant from the Church triumphant, saying that in the former the evil live mingled with the good, in the latter live saints only. But Luther wants no distinctions, being unwilling to distinguish, as I see it, between the election of which Christ said, "Many are called but few are chosen," and that election of which Christ said, "Have I not chosen you twelve, and one of you is a devil?" So that he will not have to admit that he is clearly talking nonsense, he demands that distinctions be proved from scripture, as though he would then finally believe. Yet he ridicules no less the distinction between faith formed by charity and unformed faith.

You have fashioned the most wicked fic- *Luther's words* tion of all, that of unformed faith, so that you may more easily and more safely, like the robbers of Moab, introduce your sacrileges into the scriptures of God. But Paul says to us: "What fellowship has light with darkness? What harmony is there between Christ and Belial?"

You see how, as though by Paul's authority, he declares this distinction to be not only contrived but even most wickedly contrived.

Hic refellitur Lutherus
euidente scriptura

dissimulat quod apostolum ipsum nequitiae insimulat nebulo. Quid enim frequen-
tius in ore Pauli: quam haec distinctio?
Quod multis in locis inculcat, quam multum intersit inter eam fidem
5 quae caret charitate et bonorum operum uita, et eam quae per
dilectionem operatur. Sed Luthero satis fuit, alterum clamare,
alterum dissimulare silentio.

IAM, quum Catharinus allegaret interdum quaedam: quae
diuinitus ecclesiae tradita, scribunt omnes sancti patres, et totus
10 credit christianus orbis: clamat Lutherus
Non omnia posse scripturis nihil recipio praeter euidentem scrip-
ostendi: cum multa sint nullis turam. Caeterum quod omnia scribi curarit
scripturis prodita Christus, quae uult Christianos credere, id
constanter negant fideles omnes: nec adhuc ullo scripturae uerbo
15 probat Lutherus.

QVVM de cuiuspiam scripturae sensu uerteretur quaestio, et
Catharinus pro interpretatione quam asserebat ipse, constantem
afferret sanctissimorum patrum, antiquissimorum interpretum, erudi-
tissimorum uirorum consensum, clamat Lutherus non curo sanctos
20 patres: non curo ueteres interpretes: non curo doctos illos doctores:
omnes errauerunt, ut homines: nec interim fere quicquam affert pro
se: nisi quod clamat uerum esse quicquid dicit: et quod ipse non
errat: [H₄] nec errare potest utpote non homo, sicut erant sancti
patres: sed extra sortem humanam infallibilis asinus.

25 QVVM Catharinus probaret ex Lutheri
Quam inepte respondeat Lutherus positione, multa sequi absurda, et in-
ad dicta Catharini conuenientia clamat Lutherus: Allegatio
inconuenientis non soluit argumentum: quum deductio ad in-
conueniens fortissimum sit, et probandi genus, et confutandi. Sed
30 Luthero nihil dicit, etiam si quis ex eius dogmate probet consequi
hominem esse asinum. Non magis profecerit: qui probet istud
Luthero: quam, si quis idem probet asino.

QVVM Catharinus diceret, in illis uerbis, Matth, xvi. Tibi dabo
claues regni caelorum, promissas esse claues, non datas: sed ex eo

---

5 eam quae] eam qua *RL*   6 Luthero] *L*, luthero *R*   17 constantem] *L*, constanten *R*
18–19 eruditissimorum] *L*, erudissimorum *R*   23 potest] *L*, patest *R*

Yet at the same time the scoundrel conceals the fact that he is accusing the apostle
himself of wickedness. What is more
frequently on the lips of Paul than this distinction? In many passages he insists on the great difference which exists between that faith
which lacks charity and the life of good works and that which works
through charity. But it is enough for Luther to shout one thing and to
conceal the other by silence.

Here Luther is refuted by evident scripture

Now Catharinus occasionally brought up certain points which,
being divinely taught to the church, all the holy fathers write and the
whole Christian world believes. To this Luther cries out: "I accept
nothing but evident scriptures." Yet all the
faithful steadfastly deny that Christ took
care to have everything written down
which He wishes Christians to believe; nor
has Luther proved this till now by any word
of scripture.

Not everything can be proved by the scriptures since many things are not recorded in the scriptures

When the point under discussion was the interpretation of some
scriptural text, Catharinus alleged in behalf of the interpretation which
he himself affirmed the constant agreement of the most holy fathers,
of the most ancient interpreters, of the most learned men. To this
Luther shouts: "I have no use for the holy fathers; I have no use for
ancient interpreters; I have no use for those learned doctors; all, being
men, have erred." Meanwhile, he introduces no argument on his own
behalf except to shout that whatever he says is true, and that he neither
errs nor can err inasmuch as he is not a man as the holy fathers were,
but is outside the human condition, an infallible ass.

Catharinus proved that many absurd and inconsistent conclusions
flowed from Luther's position. To this
Luther shouts: "The charge of inconsistency does not solve the argument,"
although deduction to an inconsistency is the strongest method both
of proof and of rebuttal. Luther is not impressed even if someone
should prove that from his teaching it follows that man is an ass.
Whoever should prove this to Luther would accomplish no more than
if someone should prove the same point to an ass.

How foolishly Luther answers the words of Catharinus

Catharinus said that in the words of Matthew 16, "To you I will
give the keys of the kingdom of heaven," the keys were promised, not
given, but that from this text it is necessarily proved that the keys were

probari necessario datas esse: quod dubium non sit quin Christus
uerax impleuerit promissionem, respondet Lutherus, etiam si
promisit Christus non esse credendum: quod promissa praestiterit:
nisi in scriptura legatur impleuisse.

5   *Verba Lutheri*   Nam, opus est locum, personam, et
                              tempus exhibitae promissionis, non nostra
suspicatione, sed illius testimonio nobis certificari. Si enim in scripturis
ista exhibitio clauium non poterit ostendi, in hodiernum usque diem
                              erimus incerti: quo tempore Petrus eam
        Praeclarus Lutheri scrupulus
10   acceperit. Absit autem, ut nos Christus
sic incertos reliquerit: ut nesciamus, quo tempore, quo loco Petrus
claues acceperit.

O MAGNVM periculum: si nesciamus: quo tempore, quo loco
Petrus claues acceperit. Nam istud nescire, profecto non multo minus
15 periculi fuerit: quam si quis nesciat quo die, et quo loco Petrus
baptisatus sit. [H₄v]

                              PRAETEREA, quum Lutherus inter-
        Quam iniquus sit Lutherus prae
              studio suae partis   dum scripturae textum quempiam detor-
                              queret in partem suam, Catharinus eius
20 interpretationem falsam refellens, quum ueriorem sensum suffragan-
tibus antiquis interpretibus confirmasset, refert ex abundanti, alios
etiam sensus: quorum quemlibet ostendit esse magis probabilem:
quam sit ille quem Lutherus, solum uerum euidentemque contendit.
Istud uero Lutherus sic eludit.

25   *Verba Lutheri*   Non tibi permitto ut scripturae plures
                              quam unum sensum tribuas. Nihil apud
me ualet: quod toties tentas. Potest etiam sic dici: potest etiam sic
intelligi: potest etiam sic responderi. Potest mi Catharine: haec
omnia sunt argumenta falsitatis, et mera effugia, et plane robora meae
30   sententiae.

SCILICET Luthere. Quid ni? ut si quis ostendat, te proferre talem
pro sensu, indubie, uero: qui sit e multis minime uerisimilis: quo
pluribus modis ostenderis esse stolidus: eo uicissim magis gloriere tu,
uelisque multo uideri sapientior.

17 PRAETEREA] *L*, PREATEREA *R*   33 gloriere] gloréire *L*

given because there is no doubt that Christ, being truthful, has fulfilled His promise. To this Luther answers that even if Christ made
the promise, one did not have to believe that He kept His promises
unless one should read in scripture that He did fulfill them.

> It is necessary that the place, the person   *Luther's words*   5
> and the time of the fulfillment of the prom-
> ise be confirmed for us not by our conjecture but by the testimony of
> scripture. For if this presentation of the keys cannot be shown in
> scripture, we will be uncertain even to this day as to the time when
> Peter received them. Far be it from   *Luther's remarkable scruple*   10
> Christ, however, to leave us so uncertain
> that we would not know the time, the place in which Peter received
> the keys.

O great danger, if we should not know the time, the place in which
Peter received the keys! Not to know this will surely be little less   15
dangerous than not to know the day and the place where Peter was
baptized.

Furthermore, since Luther occasionally   *How unfair Luther is in his*
twisted some text of scripture to his   *zeal for his own side*
own advantage, Catharinus, in refuting his false interpretation,   20
first proved the truer meaning from the agreement of ancient
interpreters, then recounted multiple other meanings also, showing
that any one of them was more probable than that which Luther
argues is the only true and evident meaning. But Luther escapes this
argument as follows: 25

> I do not allow you to attribute more than   *Luther's words*
> one meaning to scripture. I do not con-
> sider valid the argument that you try so often: "It can also be stated
> thus; it can also be understood thus; it can also be answered thus;
> literally it can mean this; mystically it can mean this." Away with   30
> this "It can," my dear Catharinus; all these are arguments of false-
> hood and mere evasions and clear defenses of my interpretation.

But of course, Luther. Why not? So that if someone should show
that you present as the indubitably true meaning one which is the
least probable of many, you in turn may boast the more and wish to   35
be thought so much the wiser, the more ways you are shown to be a
dolt.

Verba Lutheri　　　Sic, dicito. Hoc sic, et non aliter intelligi
debet: ut afferas unum constantem sim-
plicemque sensum scripturae: sicut et ego facio, hoc est enim theologi,
sicut illud sophistae.

5　　CERTE Luthere ut literalem sensum, fateor esse fere semper unice
efficacem ad probandum quippiam: si quando sit perspicuus: ita
quum saepe accidat ut res dicatur obscurius: quam ut unicus ille
sensus ex ambiguis uerbis eniteat eruditissimus quisque, et sanctissimus theologorum ueterum solitus est diuersos sensus elicere rem in
10　　　　　　　　　　　　medio relinquens expendendam. Nimi-
Quod Lutherus sophistae uocat
facinus maxime esse theologi　　rum, arbitrati sunt tutum illud esse, et
modesti uereque deo digni theologi, non
so[H₅]phistae quemadmodum scribis officium. Istud uero, quod
solum tu clamas theologi esse officium, theologi illi ueteres et ueri,
15　partes existimabant esse, uere mereque stolidi, superbique nebulonis
temeritatem: qui sensum scripturae dubium, et inter eruditos
controuersum, aut ex suo sensu solo commentum, solum contendat
esse genuinum. Cuiusmodi stultorum genus admonet, ac taxat
sapiens ille quum dicit, Ne innitaris prudentiae tuae, et ne sapiens
20　uideri uelis in oculis tuis. At Lutherus in oculis suis solus sapiens,
exclamat.

Verba Lutheri　　　Nolo Catharine usum longum, et multitudinem tecum sentientium inuoces,
uerbum Christi hic me urget. Huic credendum est uni prae omnibus
25　　sanctis, etiam angelis.

CREDENDVM est procul dubio Luthere plus uni Christo, quam
sanctis omnibus, et omnibus angelis. Verum, quum deus loquatur in
sanctis suis, iuxta illud: Non estis uos, qui loquimini: sed spiritus
sanctus qui loquitur in uobis: quum tot sancti, tam docti consentiant,
30　uerba Christi non in eam dicta sententiam: quam tu solus, contra tot
sanctos, tam doctos contendis. Iam non quod tu iactas, Christo
consentit: qui consentit tecum: sed contra ueritatem quam deus tot
sanctis suis inspirauit, consentit mendaciorum patri diabolo: qui per
te ueritatem conatur interuertere. Nam quum tu pro tuo more,

---

5 sensum] *corr. err. L*, sunsum *R*　　11 arbitrati] *L*, arbritrati *R*　　23–24 sentientium
inuoces, uerbum Christi hic] *corr. err. L*, sentientium. Innocens uerbum Christi, hic *R*
31 contendis. Iam] contendis, iam *L*　　32 quam] *L*, qnam *R*

Say this, "This text is to be understood
thus and in no other way," so that you
Luther's words
may allege one constant and simple meaning of scripture even as I do;
for this is the office of a theologian as the other is the office of a sophist.

Certainly, Luther. Although I grant that the literal sense, if it   5
should ever be evident, is almost always the only one effective for
proving anything; still, since it often happens that a matter is
expressed too obscurely for that single meaning to flash out from the
ambiguous words, all the most learned men and the holiest of
ancient theologians have usually ascertained various meanings,   10
leaving the matter open for careful consideration. Doubtless they
judged this was a safe procedure and the
office, not of a sophist as you say, but of a   *What Luther calls the office of a*
sophist is above all that
sober theologian truly worthy of God. But   *of a theologian*
this that you declare is the sole office of a   15
theologian, those ancient and true theologians judged to be the role
of a true and unadorned blockhead, and the rashness of a conceited
scoundrel, who argues that an interpretation of scripture which is
doubtful and disputed by learned men, or one contrived solely from
his own understanding, is the only genuine interpretation. The wise   20
man warns and reproaches this class of fools when he says: "Lean not
upon thy own prudence, and do not wish to seem wise in your own
eyes." But Luther, in his own eyes the only wise man, cries out:

I do not want you, Catharinus, to invoke
long-standing usage and the multitude of
Luther's words
those who agree with you. The word of Christ urges me in this
matter; He alone must be believed before all the saints, even before
the angels.

Without a doubt, Luther, Christ alone must be believed more than
all the saints and all the angels. But since God speaks in His saints,   30
according to the text: "It is not you who are speaking, but the Holy
Spirit who speaks in you," since so many saints, so many learned men
agree that the words of Christ were not spoken with that intention
which you alone argue against so many saints, such learned men, then
he who agrees with you does not, as you boast, agree with Christ, but   35
contrary to the truth which God has inspired in so many of His saints,
he agrees with the devil, the father of lies, who tries through you to
pervert the truth. When, according to your habit, you distort the

scripturam detorqueas, dicens: De quo enim angelorum aliquando
dixit: hunc audite? quasi ex illo uerbo, nihil debeas credere: quod
quisquam dicit alius: Cur non illius etiam uerbi meministi: quod
Christus ipse dicit apostolis, ac per illos caeteris: [H₅v] haud dubie
5 sanctis: quibus ipse dignatus est suum spiritum infundere? Qui uos
audit me audit. Quem spiritum suum, quum habunde Christum
constet inspirasse sanctis ecclesiae doctoribus: quorum et doctrinam
et uitam multis comprobauit miraculis, etiam si nemo unus non
aliquando sit lapsus ut homo, quod tu quoque predicas ipsis con-
10 tigisse apostolis, tamen in quo tam frequentes per tot aetates con-
spirauere, est non dubitandum in illud eos diuini spiritus aspiratione
consensisse, qui facit unanimes in domo: et te, quum eorum consensum spernas, et saepe blasphemus exclames: Non curo centum
Hieronymos, non curo mille Cyprianos, Augustinos, Ambrosios: in
15 illas Christi minas impingere: Quis uos spernit me spernit.

QVVM Catharinus ei concessit, uerum id quidem esse: quod
Christus sit uera et solida petra, et uerum caput ecclesiae: sic tamen
ut petrus etiam, et petra sit et ecclesiae caput sub Christo, hic mirifice
sibi plaudit Lutherus: et sibi uidetur perquam festiue scurrari.

20   Non sentit stolidum hoc caput: quod
            Verba Lutheri   si mea disputatio uno aliquo sensu uera
conceditur, presertim in spiritu: quod mihi concedit Catharinus, iam
plane uici etiam aduersarii accedente calculo.

DEINDE pergit homo festiuus facete scurrari iactitans crasse sibi
25 philosophandum esse, coram crasso et pituita laborante capite: quia
nihil esset asinus ad lyram, et ideo Catharinum Lutherus, omissa lyra
lepidus illudit literis, et uelut puerum, docet per .A. et .B: tanquam
demonstra[H₆]tione geometrica rem probaturus sic enim scribit:

                                        Quod si A. disputet cum B: et eo res
            Verba Lutheri
30   procedat: ut A. concedat B. optime, et
in spiritu locutum esse, se uero alium sensum externum sequi: et tamen

---

8 comprobauit] *corr. err. L*, comprobauii *R*   11 est non] *corr. err.*, est *om. R*, non est *L*
14 Augustinos] *L*, Augstinos *R*   28 scribit] *corr. err. L*, scribis *R*

scripture, saying, "Of which of the angels has He ever said, 'Hear this man'?" as though according to that text you ought to believe nothing that anyone else says, why do you not also remember the words which Christ Himself says to the apostles, and through them to other un- doubtedly holy men on whom He deigned to pour out His Spirit: "He who hears you hears me"? It is abundantly evident that Christ breath- ed out His Spirit on the holy doctors of the church, whose teaching and life He has confirmed by many miracles. Therefore, even if not a single one, being human, has not at some time been in error, a thing which you also proclaim happened to the apostles themselves, nevertheless, when they have agreed on a point in such great numbers through so many ages, it must not be doubted that they reached this agreement by the inspiration of the divine Spirit who makes those who dwell in a house to be of one mind, and that when you despise their agreement and frequently blaspheme them, saying, "I do not care about a hundred Jeromes, I do not care about a thousand Cyprians, Augus- tines, Ambroses," you are exposing yourself to the threats of Christ, who said: "He who despises you despises me."

Because Catharinus agreed with him that it was indeed true that Christ is the true and solid rock and the true head of the church, but in such a way that Peter also is both rock and head of the church under Christ, Luther is exceedingly self-complacent and thinks that he plays the buffoon very wittily.

> This blockhead does not perceive that if
> my argument is granted as true accord-   *Luther's words*
> ing to any one interpretation, especially the spiritual one, which
> Catharinus does grant me, then clearly I have conquered even by the
> decision of my opponent.

Then the merry fellow continues to play the witty buffoon, pro- claiming that he must philosophize dully before a dull and blear-eyed blockhead since an ass does not respond to a lyre; and so Luther, laying aside his lyre, plays liltingly with letters at Catharinus' expense, and teaches him as he would a boy by means of the alphabet, as if he were about to prove the matter by a geometric demonstration. He writes as follows:

> But if A should argue with B, and the
> matter should proceed to the point where   *Luther's words*
> A would grant that B had spoken very well and according to the

hoc ipso facto, A glorietur sese uicisse, illumque confutasse, deinde
conuiciis totum agat triumphum. Quid hic spectator iudicabit? An
non Bacchas, aut Corybantes insanire putabitur?

HA. HA. he, facete, laute, lepide Luthere, nihil supra. Catharinus
5 plane perditus. Risu omnes qui audiunt emoriri. Denique metuunt
omnes iam te. Sed, quaeso te Luthere bona cum uenia tua, liceat
nobis hominibus crassis, istam demonstrationem tuam, ut ipse fateris
crassam, crassius adhuc excutere. Fac igitur disputent inter se .A. et
.B: et dicat. A. Mosen fuisse ducem filiorum Israel ex Egipto: B uero
10 illud omnino perneget. Deinde dicat ipse B. deum fuisse ducem, et id
ei concedat A. et fateatur ipsum .B. in hoc optime et uerissime dicere,
et maxime in spiritu, et tamen id nihilo minus uerum esse, quod dicit
ipse. A. uidelicet ducem filiorum Israel fuisse Moisen. Iam si .B.
propterea quod .A. concedat ei uerum illud esse, quod dicit ipse, et
15 maxime in spiritu glorietur ex eo se uicisse, et conuicijs totum agat
triumphum, quid hic Luthere spectatores sentient? An non uere
bestiam esse B? an non fuste dignum sentient eius uere crassum et
pituitosum caput?

IAM, quale est illud: quod ais: praesertim in spiritu? Nuper
20 dicebas non spiritualem sensum, et mysticum probare quicquam: sed
literalem tantum. At nunc subito quum tibi Catharinus concederet
uerum esse spiritualiter, quod Christus sit petra: sed Christum tamen
illo apud Mattheum loco, non de sua praecellentia loquutum: sed de
preficiendo [H₆v] suo gregi uicario, placet ilico tibi sensus spiritualis,
25 et ad rem probandam prefertur literali. Nam ex eo quod te concedit,
aliquo sensu uerum dicere, praesertim in spiritu, concludis eum
falsum dicere: quum sanctorum patrum calculis obsistat tibi sub-
uertenti literam. Nam etiam si uerum sit, ut est: quod Christus est
uerissima et solidissima petra, uerissimum caput ecclesiae et uerissi-
30 mum ecclesiae fundamentum lapis angularis: qui fecit utrumque
unum: tamen in illo loco non de sua praesidentia loquutum Christum: sed de substituendo in ecclesia sua primatu, non solum sancti

---

1 illumque] *L*, illamque *R*   3 aut] *L*, aut. *R*   10 perneget] *L*, pergenet *R*
11 uerissime] verissime *L*, uirissime *R*   17 esse B?] *L*, esse? B. *R*   19 quod] quos *L*
25 literali] *corr. err. L*, literalis *R*

spiritual meaning, but that he himself follows another outward meaning, and if, with this granted, A should nevertheless boast that he has
conquered and confuted B, and should then celebrate the triumph
entirely by railing, what will the spectator judge at this point? Will he
not think that the Bacchae or the Corybantes are raging?   5

Ha! Ha! He! Clever, neat, smart, Luther, incomparable! Catharinus is clearly done for. Everyone who hears this will die laughing.
Now at last everyone is afraid of you. But please, Luther, in your kind
indulgence allow us dullards to examine still more dully this demonstration of yours which you yourself admit is dull.   10

Suppose, then, that A and B are disputing among themselves, and
A should say that Moses led the children of Israel out of Egypt, while
B should utterly deny this. Then this B would say that God was the
leader, and A would grant him that and admit that B speaks very
well and very truly on this point, especially according to the spiritual   15
meaning, and yet that what A himself says is no less true; namely,
that Moses was the leader of the children of Israel. Now suppose that
B, because A grants that what he says is true, especially according to
the spiritual meaning, should boast that he has thereby conquered
and should celebrate the triumph entirely by railing, what would the   20
spectators judge at this point, Luther? Would they not judge that B
is truly a beast? Would they not judge that this truly dull and blear-
eyed blockhead was fit to be cudgelled?

Now what is the nature of your words, "especially according to the
spiritual meaning"? Recently you were saying that not the spiritual   25
and mystical but only the literal meaning proves anything. But now
suddenly, since Catharinus granted that it is true spiritually that
Christ is the rock, but that in that passage of Matthew Christ was
nevertheless not speaking about His own preeminence but about
placing a vicar in charge of His flock, you immediately take a fancy to   30
that spiritual meaning and prefer it to the literal for proving your
point. From his granting that you speak the truth in some sense,
especially in the spiritual sense, you conclude that he speaks falsely
when by means of the decisions of the holy fathers he resists your
distortion of the letter. Even if it is true, as it is, that Christ is most   35
truly and firmly the rock, most truly the head of the church and most
truly the foundation corner stone of the church who has made both
one, nevertheless, in that passage Christ was not speaking about His
own sovereignty but about substituting the primacy in His church.

testantur, et christianus orbis consentit: sed etiam ipse contextus
literae aperte uidetur ostendere: neque enim admodum belle quad-
rare uidetur sensus: quem assignas ipse: tanquam Christus ita
loqueretur. Tu es petrus, et ideo ego aedificabo ecclesiam meam
5 super me ipsum.

AT non est, inquis, nisi unus sensus: ergo si meus est uerus: falsus
est Catharini. Ipse non negas alium interdum esse mysterij sensum,
alium literae: quem tu solum dicis efficacem ad probandum. Hunc
igitur sensum assentientibus interpretibus plaerisque omnibus,
10 Catharinus asserit sibi, tibi concedit mysticum: qui nihil praeiudicat
literae. Sed hic rursus obblateras, et clamare non desinis.

Verba Lutheri   Tu Catharine non negas meam dispu-
                        tationem esse in aliquo sensu ueram: ergo
       tua est falsa. Nam si aliquid est uerum quod ego dico: totum est
15   falsum quod dicis tu. Nam aut mea funditus et in totum nega aut tua
       funditus inania esse concedas.

QVAM aequam legem offers Luthere. An non apud Vergilium,
aliquid ueri dixit et Synon? et tamen magno stetit [H₇] Troianis qui
ueris illecti crediderunt assutis mendacijs. Nihil ne contra te dicit, nisi
20 qui tua omnia funditus et in totum sustulerit? Ergo si tuis mendacis-
simis dogmatis intermisceas apostolorum symbolum: aut negandum
est, quicquid illi dicunt ueri: aut simul concedendum quicquid ipse
mentiris. O acumen Lutheranum.

SED ILLVD uidelicet est ineuitabile telum, et gladius fortunatus:
25 quo Catharinum confodias: quod etiam si Petrus ecclesiae primas
institutus fuerit: papa tamen non possit primas esse, nec Petro
succedere possit in officio: nisi qui Petro succedit in moribus. Hic
regnas, rides, gestis, illudis, et omissis omnibus sanctis uiris: qui in
sacrosancta sede praesiderunt, uelut coruus et uultur, sola inuolas ac
30 depascis putrida: nisi quod non raro sanctissimos quosque uelut
rabidus canis arrodis, et dente tabifico, mel ipsum et antidotum, tibi
uertis in uenenum. Sed altum interim tibi silentium est, de illis
omnibus: quae tibi ad illa responderat ante Catharinus: qui tibi
probauit euidentissime sic seiunctam esse causam hominis, et officij,

25 confodias] *L*, cofodias *R*

Not only do the saints testify and the Christian world agree to this, but
even the sequence of the line itself seems to demonstrate it clearly; nor
does the sense which you assign seem to fit very exactly. It is as though
Christ were saying, "You are Peter, and therefore I shall build my
church upon myself."   5

"But," you say, "there is only one meaning. Therefore, if my
meaning is true, that of Catharinus is false." You yourself do not deny
that at times there is one sense that is mystical, another that is literal.
You say that the second alone is effective as proof. This mystical sense,
therefore, agreed on by almost all exegetes, Catharinus alleges for   10
himself and grants to you as being not at all prejudicial to the literal
sense. But at this point you start gibbering again and keep shouting:

> Catharinus, you do not deny that my   *Luther's words*
> argument is in some sense true; therefore
> yours is false. For if anything that I say is true, then everything that   15
> you say is false. You must either deny my arguments utterly and
> completely or you must grant that your own are utterly worthless.

What a fair condition you offer, Luther! Did not Sinon in Virgil
also say something true? And yet he cost the Trojans dear; allured by
what was true they believed the lies that were patched on to it. Does   20
one not refute you on any point unless he overthrows all your arguments completely and wholly? Therefore, if you mingle your utterly
false teachings with the apostles' creed, either one must deny whatever
truth the apostles say or he must grant along with it whatever lies you
tell. Oh, the shrewdness of Luther!   25

But that is clearly an inescapable weapon and a charmed sword
with which you transfix Catharinus in saying that even if Peter should
have been authorized as primate of the church, nevertheless the pope
could not be primate nor could he succeed Peter in office unless he
succeeds Peter in conduct. Here you have the mastery, you laugh, you   30
exult, you jeer, and ignoring all the holy men who have governed the
holy see you swoop down like a raven and a vulture to feed only on
decay; except that you usually gnaw like a rabid dog on all the most
holy men and with your rotting teeth turn honey itself and an antidote into your own poison. But at the same time you maintain a   35
profound silence about all the answers which Catharinus had previously given you on these arguments. He proved to you most clearly
that the case of a man and his office, of conduct and authority, of

morum et magistratus: uirtutis, et potestatis: ut malis etiam et
flagiciosis uiris quamuis tollatur in caelo uita: quam deus despondit
uirtutibus, in terra tamen non tollatur authoritas quam deus coniunxit officio. Quamobrem Luthere si uir uideri uis, abeas oportet
5   prius atque ad illa respondeas Catharino: cui postquam non more
simij gesticulis et nugamentis, sed quod hominem decet solida ratione
responderis: tum demum redeas licet ac rideas ad Calendas graecas.
Interim profecto insanus, et Aiacis risu furiosior est iste risus tuus:
quo tacitis, et dissi[H₇v]mulatis aduersarij rationibus, tanquam nihil
10 audires, nihil respondes: sed nugaris tantum ac uelut amens, et
insanus irrides, et mirifice te facetum putas dum in id iocaris, nugaris,
scurrarisque: quod si Petrus dici posset petra: qui sanctus erat ac
pius, aliquis ita desiperet ut petrae nomen putet in papam quempiam
posse competere: qui Petri non respondeat uirtutibus. O perplexum
15 nodum, et explicatu difficilem. Quum Christus, Petrum propter fidei
suae firmitatem, tanquam petram aliquam sibi substitueret ecclesiae
suae caput, et primatem, non qui immortalis esset: ut aeternum
potiri posset officio: sed in quod per uices multi succederent, nec
omnes aequalis meriti etiam si petrae nomen in illos non quadraret,
20 an ideo non est eadem potestas officij? Quid si sic dixisset Christus?
Ego te Petre bonum et sanctum uirum ob egregias uirtutes tuas,
ecclesiae meae primum praeficio: ut tu sis exemplo cuiusmodi uelim
tibi successores suffici: certe si successor eius aliquis esset talis: de quo
neque boni neque sancti nomen posset praedicari: tamen eadem esset
25 authoritas in officio: nisi nemo fuit sacerdos in Israel post Moisen, et
Araonem: nisi qui utrumuis eorum aequipararit sanctimonia: aut
nisi nemo sit episcopus: qui non sit omnino talis: qualem discribit
apostolus: certe Paulus ipse detulit episcopo etiam impio, et Caiphae
scribit euangelista, et impio, et ignoranti, prophetiae datum spiritum,
30 propter episcopatus officium. Quin Christus ipse quum pronunciat
scribas et phariseos, uiros nimirum et impios et improbos: qui aliorum
humeris graues imponerent sarcinas: quas ipsi digito suo nolebant
attingere: sed interea supine uiuebant et male: Christus tamen, ut

---

2 quamuis] *L*, qamuis *R*; tollatur] *corr. err. L*, tollotur *R*   3 uirtutibus, in terra tamen]
corr. err. L, uirtutibus in terra: tamen *R*   16 ecclesiae] *L*, ecclisiae *R*   19 nomen in]
corr. err. L, nomin *R*   23 quo] *L*, qno *R*   30 officium.] officium *R*, officium: *L*
31 nimirum et] et *om. L*

virtue and power is so distinct that, even though the heavenly life which God has promised to virtue is taken away from wicked and criminal men, nevertheless the earthly authority which God has joined to their office is not taken away. And so, Luther, if you wish to be thought a man, you should first leave off and answer these arguments of Catharinus. When you have answered him, not like an ape with gesticulation and nonsense, but with sound reason as becomes a man, then finally, at the Greek kalends, you may return and laugh.

Meanwhile, this laughter of yours is insane and madder than the laughter of Ajax; with it you pass over in silence and dissimulate the reasonings of your opponent and, as though you heard nothing, answer nothing, but only trifle and jeer like a senseless madman and consider yourself wonderfully witty when you jest and trifle and play the buffoon on the problem that if Peter, who was holy and virtuous, could be called a rock, anyone would be so foolish as to think that the name "rock" could fit a pope who does not reflect the virtues of Peter. What an intricate knot, and how difficult to untie it! Because of the steadfastness of Peter's faith, Christ made him the head and primate of His church, as a rock standing in His own place, not as though Peter were immortal and so could hold office forever, but many would successively follow him into that office, and these not all of equal merit. Since this is so, even if the name "rock" does not fit them, is the power of the office for that reason not the same? What if Christ had said: "Peter, because of your eminent virtues, I constitute you, a good and holy man, as the initial head of my church, so that you may be an example for the kind of men I wish to be appointed as your successors." Certainly, if his successor were the kind of man to whom one could apply neither the name of good nor that of holy, the same authority would nevertheless reside in the office. Unless no one was a priest in Israel after Moses and Aaron except one who equalled either of those men in sanctity; or unless no one would be a bishop who was not altogether the kind of man the apostle describes. Paul himself certainly submitted even to a wicked bishop; and of Caiphas the evangelist writes that even though he was unholy and ignorant, the spirit of prophecy was given him because of the office of the episcopacy. In fact, although Christ Himself calls the scribes and pharisees impious and wicked men who place heavy burdens on the shoulders of others which they themselves do not wish to touch with a finger, while at the same time living proudly and wickedly, nevertheless

dixi propter officium iussit illis obtemperare populum.[H₈]

QVAM ualidum et illud: quod tibi
Quid magis ridiculum uidetur absurdum: ut petrae uocabulum,
hac opinione qui significabat pium, in eum aliquando
5 competeret: qui sit impius. Opto tibi mentem, uel tantisper sanam,
dum possis perpendere eam rem quam ridicule derideas. Nam
quaeso te Luthere, petrae nomen sanctius ne censes esse quam
Christi? At Christi uocabulum etiam in malum competebat, et
reprobum: nisi Luthero sit ridiculus Dauid: qui de Saul dixit peccaui
10 tangens Christum domini.

MIROR Luthere tibi, qui solus uideri uis legisse scripturas, adeo
uideri nouum: si quod figuratum uocabulum diuersis interdum rebus
competat. Rogo te an non gygantes in scriptura sacra, uelut superbi
et uiolenti uitio dantur: et tamen Christus ipse gygas dicitur? Quid
15 serpens, quoties in scriptura designat diabolum? An non idem exal-
tatus in deserto, figurabat Christum: etiam si non nesciam cuidam et
ex doctissima et sanctissima classe theologorum, uideri serpentem,
ibi quoque designare diabolum: quod in Christi crucem sublatus,
affixus et mortuus uenenum et nocendi uires amiserit. Sed mihi
20 fortius est: quod ad se figuram Christus traxit ipse: quum dixit:

Sicut Moses exaltauit serpentem in deserto:
Nunquid Luthere et Christus sic exaltari oportet filium hominis: Iam
ipse hic errat illud opinor non est ambiguum, leonis
uocabulum non semel in scripturis inditum esse diabolo: et tamen
25 nihilo minus de Christo dicitur. Vicit leo de tribu Iuda. Electus et
apostolus an non sancta sunt nomina: et tamen utrunque competebat
in fratrem tuum Iudam, etiam tum cum in eum competebat nomen
diaboli: ut uideas quam argutus sis: qui disputes absurdum esse: ut
aliquid petra dicatur nisi sanctum: [H₈v] quum uideas Christum
30 dici: qui non sit sanctus, et apostolum dici: qui sit diabolus: et idem
uocabulum et deo datum et daemoni: et eiusdem animalis figura sit
designatus et seruator et Sathanas. I nunc Luthere, et gloriare cum
tuis: quod de primatu pontificis, Ambrosio Catharino fortiter et
festiue respondeas.

21 *gloss* Nunquid] *L*, Nuuquid *R*

Christ, as I have said, commanded the people to obey them on account of their office. How forceful also is the point which to you seems absurd: that the word "rock," which usually signified a virtuous man, would sometimes apply to a man who is not virtuous. I wish that you had a mind that would be balanced at least long enough for you to be able to weigh carefully the point which you ridiculously deride. Tell me, Luther, do you think that the name "rock" is holier than the name "Christ"? But the word "Christ" is applied even to an evil and wicked man; unless Luther considers David ridiculous for saying of Saul: "I have sinned in touching the Christ of the Lord."

What is more ridiculous than this opinion?

I am surprised at you, Luther, that you wish to appear the only one who has read the scriptures, and that you wish it to seem so novel if any figurative word occasionally applies to opposite things. I ask you whether or not giants are described in sacred scripture as proud and violent, and yet Christ Himself is called a giant? What about the serpent which so often in scripture indicates the devil? Did not the same animal when raised up in the desert represent Christ, even though, as I am aware, one of a most learned and holy group of theologians thinks that the serpent there also represents the devil, because when raised onto the cross of Christ, fixed there and dead, it lost its poison and power to harm? But to me it is a stronger argument that Christ applied this figure to Himself when He said: "As Moses lifted up the serpent in the desert, even so must the Son of Man be lifted up." Now I think that there is no doubt that the word "lion" is applied more than once in scripture to the devil, and yet it is said nonetheless of Christ: "The lion of the tribe of Juda has overcome." Are not the words "elect" and "apostle" holy names, and yet both of them were applied to your brother, Judas, even at the time when the name "devil" fitted him. Thus, you see how subtle you are when you argue that it is absurd to call anything a rock unless it is holy, although you see a man who is not holy called "Christ," and a man who is a devil called an "apostle," and the selfsame word applied to both God and the devil, and the representation of the same animal designating both the Savior and Satan. Go on now, Luther, and glory with your followers that you answer Ambrose Catharinus courageously and cleverly on the primacy of the pope.

Did even Christ Himself err here, Luther?

MIHI lector non erat propositum hoc in loco, de pontificis quicquam potestate tangere: nec tam huc illexit me libido docendi: quam
similis semper sit Lutherus sui: quam pertraxit inuitum confusanea
uiri tractatio: qua sic intricauit ecclesiae quaestionem, cum quaes-
5 tione pontificis: ut ei respondere de altero non potuerim: nisi aliquid
de utroque attingerem. At de ecclesia, quae nam sit hic in terris,
quum uel maxime res tractari postulet, non erat consilium eorum
quicquam intactum praeterire: quae Lutherum senseram, nec sine
Theseo ea de re tam acute tractasse: ut nullo usquam loco aut saepius
10 glorietur aut impudentius. Nam et hoc quoque habet perpetuum: ut
semper gloriosissime triumphet uerbis: ubi re ipsa turpissime se
uictum uidet. De ecclesia igitur tractaturus abstinere uoluissem
libenter, non solum a causa pontificis, sed etiam a quouis alio Lutheri
dogmate, quatinus pateretur praesens argumentum: quo non aliud,
15 quam eas nugas eius desumpsi refellere: quas in istum congessit
librum: quo nebulo respondet principi. Nam scelerata eius dogmata,
Qui uicerint Lutherum in his quae apud aequos ac bonos uiros, satis se
supra commemorauit author refellunt ipsa, et a multis eruditissimis
uiris habunde confutata sunt, A Prierate,
20 Catharino, Eccio, Gaspare, Cocleo, Empsero, placentino Radino,
Fabro, multisque itidem alijs: quos partim [H₉(numb. H₆)] audio,
partim uideo, solidis et ueris rationibus hominis amentiam pulcherrime traduxisse. Cuius assertiones, ita retexuit ac reuicit reuerendus pater Ioannes Fyscherus, episcopus Roffensis, uir eruditionis
25 ubertate clarus et uitae puritate clarissimus: ut, si quid est frontis
Luthero: magno iam sit empturus, assertiones suas olim iam com-
bustas a se: immo uel secum quoque: potius, quam cum tanta et tam
aeterna infamia sua, monstrosum foetum suum et spurcum Eryc-
thomim conspiceret christianus orbis. Certe quod ad pontificis
30 *Ioanes episcopus Roffensis* primatum pertinet, ita rem dilucidam
reddidit idem reuerendus episcopus, ex
euangelijs et actis apostolorum, et toto corpore ueteris testamenti, et
omnium consensu sanctorum patrum, non latinorum modo, sed quos

---

2 quam] qua *L*   3 Lutherus] *L*, Luherus *R*   16 principi.] *L*, principi *R*   17 *gloss*
uicerint] vicerint *L*, nicerint *R*   19 confutata] *L*, coufutata *R*; A Prierate] Aprierate *R*,
Apprierate *L*   20 Empsero, placentino] Empsero placentino, *RL*   26 assertiones] *L*,
assortiones *R*   28 foetum suum] *corr. err. L*, foedum *R*   28–29 Erycthomim] Ery-
ctomim *L*   31 reddidit] reddit *L*

I had not intended, reader, to say anything at all in this passage on the power of the pope, nor was I so much drawn to this by the urge to teach how Luther is ever the same, as forcibly dragged here against my will by the fellow's confusing discussion in which he has so entangled the question of the church with the question of the pope that I could not answer him on the one without touching somewhat on both. But since he most insistently demands that the question of the identity of the church on earth be discussed, it was not my intention to leave untouched any of those arguments on the question which I had noticed that Luther, not without the help of a Theseus, had handled so subtly that in no other passage does he boast more frequently or more shamelessly. This also is his constant practice, always to triumph most boastfully in word when he sees himself most disgracefully overcome in actual fact.

When I was about to discuss the church, therefore, I would gladly have refrained not only from the question of the pope but also from any other teaching of Luther's, so far as the present subject would permit, in which I have undertaken to refute nothing but the trifling remarks with which the scoundrel stuffed the book in which he answers the prince. Among just and good men his impious doctrines sufficiently refute themselves, and they have been fully disproved by many of the most learned men: by Prierias, Catharinus, Eck, Caspar, Cochlaeus, Emser, Radinus of Piacenza, Faber, and many others likewise. Partly through report, partly through my own reading, I perceive that these men have most skillfully exposed the fellow's madness with sound and true reasoning. The Reverend Father John Fisher, Bishop of Rochester, a man distinguished for his wealth of learning and above all for the holiness of his life, has so exposed and exploded his assertions that if Luther has any sense of shame he will buy up now at a high price his assertions, consigned to the flames long ago by himself, in fact together with himself, rather than have the Christian world behold, to his deep and everlasting disgrace, his monstrous offspring and foul Erichthonius. Certainly, as far as the primacy of the pope is concerned, the same venerable bishop rendered the matter very clear from the gospels, from the Acts of the Apostles, from the whole body of the Old Testament, from the agreement of all the holy fathers, not only the Latin but also the Greek, of

Those who have refuted Luther on those points which the author mentioned above

John Bishop of Rochester

maxime repugnasse iactare solet Lutherus etiam graecorum, postremo generalis difinitione concilij uictis, et uictos se fatentibus, qui
pertinacissime tum restiterant, armenis et graecis: ut frustra mihi
facturus uiderer, et rem actam acturus: si de pontificis primatu
5 scribere, de integro rursus ordirer. Cui sedi ut obedienter obtemperem
cum illa mouent omnia: quae docti sanctique in eam rem college-
runt: tum illud profecto non mouet minime: quod toties sumus
experti, non modo neminem inimicum fuisse christianae fidei: qui
non illi sedi bellum simul indixerit: sed etiam neminem unquam
10   *Nullum recalcitrasse Romanae*   extitisse qui se professus sit eius sedis
    sedi: qui non Christi quoque   inimicum: quin idem paulo post se
       iugum excusserit   declararit insigniter, Christique, et reli-
gionis nostrae capitaliter hostem, et pro-
ditorem esse. Valde me mouet et illud quod si ad istum modum
15 hominum uicia imputentur officijs, non modo non consistet papatus,
sed et [H9v] regnum, et dictatura, et consulatus, et omnis omnino
magistratus corruet et erit populus absque rectore, sine lege, et
ordine. Quae res, si aliquando contingat, id quod aliquot Germaniae
locis uidetur imminere, tum demum magno cum damno sentient,
20 quanto magis intersit mortalium, uel malos habere rectores, quam
nullos. Certe quod ad papam pertinet quid mali fuerit caruisse nouit
deus: qui eum suae praefecit ecclesiae: nec optandum puto ut res
christiana periculo perdiscat. Quanto magis optandum: ut tales deus
faciat esse pontifices quales e re christiana et apostolici muneris
25   *Talis potius optandus pontifex*   dignitate fuerit, ut sua sponte contemptis
    quam pontificium eijciendum   diuitijs et terrenis honoribus toti caelum
spirent, pietatem in populo promoueant,
pacem procurent, et authoritatem quam acceperunt a deo aduersus
mundi satrapas et robustos uenatores exerceant, diris omnibus
30 persequentes et tradentes Sathanae: si quis aut alienam ditionem
inuadat, aut male tractet suam, breui sentiret christianus orbis, ab
uno aut altero tali pontifice, quanto fuerit satius emendari papas:

---

10 professus] *L*, professius *R*   13 hostem, et] *corr. err. L*, et *om. R*   28 pacem pro-
curent] *corr. err. L*, pacem *om. R*

whose extreme opposition Luther likes to boast, and finally from the
fact that the Armenians and Greeks were defeated, and admitted
themselves defeated, by definition of a general council after the most
stubborn resistance. Consequently, I considered that I would be
acting uselessly and opening a closed issue if I were to weave a fresh 5
web of writing about the primacy of the pope.

I am moved to obedient submission to this See by all those arguments which learned and holy men have assembled in support of this
point; moreover, I am indeed moved not least by a fact which we
have so often noticed; that not only has no one been hostile to the 10
Christian faith without at the same time declaring war on that See, but
also there has never been anyone who de-
clared himself an enemy of that See without   *That no one has resisted the*
shortly afterwards declaring himself also a   *Roman See who did not also*
                                                  throw off the yoke of Christ
notorious and foremost enemy and traitor   15
both to Christ and to our religion. I am also much moved by the
consideration that if the faults of men should be imputed to their
offices in this manner, not only will the papacy not endure but also
royal power, and supreme magistracy, and the consulate and every
administrative office whatever will fall into ruin and the people will 20
be without a ruler, without law and order. If this should ever happen,
and it seems to threaten in several places of Germany, then men will
finally realize at great loss what a profound difference there is in
human affairs between having even bad rulers and having no rulers.

Surely, as regards the pope, God who put him in charge of His 25
church knew what an evil it would have been to have lacked a pope;
and I do not think one should desire the Christian world to learn this
by experience at its own risk. How much more should we desire God
to make such men popes as will befit the Christian commonwealth
and the dignity of the apostolic office, so that, freely spurning riches 30
and earthly honors, they may breathe a
wholly heavenly spirit, promote piety   *We should rather desire to have*
                                            such a pontiff than throw
among the people, procure peace and   *out the pontificate*
exercise the authority which they have
received from God against the satraps and strong hunters of the 35
world, pursuing with the most terrible punishments and delivering
up to Satan anyone who either usurps another's authority or misuses
his own. The Christian world would shortly realize, from one or two
such pontiffs, how much more satisfactory it is for the popes to be

quam auferri. Nec dubium est, quin iam olim pastorem sui gregis
respexisset Christus: si christianus populus salutem patris potius
precari, quam persequi, et nuditatem patris tegere, quam pudenda
ridere maluisset. Sed non deseret Luthere uicarium suum deus.
5 Respiciet aliquando: et nunc fortasse respicit: quum patrem, dolore
quem patitur a perditissimo filio, flagellat. Nam plane, te Luthere
puto flagellum dei esse, magno sedis illius bono, magno cum malo
tuo. Faciet enim deus, quod pia mater solet: quae quum uerberarit
filium, lacrymas eius abstergit: et quo puerum placet, perosam
10 [H₁₀(numb. H₇)] uirgam, protinus in ignem abijcit. Sed omisso
papatu, quem nisi Lutherus immiscuisset ecclesiae, non fueram hoc
loco tacturus, ueniamus nunc ad Lutheri machinam illam totam qua
se gloriatur ecclesiam Christi funditus euertisse et qua Catharinum
iactat impietatis et haereseos demonstratiue conuictum: sed eo in
15 loco uidebis Lutherum lector: qui multis in locis alijs impium sese
demonstrauit, ac stolidum, sedulo nauasse operam: ne id usquam
alias uideretur demonstrasse manifestius. Itaque hunc in modum
scribit.

Verba Lutheri   Christus, quod Catharinus fatetur, Primo
20   de petra et ecclesia, Secundo fatebitur,
quod Christus promittat portas inferi, non praeualituras aduersus
eam. Clara ne sunt haec Catharine? Non enim bestia, sed Christus
ea dicit. Stet ergo, portas inferi non praeualere aduersus, neque
petram neque ecclesiam. Portae autem inferi tunc praeualent:
25   quando in peccatum perpellunt. Aut dic tu quid sit portas inferi
praeualere aliud. Sicut econtra. Edificari super petram, est in gratia
et bonis operibus crescere, ut dicere possis, hoc esse portas Sion
praeualere. Sic. 1. Pet. ii. dicit. Vos tanquam lapides uiui super-
aedificamini domus spiritualis. Et Ephe. ii. In quo et uos coaedifi-
30   camini, in habitaculum dei in spiritu sancto. Et ne mihi elabaris.
Esto, fidem informem habeat, Papa, uel petra tua, uel ecclesia tua:
nihilominus, si in charitate non fuerit: sub potestate diaboli, et portis
inferi fuerit, Quia Ro. viij. dicit. Qui spiritum Christi non habet, hic
non est eius. Et Matth. vij. Qui fide informi fuerant, et miracula

---

9 perosam] perosa *RL*   12–13 machinam illam totam qua se gloriatur ecclesiam Christi
funditus euertisse et] *corr. err. L*, machinam totam funditus euersam et *R*   14 conuictum:
sed] *L*, conuictum sed *R*   16 usquam] *corr. err. L*, usque *R*   20 ecclesia] Ecclesia
L, eclesia *R*

reformed than to be removed. Nor is there any doubt that Christ would long ago have been mindful of the pastor of His flock if the Christian people had preferred to pray for the salvation of their father rather than persecute him, and to cover the nakedness of their father rather than laugh at his exposure. But God, Luther, will not abandon His vicar. He will one day be mindful of him and is perhaps mindful of him now as He scourges the father by means of the anguish which he suffers from his most profligate son. For I think, Luther, that you are clearly the scourge of God, to the great good of that See, but to your own great harm. God will act as a devoted mother is wont, who when she has whipped her son wipes away his tears and, to satisfy the boy, immediately throws the hated rod into the fire.

But setting aside the question of the papacy, which I would not have dealt with in this passage if Luther had not intermingled it with his discussion of the church, let us come now to that whole stratagem of Luther's with which he boasts that he has overthrown the church of Christ from her foundation and by means of which he brags that Catharinus has been conclusively convicted of impiety and heresy. But you will see, reader, that, whereas in many other passages Luther has proved that he is impious and stupid, in this passage he has taken great pains lest he seem to have proved this fact more clearly elsewhere. And so he writes as follows:

First of all, as Catharinus admits, Christ is *Luther's words*
speaking about the rock and the church.
Secondly, he will admit that Christ promises that the gates of hell will not prevail against her. Are these points clear, Catharinus? No beast, but Christ says them. Let this hold then, that the gates of hell do not prevail against either the rock or the church. But the gates of hell prevail whenever they force one into sin. Otherwise, you tell me what else it means for "the gates of hell to prevail." And the contrary holds also. "To be built upon a rock" is to grow in grace and good works, so that you can say that this is what it means for "the gates of Sion to prevail." Thus, I Peter 2 says: "Be you yourselves as living stones built thereon into a spiritual house." And Ephesians 2: "In Him you too are being built together into a dwelling place of·God in the Holy Spirit." And, lest you escape from me, suppose that the pope or your rock or your church have an unformed faith; nonetheless, if he is not in charity he is subject to the power of the devil and to the gates of hell. Romans 8 says: "But if anyone does not have the Spirit of Christ, he does not belong to Christ." And in Matthew 7, those who had had an

fecerant, et recte docuerant audiunt sibi dici: Discite a me omnes
operarij iniquitatis. Obsecro te Catharine homo Itale, Tomista,
digneris hic, bestiam parumper audire. Concedere cogo te per haec
dicta, eum qui sine charitate est sub diabolo esse, et ad Christum non
5   pertinere, ac per haec portas inferi in eum praeualuisse et dominari,
tanquam in seruum peccati. Sicut Christus dicit Ioannis. viij. Qui
facit [H₁₀v] peccatum seruus est peccati. Sunt ne etiam haec satis
clara? An hic Origene, Chrysostomo, aut etiam toto patrum Catalogo
opus est? Vltimo id quoque concedis, papam quem tu petram uocas,
10   et aedificatos super hanc petram, ei subiectos uisibili administratione
ecclesiam appellas, aliquando peccare et peccasse. Nonne concedis?
Immo si uerum fateri uoles, non est sceleratior gens in terra: quam ea,
quae papae hodie pertinacissime adhaeret: et qui maxime super eum
sunt aedificati: ac per hoc portis inferi subiecti, et omnium scelerum
15   serui. Responde nunc. Vbi est tua uerbosissima farrago, totius huius
disputationis? da ecclesiam illam, da petram in quam non praeualent
portae inferi. Quin das? Audin Catharine? Non papam dabis, scio,
neque papistas. Quam ergo dabis? Nullam externam ecclesiam,
nedum Romanam. Quia hanc solam dabis, si Christum audis, quae
20   sine peccato est domina scilicet portarum inferi. Quamcunque enim
dederis, incertum est, an sit in peccato et sub portis inferi. Si Romam
dederis ipsamet testabitur se esse scelerum lernam. Concludo ergo
aduersus te, demonstratiue conuictum uerbum Christi Matth. xvi. ad
nullam personam pertinere, sed ad solam ecclesiam in spiritu aedifi-
25   catam super petram Christum: non super papam, nec super Romanam
ecclesiam. Quam cito enim non dederis papam sanctum, tam cito non

*Quae sit petra Lutheri sententia
super quam aedificata est
ecclesia Christi*

dedisti petram neque ecclesiam, sed
sentinam peccati, et Sathanae synagogam. Cum autem etiam Sanctus Petrus
30   si praesens esset non possit sciri an
sanctus esset, et permaneret sine peccato, ideo necesse est, nec ipsum
esse petram sed solum Christum, quem solum sine peccato esse et
permanere certissimum est, et cum eo ecclesiam suam sanctam in
spiritu. Reuertamur ad conditionis pactum. Vno ego te Catharine hoc

10 ei] et *L*   11 peccasse] *L*, pecasse *R*

unformed faith and had worked miracles and had taught rightly, hear
these words addressed to them: "Depart from me, you workers of
iniquity." I ask you, Catharinus, man, Italian, Thomist, to deign to
listen here for a little while to the beast. Through these texts I force
you to grant that he who is without charity is subject to the devil and   5
does not belong to Christ, and that as a result the gates of hell have
prevailed against him and have dominion over him as over a slave of
sin. As Christ says in John 8: "Everyone who commits sin is a slave of
sin." Are not even these words clear enough? Or do you need here
Origen, Chrysostom, or even the whole catalogue of the fathers?   10
Finally, you also grant that the pope whom you call the rock, and
those built upon this rock subject to his visible administration whom
you call the church, do at times sin and have sinned. You grant this,
do you not? In fact, if you would confess the truth, there is no more
vicious race on earth than that which today adheres most obstinately   15
to the pope; these especially are built upon him and for this reason
are subject to the gates of hell and are the slaves of every crime. Answer
now. Where is the most verbose farrago of this whole disputation of
yours? Indicate to me the church, the rock against which the gates
of hell do not prevail. Why do you not indicate it? Do you not   20
hear, Catharinus? You will not indicate the pope, I know, or the
papists. Which, then, will you indicate? Not any external church,
still less the Roman. Because, if you listen to Christ, you will indicate only that church which is without sin; namely, the mistress of
the gates of hell. No matter which one you indicate, it is uncertain   25
whether or not she is in sin and subject to the gates of hell. If you
indicate Rome, she herself will testify that she is a Lernian quagmire
of crimes.

Therefore, I conclude against you, with demonstrative proof, that
the words of Christ in Matthew 16 do not pertain to any one person,   30
but only to the church built in the Spirit upon the rock, Christ, not
upon the pope or upon the Roman church. As soon as you indicate
an unholy pope, so soon do you indicate
not the rock or the church, but the sludge   *Which in Luther's opinion is the*
of sin and the synagogue of Satan. But   *rock upon which the church*
                                                           of Christ is built?   35
since it could not be known even of Saint
Peter, if he were present, whether he were holy and would remain
without sin, it is therefore necessary that not even he is the rock, but
only Christ is, who alone is and remains most certainly without sin,
and with Him His holy church in the Spirit.   40

Let us return to the stipulated agreement. I have caught you in
this one error, Catharinus, and I have fettered you with an unbreakable

Tibi ne licet, in hominem bonum quod ais non licere papae in haereticum?

errore comprehendi, et indissolubili uinculo constrinxi, quare te haereticum proclamo conuictum, et cum tanto libro condemnatum et maledictum. Habes

5 quod hic mutias, Catharine? Surge homo Tomista, et contere bestiam hanc maledictam: quae tam subito ad uniuersa tua portenta, non solum respondit: sed etiam ea ad nihilum redegit. [H₁₁ (numb. H₈)] Igitur sicut petra ista, sine peccato inuisibilis et spiritualis est, sola fide perceptibilis: ita necesse est ecclesiam sine peccato inuisibilem et

10 spiritualem, sola fide perceptibilem esse: Oportet enim fundamentum esse cum aedificio eiusdem conditionis sicut dicimus. Credo ecclesiam sanctam catholicam, at fides est rerum non apparentium. Quare hoc uerbum. Matthei. Tu es Petrus, perdis diapason a papatu, et uisibili ecclesia eius distat, immo eam funditus subuertit et synagogam

15 Sathanae facit. Vlterius si per petram papa, et per ecclesiam aedificatam, intelligeretur obediens papae congregatio, sequitur papam non esse papam, nec ecclesiam esse ecclesiam. Quod euidenter probo sic. Quia petra et ecclesia sine peccatis esse debent, non subiectae portis inferi. At cum nullus in mundo possit esse talis, certo et infalli-

20 biliter, et tamen certa debet esse petra

Ergo Christus nusquam aedificauit quam promiserat

certaque ecclesia sequitur nullum esse papam nec ecclesiam. Cum ergo haec Christi authoritas repugnet papae et ecclesiae papisticae: manifeste patet, Catharini et sui Thomae et omnium quos inducit opinionem

25 esse extreme haereticam. Quia haereticus est: qui scripturas sanctas alio sensu quam spiritus flagitat exponit, at Catharinus non modo id facit, cum Thoma suo haeretico, sed

Diuum Thomam haereticum Lutherum

etiam blasphemum sensum eis tribuit appellans petram hominem peccati,

30 diaboli seruum.

EN lector uere maledictam bestiam: de qua dicitur Apocalypseos. xiij. Quis similis bestiae, et quis poterit pugnare cum ea. Et, datum est ei os loquens magna, et blasphemias. Et aperuit os suum in blasphemias ad deum blasphemare nomen eius, et tabernaculum

35 eius, et eos qui in caelo habitant. Sed ueniet tempus quum bestia mittetur in stagnum ignis ardentis, et sulphuris. Interea bene habet:

---

1 *gloss* hominem] homine *L*   3 *gloss* haereticum?] haereticum. *L*   5 mutias, Catharine] mutias. Catharine *R*, mutias Catharine *L*   6 maledictam] *L*, meledictam *R*   15 ecclesiam] ecllesiam *R*, Ecclesiam *L*   24 opinionem] *L*, epinionem *R*   26 flagitat] flagitat, *L*   29 peccati] *L*, pcccati *R*   31 EN] *corr. err. L*, EM *R*; Apocalypseos] *L*, Apocaliseos *R*

bond, whereby I proclaim you a convicted heretic, and, together with this great book of yours, condemned and cursed. Do you have anything to mutter here, Catharinus? Arise, man, Thomist, and crush this *Are you allowed to declare against a good man what you say the pope is not allowed to declare against a heretic?* accursed beast which so suddenly not only answers all your fictions but also reduces them to nothing. Therefore, as this rock without sin, invisible and spiritual, is perceptible by faith alone, so also necessarily the church without sin, invisible and spiritual, is perceptible by faith alone; for the foundation should have a superstructure of the same character as itself. Thus we say: "I believe in the holy catholic church." But faith is "the evidence of things that are not seen." Consequently, the words in Matthew, "Thou art Peter," are removed as far as possible from the papacy and its visible church. In fact, this text overthrows it from its foundation and makes it a synagogue of Satan.

Further, if by the "rock" were understood the pope, and by the "church built on the rock" were understood the congregation obedient to the pope, it follows that the pope is not a pope nor is the church a church. I will clearly demonstrate this as follows. The rock and the church ought to be without sin, not subject to the gates of hell. But since no one on earth can certainly and infallibly be *Therefore, Christ never built what He had promised* thus, and yet we ought to be certain about the rock and the church, it follows that there is no pope and no church.

Since, then, this authority of Christ opposes the pope and the papist church, it is plainly evident that the opinion of Catharinus and of his Thomas and of all his authorities is heretical in the utmost degree. For that man is a heretic who explains the holy scriptures in a sense different than the Spirit demands; *Thomas a saint, Luther a heretic* but Catharinus not only does this along with his heretical Thomas, but he even attributes to the scriptures a blasphemous sense by calling the rock a man of sin, a slave of the devil.

Behold, reader, the truly accursed beast of which the Apocalypse 13 says: "Who is like to the beast, and who will be able to fight with it? And there was given to it a mouth speaking great things and blasphemies. And it opened its mouth for blasphemies against God, to blaspheme His name and His tabernacle, and those who dwell in heaven. But the time will come when the beast shall be cast into the pool of burning fire and sulphur." Meanwhile, as God foresaw, it is

quod prouidit deus: ut haec tam inuicta et maledicta bestia, semper
pugnaret secum. Nam quae fatetur ecclesiam esse certam: sic tamen
tractat: ut reddat incertissimam: et quae non contenta [H₁₁v] est
humano more sentire, dum sectatur et ostentat abstrusam quandam
5   *Quo Lutherus redigat ecclesiam*   ac reconditam sapientiam: crassam istam,
                                   et uulgo notam ecclesiam traducit ad
inuisibilem, ab externa ad internam, ab interna prorsus deducit ad
nullam: id quod statim uidebis manifestum. Sed primum Luthere, ut
tecum ad initium redeam, ex quo praeclaros istos syllogismos
10   deducis, quum Christus promittit portas inferi non praeualituras
aduersus ecclesiam, quid si quis neget hoc eum promittere, quod tu
tibi uelut manifestum sumis, nempe diabolum non futurum tam
potentem: ut ecclesiam perpellere possit in peccatum? Sed dicamus
proba nobis istud Luthere: quid aliud respondebis: quam ut uicissim
15   quaeras a nobis quid significare possit aliud? Nam si aliud significare
potest, interea nihil dixisti: quoad ratione aut scripturis ostenderis
interpretationem tuam esse ueriorem. Dico igitur primum, portas
inferi non significare diabolum: neque enim idem esse portas domus,
quod dominum: et portas inferi quod daemonem. Aliud igitur
20   quippiam hoc figurato sermone sensisse Christum: et licet hoc uerum
sit, quod neque aduersus Petri fidem neque Petro datam soluendi
ligandique perpetua succesione propagatam potestatem, diabolus
praeualebit: atque id Christus alibi sit non uno loco pollicitus: tamen
hoc in loco ubi non Sathanam nominat, non inferos, sed portas inferi:
25   non tam probabile sit eum dixisse de diabolo: quam de quopiam alio
aduersus ecclesiam suam, non praeualituro: neque enim daemonem
magis dixerim inferi portas esse quam uiam. Quod si quaeras, quid
aliud esse possit inferi porta, quam Sathan: duas tibi non ex commento meo, [H₁₂(numb. H₉)] sed ex ueterum interpretatione de-
30   promam. Alteram praesides et tyrannos
   Quae sint inferae portae illae a   mundi: qui nascentem persequebantur
         Christo commemoratae   ecclesiam: nec praeualuere tamen aduer-
sus eam. Alteram portam esse dico, te tuique similes, si quis unquam
similis tui fuit, haereticos et antichristos: qui inter triticum unanimis

---

8 nullam] *L*, nulllam *R*   27 quam] *corr. err. L*, quod *R*   28 Sathan: duas] *corr. err.*,
Sathan duas *L*, Sathanam: duas *R*   29–30 depromam] *L*, depromptam *R*   30 *gloss*
illae] illa *RL*

well that this unsubdued and accursed beast should always contradict
himself. He admits that the church is certain, yet discusses her in such
a way as to render her most uncertain; and he is not content to judge
in a human manner; while pursuing and manifesting a kind of con-
cealed and hidden wisdom, he reduces the   5
palpable and commonly known church to   *To what point Luther reduces
                                                  the church*
an invisible one, from an external to an
internal one, from an internal one he utterly reduces her to no
church at all, as you shall immediately see proved.

But first, Luther, to return with you to the first premise from which   10
you deduce these splendid syllogisms: Christ promises that the gates
of hell shall not prevail against the church; now, what if someone
should deny that He promises that which you assume as manifest,
namely, that the devil will not be so powerful that he can force the
church into sin? But if we should say: "Prove this to us, Luther,"   15
what else will you answer but to ask of us in turn what else this text
can signify? If it can signify anything else, you have said nothing until
you have demonstrated by reason or by the scriptures that your
interpretation is the truer one. And so, I say in the first place that the
gates of hell do not signify the devil, for the gates of a house are not the   20
same as its master, nor are the gates of hell the same as the devil.
Christ, therefore, meant something different by this figurative language; and although it is true that the devil will not prevail against
the faith of Peter or against the power given to Peter of binding and
of loosing which has been passed on in an unbroken succession, and   25
although Christ promised this elsewhere in more than one passage,
nevertheless, in this passage, where He does not name Satan or hell,
but the gates of hell, it may not be so probable that He was speaking
of the devil as of someone else who would not prevail against His
church; for I would say that the devil was not the gates of hell so   30
much as the way to hell.

But if you ask what else the gates of hell can be besides Satan, I will
present to you, not by my own contrivance but in accordance with
the interpretation of the ancients, two
kinds of gates: one the rulers and sovereigns *How those gates of hell mentioned*
of the world who persecuted the infant   *by Christ are to be*   35
church but did not prevail against her; the   *interpreted*
other gate, I say, is you and men like you, if there ever has been anyone
like you, heretics and antichrists who amid the wheat of a unanimous

et concordis fidei, non desinunt seminare zizania sectarum et schis-
matum: nec solum diuidere student inconsutilem Christi tunicam:
sed et nomen eius fidemque, subdole per cuniculos euertere. Nam et
per haereticos, miseri quos decipitis uelut per apertas et patulas
5　inferorum portas ingrediuntur ad inferos. Sed tamen stabit uerbum
Christi. Quantumuis impugnetis ecclesiam, non praeualebitis
aduersus eam. Restabit frementibus et frendentibus uobis ecclesia
Christi.

　　VIDES hic bone uir, praeclaram istam demonstrationem tuam,
10　nihil demonstrare nisi demonstres prius in isto loco, Christum per
inferi portas designasse diabolum: quas ueteres interpretati sunt illos
corporales ecclesiae persequutores tyrannos: et uos spirituales
impugnatores haereticos. Sed nunc ut demus tibi, portas inferi
significare diabolum adhuc liceret negare id quod ais portas inferi
15　praeualere, eo in loco pertinere quicquam ad peccatum: sed id
promisisse Christum, nullas diaboli machinas satis ualentes fore: ut
fidem ecclesiae, cui Petrum praeficiebat, extinguerent: aut ipsius
authoritatem ac potestatem ligandi soluendique possent infringere:
sicut adhuc usu uenisse uidemus. Atque istud, quum uerius uero sit:
20　tamen ut multis modis uideas quam nihil omnino dicas, quum tibi
uideris dixisse bellissime, demus adhuc tibi, si uoles, [H$_{12}$v] non solum
portas inferi significare diabolum: sed eam rem, ad peccatum totam
pertinere: negabo tamen etiam sic, in illo Christi uerbo, hoc esse
praeualere: quod tu interpretaris: uidelicet ut praeualere sit, in
25　peccatum quomodocunque perpellere. Neque enim praeualuit inferi
porta contra quemlibet: quem diabolus deiecit: sed aduersus eum
dumtaxat praeualet: qui tandem sic deijcitur: ut non resurgat in
pugnam. Nam nec in duello uictus dicitur qui prostratus in terram
rebellat tamen: et in pugnam conatur assurgere. Quid, quod hoc
30　ipsum uidetur portae nomen ostendere: nisi quis ociose, positam
putet. Nam quum portae sit officium duplex: ut uel intrare conantes
excludat, uel inclusos coerceat: et non patiatur exire: nec inferi portae
quemquam excludant, nam uolentibus intrare. Noctes atque dies

6 Quantumuis] *L*, Quantumnis *R*　　　18 possent] *L*, posset *R*

and harmonious faith do not cease to sow the weeds of sects and
schisms, who strive not only to rend the seamless robe of Christ but
even to destroy His name and faith by craftily undermining it. For
through heretics, as through the wide-open gates of hell, the wretches
whom you deceive enter into hell. Yet the word of Christ will stand   5
firm. However much you attack the church, you will not prevail
against her. The church of Christ will stand firm before your raging
and gnashing.

You see here, my good fellow, that your excellent demonstration
demonstrates nothing unless you first demonstrate that in this text   10
Christ was designating by the gates of hell the devil; for the ancient
writers interpreted them to mean those who persecuted the church
physically, the tyrants, and those who assault her spiritually, you
heretics. But now, suppose that we grant you that the gates of hell
signify the devil; we could still deny your statement that in this   15
passage the expression, "the gates of hell prevail," has anything to do
with sin; rather, Christ was promising that no wiles of the devil would
be powerful enough to extinguish the faith of the church which
He was committing to the care of Peter, or be able to impair his
authority and power of binding and loosing; we see that this promise   20
has been realized up till now.

Although this statement is truer than truth itself, nevertheless, in
order that you may perceive in many ways how you say nothing at all
when you think you have spoken most prettily, we will grant you still
more, if you wish: not only that the gates of hell signify the devil but   25
that this whole passage does pertain to sin. Yet even so I will deny
that in these words of Christ the phrase, "to prevail," means what
you interpret; that is, that "to prevail" means to force into sin in some
way. The gate of hell has not prevailed against everyone whom the
devil has overthrown, but it prevails only against the man who is   30
finally so completely overthrown that he cannot rise again to the
fight. In warfare no one is said to be conquered who, though prostrate
on the earth, still fights back and tries to rise again to the fight. Why,
this is what the very name "gate" seems to show; unless one thinks
that the name was thoughtlessly established. For the function of a gate   35
is twofold: it either shuts out those who try to enter, or it confines
those who are shut in and does not allow them to go out. But the gates
of hell do not shut out anyone, since to those who wish to enter, "the
door of Pluto's court lies open night and day; but to retrace one's step

patet atri ianua ditis. Sed reuocare gradum, superasque euadere ad
auras, hoc opus, hic labor est, patet profecto quod non aduersus
quemlibet quem daemon pellexit, praeualent portae inferi: sed dumtaxat aduersus eum: quem sic tenet inclusum: ut nunquam possit
5   erumpere. Nam qui se proripuit foras, praeualuit aduersus portas.
Itaque non praeualere portas inferi aduersus quemlibet, quem adijcit
in peccatum, uel illud indicat: quod septies in die cadit etiam iustus.
Manifestum est igitur aduersus nullum praeualere portas inferi,
praeterquam aduersus eum, quem sic incluserint, ut nunquam possit
10   exire: quod, quum nemini contingat in hac uita, patet illud Christi
uerbum non obsistere: quo minus et peccatores in hac uita possint esse
de ecclesia. En bone uir praeclaram demonstrationem tuam. Cuius
nulla pars quicquam demonstrat aliud quam stolidam et scurrilem
impietatem tuam. [H$_{13}$(numb. H$_{10}$)]
15   NAM, et ostendi nunc istorum uerborum interpretationem,
ueterum sanctorum sententijs et scripturis ipsis consentaneam: quae
plane refellit et confutat tuam. Nunc illud addam: quod si faterentur
etiam quicunque legerunt unquam sacras literas, non satis intelligere
se quid sibi uoluerit Christus in eo, quod dixit inferi portas aduersus
20   ecclesiam suam non praeualituras: nemo tamen possit nescire sensum
quem affers ipse falsissimum esse, et doctrinae Christi repugnantissi-
mum.
QVAESO te candide lector, istud considera (ut ab isto nebulone
reuertar ad te) quod Lutherus non hoc solum dicit neminem esse de
25   ecclesia, quamdiu est in peccato: qui si tantum istud diceret, et falsum
diceret et impium, sed multo dicit impudentius et magis impie: quod
qui est de ecclesia non peccat: imo nec peccare potest. Ait enim portas
inferi non praeualituras, idem esse quod in peccatum non posse
perpellere: ex quo plane sequitur: quod qui semel sint de ecclesia:
30   nunquam possint in peccatum perpelli: et qui in peccatum perpulsi
sunt eos nunquam fuisse de ecclesia. Et, ne quid dubites eum istud
plane sentire, non aliud omnino dicunt celebres ille collectiones:
quibus hoc pacto lutulente syllogisat sus.

Verba Lutheri   Nullum cedens portis inferi, est ecclesia
35   supra petram aedificata: sed secta paparum, cedit portis inferi: ergo secta paparum non est ecclesia.

---

21 falsissimum] *L*, fallissimum *R*   32 ille] illae *L*   34 Nullum] Nullus *L*

and escape to the upper world, this is work, this is toil." Accordingly, it is indeed clear that the gates of hell do not prevail against everyone whom the devil has allured, but only against the one whom the devil holds so confined that he can never break out. He who forces his way out has prevailed against the gates. That the gates of hell do not 5 prevail against everyone whom the devil casts into sin is indicated also by this text: "The just man falls seven times a day." It is clear, then, that the gates of hell prevail against no one except him whom they so enclose that he can never get out. Since this does not happen to anyone in the present life, it is clear that these words of Christ do 10 not prevent even sinners from being able to belong to the Church in this life.

Behold, my good man, your excellent demonstration! No part of it demonstrates anything else than your doltish and scurrilous impiety. For I have now indicated an interpretation of these words consonant 15 with the opinions of ancient holy men and with the scriptures themselves which clearly refutes and disproves your interpretation. Now let me add this: that even if all of those who have ever read the sacred writings should admit that they do not clearly understand what Christ meant in saying that the gates of hell would not prevail against 20 His church, still, no one can be unaware of the fact that the meaning which you yourself allege is completely false and utterly contrary to the teaching of Christ.

To return from that scoundrel to you, honest reader, I ask you to consider this fact: Luther not only says in this argument that no 25 one belongs to the church so long as he is in sin—this statement alone would be false and impious—he makes the far more impudent and impious statement that one who belongs to the church does not sin, indeed, cannot sin. For he says that "the gates of hell shall not prevail" is the same as "not to be able to force one into 30 sin"; from which it clearly follows that those who once belong to the church can never be forced into sin and that those who have been forced into sin have never belonged to the church. In case you doubt that he means precisely this, nothing else at all is expressed in those famous deductions in which the swine syllogizes filthily as follows: 35

> That which does not yield to the gates of   *Luther's words*
> hell is the church built upon the rock. But
> the sect of the popes yields to the gates of hell. Therefore the sect of
> the popes is not the church.

CEDERE portis inferi, nihil appellat aliud: quam peccare: quod alio declarat syllogismo sic.

Omnis ecclesia peccans cedit portis inferi: sed ecclesia papistarum peccat: ergo
5   ecclesia papistarum cedit portis inferi.

VIDES hic lector, eum manifeste dicere: quod ecclesia quae peccat non est ecclesia Christi: neque de peccato quicquam [H₁₃v] distinguit: sed ponit simplicissime, aduersus eum praeualere portas inferi: quem in quodcunque peccatum perpulerint: quod quum
10 dicat, manifeste ponit, omne peccatum esse mortale: et eos qui sunt de ecclesia, in nullum omnino peccatum posse perpelli: et qui perpellun-tur, de ecclesia non fuisse etiam antequam perpellerentur, de qua eius sententia, si quis adhuc dubitet, expendat et istud quod ait.

Quam cito enim non dederis papam
15   sanctum, tam cito non dedisti petram,
neque ecclesiam, sed sentinam peccati et Sathanae synagogam.

EN interim seueritatem censoris huius: apud quem non satis est, aliquem mediocribus esse uirtutibus: sed aut omnino sanctum, aut omnino Sathanam, quales hic syllogismos offert occasionem hoc in
20 loco colligendi de se, quem, quum non admodum sit difficile probare, non esse sanctum: ipse iam absoluit et conclusit reliquum, peccati se sentinam esse, et sedem Sathanae. Sed relinquamus eius sanctitatem in sentina Sathanae, tu lector expende quod sequitur.

Etiam sanctus Petrus si praesens esset
25   quia non posset sciri an sanctus esset et
permaneret sine peccato ideo necesse est nec ipsum esse petram.

QVOD de petra dicit Lutherus idem dicit et de ecclesia nam eiusdem ait conditionis esse oportere petram et ecclesiam funda-mentum et aedificium.

30 Sicut petra ista nempe Christus sine
peccato est et ita necesse est et ecclesiam
sine peccato esse: oportet enim fundamentum esse cum aedificio eiusdem conditionis.

"To yield to the gates of hell" he terms nothing other than "to sin," which he declares in another syllogism, thus:

> Every church which sins yields to the gates *Luther's words*
> of hell. But the church of the papists sins.
> Therefore the church of the papists yields to the gates of hell.   5

You see here, reader, that he clearly says that the church which sins is not the church of Christ, and he makes no distinction whatever as to the sin but quite simply asserts that the gates of hell prevail against one whom they have forced into any sin whatever. Since he says this, he clearly asserts that every sin is mortal and that those who belong to   10 the church cannot be forced into any sin at all and that those who are forced into sin did not belong to the church even before they were forced into sin. If anyone still doubts that this is his opinion, let him consider also the following statement.

> As soon as you point out an unholy pope,   *Luther's words*   15
> so soon have you pointed out not the
> rock nor the church but the sludge of sin and the synagogue of Satan.

At the same time consider the severity of this censor in whose judgment it is not enough for a man to be moderately virtuous but he must be either wholly a saint or wholly Satan. In presenting syllogisms   20 such as that, he offers at this point an opportunity to draw a conclusion about himself, since it is not so very difficult to prove that he is not a saint; he himself has thereby deduced the logical conclusion: that he is the sludge of sin and the sanctuary of Satan. But let us leave his sanctity in the sludge of Satan; consider, reader, what follows.   25

> Since it could not be known even of   *Luther's words*
> Saint Peter, if he were present, whether he
> was a saint and would remain without sin, it is therefore necessary
> that not even he is the rock.

Luther says the same thing of the rock as he says of the church, for   30 he says that the rock and the church, the foundation and the building, should be of the same character.

> As this rock, namely Christ, is without   *Luther's words*
> sin, even so it is necessary that the church
> also be without sin, for the foundation should have a building of the   35
> same character as itself.

ET alibi.

Verba Lutheri Necesse est solum Christum esse petram
quem solum sine pec[H₁₄]cato esse et
permanere certissimum est et cum eo ecclesiam suam sanctam in
5 spiritu.

QVID illam? nempe esse et permanere sanctam certissimum est:
quae est eiusdem conditionis cum sua petra: et ideo certum esse
contendit, illam et esse sanctam et permanere: quaecunque sit illa:
sed non esse certum de ullo homine utrum sit de illa. Et ideo mani-
10 feste uides ex his locis et ex eo quod ait, eos qui de ecclesia sunt non
posse perpelli in peccatum: Lutherum aperte ponere non aliter esse
christianos de ecclesia: quam si non solum sancti sint uerum etiam
sancti permansuri sint: nam alioqui ne interea quidem dum sancti
sunt esse ecclesiam. Nam si sanctus petrus adhuc uiueret: incertum
15 esset an esset petra: non tantum quia incertum esset, an sanctus esset:
sed etiam quia incertum esset an sanctus permansurus esset.

QVAESO te lector, quum istud dicit quam ecclesiam relinquit in
terris? An non omnem tollit funditus, et externam et internam, uisi-
bilem et inuisibilem, spiritualem et carnalem? Nam quis est usquam
20 qui non peccat? quis tam spiritualis est: ut in eo nihil delinquat
infirmitas carnis? quis tantum habet diuini spiritus: ut eum nunquam
quoquam perpellat diabolus? An non omnes peccauimus et egemus
gratia dei? An non si dixerimus quod peccatum non habemus ueritas
in nobis non est? Iam istud miror: quo fugit interim celebre illud
25 dogma Lutheri: quod iustus etiam benefaciendo peccat. Nisi hoc
uerum est: et illud item: quod tam diu tanto conatu defendit: Omne
opus bonum peccatum esse: sequitur certe: ut aut nulla sit omnino
ecclesia in terris: aut [H₁₄v] usque adeo falsum esse, quod dicit eam
non peccare: ut contra sit necessarium eam et peccare totam et
30 peccare perpetuo. Nam cum alio dogmate tollat actus omnes in-
diferentes: quicquid faciat quisquis est de ecclesia, bonum opus faciat
oportet aut malum. In opere malo quin peccet non est dubium: quod
si peccat etiam in omni opere bono: quis non uidet consequi necessario: neminem esse in ecclesia qui non peccet perpetuo? tantum

---

14 Nam] *L*, Nan *R*   20 ut] *L*, ut ut *R*   21 diuini] *corr. err. L*, diuiui *R*   23 dei?]
Dei? *L*, dei. *R*   25 Nisi] *L*, Ni si *R*

And elsewhere:

> It is necessary that Christ alone be the *Luther's words*
> rock since it is most certain that He alone
> is and remains without sin, and together with Him His holy church
> in the Spirit.   5

What does he say about her? That it is most certain that she is and
remains holy, since she is of the same character as her rock; and so he
argues it is certain that, whatever she may be, she both is and remains
holy, but that it is not certain concerning any man whether he belongs
to her. And so you see clearly from these passages and from his state-   10
ment that those who belong to the church cannot be forced into sin,
that Luther openly asserts that Christians belong to the church only
on condition that they not only are holy but also will remain holy; for
otherwise not even while they are saints do they constitute the church.
If Saint Peter were still living, it would be uncertain whether he were   15
the rock, not only because it would be uncertain whether he were
holy, but also because it would be uncertain whether he would
remain holy.

I ask you, reader, when he says this, what church does he leave on
earth? Does he not completely abolish every church, external and in-   20
ternal, visible and invisible, spiritual and physical? What man is
there anywhere who does not sin? Who is so spiritual that the weak-
ness of the flesh is utterly lacking in him? Who has so much of the
divine spirit that the devil never prevails on him to any extent? Have
we not all sinned and do we not all need the grace of God? Is it not a   25
fact that if we say that we do not have sin, the truth is not in us?

Now I am wondering about this: where during all this time has that
famous teaching of Luther's fled, that the just man, even by doing
good, commits sin? If this is not true, as well as that statement which
he defended for so long with such great effort, "that every good work   30
is a sin," it surely follows either that there is no church at all on earth
or that his statement that she does not sin is so false that on the contrary she of necessity sins entirely and sins incessantly. With the one
teaching he abolishes all indifferent actions; whatever anyone belong-
ing to the church does must be either a good or an evil action. In the   35
case of an evil act there is no doubt that one sins; but if he sins even in
every good work, who does not see that it follows of necessity that
there is no one in the church who does not sin incessantly? So far are

abesse ut qui sint ecclesia non cedant portis inferi, si portis inferi cedere sit, id quod dicit iste, nihil aliud quam quomodocunque peccare.
Sic enim nemo non cedit.

    SED propemodum diuino quid uelit. Vult opinor omnino omne
5 opus bonum peccatum esse: quia potest esse occasio superbiae: et
contra omne opus malum uirtutem esse: quia sit occasio humilitatis:
et quum quodcunque malum fiat a fidelibus, fidelibus inquam fide
non informi sicut est papistica: sed fide formata secundum formam
quam docet Lutherus, hoc est fidendo firmiter: quod nullum
10 peccatum potest damnare christianum praeter incredulitatem solam:
tunc illud malum qualecunque sit, si stet aut redeat fides absorbetur
in fide sine satisfactione, sine contritione, sine confessione: nisi si quis
(ut ait ille) consolationis causa confiteri uelit mulieribus. Nam et has
etiam sacerdotes nobis consecrat Lutherus. Luthero igitur omnia bona
15 opera sunt peccata: et tamen ecclesiae suae nulla sunt peccata nam
non solum non imputantur sed etiam donantur premio. Nam iustis
omnia cooperantur in bonum: et ideo papistarum bona opera uigiliae,
eleemosynae, orationes, castitas, ieiunia atque id genus alia nihil
aliud sunt quam mera peccata propter infirmam fidem: qua non
20 confidunt [H$_{15}$] solam fidem sine bonis operibus sufficere sed
Lutheristarum opera mala ebrietas, adulterium, rapina, blasphemia,
et denique totus huiuscemodi malorum catalogus propter eorum
fidem firmam qua confidunt firmiter solam fidem sufficere, et bonis
operibus nihil opus esse, nihil sunt aliud: quam uirtutes merae. Nihil
25 igitur opus est ecclesiae Lutheranae: ut pro peccatis suis precentur:
non enim peccant. Sed ecclesia Christi, quam Lutherus disputat
peccare non posse, docetur ab ipso Christo peccata sua precibus
expianda: Clamatque quotidie, dimitte nobis debita nostra.

    IAM si Lutherus diceret, ex hac promiscua multitudine christi-
30 anorum, qui subinde peccant, et subinde a peccato resurgunt, eos
dumtaxat esse ecclesiam, non qui nunquam peccant (nam tales nulli
sunt) sed qui sunt extra peccatum, etiam si et peccarint saepe et saepe
peccaturi sint, et eosdem homines in hac uita, mutatione crebra, nunc
esse de ecclesia, nunc de ecclesia non esse, suo peccato etiam quantulo-
35 cunque deiecti, quamquam nulla humana denuntiatione depellantur,

---

15–16 peccata nam non] *corr. err. L*, peccata: non *R*   32 peccarint saepe] *corr. err. L*,
saepe *om. R*

those who form the church from not yielding to the gates of hell, if, as
this fellow says, to yield to the gates of hell be nothing else than to sin
in any manner whatever. There is no one who does not yield in this
way.

But I almost divine what he means. He means, I think, that every   5
single good work is a sin because it can be the occasion of pride, and
on the other hand every bad work is a virtue because it is the occasion
of humility; and since every kind of evil may be done by the faithful—
I mean the faithful with a faith not unformed as is the papist faith
but with a faith formed according to the form which Luther teaches,   10
that is, by trusting firmly that no sin can damn a Christian except lack
of faith alone—then that evil, whatever kind it may be, if his faith
remains firm or returns, is swallowed up in faith, without satisfaction,
without contrition, without confession; unless someone should wish,
as he says, for the sake of consolation to confess to women. Even these   15
Luther consecrates as our priests. To Luther, then, all good works are
sins; and yet his church has no sins, for not only are sins not imputed
to her but they are even rewarded. "For to the just all things work
together unto good"; and so the good works of the papists, vigils, alms,
prayers, chastity, fastings and other works of that kind are nothing   20
else but unmixed sins because of weak faith, by reason of which they
do not trust that faith alone without works suffices; but the evil works
of the Lutherists, drunkenness, adultery, robbery, blasphemy, and in
fine a whole catalogue of such evils, because of their firm faith, by
reason of which they trust firmly that faith alone suffices and that   25
there is no need of good works, are nothing else but unmixed virtues.
The Lutheran church, therefore, does not need to make supplication
on behalf of their sins, because they do not sin. The church of Christ,
on the other hand, which Luther argues cannot sin, is taught by
Christ Himself that her sins must be expiated by prayers: "And she   30
cries out daily, 'Forgive us our trespasses.' "

Now if Luther were saying that out of this common multitude of
Christians who repeatedly sin and repeatedly rise from sin, only those
form the church, not who never sin—for there are none such—but
who are without sin, even though they have sinned often and often will   35
sin, and that in this life these same men through a frequent change
now belong to the church, now do not belong to the church, having
been driven out of it by their sin, however slight, even though they
are not banished by any human decree, he would still be talking

adhuc absurde diceret. Nam nos, quum quaerimus, quae sit illa
ecclesia: cuius authoritate fatetur Lutherus commendatam nobis esse
scripturam sacram, an dumtaxat illos dicet qui sunt extra peccatum?
Nam his, qui in peccato sunt, nihil esse credendum: tantisper enim,
5 non esse de ecclesia. Hac ratione, eidem homini eadem de re crederemus hodie, cras non crederemus, crederemus in aurora, non crederemus uesperi. Imo adeo nemini crederemus omnino: neque enim
scire possemus de alijs, quis esset in peccato, quis extra, quum nemo
de se ipso satis sciat, utrum sit odio dignus an amore. Lutherus
10 inuehitur in episcopos: quod [H₁₅v] tam cito christianos excommuni-
cent, quum ipse neminem non excommunicet citius, siquidem extra
ecclesiam illico eijciat quemlibet: qui quoquo modo peccarit. Qua in
re, quis non miretur Lutheri sententiam: quum Lutheri fratrem
uideat Iudam traditorem, etiam post conceptum, et perpetratum
15 scelus, adhuc fuisse tamen de ecclesia: neque quoad uixit ex aposto-
latu depulsum: quamquam ipsius Christi uoce diceretur esse diabolus.
At Lutherus, uir aequissimus, non modo fratrem suum Iudam ab
ecclesia depellit post peccatum: sed nec ipsum, nec sanctum Petrum
admittit in ecclesiam, etiam antequam peccaret. Nam si ante fuissent
20 de ecclesia, portae inferi non potuissent eos, ut disputat, in peccatum
perpellere. Ergo si uerum Lutherus dicit: ne tum quidem Petrus erat
in ecclesia: quum ei dixit Christus beatus es Simon Bar Iona, et tu es
Petrus et super hanc petram aedificabo ecclesiam meam. Nam postea
aduersus eum praeualuerunt portae inferi, si praeualere est, quod
25 Lutherus ait, in peccatum perpellere. Nam paulo post, Christo
consuluit ne pateretur, et audiuit ab illo. Vade retro me Sathana.
Post et ter abnegauit dominum. Quare, si praeualent portae inferi
aduersus omnes qui peccant, nemo uero non peccat maxime, si
uerum sit dogma Lutheri, perspicuum est in terris ecclesiam omnino
30 nullam esse.

SED opere precium est uidere: quam sibi tenuiter obijciat, quid
sequeretur absurdi, si ecclesia nihil esset nisi quiddam spirituale, nec
sciri posset ubi esset, quanto magis tenuiter illud soluat, quod sibi
obijcit ipse.

3 sacram, an] *corr. err. L*, an *om. R*   3 peccatum?] *corr. err. L*, peccatum. *R*   8 possemus]
L, possemns *R*   31 est uidere] est uidere *L*, uidere *om. R*

nonsense. When we ask which is that church by whose authority Luther admits that the sacred scriptures have been committed to us, will he say that it is only those who are without sin? That those who are in sin must not be believed at all, for during such time they are not of the church? According to this reasoning we would, on a particular matter, believe the same man today, not believe him tomorrow, believe him at sunrise, not believe him at sunset. Or rather, indeed, we would not believe anyone at all, for we could not know of other men which one was in sin, which was out of it, since no one may be sure even concerning himself whether he is worthy of hatred or love. Luther rails against the bishops because they so readily excommunicate Christians, whereas he himself excommunicates everyone still more readily, since he casts out of the church on the spot anyone who has sinned in any manner whatever.

Who would not wonder at Luther's judgment on this point, when he sees that Luther's brother, Judas the traitor, even after his crime was plotted and perpetrated, still nevertheless belonged to the church and so long as he lived was not expelled from the apostleship, although he was called a devil by the mouth of Christ Himself. But Luther, an eminently just man, not only expels his brother Judas from the church after his sin but does not admit either him or Saint Peter into the church, even before he sinned. If they had previously belonged to the church, the gates of hell could not, so he argues, have forced them into sin. Therefore, if Luther is speaking truly, Saint Peter did not belong to the church even at the time that Christ said to him, "Blessed art thou, Simon Bar Jona," and, "Thou art Peter and upon this rock I will build my church." For the gates of hell later prevailed against him, if "to prevail" is, as Luther says, to force into sin. For a little later, Peter advised Christ not to endure suffering and heard from Him: "Get behind me, Satan." Later also he denied his Lord three times. Therefore, if the gates of hell prevail against all those who sin, yet no one does not sin exceedingly if Luther's doctrine is true, then it is clear that there is no church at all on earth.

But it is worth observing how feebly he poses to himself the objection of the absurdity that would follow if the church were nothing but a kind of spiritual entity and her whereabouts could not be known; and how much more feebly he solves that self-posed objection.

Verba Lutheri 　　　　Dices autem. Si ecclesia tota est in
　　　　　　　　　　　spiritu, et res omnino spi[H₁₆]ritualis.
Nemo ergo nosse poterit, ubi sit ulla eius pars in toto orbe: quod uehementer absurdum est. Nam ideo papam asserimus: ut certo loco eccle-
5　　siam inueniri liceat. Alioquin, quid docet Christus oues pascere, et
Paulus ecclesiam regere, et Petrus gregem Christi pascere: si nusquam
in orbis certis poterunt locis inueniri habitantes, corporaliter fideles?
Quis enim spiritibus praedicet, aut quis spiritus uobis praedicat.
Corpus ergo et locum necessario habebit ecclesia, deinde inter
10　　corpora et loca, aliquem primum locum et primum corpus.

AVDISTI lector, quam tenuiter obijciat sibi: quasi ideo tantum
cognosci deberet ecclesia: ut sciri posset cui congregationi praedicetur
euangelium: quum contra multo magis cognoscenda sit ecclesia: ut
sciri possit a quo praedicetur euangelium: ut si alius aliud praedicet,
15　　authoritas ecclesiae certum faciat auditorem de uero euangelista: et
reijciat falsum: sicut eius authoritas, etiam fatente Luthero, certum
facit lectorem quae sint uerae scripturae sacrae. Nam, quod ille sibi
tanquam ex nobis obijcit, ideo ecclesiam cognosci debere: quo in loco
possit reperiri: ut certa sit congregatio Christi: cui praedicari debeat
20　　euangelium: istud nescio quis ei fuisset obiecturus nisi ipse: quum
nemo tam stolidus sit praeter eum: quin intelligat uerbum dei
praedicandum esse, etiam extra ecclesiam Christi: et benefacturum, si
quis illud praedicet infidelibus. Alioqui male fecissent apostoli: qui
fidem sua praedicatione propagarunt apud gentes. Sed istud ipsum,
25　　quum tam tenuiter obijciat, audi quanto adhuc magis tenuiter
soluat.

Verba Lutheri 　　　　Respondeo. Quanquam ecclesia in carne
　　　　　　　　　　　uiuat: tamen non secundum carnem
uiuit, ut Paulus dicit Gal. i. et Corin. i. Ita in loco, rebus operibusque
30　　mundi uersatur: sed non secundum haec aesti[H₁₆v]matur. Christus

　　1 ecclesia] ecclesio *R*, Ecclesia *L*　　21 quin] *corr. err. L*, cur *R*

But you will say: If the church is wholly   *Luther's words*
in the spirit and a thing altogether
spiritual, then no one will be able to know the whereabouts of any
part of her in the whole world; a thing which is extremely absurd. The
reason we claim a pope is that the church may be found in a definite   5
place. Otherwise, why does Christ teach that His sheep should be fed,
and Paul that the church should be ruled, and Peter that the flock of
Christ should be fed, if the faithful can never be discovered dwelling
bodily in definite places on the earth? Who would preach to spirits;
or what spirit preaches to you? The church, therefore, will necessarily   10
possess a body and a location, and then among these latter, some
principal location and principal body.

You have heard, reader, how feebly he poses this objection to himself, as though the church should be recognized only in order that one
can know to what congregation the gospel is being preached, whereas   15
on the contrary the church needs to be recognized much more so that
one can know by whom the gospel is being preached, so that if
different persons preach different things, the authority of the church
may give the listener certainty as to the true preacher of the gospel
and reject the false one, just as her authority, even by Luther's   20
admission, gives the reader certainty as to the identity of the true
scriptures.
As for the objection he poses to himself as though it were from us,
namely that one should recognize where the church can be found so
that there may be a definite congregation of Christ to whom the   25
gospel should be preached, I do not know who but he would have
posed that objection to him, since no one but he is so dull-witted as not
to understand that the word of God must be preached even outside
the church of Christ and that anyone who should preach it to unbelievers would be doing a good work. Otherwise, the apostles would   30
have acted wrongly in spreading the faith among the gentiles by their
preaching.
But hear how, after so feebly posing this very objection, he solves it
still more feebly.

I answer: Although the church lives in   *Luther's words*   35
the flesh, nevertheless she does not live
according to the flesh, as Paul says in Galatians I, and Corinthians I.
Thus, with the attribute of location she engages in the activities and
works of the world, but she is not valued according to them. For Christ

enim omnem locum tollit, dum dicit. Regnum dei non uenit cum
obseruatione, neque dicent hic aut hic est. Et ecce, regnum dei intra
nos est. Paulus omne corpus tollit, dum dicit. Non est personarum
acceptio apud deum. Sicut enim ecclesia, sine esca et potu non est in
5 hac uita, et tamen regnum dei non est esca et potus secundum Paulum:
ita sine loco et corpore, non est ecclesia: et tamen corpus et locus, non
sunt ecclesia neque ad eam pertinent. Sicut ergo non est necesse,
certum panem, certum potum, certam uestem esse ecclesiae, et
fidelibus omnibus, licet sine pane, sine potu, sine ueste non queant
10 uiuere in hoc seculo. Sed omnia sunt libera, et indifferentia: ita, non
est necesse, certum locum, certamque personam habere, licet sine
loco personaque esse non queat. Sed omnia sunt indifferentia et
libera, omnis locus christiano quadrat, et nullus locus christiano
necessarius est, omnis persona pascere eum potest, et nulla certa
15 persona necessaria est quae pascat, libertas enim spiritus hic regnat:
quae facit omnia indifferentia, nulla necessaria quaecunque corpor-
alia et terrena sunt. Et quid hoc mirum? cum ad hoc ut sis, homo
corporaliter nullo loco certo, nulla certa persona indiges, sed omnibus
locis, omnibus personis homo esse potes. Immo quae res mundi
20 necessario alij adhaeret et alligatur: ac non potius libere, et indifferenter, se quaelibet ad quamlibet habetur: ut libertate spiritus
plena appareat tota creatura, sicut canimus, Pleni sunt caeli et terra
gloria tua. Quis ergo furor papistarum impijssimorum, ut ecclesiam
dei, quae omnium maxime libera est, loco suo et personae suae certis
25 et necessarijs alligent: ut christianum esse negent: qui non hunc
papam etiam impium, hoc loco habitantem adorarit. Nec iuuet
quemquam, si quemlibet pastorem indifferenter, quolibet loco
habuerit. Haec est illa abominatio stans in loco sancto et operatio
erroris. Sed de hoc alias.

30 QVAESO te lector quid unquam audisti tale. Nam ut omittam
scripturas, tam absurde citatas: ut nihil allegari [H_{17}(numb. H_{11})]
possit absurdius: nonne sic tractat hunc locum, quasi nos exigeremus:
ut sic assignetur ecclesiae certus locus: ut alio in loco ecclesia esse non
possit? At quaeso te, quis unquam sensit sic certum esse debere, quo
35 in loco reperiatur ecclesia: ut idem senserit aliquem esse locum: in
quo ecclesia non possit coalescere? quum contra potius credamus

does away with all place when He says: "The kingdom of God comes unawares, and they will not say it is here or there"; and, "Behold, the kingdom of God is within us." Paul does away with all body when he says: "With God there is no respect of persons." As the church does not exist in this life without food and drink, and yet the kingdom of God does not consist of food and drink, according to Paul, so the church does not exist without place and body, and yet body and place do not constitute the church and are not proper to her. Therefore, as it is not necessary for the church and all the faithful to have particular food, particular drink, particular clothing, although they cannot live in this world without food, without drink, without clothing, but all things are optional and indifferent, so it is not necessary to have a particular place and a particular person, although she cannot exist without place and person, but all things are indifferent and optional: every place suits the Christian, and no place is necessary for the Christian; every person can feed him and no particular person is necessary to feed him; for here reigns liberty of spirit, which makes all corporal and earthly things indifferent, none of them necessary.

And why should this be strange, since in order to exist as a man you do not require from a physical aspect any particular place, any particular person, but you can be a man in any place and with any person. Indeed, what earthly thing clings and is bound by necessity to any other; does not everything rather relate freely and indifferently to everything else, so that the whole of creation appears full of the liberty of the spirit, as we sing: "The heavens and the earth are full of thy glory." What, then, is the madness of the utterly impious papists that they bind to particular and necessary persons and places the church of God, which of all things is most free as to its place and person. Thus they say that a man is not a Christian who has not adored this pope, even though impious, dwelling in this place. Nor is it of any use for a man to have indifferently any pastor he chooses in any place he chooses. This is that abomination standing in the holy place and the working of error. But of this elsewhere.

I ask you, reader, have you ever heard the like? To pass over the scriptural texts cited so absurdly that nothing more absurd can be alleged, does he not handle this argument as though we were demanding that a particular place be assigned to the church in such a way that the church cannot exist in any other place? But I ask you: Who ever thought that the location of the church had to be so definite that he thought there was some place in which the church could not take

aliquando fore: ut nullus in orbe locus sit: in quo ecclesia Christi non
sit futura, quum tempus uenerit in quo fiet unum ouile, et unus
pastor. Deinde ita rem tractat pontificiam, tanquam hij qui papae
primatum asserunt, sic illud sentiant: quod sit ecclesiae caput,
5 tanquam Romanus: non tanquam successor Petri: quum nemo
nesciat eam sedem alias fuisse alibi. Et quamquam urbem Romam,
uelut locum totius orbis celeberrimum uidetur delegisse deus: nemo
tamen ex his qui sedis eius primatum asserunt, habet pro dubio: quin,
quocunque transferatur Petri sedes: eodem etiam Petri transferatur
10 authoritas. At, nec istud quisquam dubitat, etiam si uerum est nullum
esse locum in toto orbe terrarum: in quo non possit esse congregatio
fidelium: tamen oportere necessario aliquem esse locum: in quo
ecclesia certa sit cognobilis et indubia. Alioqui, fore ut neque certum
cuiquam sit, quae sint uerae scripturae: neque scire possit: quo
15 pedem tendat: qui adhuc infidelis, fide cupiat imbui, et dogmata
christiana perdiscere.

SED iam opere precium fuerit, scripturae loca perpendere: quae
supra citauit pro se: tanquam ex his manifeste probaturus, ecclesiam
in terra militantem, non esse cognitam, istam crassam et sensibilem:
20 sed aliam christianorum multitudinem quandam, nescio quam,
insensilem et mathematicam, [H₁₇v] Platonis ideis cognatam: quae,
et in loco sit, et in nullo loco sit, in carne sit, et extra carnem sit:
quae tota sit obuoluta peccatis, et tamen omnino non peccet. Nam
hic, utrunque pariter ponit: quum omne bonum opus asserit esse
25 peccatum: et ecclesiam facit homines, qui non peccant. Sed iam
scripturas eius expendamus.

Verba Lutheri   Paulus, inquit. Gal. i. et Corinth. i.
                    dicit: quod, quamuis ecclesia in carne
uiuit: tamen non secundum carnem uiuit.

30 ROGO te Luthere, an tu aliquando peccare uocas, secundum
carnem uiuere? Certe, quisquis sapit, dixerit, secundum carnem
uiuere, non illum qui dum obluctatur carni, et conatur seruire spiritui,

---

6 eam sedem] eam sedem sedem *L*   7 celeberrimum] *L*, celeberrimam *R*   15 infidelis,
fide] *L*, fide *om. R*, infideles, fide *corr. err.*   21 insensilem] insensibilem *L*; ideis] id eis *L*
32 non illum . . . spiritui] non & conatur illum, qui dum obluctatur carni seruire spiritui *L*

root, since, on the contrary, we believe that someday there will be not a place on earth in which the church will not exist, when the time shall have come in which there will be formed one flock and one shepherd.

Secondly, he treats the question of the pontifical office as though those who maintain the primacy of the pope judge that the pope is head of the church as a Roman, not as the successor of Peter; whereas everyone knows that the see referred to has been in other places at other times. And although God seems to have chosen the city of Rome, as the most renowned place in all the world, nevertheless no one of those who maintain the primacy of its see has any doubt that wherever the see of Peter may be transferred, there also would be transferred the authority of Peter. But neither does anyone doubt, even if it is true that there is no place in the whole world where there cannot be a congregation of the faithful, that there must still necessarily be some place in which a definite church may be recognizable and certain. Otherwise no one could be certain which are the true scriptures, nor could anyone know where to turn who, as yet an unbeliever, wishes to be instructed in the faith and to learn thoroughly the Christian teachings.

But now it will be worth while to consider carefully the scriptural passages which he has cited above in support of his position, as though ready to prove clearly from them that the church militant on earth has not been recognized in this palpable and perceptible church, but in some other multitude of Christians, somehow imperceptible and mathematical—like Platonic Ideas—which is both in some place and in no place, is in the flesh and is out of the flesh, which is wholly involved in sins and yet does not sin at all. This fellow posits each proposition with equal force when he claims that every good work is a sin and considers the church as men who do not sin. But now let us carefully consider his scriptural texts.

Paul, he says, states in Galatians I and *Luther's words*
Corinthians I that, although the church
lives in the flesh, nevertheless she does not live according to the flesh.

I ask you, Luther: Do you call an occasional act of sin "living according to the flesh"? Certainly whoever has any sense will say that living according to the flesh refers not to one who, while struggling against the flesh and trying to serve the spirit, nonetheless

tamen aliquando carni cedit, ac uincitur conditione fragilitatis
humanae: sed qui uoluptatem quae-
Quid sit secundum carnem uiuere
rens carni se seruum dedit: et carnis
operibus dedicat uitam: hoc est Luthere secundum carnem uiuere,
5 non aliquando peccare. Quamobrem, non secundum carnem uiuit
ecclesia, etiam si nemo uiuat sic, quin opus habeat assidue precari: ut
debita sua sibi remittantur. Et tamen sunt in ecclesia: qui secundum
carnem uiuunt: non futuri, quum ecclesia uiuet in caelo: quos
interim saepe monet, ac taxat apostolus. Apud Corinthios eiecit etiam:
10 qui nouercam stuprauerat, et recipit postea poenitentem. Et idem
tamen erat de ecclesia, post patratum facinus, quoad eum eiecit
apostolus.

IAM illud quam ualidum est, quod ais: Christus tollit omnem
locum, dum dicit. Regnum dei non uenit cum obseruatione: neque
15 dicent: ecce hic est: aut ecce illic est. Saepe clamas, Catharinum
loqui in equiuocis: et tamen derides distinctiones: ut tibi liberum sit
ludere in equiuocis. Nam [H_{18}(numb. H_{12})] quid longius abest a
proposito: quam hic scripturae textus: qui loquitur de aduentu
Christi ad iudicium? quando ecclesiam tollet in caelum: quum nobis
20 quaestio sit de ecclesia, quae iam peregrinatur in terris. Sed illud
quanto adhuc citas absurdius: Regnum dei intra uos est: quod haud
dubie dictum est de quolibet bono, et syncere christiano pectore:
intra quod non est opinor ecclesia: quae est congregatio fidelium.

SIMILIS est uigoris et illud, quod ais: Paulus tollit omne corpus
25 dum dicit: Non est personarum acceptio apud deum: quasi, quoniam
deus et ex iudaeis et graecis uocauit ecclesiam ad fidem, ideo deus nec
Petri personam praeposuit ecclesiae, nec ipsius Christi, et quia non
est acceptio personarum apud deum, ideo multitudo christianorum
non est ecclesia: et quia deus neminem accipit in caelum acceptione
30 personae, sed meriti: ideo nemo tenetur in terra suis obedire praepositis. Lutherus initio cum scriberet, promisit se sua probaturum, aut

2 *gloss* Quid] *L*, Qnid *R*   9 apostolus. Apud] apostolus apud *L*

yields occasionally to the flesh and is overcome by the condition of human frailty, but rather to one who, seeking pleasure, surrenders himself as a slave to the flesh and devotes his life to the *What "living according to the flesh" means* works of the flesh. This, Luther, and not an occasional act of sin, is "living according to the flesh." Consequently, the church does not live according to the flesh, even if no one lives in such a way as not to need to pray constantly that his sins may be forgiven him. And yet there are those in the church who do live according to the flesh; they will not be in the church when she will live in heaven; in the meantime the apostle frequently warns and chides these men. In the epistle to the Corinthians he even cast out the man who had dishonored his stepmother, and afterward receives the penitent back again. And yet that same man belonged to the church after the commission of his crime until the apostle cast him out.

Then, how valid is your statement that Christ does away with every kind of place when He says: "The kingdom of heaven comes unawares. Neither will they say, 'Behold, here it is,' or, 'Behold, there it is.' " You often protest that Catharinus speaks in equivocations, and yet you deride distinctions so that you may be free to sport with equivocations. What is farther from the point at issue than this text of scripture which speaks of Christ's coming for judgment when He shall exalt the church to heaven; whereas our inquiry is about the church which now sojourns on earth? But how much more absurdly you quote: "The kingdom of God is within you," which undoubtedly refers to any good and genuinely Christian heart; within which there is not, in my opinion, the church which is the congregation of the faithful.

Of similar force is your statement that Paul does away with every kind of body when he says: "With God there is no respect of persons"; as if, because God called the church to the faith from among both Jews and Greeks, God therefore did not place the person of Peter, nor of Christ Himself, in charge of the church; and as if, because with God there is no respect of persons, the multitude of Christians is therefore not the church; and as if, because God receives man into heaven, not through regard to his person, but through regard to his merit, no one is therefore bound while on earth to obey his superiors.

When Luther began writing, he promised that he would prove his

scripturis euidentibus, aut euidenti ratione, aut interpretatione
sanctorum patrum, aut decretis pontificum: postea eo furoris adactus
est: ut interpretationem sanctorum, tanquam fallacem, contemneret:
naturalem rationem, tanquam fidei et religioni aduersariam,
5 sperneret: pontificum leges et decreta, quoniam ipsius haeresibus
aduersabantur, exureret: nunc, ne nihil seruare fateatur, iactat se solis
credere scripturis: et tamen inspice scripturarum textus: quos citat:
et expende loca: nec dubito, quin facile sentias, eum non magis cum
pontificum decretis, quam cum ipsis pugnare scripturis: nec magis
10 pugnare cum scripturis: quam pugnat cum sensu communi. Nam
quaeso te Luthere, qualis est haec ratio.[H₁₈v]

Verba Lutheri   Si locus et persona necessaria sunt ad
salutem: tunc qui eiusmodi habent et
colunt, salui et sancti sunt. Nam in his consequentia a particulari
15 optime ualet, cum posterioristicis constet propositionibus: cogor enim
et meam dialecticam ostentare istis admirandis dialecticis. Impossibile
est enim, ut qui unum necessarium ad salutem habet, non etiam
omnia necessaria simul ad salutem habeat. Et impossibile est: ut qui
unum non habet, aliquod ad salutem necessarium habeat. Quod
20 facillimum est inductiue probare. Sed de hoc alias.

CVM TV Luthere hoc alias aliter probabis, tum nos alias aliter
tibi respondebimus. Interea neminem esse puto, qui sapiat: quin te
plane uideat desipere, nisi non satis sapiebat apostolus: nam is et
fidem putabat esse necessariam ad salutem, cum dixit: sine fide
25 impossibile est placere deo: et tamen idem non tecum sentit: quod qui
fidem haberet, quam necessariam dixit esse ad salutem: idem protinus haberet charitatem: quam uel amplius fide ad salutem sensit
esse necessariam. Nam, si protinus habita fide, sensisset consequi
charitatem, cur istud scripsit? si fidem habeam, adeo ut montes loco
30 dimoueam, charitatem autem non habeam, nihil sum. Sed istud
uidelicet erat in re, quod in eo tempore natus nondum est Lutherus:
qui suam ostentaret dialecticam, et docere posset apostolum, talem
consequentiam a particulari ualere, propterea quod, propositionibus
constet posterioristicis. Sed hoc alias.

---

6 exureret] *L*, exurerer *R*   9 pugnare] *L*, pugnere *R*   20 probare] *L*, ptobare *R*
21 aliter probabis, tum nos alias aliter] *L*, aliter, probabis tum nos alias, aliter *R*
29 adeo] *L*, a deo *R*

arguments either by evident scriptures or by evident reason, or by the
interpretation of the holy fathers, or by the decrees of the pontiffs;
later he was driven to such a degree of madness that he contemned the
interpretation of holy men as deceptive, he spurned natural reason as
opposed to faith and religion, he burned the laws and decrees of the   5
popes because they opposed his own heresies; now, in order not to
admit that he has held on to nothing, he boasts that he believes only
in the scriptures; and yet, examine the scriptural texts that he cites
and consider the passages carefully; I have no doubt that you will
easily perceive that he contradicts the decrees of the popes less than   10
he does the scriptures themselves, and that he contradicts the
scriptures less than he contradicts common sense. Tell me, Luther,
what sort of reasoning is the following:

> If place and person are necessary for   *Luther's words*
> salvation, then those who possess and   15
> venerate this sort of thing are the saved and the saints. In these matters
> the conclusion from a particular is of the utmost validity, since it is
> established by posterioristic propositions; for I am forced to show off
> my dialectic also to these admirable dialecticians. It is impossible that
> he who has the one thing necessary for salvation does not also have at 20
> the same time everything that is necessary for salvation. And it is
> impossible that he who does not have the one thing should have any-
> thing necessary for salvation. This is very easy to prove inductively.
> But of this elsewhere.

When you will prove this elsewhere, Luther, we will answer you   25
elsewhere. Meanwhile, I suspect that there is not a man of sense who
does not clearly see that you are without sense, unless the apostle did
not have much sense; for he too considered faith necessary for salvation when he said: "Without faith it is impossible to please God";
and yet he does not agree with you that whoever would have the faith   30
which he declared necessary for salvation would by that very fact
have the charity which he deemed even more necessary than faith for
salvation. If he had thought that charity followed immediately on the
possession of faith, why did he write the following: "If I have faith so
that I can remove mountains but have not charity, I am nothing"?   35
But of course the reason for this was that Luther had not yet been
born at that time to show off his dialectic and to be able to teach the
apostle that such a conclusion from a particular is valid because it is
established by posterioristic premises. But of this elsewhere.

QVONIAM igitur certum est, incertum esse qui sint boni: con-
sequitur ut haec multitudo quae facit ecclesiam catholicam: istam
dico, ex qua fides discitur, et scriptura discer[H₁₉(numb. H₁₃)]nitur,
sit multitudo promiscua profitentium Christi nomen et fidem, etiam
5 si professioni non respondeat uita. Iam istud lector, adeo uerum est:
ut nec Lutherus, qui libenter dissimulat quicquid non potest soluere,
potuerit subticere. Fatetur enim, ecclesiam certam esse oportere. Sed
ne cogatur illud item fateri: quod uerum est istam multitudinem esse
ecclesiam, quam nunc omnes noscimus, nomine christiani populi: qui
10 fere omnes agnoscunt primatum pontificis: uertit omnem lapidem, et
ecclesiae suae spiritualis, signa quaedam dat, per quae uult eam satis
certam reddi: quae signa omnia nec satis certam reddunt ecclesiam,
quam praescribit ille et competunt omnia in hanc ipsam, quam ille
ueram negat: et uocat papisticam. Ita, bis stultus est: qui nec eo
15 peruenit, quo tantopere tendit: et in illud incidit: quod maxime
conatur effugere. Ait enim hoc pacto.

Verba Lutheri   Si per petram papa, et per ecclesiam
                            aedificatam intelligeretur obediens papae
congregatio: sequitur papam non esse papam: nec ecclesiam
20 esse ecclesiam, quod euidenter probo sic: Sine peccatis esse debent,
non subiectae portis inferi. At quum nullus in mundo possit esse talis,
certo et infallibiliter: et tamen certa debet esse petra, certaque
ecclesia: sequitur nullum esse papam nec ecclesiam.

VIDES lector, ut hic fateatur, non solum petram sed ecclesiam
25 quoque certam esse oportere. Sed illud obiter quaeso te perpende
diligenter. An non hic manifeste colligit illud: quod si tam euidenter
uerum esset: quam euidenter falsum est: non modo ecclesiam istam
quam impugnare nititur: sed quantum ad terram attinet, omnem
omnino tolleret. Nam pone Luthere, quamcunque uelis, et eam, unica
30 ratione tua, bis probo nullam esse. Quod ut tuis uerbis utar, [H₁₉v]
euidenter probo sic. Ecclesia sine peccatis esse debet, non subiecta
portis inferi. At quum nullus in mundo possit esse talis, certo et
ineffabiliter: et tamen certa debet esse ecclesia: sequitur igitur nullam
esse ecclesiam.

8 item] idem *L*   13 ille et competunt omnia in hanc ipsam, quam ille] *corr. err. L,*
et . . . ille *om. R*; ipsam,] *L,* ipsam *corr. err.*   16 pacto] *L,* pocto *R*   19 congregatio]
L, congregregatio *R*   20 sic: Sine] *L,* sic Sine *R*; peccatis esse] *L,* peccatis essc *R*;
debent] debent petra & ecclesia *L*   26 manifeste] *L,* maniseste *R*

Because it is certain, then, that it is uncertain who are good men, it follows that this multitude which constitutes the catholic church, this church, I say, from which the faith is learned and the scripture determined, is the common multitude of those who profess the name and faith of Christ, even though their life may not correspond to their profession. Now this is so true, reader, that not even Luther, who readily conceals whatever he cannot solve, could keep silent. For he admits that the church should be known for certain. But, lest he be forced to admit likewise the truth that the church is this multitude which we all know now by the name of the Christian people, almost all of whom acknowledge the primacy of the pontiff, he turns every stone and gives some signs of his spiritual church through which he would have her rendered sufficiently well known; all these signs are not enough to render sufficiently well known the church he describes, and they all apply to this very church which he says is not true and which he calls papist. Thus, he is doubly foolish, since he neither arrives at the goal toward which he strains so mightily, and he falls into the position which he is above all trying to escape. For he makes the following statement:

If by the rock is understood the pope, and *Luther's words* by the church built on it is understood the congregation obedient to the pope, it follows that the pope is not a pope, nor is the church a church; which I clearly prove thus: The rock and the church ought to be without sin, not subject to the gates of hell. But since no one on earth can certainly and infallibly be thus, and yet the rock ought to be certain and the church certain, it follows that there is no pope and no church.

You see, reader, how he here admits that not only the rock but also the church ought to be certain. But incidentally I ask you to consider this statement very carefully. Does he not here clearly reason to a conclusion which, if it were as evidently true as it is evidently false, would abolish not only this church which he endeavors to assault but every church altogether insofar as it is earthly? Suppose any church you will, Luther, and by means of this single reasoning of yours I will twice prove that it is no church; which, to use your words, I clearly prove thus: The church ought to be without sins, not subject to the gates of hell. But since no one on earth can certainly and infallibly be thus, and yet the church ought to be certain, it therefore follows that there is no church.

VIDES LVTHERE, QVOD HOC praeclarum argumentum
tuum, non magis aduersarium tuum petit: quam te: imo illum nihil
petit: te uero perfodit penitus. Nam nos in tuto sumus: ut qui
negemus id necessarium esse: ut ecclesia, dum in terra militat: sit
5 absque peccato: sed tu qui sentis id oportere, et tamen fateris neminem esse sine peccato: et praedicas etiam bona opera esse peccata: et
iustum benefaciendo peccare, tu inquam, etiam si non oporteret
ecclesiam esse certam: tamen aperte reuinceris, omnem e terris
ecclesiam sustulisse: quod rursus ut uerbis tuis utar euidenter probo sic.
10 Ecclesia debet esse sine peccato: sed nemo est sine peccato: ergo nulla
est ecclesia. Extrica tete Luthere, ex hac trica, qua tua te stoliditas
intricauit. Sed istud obiter: quum propositum mihi non aliud fuerit:
quam ut ostenderem etiam Lutherum fateri ecclesiam debere esse
certam. Igitur ad id reuertor, ut ostendam per quae signa Lutherus
15 conetur efficere, ut certa uideatur ecclesia illa interna spiritalis, et
occulta: quam solam definit ecclesiam. Scribit enim hunc in modum.

Verba Lutheri   Quo ergo signo agnoscam ecclesiam:
oportet enim aliquod sensile signum dari:
quo congregemur in unum ad audiendum uerbum dei. Respondeo.
20 Signum necessarium est: quod et habemus, Baptisma, scilicet, panem,
et omnium potissimum euangelium. Tria haec sunt christianorum
symbola, tesserae, et caracteres. Vbi enim baptisma et panem et
euangelium esse uide[H$_{20}$(numb. H$_{14}$)]ris, quocunque loco, quibus-
cunque personis, ibi ecclesiam esse, non dubites. In his enim signis,
25 uult nos Christus concordare, ut Ephe. iiij. dicit. Vna fides, unum
baptisma, unus dominus. Vbi idem euangelium est, ibi eadem fides,
spes, eadem charitas, idem spiritus est: et reuera omnia eadem. Haec
est unitas spiritus, non loci, non personae, non rerum, non corporum,
de qua seruanda, Paulus nos praecepit esse sollicitos. Vbi uero
30 euangelium non esse uideris (sicut in synagoga papistarum, et
Thomistarum uidemus) ibi non dubites ecclesiam non esse, etiam si
baptisent et uescantur de altari: nisi paruulos et simplices exceperis:
sed Babylonem ibi esse scias, plenam lamijs pilosis, Vlulis, onocrotalis,
alijsque monstris, id est magistris nostris eximijs refertam. Euangelium
35 enim prae pane, et baptismo, unicum certissimum et nobilissimum
ecclesiae symbolum est, cum per solum euangelium concipiatur,
formetur, alatur, generetur, educetur, pascatur, uestiatur, ornetur,

3 qui] *L*, qui, *R*   5 tu] *L*, tn *R*   9 rursus ut uerbis tuis utar] *corr. err. L*, rursus uerbis
tuis *R*   14 ostendam per quae] *corr. err. L*, ostendam per per quae *R*   16 Scribit] *L*,
Sctibit *R*   21 omnium] *L*, omium *R*; sunt] *om. L*   31 uidemus)] videmus) *L*, uidemus:
R   34 Euangelium] *L*, Fuangelium *R*

You see, Luther, that this brilliant argument of yours attacks your
adversary less than it attacks you; indeed it does not attack him at all,
whereas it stabs you to the heart. We, who say that it is not necessary
for the church while she is fighting on earth to be without sin, are in a
position of safety; but you, who judge that this is necessary, and yet   5
admit that no one is without sin, and who declare that even good
works are sins and that the just man sins by doing good works, you, I
say, even if the church did not need to be certain, are nevertheless
clearly convicted of having abolished every church from the whole
earth; which, to use your words again, I clearly prove thus: The   10
church ought to be without sin, but no one is without sin, therefore
there is no church. Disentangle yourself from this web, Luther, in
which your stupidity has entangled you.

But this is incidental, since I had no other intention than to show
that even Luther admits that the church ought to be known for   15
certain. I return, then, to my exposition of the signs by which Luther
tries to render certain that internal, spiritual, and hidden church
which he defines as the only church. He writes as follows:

By what signs, therefore, shall I recognize
the church, for some sensible sign should   *Luther's words*   20
be given by which we may be gathered together into one to hear
the word of God? I answer: A sign is necessary, and we have it;
namely, baptism, the bread, and above all the gospel. These are the
three signs, tokens, and marks of Christians. Where you see baptism
and the bread and the gospel, in whatever place, among whatever   25
persons, there you will undoubtedly find the church. For on these signs
Christ wishes us to agree, as Ephesians 4 says: "One faith, one baptism,
one Lord." Where there is the same gospel, there is the same faith,
hope, the same charity, the same spirit, and in fact everything is the
same. This is the unity of the spirit, not of place, not of person, not of   30
things, not of bodies, for the preservation of which Paul commands us
to be anxious. But where you do not see the gospel (as we see in the
synagogue of the papists and Thomists), there you may know without
a doubt that the church does not exist, even if they baptize and partake
of the altar, unless you except children and simple folk; but you may   35
know that Babylon is there, full of sorceresses, satyrs, owls, ostriches,
and other monsters; that is, stuffed with our unusual teachers. For the
gospel, before the bread and baptism, is the single most certain and
most excellent sign of the church, since through the gospel alone is she
conceived, formed, nourished, begotten, brought up, fed, clothed,   40

roboretur, armetur, seruetur, breuiter, tota uita et substantia
ecclesiae, est in uerbo dei, sicut Christus dicit. In omni uerbo quod
procedit de ore dei uiuit homo. Non de euangelio scripto sed uocali
loquor. Nec de quauis contione, quae in templis de suggestu declamatur, sed de germano et genuino uerbo quod fidem Christi ueram, non
informem, et Thomisticam doceat: quod per papam et papistas
extinctum et suffocatum, per orbem totum conticuit. Ideo enim,
Christus nihil tanta instantia exegit ab apostolis: quam ut euangeli-
sarent. Sic a Petro in persona omnium pastorum exegit: ut pasceret
oues: id est euangelium doceret, uiua uoce. Quod uerbum Catharinus, uere Catharinaliter, exponit, non de euangelio, iterum faciens e
simplici sensu uerborum Christi, quotuplicem uisum ei fuerit: quia
sciebat euangelizandi significationem quae sola in eo uerbo est, non
posse conuenire tot occupationibus mundi oppresso pontifici, ideo
fingenda fuit alia significatio, de regimine dominante, sicut. ij. Pet. ij.
Praedixit, et fictis uerbis, in auaritia de uobis negotiabuntur: de qua
re nunc supersedeo, abunde alias tractata. [H$_{20}$v]

QVID ais lector, an non pulchre se nunc expediuit dominus
doctor? An non ecclesiam suam, dilucide certam reddidit? Ponit
ecclesiam ex solis bonis constare, eam congregationem ait esse certam
his tribus signis, baptismo, pane, et euangelio: sed non illo scripto,
nam illud habent et papistae sed uocali, nec tamen quauis concione, qualis in templis papistarum de suggestu declamatur: sed de
germano et genuino uerbo loquitur, quod fidem Christi ueram, non
informem et Thomisticam doceat: sed Lutheranam istam, uidelicet
solam fidem sufficere sine bonis operibus: et quod nihil quemquam
damnare potest, praeter solam incredulitatem: quia omnia peccata
absorbentur a fide: et quod nullae leges obligant christianum quemquam: et quod nulla sit libertas arbitrij: sed diuina bonitas necessaria
causa sit humanae maliciae: et mille articulos huiusmodi: quos papa
et papistae per orbem totum, perperam conantur extinguere. Certe
tali praedicatione certa est ecclesia malignantium.

adorned, strengthened, armed, preserved; in short, the whole life and being of the church is in the word of God, as Christ says: "Man lives by every word which proceeds from the mouth of God."

I am not speaking of a written gospel but of a spoken one; not about just any sermon preached from the pulpit in the churches, but about the genuine and authentic word which teaches the true faith of Christ, not a misshapen and Thomistic faith; the word which, having been snuffed out and suffocated by the pope and the papists, has fallen silent throughout the world. It was for this reason that Christ required nothing of His apostles with so much insistence as that they preach the gospel. Thus He required of Peter as representative of all the shepherds that he should feed the sheep; that is, teach the gospel with the living voice.

Catharinus explains this expression, quite Catharinally, as not referring to the gospel, fashioning once more from the simple meaning of Christ's words as many meanings as he pleased, because he knew that the meaning, "preaching the gospel," which is the sole meaning of that expression, could not fit a pontiff burdened with so many worldly preoccupations, so that another meaning had to be contrived referring to the ruling power, according to the prediction of II Peter 2: "And through covetousness shall they with feigned words make merchandise of you." I now pass over this matter, since I have treated it fully elsewhere.

What do you say, reader? Has not the honored doctor now extricated himself neatly? Has he not clearly rendered his church well known? He assumes that the church consists only of good men; he says that that congregation is known for certain by means of these three signs, baptism, the bread, and the gospel; yet not a written gospel, for the papists also have that, but a spoken one; nor yet just any sermon such as is preached from the pulpit in the churches of the papists; rather, he is speaking of the authentic and genuine word such as teaches the true faith of Christ, not a misshapen Thomistic one, but this Lutheran one; namely, that faith alone suffices without good works, and that nothing can damn a man but lack of faith alone because all sins are swallowed up by faith, and that no laws bind any Christian, and that there is no freedom of will but that the divine goodness is the necessary cause of human malice, and a thousand articles of this sort which the pope and the papists throughout the whole world are falsely trying to snuff out. Certainly by such preaching the church of the wicked is known for certain.

Verum initio, quem non miserae sortis nostrae miserescat? quos tu
uelut margitas et corebos irrides: et tuo lepidus arbitratu ludis. Dum
persuasisti tibi, papistam nullum, per stuporem posse potistae
repugnantias apertissimas deprehendere. Nam primum dicis, ob id
5   oportere certam esse ecclesiam: ut possit esse certum: ubi praedicari
debeat euangelium: nam dicis nec debere praedicari, nec posse
sonare, nisi in ecclesia: ex quo uides consequi, prius oportere
cognosci ecclesiam: quam praedicetur euangelium. Postea dicis,
signum per quod unicum, ecclesia certo cognoscitur, esse praedica-
10 tionem euangelij: nam reliqua signa, fateris esse etiam apud papistas:
apud quos negas esse ecclesiam: ex [H$_{21}$(numb. H$_{15}$)] qua positione
tua sequitur, prius euangelium praedicari oportere: quam cognosci
possit ecclesia: quum ea praedicatio per te, sit unicum signum: per
quod ecclesia certo cognoscitur. Vides ergo pater prudentissime, qui
15 nunquam tibi repugnas, quam constanter et circumspecte, duo sibi
inuicem contraria connectes: uidelicet et prius cognoscendam ecclesiam, quam praedicetur euangelium: et prius praedicandum euangelium, quam cognoscatur ecclesia. Iam quaeso te doctor insignis, ac
posteriorista peritissime, quum demonstras ecclesiae certitudinem,
20 per certitudinem euangelij: et uiceuersa, demonstras euangelij
certitudinem, ex certitudine ecclesiae, liceat ex te scire quo canone
posterioristico, posterior propositio in hac demonstratione tua
posterioristica, ex priore sequatur. Quippe si hoc tibi satis explicatum
ducis, quum primum perdiscendum praecipis, quaenam sit uera
25 ecclesia, ut huic dumtaxat praedicetur euangelium: dein rursus
inquirentibus ecclesiam, constare eam censes ex euangelij praedicatione: aut tibi sit necesse est alia posterioristice quam hactenus fuit
omnibus alijs, aut te parum posterioristices peritum esse. Nempe cum
etiamnum incertum relinquas, quibus sit euangelium declamandum,
30 nec uerum uis, nisi quod praedicetur quibusdam, nescio quibus, quos
tu non satis definis: sed tanquam ideas Platonicas animo concipis, et
dum id tua ratione demonstrandi requirimus, redibit ad caput

15 circumspecte] *L*, circumspectae *R*

But in the first place, who will not commiserate with the miserable lot of us whom you deride as madmen like Margites and Coroebus, and whom you mock wittily at will, so long as you have persuaded yourself that no papist in his stupidity can detect the most obvious contradictions of a potist? First you say that the church should be certain so that it can be known for certain where the gospel should be preached, for you say that it ought not to be preached, nor can it resound except in the church; from which you see the consequence that the church must be recognized before the gospel may be preached. Next, you say that the sole sign by which the church is recognized with certainty is the preaching of the gospel, for you admit that the rest of the signs are possessed by the papists also, among whom you say that the church does not exist. From this assumption of yours it follows that the gospel ought to be preached before the church can be recognized, since such preaching according to you is the sole sign by which the church is recognized for certain. You see then, O most prudent father, who never contradict yourself, how consistently and carefully you join two mutually contradictory propositions; namely, that the church must be recognized before the gospel may be preached, and that the gospel must be preached before the church may be recognized.

Now, distinguished doctor and most proficient posteriorist, since you demonstrate the certainty of the church from the certainty of the gospel and vice versa demonstrate the certainty of the gospel from the certainty of the church, please inform me by what posterioristic rule the posterior premise in this posterioristic demonstration of yours follows from the prior premise. For if you think you have sufficiently explained this as soon as you enjoin that one must first get a sure knowledge of the identity of the true church so that the gospel may be preached to her alone, and then again when men inquire about the church hold that she is known for certain through the preaching of the gospel, either you necessarily have a different posterioristic premise than everyone else has had up till now, or you are poorly practiced in posterioristics. For since you still leave uncertain to whom the gospel must be preached, and since you do not consider the gospel true unless it is preached to some persons or other whom you do not sufficiently specify, but conceive in your mind like Platonic Ideas, even when we seek to know it by your method of demonstration, the chariot will return to the starting point; and if we undertake a

currulus: ac si centies colligere, ac recolligere aggrediamur: easdem
semper propositiones, ultro citroque ueluti labyrinthi errores
repetemus: dicemusque cognoscere nos euangelium: propterea quod
ecclesiam cognoscimus: deinde illam nosse, eo quod euangelium
5   scimus: porro iterum euangelium, quia ecclesiam sciamus. Itaque his
claustris perpetuo septi, dum quaerimus egressum, et certam [H₂₁v]
tandem metam optamus attingere, cogimur eodem recurrere. Atque
haec est domini doctoris posterioristice qui, quum sibi iam prius fas
esse scripserit, coronam regiam conspergere et conspurcare stercori-
10 bus: an non nobis fas erit posterius, huius posterioristicae linguam
stercoratam, pronunciare dignissimam: ut

Digna retalio eo viro: qui reges   uel meientis mulae posteriora lingat suis
stercoribus consparsurum
se minetur   prioribus: donec rectius ex prioribus, didicerit posteriores concludere, propositioni-
15 bus. Qui ideo se certum de ecclesia iactitet: quia certus sit de uero
euangelio: certum autem de euangelio: quod certus est de ecclesia.
Rursusque de ecclesia sibi constare ex euangelio: et tamen ecclesiam
prius inquirendam: ut ei soli euangelium praedicetur. Caeterum eam
inuestigari non posse, nisi per euangelij praedicationem. Quis non
20 credat hunc hominem, aut insanire ipsum, aut alios prorsus omnes
insanire putare: qui nihil habet considerari, quid, apud quos, in quos,
ubi, quando, uel quomodo eblateret: extra omnem locum et rationem, citra omne pensum, quicquid in buccam uenerit effutiat: atque
quaelibet in quemuis eiaculetur opprobria, more Cynicorum, si quis
25 uel ausit hiscere contra eius placita, etiam absurdissima?

SED quaeso te Luthere, satin tibi sanus uideris: quum scribas
ecclesiam ueram, hoc est per te bonorum dumtaxat: et qui sine
peccato sunt, et sine peccato permanebunt, hoc est etiam per te
nullorum, quum neminem ponas absque peccato. Sed istud omitto.
30 Sint ista simul uera, et aliquam in terris esse ecclesiam, et de ea
neminem esse: nisi qui sit absque peccato: et neminem esse sine

---

31 et neminem] *corr. err. L*, atqui neminem *R*

hundred times over to make this inference, we will always return to
the same propositions by one way or the other, like the mazes of a
labyrinth, and we will say that we recognize the gospel because we
recognize the church, then that we know her because we know the
gospel, then again that we know the gospel because we know the 5
church. And so, fenced in continually by these barricades, when we
seek an exit and desire to reach a definite goal at last, we are forced to
return to the same place; that is, the posterioristic premise of the
honored Doctor. Since he has written that he already has a prior
right to bespatter and besmirch the royal crown with shit, will we not 10
have the posterior right to proclaim the beshitted tongue of this prac-
titioner of posterioristics most fit to lick with his anterior the
very posterior of a pissing she-mule until
he shall have learned more correctly to
infer posterior conclusions from prior
premises?

*A fit retort for the man who
threatens to bespatter kings
with shit* 15

When a fellow declares that he is certain about the church because
he is certain about the true gospel, but that he is certain about the
gospel because he is certain about the church, and again that he is certain about the church from the gospel and yet that the church must 20
first be sought so that the gospel may be preached to her alone, but
that she cannot be discovered except through the preaching of the
gospel, who would not believe that this fellow is either raving mad
himself or that he thinks absolutely everyone else raving mad, since he
has no consideration as to what, among whom, against whom, where, 25
when, or how he blathers, but without any occasion or reason blurts
out unthinkingly whatever fills his cheeks and, like the Cynics, hurls
out any abuse whatever against any person whatever, if anyone has so
much as dared to open his mouth against his whims, even the most
absurd? 30

But tell me, Luther, do you think you are in your right mind when
you describe the true church; that is, according to you a church consisting only of good men and of those who are without sin and will
remain without sin; that is, also according to you, a church of no
men, since you assert that no one is without sin? But I pass over this 35
matter.

Suppose that these statements of yours are both true: that there is
some church on earth and that no one belongs to it unless he is without sin; and that no one is without sin. Nevertheless, as I have said,

peccato: et tamen, ut dixi, quandoquidem tu ita uis, sit aliqua in
terris ecclesia talium, quales in terra nusquam sunt. An tu nunc [H$_{22}$]
censes ecclesiam istam tuam, bonorum et impeccabilium uirorum,
satis certam et perspectam esse, tribus hisce signis, baptismo, pane, et
5 uera praedicatione euangelij? Primum ista tria signa, manifeste sunt
in ecclesia nostra: quam tu uocas papistarum. Nam de baptismo, et
pane, nec ipse dubitas, haec duo esse apud nos: et ideo tertium dicis
esse signum, longe certius: nempe ueram euangelij praedicationem,
hanc omnino negas esse apud nos. At nos interpretamur et praedica-
10 mus euangelium, ex sententia sanctorum patrum, quamobrem si illi
uere praedicabant, et in hac ecclesia uere praedicatur: in qua tu
neminem dicis esse de ecclesia uera: nisi si quis forte paruulos
excipiat et simplices. Nam paruulos et simplices, non prorsus affirmas
eiectos ex ecclesia Christi: quamquam sunt de ecclesia papae, hoc est
15 per te de synagoga Sathanae: et tamen eos excipi pateris ab his: qui
non sunt de ecclesia Christi: ratus quod illi fortasse sine peccato sint,
et sine peccato quoque permansuri sint: et ideo in ecclesia Christi,
numerentur etiam sine uero, ut ais, euangelio: quod unum ponis
certissimum signum ecclesiae: et quod nusquam esse contendis in
20 ecclesia papae, de qua sunt illi simplices et paruuli: quia nos papistae,
in perpendendo scripturae sacrae sensu innitimur uestigijs sanctorum
patrum. Sed tu solus uere praedicas euangelium, et ante te nemo.
Nam tu scripturas expendis, et de sensu soli credis tibi: nec sanctis
quicquam credis patribus: gnarus, eos quamtumuis sancti fuerint,
25 fuisse tamen homines et errasse saepe, ita enim tu saepe iactas: quum
interim, opinor te scias hominem omnino non esse, sed doctrinam
tuam certus es habere te de caelo: et certus es te non magis errare
posse, quam asinum, angelum uolui dicere. Verum istud, abs te
Luthere quesierim: quo nam signo di[H$_{22}$v]scernis eum scripturae
30 sensum ueriorem esse: qui uidetur tibi: quam eum quem uides uisum
esse tam multis, tam doctis, et tam sanctis patribus? ex collatione
locorum inquis. An igitur, non conferebant illi? An tu illis rationem
censes, et iudicium defuisse, quod nunc supersit tibi? quum illi

---

11 praedicatur] *corr. err. L*, praedicantur *R*   27 magis] *corr. err. L*, magi *R*

since you will have it so, suppose there is on earth a church composed
of such men as are nowhere on earth. Do you think now that this
church of yours, consisting of good and sinless men, is sufficiently
certain and evident by these three signs: baptism, the bread and the
true preaching of the gospel? In the first place, these three signs of 5
yours are clearly in our church, which you call the church of the
papists. For, concerning baptism and the bread, not even you doubt
that we have these two, and so you say that the third sign is far more
certain; namely, the true preaching of the gospel; this you absolutely
deny that we have. But we interpret and preach the gospel according 10
to the mind of the holy fathers; and so, if they preached truly, then
there is true preaching even in this church, no member of which, you
say, belongs to the true church, unless one perhaps excepts children
and simple folk.

You do not assert outright that children and simple folk are cast 15
out of the church of Christ although they belong to the church of the
pope, that is, according to you, to the synagogue of Satan; and yet you
allow them to be excepted from those who do not belong to the
church of Christ, considering that they are perhaps without sin and
will also remain without sin; and so they are numbered in the church 20
of Christ even without what you call the true gospel, which you posit
as the single most certain sign of the church and which you argue
exists nowhere in the church of the pope to which these simple folk
and children belong, since we papists in carefully considering the
meaning of the sacred scripture walk in the footsteps of the holy 25
fathers. But you alone preach the gospel truly, and before you no one
did so. For you carefully weigh the scriptures and rely on yourself
alone in regard to their meaning; nor do you rely on any of the holy
fathers, knowing that, however holy they were, they were nevertheless men and often erred, as you often proclaim; whereas all the while 30
you know, I suppose, that you are not a man at all, but you are
certain that you have your doctrine from heaven, and you are certain
that you can err no more than an ass—I meant to say an angel.

But I would like to ask you this, Luther: by what sign do you
determine that the interpretation of scripture which seems right to 35
you is truer than that which you see has seemed right to such
numerous, such learned, and such holy fathers? You answer: from a
comparison of texts. Did they then not compare texts? Do you think
that they lacked such reason and judgment as now superabound in

rationem rectam sint secuti, uos eam propemodum studeatis extinguere: sed deus uidelicet aperuit petenti tibi, iuxta illud: Petite et accipietis: nam id iactare soles, certum te esse doctrinam tuam habere te de caelo: petisti uidelicet certa cum fiducia homo spiritualis: ut
5 duplex Heliae spiritus inspiraretur in te: in quem perspicuum est spirituum nequam aliquot, sese intrusisse, myriadas. Quid ergo censes de sanctissimis patribus, aut uoluntatem defuisse, aut opem dei non implorasse, aut in deo non habuisse fiduciam? Si deum contendis tam multa, tam utilia, tam necessaria, nunc indicare tibi, cur illum
10 putes cum tanto totius ecclesiae suae detrimento, illa omnia tam diu celasse tam sanctos? Sed non caelauit Luthere. Imo aperuit eorum oculos deus, et se accomodauit eorum modestiae: quum tuam auersatus arrogantiam, patitur te sapientem uideri in oculis tuis, ut cum philosophis, quos toties improbas, dicens te esse sapientem, stultus
15 fias: et euanescas in cogitationibus tuis: et itidem fiat, et euanescat tecum: quisquis in quaestione uirtutis, et fidei, non malit animam suam periclitari cum tot sanctorum cuneis: quos in caelis esse non dubitat: quam cum uno scurra blasphemo: quem, ualde caecus est quisquis non uidet, ad inferos ire praecipitem. Igitur Luthere, si
20 uerum est, quod ipse dicis, quod ubicunque haec tria sunt, baptismus, pa[H₂₃]nis, et uerum uerbum dei, ibi non est dubitandum ueram esse ecclesiam, quia signum uerbi, ut dicis, impossibile est sonare, nisi in ecclesia per spiritum sanctum: certe quum in ecclesia nostra sit uerum euangelium scriptum, et sancti patres illud uere sint inter-
25 pretati, et multi apud nos in templis, ut uocas papistarum: et idem euangelium scriptum legant, et ex sanctorum patrum interpretatione praedicent. necessario sequitur, etiam per te, id uerum esse: quod tu tantopere pernegas: ecclesiam istam quam appellas papisticam, ecclesiam esse uere Christi catholicam. Sed et istud ex te quaero: si
30 in his populis, qui parent pontifici, et tam diu paruerunt, toto hoc tempore non fuit ecclesia: dic ubi fuerit his annis quingentis proximis, ante natum te. Nam nunc, tu uidelicet noua progenies caelo demitteris alto, ut ecclesiam malorum instituas, in bona, et ante te

---

6 aliquot, sese intrusisse,] aliquot sese intrusisse *L*   7 defuisse] *L*, desuisse *R*   17 suam]
corr. err. L, sua *R*

you, whereas they followed right method, while you strive almost to destroy it? But God has of course opened to your seeking, according to the text: "Seek and you shall receive," for you are accustomed to boast that you are certain you have your teaching from heaven; spiritual man that you are, you have, of course, sought with sure confidence that the twofold spirit of Elias might be breathed into you, a man into whom it is clear that several myriads of evil spirits have thrust themselves. Why, therefore, do you think that the holy fathers either lacked good will or did not implore the help of God or did not have trust in God? If you argue that God is indicating to you at the present time so many, such useful, such necessary truths, why should you think that He concealed all these truths for such a long time from such holy men to the great detriment of His whole church? But He did not conceal them, Luther. Rather, God opened their eyes and responded to their humility, whereas, rejecting your arrogance, He allows you to appear wise in your own eyes, so that, together with the philosophers whom you so often deride, while saying that you are wise, you may become foolish and vanish in your own reflections; and everyone likewise may grow foolish and vanish with you who, in the matter of virtue and faith, instead of preferring to risk his soul with so many troops of saints who he does not doubt are in heaven, would rather do so with a single blasphemous buffoon whom only a blind man does not see rushing headlong to hell.

Therefore, Luther, if it is true, as you say, that wherever there are these three, baptism, bread, and the true word of God, there undoubtedly is the true church, because the sign of the word, so you say, cannot possibly resound except in the church through the Holy Spirit, then certainly, since the true gospel has been written in our church and the holy fathers have truly interpreted it, and many men read this same written gospel to us in the churches that you call papist, and preach it according to the interpretation of the holy fathers, it necessarily follows, also according to you, that that is true which you so vehemently deny: that this church which you call papist is truly the catholic church of Christ.

But I also ask this of you: If the church has not existed during this whole time among these people who obey the pope and have so long obeyed him, tell me where has it been these past five hundred years before you were born? For now of course you have been sent down, a new offspring from high heaven, to establish a church of evil men in

incorrupta Saxonia. Quae et ipsa, et Germania tota, si tu uerum dicis, hactenus fuit extra ecclesiam, et maiores eorum omnes descenderunt ad inferos. Verum illi, nunc in superis male praecantur tibi: qui eorum posteros ne illuc sequantur eos, per maliciam conaris auertere.

5 Sed, quoniam probauimus ex Lutheri positione sequi, ut si sua signa certam faciant ecclesiam, necessario certum sit, ecclesiam ueram esse quam ille falsam uocat, nunc examinare libet: quam prudenter ista tria signa statuat: uelut infallibilia ecclesiae uerae indicia: Memineris Luthere, te ecclesiam ponere dumtaxat tam sanctorum: ut sint

10 sine peccato. Age igitur, pone ob oculos quamcunque uelis congregationem: et quoniam tibi libuit literis ludere: et uelut per demonstrationes agere, per A. et .B. dum [H₂₃v] dicis tibi crasse philosophandum esse, cum crasso et pituita laborante capite, atque ita colligis: Si A. disputet cum B. et caetera quae tu praeclare connectis: eodem modo

15 nos homines crassi, et pituitosi, proponemus tenui et splendidae bili tuae. Esto igitur, tu sis A: auditores tui. B. C. D. sit aliquis, qui cupiat certus esse de aliqua uera ecclesia: quam sit persuasus non aliam esse: quam quae sit absque peccato: et audierit eam tribus signis, certo posse cognosci, baptismo, pane, et uera praedicatione

20 euangelij. Sed ut pergamus per literas. Sit hic si uoles .E. pone igitur, quod .E. ueniat in ecclesiam A. B. C. D. quos nouit esse baptisatos, et uidit usos eucharistia: audiat preterea ipsum A. suo more praedicantem euangelium, apud B. C. D. et pone per impossibile: quod praedicatio quam praedicat A. uera sit, et syncera praedicatio.

25 Vtrum ex his signis certo sciret E. quod A. B. C. D. sunt uera ecclesia, eo modo quo ille accipit ecclesiam ueram, hoc est quod A. B. C. D. sint uiri boni, et sine peccato: et respondeo, quod non: quod, ut tuis uerbis utar, euidenter probo sic. E, aut nouit ipse scripturas, et dogmata christianae fidei, et uenit ut nota rursus audiat, et crebra

30 auditione pietatem augeat: aut illa nondum nouit: sed audito Christi nomine quaerit ecclesiam, a qua perdiscat fidem. Si scripturas nouit, et christianae fidei dogmata: iam certo sciet E. istam ecclesiam .A.

---

32 ecclesiam .A.] *L*, ecclesam. A *R*

good (and before your time incorrupt) Saxony. Both Saxony and all
Germany, if you speak the truth, have till now been outside the
church, and all their ancestors have descended into hell. The truth is
that in heaven the latter now call down a curse upon you, who
through malice try to turn away their posterity from following them 5
there.

But since we have proved as a consequence from Luther's position
that if his signs make the church certain it is necessarily certain that
the true church is the one which he calls false, we may now consider
how cleverly he sets up these three signs as infallible marks of the true 10
church. You remember, Luther, that you posit a church consisting
only of men so holy that they are without sin. Come then, set before us
any congregation you will, and since it has pleased you to play with
letters and to argue by means of A and B as by proofs when you say
that you must philosophize dully with a dull and phlegmatic block- 15
head and thus make your deduction: "If A should dispute with B,"
and so on with your brilliant inference; in the same manner we dull
and phlegmatic fellows shall set forth a proposition for your thin and
shiny black bile. So, then, you be A; your hearers B, C, D; let there be
someone who longs to be certain about some true church, which he is 20
persuaded is none other than that which is without sin, and let him
have heard that this church can be recognized with certainty by
three signs: baptism, the bread, and the true preaching of the gospel.
But to proceed by means of letters: let this man be E, if you will.
Suppose, then, that E comes into the church of A, B, C, D, who he 25
knows have been baptized and who he perceives have received the
eucharist; let him moreover hear A himself preaching the gospel in
his usual manner before B, C, D; and suppose, by an impossibility,
that the preaching which A preaches is true and sincere preaching.
Would E know for certain from these signs that A, B, C, D, are the 30
true church, according as he understands the true church; that is,
that A, B, C, D should be good men and without sin. And I answer,
"No"; which, to use your words, I clearly prove thus. Either E himself knows the scriptures and teachings of the Christian faith and
comes in order to hear again teachings which he knows and to increase 35
his devotion by hearing them frequently, or he does not yet know
those things, but, having heard the name of Christ, is seeking the
church from which he may thoroughly learn the faith. If he knows
the scriptures and the teachings of the Christian faith, then E will

B. C. D. per ista signa, certam esse non posse. Incertum enim
adhuc esse sibi, utrum .A. B. C. D. boni sint an mali.

Nam et dissimulari uitia possunt, et simulari uirtutes. Cognoscet
praeterea, et apud malos bene praedicari posse, sicut Christus ipse
5 praedicauit saepe Scribis, et Pharisaeis, et non [H$_{24}$] solum a malo
uiro posse praedicari ueritatem, sed etiam a diabolo: et illud falsissimum esse, quod dicis tu, uidelicet uerum uerbum non posse sonare,
nisi in ecclesia uera: quae sit absque peccato, nisi mentitur propheta:
quum ex persona dei dicit: Peccatori autem dixit deus, quare tu
10 assumis testamentum meum per os tuum. Aut nisi falsum fuit: quod
dixit diabolus: quum per os hominis insani Christum confessus est,
esse filium dei. Vides ergo Luthere: quod si E. scripturas intelligat, et
dogmata fidei christianae: iam ex ipsis, ipse certus erit, se incertum
esse de ecclesia, A. B. C. D. utrum sit uera, an falsa: hoc est utrum sit
15 bona an mala: quia quantum ad uirtutem pertinet ac uitium, E. per
nullum istorum signorum tuorum potest esse certus, utrum A. sit albus
an ater: utrum B. sit bonus an bufo: utrum C. sit creta an carbo:
utrum D. sit deus an diabolus. Atque haec Luthere, uides esse uera,
etiam posito per impossibile, quod praedicatio, quam praedicat A.
20 recta foret et indubie uera. Ex quo facile uides: quam longe tibi retro
res nunc labatur, apud E. uidelicet intelligentem, et pium: quum
praedicatio quam praedicat A. uere sit et indubie falsissima.

SED iam uideamus alteram partem. Si .E. nesciat adhuc neque
quae sint scripturae uerae, neque quae sint uera christianae fidei
25 dogmata: sed de sua salute sollicitus, audita Christi fama, uelit eius
fidem religionemque cognoscere: tunc dico quod E. ueniens in
ecclesiam .A. B. C. D. et audiens A. more suo praedicantem talia:
qualia solet apud .B. C. D. et uidens B. C. D. assentientes, et asse-
rentes hanc esse ueram praedicationem. Primum si illa talia essent
30 uera: tamen E. non posset [H$_{24}$v] habere rem pro explorata: propterea quod audierit A. B. C. D. non esse nisi minimam particulam
eorum: qui profitentur fidem Christi: nec posset ipsis solis auditis
certus esse: utrum .A. B. C. D. aut ueras scripturas profiterentur, aut
ueras uere interpretarentur: nec iudicare posset: utrum id quod apud

---

8 mentitur] mentiatur *L*   16 A.] *L*, A *R*   19 per impossibile] *L*, peri mpossibile *R*
19 A.] *L*, A, *R*   21 apud E.] *corr. err. L*, E. *om. R*   22 A.] A, *RL*   32 profitentur]
L, profitenrur *R*   33 esse: utrum] esse verum *L*

know for certain that this church of A, B, C, D, cannot be known for
certain through these signs. For he is still uncertain whether A, B, C,
D, are good or evil. For they can dissimulate vices as well as simulate
virtues. He will recognize, moreover, that there can be good preaching among wicked men, as Christ Himself often preached to the   5
Scribes and Pharisees; and that the truth can be preached not only
by a wicked man but even by the devil; and he will recognize as
utterly false your statement that the true word cannot resound except
in the true church, such as is without sin; unless the prophet is lying
when in the name of God he says: "But God said to the sinner, 'Why   10
do you profess my covenant with your mouth?' " Or unless the devil
spoke falsely when through the mouth of a raving madman he confessed that Christ is the Son of God.

You see, therefore, Luther, that if E should understand the scriptures and doctrines of the Christian faith, then from them he will be   15
certain that he is uncertain whether the church of A, B, C, D, is true
or false; that is, whether it is good or evil, because insofar as virtue
and vice are concerned, E cannot be certain by means of any of these
signs of yours whether A is black or white, whether B is a good man
or a toad, whether C is chalk or charcoal, whether D is deity or devil.   20
And you see that this is true, Luther, even given the impossible
supposition that the preaching of A were accurate and undoubtedly
true. From this you have no trouble seeing how far your case is
losing ground in the estimation of E, clearly an intelligent and
virtuous person, since the preaching which A preaches is truly and   25
without doubt utterly false.

But now let us consider another possibility. Suppose that E should
not yet know either which are the true scriptures or which are the
true teachings of the Christian faith but, being concerned about his
salvation and having heard reports of Christ, he should wish to   30
become thoroughly acquainted with the latter's faith and religion. E,
then, as I say, comes into the church of A, B, C, D, and hears A
preaching in his usual manner his usual teachings before B, C, D, and
he sees B, C, D agreeing and declaring that this preaching is true. In
the first place, if such teachings were true, E could still not consider   35
the case as proven because he has heard that A, B, C, D are only a
minimal fraction of those who profess the faith of Christ, nor could he
after listening only to them be certain whether A, B, C, D were either
professing the true scriptures or interpreting the true ones truly; nor

eos audiret uerum esset euangelium an non: nec de tanta re tam
paucis esset crediturus, nullo permotus miraculo. Ergo, quum E.
postea, tot nationes christianas perlustraret: et quantum ad salutis
necessitatem pertinet, ubique uideret eandem fidem, eadem dogmata.
5 Quum ex ueterum sanctorum scriptis intelligeret, ijsdem de rebus
eadem sensisse constanter omnes doctores sanctos: quicunque fuerunt
a Christo passo, in haec usque tempora: iam non dubitaret E. si qua
sit in terris ecclesia Christi uera, hanc esse congregationem quae per
Christum coepta, propagata per apostolos, edocta per sanctos,
10 speciali dei cura perpetuo, per tot secula permansit in unitate
christianae fidei. Ergo, si postea redeat rursus E. in ecclesiam
.A. B. C. D. et rursus audiat A. suo more, qualia solet, apud .B. C. D.
praedicantem, et asserentem se praedicare uerum, et genuinum
uerbum dei: et illos omnes christianos: quos E. in tot populis audiuit
15 alibi, decipi prorsus, et errare damnabiliter: fieri certe non potest:
quin E. quum uideat ecclesiam .A. B. C. D. non nisi riuulum quendam esse, ab illa magna dimanantem: et nunc ab ea diuulsam: et
quum non aliud quam scripturas admittat: alias tamen scripturas
non habeat: sed aliter eas, contraque, tractet: quam tota illa, tot
20 terrarum, tot aetatum tractet ecclesia: et de earum sensu sibi arroget,
contra [H$_{25}$(numb. H$_{16}$)] tot aetatum, tot et tam doctos, tam sanctos
interpretes, contra totius orbis christiani consensum: quem consensum, ex scripturis iam didicit .E. spiritu Christi coalescere: quumque uideat .E. apud .A. B. C. D. maximis de rebus, multa perabsurda
25 dogmata, non solum ecclesiae illi catholicae contraria: sed in publicos
etiam mores perniciosissima. Fieri, inquam, non potest: quin .E. certo
sit intellecturus ecclesiam .A. B. C. D. non esse ecclesiam Christi, nec
bonorum coetum: sed pessimorum scurrarum gurgustium, et conciliabulum Sathanae: et iam ex his interpretaretur .A. uel alpha esse
30 haereticorum, uel Antichristum. Sed nec fieri potest: quin .E. quum
certo iam et pernorit ecclesiam illam ueram: quae perpetua quadam

---

15 fieri] *L*, fieti *R*   26 perniciosissima.] perniciosissima, *L*   31 ecclesiam] Ecclesiam
L, ecciesiam *R*

could he judge whether that which he was hearing among them was the true gospel or not; nor would he be ready to believe so few men on a matter of such profound importance without being persuaded to do so by a miracle. Therefore, when E would later travel through so many Christian nations and would perceive everywhere the same faith, the same teachings regarding what is necessary for salvation; when he would perceive from the writings of ancient holy men that all the holy doctors from the time of Christ's passion even to the present time have consistently agreed on these same points; then E would have no doubt that, if there is any true church of Christ on earth, it is this congregation which, begun by Christ, spread by the apostles, taught by the saints, has by God's special care persisted unceasingly through so many ages in the unity of the Christian faith.

Therefore, if E should later return into the church of A, B, C, D, and again hear A preaching in his usual manner his usual teachings before B, C, D, and declaring that he is preaching the true and genuine word of God and that all those Christians whom E has heard elsewhere among so many peoples are utterly deceived and damnably in error, surely it cannot but happen that E, since he sees the church of A, B, C, D to be nothing but a kind of rivulet trickling off from that great church and now violently separated from her; and since it admits nothing but the scriptures, yet does not have different scriptures but interprets them in a way different from and contrary to that in which that whole church of so many lands and so many ages interprets them; and since it arrogates their interpretation to itself in opposition to so many and such learned and such holy interpreters of so many ages, in opposition to the agreement of the whole Christian world, an agreement which E has already learned from the scriptures takes root through the Spirit of Christ; and when E sees among A, B, C, D, many extremely absurd teachings on most important topics, which are not only contrary to that catholic church, but also utterly destructive of public morals, it cannot but happen, I say, that E will understand with certainty that the church of A, B, C, D is not the church of Christ nor an assembly of good men, but that it is the hovel of the most corrupt buffoons and the brothel of Satan; and then from these facts he would recognize A either as the alpha of heretics, or as Antichrist. On the other hand, it cannot but happen that, since E is now certainly and thoroughly acquainted also with that true church which has been continued by a certain unbroken

serie propagata est, ab ea: quam olim instituit Christus: et semper
incorrupta mansit in fide stirpis, facile sit cogniturus, quantacunque
pars ab ea se diuulserit: ramum arefactum fore, diuini spiritus exper-
tem: qui nusquam manebit, nisi in sua uinea, in quantulamcunque,
5 rescissis palmitibus, sit redacta. Ecce Luthere: qui te tam impudenter
exclamas Ambrosium demonstratiue conuincere: habes ne quicquam,
quod hic possis hiscere: quo minus te fatearis, tui generis demonstratione, uictum ac reuictum euidentissime, probatumque nobis, et
tuam ecclesiam conciliabulum esse Sathanae, et promiscuam
10 christianorum multitudinem, uulgo notam et sensibilem ecclesiam
esse Christi catholicam: cuius milites modo uincunt modo uincuntur:
dum adhuc ecclesia militat in terris.

IAM quum Lutherus tam pulchre pronunciet, de tot chri[H₂₅v]sti-
anis gentibus: quae obediunt papae: ut eas omnes asserat esse om-
15 nium sceleratissimos: nec dubitandum esse quin ibi ecclesia non sit:
nisi quis ut ait paruulos excipiat et simplices, libenter ab illo
quesierim, ubinam gentium sint illi grandes et duplices: qui nunquam peccant: quos ueram uocat ecclesiam. Nam sceleratissimam
plane, et Sathanae synagogam esse, totam dicit Italiam, totam
20 Angliam, Scotiam, Hiberniam, totas Hyspanias, ac lusitaneam, et
usque ad suum euangelium, totam fuisse Germaniam. Nam has
gentes omnes, satis constat reuerenter hactenus agnouisse successorem
petri. Nos tamen benignius sentimus de Saxonia: quam serpentis
istius pestifer infecit halitus. Nam et ibi quoque, speramus deum
25 reseruasse sibi grandium et sapientum septies septem millia: quae non
curuarunt genua sua ante Baal. Sed age, magna parte temporis, quod
Christi salutiferam mortem, et Lutheri mortiferum ortum intercessit,
si istae nationes, non faciebant maximam saltem partem ecclesiae:
dic quibus in terris erat ecclesia. Nam etiam si ecclesia non obligatur
30 ad ullam partem terrae, necesse est tamen aliqua in parte sit. Certe,
si in istis partibus terrae non fuit iamdiu aut mire pusilla fuit, aut
nusquam fuit. Constat igitur, etiam si ecclesia non sit christianorum
multitudo promiscua, sed bonorum hominum numerus, aut qui sic

---

7–8 demonstratione, uictum ac reuictum] demonstratione victum, ac reuictum *L*
13 pronunciet] *corr. err.*, pronunciet *L*, producat *R*   16 excipiat et simplices,] *L*,
excipiat, et simplices *R*   20 lusitaneam] Lusitaniam *L*

succession from the one which Christ long ago established and which
has ever remained uncorrupted in the faith of its origin, he will easily
recognize that, however great a part has violently torn itself away
from her, it will be a withered branch, lacking the divine Spirit who
will remain only in His own vine, however much it may have been   5
reduced by the pruning of its branches.

Look, Luther, you who so shamelessly proclaim that you demon-
stratively refute Ambrose, have you anything to mutter here to
prevent your having to admit that you have been most evidently
defeated and refuted by your own mode of demonstration, and that   10
we have proved both that your church is the brothel of Satan and
that the common multitude of Christians is the universally known
and perceptible catholic church of Christ whose soldiers now conquer,
now are conquered, so long as the church still battles on earth?

Now, since Luther makes such a fair proclamation about the many   15
Christian nations that obey the pope as to declare positively that they
are all the most wicked of all men and that the church is undoubtedly
not among them, unless, as he says, one excepts children and simple
folk, I should like to ask him where in the world are those grown-ups
and unsimple people who never sin, whom he calls the true church.   20
For he says that all Italy, all England, Scotland, Ireland, all of Spain
and Portugal are, and until the time of his own gospel all Germany
was, clearly most wicked and the synagogue of Satan. For all these
nations, it is well enough known, have up till now reverently acknowledged the successor of Peter. We nevertheless judge more kindly of   25
Saxony, which the pestiferous breath of this serpent has infected. For
we hope that there also God has preserved for Himself seven times
seven thousand mature and wise men who have not bent the knee to
Baal.

But come, if, during the long period of time intervening between   30
the healing death of Christ and the death-dealing birth of Luther,
these nations did not form at least the greatest part of the church, tell
me where on earth was the church. Even if the church is not confined
to any part of the earth, nevertheless she must necessarily be in some
part of it. Certainly, if she has not been in these parts of the earth,   35
then for a long time now she has been either remarkably small or she
has been nowhere. It is evident, then, that even if the church should
not be the common multitude of Christians but the number of good
men, whether of those who have been so thoroughly converted that

resipuerint: ut nunquam denuo peccaturi sint, aut qui subinde
resurgentes, subinde casuri sint: tantisper in ecclesia censendi: quam
diu steterint, eiecti quum ceciderint, recepti quum redierint: tamen
ne sic quidem quicquam confecisse te. Nam, et horum certum est
5　multo maximam partem, longo iam tempore in his fuisse genti [H$_{26}$
(numb. H$_{17}$)]bus: quae sedem Petri reuerentur ut matrem. Neque
enim usquam est, aut diu fuit alibi, tantum populorum profitentium
fidem Christi. Sequitur igitur, ut si non hae nationes sint ecclesia:
saltem in his nationibus sit ecclesia: aut quod negari non potest,
10　multo maxima pars ecclesiae. At hactenus in his nationibus, optimi
quique maxime paruere pontifici, pessimi quique maxime rebellarunt
pontifici, leges sanctissimi uiri condiderunt: optimi quique maxime
seruauerunt: pessimi quique maxime contempserunt. Sacramenta
concorditer uenerabantur uniuersi, uix unus aut alter e tot populis, in
15　tot aetatibus exortus est: qui quicquam contra mutierit: et ijdem
semper notae nobilisque maliciae. Quaecunque ergo uera sit ecclesia,
quae quidem sit aut fuerit, diu in his populis, qui maximi sunt in
professione christianae fidei, dogmatis aduersatur et semper est
aduersata tuis. Quod si tibi parum uidetur istud, quod plane tua plus
20　quam pessundat omnia, profer tu gentem aliquam, ubi unquam in tot
aetatibus, ante natum te, tue probatae sunt haereses. Ostende apud
quos christianos, sacerdos nihil distarit a laico: apud quos christianos,
mulieres admissae sint ad audiendas confessiones: ubi credite sint
foeminae sacerdotes esse: et idoneae quae conficerent eucharistiam:
25　ubi sit receptum nullas leges obligare christianos: et mille absurditates
eiusmodi. Quod si non potes, ut certe non potes, non est quod
amplius arguteris de ecclesia. Nam, quaecunque tot aetatibus uera fuit
ecclesia, siue illa fuit bonorum malorumque multitudo promiscua,
siue numerus dumtaxat bonorum, siue in his regionibus quae parent
30　Romano pontifici, siue alibi ubicunque terrarum, semper contra te
sensit illa: et tua damnauit [H$_{26}$v] insanissima dogmata. Nam, quod

1 resipuerint] *corr. err L*, respuerint *R*　　10 ecclesiae] *L*, ecelesiae *R*　　16 maliciae]
miliciae *L*　　23 admissae] *corr. err. L*, adnussae *R*　　27 quaecunque] *L*, quecunque *R*

they will never sin again or of those who while frequently rising will frequently fall, who are to be considered in the church so long as they stand firm, being cast out when they have fallen and received back again when they revive, yet not even so have you proved anything. For, even of these men, it is certain that by far the greatest portion 5 have for a long time now been among those nations which revere the See of Peter as the mother see. For there is not anywhere, nor for a long time has there been elsewhere, such a great number of peoples professing the faith of Christ. It follows, therefore, that if these nations are not the church, at least the church is within these 10 nations; or, and this cannot be denied, by far the greatest part of the church is among them. Yet up till now in these nations, all the best men have been especially obedient to the pontiff, all the worst men have been especially rebellious against the pontiff. Men of the greatest holiness have established laws; all the best men most care- 15 fully observed the laws; all the worst men most carelessly scorned them. With one heart they all venerated the sacraments; hardly one or the other of so many people arose during so many ages to murmur anything against them; and those who did were always of known and notorious wickedness. Whichever may be the true church, therefore, 20 such as indeed exists or has existed a long time among these peoples who are foremost in the profession of the Christian faith, it opposes and always has opposed your teachings.

But if this statement, which, clearly, more than destroys all your arguments, seems negligible to you, then mention any people among 25 whom at any time during all the ages before your birth your heresies have been approved. Show us among which Christians there was no difference between priest and layman; among which Christians women were allowed to hear confessions; where females were believed to be priests and fitted for consecrating the Eucharist; where 30 it was accepted that no laws bind the Christians; and a thousand similar absurdities. If you cannot do this, as you certainly cannot, then you have nothing further to prate about the church. For which- ever has been the true church through so many ages, whether that has been the common multitude of good and bad men, or only 35 the number of good men, whether in those regions which obey the Roman pontiff or anywhere else on earth, that church has always disagreed with you and has condemned your utterly insane teachings.

ais papistarum esse figmentum: quod aliud sit iurisdictionis, aliud
fraternae charitatis officium: et dicis euangelium et ecclesiam nescire
iurisdictiones (nam eas non ais esse, nisi tyrannicas inuentiones
hominum) certe nisi tu totus esses potista, facile cerneres non esse
5 prorsus idem iurisdictionem et charitatis officium: etiam si uerum est
nullam esse iurisdictionem christianam: quae non ex charitate sit
instituta. Sed tamen multa potest et debet praesidentis authoritas:
quae sibi, nec potest nec debet arrogare, cuiusque priuati hominis
charitas. Alioqui si iurisdictio nihil est omnino, cur Paulus iurisdic-
10 tionem exercuit? Cur hominem tradidit Sathanae in interitum carnis?
Cur planissime proponit. Qui potestati resistit ordinationi dei resistit.
Cur seruari praecipit, quae tradidit ipse? Cur praecepit obedire
praepositis? Cur ipse Christus obedire iussit Scribis, et Phariseis super
cathedram Moysi sedentibus? Cur ipse praebuit iurisdictionis
15 exemplum, et flagello uendentes eiecit e templo? Imo cur ipse turpiter
dissimulas, inter ipsa uerba Christi pasce oues meas, uerbum esse,
quod te confutat? Neque enim ignoras, sed dissimulas turpiter: quod
uir citra ullam controuersiam eruditissimus, et de ecclesia Christi
optime meritus, Erasmus Roterodamus annotauit, esse in illa repeti-
20 tione uerbi ποιμαίνειν, quod significat regere: sed quum istud nemo
non uideat, tibi satis est, si te dissimules cernere. Non opinor expec-
tare quenquam, ut ad praeclaram allegoriam tuam respondeam, qua
scribis tria signa figurari, per duo capita uectium, in templo Solo-
monis extra arcam extantia: quippe quum nihilominus concinne
25 potuisses, eadem figurare per duas Moysi tabulas, aut duo Moysi
cornua. [H₂₇(numb. H₁₈)]

IAM istud, nescio quanti facias ipse: quod bis immittis in nos,
nempe quod in symbolo confitemur, nos ecclesiam sanctam catholicam credere. Ex quo colligis, quum fides argumentum sit rerum non
30 apparentium, si ecclesia creditur, et est materia fidei, nullo modo
ecclesiam esse sensibilem istam bonorum et malorum multitudinem:
quae cuiuis apparet et humano sensu percipitur. Hoc telum, bis in

17–19 quod uir . . . annotauit] *om. L*   22 tuam respondeam, qua] *L,* tuam, respondeam
qua *R*

As for your statement that it is a fiction of the papists that the function of jurisdiction is one thing, that of fraternal charity another —and your statement that the gospel and the church know nothing of jurisdictions, for you say that these latter exist only through the tyrannical inventions of men—surely, if you were not an utter toper, 5 you would easily perceive that jurisdiction and the function of charity are not altogether the same; even if it is true that there is no Christian jurisdiction which has not been instituted out of charity. But still, the authority of a ruler can and ought to do many things which the charity of any one private individual neither can nor ought to arro- 10 gate to itself. Otherwise, if jurisdiction is nothing at all, why did Paul exercise jurisdiction? Why did he deliver a man over to Satan for the destruction of the flesh? Why did he declare most clearly that he who resists authority resists the ordinance of God? Why did he command that what he himself taught should be observed? Why did he com- 15 mand men to obey their rulers? Why did Christ Himself order the people to obey the Scribes and Pharisees who sat in the seat of Moses? Why did He Himself present an example of jurisdiction and drive the sellers out of the temple with a whip? For that matter, why do you yourself basely conceal that in the very words of Christ, "Feed my 20 sheep," there is a word which refutes you? You are not unaware, but you basely conceal the fact that Erasmus of Rotterdam, a man extremely learned beyond all cavil and one who has deserved very highly of the church of Christ, has noted the fact that there is in the repeated word *poimainein* the meaning "to rule"; but although every- 25 one sees this, it is enough for you to pretend that you do not perceive it. I do not suppose anyone expects me to answer your extraordinary allegory in which you write that the three signs are represented by the two heads of the carrying-poles appearing outside the ark in the temple of Solomon, since you could of course have represented the 30 same signs no less appropriately by the two tablets of Moses or by the two horns of Moses.

Now I do not know how much importance you attach to this fact which you twice let loose against us, namely that in the creed we confess that we believe in the holy catholic church, from which you 35 infer that, since faith is the evidence of things not seen, if the church is believed in and is a matter of faith, then the church is in no way that perceptible multitude of good and bad men which is apparent to everyone and is perceived by human sense. This weapon you twice

manum sumis: bis intorques fortiter: siue quod tibi uidebatur
splendidum, et quod contrectare delectabat: siue quod sentiebas esse
tam obtusum, ut saepius oporteret incuti. Hac in re, primum miror
symbolum, quod ut est, ita debet esse magni ponderis apud omnes
5 fideles, quicquam habere ponderis apud te. Nam symbolum constat
opinor traditionem esse, non scripturam: nam nec intra scripturam
canonicam numeratur: nec sanctorum patrum quisquam, quod
sciam, quum ei propositum fuisset, aliquid probare scripturis, unquam probauit ex symbolo. Quare, si tu Luthere, qui toties aduersus
10 traditiones exclamas: qui te toties clamas nihil recipere praeter
euidentes scripturas, ecclesiam credis propter authoritatem symboli
manifeste profecto, decedis de sententia: et traditionibus credis, non
scripturis. Nec istud eo dico: quod te hac in parte uituperem. Imo
adeo laudo: uellemque idem ut faceres saepius. Esset enim plauden-
15 dum: si incipias aliquando in melius esse mutabilis: qui quauis aura
incertior, et quouis folio leuior, subinde te mutas in peius.

SED interim, te quaeso, quid lucraris in causa? Nam quum planum
sit, aliam esse ecclesiam triumphantem in caelo, aliam hic militantem
in terris: quid probasti tu, de hac? si ar[H$_{27}$v]ticulus loquatur de illa:
20 ut quum percensuisset quae de diuina trinitate credenda sunt, et
humanitate Christi: tandem speratum credentium premium proponat: credendum etiam illud: quod alioqui certo sperari non possit:
admonitos itaque mortales, qui fidem profiteri uelint: ut indubitanter
crederent ecclesiam fore catholicam: quae sancta societate, remissis
25 peccatis, rediuiua carne, redditisque corporibus, uita frueretur eterna.
Sed et in terris quoque, tametsi non sit incertum quae sit: aut ubi sit
ecclesia Christi catholica, cuius consentientis authoritas, certum
quemque facit et de scripturis ueris, et de necessarijs articulis fidei,
atque ita certum, sit istud: ut hac ratione sit ecclesia sensibilis: tamen
30 et ipsa multis modis pendet a fide. Nam, etiam si sensui patet: quae
sit illa: quae de fide consentit: sensui tamen non patet, hunc con-

---

take in hand; twice you hurl it forcefully, either because it seemed to you a splendid weapon and you delighted to handle it, or because you sensed that it was so dull that it needed to be hurled more frequently. On this point I am surprised first of all that the creed, which is, as it ought to be, of great weight with all the faithful, has any weight with you. For it is well known, I think, that the creed is tradition, not scripture; it is not listed in the scriptural canon, nor did any of the holy fathers, so far as I know, when he proposed to prove something from the scriptures, ever prove it from the creed. Therefore, if you, Luther, who so often cry out against tradition, who so often declare that you accept nothing but evident scriptures, if you believe in the church on the authority of the creed, then you are evidently indeed departing from your opinion and you are believing traditions, not scriptures. And I do not say this to reproach you in this matter. Indeed, I praise you exceedingly, and I would wish you did the same thing more often. It would be a matter worth applauding if you should ever begin to be capable of changing for the better, you who, more unstable than any wind, and more flighty than any leaf, repeatedly change yourself for the worse.

But meanwhile I ask you: What are you gaining for your case? Since it is clear that the church triumphant in heaven is one thing, the church militant here on earth is another, what have you proved about the latter, if the article of the creed speaks of the former, in that, having enumerated what must be believed about the divine Trinity and about the humanity of Christ, it finally presents the hoped-for reward of those who believe as something itself to be believed, since otherwise it could not be hoped for with certainty, and thus mortals who would wish to profess the faith are reminded that they should unhesitatingly believe that there will be a catholic church which, in holy fellowship, with sins forgiven, with flesh revivified, and with bodies restored, will enjoy life everlasting?

But on earth also, even if there be no uncertainty about the identity or the location of the catholic church of Christ, whose unanimous authority gives everyone certainty about the true scriptures and about necessary articles of faith, and even if it be so certain that for this reason the church is perceptible to sense, nevertheless she herself depends in many ways on faith. For, even if the identity of that church which agrees on matters of faith is evident to sense, yet it is not evident to sense that this agreement does not come about by

sensum, non humana conspiratione fieri: sed nasci atque inspirari
diuinitus: nam id, nemo nisi fide concipit. Iam, quamquam ecclesiae
corpus sit sensibile: tamen, quod Christus eius mysticum caput sit:
id quoque non sensus ostendit, sed fides. Quin et istud, quod quicun-
5　que sanctus est in terra, pars est huius ecclesiae: quae etiam hic adeo
sancta dicitur, non quod nemo sit in ea, qui peccat: sed quod nemo
est in terra sanctus: qui non est membrum huius ecclesiae: istud
inquam fide docemur non sensu. Quamobrem, et recte credimus
ecclesiam catholicam, propter multa, quae sensui non apparent, sed
10　omnino pendent a fide: et tamen nihilo minus constat euidenter,
hanc promiscuam et sensibilem multitudinem, profitentium nomen et
fidem Christi, esse ecclesiam catholicam: qua docente, scriptura
discernitur: et certo discitur, et cognoscitur fides. Sed decies ad id
recurrit: quod ecclesia non potest esse multitudo ista promiscua: quia
15　[H₂₈] peccatores non sunt de ecclesia: nec meminit, quod in archa
Noe, quae praefigurabat ecclesiam, animalia immunda commixta
sunt mundis. Quaeso te Luthere, quum apostolus scriberet Corinthijs, an non scripsit ad ecclesiam? An igitur, nihil peccati taxat in
ecclesia. Quid, quum scribit ad Galathas non ibi quoque scribit ad
20　ecclesiam? et tamen insensatos uocat, et usque adeo clamat errare,
ut miretur etiam, quis eos fascinauerit. Iam in reuelatione Ioannis
euangelistae, quum septem ecclesijs loquitur spiritus, nihil ne reperit
usquam uicij? Quam seuere minatur, quosdam eiecturum se ni
resipiscant? Caeterum, quamquam peccantes, et si perstiterint
25　euomendos: interea tamen numerat in ecclesia. Quin Christus ipse,
de ecclesia sua praesens praesente pronunciauit: non omnes esse
bonos. Vos, inquit, mundi estis: sed non omnes. Et iterum. Nonne
duodecim elegi uos: et unus ex uobis diabolus est? Quod si commemorare uellem sanctorum patrum sententias: quae huic sententiae
30　subscribunt: et longum esset, et apud te superuacuum: qui flocci facis
unus uniuersos: apud quem, nec totius ecclesiae consensus quicquam
habet ponderis: quae non aliquos habere peccatores, sed se confessa
peccatricem totam quotidie clamat ad dominum: Ecclesiae tuae deus,

---

9 sed] *corr. err. L*, si *R*　　17–18 Corinthijs] Corrinthijs *R*, Corin. *L*　　19 ecclesia.] ecclesia?
L　　26 praesens praesente] praesente praesens *L*　　30 esset] *L*, esser *R*

human conspiring but that it is divinely born and inspired, for this no one grasps except by faith. Moreover, although the body of the church is perceptible to sense, yet the fact that Christ is her mystical head is likewise shown not by sense but by faith. Indeed, this fact also, that whoever is holy on earth is part of this church, which is 5 called holy even here on earth not because there is no one in her who sins but because no one on earth is holy who is not a member of this church; this fact, I say, is taught us by faith, not by sense. Thus, we rightly believe in the catholic church because of the many things which do not appear to sense but which depend wholly on faith, and 10 yet it is nonetheless manifestly certain that this common and perceptible multitude of men professing the name and faith of Christ is the catholic church by whose teaching the scripture is determined and the faith is learned and recognized with certainty. Luther, however, reverts ten times to the statement that the church cannot be this 15 common multitude, because sinners do not belong to the church; nor does he remember that in Noah's ark, which prefigured the church, unclean animals were mingled with clean ones. I ask you, Luther: When the apostle was writing to the Corinthians, did he not write to the church? Or does he, for this reason, censure no sin in the church? 20 What about when he writes to the Galatians? Is he not there also writing to the church? And yet he calls them senseless men, and he protests that they are so much in error that he wonders who has bewitched them. Moreover, in the Revelation of John the evangelist, when the Spirit speaks to the seven churches, does He find no fault 25 anywhere? How severely He threatens to cast out certain men unless they repent! But although they are sinning and must be vomited out if they persist in their sin, He nevertheless numbers them meanwhile within the church. Indeed, Christ Himself, while dwelling personally with His church, said of her that not all were good: "You," He said, 30 "are clean but not all of you." And again: "Have I not chosen you twelve and one of you is a devil?"

But if I wished to recall the opinions of the holy fathers which support this opinion of mine, it would take a long time and would be useless with you who, as a single individual, make light of all men 35 taken together; in your mind not even the agreement of the whole church has any weight whatever when she confesses, not that some sinners belong to her, but that she herself is wholly a sinner and cries out daily to the Lord: "Forgive the sins of thy church, O God." Nor

peccatis ignosce. Nec id humano docta consilio: sed ab ipso docta
Christo: qui et apostolos suos orare docuit: ut deus eis debita sua
dimitteret. Itaque ecclesia Christi, dum uersatur in terris, non adeo
adhuc depurata est: quin et peccata quaedam assidue maculent
5   bonos: et inter bonos ubique uiuant mali: qui interea, non aliter sunt
in ecclesia: quam morbidae partes in ulceroso corpore. Nam adhuc,
etiam si sani non sunt: tamen utcunque uiuunt, et aluntur calore
quodam di[H_{28}v]uini spiritus: qui animat et conseruat ecclesiam,
penetrans omnia fortiter, et disponens omnia suauiter. Nec desinet
10   aegras partes circumferre secum: quam diu in terris peregrinatur
ecclesia, nec desinet Christus pro partibus aegris interpellare patrem:
qui mystici corporis morbos ingemuit, ac deplorauit in cruce: longe
sunt, inquiens, a salute mea, uerba delictorum meorum. Verum quum
ueniet dies, in qua corruptione deposita uestietur immortalitate, tum
15   defluentibus tabidis illis, et putrefactis uisceribus, restabit ecclesiae
corpus undique purum ac nitidum: quod interea gestat gestabitque
morbidum: sed quantumuis morbidum, nunquam gestabit mortuum.
Erit enim cum eo Christus, et uerbum eius quod siue scriptum sit,
siue sine scripto traditum, utroque modo spiritus est et uita cum fide
20   quae per dilectionem operatur, credentibus: quod genus fidei, ne
deficiat unquam, aut desit ecclesiae, cui Christus praefecit Petrum,
Christus ipse rogauit patrem. Praefecit autem, non Romanae solum,
sed uniuersae ecclesiae: quae et hodie successorem Petri non
dedignatur obedienter agnoscere. Nam, et si, quidam se separant, ac
25   diuellunt ab illo, quemadmodum Dathan, Abyron, et Chore cum suis
complicibus, magno cum malo suo se separarunt a Moyse: tamen
omnes ferme populi, qui syncere profitentur fidem Christi, Petri
successorem uelut Christi uicarium suspiciunt ac uenerantur. Quod si
isti populi, noti nobis et christianae fidei professione coniuncti, non
30   sunt ecclesia catholica, nec ulla pars horum sit ecclesia Christi, sed
hinc inde conuentus aliquot oculti, atque incogniti: qui et ab ecclesia
reliqua, et inter se quoque de fide Christi dissentiunt, apud quem
illorum queretur is cui dictum est? Si nolit emendare: dic ecclesiae.

19–20 fide quae per dilectionem operatur] *corr. err. L*, dilectione *R*   32 et inter se] *B*
resumes here; *B adds gloss* Nempe apud Lutheranam; dissentiunt] dissentiant *B*; quem]
quam *B*   33 illorum] *L*, illorumu *R*, illarum *B*; queretur] quaeretur *BL*; is cui dictum
est? Si] is: cui dictum est Si *B*, is cui dictum est, Si *L*; emendare] *BL*, em enda re *R*

was she taught this by human counsel; but she was taught by Christ
Himself, who taught His apostles also to pray that God would forgive
them their sins. And so the church of Christ, while she dwells on
earth, is not yet so cleansed that some sins do not constantly taint
good men; and among the good men everywhere there live the 5
wicked, who for the time being are in the church, in the same way as
diseased parts are in an ulcerous body. For even though these men are
not healthy, yet they are somehow still alive and are nourished by a
certain warmth of the divine Spirit who animates and preserves the
church, penetrating all things mightily and disposing all things 10
sweetly. Nor, so long as the church is a wayfarer on earth, will she
cease bearing sick members about with her; nor will Christ cease to
intercede with the Father for the sick members, He who mourned
over the ills of His mystical body and who wept bitterly for them on
the cross, saying: "Far from my salvation are the words of my sins." 15
But when the day shall come on which, laying aside corruption, she
shall be clothed with immortality, then, those rotten and decaying
members disappearing, the body of the church will be left utterly
pure and gleaming, which in the meantime goes about and will go
about diseased, but however diseased, will never go about dead. For 20
Christ will be with her and His word, which, whether written or
handed on without writing, is in either case spirit and life, together
with the faith which works through love for those who believe; Christ
Himself prayed to the Father that this kind of faith might never fail
or be lacking to the church which Christ committed to Peter's charge. 25
But He put Peter in charge not only of the Roman but of the
universal church, which even today does not refuse to acknowledge
obediently the successor of Peter. For even if some men separate and
tear themselves away from him as Dathan and Abyron and Chore
with their associates separated themselves to their own great harm 30
from Moses, nevertheless almost all the peoples who sincerely profess
the faith of Christ look up to and venerate the successor of Peter as the
vicar of Christ. But if these peoples, known to us and joined with us in
the profession of the Christian faith, are not the catholic church, nor
is the church of Christ any part of them, but is a number of secret 35
and unknown assemblies from hither and yon who disagree both with
the rest of the church and also among themselves about the faith of
Christ, then to which of those groups will that man complain who
has been told: "If he does not wish to reform, tell the church"? By

Cui quaeso, ecclesiae, non obtempe[H₂₉]rando, fiet tibi sicut ethnicus
et publicanus? an aliam dicit Christus quam notam illam ac publicam? an quaeri iubet alicunde duos aut tres haereticos: qui Donatistarum more denegent ecclesiam catholicam esse catholicam? Sit
5 igitur e turcis quispiam: qui uenire uelit in fidem Christi: persuadea-
tur illi, non hanc ecclesiam ueram esse: quam nos appellamus
catholicam: hoc est, omnium gentium congregationem, Christi
nomen ac fidem undiquaque profitentium: etiam si plaerique professioni parum moribus et uirtute respondeant, sed ecclesiam ueram
10 esse hinc atque illinc duos aut tres, in Christi nomine congregatos
bonos: illic inter uirtutes uigere fidem ueram. Hanc uero nostram,
notam atque uulgatam, non esse ueram: sed ut moribus malis
inficitur, ita uerae fidei loco, falsis opinionibus erroribusque seduci.

Is, ad se, dicet   Dic iam Luthere quaeso, quo perget, ut
15   discat fidem? ad eos ne, quos, qui sint,
scire non potest? Neque enim scire potest, qui sint boni. Scripturas
igitur in manum sumet ipse? atque hinc eliciet omnes articulos fidei?
quum nec scriptura comprehendat omnes: et quaedam comprehendat sic: ut sine doctore legenti facile obrepat error: doctorem uero,
20 qui discernet orthodoxum ab haeretico? An deus docebit intus?
doceret certe: nisi reliquisset ecclesiam: ad quam docendos remittit.
Quam qui contemnit, persuadens sibi tam unicum esse dei delicium
se: ut seorsum solus doceatur a deo, aliud quam publice credit, ac

Non sentis te hic appellari   profitetur ecclesia: is quantumuis sibi
25   *Luthere?*   uidetur humilis: arrogantiae certe dam-
                                         natur apud deum: qui se maiori curae deo
credit esse, quam ecclesiam totam: et deo dicit: non ut docet Christus
Pater [H₂₉v] noster, sed ut superbus ait quidam amicus Iob, Pater mi:
et deo non credit ecclesiae pollicenti: Ego uobiscum sum usque ad
30 consummationem seculi. Nec meminit, aut reformidat quicquam:
quod sicut omnia, quae scire sit opus: spiritus dicit ecclesiae: sic
ecclesiam, qui non audierit: iubet Christus pro ethnico habendum et

---

2 Christus] *om. B*   8 plaerique] *RL*, plerique *B*   28 superbus ait quidam amicus]
superbis ait amicis *B*

disobeying which church, I ask, will a man become to you as a
heathen and a publican? Does Christ say it is a different one from
that which is well-known and public? Or does He order that two or
three heretics be sought somewhere, who, like the Donatists, deny
that the catholic church is catholic?   5

Suppose, then, that there is some Turk who should wish to come
into the faith of Christ; suppose him persuaded that the true church
is not this one which we call catholic; that is, the congregation of all
peoples from any place whatever who profess the name and faith of
Christ, even though most of them may not correspond in their   10
morals and virtue to their profession of faith; but suppose him persuaded that the true church consists of two or three good men
gathered together from hither and yon in the name of Christ, that the
true faith thrives there in the midst of virtues, but that this well-
known and universal church of ours is not the true one, but, as it is   15
infected with bad morals, so it is led astray by false opinions and
errors instead of possessing the true faith. Now please tell me, Luther,
where will he go to learn the faith? Will he
go to those whose identity he cannot know? *He will say, "To himself"*
For he cannot know which men are good. Shall he then take the   20
scriptures in hand himself? And shall he draw from them all the
articles of faith, although scripture does not contain all of them and
contains some of them in such a way that without a teacher the reader
easily slips into errors? But who will distinguish the orthodox teacher
from the heretic? Or will God teach him inwardly? He certainly   25
would so teach him had He not left a church to whom He sends those
who need to be taught. The man who contemns her, persuading
himself that he alone is such a darling of God that he alone is especially taught by God something different from what the church publicly
believes and professes, then, however humble he may think himself, 30
he is surely convicted of arrogance before
God, since he believes himself to be of   *Do you not perceive that you are*
greater concern to God than the whole   *being named here, Luther?*
church is, and addresses God, not, as Christ teaches, "Our Father,"
but, as a certain proud friend of Job, "My father"; and he does not   35
believe God's promise to the church: "I shall be with you till the
consummation of the world." Nor does he remember or stand in any
awe of the fact that since the Spirit tells the church all that she needs
to know, Christ orders that the man who will not hear the church

publicano. Nam si quis, inquit, admonitus coram testibus duobus aut
tribus, non emendatur, dic ecclesiae. Non dicit, dic duobus aut
tribus. Non ergo duos aut tres appellat ecclesiam: nam totidem testes
erant quos ab ecclesia distinguit. Quod si ecclesiam contendas a
5   testibus non numero differre, sed merito: ut in alteris sufficiat
numerus: in altera spectetur pietas, rursus te rogo: quonam signo
discernes ecclesiam illam bonorum trium a tribus qualibuscunque
testibus? nam et dissimulari uitia possunt: et simulari uirtutes.

Verba fiunt mortuo

Quibus ergo tribus dices: quum sis
10   dicturus ecclesiae? Alia est igitur, uelis
nolis, ecclesia catholica, quam ea, quam fingis tu: nec ob aliud fingis:
quam quo licentius contemnas, ecclesiam uere catholicam: quae nisi
esset cognobilis ac nota, non esset certe, apud quam de proximi
peccato queri possis. Apud quam, si Christus queri iubet de moribus:
15 certe multo magis iubet de fide: cuius iudicio, qui non audierit: sit,
inquit, tibi sicut ethnicus et publicanus: quorum alter peccat in

Vnde morum et fidei
petenda censura

moribus: alter aberrat in fide. Vides ad
ecclesiae iudicium in fidei causa, morum-
que recurrendum. Cuius ecclesiae iudi-
20 cium, quum tu de fide non audias: imo scurriliter illudas, subsannes,
irrideas, et opera bona contemnas: ad mala praeps prouoles: et ad
pessima quaeque currentibus addas calcaria: promissa per solam
fi[H$_{30}$]dem, sine bonis operibus, impunitate pessimorum scelerum:
merito christianis omnibus, ipsa Christi uoce denunciatus es ethnicus:
25 et digne eiectus ex ecclesia catholica, quam discindere conaris: et
comminuere in duos aut tres haereticos: qui si fors conspirent diem
non honorare dominicam, et dominicae diei loco, mercurij diem aut

Haec licentia non libertas est

ueneris sibi festum facere, contendent
nimirum praecepto se satisfacere, colere
30 uidelicet diem festum, nempe diem illum, quem ipsi sibi sumpserunt

---

9 *gloss* Verba fiunt mortuo] *BL*, Verba fiuut mortno *R*   13 esset cognobilis ac nota,
non esset certe,] esset cognoscibilis . . . certe *L*, esset: ac nota non esset: certe *B*   17–18
gloss fidei . . . censura] *BL*, sidei . . . ceusura *R*   21 prouoles] prouolas *B*   28 *gloss*
licentia] *BL*, licantia *R*; facere, contendent] facere contendent: *B*

should be considered as a heathen and a publican. "If anyone," He says, "who has been rebuked before two or three witnesses should not reform, tell the church." He does not say, "Tell two or three men." And so He does not call two or three men the church; for it is precisely this number of witnesses whom He distinguishes from the church.

But if you should argue that the church does not differ from the witnesses in number but in merit so that in the one case number suffices, but in the other piety is sought, then I ask you once again: By what sign will you distinguish that church of three good men from any three witnesses whatever? For they can both dissimulate their vices and simulate virtues. To which three, then, will you speak when you are about *The words are spoken to a corpse* to speak to the church? Therefore, the catholic church is different, willy-nilly, from that which you represent; nor do you represent it for any other reason than that you may more freely contemn the truly catholic church, which, unless it were recognizable and well-known, would certainly not be the one before whom you can complain about the sin of your neighbor. If Christ orders us to submit complaints about moral matters to her judgment, surely much more does He order us to do so in matters of faith. "He who does not hear her judgment," He says, "let him be to you as the heathen and publican"; of these the one sins in morals, the other errs in faith. You see that recourse must be had to the judgment of the church in matters of faith and of *Where the judgment of morals and faith must be sought* morals. Since you do not listen to the judgment of this church in matters of faith, but on the contrary scurrilously ridicule, deride, jeer at, and contemn good works, since you fly swiftly toward evil works and add spurs to those who rush toward all the worst actions, promising them impunity through faith alone without good works for the worst crimes, you are deservedly denounced as a heathen by all Christians, by the voice of Christ Himself, and you have justly been cast out from the catholic church which you try to rend asunder and to reduce to two or three heretics who, if they should perhaps agree not to honor the Lord's day and in place of the Lord's day to establish as a feast the day of Mercury or of Venus, will doubtless argue that they clearly fulfill the precept, namely to keep *This license is not liberty* the feast day; that is, that day which they themselves have taken as

pro festo. Liberum enim istud esse, quod nullus dies certus ulla sit
scriptura definitus, nisi forte sabbatum. Quod si quis dicat, ad
ecclesiam pertinere, spiritu sancto gubernatam, determinare: quis
potissimum dies deo dedicandus sit:

Hanc ubique cantilenam
canit Lutherus
5
eamque statuisse dominicam, responde-
bunt istud statuisse papisticam. Ecclesiam
enim ueram atque catholicam esse sese tres uidelicet congregatos in
nomine Christi. Atque hoc pacto futurum est: ut colere diem festum
non sit aliud, quam uerum prophanare festum, ac festum facere:
10
Tychonij dictum
quem cuiusque libido uoluerit: ut iuxta
Tychonij dictum, id demum sanctum sit:
quod cuique sanctum sit. Sed cui nauseam non faciat haec tam
absurda finitio ecclesiae catholicae? Nam quum apostolus dicat: quae
extra nos nihil ad nos: extra quos nos dicit? an non extra notam illam,
15
quae tunc nota erat, ecclesiam? Quum idem scripsit. Qui contemptibiles sunt in ecclesia: eos constituite ad iudicandum: de qua dicit
ecclesia: an de alia uidelicet, quam quae tum nota erat Christi
ecclesia? Quae quantumuis diffundebatur: una Christi professione et
iungebatur: et catholicae nomine cognoscebatur. In qua quicunque
20
aliam profiteban[H₃₀v]tur fidem, quam publicam: semper habiti
sunt haeretici: nec eorum conuentus Christi fuit ecclesia: nec unquam in eum numerum creuere: ut reliquum gregem superarent,
idem Christi nomen profitentem. Nam licet infideles et ethnici in
tantam molem aucti sint: ut eorum collatione Christiani uideantur
25
pusillus grex: nunquam tamen sic excreuerunt haeretici, profitentes
Christi nomen, et sibi uendicantes ecclesiam: ut dubium cuiquam
relinquerent: ubi censeretur ecclesia catholica. Nam licet in ecclesiae
uitia, homo et extra ecclesiam et uitiosissimus insultet: nunquam
efficiet tamen: ut ager domini desinat eius esse: propterea quod in
30
hoc crescendi tempore, zizaniae multum ferat inter triticum: aut
Christi rete desinat esse Christi: propterea quod dum in hoc mari
trahitur: malos pisces mixtos habet cum bonis: quousque dominus et
Lutherus piscis inutilis
triticum colliget, et pisces bonos: ac
seponet sibi: Lutherum uero, ac suos

---

4 potissimum] *BL*, potrssimum *R*   10 *gloss* Tychonij] Tythonij *BR*, Tyconij *L*
11 Tychonij] *corr. err. L*, Tythonij *BR*; id demum] *BL*, iddemum *R*   12 cui] cur *B*
14 quos nos dicit] nos *om. L*   20 profitebantur] *L*, profitebatur *BR*   30 zizaniae]
corr. err. L, zizanij *R*, zizannij *B*

their feast. They will argue that this is an optional matter, since no
particular day has been defined by any scripture, except perhaps the
sabbath. But if someone should say that it is the business of the church,
governed by the Holy Spirit, to determine which day should be
especially dedicated to God and that she has decided on Sunday,   5
they will answer that the papist church
has decided this. For the true and catholic   *Luther sings this trite song*
church is themselves; that is, three men   *everywhere*
gathered together in the name of Christ. And the result will thus be
that to keep the feast day is nothing else but to profane the true feast   10
and to make a feast which the whim of each one has chosen; so that,
according to the saying of Tyconius: "In
the long run that is holy which is holy to   *The saying of Tyconius*
each one." But who will not be nauseated by this utterly absurd
definition of the catholic church? For when the apostle says: "That   15
which is beyond us does not concern us," beyond which "us" is he
speaking of? Is it not beyond that known church which was then
known? When the same apostle wrote: "Appoint those who are rated
as nothing in the church to judge," of which church is he speaking?
Is it indeed of some other church than that which was then known as   20
the church of Christ? However widely she was scattered, she was
united by the one profession of Christ and recognized by the name of
catholic. In this church whoever professed a faith different from the
common faith were always considered heretics; nor was their assembly
the church of Christ, nor did they ever grow to such a number that   25
they surpassed the rest of the flock professing the same name of Christ.
For, although infidels and heathens have increased to such numbers
that by comparison with them the Christians seem an insignificant
flock, yet the heretics professing the name of Christ and claiming the
church for themselves never increased to such a degree as to leave   30
anyone in doubt where the catholic church might be found. For,
although a man outside the church and utterly vicious may rail
against the vices of the church, yet he will never bring it about that
the field of the Lord will cease to belong to the Lord because in this
time of growth it brings forth much cockle among the wheat, or that   35
the net of Christ will cease to be Christ's because while it is dragged in
this sea it has bad fish mixed with the good, until such time as the
Lord will gather both the wheat and the
good fish and set them aside for Himself,   *Luther is a worthless fish*

complices, foras ablegabit in ignem. Interea uero ecclesiam sponsam suam, cum qua se futurum promisit, usque ad finem seculi: quamquam alias peccantem, et saepe castigatam: ita tamen seruat sua praesentia: ut eam per infidelitatis fornicationem, in aliorum deorum

5 cultum non patiatur incidere: sed suo spiritu sancto, qui ducat eam in omnem ueritatem: sic eam fouet, et instruit: ut neque in fide sinat, neque sacramentis errare. De qua, si adhuc moueas controuersiam, et quaeras, quaenam sit illa: respondebo rursus, illa eadem ecclesia, per quam cognouisti euangelium esse euangelium: eadem, inquam,

10 ecclesia est illa catholica: quae te docet sacramenta septem esse sacramenta: quae docere non potes: cur in altero magis falli possit, quam in [I$_1$] utroque. Si nihil omnino fuisset scriptum, ecclesiae credidisses de omnibus: quae iam scripta sunt? Ecclesiae credis ueros Euangelistas fuisse, ueros apostolos, qui scripserunt ea: quae scripta

15 sunt: ex his, qui scripserunt: nemo scripsit scripta esse omnia. Imo

Non omnia scripta esse, quae
ad fidem nostram pertinent
authoribus euangelistis

scribunt aperte: quod omnia scripta non sunt. Cur igitur de reliquis, quae adhuc scripta non sunt: non credis ecclesiae cui fueras alioqui crediturus, de omnibus:

20 quae iam scripta sunt? An, quia quaedam scripta sunt: ideo contemnenda sunt reliqua? Cur ecclesia minorem apud te fidem habet de parte: quam fuerat habitura de toto? an quia quatuor aut quinque scripserunt: qui se fatentur quaedam scripsisse, non omnia: ideo fidem amiserunt uniuersi? Quos alioqui dignos habuisses: quorum

25 fidei, sine scripto, de his etiam rebus, quae iam sunt scriptae: credidisses?

---

7 adhuc] *B corr. err. L*, ahduc *R*; controuersiam] controuersum *B*   12–13 scriptum, ecclesiae credidisses] *L*, scriptum, ecclesiae credit *corr. err.*, scriptum ecclesiae: credidisses *BR*   13 sunt? Ecclesiae] *corr. err.*, sunt ecclesiae? *BR*, sunt? ecclesiae *L*   14 Euangelistas] *corr. err. L*, Euangelistos *BR*; apostolos,] *corr. err. L*, apostolos? *BR*   17 sunt. Cur] *corr. err. L*, sunt? Cur *BR*   18 ecclesiae cui] *corr. err.*, ecclesiae? cui *BR*, ecclesiae, cui *L*   20 sunt?] *corr. err. L*, sunt. *BR*

but Luther and his associates He will cast out into the fire. But meanwhile, the church, His spouse, with whom He has promised to abide until the end of the world, although she sins at times and is often chastised, He nevertheless so preserves by His presence that He does not allow her through the fornication of infidelity to fall into the worship of other gods but by His Holy Spirit, who leads her into all truth, He so cherishes and instructs her that He allows her to err neither in the faith nor in the sacraments. If you should still stir up controversy about her and question her identity, I will answer once again: that same church through whom you have known that the gospel is the gospel, that same church, I say, is that catholic church who teaches you that the seven sacraments are sacraments; you cannot show why she can be deceived on the one point more than in both points.

If nothing at all had been written, would you have believed the church concerning all the things which actually have been written? You believe the church that those men were true evangelists, true apostles, who wrote those things which have been written; of those men who have done the writing not one has written that every detail was committed to writing. On the contrary, they openly write that not everything was written. Why then do you not believe the church concerning the rest of the things which have not yet been written, since you would have been ready to believe her otherwise about all the things which have actually been written? Or, because certain things have been written, are the rest for that reason to be contemned? Why do you consider the church less reliable concerning a part than you would have been ready to consider her concerning the whole? Just because four or five individuals have written, who admit that they wrote down some details but not everything, has the entire group of these men lost their credibility, whom you would otherwise have judged worthy of your credence even without their writing the details which have actually been written?

That, on the authority of the evangelists, not everything was written which pertains to our faith

Ostendit, quam inepte Lutherus nugetur: et quam impudenter mentiatur. Cap. XI.

NIMIVM diu uideor, in re tam aperta, cum isto nebulone contendere. Qui, si quid obijcitur: id dissimulat: aut si quid commemorat:
5 false recitando deprauat: et contra sua uerba, tanquam aduersarij, potius nugatur, quam disputat. Ait nos, articulos fidei facere, ex

Nam quid faciat impudens?   quouis uerbo patrum: nec pudet tam aperte mentiri nebulonem. Quis, tanquam necessarium articulum fidei, protulit unquam tibi Luthere, unum
10 dictum cuiusquam patrum? Certe tanquam probabile proferimus: ac multo magis probabile, quam tuum, uel ob hoc, quod illis pietas

Lutherus quid antiquis patribus intersit   aperuit oculos: quos tibi claudit im[I₁v]-pietas. Illi studuerunt intelligere: tu laboras intellecta corrumpere. Quod si qua
15 in re constet, ueteres olim patres omnes idem sensisse: tantum bonorum consensum uni stolidissimo nebuloni non dubitamus opponere: quando planum est, per illum spiritum eos idem sensisse: qui facit unanimes in domo. Eodem modo nugatur: dum tenedia bipenni rem in duo genera partitur, hoc modo.

20   *Verba Lutheri*   Si usum uel authoritatem hominum, quae manifeste pugnat contra scripturas allegasses, quale est, inquit, quod stolidus rex producit, de altera parte sacramenti, anathema sit, usus, authoritas, rex Thomista, satan, et angelus de caelo.

25 Imo anathema sit iste abusor, exauthoratus fraterculus, Hussista, Satanista, de tartaro: qui scripturam Christi sacram in sensum sacrilegum, aduersus Christi sacramenta detorquet: Et hominum

Vt falsus es miser fratercule   bene dicta, male narrando deprauat. Nam quod hic uanissimus nebulo cupit, ignora-
30 tione lectoris abuti: nihil ei proderit: quum ad locum fuerit peruentum: in quo uidebis lector apertissimam nebulonis sycophantiam: qui

He shows how foolishly Luther trifles and how shamelessly he lies. Chapter 11.

I think I am spending far too much time arguing with this scoundrel about such a clear matter. If any objection is brought up, he conceals it; or if he does mention any, he distorts it by misquotation; and against objections proposed by himself as though they were his adversary's he gibbers rather than deliberates. He says that we make articles of faith out of any saying of the fathers, and the scoundrel is not ashamed to tell such a bare-faced lie.
Who ever presented to you as a necessary *What else would a shameless fellow do?* article of faith, Luther, a single statement of any father whatever? Certainly we present it as probable, and much more probable than your statement, especially because piety opened their eyes while impiety closes yours. They were eager to understand; *How Luther differs from the ancient fathers* you labor to pervert what is understood.
But if it is certain that on any one point all the ancient fathers long ago agreed, we do not hesitate to oppose such thorough agreement of good men to a single dull-witted scoundrel, when it is clear that they reached agreement through that Spirit who makes those who dwell in a house to be of one mind.

He gibbers in the same way when with a Tenedian two-edged ax he splits one thing into two kinds, as follows:

> If you had alleged any usage or human *Luther's words* authority which clearly contradicts the scriptures, such as, he says, the dull-witted king produces on the matter of the second species of the sacrament, then let usage, authority, the Thomist king, Satan, even an angel from heaven be anathema.

Rather, let this fellow be anathema, this abuser, this cashiered friarlet, this Hussite, this Satanist from hell, who twists the sacred scripture of Christ into a sacrilegious sense opposed to the sacraments of Christ and distorts by misquotation the correct statements of men. For the fact that *So false you are, you wretched friarlet* this most deceitful scoundrel longs to take advantage of the ignorance of his reader will do him no good when we have come to the passage in which you, reader, will see the transparent craftiness of the scoundrel who pretends that the king

regem fingit obijcere authoritatem hominum: qui aperte obijcit
authoritatem spiritus sancti, non hominum.

Verba Lutheri

Sin autem eum, inquit, usum, uel
authoritatem hominum allegat: quae non
5   pugnent scripturis, non damno: sed tollerari uolo: Hoc tantum
adiecto, ut libertas christiana salua sit, et in arbitrio nostro sit ea
sequi, tenere, mutare, quando, ubi, quo-

*Verum quae sunt ista, num
quaecunque non sunt scripta?
Ne seui tantopere bone pater*

modo placuerit. Quod si hanc libertatem
nobis captiuare uolent, et necessarios fidei
10   articulos statuere, anathema sit, qui hoc
praesumpserit, siue sit insulsus Thomista, siue stupidus papista, siue
rex, siue papa, tale est, quod dominus noster rex urget, pro articulis
fidei sua sacramenta confirmationis, matrimonij, ordinis, unctionis, et
mixturae aquae in uinum. [I₂]

15   EXPENDE lector, ea, quae scripsit rex de sacramentis istis: et
facile uidebis, ac ridebis improbam nebulonis calumniam: qui nihil
omnino respondens ad ea, quae rex probauit: tantum mentitur regem
obiecisse authoritatem hominum: pro quibus allegauit princeps
authoritatem sancti spiritus. Contra cuius ordinationem, qui recalci-
20   trat: ac sacramenta, quae Christus in sacrosancta consecrauit
ecclesia: blasphemat: anathema sit: qui hoc praesumpserit: siue sit
insulsus satanista, siue stupidus potista, siue frater, siue apostata.

Pulcherrime declarat, quam inepte, imo quam
prorsus amenter Lutherus adducat atque applicet
25   scripturas. Ca. XII.

SED NVNC operaeprecium est uidere: qui nihil admittit praeter
scripturas, et easdem etiam euidentes: quam pulchre scripturas
proponat ipse: quas euidenter quisque uideat neque caelum (quod
aiunt) neque terram attingere.

30   *Verba Lutheri*

Nobis, inquit, aduersus has stipulas, et
stuppas Thomisticas, plusquam nimis
sunt diuina fulmina: ubi Christus Matthaei.xv. decernit, super omnes

9 *gloss* bone pater] bo *only B*   13 confirmationis] confitmationis *B*

opposes to him the authority of men, whereas he clearly opposes to
him, not the authority of men, but that of the Holy Spirit.

But if, he says, one alleges such usage or *Luther's words*
human authority as does not contradict
the scriptures, I do not condemn this, but I wish it to be tolerated,   5
provided only that Christian liberty be safe, and that it be a matter of
our free choice to follow, maintain,
change those points when, where, how,   *But what are these things? Are*
we shall choose. But if they wish to take   *they not whatever is now*
captive this liberty of ours and to establish   *written down? Do not rage*
so fiercely, good father   10
necessary articles of faith, then let him
who will presume to do this be anathema, whether he be a silly
Thomist, or a stupid papist, or a king or a pope; such is what our lord
the king does in urging as articles of faith his sacraments of confirmation, matrimony, orders, extreme unction, and the mingling of   15
water and wine.

Consider carefully, reader, what the king has written on these
sacraments, and you will readily recognize and ridicule the wicked
calumny of the scoundrel who, answering nothing at all to what
the king has proved, only says lyingly that the king opposes to him the   20
authority of men for matters for which the prince has alleged the
authority of the Holy Spirit. Let that man be anathema who will have
presumed to resist the ordinance of this Spirit and to blaspheme the
sacraments which Christ has consecrated in His most holy church;
whether this man be a silly satanist, or a stupid potist, or a friar, or an   25
apostate.

He very skillfully declares how ineptly, indeed how utterly
senselessly Luther cites and applies the
scriptures. Chapter 12.

But now it is worth seeing how cleverly this fellow, who admits   30
nothing but the scriptures and evident ones besides, himself cites
scriptural texts which everyone evidently sees touch, as the saying
goes, neither heaven nor earth.

We have, he says, more than enough   *Luther's words*
divine thunderbolts against these Tho-
35
mistic straws and bits of tow, where Christ, in Matthew 15, passes

traditiones hominum, dicens. Sine causa colunt me doctrinis, et
mandatis hominum. Quid est uniuersa
Quam sobrie semper loquitur   fex huius laruatae Thomistae aduersus
hic pius pater
unam hanc uocem Christi, ut alia

5   plurima transeam alias memorata? Si frustraneum est, quicquid
hominum mandatum est, qua fronte stolidus rex, nobis articulos fidei
ex eo faciet? Itaque hac sola uoce Christi, prostratus iacet, infélix
et miserabilis defensor Ecclesiae Henricianae, cum toto suo libello.

CVIVS expectationem non superat impudens istius [I₂v] nebulonis
10   stultitia: qui Christi uerba illa, Sine causa colunt me doctrinis et
mandatis hominum: fulminat, uidelicet homo nugax, et Antichristus,
aduersus eum: qui dixit, ac probauit, sacramenta traditiones esse dei,
non hominum. Et tam impudentis amentiae conuictus, iam uelut
uictor ac triumphator exultans,

15   Hac, inquit, sola uoce Christi prostratus iacet infelix et miserabilis
defensor ecclesiae Henricianae cum toto suo libello.

Et ista prae furore clamat Lutherus, conscius interim sibi, neminem
non uidere tam stolide citata scriptura, quam turpiter prostratus
iaceat, infelix et miserabilis impugnator ecclesiae catholicae, cum toto
20   suo stolidissimo cerebello. Quod cerebellum tam stupidum est: ut in
ea re in qua stultitiam eius omnes rident:
Videlicet saltator camelus   adhuc se putet perquam festiue ludere.

Vbi estis, inquit, domine Henrice?
Verba Lutheri. Istic uester stilus   producite uestrum aegregium contra
est domine frater
25   Lutherum libellum. Quid asserit domina-
tio uestra? septem sacramenta? Quibus doctrinis? Dei an hominum?
Audiat ergo Thomistica uestra dominatio iudicium, non Lutheri, sed
eius, quem tremunt cardines orbis, frustra colunt me doctrinis
hominum.

30   VIDISTI lector aliquando caecum: qui pugno se cuperet irritatus
ulcisci? Verum ut scire possit: quam in partem dirigat ictum: elicit

---

8 Henricianae] Heuricianae *B*   22 putet] *corr. err. L*, putat *BR*   26 uestra] uesira
BR, vestra *L*

judgment on all the traditions of men, saying: "Without cause do they worship me with the doctrines and commandments of men." What is all the sludge of this masked Thomist against this one saying of Christ, *With what restraint this pious priest always speaks* to pass over many others mentioned elsewhere? If everything which man has commanded is vain, with what boldness does the doltish king make of it articles of faith for us? And so, by this single saying of Christ he lies prostrate, this unhappy and wretched defender of the Henrician church, together with his whole little book.

Does not the shameless folly of this scoundrel exceed anyone's expectation, in that he, clearly a trifler and an Antichrist, thunders Christ's words, "Without cause they worship me with the doctrines and commandments of men," against one who has declared and proved that the sacraments are the traditions of God, not of men? Even convicted of such shameless stupidity, he says, already exulting as a victor and conqueror:

> With this single saying of Christ he lies prostrate, this unhappy and wretched defender of the Henrician church, together with his whole little book.

And these words Luther shouts because of his raging madness, conscious meanwhile that everyone sees that he cites the scriptural text with a stupidity as great as the shamefulness of his defeat and prostration, this unhappy and wretched assailant of the catholic church, together with the whole of his most dull, diminutive brain. This witling is so dull that in the very matter in which everyone laughs at his *A camel dancer, indeed!* folly he still thinks he is carrying off a very witty jest.

> Where are you, Lord Henry? he says. Bring out your illustrious book against *Luther's words. This is your style, honored brother* Luther. What does your lordship defend? The seven sacraments? By whose teachings? God's or men's? Let your Thomistic lordship hear then the judgment, not of Luther, but of Him before whom the poles of the earth tremble: "In vain do they worship me with the teachings of men."

Have you ever seen a blind man, reader, who when provoked was eager to avenge himself with his fists? In order to know where to

ab aduersario uocem: quam prolatam protinus prosequitur uerbere: nisi citius alter se subduxerit: quam ut a caeco possit attingi. Hunc caecum mihi uidetur agere Lutherus: sed ita, ut nemo unquam magis egerit ridicule. Nam quum rex appellatus

Lutherus ipsis caecis caetior

5   ei respondet ad dextram: ille contra ictum proijcit in sinistram. Itaque, specta quaeso, quam festiuiter Lutherus hunc ludit ludum. Cogita nunc uide[I₃]re te illum, obcaecatis oculis intentum stare, ad ingerendum colaphum. Vbi estis, inquit, domine Henrice? Hic in proximo. Adhuc inuitat: ut accedat propius: nempe
10   ut feriat certius. Producite, inquit, uestrum aegregium contra Lutherum libellum. Produco. Adhuc propius. Quid asserit uestra dominatio: an septem sacramenta? Assero. Adhuc propius paululum. Quibus doctrinis? dei an hominum? Dei. Iam feriendi certus scilicet, en quam recte librat ictum. Audiat, inquit, ergo dominatio uestra.
15   Frustra colunt me doctrinis hominum. Spectatum admissi risum teneatis amici: qui uidetis hunc caecum inscium, quam longe aberrarit in diuersam partem: sic exultare prae gaudio, ut compos non sit sui: quasi aegregium colaphum infregerit aduersario?

Lutheri uerba

20

Quin tu os istud impium abstines a fide Christi

Eat, inquit, nunc dominatio uestra, et doceat dominationes papales hanc frustraneam fidem, et religionem, eamque sicut optime nouit strenue defendat. Verum ab ecclesia dei, os uestrae dominationis impurum, et sacrilegum abstinete, quae non nisi uerbum dei
25   admittit.

IMO reuerende pater potator, eat dominatio uestra: et dominabus sororibus, quibus predicatis confitenda uirorum peccata: praedicate

direct his blow he gets his opponent to say something; on hearing him
he immediately goes after him with a rain of blows, unless the other
retreats too quickly for the blind man to be able to reach him. It
seems to me that Luther acts the part of this blind man, but in such a
way that no one has ever acted more ridiculously. For when the king   5
on being called by name answers him on
the right, Luther strikes out in return with   *Luther is even blinder than*
                                                              the blind
a blow toward the left. And so, observe,
please, how wittily Luther plays out this play. Imagine now that you
see the fellow, his eyes blinded, standing determined to deliver a box   10
on the ear.

"Where are you, Lord Henry?" he says.

"Here, next to you."

He invites him to approach still closer, so that of course he may
strike more surely. "Bring forward," he says, "your illustrious book   15
against Luther."

"Here it is."

"Come still closer. What does your lordship defend? The seven
sacraments?"

"I do."   20

"Stand closer yet. By whose teachings? God's or men's?"

"God's."

Now, clearly certain of hitting his mark, see how accurately he
delivers his blow. "Listen, then, your lordship: 'In vain do they
worship me with the teachings of men.' " Friends, would you be able   25
to restrain your laughter if you were admitted to such a sight, you
who see this blind man, unaware of how far he has shifted in the
opposite direction, so exult for joy that he is beside himself, as though
he has cracked a mighty box on the ear of his opponent?

Now let your lordship go, he says, and   *Luther's words*   30
teach their papal lordships this fruitless
faith and religion, and defend it vigorously, as he best knows how. But
let your lordship keep his filthy and sacri-
legious mouth away from the church of   *See that you keep your impious*
                                                mouth from the faith of Christ
God, which admits nothing but the word   35
of God.

On the contrary, Reverend Father Tosspot, let your lordship go,
and to your sister ladyships, to whom, you preach, men must confess

perfidam fidem uestram, et religionem ruris Bohemici, ubi matrimonium nihil est aliud, quam crescere et
In quorum gratiam Lutherus multiplicare: et tanquam canes cateruatim
neget sacramentum matrimonij
coire in ecclesia. Haec est ecclesia: in
5 cuius gratiam uestra paternitas, quae procul exulat a Christi gratia:
negat matrimonium esse sacramentum: et ei prorsus tollit omnem
gratiam. Hanc ecclesiam indicat uestra paternitas, ecclesiam dei: et
per os illud impurum, et sacrilegum, ueram ecclesiam Christi
blasphemat: et uerbum dei labijs mendatio pol[I₃v]lutis, contaminat:
10 et illa Christi uerba, Frustra colunt me doctrinis hominum, uelut
fulmen et tonitrus, aduersus eos iaculamini: in quos non misit
Christus, ita fulminatis et intonatis ficticijs fulminibus et tonitribus
aduersus regem: ut olim simili praestigio Cacus aduersus Herculem.
Quamobrem seposito reuerenter fulmine
15 *Quid opus est quod* dei, dominatio uestra, quae Caci gygantis
cacodaemon quis satis
concacarit maledicentia in morem, fictile fulmen efflauit: digna
profecto fuerit, in cuius os impurum, et
fulminibus efflandis patulum, Cacus debeat aliquis incacare.

Lepide refellit insulsum Lutheri lemma impugnantis
20   diuturnitatem fidei catholicae, illata
pariter diuturnitate superstitionis
iudaicae Turcharum et
gentilium. Cap. XIII.

SED postquam ita fulminauit scripturis: ilico ratione pugnat haud
25 minus corusca. Ait enim.

Verba Lutheri   Denique adeo stultum est hoc regis propositum, ut et communi hominum sensui
repugnet. Quis enim non rideat, pro fide nostra christiana
nihil afferri roboris per tantos Sampsonas, nisi longitudinem tem-
30 *Recte mentitus es in caput tuum* porum, et multorum hominum usum?
Qua ratione probabimus Turcarum
fidem esse erroneam, quae iam ad millesimum fere annum durat, ante

11 tonitrus] *corr. err.*, tonitru *BRL*   14 *gloss om.* L

their sins, preach your faithless faith and
the religion of the Bohemian back country, *For whose favor Luther denies*
                                             the sacrament of matrimony
where matrimony means nothing but to
increase and multiply and to mate in church like a pack of dogs.

This is the church for whose favor your paternity, who is exiled far 5
from the favor of Christ, denies that matrimony is a sacrament and
takes away from it absolutely all grace. This church your paternity
points out as the church of God, and with that filthy and sacrilegious
mouth blasphemes the true church of Christ, and with lips polluted
by lying defiles the word of God, and against those whom Christ did 10
not have in mind you hurl, like a lightning flash and thunderbolts,
the words of Christ: "In vain do they worship me with the doctrines
of men." You flash and thunder with fictitious flashes and thunders
against the king just as Cacus once did with a similar stratagem
against Hercules. And so, after reverently   15
laying aside the thunderbolt of God, your   *Why it is necessary for some*
                                            cacodaemon to have shit
lordship, who, like the giant Cacus, has   *out such abuse*
blasted out a fictitious flash of lightning,
will indeed merit that, as you extend your filthy mouth wide open to
flash forth lightning, some Cacus should crap into it.   20

He wittily refutes Luther's silly premise attacking
the long duration of the catholic faith by referring
to the equally long duration of the superstition of the Jews, Turks, and heathens.
Chapter 13.   25

But after he has thus flashed lightning by means of scriptural texts, he
immediately gives battle with a reasoning no less flashing. For he
says:

Finally, this proposition of the king is so
foolish that it contradicts even the com-   *Luther's words*   30
mon sense of men. Who would not laugh to see that such great Sampsons
bring forward no argument in defense of our Christian faith but
duration in time and the usage of many men? By what reasoning will
we prove that the faith of the Turks is
erroneous, which has lasted now for   *You have lied directly against* 35
                                                your own head
almost a thousand years, having arisen

orta quam Germania ad fidem conuersa est? An hoc satis est, quod
dum per interualla terrarum semoti, non cogimur cum illis disputare,
interim in nostris angulis, quicquid uisum fuerit, licet nugari? Sic et
iudaeos quis non merito iustificet, huius inuicti Thomistae exemplo,
5   cum tanta nos superent longitudine temporum? Et cur gentes per
orbem nouam Christi fidem non dicentur, authore Henrico [I₄]
Angliae merito fuisse persecutas, cum idolatria eorum hoc pulcherrimo, et Thomisticissimo argumento, recta et sana fides censeri
debuerit, quod tot millibus annorum, tot regionibus populorum, tam
10   constanti usu firmabatur? Atque eodem Henrico magistro etiamnum
asseramus impiorum hominum errores, esse sanam fidem, quod ab
initio mundi illorum superarit multitudo, et diuturnitas, et potentia
piorum paucitatem et ignobilitatem. Summa. Si hominum dicta
ualent articulos fidei, cur non et mea uerba faciunt articulos fidei?
15   *Quia tu omnem fidem*   An ego non sum homo? Quin noua regis
merito perdidisti   sapientia, omnes homines omnium homi-
                               num uerbis credere cogamus. Et ipse rex
quoque, ut leuetur cura scribendi, sequatur suum principium, et dicat,
Homo sum, qui sic loquor, ergo oportet sic esse, Non potest aliter esse.
20   Stulta, ridicula, et uerissime Henriciana
An te credis ignorarier qui sic   et Thomistica sunt haec, quasi res
contra tua figmenta blateres?   spiritualis metienda sit praescriptionibus
temporum et usu, aut iure hominum, ceu fundus aut pratum aliquod
sit.

25   ECCE lector inuincibilem rationem, quam magnificis uerbis, quam
Phormiana fiducia phaleratam, cuius summa est: Publica Turcarum
fides, per aliquot aetates, et gentilium per aliquot annorum millia
                               perdurans est erronea: et item iudaeorum:
Agnoscis hanc disputandi   ergo et ecclesiae catholicae fides publica,
formam pater argutator
30   per quantumlibet multas aetates continuata, potest esse erronea. O acumen iudaeis, turcis, et ethnicis
plaudendum: Sed quod Christianorum quiuis uidet, obtusius esse
pistillo. Nam quum infidelium superstitio regatur a diabolo: et
ecclesiae catholicae fides a deo: haec est nimirum argumentatio
35   reuerendi patris, fides populi spiritu mendace gubernati, potest esse

---

6 nouam] nouam, *BR*, nouum, *L*   7 idolatria] idolatriae *B*, idololatria *L*   7–8 pul-
cherrimo] *corr. err. L*, pulcherrime *BR*   20 *gloss* An] *L*, an *BR*   26 est: Publica] *corr.*
err., est publica *BR*, est: publica *L*

before Germany was converted to the faith? Or is it enough that
while, separated by distances of space, we are not forced to dispute
with them, we may meanwhile utter in our corners whatever nonsense
we think right? Likewise, who would not justly vindicate the Jews by
the example of this invincible Thomist, since they surpass us by such a   5
length of time? And why should not the heathens throughout the
world, on the authority of King Henry of England, be said to have
justly persecuted the new faith of Christ, since their idolatry, according to this very neat and very Thomistic argument, should have been
judged the right and sound faith, because it was confirmed by so many   10
thousands of years within the territories of so many peoples by such
constant use? And with the same Henry as our teacher let us even
now declare that the errors of irreligious men are sound faith, because
from the beginning of the world their numbers and duration and
power have surpassed the scarcity and obscurity of religious men. In   15
sum, if the words of men have the force of
articles of faith, why do not my words also   *Because you have deservedly lost*
make articles of faith? Am I not a man?   *all reason to be trusted*
Nay more, according to the new wisdom of the king, all of us men are
forced to believe the words of everyone. Let even the king himself, that   20
he may be relieved of the trouble of writing, follow his own first
premise, and say: I am a man who speaks thus; therefore it must be
so; it cannot be otherwise. Foolish,
ridiculous, and most truly Henrician   *Do you believe that you are not*
and Thomistic are these words; as if a   *detected when you blather so*   25
spiritual matter is to be measured by   *against your own fictions?*
prescriptions of time and usage or the law of men, like an estate or
some plot of land.

Behold, reader, the irrefutable reasoning, tinselled with what
pompous words, with what Phormian assurance! And the sum of it   30
is: The public faith of the Turks lasting through several ages and of
the heathens lasting through several thousands of years is erroneous,
as well as that of the Jews; therefore, the
public faith of the catholic church, main-   *You recognize this form of*
tained through however many ages, can be   *disputing, Father Subtle*   35
erroneous. Oh, the keenness of it, deserving the applause of Jews,
Turks, and heathens; but any Christian sees it is duller than a pestle.
For, since the superstition of infidels is governed by the devil, and the
faith of the catholic church by God, this is an amazing line of
argument for the reverend father to take: the faith of a people   40

falsa: ergo etiam fides populi gubernati spiritu ueritatis potest esse
falsa. Haec ratio talis est et tam fortis Achilles: ut ego non audeam
congredi. Hac ratione, plane prostrati iacent omnes defensores
ecclesiae. Illa tamen ratio, [I₄v] quam subiungit Lutherus, et argu-
5 mentatur a simili: aliquanto est imbecillior: quum ita quaerendo
colligit. Si hominum, inquit, dicta ualent articulos fidei: cur non et
                         mea uerba faciunt articulos fidei? nunquid
      Vix, aut certe nequam
                         ego sum homo?

Huic argumento saltem responderi potest: quod reuerendus pater
10 non est homo: quia nullus asinus est homo: quum ille uere sit asinus:
qui adhuc non intelligit, aliud esse hominum dicta: qui ex se loquuntur: aut (quod ille facit) loquuntur ex diabolo: aliud, quod ecclesia
Christi loquitur: quae loquitur ex spiritu sancto. Non estis, inquit, uos:
qui loquimini: sed spiritus patris uestri: qui loquitur in uobis. Alioqui
15 quoniam Paulus erat homo: iam nisi Lutherus esset asinus: uidetis
plane consequi, ex asinino Lutheri lemmate: quod aequalis authoritatis
esset Lutheri uerbum, cum uerbo Pauli. Sed hoc tamen loco, a solito
sibi more deflexit. Consueuit enim, quicquid potest objici dissimulare
totum: et praeterire silentio. Hic uero, sibi confisus, ausus est id
20 commemorare: quod sibi uidebat obstare. Quod eum facile uidetis
nunquam fuisse facturum: si non habuisset in promptu machinam:
qua posset obicem illum protinus amoliri. Audiamus igitur, quid ait.

             Verba Lutheri   Si dixerint, inquit, suam praescriptionem
                                     in hoc differre, ab illorum praescriptione,
25   quod papistarum sit ex spiritu sancto, illorum ex hominibus.

Hoc plane dicimus Luthere nos, quos tu papistas uocas: sed ecclesiae
                              fidem ex spiritu sancto, turcarum non ex
      Turca Luthero fidei iudex
                              hominibus sed ex diabolo: quid tu nunc ad
ista respondes? Ridebit hoc, inquit, Turca. Ain uero? et tu, religiose
30 pa[K₁]ter, habes pro ridiculo quicquid ridebit turca? Tam belle tuae

governed by a lying spirit can be false; therefore also the faith of a people governed by the Spirit of truth can be false. Such is this reasoning and so bold an Achilles that I dare not engage in conflict with it. By this reasoning all the defenders of the church clearly lie prostrate. Yet that reasoning which Luther subjoins and argues by 5 analogy is still more feeble, when he makes his inference by asking the following: "If the words of a man have the force of the articles of faith, why do not my words also make *Hardly; or at least a worthless one* articles of faith? Am I not a man?"

To this argument at least one can answer that the reverend father 10 is not a man, because no ass is a man; since that man is truly an ass who still does not understand that what is said by men who speak on their own authority, or, as he does, who speak on the authority of the devil, is one thing; what is spoken by the church of Christ who speaks on the authority of the Holy Spirit is another thing. Christ said: "It 15 is not you who speak, but the Spirit of your Father who speaks in you." Otherwise, because Paul was a man, then—if Luther were not an ass— you see that it clearly follows from Luther's asinine assumption that the word of Luther would be of equal authority with the word of Paul. In this passage, however, he has nevertheless turned aside from 20 his accustomed manner. For he has been accustomed to conceal wholly whatever can be objected and to pass it over in silence. But here, confident of himself, he has dared to recall something which seemed an obstacle to him. You easily see that he would never have been ready to do this had he not had a trick at hand by which he 25 could immediately remove that obstacle. Let us hear, then, what he says.

If they say that their own precept differs   *Luther's words*
from that of others in that the precept of
the papists is from the Holy Spirit, that of the others from men, the 30
Turk will laugh at them.

We whom you call papists, Luther, clearly do say this, but we say that the faith of the church is from the Holy Spirit, that of the Turks not from men but from the devil; now   *The Turk is the judge of faith*
what do you answer to this? He says that   *for Luther*   35
the Turk will laugh at this. Really? And
you, pious father, do you consider ridiculous whatever the Turk ridicules? So well does a thing suit your faith when it suits the faith

fidei, cum turcae fide conuenit. O christianum pectus: qui nihil
probat: nisi quod turca comprobat. Nunc uideo, quare sacramenta
subsannas: uidelicet ne turcis uideare, non satis sapere. Ideo panem
restare uis et uinum in eucharistia: ne te

Non dissimile uero

5   turca derideat. Eadem ratione, propediem
corpus et sanguinem ibi negabis in totum: quod alioqui certum est
fidem tuam non posse te satis probare turcis.

FIDEM et religionem, reuerendi patris, abunde iam uides lector:
quum uideas ad quam normam, fidei componat articulos: uide nunc
10   isti religioni plane parem sapientiam.

Verba Lutheri   Dicet, inquit, Turca tibi: quum tu hoc
asseras absque scripturis, et sine signis,
mera hominum authoritate, nihil magis efficis, quam si ego meam
quoque fidem esse ex deo dixero. Et qua

Quasi uero is scripturis
assentiret

15   facilitate tu meam contemnis: et ego
tuam contemno: et qua authoritate tu
tuam probas, ego meam probo. Quid hic, inquit, fiet? nisi ut moriones
etiam intelligant, Henricianos Thomistas, pro sua insigni inscitia,
fidem nostram ludibrio exposuisse: et

Tu uero dignus es, cui et
lingua exsecetur, et
excutiantur dentes

20   omnium gentium impietatem stabili-
uisse, dignos quibus os, lingua, et manus
praeciderentur, ne in aeternum aliquid,
aut dicerent aut scriberent.

DIXI ne diuinum prorsus esse hominis istius ingenium: qui
25   uiderit: quid turca dicturus sit, aduersus eos: qui fidem ecclesiae
proponerent absque scripturis? Nam si quis afferat aliquid ex
scripturis: tunc facile uidet reuerendus

O prudentiam uenerabilis patris

frater, nihil habiturum turcam: quod
contra possit hiscere. Ita semper consueuit scilicet scripturis christian-
30   orum credere: praesertim si quis eas alleget, ita commode: sicut solet
iste reuerendus pater. Etenim quamquam alleganti consuetudinem
nostram, turca non dubitaret allegare consuetudinem suam: [K₁v]
tamen alleganti scripturas nostras, nunquam auderet scilicet allegare
scripturas suas, et aduersus euangelium obijcere Alchoranum: non
35   quin praeferat Alchoranum Machometi euangelio Ioannis: quod a

---

1 cum] *corr. err. L*, quum *BR*; conuenit.] conuenit? *L*   1–2 nihil probat] *corr. err. L*,
nihil non probat *BR*

of a Turk! What a Christian heart, that approves nothing but what the Turk approves along with you! Now I see why you deride the sacraments; it is, of course, so that you may not seem so silly to the Turk. You wish the bread and wine to remain in the eucharist lest the Turk mock you. By the same reason-ing, you will very shortly deny altogether *Not unlikely, indeed* that the body and the blood are present because otherwise it is certain that you cannot satisfactorily justify your faith to the Turks.

Now you see in full measure, reader, the faith and religious spirit of the reverend father, since you see according to what norm he constructs his articles of faith; now see his wisdom, clearly equal to this religious spirit of his.

The Turk, he says, will say to you: When you assert this without scriptures and *Luther's words* without signs, on mere human authority, you effect nothing more than if I said that my faith also is from God. I contemn your faith with the same facility with which you contemn mine; and I prove my faith *As if he actually agreed with the scriptures* with the same authority with which you prove yours. What will happen here, he says, except that even fools will understand that the Henrician Thomists in their infamous ignorance have exposed our faith to ridicule and have fortified the impiety of all the heathens; they deserve to have their mouth, tongue, and hands *You certainly deserve to have both your tongue cut out and your teeth knocked out* cut off to prevent their ever saying or writing anything.

Did I not say that the genius of this fellow is utterly divine, since he saw what the Turk would say against those who would set forth the faith of the church without scriptures? If anyone should cite any text from the scriptures, then the reverend father easily sees that the Turk will have *Oh, the shrewdness of the venerable father!* nothing to mutter against it. The Turk, of course, has always been thus accustomed to believe the scriptures of the Christians, especially if anyone cites them as appropriately as this reverend father is accustomed to do. For, although to a person citing a custom of ours, the Turk would not hesitate to cite a custom of his own, nevertheless to a person citing our scriptures he would never, of course, dare to cite his own scriptures, and to oppose the Alcoran to the gospel, not because he does not prefer the Alcoran of Mahomet to

nobis ait esse uitiatum: sed ne pudefaceret reuerendum patrem,
hominem suae fidei consonum apud papistas: qui fuerit tam stolidus,
et asinus ipsa asininitate asininior: ut crediderit Turcam crediturum
esse scripturis christianorum. Iam quicunque scribunt, quod turca
5   riserit, hos reuerendus pater zelator fidei dignos clamat, quibus os,
lingua, manus praeciderentur: ne quid in aeternum aut dicant aut

Encomium patris uenerabilis   scribant. Quis illum contra non dignum
                                putet: cuius os aureum, et lingua mel-
liflua, ipsum suadelae domicilium, nunquam conticescat: et manus ei
10   subseruiens aureis ornetur annulis: ut semper aliquid aut dicat, aut
scribat huiusmodi: quod miseros mortales inter erumnas et labores
exhilaret: ac relaxet risu? modo sic usquam abesset impietas: ut adest
ubique stultitia. Sed tamen admiror: quo pacto hic acciderit: ut homo
natura clemens ac placidus, hoc loco praeter morem suum, sic
15   excandescat inclementer: ut os, linguam, ac manus praecidere uelit
omnibus fidelibus: quicunque dicant aut scribant quicquam: quod
tanquam stultum rideant infideles. Nec interea quicquam aut linguae

Quam parum perspicax estis   aut digitis Pauli prospexit apostoli: qui se
ubique domine frater?   fatetur, non tantum aliquid praedicare:
20   quod stultum uideatur gentibus: uerum
etiam nihil praedicare praeterea. Nos, inquit, nihil praedicamus
aliud, quam Iesum Christum, Iudaeis quidem scandalum: gentibus
autem stultitiam. At id quod in Luthero sequitur: haud facile dixeris,
magis ne stultum sit, [K₂] an magis impium.

25   *Verba Lutheri*   Sed hoc agit, inquit, inquietus satan: ut
                                nos a scripturis auocet per sceleratos
Henricos, et sacrilegos Thomistas: et fidem nostram super hominum

Id in te agit iam diu satan   mendatia collocet. Neque enim iam
                                scriptura sancta opus est: si sufficit nouis
30   hominum dictis, extra scripturam roborari.

Sagatiam esse putas lector: quod satanae propositum Lutherus
deprehendit? stupidior est: quam qui tantum possit. Sed diabolus
ipse dixit ei. Neque enim intimior Christo fuit eius euangelista

---

5 riserit, hos reuerendus] *corr. err. L*, riserit hos, reuerendus *BR*   13 hic] hoc *L*
33 ei] *om. L*

the gospel of John, which he says has been corrupted by us, but lest he embarrass the reverend father, a fellow from among the papists who agrees with his own faith; a fellow so dull-witted, and an ass more asinine than asininity itself, that he believed the Turk was ready to believe the scriptures of the Christians. Now the reverend father, zealous for the faith, declares that those who write anything the Turks will deride deserve to have their mouth, tongue and hands cut off to prevent their ever saying or writing anything. Who would not rather think this fellow deserving that his golden mouth and honey-smooth tongue, a very domicile of per-

Eulogy of the venerable father

suasion, should never grow quiet and that his gesturing hand should be adorned with golden rings, so that he may always be either saying or writing something such as may cheer up wretched mortals in the midst of their tribulations and labors and relax them with laughter; if only his impiety were as absent on any point as his folly is present at every point.

But yet, I wonder how it came about that at this point a man gentle and mild by nature should in this passage, contrary to his custom, burn with such merciless anger as to wish to cut off the mouth, tongue and hands of all the faithful who may say or write anything which the infidels would mock as foolish. Meanwhile he has not considered the tongue and fin-

How little foresight you show at any point, honored brother!

gers of the apostle Paul, who confesses that he not only preaches the kind of thing which seems foolish to the gentiles but even that he preaches nothing else. "We," he says, "preach nothing else but Jesus Christ, to the Jews indeed a stumbling block, but to the gentiles foolishness." But as for what follows in Luther, you could hardly tell whether it shows more of folly, or of impiety.

But, he says, a restless Satan does this in order to call us away from the scriptures

Luther's words

through criminal Henries and sacrilegious Thomists and to found our faith on the lies of men. For there is now no need of holy scripture if the novel sayings of men are a sufficient argument apart from scripture.

Satan has been doing this in you for a long time

Do you think it is shrewdness, reader, that Luther has detected the design of Satan? He is too stupid to do such a thing. No, the devil himself has told him this. For John was no more intimate with Christ

Ioannes: quam internus est satanae ipsius

Cacangelista Lutherus

cacangelista Lutherus: qui non una coena,
sed diebus ac noctibus incubat, super pectus diaboli: imo diabolus
non incumbit: sed infigitur ipsius pectori. Alioqui non potuisset tanta
5   cum authoritate pronunciare: quod fides catholica de sacramentis
super hominum mendacia collocetur: quamquam iam euicit: ne
collocari possit super spiritum sanctum: nisi quatenus id probatur
apertis scripturis: uidelicet ne id non approbet turca: qui nihil
admittit absque scripturis nostris. Caeterum prolata scriptura
10 Christianorum, protinus Turca sese sentit et fatetur uictum. Qua in
re si Luthero non credas: paratus erit iusiurandum dare: Turcarum
quemlibet omnia Christianorum sacramenta, articulos omnes fidei
christianae, quatenus probari possunt scripturae christianae testimonijs: non minus credere ac uenerari: quam credit ac ueneratur
15   Lutherus ipse. Neminem ego certe credo

Id non est difficile

tam incredulum: qui istud Luthero non
modo iuranti, sed uel iniurato non sit crediturus. Verum sine
scripturis, neque Turca quicquam credit, neque Lutherus: ita ipsis
inter se belle conuenit. Quam in rem hanc pro se rationem red[K₂v]-
20 dit: quod iam scriptura sancta non esset opus: si sufficiat nouis
hominum dictis extra scripturam roborari.
Hic cogit me reuerendus pater addubitare: an quisquam sit usquam
turca tam stultus: ut dignetur hac sane parte, socius esse Lutheranae
stultitiae: qui non uidet: cuiusmodi sit ista consequentia. Ecclesia
25 Christi gubernata spiritu Christi, tradita certa fide, seruat Christi
sacramenta: ergo ecclesiae Christi nihil opus est scripturis. Si
Lutherus fuisset euangelistarum temporibus: hac ratione deterruisset
eos a scribendis euangelijs. Nam si tum ea, quae audiebant homines:
ab hominibus tradita credebantur illis: qui ea narrabant a deo: atque
30 ita fidem faciebant audientibus: quid opus foret euangelistas, eorum
quicquam scriptis comprehendere? An ideo uidelicet, quia Christus,
qui hanc operabatur in ecclesia sua fidem: aut aliquando foret prorsus deserturus ecclesiam, aut fidem: quam sine scripto fecerat: sine

as His evangelist than Luther is interior
to Satan as his very own cacangelist; not   *Luther a cacangelist*
only at one meal, but day and night he reposes on the bosom of the
devil; or rather, the devil does not recline upon him but is stuck fast
in his very bosom. Otherwise he could not have declared with so   5
much authority that the catholic faith concerning the sacraments is
founded on the lies of men, although he has already succeeded in
proving that it cannot be founded on the Holy Spirit except insofar
as this may be proved by evident scriptures, lest, of course, the Turk,
who admits nothing apart from our scriptures, will not approve it. But   10
when the scripture of the Christians is cited, the Turk immediately
senses himself overcome and admits it. If you do not believe Luther
in this matter, he will be ready to swear that any one of the Turks
believes and venerates all the sacraments of the Christians, all the
articles of Christian faith insofar as they can be proved by the   15
testimonies of Christian scripture, no less than Luther himself believes
and venerates them. I certainly do not
believe that anyone is so incredulous as to   *That is not difficult*
be unready to believe this not only on the oath of Luther, but even
without his oath. But without the scriptures neither does the Turk   20
believe anything, nor does Luther; so prettily do they agree with one
another. To support this point he gives the following reason as his
defense: that there would be no need of sacred scripture now if the
novel statements of men are a sufficient argument apart from
scripture.   25

At this point the reverend father forces me to doubt whether any
Turk is ever so foolish as to deign, especially in this matter, to be an
ally of the Lutheran folly, not perceiving the nature of the following
inference: the church of Christ, governed by the Spirit of Christ, with
a certain faith passed on to her, preserves the sacraments of Christ;   30
therefore the church of Christ has no need of the scriptures.

If Luther had lived at the time of the evangelists he would have
deterred them by this reasoning from writing the gospels. For if those
things, which men at that time heard from men, were believed to be
handed down from God to those who related them, and thus created   35
faith in those who heard, what need was there for the evangelists to
include any of those things in writing? Was it, indeed, either because
Christ, who was working this faith in His church, would some day
utterly abandon the church, or because He could not preserve

scripto conseruare non poterat: quum ipse priusquam nasceretur:
legem promisisset semet, inscripturum cordibus: et in carne natus,
cum ecclesia futurum, usque ad consummationem seculi? Hac
ratione non puto futuros fuisse, sic deterritos euangelistas: ut fuerint
5 supersessuri a scribendis euangelijs. Imo et alia multa, et hoc fortassis
etiam respondissent. Nunquam defuturum quidem ecclesiae suae

Christi certissimum pollicitum

Christum: cum qua se promisit ipse, ad
finem usque seculi permansurum. Nun-
quam defuturum spiritum paracletum, qui ecclesiam ducat in omnem
10 ueritatem. Ita uera sacramenta, nec ueros articulos fidei ullo unquam
tempore perituros ecclesiae catholicae: nec errorem in rebus tam [K₃]
necessarijs exoriturum, quod sponsae spem ac fidem in species inanes
auocet, atque deuertat, a sponso: etiam si ipsi nullam unquam literam
scriberent: se tamen haud frustra scripturos esse: etiam si omnibus
15 omissis articulis, et sacramentis fidei: quae deus sine scripto, et doceri
fecerat: et erat seruaturus uitam Christi, ac miraculorum partem
aliquam: atque e tam multis aliqua complecterentur: quae Christus
docuit, ad formandos in grege suo mores, ac uirtutes dignas Christiano
pectore.
20 DEINDE cuius impudentiae est, appellare ecclesiae sacramenta
noua dicta hominum: quum illa praeter Lutherum dubitet nemo,
ipsis esse euangeliorum libris antiquiora? Ita sacramentum ordinis
uocauit nouum. Nouum dixit: quod panis credatur in carnem uersus,
et uinum in sanguinem: et illud ait natum esse intra annos trecentos:
25 quum rex hominis impudentiam, uetustissimorum patrum testimonijs, pulcherrime redarguit in utroque: nec minus in caeteris
sacramentis omnibus.

---

15 omissis] *corr. err. L*, amissis *BR*

without writing the faith He had wrought without writing, although
before He Himself was born He had promised that He would write
the law in men's hearts, and when He was born in the flesh He promised that He would be with the church even to the consummation
of the world? I do not think the evangelists would have been so 5
deterred by such reasoning that they would have been ready to desist
from writing the gospels. On the contrary, they would have answered
among many other things perhaps also this: that Christ would indeed
never abandon His church with whom He
Himself promised that He would remain *The utterly certain promise of* 10
Christ
even until the end of the world; that the
Spirit, the Paraclete, who leads the church into all truth would never
fail her; that thus, even if the evangelists never wrote a letter, the true
sacraments and true articles of the faith would never be lost to the
catholic church at any time, nor would error arise in matters of such 15
necessity—a thing which would distract the hope and faith of the
bride to empty appearances and turn her away from her spouse—
that nonetheless the evangelists would not write in vain even though
they should leave out all the articles and sacraments of faith which
God both had caused to be taught and wished to preserve without 20
writing; they would include the life of Christ and some part of His
miracles, and some truths from among the many which Christ taught,
for the sake of forming in His flock morals and virtues worthy of the
Christian heart.

Finally, what sort of impudence leads him to call the sacraments 25
of the church the novel sayings of men, since, except for Luther, no
one doubts that the sacraments are more ancient than the books of
the gospels themselves? Thus he has called the sacrament of orders
something new. He said that it is a new thing that bread is believed
turned into the flesh and wine into the blood; and he says that this 30
teaching has arisen within the past three hundred years; although the
king has most skillfully refuted the fellow's shamelessness by the
testimonies of most ancient fathers, on both these points and no less
so on all the other sacraments.

Rursus ostendit: quam absurde Lutherus
torqueat scripturas: quibus probare
conatur, nihil certo credendum
quod probari non possit euidente
5　　　　　　scriptura. Caput. XIIII.

SED IAM rursus reuertitur ad scripturas:
Ea sunt Lutheri frequentissima　et noua praefatione anathema crepat, ac
argumenta　　　　maledictum, os eius maledicum et male-
dictione plenum, si quis aliud ponat fundamentum: praeter id quod
10　positum est. Quasi id quisquam [K₃v] faciat, praeter ipsum, qui
Christianam fidem conatur, positis fundamentis suis, e fundamento,
quod est Christus, euertere. Sed age, uideamus quale fundamentum,
quam apte concinnet ad aedificium suum.

Verba Lutheri　　　Paulus, inquit, pri. Cor. ij. magna sanxit
15　　　　　　authoritate fidem nostram, oportere niti
in uerbis dei, ubi dicit, Sermo meus, et praedicatio mea, non in
persuasibilibus humanae sapientiae uerbis, sed in ostensione spiritus,
et uirtutis fuit, ut fides uestra non sit in sapientia hominum, sed in
uirtute dei.

20　QVIS audiuit unquam morionem tam nihil cohaerentia, tam nihil
ad propositum producere? ita satis putat dicere: quicquid ei uenit in
buccam: tantum cauet, ne taceat. Probaturum sese iactitans, nihil
authoritatem obtinere certam, praeter scripturas. Producit illud apostoli: nemo potest aliud fundamentum ponere: praeter id quod posi-
25　　　　　　tum est. Quasi id fundamentum, quod
Quam aegregie Lutherus intelligat　positum est: esset scriptura: et non quod
uerba Pauli　　　apostolus ilico subiungit Iesus Christus. Et
ibi suis anathematis, ac maledictis, subtracto Christo, nititur nos
adigere: ut scripturam credamus illud esse fundamentum, non
30　Christum: Aut idem esse scripturam quod Christum: tanquam idem
sit liber de Caesare scriptus, quod Caesar. Deinde, quum nemo neget
innitendum esse uerbis dei: sed ex his dicamus, aliud esse scriptum,
aliud pari authoritate non scriptum: et utrique pari fide credendum:
quorum ille tacite contemnit alterum, alterum contemnit aperte: ille

> He again shows how senselessly Luther
> distorts the scriptures, with which he tries
> to prove that nothing is to be believed
> with certainty which cannot be proved by
> a clear scriptural text. Chapter 14.   5

But now he turns back again to the scrip-
tures and with a new formula, his foul   *They are Luther's most frequent*
mouth full of abuse, farts anathema and a   *arguments*
curse if anyone should lay any other foundation than that which has
been laid. As if anyone would do that except himself, who, having laid   10
his own foundation, is trying to overthrow the Christian faith from
its foundation, which is Christ. But come, let us see the nature of his
foundation and how aptly he fits it to his building.

> Paul, he says, in I Cor. 2, with great auth-
> ority ordained that our faith ought to rely   *Luther's words*   15
> on the words of God, when he says: "My discourse and my preach-
> ing have not been in the persuasive words of human wisdom but in
> the manifestation of the spirit and power, so that your faith may not
> be in the wisdom of men but in the power of God."

Who has ever heard a fool present anything so irrelevant, so beside   20
the point? He thus thinks it enough to say whatever comes into his
mouth; the only thing he avoids is silence. Declaring that he will
prove that nothing possesses certain authority except the scriptures,
he brings forward the following text of the apostle: "No one can lay
any other foundation but that which has been laid." As if that   25
foundation which has been laid were the
scripture and not what the apostle himself   *How singularly Luther under-*
immediately adds: "Jesus Christ." And   *stands the words of Paul*
then, with his anathemas and curses, having failed to mention Christ,
he tries to force us to believe that the foundation referred to is   30
scripture, not Christ; or that scripture is the same thing as Christ, as
if a book written about Caesar is the same thing as Caesar. Then,
although no one denies that we must rely on the words of God—but
we say that of these words some have been written, some, of equal
authority, not written, and both kinds must be believed with equal   35
faith; of these he silently contemns the one, the other he contemns

uelut rem magnam producit, ad fulciendum dei uerbum, illa uerba
Pauli: quae ne uerbum quidem ullum faciunt de uerbo dei. Sed de
ostensione spiritus et uirtutis dei. Et iam, uelut re gesta strenue,
conuitijs in[K₄]uadit regem: quod fundat humanae sapientiae
5 persuasibilia uerba. Quasi ipse toti terrarum orbi miraculis inclares-
cat: quibus an suam praedicationem approbarit Bohemis: adhuc non
audio: sed persuasibilia humanae sapientiae uerba, nemo illi (quod
sciam) potest imputare: a quibus nullus abest morio longius: quod
quo longius progreditur: eo reddit manifestius.

10   *Verba Lutheri*   Proinde nos, inquit, nostrae ecclesiae
                            defensori adhaeremus, qui dicit Mat. xvi.
Edificabo ecclesiam meam, non super longitudinem neque super
multitudinem hominum, neque super oportet sic esse, neque super
usum, aut dictum sanctorum. Denique nec super Ioannem Baptistam,
15 nec super Eliam, nec super Hieremiam, aut ullum ex prophetis,
sed super solam et solidam petram, super Christum filium dei. Hoc
est robur nostrae fidei, hic tuti sumus, aduersus portas inferi. Hic
     Cur ergo tu utrunque facis   mentiri et fallere non potest. Omnis
                            homo mendax. Et sancti cum extra hanc
20 rupem agunt, aut dicunt, homines sunt, purissimum, et solum ac
certum uerbum dei, nostrae fidei supponendum est. Si quis, inquit,
loquitur quasi sermones dei, Et omnis prophetia sit analogia fidei. Ro.
xij.

VIDE quaeso, uel ex hoc loco lector: quo rem perducat impius,
25 probaturus nihil esse credendum, praeter euidentem scripturam.
Allegat istud: quod ecclesiae fides aedificata sit, super solum Christum: et inde concludit, solum Christi uerbum esse credendum. Quod,
ne quis interpretari possit, ita dictum: tanquam nihil credendum sit:
nisi quod scriptura sacra complectitur: propterea quod nullum
30 aliud uerbum dicat certum esse: quod dicatur a deo: sensum istum
     Impia arrogantia Lutheri   plane tollit ipse fidem auferens, non solum
                          ecclesiae consuetudini, et uniuersis anti-
quis patribus: sed nominatim quoque Ioanni Baptistae, Heliae,
Hieremiae, et caeteris pro[K₄v]phetis omnibus, et rationis suae

30 istum] *corr. err. L,* istud *BR*

openly—he brings forward, as though it were a great argument to
support the word of God, those words of Paul, which say not even one
word about the word of God but about the manifestation of the
spirit and power of God. And then, as though the engagement had
been carried off vigorously, he heaps abuse on the king because, so he   5
says, the latter pours forth the persuasive words of human wisdom.
As if he himself is becoming known to the whole world by means of
miracles. Whether he has proved his preaching to the Bohemians by
miracles I have not yet heard; but no one can impute to him, so far
as I know, the persuasive words of human wisdom; no fool is farther   10
removed from them; the farther he proceeds, the clearer he makes
this fact.

Accordingly, he says, we adhere to the   *Luther's words*
defender of our church, who says, in Mat-
thew 16, "I will build my church," not on length of time nor on the   15
multitude of men, nor on, "It must be so," nor on usage, or the word
of the saints; nor finally on John the Baptist, nor on Elias, nor on
Jeremiah or any of the prophets, but on a sole and solid rock, on
Christ, the Son of God. This is the defense of our faith, here we are
safe against the gates of hell. He cannot   *Why then do you do both?*   20
lie and deceive. "All men are liars." And
the saints, when they act or speak apart from this rock, are men. The
absolutely pure and single and certain word of God must be the
support of our faith. "If anyone speaks," he says, "let it be as with the
words of God," and, "Let all prophecy be according to the proportion   25
of faith." Romans, 12.

Please observe, even from this passage, reader, where the impious
fellow is guiding the argument, intending to prove that nothing must
be believed except a clear scriptural text. He alleges that the faith of
the church is built on Christ alone, and from this he concludes that   30
the word of Christ alone must be believed. And he clearly praises the
interpretation of anyone who understands him to mean that nothing is
to be believed except what sacred scripture includes, because no other
word which may be spoken by God is certain. For he does away with
faith not only in the custom of the church   *Luther's impious arrogance*   35
and in all the ancient fathers, but also, by
name, in John the Baptist, Elias, Jeremiah, and all the other prophets,
and as a consequence of his reasoning, absolutely all the apostles. He

consequentia omnibus prorsus apostolis:
Fausti error   Haeretico Fausto longo interuallo deterior:
qui ex illo Christi uerbo omnes, qui ante uenerunt, fures sunt et
latrones, Mosen et prophetas omnes habuit pro maleficis. Hic uero
5 fidem abrogat, et antiquae legis et euangelij proceribus prorsus
omnibus nihil relinquit certum: nisi forte quae legitur Christus ipse
dixisse: idque tam euidenti sententia, ut nulla possit in uerbis esse
controuersia. Nam caeteros uniuersos reijcit, tanquam dubios: quod
et mentiri potuerint: quum essent homines: et incertum putat esse:
10 quum illa scriberent: in petra ne an extra petram steterint. Vides ergo
lector hominis impietatem summam: qui suas haereses, quum sciat
omnium sanctorum testimonio plane damnatas esse: nihil agit aliud:
                                        quam ut uicissim sanctorum omnium
Quorsum uideatur euasurus   authoritatem tollat: Christo paulisper
Lutherus
15   deferens, donec ad plenum perueniat
iniquitas: tum eius maiestatem recta proculdubio temeraturus, quam
interim quoque oppugnat oblique. Nam si sic mendax est omnis
homo, et tam incertum, an quae sancti locuti sunt, aut scripserunt:
fecerint illud stantes in petra fidei: ut etiam dubius author sit Helias,
20 Hieremias, et Ioannes Baptista: certe sequetur: ut dubius itidem
author sit Ioannes euangelista. Nam eodem omnino spiritu et illi
loquebantur et iste. Sed nunc uicissim uide mirificam Lutheri
stultitiam. Nam postquam id probauit: quod nullus unquam negauit:
Christum ecclesiam suam fundasse supra petram: a qua petra (quod
25   nemo nescit) in Barathrum Lutherus ex-
Imo uolens desilijt   cidit. Rursus ex eo, quod Christus unus
est fundamentum: probat solam scrip[L₁]turam esse fundamentum:
quasi uerbum dei unigenitum, sit uerbum quodlibet, in sacris literis
perscriptum. An non isti necesse est, aut nihil esse frontis, aut nihil
30 esse cerebri? Et tamen quum illud comma clausisset, illo Pauli uerbo:
si quis loquitur quasi sermones dei. Et item illo, omnis prophetia sit
analogia fidei: quorum neutrum quicquam ei dicto cohaeret: cui
                                      utrunque subnectit: iam uelut acie pro-
Homo uictoriae auidus   fligata suam sibi uictoriam buccinat.

---

3 uerbo omnes, qui] verbo, omnes qui *L*   7 sententia] *corr. err. L*, scientia *BR*

is worse by a long shot than the heretic
Faustus who, from Christ's words that all *The error of Faustus*
those who preceded Him are thieves and robbers, considered Moses
and the prophets as malefactors. This fellow, however, abolishes faith
and leaves no certainty in any one at all of the leaders of the old   5
law and the gospel, unless perhaps what one reads that Christ Himself has said, and this with so clear a meaning that there can be no
controversy about His words. He rejects all other men as doubtful,
both because they could have lied, since they were men, and because
he thinks it uncertain whether, when they were setting down their   10
writings, they stood on the rock or off the rock.

You see, then, reader, the supreme impiety of the man who, when
he knows that his heresies have clearly been condemned by the
testimony of all holy men, does nothing else but abolish in turn the
authority of all holy men, deferring for a   15
little while to Christ, until his iniquity   *Where Luther seems to be*
shall reach full growth; then he will un-   *heading*
doubtedly be ready to dishonor Christ's majesty directly, which in the
meantime also he attacks indirectly. For, if every man is thus a liar,
and if it is so uncertain whether, when holy men have spoken or   20
written, they did it while standing on the rock of faith, that even
Elias is a doubtful author, and Jeremiah, and John the Baptist, it
certainly will follow that John the Evangelist likewise is a doubtful
author. For both he and they spoke by exactly the same Spirit.

But now observe, on the other hand, the amazing folly of Luther.   25
For, after he has proved what no one has ever denied: that Christ
founded His church on a rock—from which rock, as everyone knows,
Luther has fallen into the abyss—then
again, from the fact that Christ alone is   *Rather, he has deliberately*
the foundation, he proves that scripture   *leaped off it*
alone is the foundation, as if the only begotten Word of God is just any   30
word written down in the sacred writings, must we not conclude that
this fellow has either no shame or no brain? And yet, after concluding
that clause with Paul's words: "If anyone speaks, let it be as with the
words of God," and likewise with the words: "Let all prophecy be in   35
proportion to faith," neither of which texts is at all relevant to the
statement to which he joins them both,
then, as if the battle line had been de-   *A fellow greedy for*
stroyed, he trumpets his own victory.   *victory*

Verba Lutheri

Haec sunt, inquit, robora nostra, aduersus quae obmutescere coguntur, Henrici, Thomistae, papistae, et quicquid est fecis, sentinae, et latrinae impiorum, et sacrilegorum eiusmodi. Neque habent, quod possint hic respondere: sed confusi et prostrati iacent, a facie uerborum istius tonitrui, et expectamus quoque, quid aduersus hec mutire audeat rex nugigerulus iste, cum omnibus suis sophistis. Stat enim fixa sententia, fidem non deberi, nisi certo uerbo dei, sicut dicit Ro. x. Fides ex auditu, auditus autem per uerbum Christi, proinde quicquid ultra uerbum dei producitur, hoc nostri sit arbitrij ceu dominorum, credere, non credere damnare probare sicut scriptum est, omnia uestra siue Apollo, siue Cephas, siue Paulus, uos autem Christi.

At tu magnorum scelerum ne dum nugarum sator es

Consideremus lector, quorsum tendat hoc totum Lutheri fulmen et tonitrus: Christus aedificauit ecclesiam suam super se. Si quis loquitur quasi sermones dei: omnis prophetia sit analogia fidei: fides ex auditu, auditus autem per uerbum Christi, quid ex his omnibus tandem confecisti Luthere? Hoc, inquit, confeci: quod stat fixa sententia: fidem non deberi nisi certo uerbo dei, et proinde quicquid ultra uerbum dei producitur: hoc nostri sit arbitrij ceu dominorum, credere, non credere, damnare, probare.

Et quis erit iudex, quodnam id uerbum sit: Lutherus, an ecclesia catholica?

VIDE iam, quam aegregius fulminator ac tonitor sis: cui, si [L₁v] quis haec concedat omnia: tuum tamen fulmen ac tonitrus neminem prorsus attingeret, praeter te. Te uero totum, tanquam Semelem subito perflaret incendio. Rex, si potes meminisse (nam nullus lupus magis obliuiosus est: si toties obliuisceris: quoties ad ea, quae te maxime tangunt: nihil omnino respondes) uerbum dei probauit aliud scriptum esse, aliud non scriptum: sed uel ab apostolis tradita quaedam, uel a

Redi in memoriam pater bone

16 tonitrus] *corr. err.*, tonitru *BRL*   17 omnis] *corr. err. L,* omnes *BR*

These are our defenses, he says, against
which they are forced to fall silent, the
Luther's words

Henries, Thomists, papists, every kind of scum, sludge, and privy of
such impious and sacrilegious men; and they have nothing to answer
here, but they lie confused and prostrate in the face of those thunder-
ing words; and we await also what the
king, this vendor of women's wares, together with all his sophists, will dare to
mutter against these arguments. For the

*But you are the sower of great
crimes, to say nothing of
trifles*

judgment stands fixed, that faith is not owed except to the certain word
of God, as Romans 10 says: "Faith depends on hearing, but hearing
on the word of Christ"; accordingly, whatever is brought forward in
addition to the word of God, let it be a matter of choice for us as
masters, to believe, not to believe, to condemn, to approve, as it is
written: "All things are yours, whether Apollo, or Cephas, or Paul,
but you are Christ's."

Let us consider, reader, where all this lightning and thunder of
Luther is tending. "Christ has built His church upon Himself"; "If
anyone speaks, let it be as with the words of God"; "Let all prophecy be
according to the proportion of faith"; "Faith depends on hearing, but
hearing on the word of Christ." What have you finally accomplished
by all these quotations, Luther? "I have accomplished this," he says,
"that the judgment stands fixed that faith
is not owed except to the certain word of
God, and accordingly, whatever is brought
forward in addition to the word of God, let

*And who will be the judge as to
which is that word: Luther,
or the catholic church?*

it be a matter of choice for us as masters to believe, not to believe, to
condemn, to approve."

See now how excellent a lightning flasher and thunderer you are;
if anyone should grant you all these arguments, your lightning and
thunder would still touch no one at all but yourself. But you it would
blast through as completely as through Semele with an unexpected
blaze. The king, if you can remember—for
no wolf is more forgetful (if you do forget
as often as you fail to answer anything at

*Recall this to mind, good
Father*

all to those arguments which particularly nettle you)—has proved
that the word of God is in one case written, in the other unwritten,
but that certain things were either handed down by the apostles, or
divinely spoken by Christ to His church, and that thus many details

Aduerte lector

Christo ecclesiae suae dicta diuinitus.
Multa itaque scripto comprehensa: et
multa adhuc nullo esse scripto comprehensa. Sacramenta septem: et
reliquos articulos fidei: partim scripto, partim non scripto, sed tamen
5 dei uerbo fulciri: utrumque uerbum ex aequo uerum, ex aequo
certum, ex aequo uenerabile. Haec si uera sunt: quamquam caetera
omnia concederentur (quod tamen non conceditur) tui esse arbitrij,
in quibus credendis, non credendis, damnandis, probandis, posses
tanquam rex ac dominus regnare: tamen de sacramentis interim, et
10 publicae fidei articulis, nihil prorsus quicquam confecisses: nisi aut ea,

Quid ni quum iam contempserit apostolum

quae dixi, falsa sint omnia: aut aliqua
saltem pars. Negabis ergo aliud dei uerbum
scriptum esse, aliud non scriptum: et
contra euangelistam contendes scripta esse omnia: contendes nihil
15 omissum, saltem e necessarijs articulis: quum praecipuum euangelistam uideas praecipuum omisisse sacramentum? quum Paulum
audias, pleraque sine scripto tradidisse: quum Iacobus clamet
apostolus: Suscipite insitum uerbum dei: quod saluare potest animas
uestras: quum scriptura testetur: Vnctio eius docebit uos. Negabis
20 utrumque ex aequo uerum, et scriptum uerbum et non scriptum:
quum sit u[L₂]trumque dei? Sed negabis uidelicet uerbum dei: quod
scriptum non est, certum esse cuiquam posse, uel cognitum. At ipse
iam olim fassus es, hoc ecclesiae datum esse a deo: quod potest
discernere uerbum dei, a uerbis hominum: Ergo cum utriusque
25 generis uerba dei sint, et scripta uidelicet, et non scripta: potest
ecclesia per te quoque in utroque genere uerba dei discernere, a
uerbis hominum: Ergo per te quoque, uerbum dei non scriptum

Verbum dei ecclesiae certum
Lutheri quoque confessione

certum est a uerbis hominum. Nec est
causa: cur certior esse possit ecclesia
30 Christi hodie: quare euangelium Ioannis
iam olim scriptum, sit Ioannis: quam quare quoduis sacramentum
habeat gratiam ex uerbo dei non scripto: quod si neges ecclesiam
catholicam quam tu uocas papisticam, hoc habere, quum aliquam

---

11 *gloss* Quid] *L*, quid *BR*   20 uerum] *corr. err. L*, uerbum *BR*

have been included in writing and many
have not as yet been included in any   *Pay attention, reader*
writing; that the seven sacraments and the rest of the articles of faith
are supported partly by the written, partly by the unwritten word,
but still by the word of God; that both words are equally true, equally   5
certain, equally venerable. If these statements are true, then, even if
it were granted (though, in fact, it is not granted) that all other
points were a matter of your own free choice and that, like a king and
master, you had the supreme right to decide what to believe and
what not to believe, what to condemn and what to approve—   10
nevertheless, you would have all this time accomplished absolutely
nothing in regard to the sacraments and the articles of public faith;
unless everything that I have said, or at least some part of it, be false.
Will you then deny that one word of God
is written, one unwritten; and will you   *Why not, since he has already*
                                            contemned the apostle?   15
argue, in opposition to the evangelist, that
everything has been written; will you argue that nothing has been
omitted, at least of the necessary articles, although you see that the
principal evangelist omitted the principal sacrament, although you
hear that Paul delivered very many teachings without writing, al-   20
though the apostle James proclaims: "Receive the engrafted word of
God which is able to save your souls," although the scripture testifies:
"His anointing shall teach you"? Will you deny that both the written
and the unwritten word are equally true, although both are of God?
But of course you will deny that the word of God which is unwritten   25
can be known for certain or recognized by anyone. Yet you yourself
have already long ago admitted that God has given the church the
power to distinguish the word of God from the words of men. Therefore, since the words of God are of both kinds, that is, both written
and unwritten, the church can, according to you, also distinguish   30
within either kind the words of God from the words of men. Therefore, also according to you, the unwritten
word of God is distinguished from the   *The word of God is distin-*
words of men. There is no reason why the *guished by the church even*
                                           by Luther's admission
church of Christ today can be more certain   35
as to why the gospel of John written long ago is that of John than as to
why any particular sacrament has grace from the unwritten word of
God; but if you should deny that the catholic church which you call
papistic has this power, then, since you do admit that some church has

ecclesiam hoc habere fatearis: profer aliquam praeter hanc, quam
appellas papisticam: quae uerba dei non scripta discreuit a uerbis
hominum. Imo profer aliquam praeter hanc quae tibi, non dico
maioribus tuis, sed tibi discreuit uerba dei scripta a scriptis uerbis
5   hominum. Sed ne te, nimium tuis uerbis

Vix fieri potest: ut peior   urgendo, reddam deteriorem: et te, quod
euadat
                               semper soles, reuocare cogam, quicquid
dixisti bene: omitto, quod tu concessisti: quaero, quid ad illud dicis:
quod confessus Petrus ecclesiae nomine: Iesum esse Christum filium
10   dei uiui: protinus audiuit a domino: Beatus es Simon Bar Iona: quia
caro et sanguis non reuelauit tibi, sed pater meus, qui in caelis est.

AGE Luthere, hoc uerbum, quod con-
At Luthero opus est euidenti   fessus est Petrus: quibus euidentibus scrip-
scriptura, ut cui deus negarit
spiritum suum   turis didicit: quum nec ulla scriptura
15   iudaeos, satis euidenter id docere potuerit:
nec Petrus [L₂v] idiota piscator, ullas ferme litteras didicisset: quum
illud certe, quod confessus est: Christus eum dicit, non scripto uerbo
foris, sed patris interius, infundente se spiritu didicisse. Non fuit ergo
certus, hoc uerbum esse dei: propterea quod sensit, non legit: quod
20   intus audiuit non extra? quod affers: ergo fides ex auditu: quaeso te,
an non intus audiuit Petrus quod intus locutus est deus? An dumtaxat
auditur: quod scribitur? An prius quam scripta sunt euangelia
Christiani non audierunt apostolos? Ecce iam nugigerule Luthere
quam nihil opus est, ad ista tua praeclara robora quenquam respon-
25   dere: quae citra nostrae causae praeiudicium, citra ullum commodum
tuae, licet uniuersa concedere. Tam acer es Luthere disputator?

tantus fulminator es: tam terribilibus in-
Is diabolicum tonitru non   tonas tonitribus? Reponantur igitur ab ore
diuinum habuit
                               sacrilego, in suum locum diuinum fulgur
30   ac tonitru. Deinde in os illud impurissimum, non tantum meiere fas
est. Quod quanto furore fertur in praeceps, uel illud ostendit: quod
sequitur.

13–14 *gloss* deus . . . suum] *L*, pater caelestis subtraxerit suam scientiam *R, om. B*
31 ostendit] *corr. err. L*, ostentit *BR*

it, bring forward some church besides this one that you call papistic which has distinguished the unwritten words of God from the words of men. Or rather, bring forward some church besides this one which has distinguished for you—I do not say for your ancestors, but for you—the written words of God from the written words of men. But, 5 in order not to render you worse by pressing you too hard with your own *It is hardly possible for him to turn out worse* words and force you to retract, as is your constant custom, whatever good you have said, I pass over what you have conceded; I ask: What do you say to the fact that when Peter 10 had confessed in the name of the church that Jesus is the Christ and the Son of the living God, he immediately heard from the Lord: "Blessed are thou, Simon Bar-Jonah, for flesh and blood has not revealed this to thee, but my Father in heaven"?

Come, Luther, this word which Peter 15 confessed: from what evident scriptures did *But Luther needs evident scripture, as one to whom God has denied His Spirit* he learn it, since no scripture could have taught it to the Jews very evidently, nor had Peter, an ignorant fisherman, had any but the slightest education, for Christ says that he had certainly learned that which he confessed 20 not from a word written exteriorly but from the Spirit of the Father pouring Himself out interiorly? Was he therefore uncertain that this was the word of God because he felt it, did not read it, because he heard it interiorly, not exteriorly?

As for your citing, "Therefore faith is dependent on hearing," I 25 ask you whether or not Peter heard interiorly what God spoke interiorly? Or is something heard only when it is written? Or, before the gospels were written, did the Christians not hear the apostles?

Now see, trifle-trafficking Luther, how unnecessary it is for anyone to answer these brilliant arguments of yours which, without any 30 disadvantage to our cause, without any advantage to yours, may be granted collectively. Are you such a fierce debater, Luther? Are you such a great lightning-flasher; do you thunder with such frightful thunders? Let lightning and thunder, therefore, be taken out of your sacrilegious *He had diabolical, not divine, thunder* 35 mouth and put back into their own divine place. Then it will be proper not merely to piss into that most filthy mouth. Even the following passage shows the degree of madness with which that mouth rushes headlong.

Lutheri uerba

Scriptum est, inquit, omnia uestra, siue Apollo, siue Cephas, siue Paulus, uos autem Christi. Si solius Christi sumus, quis est stolidus rex, qui suis mendacijs nos papae facere molitur? Nos non sumus papae, sed papa noster est, Nostrum est non iudicari ab ipso, sed ipsum iudicare. Spiritualis enim a nemine iudicatur, et ipse iudicat omnes: quia uerum est. Omnia uestra, etiam papa, quanto magis sordes istae, et labes hominum Thomistae et Henrici.

Imo tu stolide fratercule mentiris in regem. Tu satanista et haeretice

Dispeream, si phrenesis ipsa, tam phrenetica sit, aut furor ipse tam furiosus: quam sit istud lepidum Lutheri capitellum. Papa noster est, inquit: ergo nostrum non est ab ipso iudicari, sed ipsum iudicare. Eadem ratione, medicus noster est: ergo non est nostrum ab ipso curari: sed ipsum [L₃] curare. Et doctor discentium est: ergo non est ipsorum ab illo discere, sed docere eum.

Similis omnino ratio

IAM quod ait nostrum est, non iudicari a papa: sed ipsum iudicare. Quid sibi uult illud, nostrum est: an uniuersorum dicit? an singulorum? Si uniuersorum dicit: nihil pro se dicit: quia uniuersitas ecclesiae pro papa est, aduersus illum: at in sacramentorum causa multo minus iuuat illum: ubi et populus et papa tam praesentes quam praeteriti, sunt pro sacramentis aduersus illum: Sin singulorum est, iudicare de papa, de sacramentis, de uero sensu scripturae sacrae. Iam quum ex tot iudicibus, unius prope Lutheri iudicium sit ex altera parte: qua praerogatiua debet eius unius calculus, caeterorum omnium calculis praeponderare? Quia spiritualis, inquit, a nemine iudicatur: et ipse iudicat omnes: quia uerum est omnia uestra sunt: etiam papa. Non uideris tibi lector, audire deliramenta? Solus Lutherus ergo spiritualis est? aut solus papa non est spiritualis? ut aut Lutherus omnes possit iudicare: et iudicari prorsus a nemine: aut papa iudicari debeat ab omnibus: et iudicari neminem? Quem non

Potius omnium calculis damnari

---

14 *gloss om.* BL

It is written, he says, "that all things are
yours, whether Apollo, or Cephas, or
Luther's words

Paul, but you are Christ's." If we are Christ's alone, who is the dull-
witted king who strives by his lies to make
us the pope's? We are not the pope's, but
the pope is ours. It is our right not to be
judged by him but to judge him. For "the
On the contrary, you dull-witted
friarlet, you lie against the king. 5
You satanist and heretic!

spiritual man is judged by no man and he himself judges all men,"
because it is true that, "All things are yours," even the pope; how
much more these riffraff and good-for-nothing rascals, the Thomists   10
and Henries.

Confound it if frenzy itself is as frenetic or raving madness itself is
as raving mad as is this witty little noggin of Luther's. "The pope is
ours," he says; "therefore it is our right, not to be judged by him, but
to judge him." By the same reasoning: a
physician is ours, therefore it is our right,
Altogether similar reasoning   15

not to be cured by him, but to cure him; and a teacher belongs to his
students, therefore it is their right, not to study from him, but to
teach him.

Now as for his statement that it is our right not to be judged by the   20
pope but to judge him, what does he mean by the words, "It is our
right"? Is he speaking of all men taken together? Or of individuals?
If he says, "of all taken together," he says nothing in his own support,
because the totality of the church is for the pope, against him; but it
helps him still less in the case of the sacraments, where both people   25
and pope, present as well as past, are for the sacraments, against him.
But if it is the right of individuals to judge concerning the pope, concerning the sacraments, concerning the true sense of holy scripture,
then, since out of so many judges the judgment of Luther is almost
the only one on the one side, by what pre-   30
rogative should the vote of this one man
outweigh the votes of all the others? "Be-
Rather he is condemned by the
votes of everyone

cause," he says, "the spiritual man is judged by no one and he himself
judges all men, because it is true that all things are yours, even the
pope."   35
Does it not seem to you, reader, that you are listening to gibberish?
Is Luther alone, then, spiritual; or is the pope alone not spiritual; so
that either Luther can judge all men and be judged by absolutely no
one, or the pope ought to be judged by all men and judge no one?

delectet hominis tam suauiter insanientis amentia: qui se non uideat:
quicquid eblatterat in papam: idem etiam eblatterare in Petrum
ipsum ac Paulum? Nam omnia, inquit, uestra sunt: non dicit papa,
sed Apollo, Cephas, et Paulus. Quamobrem sicut Lutherus ait, nos
5   non sumus papae: sed papa noster est: nostrum est ergo, non iudicari
a papa: sed ipsum iudicare: quia spiritualis omnia iudicat: et iudicatur a nemine: ita necesse est ei dicere, nos non sumus Petri aut

Quaeso ergo Luthere, quid de   Pauli: sed Petrus et [L₃v] Paulus nostri
illis sentis   sunt: nostrum est ergo non iudicari a
10   Petro et Paulo, sed iudicare Petrum et
Paulum. Imo adeo non nostrum est, sed meum inquiet, quia spiritualis iudicat omnia: et a nemine iudicatur. Iudicabit ergo Lutherus
homo spiritualis hac ratione non Thomistas et Henricos, sed Petrum
et Paulum, et reliquos omnes apostolos.

15   I nunc lector: et nega e Iouis capite natam Mineruam unam:
quum istius caput unum uideas, tot parturire phreneses.

Verba Lutheri   Quanquam ego stultus, inquit, sum, et
satis ineptus, qui amentibus istis, et
deploratis cerebris, toties frustra inculco, et surdis, induratisque
20   capitibus, sine fructu semper incanto, Traditiones hominum, seu
diuturnum usum in rebus fidei nihil ualere.

SATIS profecto stultus es (ut dicis) nec ineptus modo, sed et
amens, et insanus, et cerebri deploratissimi: qui sine fructu uelut
cuculus eandem semper cantilenam canas: Traditiones hominum in
25   rebus fidei nihil ualere: quum ita surdus
Surdus Lutherus   sis et indurati capitis: ut millies tibi ad
aures inclamatum non audias dei traditiones esse: quas tu uocas
traditiones hominum: neque ad ea quicquam respondes: quibus ea
quae dicis fuerunt ante diluta quam dicta.

30   Quoties, inquit, dixi, etiam Augustini
Verba Lutheri   sententia solis canonicis libris eum
deberi honorem: ut firmissime credatur nihil erroris in illis esse,

---

4 Lutherus ait] *corr. err. L*, ait *om. BR*   5 est: nostrum] *corr. err. L*, est. Nostrum *BR*
7 nemine: ita] *corr. err.*, nemine. Ita *BR*, nemine: Ita *L*   20 fructu] *L*, fructru *BR*;
Traditiones] *L*, Thraditiones *BR*

Who will not be amused by the madness of a man raving so sweetly that he does not see that whatever he blathers against the pope he is also blathering against Peter himself and against Paul? "For all things," he says, "are yours"; he does not say, "the pope," but, "Apollo, Cephas, and Paul." For this reason, just as Luther says, "We are not the pope's, but the pope is ours; it is our right therefore not to be judged by the pope but to judge him, because the spiritual man judges all things and he is judged by no one"; so it is necessary for him to say, "We are not Peter's or Paul's, but Peter and Paul are ours; it is therefore our right not to be judged by Peter and Paul but to judge Peter and Paul." Indeed, he will rather say, not, "It is our right," but, "It is my right," because the spiritual man judges all things and is judged by no one. Therefore Luther, a spiritual man, will judge according to this reasoning, not Thomists and Henries, but Peter and Paul and all the rest of the apostles.

Pray, tell then, Luther: How do you judge them?

Go on now, reader, and deny that a single Minerva was born from the head of Jove, when you see the single head of this fellow bring forth so many frenzies.

Although I am foolish, he says, and not very skilled, I who drill so often without effect into these hopelessly senseless brains, and keep chanting without result to these deaf blockheads: "The traditions of men or long usage has no validity in matters of faith."

Luther's words

You certainly are foolish enough, as you say, and not only unskilled but also senseless, insane, hopelessly brainless, who like a cuckoo keep chanting without result the same trite song: "The traditions of men have no validity in matters of faith," since you are such a deaf blockhead that you do not hear what has been dinned into your ears a thousand times: that what you call the traditions of men are the traditions of God; nor do you answer anything at all to those arguments by which the arguments you state have been dissolved before they are stated.

Deaf Luther

How often, he says, I have said that even in the opinion of Augustine honor is owed only to the canonical books, so that one may most firmly believe

Luther's words

caeteros, quantalibet sanctitate doctrinaque praepolleant, non aequo
honore dignos esse.

DE diuturna ecclesiae fide, quam dixerat nihil ualere: non affert
probationem: Sufficit enim aduersus illud Christi uerbum: Ego
5 uobiscum sum usque ad finem seculi. Et item illud, quod spiritus
paracletus, ducet ecclesiam in omnem ueritatem: et quod Christus
orauit: ne deficeret fides [L₄] ecclesiae.

Quid Lutherus afferat aduersus scripturas   Aduersus haec inquam omnia sufficit,
quod talia dicturos irriserit turca. Sed ne
10 quis moueatur quicquam authoritate sanctorum patrum: affert illud
Augustini: caeteros libros extra scripturam canonicam, non aequo
honore dignos esse, quantalibet sanctitate authores eorum, doctrinaque praepolleant. Quasi quisquam sancti cuiusquam dictum sic
alleget: tanquam scripturam sacram. Et tamen haud dubito, eundem
15 Augustinum, si quid apud omnes ante se sanctos patres legisset,
praesertim cum sui temporis fide consentiens: nunquam fuisse
dubitaturum: quin id uerum esset: et Christianae fidei indubitatus
articulus. Nam eorum scripta, qui fuerunt

Sanctorum fidem ex eorum scriptis deprehendi   ante nos: suorum temporum fidem nobis
20 repraesentant. Neque enim aliter cum
defunctis loquimur: ut qua fide fuerint, possimus agnoscere. Ex
eorum ergo libris, qui uixerunt: illud deprehendimus, atque ita com-
perimus, hanc fidem, quam Lutherus impugnat: non esse, quod ille
mentitur, nouam: aut alicuius nationis propriam, sed multis seculis,
25 totius ecclesiae publicam: quam ueram esse, et in re tam magni
momenti, non posse errare et falli, promisit ille, qui dixit: Paracletus,
quum uenerit, ipse uos ducet in omnem ueritatem. At Lutherus
contra, Scriptura, inquit, exigit: ut nulli credatur, nisi soli sibi. Rogo
te Luthere, ubi hoc exigit scriptura? profer scripturam, per quam
30 spiritus sanctus prohibet, ne quis ipsi credat, nisi proferenti scripturam. Quum descendit super apostolos,

Lutherus ne deo quidem sine syngrapha credit   nihil ne docuit omnino, sine scriptura?
omnibus de rebus exegerunt ab illo

1 quantalibet] quantumlibet *L*   12 quantalibet] quantumlibet *L*

that there is no error in them, but that the rest, however much holiness and learning distinguish them, are not worthy of equal honor.

On the matter of the long-lasting faith of the church, which he had said is of no validity, he does not present any proof; for sufficient argument against the words of Christ, "I am with you even to the end of the world," and likewise against the statement that the Spirit, the Paraclete, will lead the church into all truth, and against the fact that Christ prayed that the faith of the church would not fail; sufficient argument against all these texts, I say, is the fact that the Turk would jeer at the men who would say such things. *What Luther opposes to the scriptures* But, lest anyone be influenced at all by the authority of the holy fathers, he presents Augustine's statement that the other books outside the canonical scripture are not worthy of equal honor, no matter how much holiness and learning distinguish their authors. As if anyone would thus cite the saying of any saint as though it were sacred scripture. And yet I have no doubt that if this same Augustine had read anything in the works of all the holy fathers preceding him, especially anything harmonizing with the faith of his own time, he would never have doubted that it was a true and undoubted article of Christian faith. For the writings of our predecessors represent to us the faith of their own times. Nor do we have any other *That the faith of the saints is gathered from their writings* way of speaking with the dead in order that we can know the content of their faith. Therefore, out of the books of those who have lived before us we find out that knowledge, and thus we discover that this faith which Luther attacks is not, as he falsely asserts, new or proper to any one nation, but that it is the public faith of the whole church through many ages. That this church is true and unable to err and be deceived in a matter of such great importance was promised by Him who said: "The Paraclete, when He shall have come, shall lead you into all truth." But Luther, on the contrary, says: "Scripture demands that nothing be believed except itself alone." I ask you, Luther: Where does scripture demand this? Cite the scriptural text through which the Holy Spirit forbids anyone to believe Him unless He is quoting scripture. When He descended upon the apostles, did He teach them *Luther does not believe even God without a written guarantee* nothing at all without scripture? Did they

scripturam? Vni tibi Luthere, tam male fidei est spiritus sanctus: ut
ei nihil sis cre[L₄v]diturus absque syngrapha? HAEC sunt, quae pijs
ac fidelibus, hoc est, ut ille uocat, surdis aspidibus incantator iste,
semper frustra cecinit: qui sine fine, inquit, suas nenias iterant et gar-
5 riunt. Augustinus, aut Hieronymus sic dixit: Ambrosius sic dixit: ergo
Lutherus est haereticus: quia Augustini uel Ambrosii dicta sunt
articuli fidei. Ego certe fateor illam consequentiam non ualere: sed
hanc opinor ualere. Nemo Luthero sic unquam dixit: ergo Lutherus
est impudenter mendax. At nec hanc negare potest ipse Lutherus.
10 Lutherus negat ea, quae spiritus sanctus ecclesiam docuit, esse
articulos fidei: ergo Lutherus est haereticus.

Verba Lutheri. Quanto magis te   Quin et isti porci Thomistae, inquit,
merito dicunt errare   coguntur concedere, saepius sanctos uiros
                                       errasse, ut eorum authoritas pro stabi-
15   lienda fide, et fulcienda conscientia, etiam communis sensus iudicio
satis esse non possit.

VAH uix tandem sensi stolidus: cur sibi tantum sumat Lutherus:
cur sibi magis de scripturae sensu credi uelit, ac fide: quam
uniuersis sanctis patribus. Nunc rationem reddidit: uidelicet, quia
20   illi saepius errauerunt: ille errare non
Imo ille potius semper   potest.

IDEO si quid in quaestionem trahat ipse solus, de quo caeteri
consentiant omnes: caeterorum authoritas omnium non sufficit ad
fulciendam conscientiam. Quare? quia nemo est aliorum: qui non
25 possit errare: sed authoritas Lutheri sufficit. Quare? quia ille non
potest errare: tanquam caecus aliquis diceret: Nemo est fere uident-
ium: qui non erret aliquando in rerum coloribus: ego errare non
possum. Si quis ergo nolit falli, de coloribus: diffidat caeteris
mortalibus uniuersis: atque uni credat mihi: et haec est, inquit,
30 [M₁] aduersus regia illa Thomistarum principia, generalis mea
responsio: quam non sani esse hominis: non sanus iuret Orestes.

---

13 concedere, saepius] concedere saepius, *BRL*   14 ut] et *BRL*   28 diffidat] dissidat
L   31 Orestes.] *BL*, Orestes, *R*

demand a scriptural text of Him in support of every truth? Is it to you
alone, Luther, that the Holy Spirit is so untrustworthy that you are
unready to believe Him at all without a written guarantee?

These are the arguments which this enchanter has always chanted
vainly to virtuous and faithful men; that is, as he calls them, to deaf 5
asps who, he says, incessantly repeat and chatter their ditties:
"Augustine or Jerome said so; Ambrose said so; therefore Luther is a
heretic because the sayings of Augustine or Ambrose are articles of
faith." I certainly admit that that inference has no validity; but I
think the following is valid: "No one has ever said any such thing to 10
Luther; therefore Luther is a shameless liar." But Luther himself
cannot deny this one: "Luther denies that what the Holy Spirit has
taught the church are articles of faith; therefore Luther is a heretic."

Indeed, and these Thomist swine, he
says, are forced to grant that holy men *Luther's words. With how much*
have erred rather often, so that their   *more reason do they say that* 15
authority cannot be enough, even by the   *you err*
judgment of common sense, for confirming faith and supporting
conscience.

Ah! I have just finally caught on, idiot that I am, why Luther 20
arrogates so much to himself; why he wishes himself more than all the
holy fathers taken together to be believed concerning the meaning of
scripture and concerning faith. Now he has given the reason; namely,
that they have erred rather often; he
cannot err.   *He, on the contrary, always errs*
                                                                          25
Therefore, if he, a single individual, drags into question any
matter on which everyone else agrees, the authority of all the others
does not suffice to support conscience. Why? Because there is not one
of the others who cannot err. But the authority of Luther suffices.
Why? Because he cannot err. As if some blind man were to say: 30
"There is hardly any person with sight who does not err at times on
the colors of things; I am unable to err; therefore, if a man does not
wish to be deceived about colors, let him distrust all other mortals
taken together, and let him believe me alone."

And this, he says, is my general response to those royal principles 35
of the Thomists. Let mad Orestes swear that this answer is that of a
madman.

Repetit quaedam absurda Lutheri dicta
quae ab ipso in principio
posita, author in hunc locum
distulit. Cap. XV.

5 QVANQVAM TE iam diu lector, fastidire scio totum genus, generalis responsionis istius: quam uides esse tam stupidam: ut non mirari
non possis: quae nam intemperiae temperarint hominem: quum eum
non puduerit tanta cum iactantia, tam insane respondere, tamen
orabo te: ut aliquid adhuc tedij deuores: dum uerba quaedam ab
10 illius libelli principio, in hunc dilata locum, recognoscas: ne ille me
causari possit imitari se: et si quid ille robustum putat, id praeterire
silentio: aut tu me lector censeas, uel tam obliuiosum: ut non
                                  meminerim: quod initio sum pollicitus:
Iam persoluet author quae initio   aut tam malae fidei: ut nolim, quod
est pollicitus
15   promisi praestare. Porro quo minori tibi
res fastidio sit futura, Lutheri stulticia, quae per singulas pene sillabas
asininas profert auriculas: tibi leuabit tedium. Ait igitur hunc in
modum.

                          NONDVM intelligere possunt papistae,
Verba Lutheri
20   pro qua re, mihi cum ipsis bellum sit.
Frustra tot libellis a me aeditis, et palam testantibus, hoc solum a me
quaeri, ut diuinae literae solae regnent, sicut dignum et iustum est,
humanae uero, inuentiones et traditiones e medio tollantur, ceu
nocentissima scandala, aut execto ueneno, et euulso aculeo, id est ui
25 cogendi et imperandi, et conscientias illaqueandi, erepta: liberae et
indifferentes tolerentur, ceu quaelibet alia pestis, aut infelicitas
mundi. [M₁v]

NIHIL audis hic lector noui, sed idem, quod ante decies inculcatum, in generali eius responsione: decies, ut uidisti, reuictum est
30   et confutatum: ne quid hic opus fuerit,
Tu in memoria lector habeto,
quae ante dixerit   eadem rursus repetere: tantum libuit
                                 admonere te, et sub oculis ponere:

---

3 posita, author in hunc locum] *BL*, posita author in hun clocum *R*   5 fastidire]
fastididire *B*   7 quae nam] quaenam *L*   8 respondere, tamen] respondere. Tamen
B, respondere: tamen *L*   9 deuores] *BL*, deuotes *R*   11 praeterire] preterire *B*
19 NONDVM intelligere] Nondum, inquit, intelligere *B*   21 testantibus] *L*, tectantibus
BR   22 regnent] negent *B*   24 ueneno] *B*, veneno *L*, uenemo *R*; euulso] *L*, euolso
BR; id est ui] *corr. err.*, id est, vi *L*, id est in *BR*   25 liberae] *BL*, libirae *R*   26 infeli-
citas] *B*, filicitas *R*, foelicitas *L*

He takes up again certain absurd statements
of Luther which the author initially proposed
for discussion but has put off till this section.
Chapter 15.

Although I know, reader, that for a long while now you have been   5
disgusted by the whole tenor of this general response, which you see
is so stupid that you cannot but wonder what sort of ungoverned
madness has governed the fellow, since he has not been ashamed to
answer so senselessly with so much boasting, nevertheless I will ask
you to endure patiently a bit more boredom while you recall certain   10
words from the beginning of that little book which I have put off till
this point, lest he be able to pretend that I am imitating him and
passing over in silence any argument he considers solid; or lest you,
reader, should judge me either so forgetful as not to remember what I
promised at the beginning, or of such bad   15
faith as not to want to fulfill what I have   *The author now carries out his*
promised. On the other hand, that the   *initial promise*
matter may hereafter be less disgusting to you, the folly of Luther,
which displays his asinine ears at almost every syllable, will relieve
your boredom. This, then, is how he talks: 20

    The papists cannot yet understand what   *Luther's words*
    the battle between me and them is all
    about. To no avail have I published so many books which openly
    testify that I seek only that the divine writings alone may reign, as
    is fitting and just, but that human inventions and traditions should be   25
    abolished as most harmful stumbling blocks, or with their poison cut
    out and their sting removed; that is, with their power of forcing and
    commanding and ensnaring consciences snatched away, they should
    be tolerated as optional matters, neither good nor bad, like any other
    pest or misfortune of the world.   30

You hear nothing new here, reader, but the same thing that,
having been hammered away at ten times before in his general
response, has been refuted and disproved ten times, as you have seen,
so that there was not any need of repeating
the same points again here, only I wished   *Keep in mind, reader, what he*   35
to warn you and to present for your   *has said before*

cuiusmodi res uocet ille, inuentiones et traditiones hominum. Nam
eas ipse commemorat paulo post: quum ait:

Verba Lutheri	Alterum genus de his rebus est, quae sunt extra scripturam, scilicet,
De papatu,	De consiliorum decretis,
De doctoribus,	De indulgentijs,
De purgatorio,	De missa,
De Academijs,	De uotis monasticis,
De episcopis idolis,	De traditionibus hominum,
De cultu sanctorum,	De sacramentis nouis,

Et si qua sunt similia scilicet zizania, per Satanam, principatu idoli
sui Romani, super agrum domini semi-

*Tam aegregie obsecro discernis
zizaniam a tritico*

nata: quibus ecclesia, non modo potest
saluberrime carere, uerum etiam, ne
consistit quidem, nisi careat, aut pro libero arbitrio utatur.

SAEPE audisti lector, eum omnia pro traditionibus hominum
ducere: quaecunque non sunt euidentibus comprehensa scripturis.
Nunc uelut speciminis loco, uides eum producere, non papatum
tantum, aut indulgentias, aut omnia monachorum uota: quae ipsa
tollendo, satis se sacrilegum esse docuisset:

*Hic uides lector, quae sint Luthero
traditiones hominum*

sed decreta consiliorum, sed doctores
sacros, sed sacramenta, purgatorium, cul-
tum sanctorum, et ipsam denique missam: quam alibi uocat merum
portentum, idolum, leruam, mendacium, et ipsissimam abominationem, in loco sancto stantem. Haec igitur omnia, nisi saltem libera
sint, et indifferentia: censet ne consistere quidem ecclesiam posse: sic
autem posse utrunque consistere: [M₂] non aliter tamen, quam consistit homo cum peste. Quamobrem multo fore salubrius, ut uelut
nocentissima scandala, tollantur omnino, papatus, doctores, Acade-
miae, episcopi, consilia, monachi, traditiones hominum, sanctorum
cultus, ac missa, sacramenta, spes omnis indulgentiae, et metus
purgatorij. Nam tum demum ecclesiam

*Quo pacto futurum felices
Christiani Luthero uideantur*

fore felicissimam, si sublato papatu, et
consiliorum decretis, et monasticis uotis, et

---

1 hominum. Nam] *BL*, hominum, Nam *R*   3 *gloss* Verba Lutheri] *B places gloss eight
lines later*   5 papatu,] papatu. *B*, Papatu, *L*; decretis,] *L*, decretis. *BR*   10 nouis,]
nouis. *L*   11 Satanam] Sathanam *L*; principatu] principatum *BRL*   14 uerum
etiam] verumetiam *L*   17 quaecunque] quaecumque *B*   24 leruam] lernam *L*

consideration the sort of things he calls inventions and traditions of men. For he himself mentions them a little later, when he says:

The other kind consists of those things which are outside scripture, namely:

Luther's words

the papacy	the decrees of councils	5
doctors	indulgences	
purgatory	the mass	
universities	monastic vows	
falsely named bishops	the traditions of men	
the cult of the saints	new sacraments	10

And anything similar, that is, cockle sown by Satan, through the rule of his Roman idol, in the field of the Lord; not only can the church very profitably do without them, but moreover she does not even endure unless she does without them, or uses them in accordance with free choice.

Do you, pray tell, so clearly distinguish the cockle from the wheat?

15

You have often heard, reader, that he considers as traditions of men everything that is not contained in evident scriptures. Now you see him bring forward, as though under the topic of example, not only the papacy or indulgences or all the vows of monks, by doing away 20 with which very things he would have showed that he was sacrilegious enough, but the decrees of councils, and holy doctors, and the sacraments, purgatory, the cult of the saints, and finally the mass itself, which he terms elsewhere a 25 sheer monstrosity, an idol, a spectre, a lie, and the very abomination itself standing in the holy place. Therefore, unless all these things be at least optional and neither good nor bad, he thinks the church cannot even endure, but that, given this condition, the one as well as the other can endure, yet only as a man endures with a pest. There- 30 fore, it would be much healthier that, like most harmful stumbling blocks, there should be abolished altogether the papacy, doctors, universities, bishops, councils, monks, the traditions of men, the veneration of saints, and the mass, the sacraments, all hope of forgiveness and fear of purgatory. For then at last 35 the church would be most fortunate, if, with the papacy abolished together with the decrees of councils and monastic vows and all universities and

Here you see, reader, what Luther considers the traditions of men

On what condition Christians would seem fortunate to Luther

Academijs omnibus, et omnibus omnino doctoribus, populus neque
legibus regatur: neque pareat magistratibus: neque doctores audiat:
sed adeo liber sit, et effrenis, euangelica libertate scilicet: ut neque
cogatur quisquam: neque iubeatur: neque consulatur: neque
5 doceatur quicquam: nec sanctos colat: et sacramenta contemnat:
missam uero, hoc est sanctis ceremonijs oblatum Christi corpus,
abominetur etiam: quod quo possit impunius: credat tantum horum
nihil libero se arbitrio facere: sed omnia mala imputet deo: firmam
habeat fidem in promissione dei: quicquid omnino fecerit, saluum se
10 fore per baptismum: ita si crediderit: beatus erit et felix. Namque

Fides Lutherana   metus omnes, et inexorabile fatum subiecit
                              pedibus, strepitumque Acherontis Auerni.
Nam purgatorium, nihil miror, si non metuit: non est profecto, cur
metuat: qui isthac fide fuerit: et ad istum uiuat modum.

15   Refellit Lutheri calumniam: qui mentitur, falso
              regem imputasse ei haeresim hanc: fidem
                   solam sine operibus ad salutem
                     sufficere. Cap. XVI. [M₂v]

SED HOC in loco non est omittendum: quod Lutherus calumniatur
20 principem: quasi haeresim hanc, falso imputet ei: Fidem solam sine
operibus ad salutem sufficere. Et hoc dicit, regem falso de se dicere:
quum ipse rursus idem dicat, in isto eodem libro: quo respondet regi:
in quo uerba sunt eius eiusmodi.

Lutheri uerba   Vnus furor est huius populi sacrilegi,
25   uelle per opera coram deo agere, et non
sola fide. Vnde necesse est Christum negari et fidem eius exinaniri.

QVID his uerbis apertius? et tamen iste, quum idem rursus inge-
minet: non dubitat, ac si nunquam id dixisset: uerum in contrariam

3 adeo] *L*, a deo *BR*   7 abominetur etiam:] *corr. err.*, abominetur etiam, *L*, abominetur: etiam *BR*   15 mentitur, falso] mentitur falso, *BRL*   21 sufficere] *L*, suffic ere *BR*
26 negari] *L*, negarij *BR*

absolutely all doctors, the people would neither be ruled by laws nor
obey rulers nor listen to doctors, but would be so free and unbridled,
with the freedom of the gospel of course, that no one would be forced,
nor commanded, nor counselled, nor taught anything, nor would
anyone venerate the saints; and he would contemn the sacraments;
but the mass, that is, the body of Christ offered with holy ceremonies,
he would even abominate. That he can do this with more impunity,
let him only believe that he does none of these things with a free will,
but let him impute all evil deeds to God; let him have firm faith in
the promise of God, that no matter what he has done he will be saved
through baptism; if he believes this, he *The Lutheran faith*
will be blessed and happy. All fears and the
inexorable fate he has cast under his feet, together with the roaring of
Avernian Acheron. I am not at all surprised if he has no fear of
purgatory; there is indeed no reason for a person to be afraid of it
who has had this sort of faith and lives in this manner.

He refutes the slander of Luther, who lies in
saying that the king has falsely charged him
with the heresy that faith alone without works
suffices for salvation. Chapter 16.

But I must not pass over at this point the fact that Luther slanders
the prince, as if the latter imputes to him falsely the heresy that faith
alone without works suffices for salvation. And this, he says, the king
says of him falsely, although he himself says the same thing once again
in this same book in which he answers the king; in it his words are as
follows:

> These sacrilegious people have one mad- *Luther's words*
> ness: they wish to act before God by
> works and not by faith alone; the result is that it is necessary to deny
> Christ and to make faith in Him void.

What is clearer than these words? And although this scoundrel
reiterates the same thing again, yet he does not hesitate—as if he had
never said it but had always argued for the contrary opinion—to

semper sententiam disputasset: regem nebulo conuitijs impetere: quia
dixit, eum id dixisse pridem: quod iam dicit denuo.

Verba Lutheri

Progenies, inquit, ista uiperae, ingenium
naturae refert, et parentum suorum
exemplum imitatur. Sic enim et Paulo, cum docuisset sola fide sine
operibus iustificari, omnes filios Adam: ut scribit Ro. iij. Qui dicunt
nos docere, faciamus mala, ut ueniant bona. Sed quod manet illos
iudicium? quorum, inquit, damnatio

*Istud tibi erit scripturarum
calumniator*

iusta est. Quid et ego meo Basilisco
dicam, de suo mendacio, nisi idem
damnationis iudicium?

QVIS non plane sit impius: qui Lutherum damnet, hominem
Pauli sodalem: et qui non aliter stilum temperet: quam quorum
linguam temperabat deus? Nam et rursus ait paulo post.

*Verba Lutheri. Audi lector
hunc apostolum*

Orbi toti constat me de fide, de charitate,
de operibus, semper eadem docuisse, et
scripsisse, licet usu et studio, de die in
diem magis ac magis proficerem, et easdem res nunc sic, nunc sic
tradiderim, aliquando clarius, alibi locupletius, alibi copiosius, et
uarie tractarem, quomodo et sacrae litterae easdem res tractant. [M₃]

ECCE uir sacerrimus, qui nobis nouas tradit sacras litteras: quibus
eam debeamus reuerentiam: ut si quid manifeste blasphemet deum,
aequi bonique consulamus: certi nos potius falli, et sensum tanti patris
non posse capere: quam uirum sanctum, et qui certum se dicit, suam
habere doctrinam de caelo, quicquam sentire perperam: atque idem
potius credamus, et album esse simul et nigrum, quam diuum
Lutherum sibi quicquam esse contrarium. Nam si Paulo, qui ne quis
ansam male sentiendi capiat: interpretatur se, non possit imputari:
quod male senserit: Cur non itidem Lutherus excusetur: qui damnatus malae sententiae, eandem identidem repetit? Et si de Paulo
recte sentimus: cuius pietas facit: ne dubitemus eum in uerbis dubijs,
indubie recte sensisse: cur non impetret Lutherus: ut cuius impietas

8 *gloss* scripturarum] *L*, scriptutarum *BR*   19 locupletius] *L*, lucupletius *BR*

attack the king with reproaches because the latter said that Luther had long ago said what he now says a second time.

This offspring of a viper, he says, mani-
fests his natural character and imitates
Luther's words
the example of his parents. For thus even Paul, when he had taught 5
that all the sons of Adam are justified by faith alone without works,
had those, as he writes in Romans 3, "Who say that we teach: let us
do evil so that good may come of it."
But what judgment awaits them? "The
This will be your judgment,
distorter of the scriptures
condemnation of such men," he says, "is 10
just." What should I say to my royal basilisk about his lie except
the same judgment of condemnation?

Who would not be clearly impious to condemn Luther, the com-
rade of Paul, and to restrain his pen no differently than God restrained the tongue of those men referred to? For he says again a 15
little later:

The whole world knows that I have always taught and written consistently
Luther's words. Listen to this
apostle, reader
about faith, about charity, about
works, although by reason of experience and study I advanced from 20
day to day more and more, so that I have expressed the same ideas
now one way, now another, at times more clearly, in some places
more amply, in other places at greater length, and I have discussed the
same ideas in various ways, even as the sacred writings also treat them.

Behold a most holy man, who delivers to us new sacred writings to 25
which we owe such reverence that if he should clearly blaspheme
God, we would take it patiently and in good part, certain that we are
rather deceived and unable to grasp the meaning of so great a father
than that a holy man and one who says he is certain that he has his
teaching from heaven judges erroneously; and so we would rather 30
believe that the same thing is white and black at the same time than
that Saint Luther in any way contradicts himself. For if Paul cannot
be charged with having misunderstood when, to prevent anyone's
seizing the chance of misunderstanding him, he interprets himself,
why should not Luther likewise be excused when, accused of mis- 35
understanding, he repeats exactly the same opinion? And if we judge
favorably of Paul, whose piety prevents us from doubting that in
doubtful passages he undoubtedly understood rightly, why may not

reddit non ambigua modo: uerum eius etiam benedicta propemodum
iure suspecta interpretemur in bonam partem, quaecumque scribit
aperte male.

Quam stolide Lutherus tergiuersetur, de operibus, et
5   fide, impudenter fingens, uerba sua perperam
calumniari principem. Ca. XVII.

NAM DE operibus et fide quid sentiat, ne quisquam dubitare possit:
subscribam ea: quibus prudentissimus princeps istam nebulonis
impietatem elegantissime redarguit.

10   "NON   EST,   inquit,   hoc   Luthero
    Verba regis   nouum, in rebus notis, tanquam nouis nu-
gari. Qui, postquam hanc fidem uerbis [M₃v] multis ostendit: deinde
fidei diuitias, in hoc extollit: ut nos reddat pauperes bonorum operum:
sine quibus, ut beatus Iacobus ait: fides
    Diuus Iacobus   omnino mortua est. At Lutherus sic fidem
15
nobis commendat: ut non solum permittat nobis uacationem ab
operibus bonis: sed etiam suggerat audaciam, qualiumcumque
facinorum. Ait enim.

Iam uides, quam diues sit homo christi-
20   *Verba Lutheri. Noua haec*   anus, siue baptizatus, qui etiam uolens,
    est religio   non potest perdere salutem suam, quan-
tiscumque peccatis, nisi nolit credere. Nulla enim peccata eum possunt
damnare, nisi sola incredulitas.

"O uocem impiam, et omnis impietatis
    Verba regis
25   magistram, ita per se exosam, pijs auribus:
ut non sit opus eam redarguere. Ergo non damnabit adulterium? non
damnabit homicidium? non periurium? si tantum credat, se quisquam saluum fore, per uirtutem promissionis in baptismate?
Nam hoc dicit apertissime: neque quicquam corrigunt hanc senten-
30   tiam, uerba quae statim subiungit: imo uerius augent: ait enim:

2 interpretemur] *corr. err. L*, interpretemus *BR*   12 uerbis multis] verbis multis *L*, uerbis
multis uerbis *BR*   16 uacationem] vacationem *L*, uacauationem *BR*   20 baptizatus]
L, baprizatus *BR*

Luther, whose impiety renders not only his ambiguous statements but even his well-expressed statements almost justly suspect, secure from us that we should interpret in good part whatever he has evidently written erroneously?

How stupidly Luther wavers on the matter of works and faith, 5 shamelessly pretending that the prince falsely misrepresents his words. Chapter 17.

Lest anyone can doubt what the fellow does think of works and faith, I will write below those words in which the most prudent prince excellently refuted this impiety of the rascal.   10

"It is nothing new for this fellow, *The king's words*
Luther, to talk nonsense about known
things as though they were new things. After he has described this faith in many words, he then extols the riches of faith so that he may render us poor in good works, without *Saint James* 15
which, as blessed James says, faith is utterly
dead. But Luther commends faith to us in such a way that he not only allows us a dispensation from good works but even suggests boldness in every sort of crime. For he says:

> Now you see how rich is the Christian *Luther's words. This is a* 20
> or baptized man who, even though wish- *new religion*
> ing to, cannot lose his salvation by any
> sins however great, unless he does not wish to believe. For no sins can
> damn him except lack of faith alone.

"O impious voice and teacher of all *The king's words* 25
impiety, so hateful in itself to pious ears
that there is no need to refute it. Will not adultery, then, damn a man? Will not murder damn him? Not perjury? If only a person believes he will be saved by virtue of the promise in baptism?

"For he says this most clearly; nor do the words which he immedi- 30
ately subjoins correct this opinion in any way at all; rather, they more truly exaggerate it, for he says:

Lutheri uerba. Si ita est cur
uitamus malefacta

Caetera omnia si redeat, uel stet fides,
in promissionem diuinam baptizato factam, in momento subsorbentur per ean-
dem fidem, imo ueritatem dei, quia se ipsum negare non potest, si tu
5   eum confessus fueris, et promittenti fideliter adhaeseris.

Regis uerba

"QUIBVS uerbis, quid aliud dicit:
quam quod dixit prius? si absit increduli-
tas, caetera flagitia omnia in momento absorberi in sola fide: si confessus fueris Christum: et eius promissioni fideliter adhaeseris: hoc est,
10 firmiter credideris te saluandum per fidem: quicquid feceris. Et quo
minus dubites, quo tendat:

Lutheri uerba

Contritio (inquit) et peccatorum con-
fessio deinde et satisfactio, et omnia illa
hominum excogitata studia, subito te deserent, [M₄] et infeliciorem
15 reddent, si in ipsis tete distenderis, oblitus ueritatis huius diuinae.

Cur ergo mortalia peccata
appellantur

Cuius ueritatis? nempe huius, quod
nulla peccata possunt te damnare, nisi
sola incredulitas.

Verba regis

"QVAE christiane ferent aures, pesti-
20 lentem hunc serpentis sibilum: quo baptismum non in aliud leuat: quam ut premat poenitentiam: et
baptismatis gratiam, statuat impune peccandi licentiam?"
AVDISTI lector, quid ei princeps imputet: imo uero quid sua ipsi
uerba imputent, atque id tam aperte: ut ne adhuc quidem colorem

Hoc hominis est, qui neque loqui
libens uelit neque tacere potest

25 ullum inuenerit: quem contra posset
opponere: et tamen impudens, uelut nihil
audisset: et idem dicit rursus: et simul
queritur imputari dictum: perinde acsi nunquam dixisset. Quod si

Quo confugies Luthere?

uideri uellet sensisse de fide formata
30 charitate: quam necessario sequantur
opera bona: quamquam id sensisse non potuit: qui non solum toties
clamat, sufficere fidem solam: sed etiam remouet opera nominatim,
uelut prorsus inutilia: ac manifeste clamitat, nulla peccata, nulla

---

1 *gloss* Lutheri uerba] Verba Lutheri *L*   6 *gloss* Regis uerba] Verba Regis *L*   12 *gloss*
Lutheri uerba] Verba Lutheri *L*   19 christiane] christianae *B*

If faith returns or stands firmly by the
divine promise made to the baptized,
everything else is swallowed up in a
moment by this same faith, indeed by the

*Luther's words. If this is so,
why do we avoid
wicked deeds?*

truth of God, because He cannot refuse Himself if you have acknowledged Him and faithfully clung to Him who gives the promise.

"What else does he say in these words but
what he has said before? Provided there be

The king's words

no lack of faith, all other crimes are swallowed up in a moment by
faith alone, if you have acknowledged Christ and faithfully clung to
His promise; that is, if you have firmly believed that you must be
saved through faith, whatever you may have done. And, so that you
may have less doubt about where he is heading:

Contrition, he says, and confession of
sins, as also satisfaction and all those exer-

Luther's words

cises thought out by men will suddenly abandon you and render you
more unhappy if you have wracked yourself on them, forgetting this
divine truth. Which truth? Why, this
truth that no sins can damn you except
only lack of faith.

*Why, then, are sins
called mortal?*

"What Christian ears will endure the
pestilential hiss of this serpent, by which he

The king's words

extols baptism for no other end than that he may debase penance and
set up the grace of baptism as a license for sinning with impunity?"
You have heard, reader, what the prince imputes to him; or
rather, what his own words impute to him and that so openly that
not even yet has he found any excuse to set
up in defense of it, and yet the shameless
fellow, as if he had heard nothing, says the
very same thing again and at the same
time, just as if he had never said it, com-

*This is characteristic of the
fellow who is neither
willing to speak nor
able to keep silent*

plains that the statement is imputed to him. But if he wished people
to think that he was giving an opinion on
how necessarily good works follow from

Where will you flee, Luther?

faith formed by charity—although that could not have been his
opinion, since he not only cries out so often that faith alone suffices
but he even explicitly abolishes works as altogether useless and

quantumuis ingentia scelera posse damnare christianum, preter
solam incredulitatem: princeps tamen ut nullum prorsus effugium
relinqueret haeretico, rursus audi, quid dicat.

Verba regis
5

"DEINDE quum dicit, quod per opera,
non satisfit deo, sed sola fide: si sentit, quod
non per sola opera sine fide, stulte bacchatur in sedem Romanam: in
qua nemo fuit unquam tam stultus: qui diceret, opera sine fide
satisfacere. Sin opera sentit superflua, et fidem solam sufficere:

Hoc aliquid nihil est
10

qualiacumque sint opera: tum uero dicit
aliquid: et uere dissentit a sede Romana:
quae credit diuo Iacobo: quod fides sine ope[M₄v]ribus mortua est.
Videtis igitur, quam inepte se commouet Lutherus: qui sic inuehitur
in Romanam sedem: ut semet interea, uel stulticiae retibus uel
impietatis, inuoluat. Quamquam profecto propinquius opinor est
15 uero, Lutherum sentire fidem semper absque operibus bonis, satis
esse ad salutem. Nam id illum sentire, cum ex alijs locis multis
euidenter liquet, tum ex eo, quo dicit.

Lutheri uerba

Opera deus nihil curat, nec eis indiget.
Indiget autem, ut uerax in suis promissis
20 a nobis habeatur.

Verba regis

"QVIBVS uerbis, quid senserit, Lutherus uiderit ipse: ego certe deum credo, et
fidem nostram, et opera nostra curare, et neque operibus nostris egere
neque fide. Nam ut bonorum nostrorum non eget: qui deus est: ita
25 curam habet omnium: quae faciunt homines: qui aliud ab his fieri
uetat: aliud iubet: sine cuius cura, ne unus quidem passer cadit super
terram: quorum duo ueniunt dipondio."

ECCE, quid unquam legisti candide lector apertius: quam quod ex
Luthero tibi produxit princeps? Aut quid unquam uidisti pestilen-
30 tius? Quod si Lutherus uideri uelit, aliud sensisse, quam scribit: cur

Vt ipsum libentius
sequantur plures

sua uerba ne nunc quidem interpretatur
sanius? Si non censet esse peccandum: cur
impunitatem peccandi pollicetur? cur

---

1 preter] praeter *BL*   15 uero,] *om. B*; sentire] sentire, *B*   17 quo] quod *B*
28 ECCE] *BL*, ECCF *R*

clearly clamors that no sins, no crimes, however monstrous, can damn
a Christian except lack of faith alone—then hear again what the
prince says in order to leave no escape at all to the heretic.

"Moreover, when he says that we do not   *The king's words*   5
satisfy God by works, but by faith alone, if
he means, 'not by works alone without faith,' he is raving senselessly
against the Roman See, in which no one has ever been so foolish as to
say that works without faith satisfy. But if he considers works super-
fluous and faith alone sufficient, no matter what sort the works may
be, then indeed he is saying something   *This something is nothing*   10
and is truly dissenting from the Roman See,
which believes Saint James that faith without works is dead. You see
then how foolishly Luther gets himself all worked up when he so
inveighs against the Roman See that meanwhile he entangles himself
in nets either of folly or of impiety. However, I certainly think it   15
is nearer the truth that Luther thinks faith without good works is
always sufficient for salvation. That he thinks this is clearly evident
from many other passages as well as from the following in which he
says:

> God cares nothing for works nor does He   *Luther's words*   20
> require them. But He does require that we
> consider Him true to His promises.

"Luther himself will have seen what he   *The king's words*
meant by these words; I certainly believe
that God cares both for our faith and for our works and that He   25
requires neither our works nor our faith. For, though He does not
require our good works, since He is God, yet He has care of everything
that men do, since He forbids them to do one thing, commands
another, without whose care not even one sparrow falls to the earth,
of which two are sold for two farthings."   30
Behold, what have you ever read more clear, reader, than what
the prince has quoted for you from Luther? Or what have you ever
seen more pestilential? But if Luther should wish us to think he
meant something different from what he   *So that more people will follow
writes, why does he not even now interpret   him more readily*   35
his words more sensibly? If he does not
think that we should sin, why does he promise impunity for sinning?

orbem totum ad peccandi securitatem inuitat? Si neget hoc habere
sua scripta: ecce, princeps produxit loca: quae et per se manifesta
sunt: et princeps tamen interpretatione fecit clariora. Lutherus
ostendit ista legisse se. Si princeps igitur alio torquet eius uerba, quam
5 debet: cur ipse tam timide rem tantam transilit? Cur ipse uicissim
non ostendit: quae uerba deprauet rex: quid assuat per calum[N₁]-
niam: quod ipsius uerba non habeant? Fecisset istud haud dubie
lector, homo uersipellis: nisi constrictum se uidisset angustius: quam
ut quicquam haberet effugij: quo se posset
Vltima Lutheri latebra
10   uertere. Nam quod ita quidam conantur
eum tueri: quasi non quaelibet opera censeat contemnenda, sed
dumtaxat opera legis: Si legem uocat praecepta: quae Moisi data sunt
in tabulis: in eodem luto haesitat. Neque enim sine illis etiamnum
sufficit fides: nisi se fingat infantibus ista scribere, aut morionibus:
15 quos a praeceptis implendis excusat inscitia. At de caeremonijs legis,
aut quomodo uocant legalibus, non potuit ista blaterare. Quippe qui
non ignorat neminem esse tam stultum nunc: ut ad ea sese censeat
obligari. Quamquam frustra laborant eius fautores stolidum istud
dogma, quoquam lenire glossemate: non uult Aethiops iste dealbari.
20   Nam quem colorem recipiet istud: quod
Dic Quintiliane colorem
non solum contendit, nihil ualere opera
bona, sed etiam nihil nocere quaecumque opera mala. Nulla, inquit,
peccata possunt damnare christianum, nisi sola incredulitas. Certe si
Lutherus quicquam de Christo crederet: nunquam talia fuisset ausus
25 cogitare. Sed uoluit uidelicet homo pius, mundum traducere a
bonorum operum fiducia, in fiduciam fidei: quasi populus tam assi-
duus esset in bonis operibus: ut inde periculum fuerit: ne quisque sibi
nimium uideretur sanctulus. Ei igitur malo ut mederetur: iubet: ut
tantum credant Christo se saluos fore per solam fidem: et negligant
30 prorsus non solum caeremonias, uerum etiam opera bona quaecumque. Imo quo libentius oblectentur in libertate fidei: cognoscant,
nihil nocere credenti qualiacunque scelera. Nulla enim [N₁v] peccata

---

3 interpretatione] *BL*, interpretetione *R*   6 deprauet] *B corr. err. L*, depaauet *R*; assuat]
astruat *B*

Why does he invite the whole world to security in sinning? If he should deny that his writings contain this meaning, behold, the prince has produced texts which are self-evident, and yet the prince makes them still clearer by interpretation. Luther shows that he has read these passages. If, then, the prince twists his words to another mean- 5 ing than he should, why does he himself skip over such an important matter so timidly? Why does he not in turn show which words the king distorts, what he patches on through misrepresentation that Luther's own words do not contain? The slippery fellow would undoubtedly have done this, reader, if he had not seen himself 10 hemmed in so narrowly that he had no- *Luther's last hiding places* where to turn for escape.

As for the fact that certain men try to defend him as though he does not think that just any works should be contemned, but only the works of the law; if he calls the law those precepts which were given 15 to Moses on tablets, he sticks in the same mud. For without these works, faith does not suffice even now; unless he pretends that he is writing these things for children or fools whom ignorance excuses from fulfilling the precepts. But he could not have babbled these words about the ceremonies of the law, or as they call them the legal 20 precepts, since he is not ignorant of the fact that no one is so foolish as to think he is at the present time bound by them. Although his promoters labor in vain to soften this stupid teaching by some gloss, the Ethiopian does not wish to be made white. What color of defense will this teaching take which not only 25 argues that good works have no value but *Make some defense, Quintilian* even that evil works, no matter of what kind, cause no harm. No sins, he says, can damn the Christian except lack of faith alone. Surely, if Luther believed anything at all about Christ, he would never have dared to think such things. But he, clearly a pious fellow, wished to 30 lead the world astray from reliance on good works to reliance on faith; as if the people were so constant in good works that there was thereby a danger that each one would think himself too much a little saint. In order to cure that evil, then, he orders that they should only believe Christ, that they will be saved through faith alone, and that 35 they should altogether neglect, not only ceremonies, but even all good works whatsoever. Indeed, so that they may spend their time more pleasantly in the freedom of faith, they should realize that no crimes of any kind harm the man who believes. For no sins can damn

posse damnare Christianum, praeter solam incredulitatem. O Satan Satan, aperuit regi deus astutias tuas: quas per os Lutheri moliris: ut euangelica libertas nihil sit aliud, quam infrenata licentia: qua populus Christi praeceps decurrat ad inferos.

5　　　　　Taxat, Lutheri improbam stultitiam: qui
leges omnes censeat abrogandas.
Cap. XVIII.

NAM ISTIVS haereseos, uelut appendix quaedam est, praeclara ista sententia: qua leges omnes humanas uellet extinctas. Imo iam negat,
10　earum omnium ullam obligare christianum quenquam. Sic enim scribit in captiuitate Babylonica.

> *Lutheri uerba. Hoc tibi percom-*　Dico itaque, neque papa, neque epis-
> *modum esset ad haeresim*　copus, neque ullus hominum, habet
> ius unius constituendae syllabae super
15　Christianum hominem, nisi fiat eiusdem consensu. Quicquid aliter sit, tyrannico spiritu fit. ideo orationes, ieiunia, donationes, et quaecumque tandem papa, in uniuersis suis decretis, tam multis, quam iniquis statuit, et exigit, prorsus nullo iure exigit, et statuit, peccatque in libertatem ecclesiae toties, quoties aliquid horum attentauerit.

20　Hanc nebulonis insaniam princeps his uerbis attingit.

> *Verba regis*　"DE LEGIBVS uero, demiror hominem
> prae pudore, tam absurda potuisse cogi-
tare: quasi Christiani peccare non possent: sed tam perfecta foret, tanta multitudo credentium: ut nihil decerni debeat, uel ad cultum dei, uel ad uitanda flagitia: Sed eadem opera, et eadem prudentia,
25　tollit omnem potestatem, et authoritatem principum, et praelatorum. Nam quid faciat rex, aut praelatus: si neque le[N$_2$]gem potest ponere: neque positam exequi: sed populus absque lege, uelut nauis absque gubernaculo, fluctuet. Vbi est ergo illud apostoli: Omnis creatura

a Christian but lack of faith alone. O Satan, Satan, God has revealed
to the king the subtleties which you plot through the mouth of Luther
so that the liberty of the gospel may be nothing else but unbridled
license by which the people of Christ may rush headlong to hell.

He censures the wicked folly of Luther, who   5
is of the opinion that all laws should be
repealed. Chapter 18.

This extraordinary opinion, by which he would wish all human laws
abolished, is like a kind of corollary of this heresy. Indeed, he already
denies that any one of all those laws binds any Christian. For he   10
writes thus in the *Babylonian Captivity*:

And so I say: neither pope, nor bishop,   *Luther's words. This would be*
nor any man has the right to impose a sin-   *very advantageous for*
gle syllable on a Christian man, unless this   *your heresy*
is done by the latter's consent. What-   15
ever is done otherwise, is done in a tyrannical spirit. Therefore,
prayers, fasting, donations, and in short whatever the pope has
ordained and demanded in the whole body of his decrees, as numerous
as they are wicked, he has demanded and ordained with absolutely no
right, and he sins against the liberty of the church as often as he   20
attempts to decree any of these things.

This madness of the rascal the prince touches on in the following
words:
"But I am amazed that the man has so   *The king's words*
little shame as to be able to think up such   25
absurd things about laws; as if Christians could not sin, but that such
a great multitude of believers were so perfect that nothing should be
decreed, either for the worship of God or for the avoidance of crimes;
but with the same stroke and with the same shrewdness he takes
away all the power and authority of princes and prelates. For what   30
should a king or a prelate do if he can neither establish any law nor
execute it once it has been established; but the people without law
drifts to and fro like a ship without a rudder. What then becomes of
the apostle's command: 'Let every creature be subject to higher

potestatibus sublimioribus subiecta sit? Vbi illud: Obedite praepositis
uestris, siue regi, quasi praecellenti? Et quae sequuntur. Cur igitur
ait Paulus: Bona est lex? Et alibi: Lex est uinculum perfectionis.
Praeterea, cur ait Augustinus: Non frustra sunt instituta, potestas
5 regis, et cognitoris ius, ungula carnificis, arma militis, disciplina
dominantis, seueritas etiam boni patris? Habent omnia ista, modos
suos, causas suas, rationes, utilitates: et
Verum, sed Lutherus haec tolli haec cum timentur: et mali coercentur.
uelit, ut malus impune sit
et boni quieti inter malos uiuunt. Sed de
10 regibus dicere supersedeo: ne uidear meam causam agere. Istud
quaero: si nemo, nec homo, nec angelus, potest super hominem
christianum legem ponere: cur tot leges ponit apostolus: et de
legendis episcopis, et de uiduis, et de uelandis feminarum capitibus?
Cur statuit: ne fidelis coniux, ab infideli discedat: nisi deseratur?
15 Cur audet dicere: Caeteris dico ego non
Nunquid hunc damnas Luthere? dominus? Cur exercuit tantam potestatem:
ut fornicarium Satanae iuberet tradi in interitum carnis? Cur Petrus
Ananiam et Saphiram, simili poena percussit: quod e sua ipsorum
pecunia, paulum reseruassent sibi? Si multa statuebant apostoli,
20 praeter speciale praeceptum domini, super
Dissimulas ista Luthere christianum populum: cur non idem
propter populi commodum faciant hi: qui successerunt in apostolorum locum? Ambrosius Mediolanensis episcopus, uir sanctus, et
nihil arrogans, iubere non dubitauit: ut per suam dioecesim, coniuges
25 in quadragesima coniugalibus abstinerent [N₂v] amplexibus: et
indignatur Lutherus: si Romanus pontifex, successor Petri, uicarius
Christi, cui Christus, uelut apostolorum principi, tradidisse creditur
claues ecclesiae: ut caeteri per illum intrarent, et pellerentur: ieiuni-
um indicat ac preculas? Nam quod suadet corpore parendum esse,
30 animo retinendam libertatem: quis tam caecus est: ut strophas istas
non uideat? Cur ignem gerit, et aquam, homo simplex et sanctulus?

20 *gloss* Luthere] *L*, luthere *BR*

authorities'? What about the text: 'Obey your superiors, or the king as supreme,' and what follows? Why then does Paul say: 'The law is good'? And elsewhere: 'The law is the bond of perfection'? Furthermore, why does Augustine say: 'Not without reason have there been instituted the power of the king, the right of the judge, the executioner's instruments of torture, the arms of the soldier, the discipline of the ruler, and even the severity of a good father. All these things have their own bounds, their own causes, reasons, usefulness; and when these things are feared, the wicked are restrained, and the good live in quiet among the wicked'?

True, but Luther would want these things abolished so that the wicked man may be without punishment

"But I forbear to speak of kings lest I seem to plead my own cause. I ask this: If no one, whether man or angel, can lay down a law for the Christian man, why does the apostle lay down so many laws about electing bishops, and about widows, and about women's veiling their heads? Why does he decree that the believing wife should not leave an unbelieving husband, unless she be deserted by him? Why does he dare to say: 'To the others I, not the Lord, say'? Why did he exercise such great power as to order the fornicator to be delivered over to Satan for the destruction of the flesh? Why did Peter strike down Ananias and Saphira with a like punishment because they had kept back for themselves a little of their own money? If the apostles were used to decreeing many things besides the special precept of the Lord for the Christian people, why may not those who have succeeded to the position of the apostles do the same thing for the welfare of the people? Ambrose, Bishop of Milan, a holy man, and not at all arrogant, did not hesitate to command that throughout his diocese married couples should abstain from marital embraces during Lent; and is Luther indignant if the Roman pontiff, the successor of Peter, the vicar of Christ, to whom as to the chief of the apostles Christ is believed to have given the keys of the church so that by him others might enter and be excluded, enjoins fasting and a few prayers? As for his persuading men that one must obey bodily but retain liberty of mind, who is so blind as not to see these tricks? Why does this simple and sanctimonious fellow carry both fire and water? Why does he order us, as

Don't tell me you condemn him, Luther!

These things you conceal, Luther

Cur iubet, uelut apostoli uerbis, hominum seruos non fieri? hominum statutis non subijci? et tamen parere iubet, pontificis iniustae tyrannidi? An apostolus hoc pacto praedicat: reges nihil iuris habent in uos: iniustum feratis imperium: domini ius non habent in uos: feratis iniustam seruitutem? Si Lutherus parendum esse non putet: cur parendum dicit? Si parendum censet: cur ipse non paret? Cur homo uersipellis talibus ludit technis? Cur in pontificem, cui dicit obediendum esse: conuitijs insurgit? cur tumultum suscitat? cur in illum concitat populos: cuius uel tyrannidem (ut uocat) fatetur esse ferendam? Profecto non ob aliud, opinior, quam ut fauorem sibi conciliet improborum: qui suorum scelerum impunitatem cuperent: et eum, qui pro libertate eorum iam decertat: caput ipsis instituerent: et ecclesiam Christi, tam diu supra firmam petram fundatam, diuiderent: et ecclesiam nouam, ex improbis et flagitiosis conflatam, erigerent: contra quam exclamat propheta: Odiui ecclesiam malignantium: et cum impijs non sedebo."

Hoc tantum agit: ut ne cogatur ipse parere. Acu rem tangit rex

QVID ad haec respondit iste? profecto, id quod potuit: hoc est, omnino nihil. Quis enim color dici potest, [N₃] aut fingi, pro re tam absurda? Et tamen hominem stolidissimum non pudet, eam toties asserere, tanto supercilio: tanquam aliter sentire sit nephas. At sibi uisus est, praeclare moderatus ineptissimam sententiam: quum VVormatiae responderit, ita demum legem euangelicam unam satis esse futuram, et leges humanas inutiles: si magistratus essent boni, et fides uere praedicaretur. Quasi uel optimi magistratus possent efficere: ut aut totus populus christianus uiuere uellet in communi: aut mali nolint furari: aut ulla fidei praedicatione posset impetrari: ut nulli usquam sint improbi. Si lex euangelica furtum non permittit: certe nec inutilis est lex humana: quae furtum punit: et obligat christianos lex humana: quae sola rerum proprietatem diuidit: qua sublata, nec esse quidem furtum potest. Quod si dicat inde

Stolidissimum dogma stolide moderatur Lutherus

21 *gloss* Stolidissimum] *L*, stolidissimum *BR*

though in the words of the apostle, not to become slaves of men, not
to be subject to the decrees of men, and yet order us to obey the unjust
tyranny of a pontiff? Does the apostle preach in this manner: 'Kings
have no right over you; you should put up with their unjust rule.
Masters have no right over you; you should put up with their unjust   5
slavery'? If Luther does not think the people should obey, why does
he say that they must obey? If he thinks they should obey, why does
he not himself obey? Why does the slippery
fellow trifle with such tricks? Why does he   *He does this only so that he*
rise up with abusive language against a   *himself will not be forced*   10
pontiff who he says must be obeyed? Why   *to obey. The king hits*
does he stir up a tumult? Why does he   *the nail on the head*
arouse the people against one whose very tyranny, as he calls it, must
by his own admission be endured? Indeed, it is for no other reason, I
think, than to procure for himself the favor of such wicked men as   15
would desire impunity for their crimes and who would appoint as
their chief him who already struggles for their liberty, and who
would divide the church of Christ, founded for so long upon a firm
rock, and would erect a new church gathered together from wicked
and criminal men, against which the prophet exclaimed: 'I have   20
hated the church of the wicked and I will not sit down with the
impious.' "

What does he answer to this? Exactly what he could; that is,
absolutely nothing. What excuse can be given or contrived for an
opinion so absurd? And yet this utterly stupid fellow is not ashamed   25
to declare it so often with such great arrogance, as if to think otherwise would be a crime. But he thought he
had brilliantly handled this very silly   *Luther stupidly handles a very*
opinion when he replied at Worms that the   *stupid doctrine*
law of the gospel alone would ultimately be sufficient and human   30
laws useless if magistrates were good and the faith truly preached. As
if even the best magistrates could manage either that the whole
Christian people would want to live in common or that the wicked
would not want to steal or that any preaching of the faith could
procure that no one anywhere would be wicked. If the law of the   35
gospel does not permit stealing, surely the human law which
punishes stealing is not useless; and the human law which alone
apportions ownership of goods binds Christians; if this ownership is
done away with, there cannot indeed be stealing. But if he should

argumentum trahi: quod utilius careremus ea lege: unde rerum
proprietas nascitur: atque in communitate quadam naturali uiuere-
mus: sublata furandi materia, nihil adiuuat causam eius: etiam si quis
istud ei concederet. Nam in communi quoque et si uiui posset multo
5 paucioribus: tamen uiui non posset omnino sine legibus. Nam et
certis ordinibus laborandi foret, praescribenda necessitas, et legibus
cohercenda flagitia: quae in illa quoque uita grassarentur. Nunc uero
si uerissime praedicata fide, sicut uerissime praedicabant apostoli: ad
haec optimis magistratibus undique praefectis populo Christiano:
10 tamen et manere posset rerum proprietas, et multi manerent improbi:
negare non potest: quin lex humana christianos obliget: ne quid alius
eriperet: quod lex alij diuiserit: nec inutilis pu[N₃v]niendo sit: si quis
furtum admiserit.

Responde Luthere

NAM quod ait in Babylonica, magis-
15 tratus bonos et prudentes, naturae ductu melius rem administraturos,
quam legibus: quis non uidet: quam sit
Istud Luthere dissimula
absurdum? An bonus magistratus minus
aequus erit in lege condenda, quam in reddendo iudicio: in quo plura
possunt occurrere: quae corrumpant innocentiam? Vt non illud
20 interim dicam: quod uix ullum iuste redditur iudicium: quod non ex
aliqua lege lata redditur. Nam neque lex euangelica diuidit possessiones: neque sola ratio praescribit formas discriminandi proprij: nisi
rationi consensus accedat, atque is in communi forma commercij
mutui publicus: qui consensus aut coalescens usu, aut expressus
25 litteris, publica lex est. Leges ergo si tollas: et omnia permittas libera
magistratibus: aut nihil neque praecipient: neque uetabunt: et iam
inutiles erunt magistratus: aut naturae suae ductu regent: et pro
imperio, quidlibet exequentur, et iam nihilo populus erit liberior, sed
seruitutis conditione deterior: quando parendum erit non statis et certis
30 legibus: sed incertis ac mutandis in diem uoluntatibus. Atque istud
oportet, accidat etiam sub optimis magistratibus: quibus, ut optima
praecipiant: tamen populus aduersabitur: atque obmurmurabit,

---

10 posset] *corr. err. L*, posse *BR*   12 nec] *corr. err. L*, et *BR*   22 praescribit] *corr. err.*
L, praescribat *BR*   28 quidlibet] *corr. err. L*, quibus *BR*

say that from this premise the argument is drawn that we would do
better to be without that law from which the ownership of goods
arises and would do better to live in a certain natural community
with the occasion of stealing eliminated, it does not help his case even
if someone should grant him this argument. For even if we could live
in common with far fewer laws, we still could not live altogether
without laws. For the obligation to work would have to be prescribed for certain classes, and laws would be needed to restrain
crimes which would run riot even in that kind of life. But now if, with
the faith preached most truly as the apostles used to preach it most
truly, with, moreover, the best rulers everywhere put in charge of the
Christian people, the ownership of property could yet remain, and
many wicked men would remain, he cannot deny that the human law
binds Christians so that no one might steal what the law has appor-
tioned to another, nor would the law be   *Answer, Luther*
useless in punishing anyone who committed
theft.

As for his statement in the *Babylon* that good and prudent magistrates will govern their charge better by the leading of nature than
by laws, who does not see how absurd this is? Will the good magistrate
be less just in establishing law than in con-
ducting a court of justice, in which many   *Conceal this, Luther*
things can occur which may destroy the innocent? To say nothing
meantime of the fact that hardly any judgment is rendered justly
which is not rendered according to some established law. For the law
of the gospel does not apportion possessions, nor does reason alone
prescribe the forms of determining property, unless reason is attended
by an agreement, and this a public agreement in the common form of
mutual commerce, which agreement, either taking root in usage or
expressed in writing, is public law. Therefore, if you take away the
laws and leave everything free to the magistrates, either they will
command nothing and they will forbid nothing, and then magistrates
will be useless; or they will rule by the leading of their own nature
and imperiously prosecute anything they please, and then the people
will in no way be freer, but, by reason of a condition of servitude,
worse, when they will have to obey, not fixed and definite laws, but
indefinite whims changing from day to day. And this is bound to
happen even under the best magistrates, whom, although they may
enjoin the best laws, nevertheless the people will oppose and murmur

utpote suspectis: quasi non ex aequo bonoque, sed ex libidine
cuncta gubernent. Nunc uero quum Lutherus ipse fateatur, nullos
usquam magistratus inueniri posse: qui non sint homines: hoc est, nec
ciuibus, nec sibi satis explorati: quales intra triduum sint futuri: quam
5   prudenter consulit homo sapiens omitti leges, et cuncta permitti
magistratibus, tanquam sic uicturo in [N₄] libertate populo?

IAM illud obsecro, quale est, quod ait: Neque papa, neque
episcopus, neque ullus hominum, habet ius unius constituendae
syllabae, super christianum hominem sine ipsius consensu? Taceo
10 interim de papa, et de ipsis, quibus deus potestatem dedit: ut multas
syllabas statuerent: quibus populum promouerent in cultum dei:
consideremus leges ciuium. Si nemo habet potestatem condendi unam
syllabam super hominem christianum, sine ipsius consensu: neque
rex, neque totus populus, ullam potest condere: quae ualeat in
15   quenquam: qui dissuasit rogatam. Felices
        O felices fures   ergo sunt fures et sicarij: qui nunquam sic
insanient: ut in legem consentiant: qua poenas dent. Quin hac
                                ratione non uidet prudens pater: quod si
        Stolidum Lutheri caput
                                omnes ad unum consentiant: tamen
20 diutius ualere non possit lex: quam donec nouus ciuis natus sit, aut
inscriptus in ciuitatem. Sed ille nihil aliud sentit uere praedicari
fidem, quam ita praedicari: ut saepe iam praedicauit ipse: nempe
solam fidem sufficere, non solum sine bonis operibus, sed etiam
                                cum quibuscumque sceleribus: quae nullo
        Quid apertius
25   modo (ut ait) damnare possunt Christianum quenquam: modo stet aut redeat fides: Hoc est nimirum, si uel
interea, dum committit scelus: credat tamen id, propter fidem in
promissione dei, sibi nocere non posse: Aut si minus firmiter id
crediderit in committendo scelere: atque ideo propter infirmam
30 fidem, scelus commisit timidius: redeat saltem fides, peracto scelere:
ne commisisse poeniteat: et frustra se conterendo torqueat. Certe si
istius Lutheranae fidei praedicationi populus haberet fidem: propediem ue[N₄v]rum diceret: quod nullae leges obligarent quenquam:
sed populus absque lege, quaeuis prouolaret in scelera.

6 populo?] populo. *L*   24 *gloss* apertius] apertius? *L*

against as suspect, as though they govern everything, not according
to what is just and fair, but according to caprice. But now, since
Luther himself admits that no magistrates can be found anywhere
who are not men; that is, of whom it is not very certain either to the
citizens or to themselves what sort of men they will be within three 5
days, how shrewdly does this wise man advise that laws be omitted
and that all things be permitted to the magistrates, as though the
people would thus live in liberty!

Now I ask you, what sort of statement is this which he makes:
"Neither pope, nor bishop, nor any man has the right to impose a 10
single syllable on a Christian man without the latter's consent"? I
say nothing for the time being about the pope and about those to
whom God has given power to impose many syllables by which they
may direct the people in the worship of God; let us consider civil laws.
If no one has the power to establish a single syllable for the Christian 15
man without his consent, then neither the king nor the whole people
can establish any law which is valid against anyone who opposed it at
the time it was proposed. Happy, there-
fore, are thieves and murderers, who will   *O happy brigands!*
never be so insane as to agree on a law according to which they 20
will pay penalties. Indeed, this farsighted
father does not see that according to this   *Luther's dull head*
reasoning, should everyone unanimously agree, yet the law can have
force only until a new citizen is born or someone is enrolled as a
citizen. But the fellow thinks that preaching the faith truly is nothing 25
else than preaching it as he himself has often preached it already;
namely, that faith alone suffices not only without good works but even
with crimes of any kind, which, so he says,
can in no way damn any Christian, if only   *What is clearer?*
his faith stays firm or returns; that is, of course, if even while he is 30
committing the crime he yet believes that it cannot harm him
because of his faith in the promise of God; or, if he has believed this
less firmly while committing the crime and so because of his infirm
faith has committed the crime more timidly, let his faith at least
return once the crime is carried through; let him not be sorry that he 35
has committed it and torture himself by useless contrition. Surely, if
the people had faith in the preaching of this Lutheran faith, they
would very soon say truly that no laws obliged anyone, but the
people without law would rush forth into every kind of crime.

Breuis authoris epilogus   IAM uides lector, quam sapienter homo
                                              prudens amoliri studeat, omnes leges
humanas, et quanto cum fructu populi christiani. Vides item, quanta
ratione, quibus scripturae testimonijs fulsit decretum suum, contra
5 doctorum omnium, contra bonorum omnium sententiam, contra
publicum totius orbis consensum. Vides, ut in ea re, in qua uix ulla
ratio potuit satis esse fortis: uir iste sagax nullam prorsus rationem
afferat, nullum scripturae testimonium: sed qui alijs falso imputat:
quod sibi solis credi postulent: ipse, ut sibi soli credatur, postulat,
10 contra totum orbem, contra manifestas rationes, contra sacrarum
testimonia scripturarum: idque cum populorum omnium summa et
ineuitabili pernicie. Atque haec in legibus humanis, quae uerae sunt
traditiones hominum. Nam ea, quae in ipsius catalogo recensentur,
tanquam traditiones hominum, atque ideo, ut censet, tanquam pestes
15 aliquae tolerandae sint: aut omnino tollendae tanquam nocentissima
scandala: iam ante probatae sunt, esse traditiones dei, partim scripturis ipsis comprehensae, partim uiuo dei uerbo traditae. Atque id
probatum est ratione, scripturis, et quod fortissimum est aduersus
Lutherum, ipsius confessione Lutheri. Nisi aut rursus neget: quod
20 fassus est: hoc ecclesiam habere a deo: ut uerba dei decernat a uerbis
hominum: aut aliam proferat ecclesiam catholicam: qua docente
cognouit euangelium: aut probet nobis nihil ecclesiam didicisse sine
scripturis, contra illud euangelistae: Non omnia scripta sunt in libro
[O₁] hoc. Et item illud apostoli: Seruate, quae praecepi uobis, siue
25 per sermonem, siue per epistolas. Item illud, ab eodem commemoratum apostolo: Dabo leges in cordibus eorum: et in mentibus eorum
superscribam eas. Et illud item Christi: Spiritus paracletus, cum
uenerit: ille ducet uos in omnem ueritatem. Aut nisi probet nobis
Lutherus, tot aetates sanctorum patrum temporibus, Christum
30 ecclesiam deseruisse, et fidem protinus ab apostolis defecisse: contra
illud: Orauit Christus: ne fides ecclesiae deficeret: et tanquam
Luthero similis esset ac mendax ueritas ipsa, quae dixit, se cum
ecclesia futuram perpetuo, usque ad consummationem seculi. Haec
nisi nobis euertat omnia: quae princeps ei obiecit omnia: quae

19 confessione] *L*, comfessione *BR*

Now you see, reader, how shrewdly the
sagacious fellow strives to remove all   *Brief epilogue by the author*
human laws and with how much profit for the Christian people. You
see, likewise, with how much reasoning, with what testimonies of
scripture he has propped up his decree in opposition to the judgment   5
of all learned men, in opposition to the judgment of all good men, in
opposition to the public agreement of the whole world. You see how
in that matter, in which hardly any reason could be strong enough,
this sagacious fellow brings forward no reason at all, no scriptural
testimony; rather, he, who falsely imputes to others that they demand   10
credence for themselves alone, himself demands credence for himself
alone against the whole world, against clear reasons, against the
testimonies of sacred scriptures, and this to the utter and inescapable
destruction of all peoples. And this in human laws which truly are the
traditions of men. For those items which are listed in his catalogue as 15
traditions of men and are therefore, so he judges, to be tolerated like
some pests or altogether abolished as most harmful stumbling blocks,
have long ago been proved to be the traditions of God, partly contained in the scriptures themselves, partly handed on by the living
word of God. And this has been proved by reason, by the scriptures,   20
and by what is the strongest argument against Luther, the admission
of Luther himself. Unless he either denies again his admission that the
church has from God the power to distinguish the words of God from
the words of men, or brings forward another catholic church by
whose teaching he has known the gospel, or proves to us that the   25
church has learned nothing without the scriptures, despite the evangelist's statement: "Not all things have been written in this book";
and likewise the apostle's words: "Hold on to what I have commanded you, whether by word of mouth or by letters"; likewise what
was recalled by the same apostle: "I will give my laws into their   30
hearts and in their minds I will write them"; and likewise those
words of Christ: "The Spirit, the Paraclete, when He shall have
come, will lead you into all truth"; or unless Luther proves to us that
for so many ages in the times of the holy fathers Christ abandoned
His church, and that the faith failed immediately after the apostles,   35
contrary to the text which says: "Christ prayed that the faith of the
church would not fail," and as though truth itself were a liar like
Luther when He said He would be with the church even to the
consummation of the world; unless Luther overthrows for us all the

Lutherus hactenus dissimulat omnia: nec ob aliud dissimulat omnia: quam quod sibi conscius est, nihil habere se quicquam: quod ad eorum quicquam omnium respondeat. Haec inquam omnia, nisi Lutherus plane faciat: ego planissimum tibi lector feci: imo regem
5 fecisse, plane demonstraui tibi: id quod initio promisi tibi, istum non tantum traditiones hominum tollere, etiam eas, quibus debet obtemperare: sed etiam tollere traditiones dei: quas os impurum nebulonis insanissimi contumeliosa blasphemia pestes appellat et nocentissima scandala.

10 ### Ostendit Lutherum id unum agere: ut demoliatur scripturas ipsas, pro quibus simulat se pugnare. Cap. XIX.

NVNC uideamus, an non scripturam sacram ipsam, pro qua se pugnare simulat: quibus potest machina[O₁v]mentis oppugnet.
15 Primum, ut omittam quam passim pessime, quam passim stolide scripturas torquet in defensionem perniciosorum dogmatum: quid magis potest aut manifestius euertere totam uim fructumque scripturarum omnium: quam id quod iste manibus pedibusque molitur: ut nemo quicquam de scripturae sensu doctorum cuiquam credat: nihil
20 sanctorum cuiquam patrum, nihil uniuersis credat: nihil toti credat ecclesiae, ab ipsis ecclesiae incunabulis in hunc usque diem consentienti: sed opponat omnibus sensum quisque suum? Quem fructum afferent scripturae: si tantum sibi quiuis arroget: ut in eis intelligendis suo innitatur sensui contra caeterorum omnium: ut nulla
25 prorsus authoritate moueatur: quo minus ex affectu et libidine metiatur scripturas? Hic plane aperit fenestram: qua se praecipitet populus in perniciem. Quaeso te Luthere per furorem tuum, si tu in illa tempestate uixisses: qua procellis Arrianis agitata est ecclesia: suasisses ne, quod suades nunc: ut quilibet e uulgo se putaret ido-

23 quiuis] *corr. err. L*, quaeuis *BR*

objections which the prince has brought up against him, all of which he so far conceals and dissimulates for no other reason than that he is aware that he has nothing at all to answer to any of all those arguments; unless, I say, Luther clearly does all these things, then I have made most clear to you, reader—rather, I have clearly shown you that the king has done so—that which I initially promised to show you: that this fellow not only abolishes the traditions of men, even those which he ought to obey, but that he abolishes even the traditions of God, which the filthy mouth of this utterly insane rascal with insolent blasphemy calls plagues and most harmful stumbling blocks.

He shows that Luther does only one thing:
destroy the very scriptures for which he
pretends to fight. Chapter 19.

Now let us see whether he does not by every trick possible attack the very sacred scripture for which he pretends to fight. In the first place, to say nothing of how he everywhere very wickedly, everywhere stupidly twists the scriptures to the defense of destructive teachings, what can more thoroughly or more clearly destroy the whole force and fruit of all the scriptures than the fact that this fellow strives hand and foot so that no one will believe any learned men at all concerning the interpretation of scripture; so that no one will believe any of the holy fathers at all, or all men taken together at all; not believe the whole church at all, though it has been of one mind from the very origins of the church until this day; but that each one will oppose his own interpretation to everyone? What fruit will the scriptures bring forth if anyone whatever claims such authority for himself that in understanding them he relies on his own interpretation in opposition to that of everyone else, so that he is influenced by no authority at all not to measure the scriptures according to feeling and fancy? Here he clearly opens the window by which the people may plunge into perdition.

Tell me, Luther, by your madness, if you had lived during that tempest in which the church was thrown into turmoil by Arian storms, would you have urged what you now urge: that anyone of the

neum: qui de illa lite iudicaret: et sibi quisque crederet in scripturis
intelligendis: quas legeret? et floccifaceret sanctorum patrum iudicium: qui fuerunt in consilijs: in quibus damnatae sunt haereses? ut
cum fatearis ibi Christum esse: ubicunque sunt duo uel tres congre-
5 gati in eius nomine: ibi neges esse: ubi sunt eodem nomine congregati sexcenti, idque ex omni parte christiani populi? Sed quis tam
caecus est: ut hac in parte non uideat, non

Lutheri consilium

aliud tibi consilium esse: quam ut sublata
prorsus authoritate consensus publici, possis ex temeraria priuatorum
10 dissentione tumultum suscitare? quo tibi liceat aliquos inuenire tam
[O₂] stultos: qui sibi liberum putent, impune contra fidem caeterorum omnium, uni fidere nebuloni tibi.

Id agit, quo magis licenter ipse
suum tueatur errorem

Contra quem, ne quid scripturae ualeret
authoritas: non id solum agis: ut sensum
15 sacrarum literarum quisque trahat in dubium: et contra sanctorum
patrum omnium, contra catholicam totius ecclesiae sententiam, suum
tueatur somnium: uerum etiam contra sententiam beati Pauli
apostoli.

HAEC tu fortasse lector sic intelligis: tanquam prebeat audaciam
20 Lutherus, non agnoscendi, quid sentiat

Paulo non credit Lutherus

Paulus: et dicendi non hoc sentit, hoc aut
illo loco Paulus: quod eum sentire credit ecclesia. Imo longe aliud
lector, quamquam nec illud esset ferendum: sed iste non ueretur:
quum Paulus quippiam e scriptura sacra, pertinere docet ad Chris-
25 tum: nihil ueretur inquam, rursus in dubium trahere: et controuer-
sam facere sententiam apostoli: et dicere: Paulus illud fortasse non ex
deo dixit: sed ex sensu proprio. Itaque recognosce nebulo, uerba
sacrilega: quibus in captiuitate Babylonica, uere captiuus in seruitio
daemonum tu, scripturas inuertis: et blasphemas apostolum. Sic enim
30 blateras.

Verba Lutheri   Paulus Ephes. v. uerba illa de matrimonio, Genes. ij. dicta, uel proprio spiritu

common people who pleased might consider himself qualified to
judge concerning that controversy, and that each one might rely on
himself in understanding the scriptures which he read, and that he
might make light of the judgment of the holy fathers who were
present at the council sessions in which the heresies were condemned, 5
so that, although you admit that Christ is present wherever two or
three are gathered together in His name, you deny that He was
present where there were gathered together in that same name six
hundred men, and those from every part of the Christian people?

But who is so blind as not to see that in   10
this matter you have no other intention   *Luther's intention*
than that, after abolishing completely the authority of public
agreement, you may be able to stir up a tumult from the heedless
disagreement of private individuals, in which case you may find some
men foolish enough to think themselves free to rely with impunity on 15
you, a single scoundrel, in opposition to the faith of everyone else?
Lest the authority of scripture might have
any force against you, you work so that   *He does this so that he may*
each person will drag into doubt the   *more freely defend his*
meaning of the sacred writings and defend   *own error*   20
his own fancy not only against the judgment of all the holy fathers,
against the universal judgment of the whole church, but even against
the judgment of blessed Paul the apostle.

Perhaps, reader, you understand this to mean that Luther is
showing boldness in not acknowledging   25
Paul's judgment and in saying: In this or   *Luther does not believe Paul*
that passage Paul does not mean what the church believes he means.
No, the case is far otherwise, reader, although not even that is to be
endured; but this fellow does not fear, when Paul teaches that some
text or other from sacred scripture refers to Christ, he does not fear, 30
I say, to draw into doubt once more and to render questionable the
judgment of the apostle and to say: Perhaps Paul did not say that
from God but from his own understanding. So then, you rascal,
recognize the sacrilegious words with which in the *Babylonian Captivity*
you, truly a captive in the service of demons, pervert the scriptures 35
and blaspheme the apostle. For thus you blather:

Paul, in Ephesians 5, either forcibly   *Luther's words*
applies to Christ on his own initiative

ad Christum trahit: uel generali sententia etiam spirituale matrimonium Christi in eo traditum docet.

Satan syncerius allegat scripturas
quam Lutherus

O Satan Satan, quanto syncaerius adhuc
scripturam tractas tu, quam discipulus
tuus Lutherus? Etenim, quamquam uno
textu, per fraudem conatus es abuti: tamen quae scripturae uerba
pertinebant ad Christum: ea ad Christum retulisti. Scriptum est,
inquis, de te: Angelis suis deus mandauit de te. At Lutherus, quae
scriptura pertinet ad Christum, [O₂v] eam non ipse modo Christo
10 non tribuit: uerumetiam apostolo tribuenti, minuit, quoad potest,

Inuenisti uirum secundum
cor tuum

fidem. Exulta Satan: habes discipulum:
qui Christi quoque uerbum faciat dubita-
bile. Nam quum ille dicat: Non est
discipulus supra magistrum: sed sufficit ei: si sit, sicut magister suus.
15 Luthero discipulo tuo, non sufficit: si sit mendax, et sycophanta
Satan sicut tu: sed longe contendit superare te. Itaque quum primum
conetur, eleuare authoritatem sacramenti, ex eo quod uideri uult: si
locus ille Geneseos quicquam pertineret ad Christum et ecclesiam:
non pertinere saltem, nisi tenuiter, quadam quasi generali sententia:
20 ne quid ad eam rem putetur pertinere proprie: conscius tamen,
Paulum non sic accipi posse: quum tam accurate tot modis exaggeret,
eius sacramenti magnitudinem, ex illo loco Geneseos de Adam
copulato cum Eua, tam proprie, tam germane relato ad matrimonium
Christi cum ecclesia: quid facit nebulo? quid? id quo nihil ad euerten-
25 dam uim scripturarum omnium potuit excogitare pestilentius.
Paulus, inquit, locum illum, proprio fortasse sensu, ad Christum

En quomodo scripturis deferat
Lutherus

trahit. O nebulo nebulo, scrupulum
inijcis: quasi non ex dei spiritu, sed
proprio, uidelicet humano (quem toties
30 appellas mendacem) scripturas interpretetur apostolus: nec interpretatur modo: sed etiam trahit: tanquam in diuersum obtorto collo,

3 *gloss* syncerius] *corr. err. L*, syncaerus *BR*   4 *gloss* quam Lutherus] *corr. err. L*, Lutherus
om. BR

those words on marriage quoted from Genesis 2, or else, according
to the commonly held opinion, he teaches that the spiritual marriage
of Christ is taught in that passage.

O Satan, Satan, how much more hon-
estly even you treat the scripture than does   *Satan applies the scriptures*
your disciple Luther! For, although you   *more honestly than Luther*   5
tried to misuse one text through trickery, yet you applied to Christ
those words of scripture which pertained to Him. "It is written of
you," you said, " 'God has given His angels command concerning
you.' " But Luther not only does not apply to Christ the scriptural   10
text which pertains to Christ, but he even belittles, so far as he can,
the trustworthiness of the apostle's application of the text. Exult,
Satan; you have the kind of disciple who
makes even the word of Christ doubtful.   *You have found a man according*
For, although Christ says, "No disciple is   *to your heart*   15
above his teacher, but it is enough for him if he be like his teacher,"
it is not enough for your disciple Luther if he be a liar and a schemer
such as you are, Satan, but he strives to surpass you by far. And so,
when he tries first of all to disparage the authority of the sacrament
according to the interpretation he wants accepted: that if that   20
passage of Genesis did pertain in any way to Christ and the church,
it would not, at any event, pertain to Him except superficially, as if
by some commonly held opinion, lest it be thought to pertain properly
to that point; yet, conscious that Paul cannot be so understood since
he exalts the greatness of that sacrament so explicitly in so many ways   25
on the authority of that passage of Genesis about the union of Adam
with Eve, a passage applied so properly, so truly, to the marriage of
Christ with the church, what does the scoundrel do? Why, something
more pestilential than anything he could have devised for destroying
the force of all the scriptures. Paul, he says, forcibly applies that   30
passage to Christ, possibly on his own
initiative. O scoundrel, scoundrel, you   *See how Luther defers to the*
suggest a scruple, as if the apostle would   *scriptures*
interpret the scriptures, not according to the spirit of God, but
according to his own—that is, a human—spirit, which you so often   35
call deceptive; nor does he only interpret but he even "forcibly
applies" them, as if he seizes them by the neck and twists them
resisting into a different meaning.

torqueat renitentes. Hoc est, quod scripturis defers: qui nihil te
credere iactas, praeter scripturas? Qui nihil aliud nisi scripturas
recipis: scripturas recipis sic: ut de sensu earum nec ipsis credas
apostolis: qui scripturarum sensum didicerunt a domino? At quae-
5 dam, inquis, a Chri[O₃]sto dicunt: quaedam a capite suo: et illa
                              credi necesse est: de his dubitari potest.
    Regula necessaria scripturis   Det ergo nobis regulam reuerende frater,
         intelligendis   uestra fraternitas: qua discernamus illa:
quae apostoli interpretantur e sensu dei ab his: quae trahunt ac
10 torquent, in scripturis sensu proprio. Audio uos domine doctor, dare
nobis regulam talem: quod indubie standum sit in sacris litteris
interpretationi apostolorum et euangelistarum: ubicunque addunt
interpretamentis suis: Haec dicit dominus: Caetera uero, quae dicunt,
dicere se: imo trahere, uel torquere scripturas: quo uolunt, ex sensu
15 proprio, hoc est humano. Nec illis in talibus esse credendum: quia
omnis homo mendax: quemadmodum in isto furioso libro uestro
                        blaterastis, prius de Hieremia, Esaia,
   Hieremiam, Esaiam, Heliam, Helia, et Ioanne Baptista. Ergo loca
   Ioannem Baptistam, Luthero omnia, quae ex prophetis, uel quocunque
       mendaces uideri   loco scripturae toties allegant euangelistae:
20
toties producunt apostoli, pro Christo: controuersa facit unus nebulo:
et uiam aperit omnibus: ut negent haec fuisse praedicta de Christo:
sed quae prophetae scripserunt de alijs: ea proprio sensu euangelistas,
et apostolos ad Christum detorsisse. Quid hoc est lector: si non est
25 aperte scripturas oppugnare?
    SED age tamen, sit istud, si uoles, nihil: permitto Luthere tibi: qui
deterior es: quam cui ullum pene uitium uitium sit. Permitto, inquam, tibi: ut leue sit, omnes doctores sanctos contemnere. Permitto:
                      ut documentum non sit hostilis in scrip-
   Lutherus manifeste scripturas turas animi: quod niteris ac laboras,
30   *oppugnat*   apostolorum interpretationes reddere sus-
pectas omnes. Illud saltem, nemo prorsus erit tam stupidus: ut non

6 *gloss* Regula] *L*, Reggula *BR*   17 *gloss* Hieremiam,] *L*, Hieremiam *BR*   18 *gloss*
Ioannem] *L*, Ioannem, *BR*

Is this your deference for the scriptures, you who boast that you believe nothing but the scriptures? You who accept nothing else but the scriptures, do you accept the scriptures in such a way that you do not believe even the apostles concerning the meaning of the scriptures from the Lord? But, you say, they speak some things from Christ, some things from their own head, and the former must necessarily be believed, the latter can be doubted. Let your friarity, reverend friar, give us, then, *A necessary rule for understanding the scriptures* a rule by which we may distinguish those passages in scripture which the apostles interpret according to God's meaning from those which they forcibly apply and twist according to their own personal judgment. I hear, honored doctor, that you give us such a rule: that the interpretation of the apostles and evangelists on the sacred writings must stand firm wherever they add to their interpretations, "Thus says the Lord"; but, as to the other things which they say, that they themselves speak them, or rather they forcibly apply or twist the scriptures where they please according to their own personal, that is a human, judgment. Nor should they be believed in such cases because all men are liars, as you have earlier blathered in that madly raving book of yours in regard to Jeremiah, Isaiah, Elias *That Jeremiah, Isaiah, Elias, John the Baptist seem liars to Luther* and John the Baptist. A single scoundrel, therefore, renders questionable all the passages which the evangelists so often cite from the prophets or from any passage of scripture whatever, all those which the apostles so often bring forward in support of Christ, and he opens the way for everyone to say that these passages were not predictions about Christ but that the evangelists and the apostles have on their own judgment forcibly applied to Christ what the prophets have written about other persons. What is this, reader, if it is not openly to attack the scriptures?

But come, though; let this, if you will, be nothing; I grant you, Luther, who are so wicked that hardly any vice is a vice to you, I grant you, I say, that it is a trifling matter to contemn all the holy doctors. I grant that it is not a proof of a mind hostile to the scriptures that you *Luther openly attacks the scriptures* strive and struggle to render all the interpretations of the apostles suspect. This at least not a single person will

sentiat: quam aperte, [O₃v] quam recta tendat in expugnationem
scripturarum omnium: quod scripturam indubie sacram, non dubitas
impius, uelut prophanam pellere. Imo, quod est adhuc detestabilius:
si concesseris esse canonicam, et apostoli scriptam calamo: audes
5 negare tamen, fidem adhibendam esse: et os in caelum ponens, lingua
maledica, blasphemare non uereris apostolum. Rursus itaque
recognosce nebulo, uerba sacrilega: quibus, quum te suis uerbis
urgeret apostolus Iacobus, in sacramento unctionis extremae: tu
uelut comminus congressus cum apostolo: in apostolum dei scurra
10 turpissime, oris impuri latrinam exhauris.

Lutheri uerba contra beatum
Iacobum apostolum

Omitto, inquis, quod hanc epistolam
non esse Iacobi, et apostolico spiritu dignam, multi ualde probabiliter asserant,
licet consuetudine authoritatem, cuiuscunque sit, obtinuerit. Tamen,
15 inquis, si esset apostoli Iacobi, dicerem, non licere apostolum, sua
authoritate, sacramentum instituere, id est diuinam promissionem
cum adiuncto signo dare. Hoc ad Christum solum pertinebat. Sic
Paulus sese accepisse a domino dicit, sacramentum eucharistiae, et
missum, non ut baptizaret, sed ut euangelizaret. Nusquam autem
20 legitur in euangelio, unctionis istius extremae sacramentum.

RELEGE quaeso lector, quid in haec uerba scripserit princeps. Ibi
statim reperies, in quam paucis Lutheri uerbis, quam multa princeps
repererit, atque reuicerit absurda. Ostendit enim: quod Lutherus
improbe reprehendit ecclesiam: quod impie redarguit apostolum:
25 et ipse quoque stolide contradicit sibi.

Pudendus (si quis pudor esset)
Lutheri lapsus

Atque haec tria in tribus fere uersibus
omnia, ut nullius unquam fuerit tam
admiranda prudentia: quam sit istius demiranda stulticia. Quid dices
hic Luthere? Quem cuniculum prospexisti tibi: per quem possis
30 effugere? Nega[O₄]bis eum, quisquis illam scripsit epistolam:
manifeste sacramentum describere: et ex tua ipsius sacramenti
finitione discedes: quod constare uoluisti, ex sensibili signo, et promissione gratiae aperte comprehensa in sacris literis? An quod

---

7 recognosce] recognoscere *L*　　16 promissionem] *L*, promissinem *BR*　　32 signo] *L*,
ligno *BR*

be too stupid to sense: how openly, how directly your not hesitating impiously to attack an undoubtedly sacred text as profane aims at sweeping away all the scriptures. Indeed, what is still more hateful: even if you have conceded that a text is canonical and written by the pen of an apostle, yet you dare to say that no faith should be placed in it and, setting your face against heaven, you do not fear to blaspheme an apostle with your abusive tongue. And so, you scoundrel, recognize again the sacrilegious words with which, when you were hard pressed by the apostle James' words on the sacrament of extreme unction, you, as though engaged in hand-to-hand conflict with the apostle, empty out on an apostle of God, you most base buffoon, the privy of your filthy mouth.

I pass over, you say, the fact that many persons assert with great probability that *Luther's words against blessed* this epistle is not by James and is not *James the apostle* worthy of the apostolic spirit, although whosoever it is, it has acquired authority by custom. Nevertheless, you say, if it were by the apostle James, I would say that no apostle is permitted to institute a sacrament on his own authority; that is, to give a divine promise with a sign accompanying it. This belonged to Christ alone. Thus, Paul says that he received the sacrament of the eucharist from the Lord and that he was sent not to baptize but to preach the gospel. Nowhere in the gospel, however, does one read of this sacrament of extreme unction.

Reader, please reread what the prince has written against these words. There you will immediately discover in how few words of Luther the prince has discovered and refuted how many absurdities. For he shows that Luther unjustly censures the church, that he impiously contradicts an apostle, and that he is also stupidly inconsistent with him- *The shameful (if he had any* self. And all three of these things in *shame) lapse of Luther* scarcely three lines, so that no man's wisdom has ever been so wonderful as this fellow's folly is bewildering. What will you say here, Luther? What burrow have you provided for yourself by which you can flee? Will you deny that whoever wrote that epistle is clearly describing a sacrament, and will you depart from your definition of a sacrament as such, which you wanted to consist of a sensible sign and a promise of grace clearly included in the sacred writings? Or will

fecisti, negabis illam epistolam in sacris
Atqui nihil Luthero cum ecclesia, literis numerandam? At eadem ecclesia,
cui iam pridem renunciat.
Lutherus utrinque stringitur quae inter sacras literas numerat euangelia: eadem inquam ecclesia inter sacras
5 litteras numerat hanc epistolam. Qua in re tu mentiris: siue falli
potest ecclesia: siue falli non potest. Si potest falli in dignoscendis dei
uerbis: ipse mentiris: qui eam dicas, in eo falli non posse. si falli non
potest: mentiris rursus: qui dicas probabile esse, hanc epistolam non
esse apostolicam: quam ecclesia probauit pro apostolica. Quid restat
10 igitur: nisi ut dictum reuoces: et neges
Hic auribus lupum tenes Luthere
rursus, ecclesiam posse dei uerba discer-
nere: et iam in dubium uoces etiam Paulinas epistolas, et euangelia?
Et qui nihil contendis certum esse praeter scripturam sacram: iam
ipsa scriptura sacra nihil reddas incertius. Sed illud adhuc nocentius,
15 quod ausus es etiam contemnere: si fatereris epistolam esse apostoli:
uidelicet opinor, quod nostri sunt apostoli: non nos illorum, iuxta
illud quod tam stulte profers quam saepe: omnia enim uestra sunt,
siue Apollo, siue Cephas, siue Paulus. Non
Lutherus illud dictum uellet est ergo, inquies, nostrum iudicari ab illis:
indictum
20 sed illos iudicare. Quomodo igitur dicis
Luthere, hoc agere te: ut solis credatur scripturis: qui manifestam
scripturam non admittas pro scriptura? Quod si nullam scripturam
reijceres: tamen, quum uniuersos interpretes floccifacias: eodem
reuolueris: quando nihil omnino credis: quod non clarescat scrip-
25 [O₄v]turis euidentibus. Nam quae unquam
Clauum clauo pellis Luthere
scripturae satis euidentes erunt: si possit
effici: quod tu conaris: ut nihil ualeat bonorum, atque eruditorum
sententia, aduersus interpretamenta, uel imperitorum stolida, uel
uafra improborum? Quis non uidet hoc pacto fore: ut nihil omnino
30 probari possit e scriptura sacra, homini tam amenti: ut scripturae
mentem aut nequeat, aut nolit intelligere? Imo nihil tam absurdum

---

1 *gloss* Atqui] *corr. err. L*, Atque *BR*   4 ecclesia] *corr. err. L*, ecclesiam *BR*   6 digno-
scendis] *L*, dignoscendi *BR*   10 *gloss* Hic] *L*, hic *BR*   12 et iam] iam *om. L*
15 contemnere] *corr. err. L*, contendere *BR*

you deny, as you have done, that that epistle should be numbered among the sacred writings? But the same church which numbers the gospels among the sacred writings, the same church, I say, *But Luther has nothing to do with the church, which he has long ago renounced. Luther is hemmed in on all sides* numbers among the sacred writings this epistle. In this matter you are lying, whether the church can be deceived or whether it cannot be deceived. If she can be deceived in discerning the words of God, you lie precisely in saying that she cannot be deceived on this score. If she cannot be deceived, you again lie in saying that this epistle, which the church has approved as apostolic, is probably not apostolic. What remains then but that you should retract what you have said and instead deny once again that the church can *Here you hold the wolf by the ears, Luther* discern the words of God, and then you would be calling into doubt even the epistles of Paul and the gospels? And you who contend that nothing is certain except the sacred scripture would then be rendering nothing more uncertain than sacred scripture itself.

But still more dangerous is the fact that you even dared to contemn the epistle, if you have admitted that it is the apostle's; doubtless, I suppose, because the apostles are ours, not we theirs, according to that text which you cite as foolishly as you do frequently: "For all things are yours, whether Apollo, or Cephas, or Paul." It does not behoove us, *Luther would want that saying unsaid* then, you will say, to be judged by them but to judge them. How then, Luther, do you say that you are doing this so that the scriptures alone may be believed, since you do not admit as scripture a clear scriptural text? But if you rejected no scripture at all, nevertheless, since you care not a straw for all interpreters taken together, you return to the same spot since you believe nothing at all which is not manifest in evident scriptural texts. For what scriptural text will ever be *You are driving out one nail with another, Luther* sufficiently evident if one can, as you are trying to do, cause the opinion of good men and of learned men to have no force against either the stupid interpretations of ignorant men or the crafty ones of wicked men? Who does not see that by this means it will come about that nothing at all can be proved from sacred scripture to a man so senseless that he either cannot or will not understand the sense of scripture? Indeed, that nothing is so absurd,

esse, nihil esse tam impium, quod non aliquis tui similis, homo
furiosus, et impudens, non possit contendere se probare scripturae
sacrae testimonijs. Nam uerbi gratia, si quis nebulo neget, Christum
ad inferos descendisse: iactabit se nihil admittere praeter euidentes

5 *Lutherum scripturas arbitrio suo*   scripturas: et illud negabit ulla probari
       fingere ac mutare   satis euidenti scriptura. Quod si quis
                              alleget illud ex psalmo: Caro mea requies-
cet in spe: quoniam non relinques animam meam in inferno: Afferet
contra commentum quodlibet e commentarijs iudaeorum: et negabit

10 illud, ad Christum quicquam pertinere. Quod si quis rursus objiciat
apostolum Petrum: qui psalmum illum de Christo loqui declarat,
actorum cap. 2. non dubitabit nebulo, dicere de Petro: quod iste
nebulo dixit de Paulo: nempe Petrum illud ad Christum proprio
sensu traxisse. Quod si quis alius nebulo, uolet opera bona, non exigi

15 ad salutem: afferet illud euangelij: Quicunque crediderit, et baptizatus fuerit: saluus erit: Nihil igitur ultra requirendum esse. Iam si
                              quis neget sic intelligendum: et afferat
    Sibi soli fidit in scripturis   genuinum sensum, cum testimonio doc-
          interpretandis   torum omnium: despiciet doctores omnes,

20 ac stabit interpretamento suo, tantum uociferans euidentem [P$_1$]
esse scripturam. Quod si quis illi quippiam objiciat e scriptura sacra:
nebulo protinus commento quopiam inepto, non dubitabit eludere.
Vtpote, si quis objiciat illud Iacobi: Fides sine operibus mortua est:
dicet idem, quod dixit iste, epistolam non esse Iacobi, non esse

25 cuiusquam apostoli: nihil habere dignum apostolico spiritu. Postremo
                              si probetur esse apostoli: tamen dicet
    Nimium arroganter ipse faciens   apostolum non recte dicere nimium arro-
gasse sibi: qui legem bonorum operum imponat Christianis: quos in
sola fide, liberos ab omni bonorum operum iugo fecerit Christus.

30   Nec quisquam possit ullam legem aut
    Et is nonne exigit bona opera?   ullam syllabam legis, ponere super christi-
anum quenquam, praeter unum Christum. Nam apostolos non
habuisse tantum authoritatis, ut iudicarent nos: sed nostrum esse
iudicare illos. Nam omnia nostra sunt, siue Apollo, siue Cephas, siue

---

18 genuinum] *corr. err. L*, geminum *BR*   20 suo, tantum] *corr. err. L*, suo tantum, *BR*
34 Apollo] *L*, Appollo *BR*

nothing is so impious but someone like you, a raging madman and a shameless fellow, can argue he proves it by the testimonies of sacred scripture. For example, if some scoundrel should deny that Christ descended into hell, he will boast that he admits nothing besides evident scriptures, and he will deny that this teaching is proved by 5 any sufficiently evident scriptural text. But if someone should cite that verse from the psalm, "My flesh shall rest in hope because you will not leave my *That Luther fashions and changes* soul in hell," he will cite in his turn what- *the scriptures at will* ever fabrication he chooses from the commentaries of the Jews, and 10 he will deny that that text refers in any way to Christ. But if someone objects in turn that the apostle Peter declared that that psalm speaks of Christ (Acts 2), the scoundrel will not hesitate to say of Peter what our scoundrel said of Paul; namely, that Peter forcibly applied that text to Christ on his own initiative. But if some other 15 scoundrel wants good works not to be required for salvation, he will cite that text of the gospel, "Whoever believes and is baptized shall be saved"; nothing else therefore should be required. Then, if someone should deny that this text is to be so understood and should cite the real *He relies on himself alone in* 20 meaning, together with the testimony of *interpreting the scriptures* all the doctors, the fellow will scorn all the doctors and will stick to his own interpretation, bawling only that the scriptural text is evident. But if someone keeps bringing up to him some objection or other from sacred scripture, the scoundrel will not hesitate to escape immediately 25 by means of some silly trick or other. For example, if someone brings up that text of James, "Faith without works is dead," the fellow will say the same thing as our rascal has said: that the epistle is not James', that it is not any apostle's, that it has nothing worthy of the apostolic spirit. Finally, should the epistle be proved to be an apostle's, the fellow will 30 still say that the apostle does not speak correctly, that he has arrogated too much *While he himself acts too* to himself in imposing the law of good *arrogantly* works on Christians whom Christ has made free in faith alone from every yoke of good works. Nor should any- 35 one but Christ alone be able to impose any *And does not He require good* law or any syllable of the law on any *works?* Christian. For the apostles did not have authority enough to judge us, but it is our right to judge them. "For all things are ours, whether

Paulus. Sic enim se Lutherum docuisse. Si quis igitur, omittens
discipulum tuum, rursus Luthere, sic opponat tibi: Ecclesia iudicauit
hanc epistolam esse apostoli, scriptam esse diuino spiritu, et tua tibi
uerba obijciat: Hoc saltem ecclesiam habere a deo datum: ut dei
uerba discernere possit, a uerbis hominum.

Quoties sibi dissentit, melius
rem perpendit scilicet

Iam reuocabis hoc protinus: ac dices,
melius a te nunc rem esse perpensam:
Ecclesiam nihil habere a deo, sed ecclesiam falli posse in recipienda
scriptura. Quod si subinferet quispiam, incerta igitur esse ipsa
euangelia: hoc tu nimirum concedes etiam, scripturas et euangelia,
quae leguntur, non esse fortassis euangelia

Illuc haud dubie tendit, ac
perueniet propediem

uera: sed illorum potius aliquod, quae
repudiauit ecclesia. Atque his de rebus,
unumquenque suo periculo credere. [P₁v]

QVOD si quis hic tibi obijciat inconstantiam: quod tibi toties
dissideas: atque a temet ipse dissentias: hic uero quantis tibi scom-
matibus, quantis cachinnis ac ronchis irrideretur: qui sit tam rudis,
et imperitus disserendi: ut nesciat: quid sit hominem dissentire
secum: aut eum putet leuem esse, atque instabilem: qui sit constanter inconstans: aut sicut taurus ligatur

Lutherus constanter inconstans

cornibus: ita ligari postulet suis uerbis
hominem: uti, si quid unquam dixit bene: id ei non liceat postea
reuocare: cum sit commodum: atque in malum uertere, modo nihil
immutet in melius, ex ijs, quae unquam dixit male.

VIDES hic lector euidenter: bonus hic

Quam bona fide Lutherus clamat
euangelion euangelion. Haeretici
omnes cum Luthero hoc
habent commune

uir quam bona fide, se clamare clamat
euangelion euangelion: quasi quisquam
unquam fuerit haereticus: qui non cla-
marit euangelium: quum is interea uiam
sibi struat, qua uertat in dubium: an euangelium esset euangelium:
et scripturas, quas ait solas regnare debere: falsis interpretamentis

---

5 *L places gloss one line earlier*   30 struat, qua uertat] *corr. err. L*, strueret, qua uerteret
BR

Apollo, or Cephas, or Paul." For thus the fellow has been taught by
Luther.

If anyone therefore, passing over your disciple, should object to
you once more, Luther: "The church has judged this epistle to be the
apostle's, to have been written by the divine Spirit," and should   5
bring up to you your own words: "This power at least has been given
by God to the church, that she can distinguish the words of God from
the words of men," then you will retract this statement immediately
and will say that you have now weighed
the matter more carefully, that the church   *Whenever he is inconsistent, he*   10
has no power from God but that the   *has of course considered the*
church can be deceived in accepting   *matter more carefully*
scripture. But if someone or other will add that therefore the gospels
themselves are uncertain, you will doubtless concede this also: that the
true gospels are probably not the scriptures   15
and gospels which we read but rather   *He is undoubtedly heading in*
some one of those which the church has   *that direction and will*
rejected. And concerning these matters,   *arrive there very soon*
each one believes at his own risk.

But if someone should at this point throw up to you your incon-   20
sistency, because you are so often at variance with yourself and
disagree with your own self, here indeed with how many jeers, how
many guffaws and snorts will that man be mocked who is so ignorant,
so inexperienced in arguing that he does not know what it means for
a man to disagree with himself, or considers capricious and unstable   25
a person who is consistently inconsistent,
or demands that a man's words should be   *Luther consistently*
bound fast as a bull's horns are bound fast   *inconsistent*
so that if he has ever said anything worthwhile he should not be
permitted later to retract it when it would be to his advantage and to   30
turn it into something evil, even as he changes nothing for the better
of those things which he has at any time said badly.

You see here clearly, reader, with what
good faith this good man proclaims that he   *With what good faith Luther*
proclaims: "The gospel! The gospel!"—as   *proclaims: The gospel! The*   35
if anyone has ever been a heretic who did   *gospel! All heretics have this*
not proclaim the gospel—while at the same   *in common with Luther*
time he devises for himself a way whereby he may raise a doubt as to
whether the gospel be the gospel, and by false interpretations weakens

eneruet: ac faciat cuilibet idem audendi licentiam. Quas ipse libet, non agnoscit pro sacris: denique si res urgeat: agnitas etiam contemnit: ne quid dubitare possis, ipsum probasse pro nobis: id quod initio polliciti sumus probaturos nos: illum id prorsus agere: ut

5 scripturas etiam ipsas, pro quibus se fingit pugnare: subuertat.

Declarat Lutherum, qui iactat papistas, uti uitioso
disputationis genere petendo principium, non
solum falso id obijcere alijs: sed etiam ipsi id
disputandi genus proprium esse atque

10   perpetuum totum caput istud est
amoenum. Cap. XX. [P₂]

AGE NVNC, expendamus illud: in quo mire sibi Lutherus placet:
ac se festiuum et disertum putat: quum in
Non conatur probare: uult sibi ecclesiam catholicam ludat tanquam pa-
credi dicenti

15   pisticam: et tam rudes censet omnes prae
se: ut non intelligat quisquam: aut qua de re sit quaestio: aut qua
ratione res probari debeat. Est, inquit,
Verba Lutheri. Tu scilicet felix apud eos ipsos, uitiosissimum genus dispu-
es, qui sine tuo labore de
caelo docearis tandi: quod uocant petitionem principij.

20   Hoc discunt et docent, usque ad canos,
usque ad sepulchrum, tot sudoribus, tot sumptibus miserrimi
homines.

    VIDEAMVS ergo lector, utra pars uitiosius petit principium?
nam aliquod principium petit utraque.
Postulata nostra
25   Nos petimus ab illo postulata quatuor.

         PRIMVM petimus: Lutherus ut credat
Postulatum 1
sacris literis. PETIMVS, ut credat aliqua
Secundum dicta, facta, tradita a deo: quae non sunt
comprehensa literis.

---

11 amoenum] amęnum *BR*, amaenum *L*   13 *gloss* conatur probare:] conatur: probare
BRL   14 catholicam] *corr. err. L*, cathalicam *BR*   17 *gloss* Tu scilicet] *BRL*, tu scilicet
corr. err.   26 *gloss* Postulatum 1] *L*, postulatum .i. *BR*

the scriptures which, he says, should alone reign, and gives everyone
the license of daring the same thing. Whatever scriptures he pleases
he does not acknowledge as sacred; then, if the case presses him hard,
he even contemns those which have been acknowledged; so that you
cannot have any doubt that he himself has proved for us that which   5
we initially promised we were ready to prove: that he does this only
in order to destroy the very scriptures for which he pretends to fight.

> He declares that Luther, who boasts that the papists
> use a corrupt method of disputation by begging the
> initial premise, not only makes this objection falsely   10
> against others, but also uses this as his own peculiar
> and perpetual method of disputing. This whole
> chapter is delightful. Chapter 20.

Come now, let us carefully examine that point in which Luther
strangely delights and considers himself   15
witty and skillful, when he makes sport of   *He does not try to prove; he*
the catholic church as papistic and thinks   *wishes to be believed on*
everyone in comparison with himself so   *his word*
ignorant that no one understands either what the point in question is
or by what method the point ought to be   20
proved. "There is," he says, "among these   *Luther's words. You of course*
very men a most corrupt method of dis-   *are fortunate in being taught*
puting which they call 'begging the initial   *from heaven without your*
premise.' This they learn and teach even   *own effort*
till grey hairs, even till the grave, with so much sweat, with so much   25
waste, the utterly wretched men."

Let us see, then, reader, which of the two sides begs the initial
premise more corruptly; for each side begs
some initial premise. We beg of him four   *Our postulates*
postulates.   30

First, we beg that Luther believe the
sacred writings. We beg that he believe   *Postulate I*
that some things were said, done, taught
by God which are not contained in writing.   *Postulate II*

Tertium

PETIMVS, ut credat ecclesiae datum a deo: ut possit discernere uerba dei, a uerbis hominum: et traditiones dei a traditionibus hominum: Christo uidelicet ecclesiam suam regente perpetuo, spirituque sancto, ecclesiae consensum dirigente semper in rebus fidei.

Quartum

PETIMVS denique, ut in controuerso sacrarum literarum sensu, credat potius constanti sanctorum patrum sententiae, et fidei totius ecclesiae catholicae: quam opinioni suae.

HAEC postulata quamquam nos putemus, haud minus euidentia christiano, quam illa sunt Euclidis Geometrica philosopho. Postulat tamen iste postulatorum eiusmodi rationes.

Ratio quarti

ATTVLIMVS ergo postremi, et alias rationes aliquot: et quod facilius est, ac similius ueri, unum falli atque [P₂v] hallucinari quam multos, malum uirum potius male sentire quam bonos, hominem haereticum potius errare, quam ecclesiam catholicam.

Ratio tertij

PENVLTIMVM uero probamus, multis et euidentibus scripturae sacrae testimonijs, multis praeterea rationibus, et denique ipsius confessione Lutheri.

Ratio .ij.

PORRO quod aliqua dicta, facta, tradita sunt a Christo: quae scripta non sunt, praeter euidentes rationes alias, praeter alia scripturae loca, probauimus authore Paulo: probauimus euangelio.

Cur nulla ratio primi

PRIMVM uero postulatum, quod scripturae sacrae credendum sit: speraueramus, haud exacturum quicquam probationis Lutherum: propterea quod toties per omnes libros clamat, nihil aliud exigere se: quam ut soli credatur scripturae sacrae.

Cur non concedit quartum

HAEC postulata nostra, Lutherus deridet omnia. Nam postremum putat esse stultissimum: si quis hoc petat: ut patribus, et ecclesiae potius credat

---

22 PORRO quod] *corr. err. L*, quod *om. BR*

We beg that he believe that the church
has been given the power from God to   *Postulate III*
distinguish the words of God from the words of men and the traditions of God from the traditions of men, with Christ clearly governing
His church constantly and the Holy Spirit always directing the   5
agreement of the church in matters of faith.

We beg finally that in a disputed inter-
pretation of the sacred writings he believe   *Postulate IV*
the consistent judgment of the holy fathers and the faith of the whole
catholic church rather than his own opinion.   10

Although we consider these postulates no less evident to the
Christian than the geometrical postulates of Euclid are to the
philosopher, nevertheless this fellow postulates reasons for such
postulates.

And so we have presented for the last   15
postulate, besides several other reasons,   *Reason for the fourth*
the fact that it is easier and more probable that one man is deceived
and out of his mind than that many are so, that a bad man mis-
understands rather than good men, that a heretical man errs rather
than the catholic church.   20

The second last postulate we prove
indeed by many and evident testimonies of   *Reason for the third*
sacred scripture, with many reasons besides, and finally by the
confession of Luther himself.

Next, as to the postulate that some   25
things have been said, done, taught by   *Reason for the second*
Christ which have not been written, besides other evident reasons,
besides other passages of scripture, we have proved this on the
authority of Paul; we have proved it by the gospel.

As for the first postulate, that the sacred   30
scripture must be believed, we had hoped   *Why there is no reason for*
that Luther would not demand any proof   *the first*
at all for this, because he so often proclaims throughout all his books
that he demands nothing else than that the sacred scripture alone
should be believed.   35

Luther jeers at all these postulates of
ours. He considers the last one to be   *Why he does not grant the*
utterly foolish: that anyone should beg him   *fourth postulate*
to believe the fathers and the church rather than himself. Whereas

ille, quam sibi. Quum patres (ut ait) et ecclesiae iudicium, aliquando
fallatur: ipse falli non possit. Propterea quod certus est (ut ait)
doctrinam suam habere se de caelo.

PENVLTIMVM uero quamquam olim
Cur negat tertium
5   ab ipso concessum, nunc tamen ferme
reuocat. Censet enim, illud esse ridiculum: si quis in fide, censeat
ecclesiam gubernari spiritu sancto: quoniam tale principium
petentem Turca rideret. Itaque pius pater, impius potius erit in
Christum: quam sit ridiculus Turcae.

10   SECVNDVM nihili plane facit: quia
Cur non admittit secundum
quaecunque dixit, fecit, aut tradidit
Christus: quae scripta non sunt: ea semel [P₃] omnia Lutherus habet
pro nihilo. Propterea (puto) quod nisi fuissent res nihili: non putaret
Lutherus tam negligentem futurum fuisse Christum: quin ea curasset
15 comprehendi scriptura.

PORRO primum propter authoritatem
Quomodo tractat primum
scripturae, tractat ambigue. Nam scrip-
turas saepe citat perperam: et a genuino plerumque sensu detorquet
in falsum. Ibi cum nihil habeat pro se, nisi uerba sua, eademque fere
20 semper contra conscientiam suam: quum diuersum sonent scripturae
uerba: patres constanter interpretentur: et tota, per tot aetates
consentiat ecclesia: ibi nos imperiti Thomistae, petimus illud
principium: ut credat potius uniuersis
At non est commodum
quam uni. Sed quia haec est petitio
25 principij, ab homine acuto et argumentandi callentissimo, risu
repellimur: et cachinnorum cumulis obruimur. QVOD si scripturae
textum proferas: qui sit apertior: quam ut de sensu possit esse
controuersia: tum necessitate coactus, prodit se: et scripturam negat
aperte. Ait enim (si res poscat) epistolam
Annon tu nimium tibi nimis
30 .   *impie arrogas?*   Iacobi, non esse apostolicam: aut etiam
si sit apostoli, apostolum tamen sibi
nimium arrogasse. Atque ubi Lutherus semel dixit istud: si quis in eo

---

13 putaret] *corr. err. L*, putaret (*sic*) *BR*   14 negligentem futurum fuisse] *corr. err. L*,
futurum fuisse *om. BR*   21 interpretentur] *corr. err. L*, interpretantur *BR*   23 *gloss*
commodum] comnlodum *B*

the fathers, so he says, and the judgment of the church are at times deceived, he himself cannot be deceived, because he is certain, so he says, that he has his teaching from heaven.

The next to last postulate, however, although once granted by himself, he now nevertheless retracts altogether. For he *Why he denies the third postulate* thinks it ridiculous if anyone should think the church is governed by the Holy Spirit in the faith, since the Turk would ridicule anyone begging such an initial premise. And so, the pious priest will rather be impious toward Christ than be ridiculous to the Turk.

The second postulate he clearly considers worthless, since whatever Christ has *Why he does not admit the second postulate* said, done or taught which has not been written Luther once and for all considers as of no importance, because—I suppose—if those points had been of importance, Luther did not think that Christ would have been so negligent as not to have taken care that they be included in scripture.

Next, because of the authority of scripture, he treats the first postulate ambiguously. *How he treats the first postulate* For he often cites the scriptures erroneously, and very often he twists them from a true meaning to a false one when he has no support for himself but his own words, and those almost always contrary to his own conscience. When the words of scripture express conflicting ideas, the fathers give a consistent interpretation, and the whole church through so many ages agrees; at such times we inexperienced Thomists beg the initial premise that he believe everyone taken as a whole rather than a single individual. But because *But it is not convenient* this is begging an initial premise, we are repulsed with the ridicule of this fellow, shrewd and quite artful in arguing, and we are overwhelmed by waves of roaring laughter.

But if you present a text of scripture which is so clear that there can be no question about its meaning, then, driven by necessity, he betrays himself and openly denies the scriptural text. If the situation requires, he says that the epistle of James is not apostolic, or even if it be an apostle's, still the apostle has arrogated too much to himself. And when once *Is it not you who too impiously arrogate too much to yourself?* Luther has said this, if anyone should again insist that Luther yield to the

rursus instet: ut authoritati cedat Lutherus apostoli: iam mille modis
ridebitur homo disputandi rudis: quem non pudeat uti uitiocissimo
genere disputandi, et principium petere: nempe ut scriptura putetur:
quam Lutherus negat esse scripturam: aut apostolus credatur scrip-
5 sisse recte: quum eum semel dixerit pater potator errasse. Hunc
igitur in modum lector, nos uitiose principium petimus.

LVTHERVS contra, paulo modestior est: principium enim statuit
etiam ille, sed dumtaxat unum: quod sibi con[P₃v]cedi postulat. Est
autem illud huiusmodi. Omnibus de rebus

Lutheri postulatum unicum

10 soli credendum ipsi.

HOC principium, uelut rem natura notam, non dubitat ubique
petere: imo pro suo sibi iure sumere. Sit quaestio de scripturae sensu:
profert primum, quod uel sentit ipse: uel se sentire saltem simulat. Tu
contra profer, quicquid unquam fuit Christianorum omnium: abigit
15 omnes, uelut muscas: et petit credi sibi. Negat leges humanas utiles
esse: profer tu contra, quicquid unquam fuit mortalium: deridet
orbem totum: et postulat credi sibi. Negat unctionis extremae
sacramentum: profer tu contra, apostolum Iacobum: contemnit
apostolum: et postulat credi sibi. Ita principium istud, nusquam fere
20 non petit concedi sibi: ut omnibus in rebus uni credatur sibi.

HOC postulatum eius, quamquam nemo non uidet esse in speciem
uehementer aequum: tamen, quia ueremur laqueos, et hominis
captiosi uersutias: aegre ac difficulter

Quo nitatur principio doctrina
Lutherana

adducemur: ut istud ei postulatum con-
25 cedamus: maxime, quia sentimus hoc
principio, et praeclaro Lutheri axiomate, totum niti mirabilis
Lutheranae doctrinae fundamentum. Nam eo principio concesso:
mirum dictu est: quales et quantas conclusiones sic probabit tibi: ut
prorsus negare non possis. At si neges illud axioma: nihil tibi probat
30 omnino. Cunctamur ergo illi concedere tam callidum et captiosum
principium: et quaerimus ab illo: qua ratione probas pater soli

---

8 dumtaxat] *L*, dumtaxut *BR*

authority of the apostle, then that person will be mocked in a thousand ways as a man ignorant of disputing, one who is not ashamed to use the most corrupt form of disputing and to beg the initial premise; namely, that that be considered scripture which Luther denies is scripture, or that the apostle be believed to have written correctly, 5 although Father Tosspot has said once and for all that he has erred. In this way, then, reader, we corruptly beg the initial premise.

Luther, on the contrary, is a little more modest, for he also has established an initial premise, but only one, which he demands to have granted to himself. It is, however, of 10

Luther's sole postulate

this kind: that he alone must be believed on all matters.

This initial premise, as a matter known by nature, he does not hesitate to beg everywhere; in fact, to assume as by his own right. Suppose there is a question about the meaning of a scriptural text; he 15 first presents what he himself either thinks or at least pretends to think; you in turn present whatever has always been the judgment of all Christians; he drives everyone away like flies and begs that he be believed. He denies that human laws are useful; you in turn present whatever has always been the judgment of mortals; he jeers at the 20 whole world and demands that he be believed. He denies the sacrament of extreme unction; you in turn present the apostle James; he contemns the apostle and demands that he be believed. Thus, almost everywhere he begs that this initial premise be granted him: that in all matters he alone be believed. 25

This postulate of his: although no one does not see that it is apparently very fair, nevertheless because we fear the snares and subtleties of this sophistical fellow, we will be prevailed upon reluctantly and with difficulty to grant

On what initial premise the
Lutheran doctrine rests 30

him this postulate, especially because we are aware that on this initial premise and brilliant axiom of Luther rests the whole foundation of the marvelous Lutheran doctrine. Once this initial premise is granted, it is amazing to relate the sort and importance of the conclusions he will prove to you in such a way that you simply cannot deny them. But if you deny 35 that axiom, he proves to you absolutely nothing. We therefore put off granting him so subtle and sophistical a premise, and we ask of him: "By what reason, father, do you prove that you alone must be believed?"

credendum tibi? Ad hoc hanc reddit causam. Quia certus sum,
inquit, dogmata mea habere me de caelo. Rursum quaerimus. Qua
ratione certus es, dogmata tua [P₄] habere te de celo? Quia rapuit me
deus, inquit, imprudentem in medias has turbas. Rursus ergo
5 flagitamus. Qui scis: quod rapuit te deus? Quia certus sum, inquit,
doctrinam meam esse a deo. Quomodo id scis? Quia rapuit me deus.
Qui scis istud? Quia certus sum. Quomodo certus es? Quia scio. At
qui scis? Quia certus sum. QVAESO te lector, an non hic locum
habet illa disputandi forma: qua, nisi mentitur Lutherus, mentitur

10   *Amsdorfij fabula de theologis*   Amsdorfius, theologos disputare Lipsenses
hoc pacto: cum respondens negasset
assumptum opponenti: probabat idem opponens hoc pacto: Oportet
sic esse. Illo iterum negante: denuo et ille: Et quomodo potest aliter
esse? Oportet sic esse.

15   HVIC mendacio Lutherus, uelut unum dictum, de dictis meliori-
bus adiunxit coronidem. Pulcherrime,
      Lutheri coronis   inquit, et Thomisticissime, quin et Lipsis-
sime, et Henricissime.

NVNC quum reuerendus pater, in hoc principio sua fundet
20   omnia: Ego certus sum: quia ego scio: et
      Lepide retaliatur coronis   ego scio: quia ego certus sum: et ideo
              Lutheri   certus sum: quia non possum errare: et
ideo non possum errare: quia certus sum: et ideo certus sum: quia
ego scio. An non nobis licet in reuerendum patrem, reuerendi patris
25 coronidem recinere, pulcherrime, et vvittenbergissime, quin et
stolidissime, et Lutherissime.

VIDES ergo hoc loco lector, nihil illius ita recitare me: quemadmodum ex regis libro ille solet omnia. Qui nihil syncere citat: sed aut

13 Illo] *L,* Illlo *BR*

To this he returns this cause: "Because I am certain," he says, "that I have my teachings from heaven."

Again we ask: "By what reason are you certain that you have your teachings from heaven?"

"Because God has seized me unawares," he says, "and carried me into the midst of these turmoils."

Again therefore we demand: "How do you know that God has seized you?"

"Because I am certain," he says, "that my teaching is from God."

"How do you know that?"

"Because God has seized me."

"How do you know this?"

"Because I am certain."

"How are you certain?"

"Because I know."

"But how do you know?"

"Because I am certain."

I ask you, reader, whether that form of disputing does not find a place here, the form by means of which (unless Luther is lying) Amsdorf lyingly says *Amsdorf's fable about the theologians* that the theologians of Leipzig dispute, as follows: when the respondent has denied his opponent's assumed initial premise, the opponent proves the same premise as follows: "It must be so." When the former again denies it, then the latter says a second time, "And how can it be otherwise? It must be so."

To this lie Luther has added, as one of his better sayings, the flourish: "Splendidly," he says, "and most *Luther's flourish* Thomistically, or rather, most Leipzigly and most Henricianly."

Now, since the reverend father founds all his arguments on this initial premise: "I am certain because I know, and I know because I am certain, *Luther's flourish is wittily retorted* and I am certain because I cannot err, and I cannot err because I am certain, and I am certain because I know," may we not re-echo against the reverend father the flourish of the reverend father: "Splendidly and most Wittenbergly, or rather, most stupidly and most Lutheranly."

You see, then, reader, that in this passage I quote none of his statements in the way that he usually quotes all the statements from

male mutat: aut ea commemorat inde: quae ibi nusquam sunt: sed
ipse dum narrat: fingit sibi monstra: quae uincat. At nos ipsa re
planum facimus, [P₄v] scripturas ab illo sic allatas, sic detortas a suo
sensu, sic ipsum sua somnia praeferre sanctorum omnium sententijs:
5   sic totam ecclesiam floccifacere prae se, sic aperte sacram scripturam
negare, et agnitam manifeste contemnere, sic sua dogmata sine
scriptura et contra scripturam statuere: ut dubitare non possis, illum
ipsa re unum illud ubique principium petere: ut contra omnes et
omnia, omnibus in rebus uni credatur sibi.

10   Ne uideri possit, haec tam absurda per calumniam
                   fingere de Luthero, Lutheri uerba ipsa
                  commemorat, atque expendit: quibus
                     clarum est, Lutherum et dicere et
                        sentire multis adhuc modis
15   absurdius. Cap. XXI.

TAMEN quo minus dubites, istud non ex ambiguis eius uerbis colligi,
sed uerbis ab ipso clarissimis praedicari. Verba ipsa nebulonis
expende.

               Verba Lutheri   Certus sum, inquit, dogmata mea
20   habere me de caelo, qui etiam aduersus
      eum triumphaui, qui in ungue nouissimo plus habet uirtutis et astutiae,
      quam omnes papae, et reges, et doctores.

      Item paulo post.

      Rapuit, inquit, me dominus imprudentem in medias has turbas.

25   Et rursus.

      Neque enim hic mihi patientiae habenda ratio est, ubi mendatijs suis

---

12 quibus] *corr. err. L,* quia *BR*   17 uerbis ab ipso clarissimis] verbis meis *L*

the king's book. He quotes nothing honestly, but he either distorts it badly or he cites from the book statements which are nowhere in the book; but while he is recounting them he is fashioning for himself monsters to conquer. But we, as a matter of fact, make clear that the scriptures are thus presented by him, thus twisted from their own 5 meaning, that this fellow thus prefers his own fancies to the judgments of all the saints, that he thus counts the whole church as straw in comparison with himself, that he thus openly denies the sacred scripture and clearly contemns the acknowledged scripture, that he thus establishes his own teachings without scripture and contrary to 10 scripture, so that you cannot doubt that in very truth this fellow everywhere begs this single initial premise: that against everyone and everything he alone be believed on all matters.

Lest it can seem that he makes up such absurd things as these about Luther through calumny, 15 he recalls the very words of Luther and examines them carefully; from which it is clear that Luther both said and thought things in many ways still more absurd. Chapter 21.

Nevertheless, that you may not doubt that this inference was not 20 drawn from ambiguous words of his but that it was proclaimed by himself in the clearest of words, consider carefully the very words of the rascal.

I am certain, he says, that I have my *Luther's words* teachings from heaven, I who have tri- 25 umphed even over him who has more strength and cunning in his little fingernail than do all the popes and kings and doctors.

Likewise, shortly after:

The Lord has seized me unawares and carried me into the midst of these turmoils. 30

And again:

Here I need have no reason for patience, when the trifling buffoon

scurra leuis, non me nec uitam meam, sed doctrinam ipsam impetit, quam certissimus sum non meam esse, sed Christi.

ATQVE haec ubi tantum dicendo probauit, iam suo iure aduersus regem nebulo debacchatur, tanquam pro fide [Q₁] corripere haereti-
5 cum: hoc demum esset blasphemare deum.

Lutheri uerba domino digna   Indulgendum esset ei, si humano modo erraret. Nunc quum prudens et sciens mendacia componat, aduersus mei regis maiestatem in caelis, damna-bilis putredo ista, et uermis: ius mihi erit pro meo rege, maiestatem
10 anglicam luto et stercore conspergere: et coronam istam blasphemam in Christum pedibus conculcare.

AH, NE seui tantopere bone pater: sed si satis debacchatus es: audi nunc iam leno. Meministi supra falso questum te: quod rex nullum in toto libro, saltem exempli causa, locum ostenderit: in quo te tibi
15 dixerit esse contrarium. Hoc tu paulo ante mentitus es: quum rex

Cur hoc minus aequum ei in te   multa loca, tuae tibi repugnantiae demon-
erit, quam tibi in eum?   strarit. Hic regem puta uicissim abs te quaerere: cur ne unum saltem locum, exempli causa protuleris: in quo eum dicas blasphemare deum. Hic
20 locus omnino quaerendus est, et paternitati uestrae proferendus. Interea uero, quam diu constabit reuerendam paternitatem uestram, tam impudenter ista mentiri: licebit alijs pro maiestate anglica, lutum et stercus omne, quod uestra putredo damnabilis egessit, in uestrae paternitatis os stercoreum, et stercorum omnium, uere sterquilinium
25 regerere: et in coronam uestram, sacerdotalis coronae dignitate

Hunc suo sibi gladio iugulat   exauthoratam, in quam non minus ac re-
giam scurrari decreuistis, omnes cloacas et latrinas effundere. Dabis mihi candide lector, pro tua aequitate

Imo ipse ita ex suis uirtutibus   ueniam: quod istius me nebulonis uerba
30   *erat ornandus*   sordidissima coegerunt respondere talia: quibus honor praefandus esset. Nunc, uero uerius illud uerbum sentio: Qui tangit picem, coinquinabitur ab ea.

---

6 esset ei,] esset, inquit, ei *B*   15 contrarium. Hoc] *BL*, contrarium, Hoc *R*   29 *gloss om. L*   30 sordidissima] *B*, sardidissima *R*, stolidissima *L*   31 esset. Nunc,] esset nunc, *L*

attacks with his lies, not me nor my life, but the very doctrine which I am most certain is not mine but Christ's.

And when he has proved this simply by saying it, then by his own right the rascal rages wildly against the king, as if to reprove a heretic on behalf of the faith were in very truth to blaspheme God.   5

He would have to be forgiven if humanly he erred. Now, since he knowingly and consciously fabricates lies against the *Luther's words, worthy of the Lord* majesty of my king in heaven, this damnable rottenness and worm, I will have the right, on behalf of my king, to bespatter his English   10 majesty with muck and shit and to trample underfoot that crown of his which blasphemes against Christ.

Come, do not rage so violently, good father; but if you have raved wildly enough, listen now, you pimp. You recall that you falsely complained above that the king has shown no passage in your whole   15 book, even as an example, in which he said that you contradict yourself. You told this lie shortly before, although the king has demonstrated to you many examples of your inconsistency. Suppose that the king here in *Why is it less fair for him to do this to you than for you to* turn asks of you why you have not pro- *do it to him?*   20 duced even one passage as an example in which you say he blasphemes God. Your paternity must by all means search out and produce this passage. But meanwhile, for as long as your reverend paternity will be determined to tell these shameless lies, others will be permitted, on behalf of his English majesty, to   25 throw back into your paternity's shitty mouth, truly the shit-pool of all shit, all the muck and shit which your damnable rottenness has vomited up, and to empty out all the sewers and privies onto your crown divested of the dignity of the priestly crown, against which no less than *He cuts the man's throat with his own sword*   30 against the kingly crown you have determined to play the buffoon.

In your sense of fairness, honest reader, you will forgive me that the utterly filthy words of this scoundrel have forced me to answer such things, for *On the contrary, he himself had to be thus adorned with*   35 which I should have begged your leave. *his own virtues* Now I consider truer than truth that saying: "He who touches pitch will be wholly defiled by it." For I am

Etenim me necessitatis etiam huius pudet: quod [Q₁v] dum os hominis merdosum detergo: digitos mihi concacatos uideo. Verum, quis
ferre potest, nebulonem talem: qui mille uitijs ostendat se possessum,
atque agitatum a legione daemonum: et tamen ita se iactet stolide?

5   *Proiicit ampullas mitissimus*   Sancti patres omnes errauerunt. Ecclesia
            pater   tota saepius errauit. Doctrina mea non
                                       potest errare: quia certissimus sum, doctri-
nam meam non esse meam: sed Christi: uidelicet alludens ad illa
                                       uerba Christi: Verba mea non sunt mea:
    Parallelon I. Lutheri de se   sed eius, qui misit me patris. Quid istud?
10
                                       Papa cadet: dogmata mea stabunt: nonne
    Secundum parellelon   certare uidetur cum illo Christi: Caelum et
terra transibit: unum iota non peribit de uerbis meis? Nam quum ait,
                                       Rapuit me dominus imprudentem in
    Tertium parellelon
15   medias has turbas. hoc plus est, quam tulit
illum diabolus: et statuit supra pinnaculum templi. Iam illud quam
gloriosum est? Ego triumphaui aduersus illum: qui in ungue nouissimo plus habet uirtutis et astutiae, quam omnes papae, et reges, et
doctores. Quanto gloriosius triumphat iste, quam Christus: qui de se
20   dixit aliquanto modestius? Ego uici mun-
    Hic superat antiparallelon   dum. Et item illud. Venit princeps mundi
            suum   huius: et in me non habet quicquam. Iste
uero quid dicit? Ergo triumphaui non aduersus mundum, sed magno
                                       interuallo sublimius, aduersus principem
    Videlicet iuxta prouerbium. is mundi diabolum. Deinde triumphum suum
25 *recte se laudat, cui nullus*   buccinat: et magnificis ornat ampullis.
    alius contingit laudator   Triumphaui (inquit) aduersus illum: qui in
ungue nouissimo plus habet uirtutis et astutiae, quam omnes papae, et
reges, et doctores. O gloriosum triumphum. Sed unde nobis comper-
30 tum? Quid hic nobis dicet: qui probat omnia scripturis manifestis?
Quid aliud, quam illud Christi (nam cum illo cer[Q₂]tare conatur)
Ego testimonium perhibeo de me ipso? Quod si quis respondeat:
                                       testimonium tuum non est uerum: recurret
    Noua Lutheri scriptura   ilico ad nouam scripturam suam. Ego
35 certus sum, dogmata mea habere me de caelo. Atque ibi, sistet in hoc

---

2 concacatos] *BL*, concatos *R*   5 *gloss om. L*   17 gloriosum] *L*, glorosum *BR*
28 omnes] *L*, omnes, *BR*

ashamed even of this necessity, that while I clean out the fellow's
shit-filled mouth I see my own fingers covered with shit. But who can
endure such a scoundrel who shows himself possessed by a thousand
vices and tormented by a legion of demons,
and yet stupidly boasts thus: "The holy *The most mild father swells*   5
with bombast
fathers have all erred. The whole church
has often erred. My teaching cannot err, because I am most certain
that my teaching is not my own but
Christ's," alluding of course to those words *Luther's first parallel concerning*
himself
of Christ, "My words are not my own but   10
His who sent me, the Father's"? What about the following: "The pope
shall fall; my teachings will stand firm"?
Does it not seem to vie with that statement *Second parallel*
of Christ: "Heaven and earth shall pass away, not one iota of my
words shall perish"? For when he says, "The Lord has seized me   15
unawares and carried me into the midst of these turmoils," this is
more than, "The devil took Him and
placed Him on a pinnacle of the temple." *Third parallel*

Then, how boastful is that statement: "I have triumphed over him
who has more strength and cunning in his little fingernail than do all   20
the popes and kings and doctors"? How much more boastfully this
fellow exults than did Christ, who said of
Himself somewhat more modestly: "I have *Here he surpasses his*
counter-parallel
overcome the world"; and likewise: "The
prince of this world comes and in me he has nothing"? But what does   25
this fellow say? "Therefore I have triumphed, not over the world, but
far more sublimely, over the prince of the world, the devil." Then he
trumpets his triumph and tinsels it with
pompous bombast: "I have triumphed," *Of course according to the proverb:*
he has a right to praise himself
he says, "over him who has more strength *whom no one else will praise*   30
and cunning in his little fingernail than do
all popes and kings and doctors." O swelling triumph! But whence
have we learned this? What will he say to us here who proves everything by evident scriptures? What else but the words of Christ (for he
tries to vie with Him): "I bear witness to myself"? But if someone   35
should answer, "Your testimony is not true," he will have recourse
immediately to his new scripture: "I am
certain that I have my teachings from *Luther's new scripture*
heaven." And there he will stand firm on this initial premise of his as

suo principio, uelut firmissimo fundamento: quod non omnes papae,

reges, doctores, homines, angeli, poterunt

Quam certus sit Lutherus, sua dogmata uera esse

euertere. Certus igitur, imo certissimus, dogmata sua habere se de caelo: sicut certi

5 sunt et certissimi, qui dormiunt, omnia uera esse: quae somniant. Imo uero certus, et certissimus mentiri se uigilantem, dogmata sua esse de caelo: quae sua sibi murmurat conscientia, daemonum illi praestigijs immissa: hominibus maledicit, et angelis: quicunque dogmatis ipsius contradicunt. Et eos clamat os in caelum ponere,

10 conspurcare sacra, blasphemare deum: quicunque non uerentur

arguere, spurcissimas ipsius blasphemias.

Cur non iuras quoque, quo facias hominibus huius rei fidem?

Tantummodo clamat, anathema sint omnes: qui impetunt dogmata mea: quia

certus sum, dogmata mea habere me de caelo.

15   HOC igitur principio a reuerendo patre petito, et a nemine concesso, sic arguit ulterius reuerendus frater, pater, potator Lutherus,

extra ordinem sancti Augustini fugitiuus,

Lepida paranomasia

unus ex magistris inertibus vvittenbergensibus, utriusque iuris bacchanalius informis, et in sacra theologia

20   doctor indoctus. Ego certus sum, dogmata

Lutheri syllogismorum series

mea habere me de caelo: ergo dogmata

mea sunt caelestia. Et tunc ulterius sic. Dogmata mea sunt caelestia: ergo quicunque contradicit dogmatis meis: os ponit in caelum: et blasphemat deum. Quoniam quidem igitur contradicunt meis dogma-

25 [Q₂v]tibus, pontifex, imperator, reges, episcopi, sacerdotes, laici, et omnes, in summa boni, mihi licebit pro dei mei maiestate, pontificem, Caesarem, reges, episcopos, sacerdotes, laicos, omnes denique bonos,

anathematizare, maledictis et conuitijs

Istud facis assidue Luthere

incessere, atque in omnium coronas, et

30 capita, licebit, ex ore meo, lutum, coenum, stercora, merdas expuere.

HAE sunt reuerendi patris conclusiones, necessario deductae, ex isto patris eiusdem principio, per eum petito: ut ipsi credatur, certum esse se, sua dogmata esse de caelo. Verum age reuerende pater: si ego

on a most firm foundation that not all the popes, kings, doctors, men, angels will be able to destroy.

Certain, then, indeed most certain that he has his doctrines from heaven, as men who sleep are certain, indeed most certain that everything they dream is true; or rather certain, indeed most certain that he lies with his eyes wide open in saying that his teachings are from heaven, whereas his own conscience murmurs to him that they have been let loose in him by the deceits of demons; he curses any men and angels who contradict his teachings. And he protests that all those who do not fear to reproach his most filthy blasphemies set their face against heaven and besmirch sacred things and blaspheme God. His only cry is: "Let all be anathema who attack my teachings, because I am certain that I have my teachings from heaven."

How certain Luther is that his teachings are true

Why do you not also swear, so that you can convince men of this matter?

With this initial premise begged by the reverend father and granted by no one, he thus argues further, this reverend friar, Father Tosspot Luther, fugitive extraordinary of Saint Augustine, one of the unskilled masters of Wittenberg, unformed ranter of both kinds of law, and unlearned doctor in sacred theology: "I am certain that I have my teachings from heaven; therefore my teachings are heavenly." And then further thus: "My teachings are heavenly; therefore whoever contradicts my teachings sets his face against heaven and blasphemes God. Because, therefore, my teachings are indeed contradicted by the pope, the emperor, kings, bishops, priests, the laity, and in fine all good men, I will be permitted on behalf of the majesty of my God, to anathematize the pope, the emperor, kings, bishops, priests, the laity, in fine all good men, to assail them with curses and insults, and against all their crowns and heads I will be permitted to spew out of my mouth muck, filth, dung, shit."

A witty pun

Luther's series of syllogisms

You do this incessantly, Luther

These are the conclusions of the reverend father, deduced by necessity from this same father's initial premise, begged by him: that we should believe him to be certain that his teachings are from heaven.

But come, reverend father, suppose I carried out the deduction

sic colligerem. Ego certus sum, reuerendum fratrem patrem esse
asinum: ergo reuerendus frater, pater est asinus. Hic si mihi concedat
reuerendus pater, istud antecedens: quam multas conclusiones mihi
licebit inferre: nimirum comedendum ei foenum: gestandas sarcinas:
5   et, quod est grauissimum: carendum esse ceruisia: quod aegre foret

Atque aegrius laturus
pater potator auditurus. Verum potius
quam eo traheretur: non dubitaret exigere:
.ut probem me certum esse, illum esse asinum: alioqui (ut est impudens) haud concessurus illud: quod omnes tamen uident esse
10 manifestum. Verum ego protinus antecedens probare non dubitem:
hoc modo. Ego certus sum: quod sicut nullum animal ridet praeter
hominem: ita nullum animal rudit praeter asinum: sed ego certus
sum: quod reuerendus frater, pater potator est aliquod animal: et
rudit rudissime: ergo ego certus sum: quod reuerendus frater, pater,
15 potator est asinus uerissime. Ecce reuerende pater, ego probaui
meum antecedens: nec postulassem mihi concedi: nisi probauissem.
Probate, precor, et uos reuerende pater, illud assump[Q₃]tum
uestrum: quomodo certa sit uestra paternitas, dogmata uestra uos

Nempe phrenesi ministra
ei sedula
habere de caelo: quo deferente, recepistis
20 illa. Nemo enim ascendit in caelum: nisi
quia descendit de caelo. Sed hic (ut audio)
respondebitis, detulisse uobis dogmata uestra de caelo: non illum
quidem, qui descendit de caelo: sed illum qui tanquam fulgur cecidit
de caelo. Bene respondetis reuerende frater. Verum non sufficio uobis
25 magister: sed uos relinquo, cum cacodaemone dogmatum inspiratore
uestrorum: cum quo manebitis in Tartaro per omnia secula seculorum.

NON SVM profecto mihi tam iniquus
Epilogus eorum, quae probata
sunt hoc primo libro
fautor: quin tibi facile lector ignoscam: si
30 minus interdum probes hanc leuitatem
meam: qua nonnunquam quaedam intersero: quae neque rei
grauitati, neque tuae seueritati respondeant. Et tamen neminem esse
usquam puto, tam toruum: qui non aequum censeat, uel conniuere
nobis interdum, uel ignoscere: quum ubique legat spurcissimam
35 petulantiam, stolidissimi nebulonis, in principem prudentissimum:
si nos ita commoueat indignatio: ut uel inuiti, uicissim cogamur

---

14 reuerendus] *L*, reuerendus, *BR*; pater,] pater *L*   30 leuitatem] *L*, lenitatem *BR*
34 nobis] vobis *L*

thus: "I am certain that the reverend friar father is an ass; therefore the reverend friar father is an ass." If the reverend father should here grant me this antecedent premise, how many conclusions I may infer: he will undoubtedly have to eat hay; he will have to bear burdens; and what is most galling, he will have to do without beer; Father Tosspot would be vexed to hear that. But rather than be *And he would be more vexed to endure it* forced to this conclusion, he would not hesitate to demand that I prove I am certain he is an ass; otherwise, shameless as he is, he will not be ready to grant what everyone nevertheless sees to be evident. But I should not hesitate immediately to prove the antecedent in this way: "I am certain that as no animal laughs but man, so no animal brays but an ass; but I am certain that the reverend friar, Father Tosspot, is some animal and that he brays most brayingly; therefore I am certain the reverend friar, Father Tosspot, is most truly an ass."

See, reverend father, I have proved my antecedent, nor would I have demanded that it be granted me had I not proved it. I pray you also, reverend father, prove that assumption of yours: how your paternity is certain that you have your teachings from heaven, from what messen- *Doubtless from frenzy, his constant servant* ger you received them. "For no one has ascended into heaven except Him who has descended from heaven." But at this point, as I hear, you will reply that your teachings were brought down to you from heaven, not indeed by Him who descended from heaven, but by him who fell like lightning from heaven. You answer well, reverend friar. Really, I do not qualify as your teacher, but I leave you with the cacodaemon who inspires your teachings, with whom you will remain in Tartarus for ever and ever.

I am indeed not so prejudiced in my own favor that I will not easily forgive you, *The epilogue of the things that have been proved in this first book* reader, if you should at times little approve of this frivolity of mine by which I occasionally intersperse certain things which suit neither the gravity of the matter nor your seriousness. And yet, I think there has never been anyone so severe as not to think it fair either to wink at us occasionally or to forgive us—when he reads everywhere the most filthy insolence of a most stupid scoundrel against a most prudent prince—if we are so stirred by indignation that, even though unwillingly, we

ineptire: et (quod ait Solomon) respondere stulto secundum stultitiam
eius. Praesertim quum eius liber, prorsus omisso negocio, totus in
scurrilibus nenijs ocietur. Nos, licet obiter, in eius insaniam ludimus:
tamen interim ita rem tractamus: ut tibi liquido constent omnia:

5 *Summa Lutherani principij*   quaecunque ab initio promisimus. Nam
cum generale responsum eius, in summa
nihil complectatur aliud: quam nihil habendum esse pro certo: nisi
quod comprehensum est, euidenti scriptura: caetera uero uniuersa
(etiamsi non aduersantibus sacris [Q₃v] literis, perpetuo totius
10 ecclesiae consensu firmata sint) uel extirpanda penitus, tanquam
traditiones hominum (quod quidem censet optimum) uel ut mini-
Conditio oblata a Luthero   mum sic tolerari libere: ut cuique relin-
quatur integrum eorum, quodque probare,
improbare, mutare, damnare, abijcere ubilibet, quando libet, quoties
15 libet. Quum in hac parte collocet omnes leges humanas, patrum
decreta, ecclesiae concilia, et sacramenta, purgatorij metum, sanctorum cultum, et cultum celebrandae missae: nos et scripturis
clarissimis, et euidentissimis rationibus, effecimus perspicuum: esse
uerbum dei absque scriptura traditum, idque non minoris authori-
20 tatis esse: quam sit ipsa scriptura. Probauimus authoritate scripturae,
atque ipsius etiam confessione Lutheri, ecclesiam in discernendo dei
uerbo, in rebus fidei, prorsus errare non posse. Probauimus ecclesiam,
quam ille uocat papisticam, esse ueram ecclesiam Christi catholicam.
Probauimus ea sacramenta, quae Lutherus appellat traditiones
25 hominum, non hominum traditiones esse, sed dei: atque ita illum,
Quanto hic uerius et modestius de se praedicat quam Lutherus   uerbum dei negare non hominum. Probauimus illum, non stolide solum tollere
leges omnes humanas, sed etiam oppug-
nare, et clanculum, et manifeste scripturas ipsas. E quibus luce clarius
30 ostendimus, illum quicquid e scripturis attulit, pro sua causa sic
allegare stolide: ut nullus morio possit allegare stolidius. Et quum de
cuiusquam scripturae sensu, neminem unum uelit uniuersis credere:
sed unumquenque sibi, planum fecimus id illum struere: ut uniuersae

33 id illum] id *om. L*

are forced in turn to act foolishly and, as Solomon says, "to respond
to the fool according to his folly," especially since the fellow's book,
leaving aside completely the subject of concern, idles about entirely
in scurrilous trifles.

We may in passing make sport of his madness; nevertheless, at the
same time we handle the matter in such a way that everything that
we promised at the beginning is made clearly evident to you. For
since his general response includes in sum
nothing else than that nothing must be   *The sum of the Lutheran*
held for certain except what is included in   *principle*
evident scriptures, but that all other things—even if they are not
opposed by the sacred writings and are confirmed by the unbroken
agreement of the whole church—either must be wholly rooted out as
traditions of men (which policy he indeed thinks best), or at least they
are to be tolerated so freely that each of
those things is left wholly to each individual   *The condition presented by*
to approve, disapprove, change, condemn,   *Luther*
reject, wherever, whenever, as often as he pleases. Since he places in
this category all human laws, the decrees of the fathers, the councils
of the church, and the sacraments, fear of purgatory, the veneration
of the saints and the rite of celebrating mass, we have made manifest
both by most clear scriptures and most evident reasons that the word
of God has been handed down without scripture and that this word
is of no less authority than is the scripture itself. We have proved by
the authority of scripture and even by the confession of Luther himself that the church cannot err at all in distinguishing the word of God
in matters of faith. We have proved that the church which he calls
papistic is the true catholic church of Christ. We have proved that
those sacraments which Luther calls the traditions of men are not the
traditions of men but of God, and that thus
he denies the word of God, not of men. We   *How much more truly and*
have proved that he not only stupidly   *modestly does he preach about*
abolishes all human laws but also attacks   *himself than Luther does*
both secretly and openly the scriptures themselves. From the latter
we have shown more clearly than light that whatever he has presented
from the scripture he cites so stupidly in support of his own case that
no fool could cite it more stupidly. And since, on the meaning of any
scriptural text, he would want no one to believe all men taken as a
whole but every single person to believe himself, we have made clear

scripturae robur eneruet: et fructum omnem uertat in perniciem.
Denique quum scripturam indubiam, non fa[Q₄]teatur esse scripturam: sed habere neget quicquam scriptura dignum: et apostolum
non dubitet apostata reprehendere: clarissimum fecimus illum non
5   occulte modo, sed etiam palam, scripturas ipsas, pro quibus pugnare
se fingit, euertere. Postremo, praeter eius improbissima mendacia, et
stolidissimas repugnantias, et mille eius insanias, quas hinc inde
patefecimus, etiam uitiosum illud disputandi genus, in petendo
principio, quod perquam facete sibi uisus est exprobrasse caeteris: id
10   inquam ipsum probauimus illi unam, at-
       Haec lector tibi tolle memor
                            que unicam disputandi formam esse. Sic
igitur lector, plus quam tibi sumus polliciti, persoluimus: idque
fecimus probationibus, non aliunde fere, quam ex regis libello
desumptis. Et quoniam Luthero nunc, ut uides, belle processit gene-
15 rale responsum: nos iam accingimur ad eiusdem specialia: e quibus
nihil uidebis: in quo non ridebis hominis singularem stulticiam. [Q₄v]

7 stolidissimas] *BL*, stolidiffimas *R*

that he is contriving to weaken the force of all scripture and to turn all
its fruit into destruction. Then, since he does not admit that an un-
contested scriptural text is scripture but denies that it has anything
worthy of scripture, and since the apostate does not hesitate to censure an apostle, we have made it very clear that he not only secretly   5
but even openly destroys the very scriptures for which he pretends to
fight. Finally, aside from his most wicked lies, and his most stupid
contradictions, and his thousand follies, which we have exposed from
here and there, we also proved that that corrupt method of disputing
by begging the initial premise which he thought he had so very   10
wittily cast in the teeth of others; this method, I say, we proved to be
his one and only form of disputing.

Thus then, reader, we have discharged
more than we promised, and we have done   *Bear this in mind, reader*
it with proofs drawn from hardly any other source than the book of   15
the king. And since, as you see, Luther's general response has now
turned out prettily for him, we next gird ourselves to handle his
special answers; you shall not see one of them in which you will not
laugh at the singular folly of the fellow.

DOCTISSIMI VIRI GVILIELMI ROSSEI,
ADVERSVS LVTHERI
CALVMNIAS LIBER
SECVNDVS.

THE SECOND BOOK OF THE MOST LEARNED
WILLIAM ROSS
AGAINST THE CALUMNIES
OF LUTHER

REFELLIT EA: QVIBVS LVTHERVS
nugatur dum ad illa respondet: quae rex obiter
attigerat de Indulgentijs. Cap. primum.

QVVM REX, VT IPSIVS LIber ostendit, nihil sibi aliud in indulgentijs, et papatu proposuerit: quam insanam Lutheri leuitatem
perstringere, qui quum utrobique desipuisset: potius quam resipis-
ceret, optauit furere: quumque haec transeunter attigisset rex, non
aliud destinans, quam sacramenta trac-
Apparet hominem parum firmis
uestigiis nixum
tare: tamen ea ipsa quae dixit obiter ita
prostrauere Lutherum: ut ne tantulum
quidem, quod responderet, inuenerit, praeter insulsos risus in
ridiculum ipsius caput redituros.

Verba Lutheri
Veniamus nunc ad particularia Henrici
nostri, et uideamus, quam feliciter aptet
principia sua, conclusionibus.

Et postea.

Primum, indulgentias apprehendit rex defensor, quas ego asserueram
Imo magna tecum est nequitia
esse imposturas Romanae nequitiae. Has
defendit, hoc modo. Si indulgentiae sunt
imposturae, impostores erunt, non solum praecedentes pontifices, sed
et ipse Leo decimus, quem tamen Lutherus eximie laudat. O regium,
et Thomisticum acumen.

Et paulo post.

Itaque nihil mihi respondet rex Thomisticus, indulgentias damnanti,
praeter hoc uerbum, Indulgentiae non sunt imposturae, [R₁] quia
Leo est bonus uir: ergo oportet sic esse: non potest aliter esse.

HOC loco, nihil est opus respondere lector: sed ipsa regis uerba
subijcere: quae tu quum leges: et ab isto nebulone deprauata com-
peries: et illud oportet sic esse: non potest aliter esse: apud regem
nusquam inuenies: sed tam saepe quam stulte fictum ab Luthero, ut

Title 1–3 DOCTISSIMI ... CALVMNIAS] *om. L* 1 GVILIELMI ROSSEI]
FERDINANDI BARAVELLI *B*
10 prostrauere] *BL*, prostauere *R* 13 nunc ad] nunc (inquit) ad *B* 19 defendit]
defendi *L* 24 Thomisticus] *BL*, Thomesticus *R* 29 illud oportet] illud, Opotet *B*;
non] Non *B*

He refutes the trifling arguments with which
Luther answers the king's passing remarks on
indulgences. Chapter 1.

Although the king, as his own book shows, had no other intention
in discussing indulgences and the papacy than to reprove the senseless
caprice of Luther, who, although he had talked nonsense on both
these points, chose to rage madly rather than return to his senses; and
although the king had touched on these
points in passing, having in mind no intention but that of treating the sacraments,
nevertheless, those very comments which he made in passing so
prostrated Luther that he has not found anything more weighty to
answer than silly ridicule, which will recoil on his own ridiculous
head.

*It is clear that the man has
proceeded with unsteady footing*

> Let us come now to particular points of
> our Henry, and let us see how success-
> fully he fits his initial premises to his conclusions.

Luther's words

And later:

> First, the royal defender seized on indulgences, which I had declared
> to be impostures of Roman wickedness.
> He defends these as follows: "If indul-
> gences are impostures, then not only the
> preceding pontiffs but even Leo X himself, whom Luther however
> praises exceedingly, will be impostors." What royal and Thomistic
> shrewdness!

*Rather, there is great wickedness
in you*

And a little later:

> And so the Thomistic king answers me nothing when I condemn
> indulgences besides this statement: "Indulgences are not impostures
> because Leo is a good man; therefore it must be so, it cannot be
> otherwise."

At this point, reader, there is no need to answer, but to submit the
very words of the king; when you will read them and discover that
they have been perverted by this scoundrel, and that you will not find
the expression, "It must be so, it cannot be otherwise," anywhere in
the king's work, but that it has been fabricated by Luther as

haberet de suo: in quod uideretur festiue ludere: tum uere oportet sic
esse: et non potest aliter esse: quin si quis Lutherum dicat esse
bipedem, stultiorem quadrupede responsurus sis: oportet sic esse:
non potest aliter esse. Hunc igitur in modum ait princeps.

5   "QVEMADMODVM animal omne
Verba regis
                   potissimum ex facie dignoscitur: ita ex hac
quoque prima propositione, clarescit: quam suppuratum is habeat
cor: cuius os amaritudine plenum, tali exundat sanie. Nam quae de
indulgentijs olim disseruit: ea plerisque multum uidebantur adimere,

10 non modo de potestate pontificis, uerum etiam de bona spe, ac sancta
consolatione fidelium: hominesque uehementer animare, ut in
Quantam fenestram patefecerit   poenitentiae suae confisi diuitijs, ecclesiae
Lutherus ad scelera   thesaurum, et ultroneam dei benignitatem
                     contemnerent. Et tamen ea, quae scripsit,

15 omnia idcirco mitius accepta sunt: quia pleraque disserebat dumtaxat: non asserebat. Subinde etiam petens doceri, seseque pollicens
meliora docenti, pariturum. Verum istud quam simplici scripsit
animo, homo sanctulus, et omnia referens ad spiritum: qui fictum
effugit: hinc facile deprehenditur: quod simul atque a quoquam

20 salubriter est admonitus: ilicet pro benefacto regessit maledictum,
conuitijs et contumelijs insaniens: quibus ope[R₁v]raeprecium est
uidere: quo uaesaniae tandem prouectus est. Ante fassus est, indulgentias hactenus saltem ualere: ut praeter culpam etiam a poenis
absoluerent: quascunque uidelicet, uel ecclesia statuerat: uel suus

25 cuique sacerdos iniunxerat. Nunc uero, non eruditione (ut ipse
inquit) sed malicia tantum profecit: ut sibi ipsi contrarius, indulgentias in uniuersum condemnet. Ac nihil aliud eas dicat esse, quam
meras imposturas, ac nihil omnino ualere, praeterquam ad perdendum
                    hominum pecuniam, ac dei fidem. Qua
Quam consulit hominum pecuniae

30 *iste oeconomus*   in re, quam non scelerate modo, uerum
                    etiam furiose bacchetur: nemo est qui
non uidet. Nam si nihil omnino ualent indulgentiae: sed merae sunt
(ut Lutherus ait) imposturae: tunc necesse est: impostores fuerint,
                    non hic tantum Leo pontifex decimus
Leo pontifex

35   (cuius innocens, et inculpata uita,

---

3 quadrupede responsurus sis:] quadrupede, responsurus sis, *B*, quadrupede, responsurus,
sis *L*   5 *gloss* Verba regis] Veis. regrba *B*   20 ilicet] ilico *B*   27 condemnet. Ac]
condemnet: ac *B*   29 *gloss om. L*   31 est qui] est, qui *B*   34 *gloss om. L*

frequently as it has been foolishly, so that he might have a statement
about his own position which he might be thought to ridicule wittily,
then indeed it must be so and it cannot be otherwise that if someone should say Luther is a biped you would be ready to answer that
he is more foolish than a quadruped; it must be so, it cannot be   5
otherwise. The prince, therefore, says the following.

"As every living being is recognized
chiefly by its face, so also from this first   *The king's words*
proposition it becomes clear what a festering and rotten heart he has
whose mouth, full of bitterness, overflows with such diseased matter. 10
For what he once argued about indulgences seems to many persons to
detract not only from the power of the pontiff but also from the good
hope and holy consolation of the faithful, and very forcefully to
encourage men that, relying on the riches of their own penitence, they
should contemn the treasury of the church   15
and the spontaneous goodness of God. And   *How wide a window Luther has*
yet all that he then wrote was received   *opened to crimes*
more favorably on the grounds that he was merely debating, not
declaring most of the points. He was continually seeking to be taught
and promising to comply with the person who taught him something   20
better. How sincerely this promise was written by the sanctimonious
fellow who ascribes all his objections to the spirit which shuns falsehood, can easily be detected by the fact that as soon as he was
wholesomely admonished by anyone he immediately returned a
malediction for the benefaction, raging madly with revilings and   25
reproaches. It is worthwhile to see to what degree of madness these
have finally carried him. He admitted earlier that indulgences had
power at least insofar as they absolved both from guilt and from
whatever penalties the church had established or one's own priest had
enjoined on each one. But now he has progressed so far, not in learn- 30
ing as he says but in ill will, that, contradicting himself, he condemns
indulgences completely. And he says that they are nothing but mere
impostures and have no power at all except to squander men's
money and their faith in God. On this
point everyone sees how he rants not only   *How this steward looks out for*
wickedly but also madly. For if, as Luther   *the money of men. Leo*   35
says, indulgences have no efficacy at all but   *the pontiff*
are mere impostures, then it is necessary that we consider as impostors
not only the present pontiff, Leo X, whose innocent and blameless

moresque sanctissimi, ab ineunte aetate, per orbem totum, satis
explorati sunt: quemadmodum in epistola quadam ad pontificem,
Lutherus etiam ipse fatetur) uerum etiam

Ergo aut ibi turpiter adulator,
aut hic mendax est

tot retro seculis, omnes Romanos ponti-
5   fices: qui (quod Lutherus ipse comme-
morat) indulgere solebant, alius remissionem annuam, alius triennem,
quidam aliquot condonare quadragesimas, nonnulli certam totius
poenitentiae partem, tertiam puta, uel dimidiam: aliqui demum
remissionem indulserunt et poenae et

An non tenet haec consequentia
10   *domine frater*

culpae plenariam. Omnes ergo (si uera
dicit Lutherus) fuerunt impostores. At
quanta magis cum ratione creditur, hunc unum fraterculum,
morbidam esse ouem, quam tot olim pontifices, perfidos fuisse pastores."

15   Et paulo post.

"QVI, quum eousque progreditur: ut neget indulgentias [R₂]
quicquam ualere in terris: frustra cum eo disputem: quantum ualeant
in purgatorio. Praeterea, quid profuerit cum illo loqui: quibus
subsidijs liberemur a purgatorio: qui

Habet forte eam potestatem
20   *unde doctrinam*

totum ferme tollit purgatorium? Vnde
quum pati non possit: ut pontifex quen-
quam eximat: ipse sibi tantum sumit: ut neminem ibi relinquat.
Quid attinet, cum eo pugnare: qui pugnat ipse secum? Quid argumentis promoueam: si cum eo agam: ut donet: quod negauit: qui
25   nunc id ipsum negat: quod ante donauerat? Verum quantumuis
disputentur indulgentiae pontificis: necesse est, inconcussa maneant
uerba Christi: quibus Petro commisit claues ecclesiae: quum dixit.
Quicquid ligaueris super terram: erit ligatum et in caelo: et quicquid
solueris super terram: erit solutum et in caelo. Item quorum remise-
30   ritis peccata: remittentur: et quorum retinueritis: retinebuntur.
Quibus uerbis, si satis constat sacerdotem quemlibet, habere potestatem a mortalibus absoluendi criminibus, et aeternitatem poenae
tollendi: cui non uideatur absurdum, sacerdotum omnium principem, nihil habere iuris in poenam temporariam? Verum aliquis
35   fortasse dicet: Lutherus ista non admittet,

Pontifex Luthero, plebeio
sacerdote inferior

sacerdotem ullum quicquam ligare, uel
soluere, aut pontificem summum plus

---

2 sunt:] sunt, *BL*   3 *gloss om. L*   4 seculis] *L*, secuculis *BR*   9 *gloss om. L*   19 *gloss*
om. L   32 absoluendi] *L*, absouendi *BR*   35 *gloss* Luthero,] Luthero *L*, Luthero. *BR*

life and most holy conduct from the time of his youth have been quite
well known throughout the whole world, as Luther himself admits in
an epistle to the pontiff, but also all the Roman pontiffs through so
many past ages who, as Luther himself recalls, used to grant indulgences: one, a year's remission, another   5
three years'; some used to remit the pen-   *Therefore he is either there a
ance of several lents, some a definite por-   *base flatterer or here a liar*
tion of the total penance, say a third or a half; others, finally, granted
full remission both of the punishment and of the guilt. If what Luther
says is true, then all these men were im-   10
postors. But how much more reason is   *Or does this conclusion not
there to believe that this single friarlet is a   *hold, honored brother?*
sick sheep than that so many pontiffs were once faithless shepherds."
     And a little later:
     "When he goes so far as to deny that indulgences have any power   15
on earth, it would be useless for me to dispute with him on how much
power they have in purgatory. Besides, what use will it be to discuss
the means of being delivered from purgatory with one who almost
wholly does away with purgatory? Since he   *Perhaps he has that power from
cannot endure that the pontiff release   *the same place as he has*   20
anyone from that place, he takes on him-   *his doctrine*
self the great work of leaving no one there. What point is there in
fighting with him who fights with himself? What shall I achieve by
arguments if I try to persuade him to grant what he has before
denied, since he himself now denies what he had before granted?   25
     "But however much the indulgences of the pontiff may be disputed,
the words of Christ necessarily remain unshaken, by which He committed to Peter the keys of the church when He said: 'Whatever you
shall bind on earth, shall be bound also in heaven; and whatever you
shall loose on earth, shall be loosed also in heaven.' Likewise: 'Whose   30
sins you shall forgive they shall be forgiven; and whose sins you shall
retain they shall be retained.' If it is indisputable that by these words
any priest has the power to absolve men from mortal sins and to take
away an eternity of punishment, will it not seem absurd to everyone
that the chief of all priests should have no right over temporal   35
punishment?
     "But perhaps someone will say: 'Luther
will not admit that any priest binds or   *To Luther, the pontiff is inferior
looses anything or that the supreme   *to a common priest*

habere potestatis, quam alium quemuis episcopum, imo quemlibet
sacerdotem. At quid id mea, quid admittat: aut quid non admittat is:
qui quorum nihil admittat nunc, eorum pleraque paulo prius admisit:
quique omnia nunc reijcit solus: quae tota tot seculis admisit ecclesia.
5 Nam (ut caetera taceam: quae nouus iste Momus repraehendit) certe

Iam utrum mauis elege Luthere indulgentias, si pontifices pec[R₂v]cauere,
qui concesserunt: immunis a peccato non
fuit tota congregatio fidelium: qui eas tam diu, tanto consensu,
susceperunt. Quorum ego iudicio, et obseruatae sanctorum consue-
10 tudini, non dubito potius acquiescendum: quam Luthero soli: qui
totam ecclesiam tam furiose condemnat."

ECCE lector, quam scite regem tetigit Lutherus: quum rex et
euangelio probarit, et ratione, successorem Petri condonare posse
poenam purgatorij: quum rex praeterea dicat: Non solum Leonem
15 decimum (quem laudat ipse Lutherus) sed omnes retro pontifices
fuisse impostores: si indulgentiae nihil sunt aliud, quam imposturae:
et totum fuisse Christianum populum, tot aetatibus obnoxium culpae:
et se meliori cum ratione, crediturum, unum Lutherum uel stolidum
esse uel impium, quam aut omnes pontifices fuisse deceptores, aut
20 totum tot aetates populum fuisse deceptum. Lutherus contra, ad
euangelium tacet: rationes dissimulat silentio, de caeteris tot seculorum pontificibus nihil respondet omnino: nihil respondet de populo:
quem tot aetatibus defunctum, cum episcopis et clero, communi
damnatione deuoluit ad inferos. Quid ergo

25 *Rhetores uidelicet imitans in iis,* respondet? nihil respondet omnino. Tan-
quae dissoluere nequit tum cachinnos tollit homo lepidus: et
Sardonio risu, risit regem: quasi nihil aliud dicat: quam, Indulgentiae non sunt imposturae: quia Leo decimus est uir bonus. Et tamen
hoc ipsum, sic ab illo recitatum de industria, ut posset deprauatum
30 uincere: quum omnibus uiribus oppugnarit: expugnare non potuit.

Lutheri uerba Si Lutherus, inquit, tantum habet
authoritatis, ut tantus rex ei credat,

---

6 *gloss om. L*   12 quum rex] *corr. err. L*, rex *om. BR*   21 dissimulat silentio, de] *corr. err.*
L, dissimulat: silentio de *BR*   24 *gloss om. L*

pontiff has more power than any bishop, indeed than any priest at all.' But what do I care what the fellow admits or what he does not admit, since he admitted not long ago many of the truths of which he now admits nothing, and since he alone now rejects all the practices which the whole church has admitted for so many ages. For, to say 5 nothing of the other things which this new Momus censures, surely if the pontiffs sinned who granted indulgences, then the whole congregation of the faith was not free from sin, since they accepted them for so long a time *Now choose whichever you* with such thorough agreement. I have no *prefer, Luther* 10 doubt that we should accede to their judgment and to the custom observed by the saints rather than to Luther alone, who condemns the whole church so madly."

See, reader, how adroitly Luther has caught the king, since the king has proved both by the gospel and by reason that the successor 15 of Peter can remit the punishment of purgatory; since the king moreover says that not only Leo X, whom Luther himself praises, but all the past pontiffs have been impostors if indulgences are nothing other than impostures, and that the whole Christian people for so many ages have been liable to blame, and that he himself is ready with 20 better reason to believe that Luther alone is either stupid or impious than that all the pontiffs have been deceivers or that the whole people has been deceived for so many ages. Luther, on the other hand, says nothing to the gospel; he conceals the reasons by silence; he answers nothing at all about the other pontiffs of so many ages; he 25 answers nothing about the people whom, deceased now for so many ages, together with the bishops and clergy, he tumbles down to hell in a common damnation.

What, then, does he answer? He answers nothing at all. The witty fellow only raises loud guffaws and with a 30 Sardonian laugh laughs at the king as if the *Imitating, of course, the* latter says nothing but: "Indulgences are *rhetoricians concerning those* not impostures because Leo X is a good *points he cannot solve* man." And yet this very statement, thus deliberately recited by him that he might be able to refute what he had perverted, he was not 35 able to disprove although he disputed it with all his powers.

If Luther, he says, has so much authority that such a great king should believe him *Luther's words*

Leonem decimum laudanti: cur non credat eidem, indul[R₃]gentias
damnanti?

Quia non credit inconstanti
scurrae rex prudens

Hui, quam argute nobis arguit reuerendus
frater. Si negemus hoc lemma: sic nimirum probabit a simili. Si rex mihi credit
uera dicenti: cur non itidem credit aperte mentienti? Nam, quod ait
se, quum diceret, indulgentias nihil omnino ualere, sed esse meram
imposturam, muniuisse sententiam suam scripturis, et rationibus:
reuerendus pater aperte mentitur. Nam in illis libris, quibus egit serio
de indulgentijs: nihil dixit ultra, quam eas ualere dumtaxat, ad
tollendas poenas: quas aut lex inflixisset, aut homo. At nihil omnino
ualere, et meras imposturas esse, id demum, primum in captiuitate
Babylonica, sine scripturis, aut ratione, ex pectoris sui sentina, solo
furore deprompsit. Illud quoque non minus praeclarum, quod sic
ait.

Verba Lutheri

Hoc argumento regio, et Thomistico
usus, potes dicere, Romae in curia nihil
agitur mali, quia Leo decimus est bonus uir, et sic iustificabis omnem
illam abominationem, Romanae perditionis.

EN quam pulchre, quam similia connectat. Quasi, aut in Romana
curia fierent omnia: quae bonus iste pater

An tu ita stupidus es, ut non
intelligas melius, regis argu-
mentum? En Luthere quam
tu pulchre uerba connectas

mentitur: aut quae facerent omnes: omnia
sciret pontifex: aut si quaedam nesciret
illorum: ideo nescire posset: quod ullas
concedat indulgentias: aut non esset
impostor: si sciens faceret imposturas: aut bonus esset: qui impostor
esset: aut sibi non pugnaret stolidissime, prudentissimus pater: qui
dicit: Leo decimus est impostor: sed tamen est bonus uir.

3 *gloss* Quia] quia *BR, gloss om. L*   13 aut] & *L*   24 *gloss* tu pulchre] tupulchre *BR,*
gloss om. L

when he praises Leo X, why does not the king believe him also when he condemns indulgences?

Because the prudent king does not believe a fickle buffoon

Phew! How artfully the reverend friar argues with us. If we should deny this assumption, he will no doubt prove his case from a similar one: "If the king believes me when I tell the truth, why does he not also believe when I openly lie?" For as for his statement that, when he says indulgences have no power at all but are mere impostures, he has fortified his opinion by scriptures and reasons, the reverend father is openly lying. For in those books in which he dealt in earnest with indulgences he said nothing further than that they have power only to take away punishments which either the law or man had inflicted. But the statement that they have no power at all and are mere impostures, this he first drew forth in the *Babylonian Captivity* without scriptures, without reasoning, from the bilge of his own breast through madness alone. No less clear is another statement which he makes as follows:

Using this kingly and Thomistic argument you can say that nothing evil is done in the Roman curia because Leo X is a good man, and thus you will justify all that abomination of the Roman perdition.

Luther's words

See how neatly he relates such similar ideas. As if there happened in the Roman curia all the things which this good father lyingly claims; or as if the pontiff knew everything that everyone did, or that, if he did not know some of the things they did, he could therefore not know that the curia grants any indulgences; or as if a person who knowingly committed impostures were not an impostor, or as if a person who was an impostor were a good man; or as if the most prudent father did not contradict himself most foolishly when he says: "Leo X is an impostor, but nevertheless he is a good man."

Or are you so stupid that you do not better understand the argument of the king? See, Luther, how neatly you draw conclusions

Obiter pulchre tractat Lutherum, stolide argutantem
aduersus Aristotelem, quod nemo sit bonus
uir nisi qui possit esse bonus
princeps. Cap. II. [R₃v]

5 NAM QVID obtusius est illa argutia: qua sibi uidetur argute
refellere, Aristotelis (ut ipse uocat) argutiam.

Lutheri uerba. Aristoteles

Si hoc loco, inquit, argutiam illam
tractem: quod aliud sit, esse bonum
uirum, et aliud bonum principem (ut Aristoteles eorum docet) frustra
10 tractauero, coram tam stupidis et crassis truncis: quanto minus caperent, si secundum diuinas literas, hac de

*Ista ne est uestra tractatio
secundum diuinas literas?*

re disputarem. Nam re uera bonus uir
non est, qui bonus princeps esse non
potest. Spiritus enim Christi (quo solo boni sumus) reddit hominem
15 perfectum, ad omne opus bonum instructum, ut Paulus ad Timotheum
docet. Id quod et historiae probant scripturarum. Coram hominibus
locum habet argutia ista: aliud est, esse bonum uirum, nempe in
speciem: et aliud bonum principem, aeque in speciem. At Saul, ut
desijt esse bonus uir, simul desijt esse bonus princeps.

20 AN NON dum legis haec: tecum lector cogitas illud Horatij:
Quorsum haec tam putida tendunt? Nam Leo decimus, si fuit impostor: neque bonus papa fuit: neque bonus uir: Quem Lutherus
bonum uirum fuisse confirmabat: donec se declarauit Leo mali uiri
non esse fautorem. Quamobrem extra locum suum prorsus, hanc
25 argutatur argutiam: nec in aliud, quam ut suam declaret stultitiam.
Quis enim praeter Lutherum tam stupidus est, et crassus truncus: ut
id non uideat esse uerum, uel negante Aristotele, non modo non
admonente, non idem esse bonum uirum, quod bonum principem:

Inepte interpretatur apostolum

quantumuis id neget bipedum stultissimus
30 Lutherus? Qui ex illo Pauli: Spiritus
Christi reddit hominem perfectum, ad omne opus bonum instructum:
Concludit, neminem in hoc mortali statu bonum uirum esse: qui non
sic habeat spiritum Christi: ut sit instructus ad gu[R₄]bernandum

---

11 *gloss om. L*   29 *gloss* Inepte interpretatur apostolum] *BR*, Pulchre, bene, recte *L*
31 instructum] *L*, inctructum *BR*   33 habeat] habet *L*

In passing he deftly handles Luther's stupid prating
against Aristotle that no one is a good man
unless he can be a good
prince. Chapter 2.

What is duller than that subtlety with which he thinks he subtly   5
refutes the subtlety—as he calls it—of Aristotle.

If at this point, he says, I should treat
that subtlety that it is one thing to be a   *Luther's words. Aristotle*
good man and another to be a good prince (as their Aristotle teaches),
I shall have treated it in vain in the face of such stupid and dense lunk-   10
heads; how much less would they understand if I disputed on this
matter according to divine writings. For as a matter of fact one is not
a good man who cannot be a good prince.
For the Spirit of Christ, in whom alone   *Is this discussion of yours in*
we are good, renders a man perfect,   *accord with the divine*
equipped for every good work, as Paul   *writings?*   15
teaches in his epistle to Timothy. The historical books of scripture also
prove this point. In the eyes of men this subtlety has value: that it is
one thing to be a good man, that is, in appearance, and another to be
a good prince, equally in appearance. But when Saul ceased to be a   20
good man, he at the same time ceased to be a good prince.

While you read these words, reader, do you not recall those words
of Horace: "Where are these addled words leading?" For if Leo X
was an impostor, he was neither a good pope nor a good man. Luther
used to affirm that Leo was a good man until Leo declared that he   25
would not favor a wicked man. Luther, therefore, prattles this
subtlety quite irrelevantly and for no other purpose than to declare
his own folly. For who besides Luther is so stupid and dense a lunk-
head as not to see that it is true, even if Aristotle denied it instead of
not mentioning it at all, that to be a good man is not the same thing   30
as to be a good prince, however much this statement may be denied
by that most foolish of bipeds, Luther? From those words of Paul,
"The Spirit of Christ renders a man perfect
and equipped for every good work," he   *He interprets the apostle*
concludes that no one in this mortal state   *absurdly*
is a good man who does not have the Spirit of Christ in such a way   35

regnum. Et nisi quis ita sit bonus: quomodo nemo bonus est, nisi solus deus: alioqui bonus uir uocari non possit: nec bonus uir sit: qui bene credit: et bene facit, pro ingenij sui captu: si sit aliquanto simplicior: quam ut sit idoneus gubernando populo. Docet ergo nos
5 stupidos et crassos truncos, huius patris ingenium subtile, et tenui festuca tenuius, illud Pauli: Spiritus Christi reddit hominem perfectum: sic intelligi, quod nemo sit bonus: nisi idem sit optimus. Et quia spiritus Christi, reddit hominem instructum ad omne opus bonum: ideo quemlibet, cui se aliquo modo infundit: instructum
10 reddit ad quodlibet: ut nisi quis omnia omnium dona gratiarum receperit: nullius omnino receperit: nimirum iuxta illud eiusdem Pauli: Diuisiones gratiarum multaé sunt: et unusquisque proprium donum habet a deo, alius quidem sic, alius autem sic: sed idem nobis egregie probat historijs scripturarum. Nam coram hominibus locum
15 habet, inquit, argutia ista: aliud esse bonum uirum, nempe in speciem: aliud bonum principem, nempe in speciem. At Saul, ut

Pulchre, bene, recte   desijt esse bonus uir: desijt simul esse bonus princeps.

O PRAECLARVM argumentum. Sic accidit in Saule: ergo sic
20 accidere necesse est in omnibus hominibus: uelut si quis ita colligat: iste homo stultus est: ergo omnis homo stultus est. Quid impedit: quo minus is, qui priuatim aliquo laborat uitio: tamen utilior esse possit in publicum: quam quispiam nullo laborans uitio: sed minus callens

Intelligis Luthere an non   earum artium: quibus instructum oportet
25 *dum etiam*   esse principem. Neque enim deus omnia impertit omnibus. Quod si maxime [R₄v]
uerum esset, neminem esse bonum principem: nisi qui sit bonus uir: tamen altera parte non commearet ratio, neminem esse bonum uirum: nisi qui sit bonus princeps: nisi nobis persuadeat reuerendus
30 pater, hoc argumentum bonum esse: Omnis rex est homo: ergo omnis homo est rex. Et item istud. Omnis asinus est animal: ergo

Quam non commode Luthere rem   omne animal est asinus. Et hic uides lector:
diuisisti temporibus?   quam belle procedat huic reuerendo patri: id quod ille extra necessitatem, extra

---

3 sui] *om. B*   8 hominem] *BL*, homnem *R*   14 egregie] aegregie *B*   15 ista: aliud]
ista, Aliud *B*   17 *gloss* Pulchre, bene, recte] *BR*, Inepte interpretatur apostolum *L*
21 Quid] Qui *L*   24 *gloss om. L*   32 *gloss om. L*

that he is equipped to govern a kingdom. And unless a man is as good
as only God is good, he cannot otherwise be called a good man; nor
is a person a good man who believes well and acts well according to
his natural capacity, if he is somewhat too simple to be suited for
governing people. The genius of this father, therefore, subtle and 5
slighter than a slight straw, teaches us stupid and dense lunkheads
that the words of Paul, "The Spirit of Christ renders a man perfect,"
are understood to mean that no one is good unless he is likewise the
best. And because the Spirit of Christ renders a man equipped for
every good work, He therefore renders equipped for any activity 10
whatever anyone on whom He chooses to pour Himself out in any
manner, so that, unless a man has received all the gifts of all the
graces, he has received no grace whatever; doubtless according to the
words of the same Paul, "There are many varieties of gifts; and each
one has his own gift from God, one indeed in one way and another in 15
another." But he eminently proves the same point to us from the
scriptural histories. "For this subtlety has value in the eyes of men,"
he says, "that it is one thing to be a good man, that is in appearance,
another to be a good prince, that is in appearance. But when
Saul ceased to be a good man, he ceased at   *Splendid, excellent, superb!* 20
the same time to be a good prince."

What a brilliant argument! It happened thus in the case of Saul;
therefore it must necessarily happen thus in the case of all men; as if
anyone would infer: "This man is foolish; therefore every man is
foolish." What prevents a man who labors under some personal fault 25
from being nonetheless able to be more useful for the public good
than some person laboring under no fault but less skilled in those arts
with which a prince ought to be equipped?
God does not impart all things to all men.   *Do you understand, Luther, or*
But if it were quite true that no one is a   *not even yet?* 30
good prince unless he is a good man, nevertheless the proposition is
not convertible: that no one is a good man unless he is a good prince;
unless the reverend father should persuade us that this reasoning is
good: "Every king is a man; therefore every man is a king." And
likewise this: "Every ass is an animal; therefore every animal is an 35
ass." And here you see, reader, how
prettily that argument turns out for this   *How poorly you have timed this*
reverend father which without necessity,   *argument, Luther*
without occasion, without any relevance he has brought forward for

occasionem, extra locum omnem protulit: non in aliud omnino,
quam ut iactaret istud bellum inuentum suum, et triumphum aduersus Aristotelem, idem esse bonum uirum, et bonum regem.

Pergit retegere, et festiuiter refellere nugas Lutheri,
5   circa Leonem decimum. Cap. III.

RVRSVS ad id redit, quo sua se stultitia dolet urgeri.

Verba Lutheri. Audin hunc   Itaque nihil, inquit, contra me facit
Sextum Neuium?   hoc, quod Leonis decimi personam
                                 laudaui, et indulgentias damnaui. Dup-
10   lex est hic iudicium, Hominem non licet iudicare, etiam si pessimus sit,
coram deo donec foris sine crimine uiuit. Hoc enim iudicium ad eum
pertinet, qui scrutator est cordis et renum. Aliud est de indulgentiis
iudicare, quod ad doctrinam pertinet, in qua ut errare possunt, tam
                                 boni quam mali, siue sint uere aut
Tu utriusque modi es
15   ficte boni, imo et electi, ita pertinaces
in errore non sunt, nisi manifeste impii. Hoc iudicium ad omnes
et singulos pertinet, ut uocem pastoris, et alienorum discernamus. De
Leone autem ipso, adhuc hodie incertus sum, quid senserit apud sese,
                                 et an sit pertinax in [S$_1$] errore. Sed quid
Quae quaeso spiritualia?
20   ista spiritualia, et preciosa, ante porcos
proijcio? Quid capiat harum rerum, qui hunc syllogismum non capit,
longe insulsissimum esse? Leo bonus est uir: ergo indulgentiae sunt
uerae.

QVID ais lector? num se pulchre expediuit reuerendus pater, hac
25   bella distinctione: qua uidelicet effecit: ut recte laudarit Leonem:
etiamsi uocet impostorem? Nam ut se excuset a repugnantia: sic
excusat pontificem: ut quamquam pontifex non solum concesserit
indulgentias: sed etiam excommunicarit illum: qui reprehendit indulgentias: tamen dubitat: quid ille pontifex apud se senserit de
30   indulgentijs. De quibus si senserit idem, quod Lutherus: hoc est, si

---

3 *B adds* Et cum se tam prudenter gesserit in regem lepide scurratur adagiis, Aut regem aut
fatuum inquiens nasci oportere. Pape Luthere, quam commode. Nam hoc adagium
utrumque uestrum beat, et illum, quod natus est rex: et te, quod natus es fatuus. *See n.*
7–8 *gloss* Audin hunc Sextum Neuium?] *om. L*   14 *gloss om. L;* uere] ue re *B*
19 *gloss om. L*   24 num] non *L*

no other purpose at all than that he might boast of this fine discovery of his, and of his triumph over Aristotle: that to be a good man and a good king is the same thing.

He proceeds to disclose and wittily disprove
Luther's nonsense about Leo X. Chapter 3.   5

He returns once more to that point to which he is painfully urged by his own folly.

And so, he says, the fact that I have praised the person of Leo X and condemned indulgences does not work *Luther's words. Do you hear this Sextus Naevius?* 10 against me at all. There is here a twofold judgment: that it is not lawful to judge a man, even if he is very wicked in the eyes of God, so long as he lives exteriorly without offense, for this judgment belongs to Him who is the searcher of the heart and desires; it is another thing to judge about indulgences, which pertains to doctrine, in which although the 15 good as well as the wicked, whether they are truly or feignedly good, indeed even the elect, can err, yet they are not stubbornly in error unless they are clearly impious; this judgment *You are of both kinds* belongs to each and every individual so that we may distinguish the voice of the shepherd from that of 20 strangers. But as for Leo himself, I am uncertain even to this day what he thought within himself and whether he is stubbornly in error. But why do I cast these spiritual and precious *What spiritual words, please?* words before pigs? What can a person grasp of these things who does not grasp that by far the most foolish 25 syllogism is this: Leo is a good man; therefore indulgences are true?

What do you say, reader? Surely not that the reverend father has extricated himself neatly through this fine distinction by which he has of course proved that he praised Leo rightly even if he calls him an impostor? For in order to excuse himself from inconsistency, he 30 thus excuses the pontiff; that although the pontiff not only granted indulgences but even excommunicated the man who censured indulgences, nevertheless there is some doubt as to what that pontiff thought within himself about indulgences. If he thought the same about them as Luther; that is, if he thought contrary to what he 35

Responsio Lutheri super indulgentiis

contra sensit, quam scripsit: fuit bonus uir. Et haec est acuta responsio reuerendi patris de indulgentijs: Ego certus sum: quod sunt merae pontificis Romani imposturae: sed quia de occultis non debeo iudicare: et occultum est mihi: an Leo decimus fuit pertinax in contraria opinione: an et ipse quoque crediderit, eas esse meras imposturas: et eas credens nihil omnino ualere: tamen uelut multum ualituras concesserit: et me, quod contra pertinaciter senserim:

Arguta collectio scilicet

excommunicauerit: atque ita uerus impostor fuit. Ideo absque repugnantia et indulgentias, ut imposturas eius reprehendi, et ipsum tamen imposturarum factorem, ut bonum uirum laudaui: quia idem est bonus uir, et bonus princeps. Et hoc est lector

Eximium quoddam Lutheri acumen

ingenij Lutherani praeclarum specimen: quod rationibus regis omnibus omissis, frustum unum descerpserit sibi: et pro suo deprauauit commodo: quo facilius posset uincere. Et tamen quum id deprauasset maxime: tam stolidus est: ut non posset soluere. [S₁v]

Refellit deliramenta Lutheri: quibus respondit de papatu. Cap. IIII.

Verba Lutheri

VEniamus nunc, inquit, ad aliud de papatu: quem ego potentibus scripturis conuulsi. Defensor autem eius ad scripturas magis mutus quam piscis, regia fiducia praesumit, Lutherum ad solum eius nutum scripturas deserturum, et suis mendacijs accessurum. Probat autem papatum hoc modo. Oportet sic esse, quia audiui

Vt nihil pudet nebulonem mendacij

etiam Indiam sese Romano pontifici subdere. Item Graeciam. Item Sanctus Hieronymus agnoscit Romanam ecclesiam pro matre. Quid hic Lutherus dicere audebit aduersus tam aegregia, et tam Thomistica.

ECCE lector ubique similem sui Lutherum, hoc est, nebulonem improbe impudenterque mendacem. Nam quum adhuc extent libri: ex quibus eius uanitas arguitur: tamen, tanquam homines prorsus

---

1 *gloss om.* L   9 *gloss om.* L   13 *gloss om.* L   26 *gloss om.* L

wrote, he was a good man. And this is the sagacious answer of the reverend father concerning indulgences: "I am certain

Luther's answer concerning indulgences

that they are mere impostures of the Roman pontiff, but because I should not judge about hidden matters, and it is hidden from me whether Leo X was stubbornly of the opposite opinion or whether he himself also believed that they are mere impostures and, while believing that they have no power at all, nonetheless granted them as though they would have much power and excommunicated me because I stubbornly thought the contrary and thus was a true impostor. Therefore, without inconsistency I both censured indulgences as his im-

A subtle syllogism, indeed

postures and yet praised as a good man the very author of the impostures, because a good man is the same thing as a good prince." And this, reader, is an eminent example of the Lutheran genius; that, having passed over all the king's reasons, he plucked off

An example of Luther's singular sagacity

one scrap for himself and distorted it for his own advantage so that he might more easily triumph. And yet, although he had distorted it completely, he is so stupid that he could not solve it.

He refutes Luther's nonsensical answer about the papacy. Chapter 4.

Let us come now, he says, to the other point about the papacy which I have de-

Luther's words

stroyed by forceful scriptural texts. But its defender, muter than a fish in reply to the scriptures, presumes with royal assurance that at his mere nod Luther will abandon the scriptures and accede to his lies. But he proves the papacy in this manner: "It must be so because I have heard that even India subjects itself to the Roman pontiff. Likewise Greece. Likewise Saint Jerome acknowl-

How completely unashamed of lying is the scoundrel

edges the Roman church as his mother." What will Luther dare to say here against such singular and such Thomistic arguments?

See Luther is everywhere like himself, reader; namely, a wicked scoundrel and a shameless liar. For although there are still books from which his deceitfulness is convicted, nevertheless, as though men were

essent caeci: audet scurra uanissimus ea dicere: quae nemo nescit
eum improbe stulteque mentiri. Quod quo tibi faciam clarius: ipsa
regis uerba, quatenus ad hanc rem faciunt: adiungam.

"QVIS NON hic quoque, nisi qui
Verba regis. Quam hoc sit   maliciam norit: miretur inconstantiam?
5   *probabile considera lector*
Nam prius negauerat papatum esse diuini
iuris: sed humani iuris esse concesserat. Nunc uero secum dissidens,
neutrius iuris esse confirmat: sed pontificem sibi mera ui sumpsisse,
atque usurpasse tyrannidem. Sentiebat ergo pridem, humano saltem
10 concensu, propter bonum publicum, Romano pontifici, super ecclesiam catholicam, delatam esse potestatem. Idque usqueadeo sentiebat:
ut Boemorum quoque schisma detestaretur, pronuncians eos peccare
damnabiliter: quicunque papae non obtemperarent. Haec cum haud
ita pridem scripserit: nunc [S₂] in idem, quod tunc detestabatur:
15 incidit. Quin istud quoque similis est constantiae: quod quum in
concione quadam ad populum, excommunicationem doceat esse
medicinam: et obedienter patienterque ferendam. Paulo post excommunicatus ipse, idque meritissimo iure, sententiam tamen tam
impotenter tulit: ut rabie quadam furibun-
Hiccine bonus uir sit, qui   dus, in contumelias, conuitia, blasphemias,
20   *sic agat?*
supra quam ullae possent aures ferre:
proruperit: sic, ut suo furore plane perspicuum fecerit, eos, qui
pelluntur e gremio matris ecclesiae: statim furijs corripi, atque agitari
demonibus. Sed istud rogo, qui illa tam nuper uidit: unde nunc
25 subito uidet, nihil se tunc uidisse? Quos nouos oculos induit? An
acutiore cernit obtutu: postquam ad superbiam solitam, ira quoque
superuenit, et odium: et longius uidelicet prospicit, usus tam prae-
claris conspicilijs? NON tam iniurius ero pontifici: ut anxie ac
solicite, de eius iure disceptem: tanquam res haberetur pro dubia:
30   satis est ad praesens negocium: quod
Lutherum sibi fidem cupiditate   inimicus eius ita furore prouehitur: ut sibi
derogare sua
fidem deroget ipse: ac dilucide se ostendat
prae malitia, neque constare secum, neque uidere quid dicat.

---

4 *gloss* regis.] Regis. *L*, regis *BR*   30 *gloss om. L*

completely blind, the most deceitful buffoon dares to say things in which everyone knows he lies wickedly and foolishly. That I may make this clearer to you, I shall add the very words of the king insofar as they deal with this matter.

"Who would not here also marvel at his inconsistency, unless he knew his malice? *The king's words. Consider how credible this is, reader* For earlier he had denied that the papacy is a matter of divine law but had conceded that it is a matter of human law. But now, contradicting himself, he affirms that it is of neither law, but that the pontiff has by sheer force assumed and usurped despotic power. He formerly thought, therefore, that the Roman pontiff was given power over the catholic church at least by human consent for the sake of the common good. And he was so convinced of this that he even denounced the schism of the Bohemians, declaring that whoever did not obey the pope sinned damnably. Although he wrote this such a short time ago, he has now fallen into the same error which he then denounced. Indeed, the following instance shows a similar consistency: although he taught the people in a certain sermon that excommunication is a medicine and should be borne obediently and patiently, yet when he himself was shortly after excommunicated, and that for a very just reason, he bore the sentence with so little restraint that, raging with a kind of madness, he broke out into worse revilings, railings, blasphemies than any ears could endure, *Can this be a good man who acts thus?* so that he made it quite clear by his raving that those who are driven from the bosom of their mother church are immediately seized by furies and tormented by demons. But I ask this: how does he who so recently saw those things now suddenly see that he then saw nothing? What new eyes has he taken on? Or does he perceive things with a keener vision now that anger and hatred have been added to his usual pride, and does he indeed have longer range vision using such excellent spectacles?

"I will not be so unjust to the pontiff as to debate anxiously and punctiliously about his right, as though the matter were considered doubtful; it is enough for the task at hand that his enemy is so carried away by raging madness that he detracts from his own trustworthiness and shows *That Luther by his vehemence detracts from his own trustworthiness* clearly that because of his malice he is neither consistent with himself nor

Nam negare non potest: quin omnis ecclesia fidelium, sacrosanctam
sedem Romanam uelut matrem primatemque cognoscat, ac uene-
retur: quaecunque saltem neque locorum distantia, neque periculis
interiacentibus prohibetur accessu. Quamquam si uera dicunt: qui ex
5 India quoque ueniunt huc: Indi etiam ipsi tot terrarum, tot marium,
tot solitudinum, plagis disiuncti, Romano tamen se pontifici sub-
mittunt. Ergo si tantam ac tam late fusam potestatem, neque dei iussu
pontifex, neque hominum uoluntate conse[S₂v]cutus est: sed sua sibi

ui uendicauit: dicat uelim Lutherus:
Age tu Formio
10 quando in tantae ditionis irruperit posses-
sionem. Non potest obscurum esse initium tam immensae potentiae:
praesertim si intra memoriam hominum nata sit. Quod si rem dixerit
unam fortassis, aut duas aetates superare: in memoriam rem nobis
redigat ex historijs. Alioqui, si tam uetusta sit: ut rei etiam tantae
15 obliterata sit origo: legibus omnibus cautum esse nouit: ut cuius ius
omnem hominum memoriam ita supergreditur: ut sciri non possit:
cuiusmodi habuerit initium: censeatur habuisse legitimum: uetitum

esse constat, omnium consensu gentium:
Constat autem, at Lutherus
contemnit
ne, quae diu manserunt immota: mouean-
20 tur. Certe si quis rerum gestarum monu-
menta reuoluat: inueniet iam olim, protinus post pacatum orbem,
plerasque omnes christiani orbis ecclesias, obtemperasse Romanae.
Quin Graeciam ipsam, quamquam ad ipsos commigrasset imperium:
reperiemus tamen: quod ad ecclesiae primatum pertinebat: praeter-
25 quam dum schismate laborabat, ecclesiae Romanae cessisse. Beatus
uero Hieronymus quantum Romanae sedi censeat deferendum: uel
inde luculenter ostendit: quod quum romanus ipse non esset: tamen
aperte fatetur, sibi satis esse: si suam fidem, quibusuis improbantibus

alijs, comprobaret papa Romanus. Cui
Audin haec Luthere?
30 cum tam impudenter Lutherus pro-
nunciet, idque contra suam pridem sententiam, nihil omnino iuris in
ecclesiam catholicam, ne humano quidem iure competere: sed
papam mera ui, meram occupasse tyrannidem: uehementer admiror:
quod tam faciles, aut tam stupidos speret esse lectores: ut sacerdotem

18 *gloss om.* L

aware of what he is saying. For he cannot deny that every church of
the faithful recognizes and venerates the holy see of Rome as mother
and primate, at least wherever approach to her is not hindered either
by distance of place or by the dangers of the way, although if those
who come here even from India are telling the truth, the Indians also,   5
separated by such expanses of land, sea and desert, yet submit
themselves to the Roman pontiff.

"Therefore, if the pontiff has acquired such great and such wide-
spread power neither by the order of God nor by the will of man but
has claimed it for himself by force, I wish   10
Luther would tell me when the pontiff   *Come on, Phormio*
usurped such great dominion. The beginning of such boundless power
cannot be obscure, especially if it has risen within the memory of
men. But if he says that the matter perchance antedates one or two
generations, then let him recall the matter to our memory from   15
historical writings. Otherwise, if the matter is so ancient that even the
origin of such an important matter has been obliterated, he knows
that all laws provide that one whose right extends back so far beyond
the entire memory of mankind that the nature of its beginning
cannot be known is judged to have held it legally; everyone knows   20
that it is forbidden by the agreement of all
nations to change what has remained for   *Although it is well known,*
such a long time unchanged.   *Luther scorns it*

"Certainly, if anyone reads the records of history he will find that
long ago, just after peace was established in the world, almost all the 25
churches of the Christian world obeyed the Roman church. In fact,
although the imperial power passed to the Greeks, yet we will find
that in what pertained to the primacy of the church, except for the
time that Greece labored under schism, it submitted to the Roman
church. Indeed, blessed Jerome clearly showed how much he thought   30
men should defer to the Roman See by openly confessing, though he
was not himself a Roman, that whoever else disapproved of his faith
it was enough for him if the pope of Rome
approved of it.   *Do you hear this, Luther?*

"When Luther so shamelessly declares, and that contrary to his   35
own former opinion, that the pope possesses no right at all over the
catholic church, not even by human law, but that the pope has by
sheer force seized sheer despotic power, I am very much amazed that
he would hope his readers are so gullible or so stupid as to believe

credant inermem, solum, nullo [S₃] septum satellitio (qualem necesse
est eum fuisse, priusquam eo potiretur: quod eum Lutherus ait
inuasisse) uel in spem uenire unquam potuisse: ut nullo iure fultus,
nullo fretus titulo, in tot ubique pares episcopos, apud tam diuersas,
5   tam procul disiectas gentes, tantum obtineret imperium: ne dum ut
credat populos omnes quisquam, urbes, regna, prouincias, suarum
rerum, libertatis, iuris, fuisse tam prodigos: ut externo sacerdoti, cui
nil deberent: tantum in sese potestatis darent: quantum ipse uix
esset ausus optare. Sed quid refert: quid in hac re Lutherus sentiat:
10 qui prae ira atque inuidia, non sentit ipse: quid sentiat."

VIDES hic regem lector, non id agere: quod mentitur iste: ut
tanquam res esset dubia: probet papatum. Imo ex professo, abstinere
ab ea quaestione, ne uideatur habere potestatem pontificis pro
controuersa. Tantummodo reprehendit insanam leuitatem nebulonis:
15 qui quod paulo ante sic asseruerat esse legittimum: ut damnabiliter
eos peccare fateretur: quicunque contradicerent: paulo post contra-

Et merito quidem   dixit ipse: atque sua ipsius sententia in
eandem damnationem incidit: affirmans
papatum, nullo iure quicquam habere ponderis: neque aliud esse
20 quicquam, nisi meram tyrannidem: quam pontifex inuadens per uim
atque iniuriam occuparit. Quod quam uerisimile sit: pulcherrime
tetigit princeps. Quaesiuit enim, quando, quibus inuaserit uiribus:
quam uerisimile sit, tot nationes adduci potuisse: ut tantum in se
iuris externo sacerdoti, nullo iure coacti concederent. Nam planum
25 esse omnes gentes populi christiani, qui locorum distantia non pro-
hibentur: neque ui distinentur, a[S₃v]gnoscere papam Romanum,

Non enim potuit   pro generali uicario Christi. Ad haec
omnia, nihil respondet Lutherus. Quid
enim posset in tam aperta re: sed quod rex adiecit ex habundanti, de
30 Graecia et India: id uero uir disertus arripit auide: in quod caninam
facundiam suam exerceat.

Lutheri uerba   Respondeo, inquit, si ideo stabit papatus:
quia rex Angliae audiuit, Indiam et
Graeciam sese subdidisse, eadem ratione non stabit. quia Lutherus

that a priest, unarmed, alone, defended by no bodyguard—such as he
must necessarily have been before gaining possession of the power
which Luther says he usurped—could ever have even hoped that,
supported by no right, relying on no claim, he would secure such
great dominion over so many fellow bishops everywhere, among such   5
diverse, such widely scattered nations; to say nothing of anyone's
believing that all nations, cities, kingdoms, provinces were so
prodigal of their possessions, liberty, rights, that they would give to a
foreign priest to whom they owed nothing such extensive power over
themselves as he himself would hardly have dared to desire. But what   10
difference does it make what Luther's idea is in this matter, when
through anger and envy he himself has no idea as to what his idea is?"

You see here, reader, that the king does not aim, as this fellow
falsely claims, to prove the papacy, as though it were a doubtful
matter. Rather he professedly refrains from that question, lest he seem   15
to consider the power of the pontiff a matter of controversy. He only
censures the senseless caprice of the scoundrel who himself a little later
resisted what he had shortly before declared to be so legitimate that he
admitted that whoever resisted it sinned damnably, and who by his
own judgment fell into that same damna-   *And indeed deservedly*   20
tion, declaring that the papacy has no
rightful authority at all and that it is nothing else at all but sheer despotic power which the usurping pontiff has seized by force and injustice. How likely this assertion is the prince has discussed excellently.
For he asked when, by what forces, the pontiff usurped power; how   25
likely was it that so many nations could have been persuaded,
though compelled by no obligation, to yield so much right over
themselves to a foreign priest. For it is clear that all nations of the
Christian people who are not prevented by distance of place nor
hindered by force do acknowledge the Roman pope as the universal   30
vicar of Christ. To all these things Luther
answers nothing. What could he answer in   *For he could not*
such an evident matter? But what the king added over and above
about Greece and India, that indeed the shrewd fellow seizes on
greedily to exercise against it his snarling eloquence.   35

I answer, he says, if the papacy will stand
firm because the king of England has   *Luther's words*
heard that India and Greece have subjected themselves to it, by the

Et hic mentiris

certus est, neque Indiam, neque Graeciam, sub romano pontifice unquam fuisse,
aut esse uoluisse.

PRIMVM si quis ab hoc reuerendo fratre quaereret: quomodo
5 certus sit, neque Indiam, neque Graeciam, sub romano pontifice
unquam fuisse: aut esse uoluisse: Respondebit, sat scio, nobis, eadem

Eadem nimirum

certitudine se certum esse: qua certus est,
ut scribit, dogmata sua se habere de caelo.
Ergo, si ideo certus est, reuerendus pater se uerum dicere: quia
10 certus est, dogmata sua se habere de caelo: Ego ideo certus sum,
reuerendum patrem falso mentiri: quia certus sum, dogmata illum

Hoc uerisimilius

sua habere de tartaro. Et haec est forma,
formalis consequentiae, secundum regulam patris Lutheri, fratris extra regulam beati Augustini. Quam
15 regulam Augustini, et diui Benedicti, et item dominici, ac Francisci,
receperunt et Indi et Graeci, approbatam uidelicet, authoritate sedis
Romanae. Per quod, et alia multa ex annalibus, et synodis, et
Graecorum patrum commentarijs, et epistolis euidenter constare
posset, utriusque gentis ecclesiam, agnouisse sedis Romanae prae
20 cellentiam. Si aut hoc probandum sibi sumpsisset rex: aut nobis aliud
esset propositum: quam ut ostendamus: quam stolide Lutherus respondeat regi. Quod si ideo negat papatum Lutherus: quia id quod
etiam [S₄] rex fatetur, longius absunt Indi: quam ut possint, ob
quoduis negociolum Romam currere: negabit humano generi domi
25 nium tributum, in caetera animalia: quod in illis desertis degunt
multa: quae hominibus sunt inaccessa. Quod si Graeci perpetuo
repugnassent ecclesiae Romanae: tamen ne sic quidem quicquam

At hoc non concedet turca,
inquiet Lutherus

sustulisset argumentum regis: cuius robur
consistit consensu ecclesiae catholicae:
30 quae plane fuisset in reliquis nationibus:
etiam si perpetuo fecisset Graecia: quod nunc faciunt quaedam rura
Boemica. Nisi neget Lutherus Carolum esse regem, totius Hispaniae:
propterea quod aliquot oppida rebellarunt. Iam ex India, et Graecia,
tandem peruenit ad Hieronymum.

---

17 Romanae] Roma *L*   21 quam ut ostendamus] *corr. err. L,* quam *om. BR*   28 *gloss*
om. L

same reasoning it will not stand firm because Luther is certain that
neither India nor Greece has ever been
or wanted to be under the Roman   *And here you lie*
pontiff.

First of all, if anyone were to ask of this reverend friar how he is   5
certain that neither India nor Greece has ever been or wanted to be
under the Roman pontiff, he will answer us, I am quite sure, that
he is certain with the same certainty with
which he is certain, as he writes, that he has   *The same, to be sure*
his teachings from heaven. Therefore, if the reverend father is certain   10
that he speaks the truth because he is certain that he has his teachings
from heaven, I am certain that the reverend father lies falsely because
I am certain that he has his teachings from
Tartarus. And this is the form of a formal   *This is more likely*
conclusion according to the rule of Father Luther, friar outside the   15
rule of blessed Augustine. This rule of Augustine and that of Saint
Benedict, and likewise of Dominic and of Francis both Indians and
Greeks have accepted, approved of course by the authority of the
Roman see. Through this argument and many others from the annals
and synods and commentaries and epistles of the Greek fathers it   20
could be clearly established that the church of both nations acknowledged the pre-eminence of the Roman see, had the king undertaken
to prove this, or had we intended anything other than to show how
stupidly Luther answers the king.

But if Luther denies the papacy because, as the king admits, the   25
Indians are too far away to be able to run to Rome for any little
business whatever, he will deny the dominion attributed to the human
race over other animals because in those wastelands there live many
which are inaccessible to men. But if the Greeks had continually
resisted the Roman church, nevertheless not even so would the   30
argument of the king have suffered at all,
since its strength rests in the agreement of   *But the Turk will not grant*
the catholic church which would clearly   *this, Luther will say*
have existed in the rest of the nations even if Greece had constantly
done what certain Bohemian backwoodsmen are now doing. Unless   35
Luther denies that Charles is king of all Spain because several towns
have revolted. Then, from India and Greece he finally arrives at
Jerome.

Verba Lutheri. Vbi est acumen tuum domine frater?

Deinde, inquit, gloriosus dominus rex, pro suo more, satis fortiter mentitur: dum Hieronymum facit assertorem papatus, cum uir ille ecclesiam Romanam, suam dumtaxat, non nobis matrem appellasset.

QVAESO lector iudica, quam syncere pater potator hunc locum Hieronymi tractet: cum ille dicat, satis esse sibi, si suam fidem comprobaret papa Romanus: nimirum aperte significans, non dubitandum esse illum recte sentire de fide, qui cum illa sede consentiat: quo quid potuisset dicere magnificentius? istud adeo dissimulat pater

Conatur sed frustra

potator Lutherus: ut etiam tenebras lectori conetur offundere: et animos hominum uerbis alio, ne quid recordentur abducere. Sed istud est impudentissimum: quod quum papatum, nec humano saltem consensu robur accepisse contendat, sed meram uim esse pontificis, occupantis tyrannidem: insectatur principem scommatis: quod amentiam eius taxans ac intemperantiam, ad potentes (ut ait) scripturas, qui[S₄v]bus ipse uidelicet rem probauerit: magis mutus quam piscis fuerit. Quis non hunc impudentem nebulonem rideat? quando nemo nesciat, tantum abesse: ut aut scripturis, aut ratione probarit istud: ut ne conatus id quidem unquam sit: sed iactarit dumtaxat furiosus per

Tum eiectum ab ecclesia dei corripuit diabolus

conuitium: atque nec id quidem ante fecerit: quam excommunicatus e coetu fidelium, correptus a coetu daemonum, ira atque inuidia frendens, nec amplius sui potens, sibi fidem sustulit.

9 quo] *corr. err. L,* quod *BR*   10 magnificentius?] *corr. err. L,* magnificentius: *BR*
11 *gloss* Conatur] conatur *BR, gloss om. L*   13 ne quid] *corr. err. L,* ne quod *BR*
22 *gloss om. L*

Next, he says, the pompous lord king, according to his custom, lies quite boldly when he makes Jerome a defender of the *Luther's words. Where is your sagacity, honored brother?* papacy whereas that illustrious man called the Roman church only his own mother, not ours.

Please judge, reader, how honestly Father Tosspot handles this passage from Jerome; when that illustrious man says that it is enough for him if the Roman pope approved his faith, without doubt indicating clearly that no one must be doubted to have the right judgment about the faith who agrees with that see, what could he have said more grandly than this? This fact Father Tosspot Luther conceals precisely that he may try to envelop his reader also in darkness and by his *He tries, but in vain* words lead the minds of men elsewhere so that they will not remember anything. But most shameless is the fact that when he argues that the papacy has not received its power even by human agreement but that it is the sheer force of the pontiff usurping despotic power, he assails the prince with taunts, saying that in censuring his madness and insolence the king was muter than a fish in regard to the forceful scriptures, as he calls them, with which he himself has of course proved the matter. Who would not ridicule this shameless rascal, when everyone knows he is so far from having proved his case either by scriptures or by reasoning that he has never even tried to do so but has only boasted ragingly with railing; nor did he do so even before the time when, excommunicated from the assembly of the faithful, seized on by an *Then the devil seized him, cast out of the church* assembly of demons, gnashing his teeth with rage and hatred, and no longer master of himself, he destroyed faith in himself?

De communicatione laicorum, sub utraque specie,
profert ea: quae scripsit rex: et eadem comparat
in genere, cum his: quae scribit
Lutherus. Cap. V.

5   POSTQVAM dimidium libelli sui, alijs consumpsit nugis: incipit
homo nugacissimus, nugari tandem, in ipsis sacramentis: et post
deliramentorum et insanae scurrilitatis abyssum, producit aciem
argutiarum, si quis ipsi credat, inuictam.

Verba Lutheri   Age, inquit, reuelemus sceleratam hanc
10   et regiam nequitiam in prima tyrannide,
scilicet una parte sacramenti. Ego, alteram partem esse impie
Christiano populo ablatam, septem argumentis probaui: quae et tum
Sic tibi uisus es   me uincebant: nunc autem et trium-
                           phant: postquam assertor papistarum
15   gloriosissimus, regia fortitudine illa transit intacta.

AVDIN lector, Thrasonis huius magnifica uerba: et celebres ab se
sibi decretos, atque adornatos triumphos? ut argumenta sua septem,
uelut reformidantem, regem reliquisse iactat intacta? Nos ergo lector,
argumenta ista [T₁] Lutheri strenua statim producemus tibi, eadem-
20   que misere (ut uidebis) affecta. Sed interim, quia uideri uult, non
ausum ea regem tangere: nos tibi primum e regis libro, quaedam
recensebimus: quibus abs te perpensis, fiet perspicuum: quum
Lutheri septem illos duces sigillatim uidebis, a me produci mortuos,
eos olim omnes, inuictum principem uno semel ictu, mactasse.
25   Princeps igitur hac de re scribit, hunc in modum.

Verba regis   "INTERIM uero, libet excutere: quam
                           fraudulenter per speciem fauoris in laicos,
conetur eorum odium concitare in sacerdotes. Nam quum decreuisset,
ecclesiae fidem suspectam reddere: ne quid ponderis eius haberet
30   authoritas: atque ita facta uia, praecipua quaeque Christianae
religionis euertere: ab ea re sumpsit initium: cui populum sperabat
alacriter applausurum. Tetigit enim uetus ulcus: quo pridem ulcerata

---

13 *gloss om. L*   31 re sumpsit] *L*, resumpsit *BR*

Concerning the communion of the laity under both kinds he presents those arguments which the king has written and compares them as to their nature with those which Luther writes. Chapter 5.

After expending half his little book on other trifles, this arch-trifler finally begins to trifle about the sacraments themselves, and after a bottomless pit of ranting and mad buffoonery he leads out a line of subtleties which, if one would believe him, are invincible.

Come, he says, let us expose this criminal and royal wickedness in its foremost tyranny; that is, in the one part of the sacrament. That the other part has been impiously taken away from the Christian people I have proved by seven arguments which even then convinced me, but now also they triumph, when the most boastful defender of the papists with royal courage passes them over without touching them.

Luther's words

So it seemed to you

Do you hear, reader, the pompous words of this Thraso and the solemn and splendid triumphs decreed by himself for himself as he boasts that the king, as though in awe of his seven arguments, has left them untouched? We will therefore immediately lead out for you, reader, these vigorous and at the same time, as you shall see, wretchedly weak arguments of Luther. But meanwhile, because he wishes it to appear that the king has not dared to touch them, we will first recall to your mind certain arguments from the king's book; once you have considered them carefully, it will become clear when you shall see those seven leaders of Luther's set out by me one by one, dead, that the invincible prince has long ago slaughtered all of them with one blow. The prince, then, writes of this matter as follows.

"But meanwhile, I should like to examine how deceitfully, under pretext of favoring the laity, he tries to excite their hatred against the priests. For when he had determined to render the trustworthiness of the church suspect, so that her authority would not have any weight, and with the way thus opened, to destroy all the most important elements of the Christian religion, he took his start from a subject which he hoped the people would eagerly applaud. For he touched the old wound

The king's words

est Boemia: quod laici sub utraque specie non recipiant eucharistiam. Eam rem quum prius ita tractasset: ut dumtaxat diceret, recte facturum pontificem: si curaret, communi consilio statuendum: ut sub utraque specie laici communicarent: Post, ubi nescio quis, illud
5　ei negauit: non contentus in eo manere: quod dixerat: sic profecit in peius: ut totum clerum condemnet impietatis: quod istud non faciant, non expectato concilio. Ego de primo non disputo. Caeterum, etiam si causas non uiderem: cur non decernat ecclesia: ut utraque species ministretur laicis: tamen dubitare non possem: quin sint idoneae:
10　quae et olim fecerunt: ut id omitteretur: et nunc quoque faciant: ne redintegretur. Nec plane assentior, totum clerum, per tot [T₁v] secula fuisse tam stolidum: ut se obstrinxerit aeterno supplicio, propter eam rem: unde nihil reportaret commodi temporalis: imo uero, quam nihil sit talis periculi: uel hoc euidenter ostendit: quod eos, qui non
15　tantum istud fecerunt: uerum etiam qui scripserunt esse faciendum: deus non modo suscepit in caelum: uerum etiam uoluit esse uenerandos in terris, et ab hominibus honorari: a quibus honoratur ipse. Inter quos fuit (ut de alijs interim taceam) uir eruditissimus, et idem sanctissimus, diuus Thomas Aquinas: quem ideo libentius comme-
20　moro: quoniam eius uiri sanctitatem, Lutheri ferre non potest impietas: sed quem omnes Christiani uenerantur: pollutis labijs ubique blasphemat. Quanquam sunt permulti: qui etiamsi pro sanctis recepti non sunt: tamen siue doctrina, siue pietate spectentur: tales sunt: ut Lutherus eis comparari non possit: qui hac in re contrarium
25　Luthero sentiunt. Inter quos sunt magister Sententiarum, et Nicholaus de Lira, et complures alij: quorum cuilibet magis expedit christianos omnes, quam Luthero credere. At uide quaeso, quam uacillat: ac sibi repugnat Lutherus: uno loco dicit: Christum in coena omnibus omnino fidelibus, non permittendo, sed praecipiendo
30　dixisse: Bibite ex eo omnes. Postea uero, timens ne laicos, quibus in sacerdotum odium adulatur: offenderet: haec uerba subiungit. Non quod peccent in Christum: qui una specie utuntur: quum Christus

with which Bohemia was long ago wounded: that the laity do not
receive the eucharist under both forms. Although he had earlier
treated this matter in such a way as to say only that the pope would
do well to have a general council decree that the laity might communicate under both forms, later when someone or other refused him   5
that, not being content to abide by what he had said, he proceeded
to the worse point of accusing the entire clergy of impiety because they did not carry out his suggestion without waiting for a
council.

"I do not argue about his first point. But even if I did not see the   10
reasons why the church does not ordain that both forms should be
administered to the laity, yet I could have no doubt that there are
sound reasons which once caused this practice to be dropped and now
also cause it not to be renewed. And I certainly do not agree that the
entire clergy through so many ages has been so senseless as to incur   15
eternal punishment because of a practice from which it would gain
no temporal advantage. On the contrary, in fact, that there is no
danger of this being the case is clearly shown by the fact that God has
not only received into heaven both those who followed this practice
and also those who wrote that it should be followed, but has also   20
wished them to be venerated on earth and to be honored by the men
by whom He Himself is honored. Among these men—to say nothing
meanwhile of others—there was that most learned and also most holy
man, Saint Thomas Aquinas, whom I mention the more readily
because the impiety of Luther cannot bear the sanctity of this man,   25
but at every opportunity he blasphemes with his polluted lips one
whom all Christians venerate. There are very many men, however,
who disagree with Luther on this point; even if these men are not
accepted as saints, nevertheless, whether they are considered in their
learning or in their piety, they are the kind of men with whom Luther   30
cannot be compared. Among them there are the Master of the
Sentences, and Nicholas of Lyra, and many others, any one of whom
it is more fitting that all Christians believe than that they believe
Luther. But please observe how Luther vacillates and contradicts
himself: in one place he says that Christ at the supper said to every   35
single one of the faithful, not by way of permission but by way of
command, 'All of you drink of this.' But afterwards, fearing to offend
the laity whom he flatters into hatred of the priests, he adds these
words: 'Not that they would sin against Christ who receive one form,

non praeceperit ulla uti: sed arbitrio cuiuslibet reliquerit: dicens:
Quotiescunque haec feceritis: in mei memoriam facietis: Sed quod
illi peccant: qui hoc arbitrio uolentibus uti, prohibent utramque dari.
Cul[T₂]pa non est in laicis, sed in sacerdotibus. Videtis aperte, quod
5 primo dixit esse praeceptum: hic dicit non esse praeceptum: sed
cuiuslibet arbitrio relictum. Quid opus est ergo, nos illi contradicere:
qui sibi toties contradicit ipse? Et tamen quum dixit omnia: laicos
non satis defendit: si quis rem urgeret: et in sacerdotibus, quos tam
attrociter accusat: nihil probat esse peccati. Nam in eo dicit totum
10 esse peccatum: quod sacerdotes alterius speciei laicis inuitis adime-
rent libertatem. Hic igitur, si quis eum perconctetur: qui sciat, istum
ritum inoleuisse, renitente populo: non potest (opinor) docere. Cur
ergo totum condemnat clerum: quod laicis inuitis, ademerit suum ius:
quum id inuitis esse factum, nullo possit documento probare? Quanto
15 fuit aequius: si, nisi uolentibus illis, recte nequiuit institui pronunciare, pro tot saeculorum consuetudine, plebis interuenisse consensum.
Ego certe, qui uideo, quas res a plebe clerus obtinere non potest: ne
tantum quidem, quin ferme, sub ipso altari suorum condant cadauera: non facile credo, populum fuisse passurum: ut inuiti per
20 contumeliam, in tanta re, ab ulla iuris sui parte pellerentur, sed causis
aliquot idoneis, e laicorum uoluntate constitutum. At istud miror,
tam uehementer indignari Lutherum, laicis ademptam alteram, quum
illum nihil permoueat: quod utraque species adimatur infantibus:

Infantes olim communicasse

nam illos olim communicasse, nec ipse
25   negare potest. Qui mos si recte fuit omissus:
quamquam Christus dicat: Bibite ex hoc omnes: Nec quisquam dubi-
tat: quin causae fuerunt magnae: etiam si nunc earum nemo
meminisset: cur non etiam cogitemus, [T₂v] bonis iustisque rationibus, quantumuis nunc ignoratis, abolitam esse consuetudinem: qua

12 renitente] retinente *L*

seeing that Christ did not command the use of any form but left the
matter to the free choice of each individual, saying, "As often as you
do these things you shall do them in remembrance of me"; but that
they do sin who refuse to give both forms to those who wish to
exercise this freedom of choice. The fault is not in the laity but in the   5
priests.' You see clearly that first he said it was commanded; here he
says it was not commanded but left to the free choice of each individual. What need is there for us to contradict him, then, since he
so often contradicts himself?

"And yet when he has said everything, he does not sufficiently   10
defend the laity, should anyone press the matter, and he does not
prove that there is any sin in the priests whom he so bitterly reproaches. For he says that the whole sin consists in the fact that the
priests, against the wishes of the laity, took away from the laity the
freedom of the second form. If anyone, then, should here inquire of   15
the fellow how he knows that this custom has developed despite the
resistance of the people, I do not think he can tell. Why, then, does
he accuse the whole clergy of taking the laity's own right away from
them against their wishes, when he cannot prove by any evidence
that this was done against their wishes? How much more reasonable   20
it would have been, if no practice could lawfully be established except
by the will of the laity, to declare that the agreement of the people
was given for such an age-old custom.

"Indeed, when I see what things the clergy are unable to secure
from the people, not even so much as to prevent them from burying   25
their dead almost under the very altar, I do not easily believe that the
people would have permitted themselves to be unwillingly and
insultingly deprived of any part of their own right in such an important matter, but that this practice was established for some suitable
reasons and according to the will of the laity.   30

"But I am surprised that Luther is so fiercely indignant that the
one form was taken from the laity, since he is not at all disturbed that
both forms are withheld from infants, for
that they at one time received communion   *That infants once received*
communion
he himself cannot deny. If this custom was   35
rightfully dropped, although Christ says, 'All of you drink of this,'
and if no one doubts that there were serious reasons for dropping it,
even if no one now remembers them, why may we not also think that
for good and just reasons, though now unknown, the custom was

laici olim, nec id fortasse diu, sub utraque specie solebant recipere
sacramentum? Praeterea si eam rem, ad exactam euangelicae
narrationis formam reuocet: neque quicquam prorsus permittit
ecclesiae: cur eucharistiam non iubet semper in coena recipi, imo
5   uero post coenam? Denique non minus incommodi fuerit, in hoc
sacramento facere: si quid fecisse non debeas: quam si quid non
facias: quod fecisse debueras. Ergo si totius ecclesiae consuetudo,
rectum non facit: ut in laicis omittatur species uini: qua ratione
aquam in uinum audet Lutherus infundere? Neque enim tam
10   audacem puto: ut sine aqua consecret: quam tamen ut admisceret,
neque exemplum habet ex coena dominica, neque ex apostoli
traditione compertum: sed sola ecclesiae consuetudine didicit: cui si
putat hac in parte parendum: cur eam in altera tam arroganter
oppugnat? Qua de re, quicquid Lutherus obgannit: ego certe tutius
15   opinor credere, laicos recte sub altera tantum specie communicatos,
quam per tot secula totum clerum (quod iste disputat) hac una de
causa fuisse damnatum. Nam omnes appellat impios, et tales: ut in
crimen inciderint laesae maiestatis euangelicae. Quod si utri sint
(inquit) haeretici et schismatici nominandi, non Boemi, non Graeci:
20   quia euangelijs nituntur: sed uos Romani estis haeretici, et impij
schismatici: qui solo figmento praesumitis contra euidentes dei
scripturas. Si Lutherus nihil admittit aliud, quam euidentes dei
scripturas: cur non iubet eucharistiam (uti dixi) sumi a coenantibus?
Nam sic factum a Christo, scriptura [T₃] commemorat. Quanto
25   melius crederet Lutherus, non humano figmento, sed eodem authore
deo, factum in ecclesia: ne laici sub utraque specie reciperent eucharistiam: quo authore factum est: ut reciperetur a ieiunis? Placuit, ut
ait beatus Augustinus, spiritui sancto: ut corpus domini, quod post
alios cibos ab apostolis in coena receptum est: ante alios cibos, a
30   ieiunis reciperetur in ecclesia. Videtur ergo uerisimile: quod spiritus
sanctus, qui Christi regit ecclesiam: sicut eucharistiae sacramentum

abolished by which the laity at one time, and that perchance not for long, used to receive the sacrament under both forms?

"Besides, if he restores that practice to the precise form of the gospel account and leaves nothing at all to the church, why does he not order that the eucharist always be received at supper, or rather, after 5 supper?

"Finally, it is no less detrimental, where this sacrament is concerned, to do something you should not have done than not to do something you should have done. Therefore, if the whole church acts wrongly in its custom of withholding the form of wine among the 10 laity, by what reason does Luther dare to pour water into the wine? For I think he is not so bold as to consecrate without water; yet he neither has a precedent from the Lord's supper for mingling water with the wine nor has he discovered this from what the apostle taught; rather he has learned it only from the custom of the church. 15 If he thinks she must be obeyed in this matter, why does he so arrogantly oppose her in the other?

"Consequently, no matter what Luther snarls on this point, I certainly think it is safer to believe that the laity are rightly communicated under only one form than that the entire clergy through- 20 out so many ages has, as he argues, been damned for this reason alone. For he calls them all impious and such men as have fallen into the crime of treason against the gospel. But if either side, he says, must be called heretics and schismatics, it is not the Bohemians, not the Greeks, since they rely on the gospels, but you Romans are heretics 25 and impious schismatics who presume on a fabrication alone, contrary to the evident scriptures of God.

"If Luther admits nothing else than evident scriptures of God, why does he not, as I said, order the eucharist to be received by men at supper? For scripture records that this was done by Christ. How much 30 better for Luther to believe that the church's practice of not giving the laity communion under both forms was not introduced by human invention but by the same divine authority which introduced the practice of receiving communion fasting. It pleased the Holy Spirit, as blessed Augustine says, that the body of the Lord which was 35 received by the apostles at supper, after other food, should be received in the church by men fasting, before other food. Therefore, it seems probable that as the Holy Spirit who governs the church of Christ has caused the sacrament of the eucharist to be received by men

mutauit a coenantibus ad ieiunos: ita laicos, ab utraque specie
deduxit in alteram. Nam qui alterum mutare potuit: cur non alterare
potuerit et alterum?"

VIDES charissime lector, hac in parte, quam modeste se gerat
5 princeps, aduersus nebulonis istius immodestiam. Nam et modice
reprehendit eius maliciam, et in una atque eadem re, duplicem
inconstantiam, semper se in deteriora mutantem. Arguit eius impietatem: qui totam tot seculorum damnet ecclesiam: et id dicat

Rem dignam fustuario
factum malicia sacerdotum: quod factum
10 est bonitate spiritus sancti. Nam si ste-
tisset in eo Lutherus: ut diceret ecclesiam benefacturam: si communi consilio, laicis utramque speciem permitteret: rex ea de re se
disputaturum negat. Quamquam ego non dubito: quin istud, quod
per tot aetates iam factum est: dei consilio factum sit: id quod
15 luculenter ostendit rex: et nisi deo rursus idem placeat immutari:
non passurum alioqui ecclesiam, istud humano demutare consilio:
nec in sacramentis alio gubernari spiritu, quam sancto spiritu suo.
Sed rex modeste se negat hac de re disserturum. At quod iam dis-
cordiam Lu[T₃v]therus commouet: et hortatur: ut sua quisque
20 authoritate audeat, tot aetatum totius ecclesiae consensum contemnere: et Christianos omnes, per tot secula defunctos, mittit ad
inferos: quasi non spiritus dei sanctus gubernaret ecclesiam: sed
spiritus ille diaboli: qui per os Lutheri spurcissimum, sanctam
blasphemat ecclesiam, et ecclesiae sponsum Christum: id uero ferre
25 pius princeps non potuit: et tamen absque conuitijs et contumelijs
disputat, aduersum hominem conuitiantissimum, et omnibus
conuitijs et contumelijs dignissimum: atque ostendit, neque causam
esse: cur sacerdotes tollere uoluerint laicis alteram sacramenti
speciem, et animas suas perdere, propter id: unde nihil prorsus essent
30 lucraturi: neque laicos id unquam fuisse passuros: ut alteram speciem
inique praeriperent sacerdotes: quibus interdum aequa et iusta
petentibus, unde nec ipsi lucrifacerent clerici: neque perderent quicquam laici: populus tamen, uelut pro titulo sui iuris obsistit. Ostendit

11 benefacturam: si] benefacturam sit *L*   15 et nisi] *corr. err. L*, et *om. BR*; rursus] rursum
L   30 alteram speciem] *corr. err. L*, speciem *om. BR*   32–33 quicquam laici] *corr. err.*
L, laici *om. BR*

fasting instead of by men at supper, so He caused it to be received by the laity under one form instead of under both forms. Why could not He who was able to change the one practice also have been able to change the other?"

You see, my dear reader, how restrainedly the prince conducts himself in this passage against this scoundrel's lack of restraint. For he moderately reproaches both the fellow's malice and at one and the same time his deceitful inconsistency, always changing itself for the worse. He denounces the impiety of the fellow who condemns the whole church of so many ages and who says that a thing was done by the malice of priests which was done by the goodness of the Holy Spirit. For if *A matter deserving a deadly cudgelling* Luther had stood firm in his statement that the church would do well, through a general council, to allow both kinds to the laity, the king says that he himself was not ready to argue about that point. However, I do not doubt that this practice which has already been followed throughout so many ages has been followed by the counsel of God, as the king has clearly shown; and unless it should please God that the practice be changed again, He would not otherwise allow the church to change it for the worse by human counsel, nor in the matter of the sacraments to be governed by a spirit other than His own Holy Spirit. But the king modestly says that he would not discuss this matter, except that Luther now stirs up discord and exhorts each one to dare on his own authority to contemn the agreement of the whole church of so many ages, and he sends to hell all Christians, deceased for so many centuries, as if the church were not governed by the Holy Spirit of God but by that spirit of the devil who through the most filthy mouth of Luther blasphemes the holy church and Christ the spouse of the church; this indeed the pious prince was not able to bear; and yet without railing and reviling he argues against a man who rails beyond measure and who very justly deserves every sort of railing and reviling; and he shows that there was no reason why the priests wished to take away the second form of the sacrament from the laity and to destroy their own souls for the sake of something from which they would gain nothing at all; nor would the laity ever have permitted the priests wickedly to snatch the second form, for when the priests at times sought fair and just measures, from which neither the clergy themselves would derive any gain nor the laity lose anything, the people nevertheless resisted them

multa princeps: quae circa hoc sacramentum, iam multis seculis
ecclesia tota fidelium, ab exemplo Christi sacramentum instituentis,
euariat: quorum nullum Lutherus ante reprehenderat. Quaedam, ne
nunc quidem, quae tamen aut male fieri necesse sit, et damnabiliter:
5   aut fieri, quod plane uerum est, authore deo. Ostendit igitur princeps,
eius generis omnia consilio spiritus sancti, ecclesiam gubernantis esse
mutata. Aduersus hoc tam pium, tam uerum, ac modestum regis
responsum, improbus atque impius nebulo, conuitijs et stulticijs
insanit.

10   *Lutheri uerba*   Ego, inquit, alteram partem sacramenti,
                                              esse impie christiano populo ablatam,
              septem argumentis probaui. [T₄]

REX sufficienter ostendit, non ablatam per sacerdotes. Ergo si per
homines factum est: per ipsos factum est laicos. Atque ita Lutherus,
15   hanc impietatem a sacerdotibus, in quos cupit trudere, depellit homo
sapiens, in ipsos, quibus adulari studet, laicos. Et depellit inexcusabi-
liter, suo ipsius dogmate. Nam si uerum est: quod omnes laici sunt ita
sacerdotes: ut habeant aequalem potestatem, super quodcunque
sacramentum: Postquam ad hoc dumtaxat electi sunt, et elegi
20   poterunt per alios laicos (ut ait) Lutherus in sacramento ordinis, adeo
non defendit laicos, stolidissimus iste patronus: ut etiam uehementer
inuoluat damnatione: quod suae salutis incuria, neglexerint eligere
sibi sacerdotes: qui sibi ministrarent utramque speciem. Nisi laicos
dicat, hactenus ignorasse mysterium. Nunc uero, missum de caelo se:
25   qui tam sacrum dogma reuelaret hominibus: ut deus, qui solet
abscondere a sapientibus, et reuelare paruulis: iam contra credatur,
a paruulis abscondisse: quod reuelaret superbissimo nebuloni. An
ideo dicet, per sacerdotes ademptam laicis: quia de ea re cautum est in
concilijs? At si perpendas lector, ea ipsa concilia: facile uidebis hanc
30   rem, non ex illis natam esse concilijs: sed aduersus eos esse statutum:

6 consilio] *corr. err. L*, consilia *BR*   22 damnatione] *L*, dammatione *BR*

as though for the title of their own right. The prince points out many practices surrounding the sacrament which the whole church of the faithful has already for many centuries changed from the example of Christ's instituting the sacrament, none of which had Luther censured before. He points out certain practices no longer current, a thing 5
which yet necessarily either happens wrongly and culpably or happens, as is clearly true, by divine authority. The prince therefore shows that everything of that sort has been changed by the counsel of the Holy Spirit governing the church. Against this response of the king, so pious, so true and moderate, the wicked and impious 10
scoundrel rages with mad railing and folly.

> I, he says, have proved by seven argu-   *Luther's words*
> ments that the second part of the sacra-
> ment has been impiously taken away from the Christian people.

The king shows satisfactorily that it was not taken away by the 15
priests. Therefore, if it was done by men, it was done by the laity themselves. And thus Luther, the wise man, diverts this impiety from the priests on whom he desires to thrust it to the very laity whom he is eagerly trying to flatter. And he diverts it irrefutably by his very own teaching. For if it is true that all the laity are priests, so that they 20
have equal power over any sacrament whatever, after they have been simply elected to this office (and they will be able to be elected by other laymen, so Luther says, in the sacrament of orders), this utterly dull-witted patron so little defends the laity that he even involves them forcibly in damnation because, through want of care 25
for their own salvation, they have neglected to elect for themselves priests who would administer to them both forms. Unless he should say that up till now the laity did not know this mystery. But now he has been sent down from heaven to reveal so sacred a teaching to men, so that God, who usually hides things from the wise and reveals 30
them to little ones, now on the contrary is believed to have hidden it from little ones so that He might reveal it to a most conceited scoundrel.

Or will he say that the second form was taken away from the laity by the priests because this matter was provided for in councils? But 35
if you should carefully examine those very councils, reader, you will easily see that this practice did not arise from those councils but that a decree was passed against those men who, as this fellow is now

qui, quod iste nunc facit, auderent mutare: quod iam tum diu ante,
per omnem populum catholicum fuerat obseruatum, nimirum
spiritus sancti, per totam ecclesiam sese diffundente consilio. Quomodo enim in idem totus Christianus populus, per tam diuersas
5　gentes in ea re consensisset: quum uerba euangelij uideantur in
alteram potius partem uergere: nisi illo id agente, qui facit unani-
[T₄v]mes in domo: qui ducit ecclesiam suam in omnem ueritatem:
qui cum ea semper est, usque ad consummationem seculi. Qui
scripturarum, ut author est dignissimus: sic est interpres uerissimus.
10　Quamobrem quum id, quod Lutherus ablatum queritur, hoc est nihil
rei: nam et sanguis Christi est in corpore Christi: sed altera species,
non id per sacerdotes ablatum sit, non omnino per homines, sed per
spiritum dei: Qui quod rex, ut priore libro supra declaratum est:
apertissime docuit: suo flatu in rebus fidei regit et gubernat ecclesiam,
15　Lutherus dum dicit istud impie ablatum esse: non conuitiator est in
regem: sed blasphemator in deum: per quem factum est: quod impie
factum, homo ter impius asserit. Neque iam contra regem pugnat iste
bellus bellator, cum suis septem argumentis: sed uelut draco ille cum
septem capitibus, insurgit aduersus deum: et quod Satan ausus est
20　olim in deserto: scripturis pugnat aduersus scripturarum dominum.

Speciatim recitat ac refellit septem
argumenta Lutheri. Cap. VI.

AGE ERGO, producamus istos nunc Lutheri septem duces claros,
septem (puto) uictores olympiacos, imo gladiatorum septem putrida,
25　et foetoribus abominanda cadauera.

Verba Lutheri. Primus
Achilles

Primum, inquit, argumentum meum erat
authoritas euangelistarum, narrantium
constanti et uno sermone, Christum
instituisse utramque speciem, his qui memoriam sui erant facturi, et
30　signanter ad calicem adiecit: Bibite ex eo omnes. Ad hoc ni[V₁]hil
dicit rex defensor ecclesiae.

---

13 Qui quod] *corr. err. L*, Qui *om. BR*　　14–15 ecclesiam, Lutherus] *corr. err. L*, ecclesiam.
Lutherus *BR*

doing, were daring to change what had already long before that time been observed by all the catholic people, undoubtedly by the counsel of the Holy Spirit pouring Himself out through the whole church. For how would the whole Christian people throughout such scattered nations have agreed to the same practice on that matter, since the words of the gospel seem rather to incline toward the other side, except by the action of Him who makes those who dwell in a house to be of one mind, who leads His church into all truth, who is ever with her even to the consummation of the world? As He is the most fitting author of the scriptures, so He is their truest interpreter. Therefore, since that which Luther complains has been taken away is not a matter of the substance, for the blood of Christ is also in the body of Christ, but is a matter of another form, and since it has been taken away not by the priests, not by men at all, but by the Spirit of God who rules and governs the church in matters of faith by His inspiration, a fact which the king has taught most clearly, as has been declared in the first book above, then so long as Luther says that this practice has been impiously taken away, he is not a railer against the king but a blasphemer against God, through whom was done what this fellow, thrice impious, declares was impiously done. Neither, then, does this gallant warrior now fight against the king with his seven arguments, but like that dragon with seven heads he rises up against God, and as Satan once dared to do in the desert he battles by means of the scriptures against the Lord of the scriptures.

He recites and refutes in particular the seven arguments of Luther. Chapter 6.

Well, then, let us now lead out those seven noble leaders of Luther's, seven Olympian victors I suppose, or rather, seven gladiators' rotting and abominably stinking carcasses.

My first argument, he says, was the authority of the evangelists relating in a consistent and single report that Christ *Luther's words. The first Achilles* instituted both forms for those who would act in memory of him, and at the chalice He expressly added: "All of you drink of this." To this argument the king, defender of the church, says nothing.

EN simium in purpura, Thersitem in Achillis panoplia. Non est
argumentum tuum authoritas euangelistarum Luthere: neque enim
euangelista quisquam, aut haeresis author est, aut schismatis: sed
sensus adulterinus, quem tu ex euangelio confingis, et quicquid ipse
5   pestilenter assuis euangelistarum uerbis: illud est argumentum tuum.
Nam ex eo, quod illi narrant Christum consecrasse sub utraque specie
in coena: tu interpretamento capitis tui concludis, ministrandum
                                    esse laicis: quum id neque exemplum
        Lutherum non recte accipere   Christi probet: nec ullum uerbum Christi,
             uerba euangelistae
10   uel euangelistae cogat. Nam licet tibi non
libeat illud intelligere: nemo tamen est: qui nesciat, in coena Christum instituisse formam sacrificij: quod solum et unicum, loco sacrificiorum omnium legis Mosaicae, sacerdos euangelicae legis offerret,
in memoriam passionis suae. Atque idem sacrificium (quemadmo-
15 dum uere scripsit rex) quod offerendo consummauit in cruce: consecrando inchoauit in coena. Instituit item conuiuium: quo in
memoriam eius imposterum epularetur populus: ut de eodem sacramento comederet: ac pane propositionis uesceretur, utique si mundus
esset. Hoc institutum, Christus (quatenus ad sacrificij formam per-
20 tinet) perpetuo seruari fecit in sacerdotibus: ut simul et panis et uini
speciem offerret: ut figurae respondeat res: quae olim adumbrata est
in oblatione Melchisedech: qui panem et uinum obtulit Abrahae.
Populi uero conuiuium, alias apparauit aliter, non sacerdos, non
populus, sed conuiuator ipse Christus. Nam alias populum pauit, non
25 corpore solum et sanguine, [V₁v] uerum etiam sub utraque specie
panis et uini. Alias uini speciem sustulit: rem tamen ipsam, suum
uidelicet sanguinem, eis reliquit in carne. Nec utrobique eadem ratio
est. Nam duae illae species, non unum tantum conficiunt sacramen-
                                    tum, sed duo. Verum illa sacramenta duo,
        De sacramento et sacrificio   non duo faciunt integra sacrificia, sed
30   *notandum*
                                    unum. Integrum est ergo sacramentum
sub alterutra specie: sed utramque requirit integritas sacrificij. Sed
unde probas, inquit, alteram speciem, laicis ab ipso sublatam Christo:

---

11 nemo] *corr. err. L*, ne *BR*   17–18 sacramento] *corr. err. L*, sacro *BR*   18 mundus]
corr. err. L, omnibus *BR*

See the ape in royal purple, Thersites in Achilles' armor. Your argument, Luther, is not the authority of the evangelists, for no evangelist is an author either of heresy or of schism; but the adulterated interpretation which you fabricate from the gospel and whatever you yourself pestilently patch on to the words of the evangelists—that is your argument. For from the fact that the evangelists report that Christ consecrated under both forms at the supper you conclude by an interpretation from your own head that both forms must be administered to the laity, although neither the example of Christ proves this nor does any word of Christ or of the evangelist urge it. For although you choose not to understand this fact, nevertheless, there is no one who does not *That Luther does not correctly understand the evangelist's words* know that at the supper Christ instituted a form of sacrifice; this alone and only this He, as priest of the law of the gospel, offered in memory of His passion in place of all the sacrifices of the law of Moses. And the same sacrifice, as the king has truly written, which He consummated by offering it on the cross, He initiated by consecrating it at the supper. He likewise instituted the banquet at which the people might thereafter feast in His memory so that they would eat of the same sacrament and feed of the showbread, at least if they were clean. In so far as this institution pertains to the form of the sacrifice, Christ caused it to be forever preserved among priests, so that he might offer at the same time the form of both bread and wine in order that the reality, which was once foreshadowed in the offering of Melchisedech, who offered bread and wine to Abraham, may correspond to the figure. But the banquet of the people was at different times provided for in different ways, not by a priest, not by the people, but by the master of the feast Himself, Christ. For at one time He fed the people not only with His body and blood but also under the form of both bread and wine. At another time He took away the form of wine; nonetheless, He left for them in the flesh the reality itself, that is, His blood. Nor is the relation the same on both sides. For those two forms effect not only one sign, but two. But those two signs make not two integral sacrifices, but one. There is, therefore, an integral *What must be noted concerning the sign and the sacrifice* sign under either form, but the integrity of the sacrifice requires both forms.

But how do you prove, he asks, that the second form was taken

quam ego prius contendi, sublatam populo, malicia sacerdotum. Imo
tibi Luthere, prius probandum fuit: quod ipse per maliciam finxisti,
per uim, et tyrannidem sustulisse uini speciem sacerdotes. Quod
mendacium tuum impudens, et uipereum retexit, ac reuicit princeps.
5 Sed id tu tuo more dissimulas. Verum probauit id rex, a solo factum
deo: cuius unius spiritu, in sacramentis et articulis fidei gubernari
probauit, ecclesiam catholicam: per quam uniuersam, obseruatur id,
quod reprehendis. Et probauit illud princeps, non ratione solum, et
sanctorum patrum omnium sententijs, sed apertissimis etiam scrip-
10   turis. Denique (quod tibi turpissimum est)
       Nihil turpe homini per se   probauit ex uerbis tuis: ad quae omnia, ne
              impuro   uerbum quidem respondisti tu: sed omnino
surdus ad ea, quae respondentur tibi: pulchre te litigare censes: si
coccicis in morem perpetuo recinas, quod coepisti semel occinere.
15 NAM quod uideri uis, ex illo mire causam fulciri tuam: quod
Christus ad calicem signanter (ut ais) adiecerit: Bibite ex eo omnes:
quasi neminem prorsus excipi uoluerit a bibendo sanguine, sub specie
uini: quid habes ex euangelio: quo possis ad alios illa uerba trahere:
quam ad [V₂] tum praesentes apostolos: praesertim quum alius
20 euangelista commemoret idem: ac uelut interpretetur alijs uerbis:
nempe his, Accipite et diuidite inter uos? Quos, quaeso, dixit: quum
dixit inter uos? alios ne, quam inter praesentes apostolos? An non
satis aperte declarat: quos omnes iubeat bibere: quum illud, quod
bibi iussit, ostendat: inter quos iubeat diuidi? An adhuc Luthere
25 postulas: ut doceare clarius: quos omnes dixerit: quum dixit: Bibite
ex eo omnes? Ecce, potes istud ex illo saltem discere: quod euangelista
subiungit: Et biberunt ex eo omnes. Dubitas adhuc bone uir, quibus
omnibus dixerit: quum id quod omnes facere iussit, ab omnibus uides
esse completum? Quin istud Luthere libenter abs te quaererem: Quid
30 tibi uis, in eo quod ais, Christum signanter adiecisse ad calicem:
Bibite ex eo omnes? Non opinor id sentire te, quod plures uoluerit
Christus recipere speciem uini, quam panis. Quantumuis ergo

away from the laity by Christ Himself, which I earlier argued was taken from the people by the malice of the priests? Rather, Luther, you should first have proved what you yourself have fabricated through malice: that the priests took away the form of wine through force and tyranny. This shameless and poisonous lie of yours the prince has revealed and refuted. But you conceal this according to your custom. Yet the king has proved that this change was effected by God alone, whose Spirit alone, he has proved, governs in the sacraments and in the articles of faith the catholic church, throughout the whole of which is observed that practice which you censure. And the prince has proved this not by reason alone, and by the opinions of all the holy fathers, but also by most evident scriptures.

Finally, which is to your utter disgrace, he *Nothing is disgraceful to a man inherently foul* has proved it by your words; to all these proofs you have not answered a single word, but, entirely deaf to the answers given you, you think that you argue brilliantly if, like the cuckoo, you constantly re-echo what you have once begun to croak.

As to your wishing it to appear that your cause is wonderfully supported by the fact that Christ at the chalice expressly, as you say, added, "All of you drink of this," as if He wished no one at all to be excluded from drinking the blood under the form of wine, what text do you have from the gospel which enables you to apply those words to other persons than the apostles then present, especially since another evangelist records the same event and as it were interprets it in other words; that is, in these words, "Take this and divide it among you"? Of whom, I ask you, was He speaking when He said, "among you"? Among others than among the apostles present? Or does He not declare clearly enough all whom He commands to drink when He shows among whom He orders that that be divided which He ordered to be drunk? Or do you still demand, Luther, to be shown more clearly all of whom He was speaking when He said, "All of you drink of this"? Look, you can learn this at least from the fact that the evangelist adds, "And they all drank of it." Do you still doubt, my good fellow, to all of whom He spoke when you see that that which He commanded all to do was fulfilled by all? Rather, Luther, I would like to ask this of you: What do you mean by saying that Christ expressly added at the chalice, "All of you drink of this"? I do not think that you understand this to mean that Christ wished more persons to receive the form of wine than that of bread. However

signanter, omnes adiecit ad calicem: noluit tamen ad plures pertinere, quam illud, quod ante dixit de corpore: Accipite et comedite:
ut utrumque dictum perinde ualeat: acsi aut ibi dixisset: Bibite ex
eo: nec adiecisset omnes: aut hic dixisset: Accipite, et comedite
5　omnes. At nec istud puto negaturum te, non alijs illud dixisse
Christum: Accipite et comedite: aut, Bibite ex eo omnes: quam dixit
istud: Hoc facite in meam commemorationem. Ergo si illud, Accipite
et comedite, et illud item, Bibite ex hoc omnes, non dixit apostolis,
sed christianis praesentibus et futuris, citra ullam prorsus excep-
10　tionem, uniuersis: sequetur nimirum: quod uniuersis dixit et illud:
Hoc facite in meam commemorationem. Recordare iam, quod ipse
sic interpretaris haec uerba Christi: Hoc facite, id est, hoc [V₂v]
totum facite: quod ego nunc facio, hoc est, consecrate corpus et
sanguinem meum: et comedite, et bibite. Vides ergo bone uir, eo rem
15　deduxisse te: ut necesse habeas: aut illud, omnes bibite, restringere,
ad praesentes dumtaxat apostolos: aut illud, Hoc facite, dilatare

Tolle iam exanimem Luthere　prorsus ad uniuersos. E quorum altero,
tuum Achillem　sequetur interitus argumenti tui fortissimi:
ex altero sequetur illud absurdissimum:
20　quod nemo prorsus erit, neque sacerdos, neque laicus, neque uir,
neque puer, neque mas, neque foemina: quin illi demandatum sit: ut
Christi corpus et sanguinem non recipiat solum: sed etiam consecret.
Quam rem omnium absurdissimam, quamquam te tam absurdum
uideo, ut pro absurda non habeas: tamen quando non dubito, nemi-
25　nem fore tam insanum: ut hac in parte dignetur furori tuo subscribere:
mihi satis erit, eo traxisse te: ut aut necesse habeas fateri: id quod ex

Hic os comprime Luthere　argumento tuo sequitur, perquam absurdum esse: aut eam rem neges esse absur-
dam: quam nemo plane nescit esse furiosam. Et hoc est lector
30　argumentum primum: quod tanquam fortissimum, dominus doctor
collocauit in fronte: ad quod ait, regem nihil dixisse: qui tamen uno
responso, et illud, et reliqua sex, perfodit penitissime: quum probauit:
quod licet in coena sacramentum istud primo sit institutum, et

10 uniuersis . . . quod] *om. B*; et illud] *om. B*　　13 hoc est,] hoc est *B*　　27 *gloss*] *BL,*
Hic os cum prime Lnhere *R*

expressly, therefore, He added "all" to the chalice, He nevertheless did not wish this to refer to more persons than that which He had before said of His body, "Take and eat"; so that both expressions have exactly the same force as if He had said of the former, "Drink of this" and not added, "all"; or had said of the latter, "Take and eat this, all of you." But I think you are not ready to deny that Christ did not say the words, "Take and eat," or, "All of you drink of this," to any other persons than those to whom He said, "Do this in remembrance of me." Therefore, if He did not say to the apostles, "Take and eat," and likewise, "All of you drink of this," but to all Christians present and future, without any exception whatever, it undoubtedly will follow that He said to everyone these words also, "Do this in remembrance of me." Remember now, that you yourself thus interpret these words of Christ, "Do this"; that is, do this entire action that I am now doing; that is, consecrate my body and blood, and eat and drink it. You see therefore, my good fellow, to what point you have led the case, so that you necessarily must either restrict the words, "All of you drink," to the apostles only who were present or extend the words, "Do this," to absolutely everyone. From the first of these alternatives will follow the destruction of your most powerful argument; from the second will follow that most absurd con-

Haul away now, Luther, your lifeless Achilles

clusion: that there will be no one at all, neither priest, nor layman, neither man, nor boy, neither male nor female, of whom it was not demanded that he not only receive the body and blood of Christ but also consecrate it. Although I see that you are so absurd that you do not consider this most absurd of all conclusions absurd, nevertheless, since I do not doubt that no one would be so insane that he would deign to subscribe to your madness in this matter, it will be enough for me to have drawn you on to the point where you either necessarily have to admit that what follows from your argument is completely absurd, or you have to deny that that conclusion is absurd which everyone clearly knows is raging mad.

Hold your tongue here, Luther

And this, reader, is the first argument which, as his most powerful one, the honored doctor has stationed in the van; he says that the king has answered nothing to it, whereas the latter nevertheless has by one answer pierced both that argument and the remaining six to the core, when he proved that although at the supper this sacrament

sacrificium inceptum: tamen oblatum est, et consummatum in cruce:
nec tam certam sacramenti formam, in illa coena praescriptam esse
fidelibus: quin et illius sacrosancti sacramenti, sicut et ceterorum
omnium obseruatio legitima, perpetuo petenda sit ab ecclesia: quam
5   et post illam coenam docuit Christus, per spiritum sanctum: et per
eundem spiritum, quando uult in ecclesia sua [V₃] quaedam, prout
ipsi placet, immutat: causasque mutandi, ut solus deus mutat: ita
solus deus nouit. Hoc dumtaxat nemo non nouit: quicquid circa
sacramenta, per totam mutatur ecclesiam, mutari illud non alio
10 mutante, quam deo: qui, ne in rebus eiusmodi tota possit errare:
promisit suum spiritum, illam ducturam in omnem ueritatem: et se
cum illa futurum usque ad consummationem seculi.

Secundus Achilles Lutheri   Secundum erat hoc: si solis presbyteris
                                   dedisset Christus in coena sacramentum,
15   non licere ullam partem dare laicis, quia non licet institutum et
exemplum Christi mutare. Hic tacet gloriosus defensor rex Angliae.

IMO hic, non tacuit rex: sed ostendit tibi Luthere multa mutata:
sed ea mutata per illum, qui potestatem habet mutandi omnia:
nempe per ipsum deum, sine cuius instinctu probauit, ecclesiam
20 nihil in sacramentis mutasse.
Nam argumentum istud tuum quam praeclare procedit: Deus dedit
sacramentum solis sacerdotibus: ergo non licet dare laicis? Eadem
ratione dicas licet: Christus dedit tantum uiris: ergo non licet dare
mulieribus. Quod si dicas, nihil in Christo differre mares a foeminis:
25 et contra Paulum, permittas mulierem concionari: dicemus tibi, nec
laicum per te differre a sacerdote: ut adhuc contra te procedat
similitudo: ut si dari possit mulieribus: quod Christus legitur, solis
dedisse uiris: possit et dari laicis: quod Christus legitur, solis dedisse
sacerdotibus. Praeterea, quaero abs te Luthere: an quisquam in
30 coena sacramentum receperit, praeter solos apostolos? Si dicas alios:
Doctrina sua caelesti uidelicet   quaero, qua scriptura probes id? Nam
                                    tu nihil admitti uis, absque manifesta

---

3 ceterorum] caeterorum *BL*   5 spiritum] *BL*, speritum *R*   13 erat hoc:] er at, inquit,
hoc: *B*   16 tacet gloriosus] *L*, tacet, gloriosus *R*, tacet, inquit, gloriosus *B*   19 eccle-
siam] et ecclesiam *B*   24 Quod] Quam *L*   31 *gloss om. L*; probes] probas *B*

was first instituted and the sacrifice initiated, yet it was offered and consummated on the cross; and that the form of the sacrament was not prescribed for the faithful at that supper so definitely that the legitimate observance of this most holy sacrament as of all the others also need not be sought continually from the church, which even after that supper Christ has taught through the Holy Spirit; and through the same Spirit, when He wishes, He changes certain things in His church as it pleases Him; and as God alone makes the changes so God alone knows the reasons for changing. Only this does everyone know: whatever is changed throughout the whole church concerning the sacraments is changed with no one but God doing the changing, who, so that the whole church cannot err in matters of this sort, has promised that His Spirit will lead her into all truth and that He Himself will be with her even to the consummation of the world.

The second argument was this: If Christ had given the sacrament at the supper to *Luther's second Achilles* priests only, it is not lawful to give any part of it to the laity because it is not lawful to change the ordinance and example of Christ. At this argument the pompous defender, the king of England, is silent.

On the contrary, the king has not been silent here but he has shown you, Luther, many changes, but things changed by Him who has the power of changing all things; that is, by God Himself, without whose impulse, the king has proved, the church has changed nothing in the sacraments.

How brilliantly does this argument of yours proceed: "God gave the sacrament to priests only; therefore, it is not permitted to give it to the laity." By the same reasoning you may say: "Christ gave it only to men; therefore, it is not permitted to give it to women." But if you should say that in Christ there is no distinction between male and female, and if, contrary to Paul, you should permit women to preach, we will say to you that according to you neither does the laity differ from the priest, so that the comparison still works to your disadvantage, so that if what Christ is read to have given to men only can be given to women, then what Christ is read to have given to priests only can be given also to laymen. Besides, I ask you, Luther, whether anyone received the sacrament at the supper besides the apostles alone? If you should say there were others, I ask by what scriptural text do you prove *By means of his heavenly* *doctrine, of course* this? For you want nothing to be admitted

scriptura. Sin concedas, solos apostolos: id quod conce[V₃v]dere tibi
necesse est: tunc quaero, utrum, quando recipiebant sacramentum,
laicos fuisse illos dicas, an sacerdotes? nam nec erat alius aliud, nec
quisquam utrumque simul. Elige ergo utrum libet: si uis, fuisse
5 laicos: iam ex ista praeclara argumentandi forma, quam affers tu:
liceret dicere: Dedit tantum laicis: ergo non licet dare sacerdotibus:
quia non licet institutum et exemplum Christi mutare. Sin fateare
fuisse sacerdotes: iam ex argumento tuo, laicis, quibus utramque
speciem deberi disputas, utramque sustulisti: nisi falsa sit tua collec-
10 tio: quod non licet dare laicis: quod Christus in coena dedit tantum
sacerdotibus. Sed est omnino falsa ista, et furiosa collectio: nisi ualeat
haec quoque: Christus hoc modo fecit in coena: ergo instituit: ut idem
eodem modo perpetuo fieret in ecclesia. Et item haec: Christus ita
fecit in coena: ergo non licet ecclesiae, ipso iubente Christo, quic-
15 quam mutare. Christus dedit coenantibus: ergo non licet ecclesiae,
iubente Christo, dare ieiunantibus. Christus in coena legitur, in
calice consecrasse solum uinum: ergo non licet Christo iubere: ut in
ecclesia sua sacerdos immisceat aquam. Et hoc est lector secundum
argumentum Domini doctoris: quod uoluit uideri tam ualidum.

20   *Tertius Achilles Lutheri*   Tertium est. Si potest una pars laicis tolli
                                            huius sacramenti, poterit et baptismi, et
penitentiae, eadem authoritate tolli, et quicquid Christus unquam
statuit, potest partim tolli, et particulatim totum tolli. Si totum tolli
non potest, nec ulla pars tolli potest. Ad hoc obmutescit gloriosus
25 assertor sacramentorum.

REX ad istud respondit Luthere, alteram sacramenti speciem
ablatam esse laicis, dispensatione dei: et illud tibi probauit euidenter.
Nec ueretur asserere, deum, qui unam [V₄] speciem sustulit laicis,
auferre, si uelit, utramque posse: Ecclesiam uero, nisi deo sic uolente,
30 non posse: sed neque in id consentire posse: quod in sacramentis fieri

---

apart from clear scripture. But if you grant that the apostles
alone received, a thing which you must necessarily grant, then I ask
whether, when they were receiving the sacrament, you would say
they were laymen or priests? For neither was one person one thing,
another the other, nor was anyone both at the same time. Choose   5
then whichever you please; if you wish them to have been laymen,
then according to that brilliant form of arguing which you present it
would be permissible to say, "He gave it only to laymen; therefore, it
is not permitted to give it to priests, because it is not permitted to
change the ordinance and example of Christ." But if you admit they   10
were priests, then according to your argument you have taken both
forms away from the laity to whom you are arguing that both forms
are due; unless your inference is false: that it is not permitted to give
to the laity what Christ at the supper gave only to priests. But this
inference is utterly false and insane, unless the following is also valid: 15
"Christ acted in this way at the supper; therefore, He determined
that the same thing would be done in the same way forever in the
church." And likewise the following: "Christ acted thus at the supper;
therefore, the church is not permitted, even though Christ Himself
commands it, to change anything." Christ gave the sacrament to men   20
at supper; therefore, the church is not permitted, even though Christ
commands it, to give it to men fasting. We read that at the supper
Christ consecrated only wine in the chalice; therefore, Christ is not
permitted to order that in His church the priest should mingle water
with the wine. And this, reader, is according to the argument of the   25
honored doctor which he wished to seem so powerful.

> The third is: if one part of this sacrament   *Luther's third Achilles*
> can be taken away from the laity, then by
> the same authority part of baptism and penance will be able to be
> taken away, and whatever Christ has ever established can be taken   30
> away in part and bit by bit taken away wholly. If the whole cannot be
> taken away, neither can any part be taken away. To this argument the
> pompous defender of the sacraments is speechless.

The king has answered to this, Luther, that the one form of the
sacrament has been taken away from the laity by the dispensation of   35
God, and he has proved this to you clearly. Nor does he fear to declare
that God, who took away one form from the laity, can, if He should
wish, take away both forms; but the church, unless God so wills, cannot; yet neither can she give her consent to that thing in the

deo nolente non liceat. Nam deus ecclesiae suae, talibus in rebus
dirigit corda: et per spiritum sanctum, ducit in omnem ueritatem: ut
eam reddat columnam, et firmamentum ueritatis et fidei. At tibi
contra, rex ostendit pectus inspirare diabolum: per quem ausus es et
5 baptismi sacramento gratiam tollere: et fidem eius, malorum operum
securitate polluere: Poenitentiae uero duas partes tollere: tertiam
stultissimis dogmatibus inficere. Eucharistiae sacramentum, non alijs
modo substantijs miscere, sed omnium caeremoniarum honore
spoliare: et (quod omnium sceleratissimum est) in conscientiam
10 conspurcatam, quibuslibet inquinamentis immergere. Denique
matrimonij sacramentum, et confirmationis, et ordinis, et unctionis
extremae, nec authoritate, nec ratione fretus abnegare. Et non pudet

Nihil nebuloni sanctum   te ecclesiam totam conuitijs, et syco-
phancijs incessere? quasi laicis tollat unius
15 sacramenti partem alteram: cum tu nebulo miserrimus et quatuor
tollas integra: et reliqua tria foedissimis haeresibus contamines. Et
quum haec omnia tibi rex sacramentorum defensor, et uera dignus
gloria, responderit: tu ad haec omnia sacramentorum furiosus
impugnator, obsurdescis.

20   *Quartus Achilles Lutheri*   Quartum est, inquit, quod Christus dicit,
sanguinem suum fundi pro remissione
peccatorum nostrorum, eis non posse negari signum remissionis,
quod illis Christus dederit. Ad hoc, inquit, mutus est laruatus
Thomista Anglorum.

25 PRINCEPS ad hoc Luthere non erat mutus: sed tu laruate potista,
surdus, qui semper nihil audis: quod non [V₄v] libenter audis.
Alioqui recordare nebulo, quod probauit princeps uini speciem non
per homines ablatam laicis, sed per ipsum Christum: et iam propone
rursus istud argumentum tuum. Christus pro laicis fudit sanguinem,
30 in remissionem peccatorum: et hoc pacto concludas: Ergo Christus
(quamquam sub specie panis, remissionis integrum signum relinquens
in corpore) non potuit auferre laicis speciem uini: quod est signum
remissionis in sanguine. Nam sic necesse est inferas: si quicquam uelis

---

1 nolente] volente *L*   3 ueritatis et] *corr. err. L*, et *om. BR*   12 fretus abnegare] *corr. err.*, fretus, abnegare *L*, fretus auferre, abnegare *BR*   14 laicis] laici *L*

sacraments which may not be done if God does not want it done. For God directs hearts for His church in such matters, and through the Holy Spirit He leads her into all truth, so that He may render her a pillar and support of truth and faith. But as for you, on the contrary, the king shows that the devil breathes into your heart; through him you have dared to take grace away from the sacrament of baptism and to defile faith in it by lack of concern for evil works; to take away in fact two parts of penance and to infect the third with most foolish teachings, not only to mingle the sacrament of the eucharist with other substances but to strip it of the honor of all ceremonies and, what is most criminal of all, to steep it in a conscience contaminated by every kind of filth; finally, to reject the sacraments of matrimony and of confirmation and of orders and of extreme unction, relying neither on authority nor on reason. Are you not ashamed to assault the whole church with reproaches and slanders, as if she takes away from the laity one part of one sacrament when you, you *Nothing is sacred to a scoundrel* wretched scoundrel, take away four whole sacraments and corrupt the remaining three with most loathsome heresies? And although the king, defender of the sacraments and deserving of true honor, has answered you all this, you, the raving assailant of the sacraments, grow deaf to all this.

> The fourth, he says, is that Christ says that His blood is shed for the remission *Luther's fourth Achilles* of our sins; the sign of remission cannot be denied to them because Christ has given it to them. To this, he says, the masked English Thomist is mute.

To this, Luther, the prince was not mute; but you, you masked sot, are deaf, since you never hear anything you do not want to hear. Otherwise, recall, rascal, that the prince has proved that the form of wine was not taken away from the laity by men but by Christ Himself, and then set forth again this argument of yours: Christ shed blood for the laity unto the remission of sins; and you draw your conclusion as follows: "Therefore, Christ, although leaving the integral sign of remission in His body under the form of bread, was not able to take away from the laity the form of wine which is the sign of remission in His blood." For you necessarily make this inference if you wish to infer anything that is relevant.

inferre: quod tangat rem. Alioqui si concludas hoc pacto: Ergo
homines non potuerunt auferre speciem uini: quod est signum
remissionis: quid potest concludi stolidius aduersus principem: qui
tam aperte probauit, non ablatam esse per homines, sed per deum?
5 Ecce domine doctor, quam belle uobis procedat istud argumentum
quartum.

Quintus Achilles Lutheri   Quintum est, inquit, si potuit uinum
                              tollere, potuit et panem, ac per hoc totum
institutum Christi penitus euacuare: si totum non potest, nec partem
10   potest. Et inuictus rex, forte recordatus prouerbij, Silentio respondetur
multis, et ipse mihi silendo omnia respondet.

TV potator inuicte, neque meminisse potes: quid tibi responderit
rex: neque quid ipse in proximo pene uersu dixeris. Nam, quid est
aliud stolidum istud argumentum quintum, quam frustulum marci-
15 dum, ex furfuracea massa tertij argumenti decerptum. Nam quod hic
colligis de uno sacramento: ibi colligebas de omnibus: nec interim
                              uerbum facis ullum de eo: quod princeps
Cur tu silendo ad id respondisti   aduersus te probauit: istud, quod tu im-
Luthere?   pugnas, non ab homine factum esse, sed a
20 deo. Atqui Luthere, oportebat te, ad id respondere pri[X₁]mum.
Interea stolide facis: si dissimules illud: et dicas nobis: Homo non
potest uini speciem tollere: sin fateris illud: et stolide facis, et impie:
si dicas: Deus non potest mutare: quod potuit non instituere. En
quali silentio tibi respondetur ad quintum.

25 QVID mirum si partem tertij ponas pro quinto: qui sextum
omisisti totum, tam bellus arithmeticus, ut ita numeres, primum,
secundum, tertium, quartum, quintum, septimum? Sed ne quid tibi
queraris interceptum: fugitiuus ille seruus, in captiuitate Babylonica
repertus est, atque extractus huc: ut cadauer istud exangue, uel ex
30 stigmate possis agnoscere.

Sextus Achilles Lutheri   Obsecro, inquis, quae necessitas, quae
                             religio, quae utilitas laicis negare
utramque speciem, id est signum uisibile, quando omnes concedunt

---

1 Alioqui si] *corr. err. L*, si *om. BR*   6 quartum.] *L*, quartum *BR*   15 decerptum.]
decerptum? *L*   17 *gloss om. L*   30 stigmate] *corr. err. L*, stigmeat *BR*

Otherwise, if you conclude as follows: "Therefore, men were not able to remove the form of wine which is the sign of remission," what more stupid conclusion can be drawn against the prince who so clearly proved that it was not taken away by men but by God? Behold, honored doctor, how prettily this fourth argument of yours turns out. 5

The fifth is, he says, if man was able to take away the wine he was able also to take away the bread and by this means wholly to make void the entire institution of Christ; if he cannot take away the whole, neither can he take away the part. And the invincible king, perhaps recalling 10 the proverb, "Silence answers many things," also answers me by keeping silent about everything.

Luther's fifth Achilles

You, tosspot invincible, cannot remember what the king has answered you nor what you yourself said in almost the next line. For what else is this stupid fifth argument of yours than a dried-up crumb 15 plucked from the husk-like lump of your third argument. For what you here infer concerning the one sacrament, you were there inferring concerning all of them; nor do you meanwhile utter one word concerning what the prince has proved against you: that this 20 practice which you attack was not effected by men but by God. And yet, Luther, you should have answered that first of all. Meanwhile, you are acting stupidly if you conceal that argument and say to us, "Man cannot take away the form of wine"; if, on the contrary, you admit that argument, you act both stupidly and impiously if you say, 25 "God cannot change what He could have not instituted." See the kind of silence with which your fifth argument is answered.

Why have you answered this by keeping silent, Luther?

What wonder if you set down part of the third argument in place of the fifth, you who omit the whole sixth argument, such a fine arithmetician that you can count thus: first, second, third, fourth, 30 fifth, seventh! But lest you complain that anything has been stolen from you, that runaway slave has been discovered in the *Babylonian Captivity* and dragged out here, so that you can recognize this bloodless cadaver even from its brand:

I ask you, you say, what need, what religious scruple, what utility is there in denying both forms to the laity; that is, the visible sign, since everyone grants them the substance of the sacrament without the sign; if they

Luther's sixth Achilles   35

eis rem sacramenti sine signo, si rem concedunt, quae maior est, cur
signum, quod minus est, non concedunt?

OBSECRO te Luthere per stulticiam tuam, non sentis istud ipsum,
quod tu torques in clericos, regem in te retorsisse? Nam quum tu nihil
5 aliud clames, ob maliciam, quam alteram speciem impie sustulisse
sacerdotes: rex, declarans eam rem, non esse imputandam sacerdotibus, ostendit, non solum laicos tantam iniuriam non fuisse passuros:
sed illud etiam, quod ipse quoque perquam prudenter fateris: nullam
fuisse causam, cur sacerdotes illud per iniuriam facere uoluerint.
10 Quod enim commodum inde consequerentur ipsi? aut quae fuisset
inuidia: quum nemini negent rem ipsam totam? nemini negent
signum totius in corpore, signum etiam cuiuis utrumque concedere?
Aut, quamobrem uoluissent, eo concesso, quod est ultra mo-
                                    dum omnem maius, id [X₁v] subtrahere,
        Dic aliquid hic domine
15   *frater*   quod omnes sciant incomparabiliter esse
                                    minutius?

O prudentem uirum, quam scite disputas aduersus regem. Ille dicit,
id non fecisse sacerdotes: tu probaturus eos fecisse, contendis, nullam
fuisse causam, cur facerent. Rex probat id fecisse deum: et, quod ipsi
20 placitum est, non solum sacerdotibus, sed populis insuper inspirasse
fidelibus: qui ecclesiam suam catholicam (cum qua se futurum
promisit, usque ad consummationem seculi) non patitur in sacramentis errare. An tu adhuc quaeres: quare fecit? Et non desines
impugnare: quod deus fecit: nisi tibi reddatur ratio, quare fecerit.
25 An nobis respondere non licet: quis consiliarius eius fuit? Scio
multas, magnasque causas allegari posse, et prudentissimos quosdam
uiros allegasse permultas: quae populum permouere potuerint:
                                    uerum ego diuinare non dignabor de
     An non hoc pium est Luthere
              facere?   causa: quum certus sim, neque populum
30   dei sine deo, neque in populo deum sine
causa fecisse. Nam quod tu garris, hoc a deo permissum: ut esset
occasio schismatis: nempe sic est permissum a deo: ut a deo
permissum est, euangelium scribi: ex quo suscitarunt haeretici,
multa schismata. Nam boni uiri nullam ex communione coeperunt

12 concedere?] *corr. err. L*, concedere. *BR*   13 concesso] *L*, cocesso *BR*   14 *gloss* frater]
frarer *BR*; *gloss om. L*   28 *gloss om. L*   31 Nam quod] Nam quod quod *L*; permissum]
corr. err. L, promissum *BR*   32 sic est permissum] *corr. err. L*, est *om. BR*

grant the substance which is greater, why do they not grant the sign which is less?

I ask you, Luther, by your folly, do you not sense that the king has hurled back against you this very argument which you hurl against the clergy? For whereas, through malice, you shout nothing else than that the priests have impiously taken away the second form, the king, while declaring that this matter must not be imputed to the priests, shows not only that the laity would not have allowed so great an injustice but also, a thing which you yourself also very shrewdly admit, that there was no reason why the priests would have unjustly wished to do that. For what advantage would they themselves gain from it? Or, since they deny no one the total substance itself, since they deny to no one the sign of the whole substance in the body, what ill will would there have been to grant both signs also to anyone? Or, for what reason would they have wished, having granted that which is immeasurably greater, to steal away that which everyone knows is incomparably smaller?

Say something here, honored brother

O shrewd fellow, how cleverly you dispute against the king. He says that the priests did not do it; you, wishing to prove that they did, argue that there was no reason for them to do it. The king proves that God did it, and that He inspired not only the priests but also the faithful people as to what was His pleasure, since He does not allow His catholic church—with whom He has promised to remain even to the consummation of the world—to err on the sacraments. Or do you still ask, "Why did He do it?" And will you not cease attacking what God has done unless you are given the reason why He has done it? Or may we not answer: "Who has been His counsellor?" I know that many and weighty reasons can be alleged and that certain very wise men have alleged very many of them that could have influenced the people, but I will not deign to divine the reasons, since I am certain that neither would the people of God have acted without God nor would God among His people have acted without reason.

Or is it not pious, Luther, to do this?

As for your snarling remark that this was permitted by God so that there might be an occasion of schism, obviously it was permitted by God just as it was permitted by God that the gospel be written from which heretics have stirred up many schisms. For good men have

occasionem schismatis: sed ecclesia concors erat et unanimis. Neque
quisquam fere fuit e populo: qui uel peteret speciem uini: uel tam
rebellis esset spiritui: ut uel oblatam foret accepturus: donec unus aut
alter similis tui, fax inferni, in segetem domini immisit ignem: qui
5   angulum aliquem depopularetur agri dominici.

    PORRO, quod ais his uerbis, nos re sacramenti iam du[X₂]dum
amissa, iam contra rem maximam propter signum pugnare recte sane
et uere, nos illud, dicis. Nam catholici re ipsa contenti, de signo
soliciti non sunt: sed uos schismatici et haeretici, contra rem uere
10 maximam, hoc est uoluntatem dei pugnantes, pro signo solo totam
sacramenti rem, fructumque eius omnem perdidistis. Postremo, quod
ais istam ablationem alterius speciei tunc temporis incoepisse, quo
tempore pro diuicijs mundi, coepimus contra christianam charitatem
insanire: quam frigidum est. Nam quid habet haec res affine cum
15 diuitijs? an sacerdotes, ut laicis non ministrent utramque speciem:
conducuntur diuitijs. O rerum solidarum inopem, uerborum stolidorum diuitem Lutherum.

        Septimus Achilles Lutheri   Septimum est, inquit, Paulus omnium
                                obstruens ora, qui ad Corinth. undecimo,
20   non presbiteris, sed ecclesiae et omnibus fidelibus tradidit totum
    sacramentum. Hoc, inquit, argumentum dixit assertori sacramen-
    torum, Noli me tangere.

    AN IDEO Luthere non tangeris: quia tam stupidus es: ut non
sentias, quando tangeris? Certe stupidissimus es: si non sentis: quam
25 parum causam tuam probet apostolus. Nam primum, etiam si locus
ille nihil haberet ambigui: tamen uix aequum esset postulare te: ut
ora omnibus obstruat apostolus: quum apud te nullius apostoli tanta
sit authoritas: ut os obstruat tibi: ut qui linguam maledicam exertare
non solum sis ausus in apostolum Iacobum: et illi de authoritate sua
30 mouere controuersiam: sed in ipsum quoque debacchari Paulum:
qui quum te offendit, ad Ephesios quinto: quod ausus est matrimonium uocare sacramentum: non dubitas in dubium uocare: utrum id

---

1 et unanimis] *corr. err. L,* et *om. BR*   4 segetem] *L,* segerem *BR*   12 temporis
incoepisse,] *corr. err. L,* incoepisse *om. BR*   28 exertare] exercere *L*

taken no occasion of schism from communion, but the church was of one heart and mind. And there was hardly any one of the people who either asked for the form of wine or was of so rebellious a spirit that, if offered, would have accepted it, until one or the other like you, a firebrand of hell, cast fire onto the grain field of the Lord in order to   5 lay waste a corner of the Lord's field.

Moreover, as for what you say in these words: that we, having long ago lost the substance of the sacrament, now fight for the sign in opposition to the most important thing, the substance, you say that "we" correctly indeed and truly. For catholics, content   10 with the substance itself, have not been anxious about the sign, but you schismatics and heretics, fighting against the truly most important reality, that is, the will of God, have for the sake of the sign alone destroyed the whole substance of the sacrament and all its fruit.   15

Finally, as for your statement that this removal of the second form began at that time when for the sake of worldly riches we began to rage against Christian charity, how feeble it is. For what connection does this case have with riches? Or are the priests bribed by riches not to administer both forms to the laity? How poor in solid argu-   20 ments, how rich in stupid words you are, Luther.

> The seventh is, he says, Paul stopping the   *Luther's seventh Achilles*
> mouths of everyone when in Corinthians
> 11 he delivered the whole sacrament not to priests but to the church
> and to all the faithful. This argument, he says, has said to the defender   25
> of the sacraments: "Do not touch me."

Luther, are you not touched because you are so dense that you do not sense when you are touched? Certainly you are very dense if you do not sense how little the apostle proves your case. In the first place, even if that passage were not ambiguous, yet it would hardly be fair   30 for you to demand that the apostle stop everyone's mouth, since no apostle's authority is so great in your mind as to stop your mouth, since you have dared not only to stick out your abusive tongue against the apostle James and to stir up controversy about his authority, but also to rant wildly even against Paul himself; when he   35 offends you in the fifth chapter of his letter to the Ephesians because he dared to call matrimony a sacrament, you do not hesitate to call

Nemo ipsi ex deo loquitur, qui non suffragatur eius impietati

ex deo sit locutus: an ex sensu suo. Verum quoniam satis certum est, [X₂v] neminem tam impium esse, quam te: perge nihil ueritus, caeteris christianis omnibus Pau-

5   lum allegare. Sed uide tamen quatenus suffragetur tibi. Si quis aut negasset laicos olim utramque speciem recepisse: aut id factum reprehendisset in Corinthijs: recte Paulum citasses cum et factum probaret illic tantus testis: et recte factum tantus probaret apostolus. Nunc uero quum concedant omnes, et illud olim factum uolente deo:

10 et nunc illud ipsum deo dispensante mutatum, tu stolide nunc allegas apostolum: ex quo probas illud: quod nemo negat: illud, quod obstat tibi: non attingis: nisi te forte putas pulchre colligere: si rem hoc pacto concludas: Paulus utramque speciem dedit laicis olim: quando deus ita uoluit: ergo perpetuo sic facere debet ecclesia: siue uelit

15 deus, siue nolit. An non Paulus quaedam tradidit Corinthijs: quae neque tum licebat negligere: neque nunc obligatur quisquam seruare? nisi tu, qui libertatem praetendas, multis damnationibus inuoluas uniuersum orbem. Paulus circumcidit Timotheum: nec dubito: quin id recte riteque fecerit: et tamen idem paulo post interminatur alijs:

20 Si circumcidimini, Christus uobis nihil proderit. Olim ad baptismum tantum admittebantur adulti: et Christus, non antequam adoleuit, baptisatus est. Infantes baptisasse non leguntur apostoli. Cur ergo

Forte quia non succurrebat

non clamas institutum esse: ne baptisentur pueri: ut hac quoque parte calumniam

25 struas ecclesiae. Olim contra, postquam baptisari ceperunt infantes, etiam communicari consueuerant. Nunc illud uidemus abolitum. Cur utramque speciem non redarguis, tot secula iam subtractam pueris: qui alteram tantum damnes ablatam [X₃] laicis? Iam istud ipsum de uini specie, an non Christus ipse praetermisit aliquando: nisi contra

30 sanctos omnes Cleopham neges, et socium eius recepisse corpus in specie panis: quum in fractione panis cognouerunt eum: aut qui nihil

---

1 *gloss om. L*   7 Corinthijs: recte Paulum citasses] *corr. err. L*, recte . . . citasses *om. BR*
9 illud olim] olim *om. L*; uolente] *corr. err. L*, nolente *BR*   31 quum] cum *L*

into doubt whether he has spoken that
according to God or according to his own *For him, no one speaks according*
understanding. But since it is certain *to God who does not support*
his impiety
enough that no one is so impious as you,
proceed without fear to cite Paul to all other Christians. But take 5
heed, nevertheless, to what extent he supports you. If anyone had
either denied that the laity once received both forms or had reproved
that practice among the Corinthians, you would rightly have quoted
Paul, since such an important witness would prove that it was done,
and such an important apostle would prove that it was done rightly. 10
But now since everyone grants both that this practice was observed
long ago according to the will of God and that it has now been
changed by God's direction, you are now citing the apostle stupidly
to prove what no one denies; that which opposes you, you do not
touch on; unless perhaps you think you are making a clever inference 15
if you draw the following conclusion: "Paul once gave the laity both
forms when God so willed; therefore, the church ought forever to do
this whether God wills it or does not will it." But did not Paul teach
certain things to the Corinthians which he was not then permitted to
disregard and which no one is now obliged to observe? Unless you 20
who feign liberty would involve the whole world in many condemna-
tions. Paul circumcised Timothy; I have no doubt that he did this
rightly and fitly, and yet shortly after he warns others: "If you are
circumcised Christ will be of no advantage to you." At one time only
adults were admitted to baptism, and Christ was not baptized before 25
He grew to manhood. We do not read that the apostles baptized
infants. Why, therefore, do you not protest
that it has been decreed that children *Perhaps because it did not*
support you
should not be baptized, so that in this
matter also you may contrive a false charge against the church? On 30
the other hand, formerly, after infant baptism was begun, even
infants used to receive communion. Now we see that practice
abolished. Why do you not argue that both forms were wrongly taken
away from children for so many ages, since you condemn the taking
away of the one form from the laity? Then, this very matter of the 35
form of wine: did not Christ Himself omit it at one time? Unless
contrary to all the saints you deny that Cleophas and his companion
received the body in the form of bread when they recognized Him in
the breaking of the bread, or unless you who admit nothing apart

admittis absque scriptura: nobis probes absque scriptura: simul
praebitam speciem uini: quum testetur euangelista, protinus a
porrectione panis, euanuisse Christum. An non Paulum ipsum legis,
in actis panem consecrasse, porrexisse discipulis, nec interim de uino
5   uerbum ullum? Quod si pergas quaerere, qui sciam, quae mutantur
in ecclesia, circa sacramentorum formam, ea mutari placito et consilio dei: quaeram abs te uicissim: qui scias ipse, lotionem pedum
licuisse praetermittere? nec eam sic institutam a deo, siue sacramentum fidei, siue sacramentorum saltem ritum, talem qui nusquam
10 licite posset aboleri: quum Christus lotionis illius exemplum prae-
buisse non minus accurate uideatur, quam eucharistiae: Imo hoc
etiam magis accurate, quod non dixit illis, hoc facite: sed meo
exemplo hoc debetis facere. Quae uerba nullo modo suadere, sed
necessitatem uidentur imponere: praesertim quum modestiae causa
15 recusanti Petro, tam humile ac prope sordidum erga se officium
domini, sit interminatus, non habiturum eum ullam partem cum ipso:

Cur magne doctor non docuisti
hoc nos stupidos

nisi perageretur lotionis illius mysterium.
Dic ergo Luthere: qui scis istam lotionem,
aut non institutam pro sacramento, aut
20 tantum fuisse ritum temporarium? Qua scriptura discernes istud? alia
ne quam hac, qua Christus promisit ecclesiae: Spiritus paracletus,
quem mittet pater in nomine meo, ipse uos ducet in omnem ueritatem? [X₃v] Et, Ego uobiscum sum, usque ad consummationem seculi:
et si qua sit alia eiusmodi? Qui scis, licite paulo post esse mutata,

Quid aliud putet apostolorum
emulus ac hostis

25 quae per epistolam olim constituerunt
apostoli? nisi putas apostolorum quoque
concilio, quod communiter habuerunt
Hierosolymis, defuisse spiritum dei. Qui scis, apostolos absque
peccato mutasse baptismi formam, ab ipso praescriptam Christo:
30 idque in re momenti (quicquid tu garrias) maximi? Neque enim
tantum refert: an quisquam baptisetur aqua: quantum refert, in
cuius baptisetur nomine. Potest et martyr suo baptisari sanguine.

25 *gloss om. L*

from scripture would prove to us apart from scripture that the form
of wine was offered at the same time, although the evangelist testifies
that immediately after handing them the bread Christ disappeared.
Do you not read in the Acts that Paul himself consecrated bread,
handed it to the disciples, nor at the time was there any mention of   5
wine?

But if you go on asking how I know that the things concerning the
form of the sacraments which are changed in the church are changed
by the will and design of God, I shall ask you in turn how you yourself know that it was permissible to omit the washing of feet? or that   10
that practice was not thus instituted by God, whether as a sacrament
of the faith or at least as a rite of the sacraments such as could never
lawfully be abolished, since Christ seems to have presented an
example of that action no less explicitly than He did that of the
eucharist; in fact, even more explicitly than the latter, in that He did   15
not say to them, "Do this," but, "According to my example you
should do this." These words seem in no way to persuade but to
impose a necessity, especially since Christ threatened Peter, who was
refusing out of modesty such a lowly and almost disgraceful service
toward himself on the part of the Lord, that he would have no part   20
with Himself unless the mystery of that washing was carried through.
Tell me then, Luther, how do you know
that this washing was either not instituted   *Why, great doctor, have you not
as a sacrament or was only a temporary   taught this to us dolts?*
rite? By what scriptural text do you determine this? By any other   25
than this in which Christ promised His church: "The Spirit, the
Paraclete, whom the Father will send in my name, He will lead you
into all truth," and, "I shall be with you even to the consummation of
the world," and any other of the same kind? How do you know that
those things were shortly after legitimately changed which the   30
apostles once established by epistle? Unless you think that the Spirit
of God was lacking also to the assembly
which the apostles held in common at   *What else would a rival and
Jerusalem. How do you know that the   enemy of the apostles think?*
apostles changed without sin the form of baptism from that prescribed   35
by Christ Himself, and that in a matter of the greatest importance—
whatever you may prate? For it is not so important whether someone
is baptized in water as it is important in whose name he is baptized.
Moreover, a martyr can be baptized in his own blood. A person can

Potest aliquis et spiritu: sed in alio nomine nemo potest: quam in quo
praescribit deus. Quod si contendas, satis fuisse nomen Christi: ego
Luthere, ut ista fateor esse uera: sic ista uere uideo contra te facere
omnia. Nam quum Christus institueret tria nomina, patris, et filij, et
5 spiritus sancti: in quibus per lauacrum, populus regeneraretur in
fidem: nulla prorsus humana ratio potuit apostolis esse sufficiens: ut
deflecterent a praescripto Christi: neque potuerunt contra Christi
tam aperta uerba credere, magis referre: ut solius Christi nomen
redderetur illustre: quam ut tota trinitas inclaresceret orbi: et con-
10 suesceret populus in ipsis Christianismi foribus cognoscere, et colere
patrem, filium, et spiritum sanctum: quorum nominibus baptisma
recepissent. Quod si respondeas: ut respondent quidam: Christi
nomen, quum significet unctum, et patrem unctorem implicare, et
unctionem spiritum: retorquebimus in te carnem: qui subest speciei
15 panis, non implicare tantum, sed et uere continere sanguinem: qui
seorsum consecratur in specie uini: sed [X$_4$] tamen, ut tu non concedis
id, satis esse causae: cur ecclesia relinquat in laicis, uini speciem: ita
nos non concedemus tibi, illud alterum satis fuisse causae: cur apostoli
potuissent, in baptismo nomina patris, et sancti spiritus praetermit-
20 tere: nec illud eadem ratione, quod Christus deus erat, et idem deus
cum patre et sancto spiritu. Nam ut tu Christum dicis, duas instituisse
species in eucharistia: ita nos Christum dicimus: et euangelio teste
dicimus, in baptismo tria statuisse nomina, nec illud obiter aut ociose,
sed maxima de causa statuisse: ut protinus
I nunc et nega, licuisse quicquam
25 *immutare Luthere?* in baptismo personarum trinitas innotes-
ceret. Vides ergo Luthere nullam rationem
apostolos permouere potuisse: ut ex baptismi forma, patris aut spiritus
nomen expungerent: quam formam non minus expressam uides in
euangelio, quam utramque speciem in eucharistia. Quid affers igitur,
30 cuius dum accusas ecclesiam, non accuses apostolos? An hoc uidelicet
interesse dices, inter hanc causam et illam? quod illorum factum

---

14 qui] quae *L*   25 *gloss* Luthere?] *om. L*

also be baptized in the spirit, but no one can be baptized in any other name than that which God prescribed. But if you should contend, Luther, that the name of Christ was sufficient, then, while I admit this is true, yet I truly see that it works wholly against you. For when Christ established the three names, of the Father and of the Son and of the Holy Spirit, in which through washing the people would be regenerated unto faith, no human reason whatever could have been sufficient for the apostles to turn away from what was prescribed by Christ, nor could they contrary to such clear words of Christ believe that it is more important that the name of Christ alone be rendered glorious than that the whole Trinity be made known to the world and that the people grow accustomed at the very portals of Christianity to acknowledge and to worship the Father, Son, and Holy Spirit, in whose names they had received baptism.

But if you should answer, as some do answer, that the name of Christ, since it signifies the anointed, implies both the Father as anointer and the unction, the Spirit, we will hurl back at you that the flesh which is concealed under the form of bread does not only imply but also truly contains the blood which is consecrated separately in the form of wine, but nevertheless, as you do not grant that this is sufficient reason for the church to abandon among the laity the form of wine, so we will not grant you that that other answer was sufficient reason for the apostles to have been able to omit in baptism the names of the Father and Holy Spirit; nor the following one, according to the same reasoning: that Christ was God and the same God with the Father and Holy Spirit. For, as you say that Christ established two forms in the eucharist, so we say, and we say it on the testimony of the gospel, that Christ established in baptism three names, nor did He establish this incidentally and haphazardly, but for a most important reason: so that immediately in baptism the trinity of persons might become known. You see *Go now and deny that it was lawful to change anything, Luther!* then, Luther, that no reason could have persuaded the apostles to strike out from the form of baptism the name of the Father or the Spirit; this form you see no less explicit in the gospel than both forms in the eucharist. Why do you bring up, then, something for which, while you reproach the church, you do not reproach the apostles? Or will you say that of course there is this difference between the latter case and the former one: that the action of the apostles is

scriptura sacra complectitur: cui tu standum esse fateris: Ecclesiae
factum, nulla scriptura nititur, sed mera consuetudine: quam tu et
male inoleuisse, et propere censes abolendam. At hic uide, quam nihil
dicis: nam in actis apostolorum, nihil aliud legis, quam apostolos in
5 solius Christi nomine baptisasse: sicut hic uides, laicos sub altera
tantum specie per tot aetates communicasse: et in euangelio uides
magis aperta uerba Christi: quibus iussi sunt, patris et spiritus sancti
nomen adiungere: quam sunt omnia, ex quibus contendis ecclesiae
praeceptum a deo: ut utramque speciem daret populo. Rursus
10   ergo te rogo: quomodo non oppugnas
      Facit utrumque, idque animo   apo[X₄v]stolos, eisdem machinis: quibus
             gladiatorio   oppugnas ecclesiam? Qui nunc maledicis
ecclesiae, quomodo non blasphemas apostolos? quos, quid aliud
habes: quo defendas: quam quod in solo Christi nomine baptizarunt,
15 eius ipsius dispensatione: cuius ore prius aliam baptizandi formam
susceperant. Istud igitur idem rex tibi respondit de ecclesia, uidelicet
eam, quod hac in re facit, Christi spiritu gubernatam facere. Sed ubi
legit, inquis, istud rex, ecclesiam istud immutasse per spiritum dei?
Vbi legis tu Luthere, apostolis aliud postea mandasse Christum:
20 quam quod ante mandauerat? An apostolos in sacramentis non
patietur errare: quos delegit propter ecclesiam? et ecclesiam ipsam
patietur errare: propter quam ipsos delegit apostolos? An ad solos
pertinet apostolos illud Christi: Spiritus sanctus, quum uenerit: ille
uos ducet in omnem ueritatem? ut illud ad eosdem quoque tantum
25 pertinere disputes: Ego uobiscum sum, usque ad consummationem
seculi?

---

10 *gloss om.* L   21 ecclesiam ipsam] *corr. err.* L, ecclesiam *om.* BR

included in holy scripture, which you admit must stand firm, while the action of the church relies on no scripture but on a mere custom, which you think has grown rampant and should be speedily uprooted. But here see how you are saying nothing, for in the Acts of the Apostles you read nothing other than that the apostles baptized in the name of Christ alone, as here you see that the laity have received communion for so many ages under only one form; and in the gospel you see that the words of Christ by which He commanded them to add the name of the Father and of the Holy Spirit are much clearer than are all the words from which you argue that the church is commanded by God to give both forms to the people.

Again, therefore, I ask you: why is it that you do not attack the apostles with the same tricks with which you attack the *He does both, and that with the spirit of a gladiator* church? You who now abuse the church, how is it that you do not blaspheme the apostles? What other means do you have to defend them than that they baptized in the name of Christ alone by His own direction, from whose mouth they formerly had received a different form of baptizing? The king, then, gives you the same answer concerning the church; namely, that what she does in this matter she does governed by the Spirit of Christ. But where, you ask, does this king read that the church has changed this through the Spirit of God? Where do you read, Luther, that Christ commanded the apostles something after what He had earlier commanded? Or, on the matter of the sacraments, will He not allow the apostles to err whom He chose for the sake of the church, and allow the church herself to err for whose sake He chose the apostles? Or do the words of Christ pertain to the apostles alone: "The Holy Spirit when He shall have come will lead you into all truth," so that you argue that the following words also pertain only to them: "I am with you even to the consummation of the world"?

Epilogus eorum, quibus rex refellerat
argumenta Lutheri: et simul quam
incerta redderentur omnia: si
cuique liceat e quouis
scripturae uerbo conuellere
fidem publicam. Ca. VII.

NVNC igitur uides lector: quam imbecillum sit istud robur, omnium
illorum septem argumentorum: quibus
Stulta Lutheri
ratiocinatio
iste Satan conatur expugnare Christum:
quam stulte nobis arguit: qui dicit:
homines non possunt istud facere: quum princeps, et clarissime
dixerit: et non uno tantum [Y₁] loco clarissime probauerit, non
homines hoc fecisse, sed deum. Si deum fecisse Lutherus non fatetur:
cur id non negauit? Cur id a rege toties dictum, tot libri sui locis
incultatum, tam saepe tam aperte probatum, silentio dissimulat? Sin
deum fecisse fatetur (fatetur autem, qui contra nihil respondet) quam
stolida nunc atque impia sunt omnia septem argumenta: quae nihil
prorsus aliud ualent: quam si diceret: Hoc deus instituit: ergo peccat,
quisquis aliter, ipso iubente deo, fecerit. Aut si sic diceret: Hoc sonat
scripturae litera: ergo impij sunt: qui obsequuntur spiritui sancto,
contra speciem literae: quam spiritus ille sanctus melius intelligit,
quam septem millia spirituum nequam: qui Luthero ministrant sua
septem argumenta. Quamobrem lector
Ecclesiam a Christi spiritu
occulte regi
charissime, quum istud, quod Lutherus
reprehendit, uelut sacerdotum factum: rex
probauit esse factum spiritus sancti: cuius oculto spiraculo gubernari
probauit ecclesiam: cui rei, Lutherus nihil adhuc inuenire potuit:
quod responderet: Vides iam, quam stolide bacchetur in regem:
quasi non responderit ad argumenta sua, tam fortia uidelicet ac
robusta: ut uno uerbo ueritatis prostrata sint omnia. Et tamen quum
rex sustulit omnia clarissime, probans uidelicet, id quod Lutherus
uelut a sacerdotibus factum, reprehendit: non ab illis esse factum, sed
a spiritu sancto: recurrit adhuc stipes tam stupidus: ut plagam, qua ad
cor usque uulneratus est: non sentiat: ac rursus in regem torquet sua

---

8 *gloss* Stulta] Luthere Stulta *L*   15 incultatum] inculcatum *BL*   20 litera: ergo]
litera ergo *L*   23 *gloss om. L*   33 recurrit] Recurrit *B*   34 torquet sua] torqueat,
illa sua *B*

The epilogue to those arguments by which the king
had refuted the arguments of Luther; and at the
same time, how uncertain everything would be
rendered if it should be permitted to each person to
destroy the public faith on the authority of some   5
word of scripture. Chapter 7.

Now then, reader, you see how feeble is the strength of all those seven
arguments by which this Satan tries to
conquer Christ, how foolishly he re-   *Luther's foolish reasoning*
proaches us when he says that men cannot do this thing, since the   10
prince has said most clearly, and in more than one passage proved
most clearly, that men have not done this, but God. If Luther does not
admit that God has done it, why has he not denied it? Why does he
conceal by silence what has been said by the king so often, empha-
sized in so many passages of his book, proved so often and so   15
evidently? But if he admits that God did do it—but he does admit it
since he answers nothing to the contrary—then how stupid and
impious are all the seven arguments, which have absolutely no other
force than if he said: "God has instituted this; therefore, that man
sins who has done otherwise by the order of God Himself." Or, if he   20
said: "The letter of scripture signifies this; therefore, those men are
impious who obey the Holy Spirit against the appearance of the
letter which that Holy Spirit understands better than the seven
thousand evil spirits who supply Luther with his seven arguments."

Therefore, dear reader, since the king   25
has proved that this practice which Luther   *That the church is governed*
censures as the work of priests is the work   *secretly by the Spirit of*
of the Holy Spirit, by whose hidden breath   *Christ*
he has proved that the church is governed, to which proof Luther has
not yet been able to find any answer, you see now how stupidly he   30
rants against the king as if the latter has not answered his arguments,
so strong and powerful indeed that they are all prostrated by one
word of truth. And yet, although the king has destroyed all of them
most clearly, namely by proving that what Luther censures as done by
priests was not done by them but by the Holy Spirit, the dolt still   35
comes back, so dense that he does not sense the blow by which he has
been wounded even to the heart, and he hurls once more against the

Quam certus iaculator Lutherus septem, septies redarguta, argumenta: quae sua septem tela tam pulchre dirigit: ut septem millibus nunc aberrent a scopo. Nam quum res facta probatur a deo: [Y₁v] ille disputat in sacerdotes. An postquam con-

5 stat de authore spiritu dei: tamen resistet spiritui, propter corticem literae. Cuperem ergo scire: quid sentiat de salute martyrum: quos proprio sanguine baptisatos credit ecclesia. Quibus antea contigit occidi, pro fide Christi: quam sacramentum possent baptismi recipere. Non dicet (opinor) sanctissimos illos

10 *Quid ni? qui mendacij et arrogantiae insimulet apostolos Christi* martyres, omnes esse damnatos. Nec uideo tamen, quomodo possit eorum salutem asserere: si nihil recipiat praeter euidentes scripturas. Quarum si quas reperias: quae uideantur illis promittere regnum dei: non facile tamen inueniet ullam: quae promittat

15 apertius: quam haec aperte uidetur denegare: Nisi quis renatus fuerit ex aqua et spiritu sancto: non potest introire in regnum dei. Verum, quoniam haud multum est curae martyrum Luthero: ut quorum imagines, et cultum omnem contendat tollendum: cupio saltem scire ex eo: si nihil admittat omnino praeter euidentes scripturas: quidnam

20 satis euidenter esset responsurus: si quis illi tam facilem ex sola fide pollicenti remissionem peccatorum omnium, idque subitanea, et qualicunque unius momenti poenitentia, obijceret illud de peccato in spiritum sanctum: quod Christus aperte dicit, neque in hoc seculo, neque in futuro remittendum? Quid hic faciet Lutherus? Obijciet

25 uidelicet illud Prophetae. Quacunque hora ingemuerit peccator, &c. Quid ergo dicet: si is, qui proposuit, dicat illud peccatum exceptionem esse, et aliquod saltem esse peccatum: quod quale sit: nemo adhuc satis explicuit: quod nulla deleri poenitentia possit? Quis erit disputandi finis? Imo si quis objiciat illud

Quid Luthero cum apostolo?
30 apostoli, [Y₂] Voluntarie enim peccantibus nobis, post acceptam noticiam ueritatis: iam non relinquitur pro peccatis hostia. Terribilis autem quaedam expectatio iudicij, et ignis emulatio: quae consumptura est aduersarios. Et illud item eiusdem:

---

1 *gloss om.* L   7 ecclesia. Quibus] ecclesia: quibus L; contigit] corrigit L   9 *gloss* Quid] quid B, *gloss om.* L   15 renatus] tentatus L   17 multum est curae martyrum Luthero] multum curat Lutherus de martyribus B   25 Prophetae] Christi B; peccator, &c.] peccator: saluus erit B   27 aliquod] BL, aliquot R   29 *gloss* Luthero] L, Lnthero BR

king his seven arguments, seven times
refuted, which seven weapons of his he
aims so accurately that they now miss their

*What an accurate marksman
Luther is!*

target by seven thousand paces. For, when the practice is proved to
have been effected by God, the fellow argues against the priests. Or,
when the authorship of the Holy Spirit is well-known, the fellow
nevertheless resists the spirit for the sake of the shell of the letter.

I would very much like to know what he thinks about the salvation
of the martyrs whom the church believes baptized in their own
blood. They happened to die for the faith of Christ before they could
receive the sacrament of baptism. I think
he will not say that those most holy martyrs
have all been damned. Nevertheless, I do

*Why not? He falsely accuses the
apostles of Christ of lying
and arrogance*

not see how he can affirm their salvation, if he accepts nothing but
evident scriptures. If you should discover any of these scriptures
which seem to promise the kingdom of God to those martyrs, he will
still not easily find out any which makes the promise more clearly
than the following text seems clearly to refuse it: "Unless a man is
born again of water and the Holy Spirit he cannot enter into the
kingdom of God." But because Luther has so little care for the
martyrs that he argues that their images and veneration should be
wholly abolished, I desire at least to know of him—if he admits nothing at all besides evident scriptures—what sufficiently clear answer
he would give if, when he promises such easy remission of all sins by
faith alone, and that by means of any sort of sudden penitence lasting
but a moment, someone were to bring up that text about the sin against
the Holy Spirit which Christ clearly says is not to be forgiven either
in this world or in the next? What will Luther do here? He will
bring up, of course, that text of the prophet: "At whatever hour the
sinner shall lament, etc." What then will he say if the one who
brought up the objection says that this sin is an exception and that
there is at least some sin, the nature of which no one has yet
satisfactorily explained, which cannot be blotted out by any repentance? What will be the end of the disputing? Or rather, if someone
should bring up the words of the apostle,
"For if we sin willfully after receiving the
knowledge of the truth, there remains no

*What has Luther to do with an
apostle?*

longer a sacrifice for sins, but a certain dreadful expectation of
judgment and the fury of a fire which will consume the adversaries"?

Irritam quis faciens legem Mosi, sine ulla miseratione, duobus uel
tribus testibus moritur. Quanto magis putatis, deteriora mereri
supplicia: qui filium dei conculcauerit: et sanguinem testamenti
pollutum dixerit: in quo sanctificatus est: et spiritui gratiae con-
5 tumeliam fecerit? Et item illud. Impossibile est enim, eos, qui semel
sunt illuminati: et gustauerunt etiam donum caeleste: et participes
facti sunt spiritus sancti: gustauerunt nihilominus bonum dei uerbum: uirtutesque seculi uenturi: et prolapsi, sunt rursus reuocati ad
poenitentiam: rursum crucifigentes sibimet ipsis filium dei et ostentui
10 habentes? Has, inquam, scripturas si quis producat: et iam illud
Christi: Quacunque hora ingemuerit peccator: saluus erit: dicat
intelligendum esse: quacunque parte aetatis, peccatorem infidelem
posse per poenitentiam recipi, ad baptismi gratiam: caeterum post
baptismum, rursus peccanti, denuo salutis locum non esse, quis erit
15 hic Luthero finis: qui nihil admittit, praeter euidentes scripturas?
Quando faciet scripturas tam euidenter concordes: ut non remaneant
argumenta plus septem, Lutheri aduersario: quae nunquam poterit
euidenter tollere: nisi recurrat ad ecclesiae
Verum is non audiet nisi sua
fidem, dei digitis scriptam in cordibus
20 fidelium: neque minus ueram, neque minus certam, quocunque libro
scripturarum: per quam fidem, certi sumus de fidei articulo: etiam
quum de scripturae sensu saepe simus incerti: e cuius scripturae textu,
ar[Y₂v]gumentis plus septem Christum oppugnabat Arrius. Argumentis plus septem, Christi matrem sanctam impius oppugnabat
25 Heluidius. Vtriusque perfidiam expugnauit ecclesia, sita nimirum
super solidam petram fidei, qua docuit eam spiritus sanctus aduersus
Arrium, concordare scripturas aduersus Heluidium, et ab ipso
declarare productas, et citra ullum scripturae testimonium: perpetuam uirginis integritatem credere. Quum igitur et ecclesiae
30 catholicae publica fide, et consentiente scriptura certissimum sit,
ecclesiam in fidei rebus, regi spiritu Christi: non dubitamus id uerum
esse rectumque: quod spiritus dicit ecclesiae: etiam si qua litera

And likewise these words of the same apostle, "A man making void the law of Moses dies without any mercy on the word of two or three witnesses; how much worse punishments do you think he deserves who has trodden under foot the Son of God and has regarded as unclean the blood of the covenant through which He was sanctified and has insulted the Spirit of grace?" And likewise the following, "For it is impossible for those who were once enlightened, who have both tasted the heavenly gift and become partakers of the Holy Spirit, who have moreover tasted the good word of God and the powers of the world to come, and then have fallen away, to be recalled again to repentance since they crucify again for themselves the Son of God and make Him a mockery"? If someone, I say, should bring out these scriptures and then those words of Christ; and if he should say that this text, "At whatever hour the sinner laments he will be saved," must be understood to mean that at any time of his life whatever the unbelieving sinner can be received through penitence to the grace of baptism, but after baptism, if he sins again, there is no second opportunity for salvation, what will be the end here for Luther, who admits nothing besides evident scriptures? When will he make the scriptures so clearly harmonized that there will not remain more than seven arguments for Luther's adversary which he will clearly never be able to *But he will not hear any except his own* destroy unless he has recourse to the faith of the church written by the fingers of God in the hearts of the faithful, no less true and no less certain than any book of scripture, through which faith we are certain about an article of faith even when we are often uncertain about the meaning of scripture; from a text of this scripture Arius attacked Christ with more than seven arguments; with more than seven arguments the impious Helvidius attacked Christ's holy mother. The church conquered the faithlessness of both these men, being founded indisputably on the solid rock of faith by which the Holy Spirit taught her to harmonize the scriptures against Arius, against Helvidius, and to declare that the scriptures were brought into being by Himself, and to believe in the perpetual integrity of the virgin without any scriptural testimony.

Since, therefore, it is most certain both from the public faith of the catholic church and from the agreement of scripture that the church is ruled by the Spirit of Christ in matters of faith, we do not doubt that what the Spirit says to the church is true and correct even if there

scripturae sit, in speciem contraria, scientes, aut de illa dispensasse
deum, aut certe non esse contrariam, sed uideri, sicut duos interdum
scripturae textus: qui pugnare uidentur: nihil dubitamus, inter se
concordes esse: etiamsi nobis discordare uideantur. Quamobrem, aut
5 illud Lutherus tollere debuit regi, mutationem, quam uelut factam
per sacerdotes incessit factam esse per spiritum sanctum. Et item
illud. Ecclesiam in fidei rebus eodem gubernari spiritu. Ad quae duo,
nihil omnino respondet: aut salua est ecclesia Christi, non solum
aduersus argumenta septem Lutheri, sed etiam aduersus septua-
10 *Lutherus cacodaemonum organum* gesies septies septena millia cacodaemonum: qui Luthero, uelut aptissimo
daemonum organo, tam stolidas argutias aduersus ecclesiam, et
Christum sponsum eius inspirant. Igitur quum omnia Lutheri
argumenta, princeps aperte soluerit: Lutherus contra, suo more,
15 quaedam excerpens, cum quibus pugnet: ualidissima quaeque
dissimulat. Nam neque ad hoc respondet [Y₃] quicquam: quod rex
ostendit, rem, quam ille reprehendit, per eos factam non esse: quos
reprehendit. Nihil ad illud respondet: quod rex ostendit, eum laicos
non excusare: quos ille uult excusatos. Nihil ad illud respondet: quod
20 utraque species nunc aufertur infantibus: de quo nihil queritur
Lutherus. Nihil respondet ad illud: quod
Memor ipse prouerbij, silentio rex ait rem, quam ille redarguit: non ab
respondetur multis
hominibus esse factam, sed a deo: qui in
fidei rebus regit ecclesiam: qua in re, summa totius rei consistit.
25 Quum haec ita se utrinque habeant: tu nunc lector aequus, inter
utrunque iudica: quam impudens nebulo sit Lutherus: qui tam
magnifice scurratur: et scurriliter gloriatur, regem ei nihil respondere:
se uero respondere ad omnia: quum uno uerbo rex, illius argumenta
uere soluat atque euertat omnia: ille regis contra fere dissimulet ac
30 praetereat omnia.

6 sacerdotes incessit] *corr. err.*, sacerdotes incessit, *L*, sacerdotes, incessit *BR*

is an apparently contrary letter of scripture, knowing either that God
has arranged for that text, or that it is surely not contradictory but
seems so, just as we have no doubt that two texts of scripture which
at times seem to conflict are consistent with each other, even though
they seem to us to disagree. Therefore, either Luther should have   5
destroyed the king's statement that the change which Luther attacks
as made by priests was made by the Holy Spirit, and likewise the
statement that the church is governed by the same Spirit in matters
of faith, to which two statements he answers nothing at all; or else the
church of Christ is safe not only against Luther's seven arguments but   10
also against the seventy times seven times seven thousand cacodaemons who breathe into Luther, as into a
most fitting demon-pipe, such stupid *Luther the pipe of cacodaemons*
sophistries against the church and against Christ her spouse.

Therefore, whereas the prince has clearly solved all Luther's argu-   15
ments, Luther on the other hand, in his usual manner plucking out
certain points with which he may quarrel, conceals all the most forceful arguments. For he answers nothing at all to the king's demonstration that the practice he censures was not brought about by those
whom he censures. He answers nothing to the king's demonstration   20
that he does not excuse the laity whom he wishes excused. He answers
nothing to the fact that both kinds are now taken away from infants,
about which practice Luther makes no
complaint. He answers nothing to the *Himself remembering the proverb:*
king's statement that the action which the *Silence answers many*
fellow is opposing was not done by men *things*   25
but by God, who rules the church in matters of faith; in which fact
the sum of the whole matter consists. Since this is the way the matter
stands on both sides, judge now, honest reader, between the two sides:
how shameless a scoundrel is Luther who so pompously plays the   30
buffoon and buffoonishly boasts that the king answers him nothing
while he himself indeed answers everything; whereas the king with
one word actually solves and destroys all the fellow's arguments, the
latter, on the other hand, conceals and passes over almost all the
arguments of the king.   35

Retegit ac refellit duplicem, imo triplicem Lutheri
mendacissimam et stolidissimam sycophantiam. Cap. VIII.

NAM ILLA, quae uelut firmissima delegit: cum quibus luctaretur:
sic tractauit aegregius palestrita: ut perspicuum fecerit illa ipsa, quae
5 uideri uult infirma: infirmis ipsius uiribus esse firmiora.

Verba Lutheri

*Animus tibi uersatur in patinis
uentricose nebulo*

10

Elinguis, inquit, defensor in rebus necessarijs, uideamus quam linguax sit in suis
nugis, uentrem distende lector, ut mag-
nalia ista Thomistica capere possis,
probaturus licuisse alteram partem tollere
quam regaliter incedit, quasi esset rex. Ecclesia, inquit, mane communicat sacramento, quod Christus fecit uesperi, de[Y₃v]inde nos
aquam uino miscemus, de quo nihil meminit scriptura. Quare si
ecclesia hic potuit aliud facere, aut instituere, potuit et partem
15 sacramenti tollere.

ECCE lector, quam nebulonice procedat nebulo. Nam si rex
loquutus de ecclesiae, uel institutione uel consuetudine, nihil eo loco
prorsus adiecisset aliud: tamen quum tot libri sui locis, et ratione
probauerit, et scripturis, ecclesiam in sacramentis gubernari spiritu
20 sancto: quis ita sine sensu uiueret: ut non sentiret: quid sentiret rex?
aut quis tam improbe faueret Luthero: ut non damnaret in re tam
aperta, tam stolidam Lutheri calumniam? At nunc, ut uanissimum
uideas sycophantam: audi quaeso lector: princeps, illo ipso in loco,
quid dicat.

25   *Verba regis*

"SI Lutherus, inquit, nihil admittit
aliud, quam euidentes dei scripturas: cur
non iubet eucharistiam (ut dixi) a coenantibus sumi? Nam sic
factum scriptura commemorat. Quanto melius crederet Lutherus,
non humano figmento, sed eodem authore deo factum in ecclesia: ne
30 laici sub utraque specie reciperent eucharistiam: quo authore factum

---

3 NAM] *L*, NAN *BR*   8 *gloss om. L*   20 quid sentiret] quid senserit *L*

He reveals and refutes Luther's threefold most deceitful and most stupid subterfuges. Chapter 8.

Those arguments which he has selected as the most powerful to wrestle with, this singular wrestler has so handled as to make it clear that those very arguments which he wishes us to think powerless are 5 more powerful than his own powerless forces.

Let us see, he says, how eloquent about his trifles is this defender, speechless about necessary matters; swell out your belly, reader, so that you can take in these grandiose Thomistic words; when *Luther's words*

Your mind is taken up with dishes, you pot-bellied rascal 10

he is about to prove that it was permissible to take away one kind, how royally he advances, as though he were a king. The church, he says, receives in the morning the sacrament which Christ instituted in the evening; moreover, we mix water with the wine, of which practice 15 scripture makes no mention. Therefore, if the church could do something different or institute something different on this point, she could also take away part of the sacrament.

See, reader, how rascally the rascal proceeds. For if the king, having spoken about either the institution or the custom of the 20 church, had added absolutely nothing else in that passage, yet, since in so many passages of his book he has proved both by reason and by scriptures that in the sacraments the church is governed by the Holy Spirit, what man living would be so senseless as not to sense what the king meant? Or who would be so wickedly partial to Luther that in 25 such a clear matter he would not condemn Luther's very stupid slander? But now, so that you may perceive the fellow's most deceitful chicanery, please listen, reader, to what the prince says in that very passage.

"If Luther admits nothing else than evident scriptures of God, why does he not, *The king's words* 30

as I have said, order the eucharist to be received by men at supper? For scripture records that it was done this way. How much better for Luther to believe that the church's practice of not giving the laity communion under both kinds was not introduced by human invention 35 but by the same divine authority which introduced the practice of

Diuus Augustinus

est: ut reciperetur a ieiunis. Placuit enim (ut inquit Augustinus) spiritui sancto: ut corpus domini, quod post alios cibos ab apostolis in coena receptum est: ante alios cibos, a ieiunis reciperetur in ecclesia." Et protinus ita
5 rem concludit rex: "Spiritus sanctus, qui Christi regit ecclesiam: sicut eucharistiae sacramentum mutauit a coenantibus ad ieiunos: ita laicos ab utraque specie deduxit ad alteram."

QVID hic ais lector? Per quem dicit rex haec esse mutata? per homines, an per deum? An non manifeste dicit mu[Y₄]tata per
10 deum? Quo ergo nomine dignus est frater scurra Lutherus: qui nusquam non mentitur, principem disputare, haec esse mutata per homines? Nam haec est istius nebulonis perpetua forma, non disputandi, sed calumniandi scurriliter. Et nunc, quasi scirent omnes, regem id dicere: quod sciunt omnes Lutherum mentiri: pergit
15 scurrari strenue.

Verba Lutheri

Sic rotari debet, inquit, ac ferri, preceps et insana libido mentiendi, aduersus dominum gloriae.

IMO Luthere, sic rotari debet et praeceps ferri, furiosus fraterculus,
20 et insana mentiendi libido, aduersus agnitam ueritatem, desiderio despuendae gloriolae. Nam id ridiculum

Ridiculum Lutheri commentum

est: quod uideri uis regem, loqui aduersus dominum gloriae. An hoc quicquam est contra dominum gloriae: quod rex ait, deum posse sacramenta sua, prout ipsi libet, dispensare:
25 et parendum esse deo, siue per scriptum quicquam iubeat, siue sine scripto? Nam quod tu imputas regi, quasi dicat homines posse mutare: quod statuit deus: illud certe, tam impudenter et improbe mentiri conuictus es: ut oculos posthac, si quis pudor esset: nunquam auderes attollere.

30

Verba Lutheri

Quam uellem, inquit, modo possent asini et porci loqui, ut inter me et Henricum iudicarent.

HOC saltem recte facis Luthere, et in causam tuam commode: quam quoniam deo et hominibus uides esse damnatam: ad porcos

13 scurriliter] *BL*, scurrilitet *R*

receiving communion by men fasting. It
pleased the Holy Spirit, as Augustine says, *Saint Augustine*
that the body of the Lord which was received by the apostles at
supper, after other food, should be received in the church by men
fasting, before other food." And the king directly concludes the case 5
as follows: "Just as the Holy Spirit who governs the church of Christ
has caused the sacrament of the eucharist to be received by men
fasting instead of by men at supper, so He caused it to be received by
the laity under one kind instead of under both kinds."

What do you say here, reader? By whom does the king say this 10
practice was changed? By men or by God? Does he not clearly say it
was changed by God? What name then fits Friar Buffoon Luther, who
everywhere falsely claims that the prince argues that this practice
was changed by men? This is our rascal's constant form, not of
disputing, but of buffoonishly slandering. And now, as if everyone 15
knew that the king said what everyone knows is Luther's lie, the
latter proceeds to play the buffoon briskly.

> In this way there ought to be rolled and
> rushed along, he says, the headlong and *Luther's words*
> senseless lust for lying against the Lord of glory. 20

On the contrary, Luther, in this way there ought to be rolled and
rushed headlong the furious friarling and his senseless lust for lying
against the acknowledged truth, from a desire for spewing out a bit of
boasting. It is ridiculous that you wish the
king to seem to speak against the Lord of *Luther's ridiculous fiction*
glory. Is it anything at all against the Lord of glory that the king says 25
God can order His sacraments as He chooses and that God must be
obeyed whether He commands anything through scripture or without
scripture? As for your accusing the king as though he says that man
can change what God has established, here surely you are convicted 30
of lying so shamelessly and wickedly that if you had any shame you
would never dare to raise your eyes after this.

> How I would wish, he says, that asses
> and pigs could only speak so that they *Luther's words*
> might judge between me and Henry. 35

This at least you do rightly, Luther, and conveniently for your own
case: when you perceive your case condemned by God and men, you

Dignos Luthero arbitros   appellas et asinos: si forte tam spurcum aut
stolidum ullum brutum possis inuenire: ut
tibi uel adgrunnire uelit, uel adrudere. Quamquam ego profecto non
dubitem: si uel asini possent uel porci loqui: quin facile iudicarent,
5 te et spurciorem esse porco, et stolidiorem asino: qui tam [Y₄v] foede
mentiaris: et orbi te speres imponere, tam perspicuo et tam patenti
mendacio.

Verba Lutheri   Sed accipiam, inquis, alios asinos et porcos: Iudicate ergo uos ipsi sophistae
10 Parisienses, Louanienses, Colonienses, Lipsenses quoque, et uestri
similes ubiubi sint, qua dialectica ualet, ista Henricissima et Tho-
misticissima consequentia? Nam et uos signastis ad marginem libelli
huius: Hic iacet Lutherus prostratus. Et Henricum uestrum appro-
bastis.

15 *Et re uera prostratus eras*   ATAT hoc illud est. Hinc illae lachrymae.
Hoc animum tuum percellit Luthere. Hoc
uulnerat, laniat, lacerat: quod principis liber passim probatur doctis:
qui merito probant: et merito signant in margine: Hic iacet Lutherus
prostratus. Iaces profecto prostratus turpissime: si prostratus iacet:
20 qui nihil habet reliqui: quod contra possit hiscere, praeter apertum,
et nulli non compertum mendacium.

Verba Lutheri   Dicite ergo, inquis, unde locus? unde
regula istius consequentiae? Aliquid sit
extra scripturam: ergo contra scripturam est sentiendum.

25 TIBI Luthere quaerenda est regula: qua tuearis istam consequentiam. Nam ista plane tua est. Quis istam consequentiam fecit
tibi? Quis ita collegit nisi tu? Sic enim colligit princeps, Christus per
spiritum sanctum multa iubet, ac docet ecclesiam sine scriptura: ergo
Lutherus est haereticus et Antichristus: qui nihil ecclesiae credendum
30 praedicet absque scriptura.

Verba Lutheri   Vnde, inquis, regula istius consequentiae? Vinum miscetur aqua extra scrip-
turam: ergo scriptura alteram partem statuens, est damnanda, pro
haeresi habenda, et alijs blasphemijs uestris conspurcanda.

---

8 *gloss* Lutheri] Lntheri *B*   12 marginem] merginem *B*   20 contra] *BL*, contta *R*
27 princeps, Christus] princeps. Christus *B*   34 blasphemijs] *BL*, blaphemijs *R*

summon it before pigs and asses, on the
chance that you can find any brute beast *Judges worthy of Luther*
so foul or foolish that it would wish either to grunt or bray for you.
However, I have no doubt indeed that if either asses or pigs could
speak they would readily judge you to be filthier than a pig and more 5
foolish than an ass, since you so foully lie and hope to impose yourself
on the world by means of such transparent and manifest lying.

> But I will accept, you say, other asses and
> pigs. Judge therefore yourselves, you so- *Luther's words*
> phists of Paris, Louvain, Cologne, Leipzig too, and wherever your 10
> ilk are found: by what dialectic does this most Henrician and
> Thomistic conclusion have validity? For you have even made a
> marginal note in this book: "Here Luther lies prostrate." And you
> have approved your Henry.

Ah! This is it! This is the source of those 15
tears. This, Luther, strikes your mind with *And in very fact you were*
consternation. This wounds, mangles, *prostrate*
lacerates: that the book of the prince is everywhere approved by
learned men, who justly approve it and justly make the marginal
note: "Here Luther lies prostrate." You do indeed lie most shame- 20
fully prostrate, if a person lies prostrate who has nothing left to hiss in
his turn besides an evident, universally detected lie.

> Tell me then: (you say) What is the
> source of this topic? Whence the rule for *Luther's words*
> this conclusion? Should it be something outside scripture, then it must 25
> be considered to be opposed to scripture.

You must seek the rule, Luther, by which you may defend this
conclusion. For it is clearly yours. Who has made this conclusion for
you? Who has drawn such a conclusion but you? For the prince has
reasoned as follows: "Christ commands many things through the 30
Holy Spirit, and teaches the church without scripture; therefore,
Luther is a heretic and Antichrist, since he preaches that the church
must not be believed in anything without scripture."

> Whence, you say, is the rule of this con-
> clusion: Wine is mixed with water with- *Luther's words*
> out scriptural authority; therefore, the scripture decreeing the second 35
> part of the sacrament must be condemned, must be considered a
> heresy, and must be befouled by your other blasphemies?

ET statim magnifice scurra subiungis.

Imo tu es   Pudescit ne tua frons Henrice, non iam
rex, sed sacrilege la[Z₁]tro? Non sudatis
uirulenti sophistae, uos miserabiles trunci, in reprobum sensum
5   uersi?

SIC libet ac licet nebuloni ludere, et alijs obijcere capitis sui
stulticias. Nam quis tibi sic argumentatus est? Quis damnauit
scripturam ullam? Quis habendam censuit pro haeresi? Quis con-
spurcauit blasphemijs? Nemo certe, nisi tu: qui et Pauli reijcis
10 interpretationem: et epistolam canonicam reprobas: et Iacobum
blasphemas apostolum. Nam quod rex ait, huc tendit: quod sicut
deus aquam uino miscendam docuit, absque scriptura: sic et alteram
speciem auferendam docuit, absque scriptura. Quam, sicut ante
monstratum est, nulla scriptura laicis dare praecepit. Ego plus etiam
15 dicere non dubitem: quod si quando, clarissime fuisset aliquid de
sacris ritibus aut sacramentis, in scriptura mandatum: quo quippiam
non dico credi, sed fieri, hoc aut illo modo mandetur: deo tamen
postea, aliter de illo dispensante mandato, et absque scriptura iubente
contrarium, id quod eum hac in causa fecisse probauit rex: non erit
20 impius: qui sine scriptura paret, atque obtemperat deo: quemadmodum facit ecclesia: sed qui (quod Lutherus facit ac docet) scripturae
praetextu deum contemnit. Nec ecclesia tamen scripturam, si qua
uideretur aduersari, damnaret: aut haberet pro haeretica: aut con-
spurcaret blasphemijs: sed honore seruato scripturae, diuinitus
25 edocta cognosceret, mandatum illud fuisse temporarium. Alioqui

Hic Luthere scrupulus tibi iniectus est   dicat nobis elegantissimus porcus, et
prudentissimus asinus: an quisquis lotio-
nem illam pedum non seruat hodie: quam
Christus olim peregit in coena: damnat et conspurcat illud euan-
30 gelium?[Z₁v] Et tamen Christus et exemplum dedit lotionis illius, et,
si locum spectes, cum interminatione mandatum: et seruauerunt et
tradiderunt apostoli: et aliquandiu tota seruauit ecclesia: id quod
disci licet e Cypriano martyre. Et nunc tamen, absque scriptura

---

2 *gloss om. L*   13 Quam] *corr. err. L*, Qua *BR*   19 contrarium] *L*, contarium *BR*
20–21 quemadmodum facit] *L*, quemadmo-facit *BR*   31 spectes, cum interminatione]
spectes cum interminatione, *BRL*

And immediately you, you buffoon, grandly add:

> Is not your face ashamed, Henry, now no longer a king, but a
> sacrilegious robber? Do you not sweat,   *Rather, you are*
> you poisonous sophists, you wretched
> blockheads, turned toward a spurious interpretation?   5

Thus the rascal chooses and is permitted to make sport and to hurl
the follies of his own head against others. For who has argued in this
way with you? Who has condemned any scripture? Who has judged
that it must be considered heretical? Who has befouled it with
blasphemies? No one, certainly, but you, who reject even Paul's   10
interpretation and condemn a canonical epistle and blaspheme the
apostle James. For what the king says has this aim: that as God has
taught without scripture that water must be mingled with wine, so
also He has taught without scripture that the second kind must be
taken away. No scripture, as has been proved before, has commanded   15
that this kind be given to the laity. I should not hesitate to say even
more: that if ever anything concerning the sacred rites or sacraments
had been commanded most clearly in scripture so that we are
commanded, I do not say to believe but to do something in this or that
manner, nevertheless, if God afterwards dispenses otherwise concern-   20
ing that commandment and orders the contrary without scripture—
a thing which the king has proved was done in this case—a person will
not be impious who obeys without scripture and submits to God as the
church does; rather, that person is impious who—as Luther does and
teaches—contemns God under pretext of the scripture. Nevertheless,   25
if some scripture seemed contradictory, the church would not condemn it or consider it heretical or befoul it with blasphemies, but,
safeguarding the honor of the scripture, she would recognize, being
divinely taught, that the command referred to had been temporary.

Otherwise, let the most eloquent pig and   30
most prudent ass tell us whether anyone   *Here, Luther, a scruple is*
condemns and befouls that gospel who   *suggested to you*
does not preserve today that washing of the feet which Christ long ago
carried out at the supper. And yet Christ gave both the example of
that washing, and, if you consider the passage, a command with   35
a threat; and the apostles preserved and handed it on, and for some
time the whole church preserved it, as may be learned from Cyprian
the martyr. And yet now, without a new scripture, through the

noua, per Christi spiritum ad eam lotionem christianus populus
desijt obligari: nisi tu, qui quinque sustulisti de sacramentis septem,
subito reponas octauum. Nec tamen quisquam damnat, aut blasphemijs illud conspurcat euangelium. An Paulum dicis apostolum
5 blasphemijs conspurcasse deum, et hanc damnasse scripturam? Erit
pactum meum in carne uestra, in foedus aeternum: Masculus, cuius
preputij caro circumcisa non fuerit, delebitur anima illa de populo
suo: quia pactum meum irritum fecit. Nam contra illam tam manifestam, tam rigidam, tam minacem scrip-
10 *An non haec satis est manifesta*   turam, non dubitauit dicere: Si circum-
scriptura Luthere?   cidimini, Christus uobis nihil proderit. At
Christus, inquis, baptizare iussit: et baptizatus est ipse. Fateor: sed et
circumcidi iam olim iusserat: et circumcisus est ipse: et se uenisse
dixit: non ut legem solueret: et circumcisionis legem scriptura uocat
15 foedus aeternum: nec per scripturam Christus contra docuit Paulum.
Nam et ipse circumcidit Timotheum. Quid aliud habes: quam ut
Paulum dicas, absque scriptura doctum a spiritu sancto: ut contra
scripturae uerba, manifeste mandantia perpetuo circumcidi: contra
exemplum Christi, qui circumcisus est ipse: contra tam apertum
20 uerbum Christi, qui se uenisse dixit, non ut solueret legem, sed ut
impleret: non dubitaret tamen auferre circumcisionem? Memineris
ergo, regem eodem [Z₂] modo respondisse tibi: quod ecclesia
catholica, ab eodem docta spiritu, quo doctus est Paulus: uini speciem
non dubitauit auferre. Quam uini speciem praeberi laicis (quamquam
25 aliquando factum est) nulla tamen scriptura (qualem tu solam recipis)
euidens, et manifesta praecepit. At (inquies) Paulum docuit deus, et
absque scriptura: sed ecclesiam nihil docet absque scriptura. Ergo,
quod deus quicquid docet ecclesiam, docet euidentibus scripturis:
hoc tu Luthere proba nobis euidentibus
30 *Iam obmutescit uerbosus*   scripturis, contra illud euangelistae: Non
fraterculus   omnia scripta sunt. Et illud apostoli.
Collaudo autem uos fratres: quod omnia mea memoria tenetis: et
quemadmodum tradidi uobis, instituta tenetis. Praeterea illud. Huius
rei gratia reliqui te in Creta: ut quae desunt, pergas corrigere: et

12 sed et] et *om. L*

Spirit of Christ, the Christian people cease to be bound to that washing; unless you who have taken away five of the seven sacraments suddenly set up an eighth one. Still, no one condemns or befouls that gospel with blasphemies.

Or do you say that the apostle Paul has befouled God with blasphemies and condemned this scripture: "My covenant shall be in your flesh as a perpetual covenant. If any male have not the flesh of his foreskin circumcised, that person shall be cut off from his people, because he has broken my covenant"? For against that very manifest, very inflexible, very threatening scripture, he did not hesitate to say: "If you be circumcised, Christ will be of no advantage to you." But Christ, you say, ordered baptism and He Himself was *Or is not this scripture sufficiently clear, Luther?* baptized. I grant this, but He had also long ago ordered circumcision and He Himself was circumcised, and He said that He had come not to destroy the law, and scripture calls the law of circumcision an eternal covenant, nor did Christ teach the contrary to Paul through the scripture. For Paul himself circumcised Timothy. What else do you have to say than that Paul was taught apart from scripture by the Holy Spirit, so that contrary to the words of scripture clearly commanding circumcision forever, contrary to the example of Christ who was Himself circumcised, contrary to the very clear word of Christ who said that He had come not to destroy the law but to fulfill it, Paul did not hesitate nevertheless to do away with circumcision? You remember, therefore, that the king answered you in the same way that the catholic church, taught by the same Spirit by which Paul was taught, has not hesitated to take away the species of wine. Yet no clear and manifest scripture—the only kind you accept—has commanded that this species of wine be offered to the laity (although this was at one time done). But, you will say, God taught Paul even without scripture, yet He teaches the church nothing without scripture. Prove to us, therefore, by evident scriptures, Luther, contrary to the words *Now the long-winded friarling falls mute* of the evangelist, "Not all things have been written," that whatever God teaches the church He teaches by evident scriptures. Contrary also to the words of the apostle: "Now I praise you, brethren, because in all things you are mindful of me and hold fast my precepts as I gave them to you." Moreover, the following: "For this reason I left thee in Crete, that thou shouldst set right anything

constituas oppidatim presbyteros: sicut ego tibi ordinaram. Et contra illud. Seruate, quae praecepi uobis, siue per sermonem, siue per epistolam. Et illud item. Ego, quum uenero, caetera disponam. Necnon et illud prophetae. Ego dabo leges meas in cordibus eorum:
5 et in mentibus eorum superscribam eas. Et quaecunque sunt eius generis alia. Aut proba saltem scripturis euidentibus, Christum, qui cum spiritu suo affuit Paulo: ecclesiae non adesse catholicae, contra scripturam euidentem: qua contra promisit ipse: quum dixit: Ego uobiscum sum, usque ad consummationem seculi. Pudescit ne nunc
10 *Alludit ad uerba Lutheri* — tua frons Luthere? Non sudas uirulente sophista? Vere frons meretricis facta est tibi. Vere miserabilis truncus factus es, et sic in reprobum sensum uersus: ut mendacijs, sycophantijs, haeresibus, et blasphemijs instupescens miseriam tuam, prae praesentium mole[Z₂v]stiarum
15 mole, imminentium malorum terrore, et aeternae damnationis horrore, non sentias.

Verba Lutheri — Dicat, inquit, nobis gloriosus assertor sacramentorum, unde probet missam necessario mane celebrandam.

20 *Hoc nusquam non facit* — ECCE lector, ut sui semper similis est. Vt rursus nebulo, mendacem se, ut rursum se declarat sycophantam. Dic reuerende Asine, ubi dixerit rex, necessario mane celebrandum esse. Sic enim dixit rex.

"SI Lutherus, eam rem ad exactam
Verba regis —
25 euangelicae narrationis formam reuocat: cur eucharistiam non iubet semper in coena recipi, imo uero post coenam."

ECCE Luthere, rex rem non restringit ad auroram: sed (ut saepe iam dixi) ostendit ecclesiam, spiritu doctam sancto: ne se obligari
30 putaret ad uesperum. Et Augustino teste probat, sanctum docuisse spiritum, contra Christi exemplum, sumendum esse ieiunis: quod Christus dedit coenantibus. Dic iam Luthere: dic, ubi sit illud: quod

---

5 superscribam] subscribam *L*

that is defective and shouldst appoint presbyters in every city, as
I myself directed thee to do." And on the other hand this: "Keep the
teachings that you have learned whether by word or by letter." And
likewise the following: "The rest I shall set in order when I come."
Also the words of the prophet: "I will give my laws in their hearts and
in their minds I will write them." And whatever other passages there
are of this nature. Or, at least prove by evident scriptures that Christ
who sustained Paul with His Spirit does not sustain the catholic
church, contrary to the evident scripture by which He Himself promised the opposite when He said: "I am with you even to the
consummation of the world."

Is not your face now ashamed, Luther?
Do you not sweat, poisonous sophist? *He plays on Luther's words*
Surely, your face has become that of a harlot. Surely you have become
a wretched blockhead and so turned toward a spurious interpretation
that, growing numb by means of lies, deceits, heresies and blasphemies, you do not sense your own misery because of the mass of
present troubles, the terror of threatening evils and the horror of
eternal damnation.

> Let the boastful defender of the sacra-
> ments tell us, he says, whence he proves   *Luther's words*
> that the mass must necessarily be celebrated in the morning.

See, reader, how he is ever like himself,
how once more the rascal declares himself   *This he never fails to do*
a liar, once again a trickster. Tell me, reverend ass, where the king
has said that the celebration must necessarily take place in the
morning. The king said the following:

"If Luther recalls this practice to the
precise form of the gospel account, why   *The king's words*
does he not order the eucharist always to be received at supper, or
rather, after supper?"

See, Luther, the king does not restrict the practice to the morning,
but, as I have often said already, he shows that the church is taught
by the Holy Spirit not to consider herself bound to the evening. And
with Augustine as witness, he proves that the Holy Spirit has taught,
contrary to the example of Christ, that the eucharist, which Christ
gave to men at supper, must be received by men fasting. Tell me now,
Luther; tell me, where is that statement which you falsely claim the

regem mentiris dixisse, de mane. An idem est mane sumere, et ieiunum sumere? Proba nobis euidentibus scripturis, idem esse mane
sumere, et ieiunum sumere. An ideo idem est, ieiunum sumere, et
mane sumere: quia tu ieiunus sumere, nisi summo mane, non potes:
5   *Alludit ad uerba Lutheri*   quia summo semper mane potas? Hic
                                         locum habet tua quaestio: dicite sophistae
VVittenbergenses, unde locus? unde regula huius consequentiae?
pater potator summo mane semper est ebrius: ergo nemo potest nisi
mane recipere sacramentum sobrius.

10   *Verba Lutheri*   Idem, inquit, quaero de aqua miscenda
                                   uino. Quis fecit hunc articulum fidei?
quis audet dicere, peccatum esse, si sine aqua celebretur? An Henricus, dum credit sic esse, et non credit Lu[Z₃]therum sine aqua
celebrare.

15   AEQVVM est te Luthere ueniam regi dare: quod te non adeo
putauit improbum: quam tute temet esse gloriaris. Nam cuius de te
cogitationem, tua non uincat impietas? Etenim, quid in sacris
audeas: et nunc significas: et paulo post satis aperte declaras.

          Verba Lutheri   Quis fecit, inquis, hunc articulum fidei?
20   Quis audet dicere peccatum esse, si sine
        aqua celebretur?

      VT celebretur a ieiunis, et aqua fundatur in uinum: ista fideles
suos, docuit author fidei: qui in rebus, et sacramentorum et fidei,
docet ecclesiam suam omnem ueritatem: eique, quod ipsi placet,
25 inspirat. Cuius uoluntati, qui non obtemperat: peccet ne, an non
peccet: tua te stultissime damnatio docebit. Non opus est, ista tibi
dicat Henricus. Tota hoc tibi dicit ecclesia Christi, ab annis plus
mille praeteritis. Cui quicquid tamdiu inspirauit sponsus: uere
oportet sic esse: quantumuis id nouus nunc neget, et contemnat

14 celebrare.] celebrare? L

king has made about the morning? Or is it the same thing to receive
in the morning and to receive fasting? Prove to us by evident scriptures that it is the same thing to receive in the morning and to receive
fasting. Or is it the same thing to receive fasting and to receive in the
morning for the reason that you cannot receive fasting except very 5
early in the morning since you are always drinking very early in the
morning? Here your question has place:
Tell me, sophists of Wittenberg, whence is   *He plays on Luther's words*
the topic, whence the rule for this conclusion: Father Tosspot is
always drunk very early in the morning; therefore, no one can 10
receive the sacrament soberly except in the morning?

I ask the same, he says, about mixing
water with wine. Who has made this an   *Luther's words*
article of faith? Who dares say it is a sin to celebrate without water?
Is it Henry when he believes it thus to be, and does not believe that 15
Luther celebrates without water?

It is decent of you, Luther, to give the king the benefit of not having
thought you so wicked as you yourself boast that you are. Does not
your impiety surpass his opinion of you? You now indicate what you
would dare in the sacred mysteries and shortly after declare it quite 20
openly.

Who, you say, has made this an article of
faith? Who dares say it is a sin if one   *Luther's words*
celebrates without water?

That mass should be celebrated by men fasting and that water 25
should be poured into the wine have been taught His faithful people
by the author of faith, who in matters both of the sacraments and of
faith teaches His church all truth and inspires her as to His pleasure.
Whether the person who does not obey His will sins or does not sin,
your own condemnation will teach you, archdolt. There is no need 30
for Henry to tell you this. The whole church of Christ for more than a
thousand years past tells you this. Whatever her spouse has inspired
in her for so long a time surely must be so, however much a new
heretic may now deny and contemn it.

Next, no less ridiculous than your other impious statements is that 35

haereticus. IAM illud non minus est ridiculum, quam caetera impia:
quod e tuo phanatico cerebro natum, regem fingis dicere, his uerbis.

Verba Lutheri

Consuetudo (inquit) habet uim legis.
Respondeo. Habet uim legis, sed in
5   ciuilibus causis.

VT TV semper Luthere, Lutherus es. Reperias nobis in toto regis
libro, ubi dicat hoc: quod tu eum dicis dicere: Consuetudo habet uim
legis. Non te pudet istud fingere: ut possis
Bellus es Luthere rhetor extra uidelicet pulchre soluere? respondendo,
controuersiam
10   Habet, sed in ciuilibus causis. Quasi rex
tibi allegasset hominum consensum: ac non manifeste scripsisset,
Christum ista suis inspirasse fidelibus. Nos igitur (ut uideas, quam
bel[Z₃v]le tibi procedat, ista tua tam impudens sycophantia) res-
pondemus tibi, consuetudinem Christiani populi in rebus sacra-
15 mentorum et fidei, uim habere ualentioris legis: quam ulla habeat
consuetudo cuiusquam populi, in rebus ciuilibus: quum haec nitatur
consensu dumtaxat humano: illa concilietur, et coalescat inspiratione
diuina.

Lutheri uerba

Nos, inquis, in libertatem uocati sumus,
20   quae nec legem, nec consuetudinem
ferre potest, quum agamus in spiritualibus.

VERISSIME profecto pronuncias, de te et tui similibus: quos
diabolus uocauit in seruilem libertatem suam. Nam ut legibus et
moribus christiani populi, deo seruire regnare est: ita leges et mores
25 abrumpere, quos populum suum Christus uoluit obseruare: et suaue
iugum excutere, quod Christus uoluit suum gregem portare: quid
aliud est: quam seruum deo fugitiuum
Cuiusmodi sit Lutheri libertas esse, ut libere uiuas diabolo? Imo libertatis specie, seruitutem seruias miserrimam.

30   *Verba Lutheri*

Quare, inquit, dominatio et regalitas
Henrici, suam dialecticam male didicit,
et hoc loco uitiosissime petit principium, arripiens hoc pro certo,
probato, diuino, necessario articulo fidei, quod est mere liberum, et
humanum inuentum.

---

8 *gloss* Luthere] *L,* luthere *BR*   9 respondendo] respondeo *L*   24 seruire] seruire, *L*

statement which, though it was born from your mad head, you
pretend is said by the king, in these words:

> Custom, he says, has the force of law. I
> answer. It does have the force of law, but   *Luther's words*
> in civil cases.   5

Luther, how consistently you are Luther! Find for us in the whole
book of the king where he says what you say he says: "Custom has the
force of law." Are you not ashamed to
fabricate this statement, so that you can,   *Beyond question, Luther, you are*
                                                                          a splendid rhetorician
of course, neatly solve it by answering, "It   10
does have, but in civil cases"? As if the king had alleged the agreement of men and not clearly written that Christ has inspired these
things in His faithful.

In order, therefore, that you may see how prettily this very shameless cunning of yours works to your advantage, we will answer you   15
that the custom of the Christian people in matters of the sacraments
and of faith has the force of a more powerful law than has any custom
of any people whatever in civil matters, since the latter relies only on
human agreement, the former is procured and prospers by divine
inspiration.   20

> We, you say, are called to the liberty
> which can endure neither law nor custom   *Luther's words*
> since we are acting in spiritual matters.

You announce the absolute truth, indeed, about yourself and your
ilk whom the devil has called to his servile liberty. For just as to serve   25
God is to reign according to the laws and customs of the Christian
people, so, to tear away the laws and customs which Christ wished
His people to observe and to shake off the
sweet yoke which Christ wished His flock   *Of what sort is Luther's*
                                                                        liberty
to bear, what else is this than to be a slave   30
fleeing from God in order to live freely for the devil? Or rather, in
order that you may serve the most miserable slavery with the
appearance of liberty.

> Therefore, he says, Henry's lordship and   *Luther's words*
> regality has learned his dialectic badly   35
and in this passage most faultily begs the initial premise, seizing
on this as a certain, proven, divine, necessary article of faith, which is
merely a free and human invention.

DOCTORALIS magistralitas Lutheri non considerat: quod in hoc loco se declarat uitiosissimum nebulonem: qui sub nomine regis blasphemet, Augustinianus Augustinum: in cuius olim uerba iurauerat: a quo nunc, et Christo simul, perfuga periurus aufugit. Nam
5   illum allegauit princeps, aperte pronunciantem id, quod iste clamat esse merum, et liberum inuentum humanum, fuisse inuentum spiritus sancti. Et certe ex tot sanctis ecclesiae patribus, qui ad hunc usque diem a Christo passo uixerunt: nullus unquam [Z₄] fuit: qui communes uniuersae ecclesiae mores, circa sacramenta non crediderit, aut
10   traditos esse dei iussu per apostolos, aut per spiritum sanctum ino-

At Luthero peccatum est eos seruare

leuisse in ecclesia. Quos si quis interdum humana fragilitate transgressus est: inter peccata numerauit. Contra uero, ex tot impijs et insanis nebulonibus, qui ad hunc usque diem a Christo passo
15   uixerunt, tu propemodum solus exortus es: qui communes uniuersae ecclesiae mores, circa sacramenta blateres, sic esse prorsus liberos: ut quod uniuersi tam sancte, tam perpetuo seruant, et tot seruarunt seculis: id iam cuique liberum sit, quando libet, quoties libet negligere. Et audes nebulo, sub papistarum nomine totam tot aetatum
20   ecclesiam irridere.

Verba Lutheri

Quare nos, inquis, papistis istis sanctis, libenter fauemus, magnificos illos fidei suae articulos, qua credunt, Esse tantum mane communicandum, Esse tantum in loco sacro, aut portatili, quod uocant, celebrandum:
25   Esse aquam uino miscendam, et alios grauissimos, et his sanctissimis sanctis dignissimos articulos.

NEMO est petulantissime scurra: qui non sentiat blasphemas istas irrisiones tuas, recta contingere sanctissimos quosque proceres ecclesiae catholicae, nempe Cyprianum,

Quantos qualesque uiros irrideat Lutherus

30   Hieronymum, Ambrosium, Augustinum, Basilium, Gregorium, Chrisostomum, atque id genus reliquos: quorum sanctissimi libri passim declarant, eos, quae tu derides, serio sancteque seruasse, et execrabilem credidisse,

Luther's doctoral magistrality does not consider that in this passage he proclaims himself the kind of utterly vicious scoundrel who under the name of the king blasphemes, himself an Augustinian, Augustine, by whose words he had once sworn, from whom as well as from Christ he now flees as a fugitive forsworn. For the prince cited Augustine as clearly declaring that what this fellow proclaims is nothing but an optional human invention was the invention of the Holy Spirit. And certainly, of so many holy fathers of the church who have lived from the time of Christ's passion even to the present day, there has never been one who did not believe that the common customs of the universal church concerning the sacraments either were handed down by the order of God through the apostles or had developed in the church through the Holy Spirit. If anyone at times transgressed these customs through human frailty, he reckoned it among his sins. But, *But for Luther it is a sin to observe them* on the other hand, of so many impious and insane scoundrels who have lived from the time of Christ's passion even to the present day, you almost singly have risen up to blather that the common customs of the universal church concerning the sacraments are so completely optional that what all men observe so holily, so uninterruptedly, and have observed during so many centuries is now optional for each person to ignore when he pleases, as often as he pleases. And you dare, scoundrel, under the name of papists to mock the whole church of so many ages.

Therefore, you say, we willingly grant *Luther's words* to these holy papists those solemn articles of their faith by which they believe that the eucharist must be communicated only in the morning, that it must be celebrated only in a consecrated place or on a portable altar, as they call it; that water must be mixed with the wine, and other most weighty articles very worthy of these most saintly men.

There is no one, you most insolent buffoon, who does not sense that these blasphemous mockeries of yours directly touch all the most saintly leaders of the catholic church; *The importance and character of the men Luther mocks* namely, Cyprian, Jerome, Ambrose, Augustine, Basil, Gregory, Chrysostom, and the rest of that class whose most holy books everywhere proclaim that they observed earnestly and holily the practices which you

si quis illa non per incuriam praeteriret: sed quod tu facis arroganter
et contumeliose contemneret. Sed tu tibi conscius, omnibus sanctis te
esse execrabilem: uelut desperatus nebulo, uicissim sanctos omnes,
amens et insanus irrides. [Z₄v]

5   *Verba Lutheri*   Nos autem, inquis, tales fideles mere
                                    fatuos, et stolidos affirmamus.

Nimirum, quasi dicas nos haeretici, nos infideles, tales fideles mere
fatuos et stolidos appellamus. Sed quum dies illa uenerit Luthere: in
qua stabunt fideles in magna constantia: tum uos haeretici, et
10   infideles uidentes, turbabimini timore hor-
Tum tibi Luthere excutietur ista
iactantia uerborum   ribili: et gementes prae angustia spiritus
                                    dicetis: Hi sunt fideles et sancti: quos
nos infideles et impij aliquando habuimus in derisum, et in similitudinem improperij. Ecce, quomodo computati sunt inter filios dei.
15 Ergo nos errauimus a uia ueritatis: et iusticiae lumen non luxit nobis:
et sol intelligentiae non est ortus nobis. Lassati sumus in uia iniquitatis et perditionis. Quid profuit nobis superbia?

        Verba Lutheri   Nos, inquis, communionem sacramenti
                                    liberam habemus, siue per diem, siue
20   per noctem, siue mane, siue uesperi, libera sunt tempora, horae, loci,
uestes, ritus.

OMNIA tibi libera sunt: nec tua refert, ubi, quando, quomodo
sacrifices, noctu ne, an interdiu, in luce ne, an in tenebris, ebrius, an
sobrius, uestitus, an nudus, cultus, an sordidus, super altare, an super
25 foricam furcifer.

        Lutheri uerba   Apud nos, inquis, non peccat, qui
                                    modeste ederit, aut biberit ante com-
munionem, quod et Paulus confirmat. I. ad Cor. XI. dicens. Si quis
esurit, domi manducet, ut non in iudicium conueniatis ad coenam
30   dominicam.

Vtpote apud quos nullum sit   QVI ante communionem ederit aut bi-
peccatum, nisi incredulitas   berit, non peccat, apud uos haereticos, ho-
                                    mines nimirum impeccabiles. Apud quos,
nullum tam grande peccatum est: quod peccatum esse possit. Omnia
35 peccata uestra, sic absorbentur in fide: quorum animas interim totas

13 habuimus] *L*, hobuimus *BR*   33 impeccabiles] *corr. err. L*, implacabiles *BR*

deride, and that they believed a man execrable, not if he omitted those practices through carelessness, but if, as you do, he arrogantly and insultingly contemned them. But you, aware that you are execrable to all the saints, like a desperate scoundrel, senselessly and insanely deride in turn all the saints.

> But we, you say, declare such faithful men mere simpletons and dolts.

Luther's words

No doubt; as if you should say: "We heretics, we infidels, call such faithful men mere simpletons and dolts." But when that day shall have come, Luther, in which the faithful shall stand in great constancy, then you heretics and infidels, seeing it, will be shaken with dreadful fear, and groaning in anguish of spirit you will say: "These are the faithful and holy men whom we faithless and impious men once held as a laughingstock and as a type for mockery. See how they are accounted among the sons of God. We then have strayed from the way of truth, and the light of justice did not shine for us, and the sun of understanding did not rise for us. We had our fill of the ways of mischief and of ruin; what did our pride avail us?"

Then, Luther, this bandying about of words will be shaken out of you

> We, you say, hold the communion of the sacrament freely, whether by day or by night, whether in the morning or in the evening; free are the times, hours, places, vestments, rites.

Luther's words

All things are free for you; nor does it make any difference to you where, when, how you offer the sacrifice, whether by night or by day, whether in the light or in darkness, drunk or sober, clothed or naked, clean or filthy, on the altar or on the toilet, you hang-dog knave.

> Among us, you say, a man does not sin who eats or drinks moderately before communion, which Paul also confirms in I Corinthians 11, saying: "If anyone is hungry, let him eat at home, lest you come together unto judgment at the Lord's supper."

Luther's words

He who eats or drinks before communion does not sin among you heretics, men unquestionably without sin, among whom no sin is so serious that it can be a sin. All your sins are so swallowed up in faith, while at the same time, lack of faith wholly swallows up your souls.

Seeing that among them there is no sin but lack of faith

absorbet infidelitas.[AA₁] Iam quod affers ex Paulo: pone primum
illic perspicue dici, quod tu illum dicis dicere: quid aliud ex eo loco
probasti tamen: quam quod id tum licuerit? Concludes ne ex eo,
postquam tibi probauit rex, contra placuisse spiritui sancto, annis
5 iam plus mille, idem licere nunc? quia apostolus, sic dispensante
deo, permisit illud tunc? quasi non quaedam aliquando permiserit:
quae paulo post etiam ipse prohibuit: nisi nunc circumcisionem
permittas omnibus: quia Paulus olim circumcidit Timotheum. Sed
quaeso te Luthere, qui nihil admittis praeter euidentes scripturas:
10 quomodo facies illum Pauli locum tam euidentem pro te? Paulus ait:
Si quis esurit, domi edat. An ideo manifestum facies, illum dicere id
eis licere? nec ullum esse peccatum, si esurientes prius domi come-
dant: deinde saturi sumant eucharistiam? Idem quum ijsdem scribat
Audi nunc iam Luthere contra   Corinthijs: Qui contemptibiles sunt in
15   ecclesia, eos constituite ad iudicandum:
probat ne, ut constituantur contemptibiles? an id potius dicit, ad
eorum uerecundiam, qui neminem repererint satis sapientem in
ecclesia: qui dirimeret lites christianorum: sed eos litigare permittant
apud ethnicos? quamquam uelit eos potius apud quemuis litigare
20 christianum iudicem, quam Christi nomen prophanare apud gentes.
Tamen aperte pronunciat eos peccare: quod de pecunia litigent apud
se. Omnino (inquit) peccatum est: quod habetis iudicia inter uos. Et
En Luthere testimonium tuum   tu Luthere, si locum, quem affers, dili-
contra te   genter expendas: uidebis eum torte potius
25   totum contra te canere. Nam ibi manifeste
reprehendit apostolus eos, qui suas coenas afferentes secum, prae-
occupabant eas aedere: priusquam ederent [AA₁v] coenam dominicam. Et ideo, Non licet (inquit) edere coenam dominicam: quia
propriam quisque coenam praeoccupat. Ex quo non obscure colligitur,
30 ieiunos uenisse ad communionem, sed cibum quenque suum, cepisse
portare secum: quem quia quidam praegustabant: apostolus id
reprehendit: praecipiens, ut domi corpus pascerent: in templo
pascerent animam. Quod si tam effoeminati essent, aut alias sic

4 rex, contra] *corr. err. L*, rex contra, *BR*   28 Et ideo, Non] Et ideo. Non *L*

Now, as for what you bring up from Paul; suppose first of all that in that passage he clearly says what you say he says; what else have you yet proved from that passage than that the practice was then permitted? Do you conclude from it, after the king has proved to you that the Holy Spirit has willed the contrary for more than a thousand years already, that the same thing is permitted now because the apostle, by God's dispensation, permitted it then? As if the apostle did not at times permit certain things which shortly after even he himself prohibited; unless you now permit circumcision to all because Paul once circumcised Timothy.

But I ask you, Luther, who admit nothing besides evident scriptures, how will you make that passage of Paul support you so clearly? Paul says: "If anyone is hungry, let him eat at home." Will you therefore make it clear that he says this is permitted to them and that there is no sin if men who are hungry eat at home first, then when satisfied receive the eucharist? When the same apostle writes to the same Corinthians: "Appoint those who are rated as nothing in the church to judge," *Listen now in turn, Luther* does he approve that men who are rated as nothing are appointed? Or does he rather say this to the shame of those men who did not find anyone sufficiently wise in the church to settle the lawsuits of Christians, but who permit them to go to law before unbelievers, although he wishes them rather to take up the case before some Christian judge than to profane the name of Christ before pagans? Nevertheless, he clearly declares that those men sin because they quarrel over money among themselves. "It is altogether sinful," he says, "that you have lawsuits one with another." And, Luther, if you carefully examine the passage which you bring up, you will see that he is perhaps rather declaiming *See your testimony against yourself, Luther* wholly against you. For there the apostle clearly censures those who, bringing their suppers with them, hastened to eat them before they ate the Lord's supper. And so, he says: "It is not permitted to eat the Lord's supper because each one first greedily eats his own supper." From this it is inferred, not obscurely, that they came fasting to communion, but that each one began to carry his own food with him; and because certain ones were eating their supper beforehand, the apostle censures that practice, commanding that they should feed their body at home, feed their soul at church. But if they were so weak or at times so indisposed that it would be difficult for

affecti: ut grauerentur tantisper durare ieiuni: quoad conueniret
concio: continerent se potius: et comederent domi: nec ad communionem auderent, saturi et eructantes accedere: unde sibi damnationem
accerserent. Relege ergo locum rursus Luthere, uidebisque eum
5 totum tibi potius aduersari, quam suffragari. Siquidem haud ait, si
quis esurit, domi manducet, ac dein ueniat: sed si quis inediam
nequeat ferre, domi remaneat iubet, ac ibi famem sedet: nec ad
templum dei adeat: ut uentris negocium agat.

Verba Lutheri   Non quod damnem usum, mane et locis
10   sacris communicandi, sed necessitatem
repudiamus. Volumus enim, si quis ieiunare non possit, aut reumate,
uel grauedine leuari ieiunus non possit, ante comedat et bibat, quam
participet mensae domini: et hoc libere agat, quo corpore et animo
sit compositissimus. Nam quod Henricus Ecclesiam uocat, nos dici-
15   *Vos, id est haeretici*   mus meretricem purpuratam esse. Eccle-
                                    sia enim et si ritibus et caeremonijs
carere non possit, non tamen leges et laqueos animarum ex ipsis facit,
faciunt autem hoc, qui ecclesiae nomen iactant porci illi et asini,
Henricistae, Papistae, sophistae, Thomistae, et sui generis deceptores,
20   et Antichristi.

Dominus Martinus plus millies declarauit aperte, quam magnifice,
et quam regaliter, imo quam nebulonice, et quam scurriliter, omnes
ecclesiae consuetudines, omnes leges, omnes ritus, et caeremo[AA₂]-
nias omnes contemnat. Nam leges exussit etiam, ne quis dubitet,
25 quanti faciat reliqua: quibus hoc pro magno tribuitur: ut legibus,
quas exussit, aequentur. At nunc subito cepit esse circumspectus, et
moderari sententiam suam. Nam ante dixit saepe, sic esse omnia ista
libera: ut liceat omnia, quando libet, quoties libet, seruare, mutare,
probare, damnare, curare, necgligere. Nunc non damnat usum: sed
30 repudiat necessitatem communicandi mane, et locis sacris. Et qui in
Hiccine qui nunquam pugnantia   Babylone contendit, missam fore multo
dicit?   magis christianam: si uestium, cantuum,
                                   gestuum, et caeterorum rituum, et caere-

24 exussit etiam, ne] *L*, exussit, etiam ne *BR*, excussit etiam, ne *corr. err.*   31 *gloss*
om. L   32 uestium] vestium *L*, uestuum *BR*

them to wait fasting so long a time until the assembly should come together, they should rather restrain themselves and eat at home, nor should they dare to approach communion filled and belching; from this they would bring condemnation on themselves. Reread the passage therefore, Luther, and you will see that it rather opposes you entirely than supports you, since he does not say, "If anyone is hungry let him eat at home and then come," but if anyone cannot bear fasting, he commands him to remain at home and there appease his hunger, and not to approach the temple of God to take care of his stomach's need.

Not that I condemn the usage of receiving communion in the morning and *Luther's words* in consecrated places, but we reject the necessity of doing so. For we wish, if anyone cannot fast or cannot while fasting be relieved of catarrh or heaviness, that he should eat and drink before he partakes of the table of the Lord, and he should do this freely so that he may be completely at ease in body and mind. *You, that is, the heretics* For what Henry calls the church we say is the scarlet-clad harlot. Even if the church cannot do without rites and ceremonies, nevertheless she does not make laws and soul-snares of them; but those men do this who bandy about the name of church, those pigs and asses, Henricists, papists, sophists, Thomists, and deceivers of that ilk, and followers of Antichrist.

The honored Martin has openly declared more than a thousand times how solemnly, and how regally, or rather how rascally and how buffoonishly, he scorns all the customs of the church, all laws, all rites, and all ceremonies. For he has even burned the laws, lest anyone doubt how much store he sets by the rest of the things to which he attributes great significance that they be put on the same level as the laws which he has burned. But now suddenly he begins to be cautious and to temper his opinion. For before he often said that all these things are so free that it is permissible in the case of all of them, whenever one pleases, as often as one pleases, to keep them, to change them, to approve them, to condemn them, to attend to them, to ignore them. Now he does not condemn the usage, but he rejects the necessity of receiving communion in the morning and in consecrated places. And he who argued in the *Babylon* that the mass would be much more *Is this the man who never says anything contradictory?* Christian if the pomp of vestments, chants,

moniarum omnium, pompa tolleretur: contra nunc fatetur hic,
ecclesiam ritibus et caeremonijs carere non posse: Sed ecclesiam
ueram, id est Lutheranam, ritus et ceremonias habere liberas:
ecclesiam uero papisticam, id est catholicam, leges et laqueos
animarum, ex ipsis facere. Videamus ergo
5   *Animum lector aduerte*
Luthere, qui sint hi laquei: quos inijcit
ecclesia catholica: et quae sit haec libertas: in quam nos uendicat
ecclesia tua. Consideremus istud, in hac ipsa consuetudine, qua
communicamus ieiuni. Ecclesia hunc ritum accipit, et alios ritus
10 eiusmodi, perductos in consuetudinem, per occultam dispensationem
spiritus sancti: sicut sanctissimi quique patrum testantur: non tanquam sacramentorum substantiam, sed qui in honorem sacramentorum adhibentur: qui neque contemni sine peccato possunt: nec sine
magna, grauique causa debent omitti. Caeterum si quis decumbat
15   aegrotus: aut alias sit in periculo: com-
An non Luthere hoc satis est
libertatis?   municat non ieiunus: communicat uel
ter pastus: ne decedat absque uiatico.
Verum ubi neminem est commu[AA₂v]nicandi necessitas: abstinen-
dum potius censet ecclesia catholica: quam ritum et consuetudinem
20 diuinitus institutam, temere praesumas infringere. Dic igitur Luthere,
quis est hic animarum laqueus? Vbi potes implere, quod praecipitur?
et quod non potes implere, non exigitur.
Nempe cui nulla sit libertas,   Sed hoc tibi tamen, et ecclesiae tuae, non
nisi licentia
satis uidetur liberum. Sed si quis reumate
25 uel grauedine leuari ieiunus non possit: uis, ut ante comedat, et
bibat: quam attingat mensam domini: et hoc libere agat? Cur istud?
ut sit (inquis) corpore et animo quam compositissimus. Valde profecto
liberum facis illum ecclesiae ritum: si libere tibi licet eum soluere,
de qualibet causa tam facile, ob reumatis aut grauedinis paululum.
30 Nam si talibus excrementis, corpus exuberet ualdius: nocuerit potius,
quam profuerit cibus. Quin istud miror
Hic quoque nihil tecum pugnas   nunc placere tibi: ut qui communicat,
Luthere scilicet
animum habeat compositum: quum in
Babylonica placuerit: ut accedens ad communionem, haberet
35 animum, quam maxime posset, confusum, per conscientias erroneas,

18 neminem] *corr. err. L,* nullum *BR*   31 *gloss om. L*

gestures and other rites and all ceremonies were abolished, now on
the contrary admits here that the church cannot do without rites and
ceremonies, but the true church, that is the Lutheran, considers rites
and ceremonies free, whereas the papist church, that is the catholic,
makes of them laws and soul-snares.   5

Let us see, therefore, Luther: What are
these snares which the catholic church sets   *Take notice, reader*
and what is this liberty unto which your church sets us free? Let us
examine this point in regard to this very custom by which we
communicate fasting. The church accepts this rite and other rites of   10
the same kind which have been drawn out into custom by the hidden
dispensation of the Holy Spirit, as all the most holy fathers testify, not
as being the substance of the sacraments but as those elements which
are applied for the honor of the sacraments and which neither can be
scorned without sin nor should be omitted without grave and   15
serious cause. But if anyone falls ill or is at
other times in danger, he communicates   *Is this not enough liberty,*
without fasting; he communicates even if he   *Luther?*
has eaten three times so that he may not depart without viaticum.
But when there is no necessity for communicating, the catholic church   20
judges that you should rather abstain than that you should rashly
presume to infringe the rite and divinely constituted custom. Tell me,
then, Luther, what soul-snare is here, where you can fulfill what is
commanded and where what you cannot fulfill is not required?

Yet this still does not seem sufficiently   25
free for you and your church. But if any-   *Doubtless for him to whom there*
one, while fasting, cannot be relieved of   *is no liberty but license*
catarrh or heaviness, you wish him to eat and drink before he
approaches the table of the Lord and to do this freely. Why so? So
that, you say, he may be as completely at ease as possible in body and   30
mind. You certainly make that rite of the church extremely free if you
are freely permitted to relax it so easily for any cause you please,
because of a little catarrh or heaviness. If the body is so excessively
full of such excrement, food will rather harm than profit it. Indeed, I
am surprised that you should now want   *Here, of course, also, you do not*   35
the one who communicates to have his   *contradict yourself at all,*
mind at ease, since in the *Babylon* you   *Luther*
wished that on approaching communion
one should have his mind as confused as possible by distracting

et peccatorum, uel morsu, uel titillatione turbatas. Praeterea si reumate uel grauedine molestetur: quare non potius differet communicare: quam contra tam receptum totius ecclesiae morem communicet? Hoc uidelicet te mouet: quod tunc communicaretur rarius:

5 et tu communicationem illam sanctissimam uelles fieri frequentissi-

Quam haec cohaereat tu lector aestima

mam. Hoc tu curas scilicet: qui in Babylone censes eucharistiam sumendam, tantum semel in uita: nec id nisi in mortis articulo. SED tu adhuc liberiorem facis ecclesiam tuam: nempe ut

10 praeoccupet edere: si quis ieiunare non possit. Olim, qui communicabant, ad coenam usque ieiunabant: [AA₃] Quam rem, quum aliquot aut aegroti, aut delicati non ferrent: ecclesia, docente spiritu sancto, mutauit tempus: Et potius elegit a uespere ad auroram ducere, quam praetextum relinquere cuiquam: ut cogi uideatur ante communionem

15 edere. Et nunc tu tamen dicis: si quis non potest ieiunare. posses fortassis istud dicere: si communicare non liceret ante uesperum. Nunc miseret me profecto tui, et ecclesiae tuae: si perpotantes usque ad mediam noctem, non potestis postea ieiunare, usque ad summum mane. Nunc uides lector, quam belle reuerendus pater temperat

20 sermonem suum: et quam pulchre diffiniat: quatenus deferendum sit ritibus, et consuetudinibus ecclesiae.

Refellit solutiones Lutheri: quibus conatur illud soluere: quod rex obiecit, de aqua infusa uino. Cap. IX.

25 SED IAM illud, quod aqua licite miscetur uino. Quae res, ut ostendit princeps, non magis potuit fieri, quam altera species omitti, nisi per spiritum dei. Per quem et dicit et docet, utramque rem esse receptam. Operae precium est uidere, quum diu riseris, quam perplexe tractes interea: et quam ridicule tandem solueris. Ais diuersam esse rationem,

30 de specie uini tollenda laicis, et de aqua infundenda in uinum.

---

15 ieiunare. posses] ieiunare, posses *L*

recollections and agitated either by the gnawing or by the titillation of sins. Besides, if a man is troubled by catarrh or heaviness, why may he not rather put off communicating than communicate contrary to such an accepted custom of the whole church?

This, of course, is your motive: that communion would then be received less often, and you would wish that most holy reception of communion to occur most frequently. You of course are concerned about this, who in the *Babylon* think that the eucharist should be received only once in a lifetime and that not except on the point of death. But you make your church still more free, obviously so that one may hasten to eat beforehand, if he cannot fast. Long ago those who received communion used to fast even until supper; since some sick or delicate persons could not bear that, the church by the teaching of the Holy Spirit changed the time and chose rather to transfer it from evening to morning than to leave anyone the pretext of appearing forced to eat before communion. And now you still say: "If anyone cannot fast . . ." You could perhaps say this if one were not permitted to communicate before evening. Now I am surely sorry for you and your church if, guzzling your fill until midnight, you cannot afterwards fast until the very early morning. Now you see, reader, how finely the reverend father tempers his words, and how neatly he defines how far one must defer to the rites and customs of the church.

Consider how consistent these points are, reader

He refutes the solutions with which Luther tries
to solve the king's objections about the water
poured into the wine. Chapter 9.

But now, this practice that the water is lawfully mingled with the wine. This practice, as the prince has shown, could no more have come about than that the second kind be omitted, except by the Spirit of God, through whom he both says and proves that both practices have been accepted. It is worth while to see, since you have ridiculed it for so long, how confusedly you meanwhile handle the matter and how ridiculously you have finally solved it. You say that the reason for taking away the species of wine from the laity is different from that

Alterum enim ecclesiae non licere statuere: quia uini species est pars
sacramenti: de altero licite statuere potuisse: quia est res impertinens
ad sacramentum. Nam quicquid est impertinens: id plane liberum
esse dicit, et de talibus homi[AA₃v]nes posse statuere, utpote ritibus
et caeremonijs: quibus ecclesiam dicit non posse carere. Obiter ergo
lector quam festiuum illud? quod ritibus

Festiuum illud, quod nec pugnantia
dicere uult uideri

ac caeremonijs fatetur ecclesiam carere
non posse: et tamen paulo post unum-
quenque liberum esse uult, eadem statuta uel obseruare uel trans-
gredi: uidelicet ut libera sit ecclesia. In quam libertatem sic uocati
sumus, inquit, e seruitute: ut nec ulla lege, nec ulla consuetudine
teneamur: sed ita uidelicet liber quisque sit in rebus spiritualibus: ut
quicquid libet, licere debeat: quid ni? ut dum unus natale celebrat:
alius faciat pascha, et dum religiosi ieiunant quadragesimam: pater
potator interea, cum suis compotoribus, celebret bacchanalia. Et
haec est una solutio: qua soluit illud argumentum regis.

Verba Lutheri

Non ualet, inquit, similitudo: quia, ut
tolleretur altera species, non potuit ec-
clesia statuere: quia forma est instituta a Christo: sed de aqua infundenda potuit, quia non est de forma sacramenti, sed quiddam imper-

Et tu malis in peiorem peccare
partem

tinens, et quicquid est impertinens, non
solum ecclesia, sed etiam quilibet potest
libere pro suo libito facere, uel omittere.

ET tamen paulo post, idem reuerendus pater ait, non impertinens
esse, sed malum, aquam infundere uino: atque ita non licere: quia

Vnde ista regula Luthere?

habet, inquit, malam significationem: nam
significat, inquit, synceritatem scripturae,
confundi traditionibus humanis. Vides igitur, ut homo sapiens, et
nusquam sibi contrarius, unum regis argumentum soluat duabus
solutionibus, inuicem sibi contrarijs: Altera, quod cuilibet licet
aquam infundere: quia non est prohibitum: sed tantum est impertinens: nec magis ulli parti sacramenti contrarium, quam creationi
mundi, aut natiuitati [AA₄] Christi: Altera, quod licere non potest:

---

5 dicit] *corr. err. L*, dicis *BR*   6 *gloss* Festiuum] festiuus *corr. err. from* festinus, Festiuus
BR, gloss om. L   14 pascha,] *L*, pascha. *BR*   21 *gloss om. L*

for pouring water into the wine. For the church is not permitted to decide the one practice since the species of wine is part of the sacrament; concerning the other she could lawfully have decided, since the matter is not essential to the sacrament. Whatever is not essential, this the fellow says is clearly free and men can decide concerning such 5 matters as being rites and ceremonies which you say the church cannot do without.

Incidentally, reader, how amusing is his admission that the church cannot do with- out rites and ceremonies and yet shortly after his wish that each one be free either

Amusing, that he wants us to think he says nothing inconsistent 10

to observe or to transgress those same statutes, so that of course the church may be free. "Into which liberty we are called," he says, "from slavery so that we are bound neither by any law nor by any custom but each one is of course so free in spiritual matters that he 15 ought to be permitted whatever he pleases." Why not? So that while one celebrates Christmas, another may keep Easter, and while religious men fast during lent, Father Tosspot may celebrate the Bacchanalia with his pot-companions. And this is one solution with which he solves the king's argument. 20

The comparison, he says, is not valid, because the church could not decide to

Luther's words

take away the one kind since the form was instituted by Christ, but it could decide about pouring water into the wine since this does not concern the form of the sacrament but is something unessential, and whatever is unessential, not only the church but also

And you prefer to sin in the worse way 25

anyone whatsoever can freely do or omit according to his pleasure.

And yet, shortly after, the same reverend father says that it is not unessential but wicked to pour water into the wine and that it is thus 30 not permitted because it has, he says, an evil significance; for it signifies, he says,

Whence this rule, Luther?

that the purity of the scriptures is being mingled with human traditions. You see, then, how the wise fellow, never contradicting himself, solves the one argument of the king with two mutually contradictory 35 solutions: the one that each person is permitted to pour in water because it is not prohibited but is only unessential and not more contrary to any part of the sacrament than to the creation of the world or to the nativity of Christ; the other that it is not permitted

quia malam habet significationem. Et certe licere non potest: si tam
malum est: ut significet synceritatem scripturae confundi traditionibus humanis.

HIC ego tuam fidem charissime lector imploro. Id quod hic
5   nebulo modo appellat impertinens, modo consuetudinem incertae
originis, modo etiam ritum malum: cogita quaeso tecum: an ullam
originem habere censeas, praeter solam
Nullam aliam Lutherus potuit   uoluntatem immortalis dei. Nam si mor-
nominare   tales omnes conuenissent in unum: putas
10 ne tam audacem futurum fuisse quenquam: qui primus ausus esset
proponere, aquam infundendam in uinum: qua de re nihil esset
factum in exemplo Christi? Quod si quisquam fuisset tam audax: ut
proponeret: quenquam ne putas fuisse futurum tam amentem: ut in
re tanta ferret talia proponentem: ut homines ex aqua et uino rite se
15 facturos crederent: quod Christum accepissent in solo fecisse uino?
An non minus timuissent utramque spe-
Non est uerisimile   ciem omittere, quam alteram, adiuncta
tertia humana temeritate uiolare? etiamsi quid esset: quod omnes
scirent habere significationem optimam. Quanto minus si (quod hic
20 ait nebulo) res haberet significationem pessimam? NAM alioqui
nihil censet esse periculi: si quis, quum sacramentum conficit,
quicquam faciat: quod sit impertinens, et non contrarium. Ah
sceleratum scurram, quem, hac ratione, uident omnes non reueri-
turum cum pane mixtum consecrare caseum, aut sacrosanctum
25 corpus domini conscindere, atque infarcire farcimine.

SED tu lector pie, quum uideas neminem, qui quidem [AA₄v]
christianus esset, id unquam fuisse ausurum: ut aliquid adijceret
uenerando sacramento: dubitare non potes, aquam solo sancti
spiritus ordinatione infusam: uel ut repraesentet illius aquae
30 memoriam: quae simul cum sanguine de Christo fluxit in cruce: uel
quia uinum in coena quoque miscuit Christus: etiam si nihil de ea
loquantur euangelistae: qui non omnia scripserunt: quae fecit
Christus: certe quacunque de causa spiritus sanctus instituit: non
alio receptum spiritu, quam sancto, potes lector esse certissimus.
35 Quare nec id dubitare potes, quod spiritus sanctus instituit: quisquis
id malum significare dicit, illius spiritum
Is est Lutherus   a spiritu pessimo fortiter esse possessum.

---

7 *gloss om.* L   13 fuisse futurum] futurum fuisse *L*   29 uel ut] uelut *BRL*

because it has an evil significance. And certainly it cannot be permitted if it is so evil that it signifies that the purity of the scripture is mingled with human traditions.

Here I appeal to your faith, dear reader. Please consider whether that which this scoundrel calls at one moment unessential, at another moment a custom of uncertain origin, at still another even an evil rite, has any origin besides the sole will of the immortal God. For if all mortals *Luther could name no other* had met in assembly, do you think that anyone would have been so bold as to have dared to be the first to propose that water be poured into the wine, for which practice there is no precedent in Christ's action? But if someone had been so bold as to propose this, do you think anyone would have been so senseless that in such an important matter he would put up with the man who proposed such actions so that men would believe that they might lawfully do with water and wine what they had learned Christ had done with wine only? Or would they not have feared less to omit both kinds than to violate the second by *It is not likely* adding a third through human rashness, even if it were something which everyone knew had the best significance? How much less if, as this scoundrel says, the matter had the worst significance? For otherwise, he thinks there would be no danger if someone, in consecrating the sacrament, should do something which is unessential and not contrary to it. Ah, sinful buffoon, who, according to this reasoning, everyone sees would not be afraid to consecrate cheese mixed with bread, or to tear to pieces the most holy body of the Lord and to stuff it full of sausages.

Yet, devout reader, when you see that no one who was truly Christian would ever have dared to add anything to the venerable sacrament, you cannot doubt that the water is poured in only by the ordinance of the Holy Spirit, either so that it may represent the memory of that water which together with the blood flowed from Christ on the cross, or because Christ at the supper also mingled wine with water, even if this fact is not mentioned by the evangelists, who did not write all the things which Christ did. Certainly, for whatever reason the Holy Spirit instituted it, you can be most certain, reader, that it was not received from any other spirit than the Holy Spirit. Therefore you cannot doubt either that the spirit of the man who says that this practice *This fellow is Luther*

5

10

15

20

25

30

35

Quid ergo mirum est: si stolidus nebulo calumniatur principem:
quum et apostolum Iacobum, et ecclesiam totam catholicam, iam
olim contempserit: et nunc eo procedat impietatis: ut aperte
blasphemet spiritum sanctum. Quum id,

O sacrilegum nebulonem

5   quod nemo non uidet, spiritum sanctum
omnibus inspirasse fidelibus: hoc audet scurra, quouis infideli
deterior, execranda lingua et radicitus execanda, blasphemare.

Ostendit, quam impeditus sit illo argumento Lutherus,
de aqua infusa in calicem: et simul duo
10   illa stultorum genera, ab Luthero
conficta facete
retaliat. Ca. X.

SED quam misere torqueatur illo argumento de aqua infusa uino:
docet eius perplexa fluctuatio. Huc atque illuc rotat se: nec usquam
15 consistit secum: licet, inquit, ho[BB₁]minibus statuere: ut infundatur
aqua, quia est tantum ritus, et res impertinens ad sacramentum. Et
statim paulo post. Non licet aquam infundi: quia malam habet
significationem. Rursus. Ecclesia non potest carere ritibus, et caeremonijs: ex quo sequitur: quod ritus et caeremoniae seruandae sunt:
20 et ex consequente, seruanda est aquae mixtio: quem ritum esse
fatetur, et dumtaxat impertinentem: et qualem dicit ecclesiam posse
statuere. At rursus, paulo post: Nemo tenetur ad ritus aut caeremonias: quia liberi sumus ab omnibus euangelica libertate: Ergo
aquam non obligamur infundere. Sed paulo post rursus. Si quis
25   infundat aquam, malum significat: Atque

Vos uidemini male didicisse
dialecticam uestram
domine Luthere

hac ratione, prohibemur infundere. Vide,
quo pacto se ex illo extricet argumento
Dominus Martinus. Aquam tenemur
infundere. Aquam non tenemur infundere. Aquam tenemur non
30 infundere. Age age nebulo: perge sceleste, sic perplexe loqui. Sic

---

7 radicitus execanda] radicitus execranda *L*   8 impeditus sit] sit *om. L*   10 stultorum
genera] genera stultorum *L*   25 *gloss om. L*   29–30 tenemur non infundere] non
tenemur infundere *L*

instituted by the Holy Spirit signifies evil is powerfully possessed by a completely evil spirit. What wonder, then, if the stupid scoundrel slanders the prince, since he has already long ago scorned both the apostle James and the whole catholic church and now proceeds to such a degree of impiety that he openly blasphemes the Holy Spirit, since that which everyone sees the Holy Spirit has inspired in all the faithful, this buffoon worse than any infidel dares to blaspheme with his cursed tongue which should be cut out by the roots.

O sacrilegious good-for-nothing

He shows how embarrassed Luther is by that argument about the water poured into the chalice and at the same time he wittily retaliates against those two kinds of fools fashioned by Luther. Chapter 10.

But how wretchedly he is racked by that argument about the water poured into the wine, his confused vacillation shows. He whirls this way and that and is never consistent; he says it is lawful for men to decide that water be poured in because it is only a rite and a matter unessential to the sacrament; and very shortly after: it is not lawful for the water to be poured in because it has an evil significance. Again: the church cannot do without rites and ceremonies, from which it follows that rites and ceremonies must be preserved, and in consequence of this there must be preserved the mingling of the water, which he admits is a rite and only unessential, and as such, he says the church can decide it. But again, shortly after: no one is held to rites or ceremonies because we are free from all things with the gospel freedom; therefore, we are not bound to pour in the water. But shortly after again: if anyone pours in the water, he signifies something evil, and according to this reasoning we are forbidden to pour it in. See how the honored Martin disentangles himself from this argument. We are obliged to pour in water. We are not obliged to pour in water. We are obliged not to pour in water. Come, come, rogue; keep on speaking so

You seem to have learned your dialectics poorly, my honored Luther

obscuratur cor insipiens. Sic caligant impij. Sic hallucinantur
schismatici. Sic uertigine rotantur haeretici.

ET tamen affectat uideri non rixator tantum strenuus: sed si
superis placet, etiam scurra facetus. Fingit itaque duo stultorum
genera: quorum alter sit tam stultus: ut ex
facto impertinente extra scripturam, putet
tolli scripturam: ut ex eo, quod fit adul-
terium, tolli putet scripturas, prohibentes adulterium. Alter uero,
tam stolidus, ut ex uno quolibet scripturae loco, quemlibet alium
scripturae locum, quantumuis impertinentem putet haereticum esse:
ut ex eo, quod Ietro legitur consuluisse Mosi: ut statueret iudices:
credat omnes scripturas falsas esse: quae loquuntur de natiuitate
Christi. Deinde disputat suo more festiue: hoc est [BB₁v] scurriliter:
utroque stulto stultiorem esse principem: qui ex eo, quod homines
licite statuerent: ut aqua uino misceretur in sacramento: quae res est
(ut ait) ritus dumtaxat impertinens: et ideo licite potuit ab hominibus
institui: concludat etiam, licite ab hominibus institutum: ut uini
species tolleretur laicis. Quam rem talem esse contendit: ut ab
hominibus institui non potuerit: quia uini species non est res impertinens, sed pars sacramenti.

Stulta Lutheri stultorum
fictio

VERVM quum huius tam festiuae
fictionis fundamentum sit, non ullum
uerbum principis, sed stolidum ipsius
Lutheri commentum: quo nemo non illum uidet, id dictum imputare
regi: rex quod nusquam dicit, quis adeo stultus est: ut non stultum
istum, tam stulte stultos fingentem, rideat? Nam quod tam facile
nobis fingit stultos: equidem nihil miror. Naturale est enim: ut
stultus procreet stultum, similis similem, sicut asinus asinum. Nec
dubito: quin stultus iste, postquam ei iam
displicere coepit in sacerdote castitas,
multos nobis stultos geniturus sit. Verum
cum sua stultorum suorum generatione, sic glorietur, ut aut neminem
stultitiam suam uidere credat: aut id se saltem simulet credere:
fingat nobis aegregius iste stultorum figulus, unum saltem stultum

Occasio huius fictionis
Lutheri

Si tantum stultos gigneret minus
esset mali

confusedly, rascal. Thus the foolish heart is beclouded. Thus the impious are befogged. Thus the schismatics prate. Thus the heretics are whirled with giddiness.

And yet he aspires to appear not only a restless wrangler, but, should it please the gods, even a witty buffoon. And so he fashions two kinds of fools; of which the one is so foolish that because of an unessential action without scriptural authority he thinks scripture is abolished; for example, from the fact that adultery is committed he thinks the scriptures forbidding adultery are abolished. But the other is so dull-witted that because of any one passage of scripture whatsoever he thinks that any other passage of scripture whatsoever, however irrelevant, is heretical; for example, from the passage where Jethro is read to have advised Moses to set up judges he believes that all the scriptures are false which speak of the nativity of Christ. Then he argues wittily in his usual manner, that is buffoonishly, that the prince is more foolish than either fool since, from the fact that men lawfully decided that water should be mingled with wine in the sacrament—which practice is, as he says, only an unessential rite and therefore could lawfully be instituted by men— he has concluded that it was also lawfully instituted by men that the species of wine be taken away from the laity. This matter Luther argues to be such that it could not have been instituted by men because the species of wine is not an unessential element but a part of the sacrament.

Luther's foolish fashioning of fools

But since the foundation of such a facetious fiction is not any word of the prince but the dull-witted device of Luther himself, by which everyone sees that he imputes to the king a statement which the king nowhere makes, who is so foolish that he will not laugh at this fool so foolishly fashioning fools? I am not surprised, indeed, that he so facilely fashions fools for us. For it is natural that a fool should beget fools, like beget like, as an ass begets an ass. Nor do I doubt but that this fool of ours, now that priestly chastity has begun to gall him, will beget many fools for us. But since he so glories in his begetting of his fools that he either believes no one sees his own folly, or at least pretends to believe it, let this remarkable fashioner of fools fashion for us at least one fool of the kind who, when

The pretext for this fiction of Luther's

If he would beget only fools, it would be less evil

huiusmodi: qui quum inuenerit forte annulum ex orichalco, per

Huiusmodi quiddam se iam reperisse putat Lutherus

iocum deceptus a quopiam, persuadeat sibi, eum esse aureum illum annulum Gygis: qui olim imperitabat Sardibus: quo
5 illum, ferunt, solitum ire quolibet inuisibilem. Hac mirabili fortuna, superbus morio, quos ludos iocosque dabit: dum mille nugis faciet prestigij sui periculum? quam gestiet? quam ridebit?[BB₂] quam saltabit prae gaudio, spectatoribus in aliam partem auertentibus oculos, ut eius foueant stultitiam? Ima ille, se interea mirabilem
10 quempiam semideum his haberi putabit: quibus ridetur insanus. Non simius, simio similior est: quam isti stulto stultus, et stulte stultefex Lutherus. Qui tanquam nemo stultitiam eius uideat: ita se superbus effert: et quasi iam persuaserit omnibus, id regem hominibus tribuere: quod nemo nescit eum tribuisse

Morionis uidelicet ritu saltantis in rete
15

dumtaxat deo: ludit ac gestit stolidus, uelut omnibus omnium oculis nouo perstrictis praestigio, ne se ludentem conspiciant, uenuste scilicet in morem cameli saltantem. Ipse tam stultus interea, ut sannas, cachinnos, ronchos, et rinocerotas non animaduertat omnium undique riden-
20 tium, tam ridiculam stolide sibi plaudentis insaniam.

VERVM ne fors aegre ferat uenerandus pater, nomen stulti: age, fingatur alius, non plene stultus, sed pene stultus. Caeterum plene nebulo, et plusquam plene scurra parasiticus, qui fuerit aliquando frater, post curtisanus, dein rursum frater,

Tacite tangit crebras Lutheri metamorphoses
25

post apostata, tum leno rursus, postremo plagepatida: qui in aliquo Bohemiae pago, rusticorum conuiuium ingressus, scurrari coeperit: qui quum tur-pissimis gestibus, et uerbis obscoenissimis risum captarit: postquam ineptus mimus, et improbus, imitatus est rusticum, lenonem,
30 ebriosum, meretricem furiosam, tandem cupiens exhilerare conuiuas, incipiat imitari morionem: et quo primarium stultitiae specimen edat, nudus prodeat in conuiuium dumtaxat opertus rete: quasi persuaserit ei quispiam, sic incantatum esse se, ut nemini possit conspici.[BB₂v] Sic igitur ingressus, non morio stultus et innocens, sed

15 ludit] *L*, ludet *BR*

he has happened to discover a ring made of brass, being deceived by
someone's joke, will persuade himself that
it is the golden ring of Gyges, who once   *Something of this sort Luther*
governed Sardis, by means of which,   *thinks he has now found*
they say, he used to go anywhere he pleased, invisible. With this   5
marvelous good luck, what tricks and jokes the conceited fool will
play while with a thousand trifles he will try out his trick! How he
will exult! How he will laugh! How he will leap for joy, while the
spectators turn their gaze in another direction to encourage his
folly! Then he will think that he is all the while considered some   10
marvelous demigod by those who mock him as insane. An ape does
not ape an ape more than a fool is played the fool by our foolish and
foolishly fool-fashioning Luther, who, as though no one saw his folly,
is so proudly puffed up, and, as if he had now persuaded everyone
that the king attributes to men what everyone knows the latter has   15
attributed to God alone, sports and frolics,
the dolt, as though everyone's eyes were   *That is, like a fool dancing*
blinded by his new trick so that they do not   *in a net*
perceive him frolicking; that is, dancing gracefully like a camel. He
himself meanwhile is so foolish that he does not notice the derisive   20
grimaces, the roars of laughter, the jeers and sneering mockery of
everyone on all sides ridiculing the ridiculous madness of a man
stupidly applauding himself.

But lest the venerable father be irritated by the name of fool, come,
let another be fashioned, not clearly a fool but nearly a fool; what is   25
more, clearly a scoundrel and more than clearly a toadying buffoon,
who was once a friar, later a pimp, then again a friar, afterwards an
apostate, then again a pander, finally a
clout-pate, who in some hinterland of   *Implicitly he touches on Luther's*
Bohemia coming in on a feast of rustics   *frequent metamorphoses*   30
begins to play the buffoon; when he has won their laughter by the
filthiest gestures and the most obscene words, afterwards the silly and
wicked mimic, having imitated a rustic, a pander, a drunk, a raging
whore, finally eager to delight the feasters, begins to imitate an
idiot, and in order to present a prime example of folly he comes out   35
naked into the company covered only with a net, as if someone has
persuaded him that such a spell has been cast over him that he can be
perceived by no one. Having thus entered, not a foolish and innocent
idiot, but a wicked buffoon and shameless debauchee, he labors with

Haec Luthere in te belle competunt

improbus scurra, et lastaurus impudens, obscoenis gestibus laborat excitare risum, donec tam foedum spectaculum detestantibus, illius etiam ruris rusticis, qui publice coeunt in templis, ipso solo

5 qui risum captat sic ridente, quo modo ridere solet irritatus canis,

Sic tractari debet Lutherus

caeteris indigne ferentibus, auulso tandem rete, scurra flagris eijcitur. Hic scurra, scio, non displiceret Luthero: neque enim sua cuiquam forma displicet: neque quicquam Luthero tam conforme, quam huiusmodi

10 scurra: ita uterque pari modo scurratur. Nam nec illius nuditas magis conspicua est, quam Lutheri: cuius obscoena sic retegit, ac reuelat regis libellus: ut ipsius liber, quo se tectum simulat: non magis eum tegat: quam illum alterum scurram tegit rete: nec illius magis pudenda nuditas, nec magis impudens, quam nebulonis istius,

15 qui sibi conscius, turpissimam sycophantiam suam omnibus ubique patere: neque quenquam esse mortalium, qui non illum sentiat idipsum aperte sentire: tamen scurra turpissimus, tanquam sibi persuaserit, nemini se posse conspici: sic se stultum simulat: ac sub

Hoc, quo magis appareat eius stulticia

persona stulti, non in rusticorum conuiuio,
20 sed in totius orbis theatro, non in re leuicula, sed in materia religionis et fidei, tam impudenter abutitur improbe scurrandi licentia: ut plane se demonstret dignum: quem non honesti solum cuncti, uelut honestatis corruptelam publicam publice castigandum curent: sed omnes etiam

25 scurrae uirgis in foro uerberent: quod tam improbe scurrando, scurrarum ordinem ex ridiculo reddat inuisum.[BB₃]

---

19 *gloss* appareat] *L*, apareat *BR*   22 impudenter] imprudenter *L*

obscene gestures to arouse a laugh until so *This fits you prettily, Luther*
filthy a show is denounced with curses even
by the rustics of that hinterland, who publicly mate in their temples,
while he alone who seeks the laugh is laughing—just as a dog when
provoked usually laughs—and the rest, *So ought Luther to be treated* 5
indignant, finally tear off the net and the
buffoon is thrown out with a beating.

This buffoon, I know, would not displease Luther, for one is never
displeased by one's own appearance, and nothing is so like Luther in
appearance as a buffoon of this sort, so equally does each play the 10
buffoon. For the nakedness of this fellow is no more conspicuous than
that of Luther, whose obscenities the king's book uncovers and un-
veils so thoroughly that his own book with which he pretends to be
covered covers him no more than the net covers that other buffoon,
nor is that fellow's nakedness more shameful nor more shameless than 15
that of this scoundrel of ours, who, aware that his most disgraceful
trickery is evident to everyone everywhere and that there is no mortal
who does not sense that he clearly senses the same thing, nevertheless,
a most foul buffoon, as though he has persuaded himself that he can be
observed by no one, so simulates a simpleton, and under the mask of 20
a simpleton, not at a rustic feast, but in the
theater of the whole world, not in a trifling *This, so that his folly may*
matter but in a matter of religion and of *appear more clearly*
faith, so shamelessly abuses the license of playing the wicked buffoon
that he clearly proves himself deserving not only that all honorable 25
men should see to it that he is chastised publicly as a public corrupter
of honor but also that all buffoons should beat him with rods in the
marketplace because by playing the buffoon so wickedly he renders
the class of buffoons hateful for their joking.

Ostendit Lutheri in causa diffidentiam, et dissimulationem earum rerum, quibus debuit respondere: necnon aduersus beatum Ambrosium, stolidam et blasphemam sycophantiam. Caput. XI.

5   DE TRANSVBSTANTIATIONE.

Verba Lutheri

QVarto, quum ego demonstrassem, non esse necessarium credere panem et uinum transubstantiari: insurgit in me Thomista rex, duabus machinis. Quarum prima est Ambrosij uerbum: Altera Thomisticus
10   ille aries, qui uocatur Oportet sic esse. Ambrosium inducit, asserentem nihil remanere nisi corpus et sanguinem post consecrationem. Quid ergo respondeam tam insulsis, et ineptis

Id quod tam insulsus quam tu es uellet, conuitia mera

stultis? Si hic quaeram, an Ambrosij uerbum sit articulus fidei necessarius,
15   dicet rex, Oportet sic esse. Si dixero, quis dedit Ambrosio ius condendi articulos fidei, dicet, Oportet sic esse. Et non uidet stolidum caput, tale esse Ambrosij uerbum, quod se ipsum deuorat, cum impossibile sit, nihil remanere nisi corpus et sanguinem post consecrationem, nisi apud Thomistas subtilissimos uiros, forma, color, frigus, et alia
20   accidentia, nihil esse dicuntur. Nam haec uere ut non sunt nihil, ita uidemus ea remanere, ut Am-

Et tu nequis tuum uidere scelus?

brosium hic errasse palam palpemus etiam.

AVT nunquam quisquam uictus est candide lector: aut hac in re
25   profecto clarissime uictus est: et turpissime cecidit impijssimus haereticorum Lutherus: Cui, si tam aliquid esset frontis, quam nihil est omnino mentis: sic illum oppressisset pudor: ut in ignem potius fuisset coniecturus sese: quam in huius articuli mentionem unquam uenturus denuo. Sed quam nihil illum pudeat, uel hinc agnosce
30   lector. [BB₃v] Rex illius argumenta recensuit omnia fideliter: atque adeo nihil imminuit: ut quaedam etiam

At Lutherus utitur diuersa rhetorica, ut aliquid truncet

amplificet. Omnia uero tam aperte soluit: ut ne nunc quidem praeter stulta conuitia,

12 *gloss* tu] *L*, ru *BR*   21 *gloss* Et] *L*, et *BR*

He shows Luther's mistrust in his cause and his concealment of those arguments he should have answered, together with his stupid and blasphemous slander against blessed Ambrose. Chapter 11.

On Transubstantiation

Fourthly, when I had proved that it was not necessary to believe that the bread *Luther's words* and wine are transubstantiated, the Thomist king rose up against me with two stratagems. Of which the first is the word of Ambrose, the other that Thomistic battering ram which is called: "It must be so." He brings in Ambrose's assertion that nothing remains but the body and the blood after consecration. What, then, should I answer such senseless and silly *Just what a person as senseless as* fools? If I should here ask whether the *you would wish—mere insults* word of Ambrose is a necessary article of faith, the king will say, "It must be so." If I ask, "Who gave Ambrose the right of establishing articles of faith?" he will say, "It must be so." And the dull-witted blockhead does not see that the word of Ambrose is the kind that devours itself, since it is impossible for nothing but the body and blood to remain after consecration, unless among the Thomists, very subtle men, form, color, cold and other accidents are said to be nothing. For, truly, as these things are not nothing, so we see that they remain, so that here we even pal- pably feel that Ambrose has openly *And you, can you not see your* erred. *own crime?*

Either no one has ever been conquered, honest reader, or in this case this fellow has certainly been most clearly conquered and has most shamefully fallen, this most impious of heretics, Luther; if he had as much sense of shame as he has nothing at all of mind, shame would have so completely overwhelmed him that he would rather have been ready to hurl himself into the fire than ever happen to mention this article a second time. But that he is ashamed of nothing, reader, recognize even from this: the king has reviewed all this fellow's arguments faithfully and so little does he abbreviate them that he even amplified some of them. But all of them he has solved so clearly that *But Luther uses a different* not even now has Luther been able to find *rhetoric, to lop off something*

sicuti statim uidebis, quicquam potuerit inuenire Lutherus: quod
contra rursus obijceret. Denique totam rem ex ipsis Christi uerbis
probauit: quae, licet tam aperta sint, ut expositione non egeant: tamen
exposuit tam dilucide: ut si cuiquam ante fuissent dubia: post ea
5 dubitare non posset. Postremo, ne uideretur ex suo dumtaxat capite

Hos ne taceat, ridet Lutherus

quicquam dicere: sicut Lutherus e suo
dicit omnia: profert magnam antiquorum
patrum, et doctissimorum, et sanctissimorum cateruam, eadem de re,
idem omnino sentientium: quorum testimonio probauit, non modo
10 se pro suo libito non torquere scripturam dubiam: sicut Lutherus ui
in transuersam torquere solet apertam: sed nec in clarissima quidem

*At Lutherus contra, sese praefert
omnibus*

sibi cito credere, nisi secum consentire
senserit bonorum, atque eruditorum sententiam. Quin eadem opera, probauit et
15 illud: Nempe transubstantiationis fidem: quam Lutherus improbe
mentitus est, natam esse intra trecentos annos: ueterem fuisse ecclesiae
fidem ante annos plus mille. Quum ergo princeps (ut dixi) luculenter
haec probarit omnia: Lutherus ita prostratus in lutum, pudoris
dolore stimulatus, ex ira uersus in furiam, haec ferme dissimulat
20

Hoc pro suo more facit

omnia. Et omissis ossibus ac neruis, conatur, mollioris hinc inde carunculae, frus-
tum aliquod arripere: quod rodat. Nec tamen quicquam inuenit tam
fragile: quin putridos eius dentes infringat. Quemadmodum illud
ipsum de Ambrosio, in quo spectare potes, et extremae despera[BB₄]-
25

Solita Lutheri sycophantia

tionis, et duplicis sycophantiae Lutheranae
conscientiam. Ait enim regem, tantum
afferre duo, uidelicet dictum Ambrosij, et Thomistarum (ut uocat)
arietem, Oportet sic esse. Quaeso te Luthere, quum tot ueteres
produxerit rex, cur tu, qui sacrilegium clamas esse omitti tuorum
30 quicquam, atque id clamas impudenter ibi: ubi nihil prorsus
omittitur: cur inquam, hic reliquos omnes subtrahis: de solo fateris

4 post ea] postea *L*   10–11 ui in] ui *corr. err.*, in *BRL*   20 *gloss* Hoc] *L*, hoc *BR*

anything but foolish insults, as you shall see immediately, to bring up
in his turn.

Next, he has proved the whole case from the very words of Christ,
which, although they are so clear that they do not require explanation, he has yet explained so clearly that if they had been doubtful to
anyone before, that person could not doubt them afterwards. Finally,
lest he seem to say anything only from his
own head, as Luther says everything from *Rather than keep quiet about these*
men, Luther mocks them
his, the king brings forward a large
company of the ancient fathers, both very learned and very holy,
completely unanimous on the matter; by their testimony he has
proved not only that he does not twist a doubtful scripture according
to his own whim as Luther usually twists a clear text into its opposite,
but that not even in a most clear scripture does he readily trust himself unless he senses that the opinion of
good and learned men is in agreement *But Luther, on the other hand,*
sets himself above all others
with him.

Indeed, he has at the same time proved this also; namely, that
faith in transubstantiation, which Luther wickedly pretends has
arisen within the past three hundred years, was the ancient faith of
the church more than a thousand years ago. Since, therefore, the
prince, as I have said, has clearly proved all these things, Luther, thus
prostrate in the mud, goaded by the torture of shame, turned from
wrath to raging madness, conceals almost all these things. And,
passing over the bones and sinews, he tries
to seize on some little piece of soft flesh in *This he does in his usual*
manner
one spot or another to gnaw on. And yet
he does not find any morsel so tender but it breaks his rotting teeth.
As, for instance, that very text from Ambrose, in which case you can
behold a conscience marked by extremely desperate boldness, and
by double-dealing Lutheran cunning. For
he says that the king brings forward only *Luther's usual cunning*
two arguments; namely, Ambrose's statement and the battering ram,
as he calls it, of the Thomists: "It must be so."

Tell me, Luther, when the king has brought up so many ancient
writers, why do you, who protest that it is a sacrilege for any of your
arguments to be passed over and who shamelessly protest this in
instances where nothing has been passed over at all, why, I ask, do
you here fail to mention all the rest and speak of Ambrose alone? No

Itaque Lutherus eos subticuit Ambrosio? Nemo tam stupidus est: qui non intelligat tam multorum, qui et eruditi fuerunt et sancti, consensum, tempore locoque distantium plus habere momenti, quam dictum unius Ambrosij. Cur tu tantus

5 bellator, tam certus uictoriae, in causa (ut fingis) facili, non audes congredi cominus? Cur quaeris tam pudenda suffugia: ut, quod fortius est, dissimules: quod minus forte est, id selegas, tanquam solum sit: cum quo pugnare debeas? Putasti quenquam esse tam

Ita credidit stupidum: ut te non sentiat, quum ita rem

10 tractas, pugnam detrectare, et extremam desperationem tuam male tegendo, manifeste prodere?

SED age, reliquos omittamus in gratiam tuam: uideamus interim: quam belle uiceris hunc unum: quem tanquam oportunum et obnoxium, ac superatu facillimum delegisti tibi comparem.

15 *Verba Lutheri* Si quaeram, inquis, an Ambrosii uerbum sit articulus fidei necessarius, dicet rex, Oportet sic esse. Si quaeram, quis dedit Ambrosio ius condendi arti-

Audin lector hunc sycophantam? culos fidei? dicet, oportet sic esse, non potest aliter esse.

20 HORVM Luthere, princeps neutrum respondit. At si quaesieris, an qui talia quaerit, absurde nugetur: an is, qui in tanta re tam inepte nugatur, sit improbus et absurdus [BB₄v] nebulo: nemo non

Et non immerito ad utrumque respondebit: oportet sic esse: non potest aliter esse. IAM quid unquam

25 legisti lector, magis scurrile: quam id, quod sequitur: quo furiosulus iste bacchatur in beatum Ambrosium: quem uult haberi tam stultum: ut uerbum eius seipsum deuoret, propterea, quod impossibile sit, nihil

Pulchra scilicet ratio Lutheri remanere, nisi corpus et sanguinem? scilicet quia remanent accidentia: quae non

30 sunt omnino nihil. Atque ex hac ratione concludit, Ambrosium illo dicto sic errare palam: ut id palpemus etiam. Refer adhuc manum palpator eximie. Ambrosium palpa diligentius: quum dicit hoc pacto.

one is so stupid that he does not under-
stand that the agreement of so many men, *And so Luther conceals them by silence*
separated by time and place, who were
both learned and holy, has more weight than the saying of a single
Ambrose. Why do you, such a great warrior, so certain of victory, in 5
what you pretend is an easy cause, why do you not dare to join
combat hand to hand? Why do you seek such shameful subterfuges
so that you conceal what is more forceful, what is less forceful call out
as though it were the only one with which you should fight? Did you
think anyone is so stupid as not to sense *So he believed* 10
that when you handle the matter in this
way you are refusing to fight, and that by making a poor camouflage
for your extreme desperation you are clearly betraying it?

But come, we will pass over the rest for your sake; let us see
meanwhile how cleverly you have refuted this one argument which as 15
though fitting and frail and most easy of conquest you have selected
as equal to yourself.

If I should ask, you say, whether the word *Luther's words*
of Ambrose is a necessary article of faith,
the king will say, "It must be so." If I should ask who gave Ambrose 20
the right to establish articles of faith, he
will say: "It must be so, it cannot be *Do you hear this trickster, reader?*
otherwise."

The prince answers neither of these answers, Luther. But if you
will ask whether the man who asks such questions talks arrant non- 25
sense, or whether the man who talks such silly nonsense in such a
serious matter is a wicked and senseless scoundrel, everyone will
answer to both questions: "It must be so, *And not undeservedly*
it cannot be otherwise."

Now what have you ever read, reader, more buffoonish than that 30
which follows, in which this raging little madman rants against
blessed Ambrose, whom he would have us consider so foolish that his
word devours itself because it is impossible
that nothing remain but the body and the *Clever reasoning, indeed, on Luther's part*
blood? Because, of course, the accidents 35
remain, which are not nothing at all. And he concludes from this
reasoning that Ambrose errs so plainly in that statement that we may
even palpably feel it. Put out your hand once more, feeler extraordinary. Feel Ambrose more carefully; when he says the following,

Ambrosii uerba   Licet figura panis et uini, in altari uideatur: nihil tamen aliud quam caro et
sanguis Christi credendum est, dicit ne perijsse prorsus accidentia? si
dicat accidentia perijsse: quomodo dicit restare panis et sanguinis
5 figuram? An figuram sensit esse substantiam? Quomodo potuisset
apertius dicere, remanere accidentia, mutari substantiam: quam
quum diceret, adhuc ea manere: per quae
Vbi sunt Luthere illa uerba sui   manere uiderentur panis et uinum: sed
de uoratricia?   non manere quicquam, quod esset aut
10 panis aut uinum? An dumtaxat oculorum uisu, manet species panis:
et non idem reliquis item sensibus uidetur? Igitur quum dicit adhuc
uideri panem et uinum: an non aperte dicit accidentia manere, per
quae efficitur: ut panis et uinum esse uideatur? Quomodo igitur, hic
palpat palpator, beatum Ambrosium errare? Ita ne cuiusquam
15 digiti stupent: ut non palpet hunc palpatorem non errare palpando,
Lutherus quam certus palpator   sicut errauit Isaac: sed maligne calumni-
ando bacchari, nec sese deuorare beati
Ambrosij uerbum, sed furias deuorasse Lutheri cerebrum. [CC₁]

Verba Lutheri   Sed esto, inquit, Ambrosius uoluerit
20   non manere panem et uinum, dicam,
Ambrosium suo sensu habundare permitto. Neque sanctus uir, hoc
Cur ergo tu iniquior es Ambrosio   uerbo conscientiam ullius ceu articulo
cum nihilo sis certior   fidei uoluit obstringere, quum id non
possit e scripturis demonstrare, sed sicut
25 ipse libere hoc modo est opinatus: ita permisit aliter aliis opinari,
exceptis Thomistis, quos etiam ueternosis somniis suis ceu articulis
fidei, iustum est illaqueari et uexari.

QVAM acute soluit: quum non ex unius Ambrosij, sed caeterorum
quoque sanctorum omnium libris clarescat, publicam catholicae
30 ecclesiae fidem (quam uel absque scriptura certam esse, ueramque,
nec falli posse, scriptura testatur) multa secula fuisse talem: quum

---

3 credendum est, dicit] *corr. err. L*, credendum est. Dicit *BR*; prorsus accidentia? si] *L*,
prorsus accidentia: si *BR*   31 nec] *corr. err. L,* uel *BR*

"Although the appearance of bread and
wine is seen on the altar, yet nothing else   *Ambrose's words*
must be believed to be there but the flesh and blood of Christ." Does
he say that the accidents have altogether disappeared? If he should
say that the accidents have disappeared, how does he say that the   5
appearance of bread and wine remains? Or does he understand the
appearance to be the substance? How could he have said more
clearly that the accidents remain, the substance is changed, than
when he said that those things still re-
mained through which bread and wine   *Where, Luther, are those words*
                                         which devour themselves?   10
seemed to remain, but that nothing at all
remained which was either bread or wine? Or does the species of
bread remain only to the sense of sight and does not the same appear
likewise to the rest of the senses? Therefore, when he says that bread
and wine still appear, does he not clearly say that the accidents   15
remain through which it comes about that bread and wine appear to
be present? How, therefore, does our feeler here feel that blessed
Ambrose errs? Are the fingers of anyone so numb that he does not
feel that this feeler does not err as Isaac
erred in his feeling, but that he raves with   *How accurate a feeler*
                                                 Luther is   20
spiteful slandering, and that the word of
Ambrose does not devour itself but that raging madness has devoured
the brain of Luther?

But suppose, he says, that Ambrose did
not wish the bread and wine to remain; I   *Luther's words*
                                                          25
would say: "I permit Ambrose to abound in his own interpretation." Nor did the holy man wish to bind the conscience of anyone
by this word as by an article of faith,
since he cannot prove it from scriptures,   *Why then are you more unfair*
                                               than Ambrose since you are
but as he himself held this opinion freely   *not at all more certain?*   30
in this way, so he permitted others to
think otherwise, with the exception of the Thomists, whom it is fair to
ensnare and harass even by languid dreams as by articles of faith.

How keenly he has solved it, since not from the book of a single
Ambrose but from the books of all the other holy men also does it   35
become clear that the public faith of the catholic church (which the
scripture testifies to be certain and true and unable to be deceived,
even apart from scriptures) has been such for many centuries; since

eandem fidem probent etiam aperta uerba Christi: non debent haec
satis esse Luthero: qui fidem hanc natam
esse mentitur intra trecentos annos. An
aduersus Lutherum ideo non debent haec ualere: quia Lutherus
5 Ambrosium permittit abundare in suo sensu: et idem Ambrosius
tantum suum sensum aperuit: nec Luthero praecepit aperte: ut idem
crederet: quia nunquam putauit, nasciturum tam improbum haereticum: qui id, quod Christus ecclesiae pro indubitato tradidit: tracturus
esset in dubium?

Lutheri commentum de fide

10

Comparat et expendit uerba regis,
cum uerbis Lutheri: et ex
euangelijs responsum Lutheri
conuincit. Caput. XII.

Verba Lutheri. hic nos tuam
non tam stultitiam quam
audaciam miramur

IAm aliud regis robur, quod oportet sic
15 esse, quia clara sunt, inquit, uerba
Christi, dicentis: Hoc est corpus meum.
Non dicit cum hoc, aut in hoc, est corpus
meum. Hic iterum non tam lethargum regis, quam nequitiam accuso.
Sic enim detruncat latro [CC₁v] uerba Christi, et meum argumentum
20 regaliter transilit, acsi ius haberet uerba dei rapere, et ponere pro
libidine. Ipse, iuxta rudem et asininam Thomistarum philosophiam,
aptat pronomen, Hoc, ad praedicatum, corpus meum. Deinde mox
(quasi hoc uicisset) clamat, Aperta sunt uerba. Hoc est corpus meum.
Sed interim totum pondus, quo larualem illam philosophiam urge-
25 bam, tacet subdolus sophista. Hic enim,
tota disputatione egi, ne pronomen, hoc,
ad corpus meum aptari possit in eo loco. Neque enim opus erat
mihi, tam crassis porcis, qui mihi dicerent, nihil esse nisi corpus ibi, si
pronomen, hoc, non nisi corpus demonstrat. Sed quum uitiosissimus
30 petitor principij (ut est mos omnium sophistarum) debeat primum

Imo tu emotae mentis es nebulo

14–16 *gloss* hic . . . miramur] *om.* L

the clear words of Christ also prove the same faith, ought not these arguments to be enough for Luther, who pretends that this faith has arisen within the past three hundred years? Or should not these arguments have force then against Luther because *Luther's fabrication about the faith* Luther permits Ambrose to abound in his own interpretation, and the same Ambrose revealed only his own interpretation and did not clearly command Luther to believe the same, because he never thought that a heretic would be born so wicked as to drag into doubt that which Christ handed on to the church as undoubted?

He compares and carefully examines the words of the king together with the words of Luther and from the gospels refutes Luther's answer. Chapter 12.

Now the other argument of the king, that it must be so, since, he says, the words of Christ are clear in saying: "This is my body." He does not say, "My body is with *Luther's words. Here we are amazed not so much at your folly as at your boldness* this or in this." Here again I reproach not so much the lethargy of the king as his villainy. For the robber so mutilates the words of Christ, and regally leaps over my argument as if he had the right to snatch up the words of God and set them down according to his whim. He himself, according to the crude and asinine philosophy of the Thomists, fits the pronoun "this" to the predicate "my body." Then, as if by this means he had conquered, he soon shouts, "The words are clear: 'This is my body.'" But meanwhile the whole weight with which I was pressing that masked philosophy the subtle sophist passes over in silence. *On the contrary, rascal, you are mentally disturbed* Here I have been arguing throughout the whole disputation that the pronoun "this" cannot be fitted to "my body" in that passage. Nor did I need to do this with such fat pigs as were saying that nothing but the body was there if the pronoun "this" indicates nothing but the body. But although the most corrupt beggar of the initial premise—as is the custom of all sophists—ought first to

ostendere pronomen, hoc, ad praedicatum pertinere, et meas
rationes diluere, horum nihil facit, et
Imo omnia facit Luthere: quae garrit ridicule Christum non dixisse, in
tu eum negas facere
hoc, uel cum hoc, sed hoc est corpus
5   meum. Nonne et ego ista subtilissima subtilitate Thomistarum,
possem dicere, Christus non dixit panis substantiatur in corpus: ut uos
fabularum magistri fingitis? Sed hic fuerit regi laborandum, ubi ex
filo sermonis ostendi, pronomen, hoc, ad
Egregie sane demonstratis
panem aptari: et sic sonare aperte uerba.
10   Hoc est corpus meum, id est, hic panis est corpus. Nam textus sic
habet. Accepit panem, benedixit, fregit, et dixit, Hoc est. &c. Vides
hic, ut omnia illa uerba, accepit, benedixit, fregit, de pane dicantur.
Et eundem demonstrat pronomen, hoc, Quia illud ipsum, quod
accepit, benedixit, fregit. hoc inquam acceptum, et benedictum, et
15   fractum, significatur, quum dicitur, Hoc
At iam apparet uos male intelligere est corpus meum, non praedicatum sed
grammaticam uestram
subiectum demonstrat. Non enim corpus
suum accepit, benedixit, et fregit, sed panem: ideo non demonstrat
corpus, sed panem. Haec sunt clara uerba, quae rex nequitiosus
20   oculit, et nudam illam propositionem urget, Hoc est corpus meum, et
pronomen, hoc, ad corpus temeritate propria aptat.

SI QVIS usquam locus est lector: cuiusmodi sunt supra mille: qui
manifeste probent, Lutherum esse morta[CC₂]lium omnium maxime
impudentem: hic certe locus id docet clarissime. Queritur principem,
25   Christi uerba temerasse, ipsius argumenta praeterijsse: quum rex
integre Christi uerba recenseat, ex euan-
Quomodo rex praetereat Lutheri gelistis omnibus: Lutheri argumenta mel-
argumenta. Lutherus ipse id
facit quod regi exprobrat ius recitet, quam Lutherus. Deinde sic rem
tractet: ut hoc libello plane se demonstret
30   Lutherus, suam se causam prorsus habere pro uicta: ita regis argumenta prorsus relinquit intacta: cum uno dumtaxat aut altero
argumenti frustulo rixatur: nihil prorsus affert: quo labantibus
argumentis suis succurrat. Quamobrem hac in re nihil erit mihi cum
Luthero negocij: subiungam tantum quaedam ex libello principis:
35   quae quum lector, cum Lutheri responso contulerit: facile deprehen-
det: quam deploratam causam Lutherus habeat. Quam nunc, post

---

14 accepit] *L*, acccepit *BR*   18 benedixit] *L*, be-dixit *BR*   30 causam prorsus] *corr.*
err. L, causam *om. BR*

show that the pronoun "this" belongs to the predicate and weaken my reasoning, he does none of these things and prattles absurdly that Christ did not say "in this," or "with this," but, "This is my body." Could not I also say by means of this most subtle subtlety of the Thomists: Christ did not say, "The bread is changed substantially into the body," as you masters of fables pretend? But here the king will have to work, when from the context of the speech I show that the pronoun "this" is fitted to the word "bread"; and thus the words clearly signify: "This is my body"; that is, "This bread is body." For thus the text has it: "He took bread, blessed, broke, and said, 'This is, etc.'" You see here how all those words, "took," "blessed," "broke," are spoken of the bread. And the pronoun "this" indicates the same thing, because that very thing which He took, blessed, broke, this, I say, is signified as taken, blessed, broken when the statement is made: "This is my body"; it indicates not the predicate but the subject. For He did not take His body and bless and break it, but bread; therefore, He does not indicate the body but the bread. These are clear words which the villainous king conceals, and urges that bare proposition, "This is my body," and by his own rashness fits the pronoun "this" to "body."

On the contrary, Luther, he does everything you deny that he does

With truly singular proofs

But it is already clear that you poorly grasp your grammar

If there is any passage anywhere, reader, of which sort there are above a thousand which clearly prove that Luther is the most shameless of all mortals, surely this passage teaches it most clearly. He complains that the prince has desecrated the words of Christ, passed over his own arguments; whereas the king quotes the words of Christ exactly from all the evangelists; he recites Luther's arguments better than Luther does. Moreover, he handles the case in such a way that in this book Luther plainly represents himself as considering his case completely conquered. He thus leaves the arguments of the king completely untouched; he wrangles over only one or the other crumb of an argument; he presents nothing at all to support his own stumbling arguments. For this reason I will have nothing to do with Luther in this matter; I shall only subjoin certain words from the book of the prince; when the reader compares them with Luther's answer, he will easily grasp how hopeless a cause Luther maintains,

How the king passes over the arguments of Luther. Luther himself does that of which he accuses the king

tam gloriosam iactantiam, tandem sic reliquerit indefensam. Sic
igitur inquit rex.

Verba regis

"SECVNDAM captiuitatem facit, quod
quisquam uetetur credere uerum panem,
5 uerumque uinum restare post consecrationem. Qua in re, contra
quam, totus iam credit Christianus orbis: ac multis retro saeculis
credidit: persuadere conatur Lutherus, in

*Is sibi captus uidetur, nisi
quidlibet liceat facere*

eucharistia sic esse Christi corpus et
sanguinem: ut tamen substantia ueri
10 panis, uerique uini remaneat: posthac opinor, quum libebit, corporis
aliquando substantiam sanguinisque negaturus, tanquam post in
melius mutata sententia, quemadmodum ter, ante iam fecit, nempe
in indulgentijs, in potestate pontificis, et communione laicorum.
Interea se fingit ista docere, motum uidelicet misericordia captiui-
15 tatis: qua populus Israeliticus seruiat Babyloni. Ita totam ecclesiam
appellat Ba[CC$_2$v]bylonem: Ecclesiae fi-

*Quam Lutherus proponat
libertatem*

dem uocat seruitutem: et homo misericors
offert libertatem omnibus: qui uelint ab
ecclesia seperari, et istius putridi et abscissi membri contagione
20 corrumpi. At quibus modis, inuitat in hanc plus quam seruilem
libertatem, operae precium est cognoscere. Magnam censet ac
primariam rationem: quod uerbis diuinis non est ulla facienda uis,
neque per hominem, neque per angelum:

Verba Lutheri

Sed quantum fieri potest (inquit) in
25 simplicissima significatione seruanda
sunt, et nisi manifesta circumstantia cogat, extra grammaticam, et
propriam, accipienda non sunt: ne detur aduersarijs occasio, uniuersam scripturam eludendi. At uis fit uerbis diuinis, si quod Christus
ipse uocat panem: hoc nos dicamus

*At maior fit uis, si quod ille corpus
suum tu per contemptum
panem uoces*

30 intelligi panis accidentia, et quod ille
uinum uocat: hoc nos dicamus esse
tantum uini speciem. Omnibus ergo mo-
dis, uerus panis, ac uerum uinum restat in altari, ne uerbis Christi fiat
uis, si species sumatur pro substantia. Nam quum euangelistae clare
35 scribant, Christum accepisse panem, ac benedixisse. et actuum liber,

---

10 posthac opinor,] posthac, opinor, *L*   15 Israeliticus] *L*, Israelititicus *BR*   17 *gloss*
libertatem] *L*, libertem *BR*   29 *gloss om. L*

which now, after such pompous boasting, he has finally left so defenseless. The king then says the following:

"He considers as the second captivity that anyone should be forbidden to believe that the true bread and true wine remain after consecration. In this matter, contrary to what the whole Christian world now believes and has believed for many centuries past, Luther tries to persuade us that the body and blood of Christ are in the eucharist in such a way that the substance of true bread and true wine still remains. I suppose that later on, when he chooses, he will be ready to deny the substance of the body and the blood, as though he had changed his opinion for the better, just as he has done three times already; namely, on the questions of indulgences, the power of the pope, and the communion of the laity. At the same time he pretends that his motive for teaching these doctrines is indeed his pity for the captivity by which the people of Israel are enslaved to Babylon. Thus, he calls the whole church Babylon; he calls the faith of the church slavery; and this merciful fellow offers liberty to all who wish to be separated from the church and to be corrupted by the contagion of this rotting and lopped-off member. But it is worth our while to recognize the reasons for which he invites men to this more than slavish liberty. He judges that the great and foremost reason is that the divine words must not suffer any violence either at the hands of men or at the hands an angel.

The king's words

He considers himself captive unless he is permitted to do whatever he pleases

What sort of liberty Luther proposes

But insofar as can be done, he says, they should be preserved in the most simple signification possible, and unless the context clearly requires it, they should not be accepted beyond their grammatical and proper sense, lest occasion be given to the adversaries for making sport of all scripture. But violence is done to the divine words, if we should say that what Christ Himself calls bread is understood as the accidents of bread and what He calls wine is only the appearance of wine. In all ways, then, do the true bread and the true wine remain on the altar, lest violence be done to the words of Christ, if the appearance is taken for the substance. For since the evangelists clearly write that Christ took bread

Luther's words

But greater violence is done if what He calls His body you through contempt call bread

et Paulus, panem deinceps appellent, uerum oportet intelligi panem, uerumque uinum, sicut uerum calicem. Non enim calicem transubstantiari etiam ipsi dicunt.

Regis uerba. Lutheri
argumentum diluitur

5   "HAEC est ergo magna, et (quemadmodum ait ipse) primaria Lutheri ratio: quam ego me spero facturum: ut omnes quam primum intelligant, nihil magni habere momenti. Nam primum, id quod ait, euangelistas clare dicere, quantumuis clare dicant: pro Luthero tamen nihil clare probat: contra uero, quod pro
10 illo probaret: hoc nusquam dicunt. An non scribunt (inquit) accepisse panem et benedixisse? Quid tum postea? Accepisse panem et benedixisse, etiam nos fatemur. Panem uero dedisse discipulis, postquam inde suum corpus confecerat: hoc et nos instanter [CC₃] negamus: et euangelistae non dicunt. Quae res, quo fiat apertior, et
15 tergiuersandi minus pateat locus: Euangelistas ipsos audiamus. Matthaeus ergo sic narrat. Coenantibus autem eis, accepit Iesus panem, et benedixit, et fregit, deditque discipulis suis: et ait: Accipite et comedite: hoc est corpus meum. Et accipiens calicem, gratias egit: et dedit illis, dicens: Bibite ex hoc omnes: hic est sanguis
20 meus noui testamenti: qui pro multis effundetur, in remissionem peccatorum. Marci uero uerba sunt ista. Et manducantibus illis: accepit Iesus panem, et benedicens fregit, et dedit eis, et ait: Sumite: hoc est corpus meum. Et accepto calice, gratias agens, dedit eis, et biberunt ex illo omnes: et ait illis: Hic est sanguis meus noui testa-
25 menti: qui pro multis effundetur. Lucas denique narrat hoc pacto. Et accepto pane, gratias egit, et fregit, et dedit eis, dicens: Hoc est corpus meum: quod pro uobis datur. Hoc facite in meam commemorationem. Similiter et calicem postquam coenauit, dicens: Hic est calix, nouum testamentum in sanguine meo: qui pro uobis fundetur.
30   "EX omnibus euangelistarum uerbis, nullum uideo locum: in quo post consecrationem, sacramentum uocetur panis aut uinum, sed tantum corpus et sanguis. Dicunt in manus Christum sumpsisse panem: id quod nunc fatemur omnes: at quum reciperent apostoli: non panis nominatur, sed corpus. At Lutherus euangelistae uerba, in
35 suam partem conatur, interpretatione torquere. Accipite. Manducate.

---

5 *gloss* argumentum] argumentu *B*   10 probaret:] probarat, *L*; (inquit)] ,ait, *L*

and blessed it, and the book of Acts and Paul in turn call it bread, it ought to be understood as true bread and as true wine, just as there is understood a true chalice. For not even they say that the chalice is transubstantiated.

"This, then, is Luther's great and, as he himself says, foremost reason. I hope to cause everyone to grasp as soon as possible *The king's words. Luther's argument is weakened* that it has no great importance. To begin with, however clearly the evangelists say what he quotes, it nevertheless proves nothing clearly for Luther; on the contrary, they nowhere say anything which would prove his point. But do they not write, he says, that He took bread and blessed it? Well, what follows? That He took bread and blessed it, we also confess. But that He gave bread to the disciples after He had made it His own body, this we flatly deny, nor do the evangelists say it.

"That this fact may become clearer, and that there may be less opportunity for evading the issue, let us hear the evangelists themselves. Matthew's account is as follows: 'And while they were at supper, Jesus took bread, and blessed, and broke, and gave it to His disciples, and said, "Take and eat; this is my body." And taking a cup, He gave thanks and gave it to them, saying, "All of you drink of this; for this is my blood of the new covenant, which is being shed for many unto the forgiveness of sins." ' And the words of Mark are these: 'And while they were eating, Jesus took bread, and blessing it, He broke, and gave it to them, and said, "Take, this is my body." And taking a cup and giving thanks, He gave it to them and they all drank of it; and He said to them, "This is my blood of the new covenant, which is being shed for many." ' Finally, Luke tells it in this manner: 'And having taken bread, He gave thanks and broke, and gave it to them, saying, "This is my body, which is being given for you; do this in remembrance of me." In like manner He took also the cup after the supper, saying, "This cup is the new covenant in my blood, which shall be shed for you." '

"From all the words of the evangelists, I see no place in which, after the consecration, the sacrament is called bread or wine, but only body and blood. They say that Christ took bread into His hands, a thing which all of us also admit; but when the apostles received it, it is not called bread but body. Yet Luther tries by his interpretation to twist the words of the evangelist to his own advantage. 'Take. Eat. This

Argutula Lutheri interpretatio Hoc, id est, hic panis, (inquit is) quem acceperat, et fregerat, est corpus meum. Sed haec est interpre[CC₃v]tatio Lutheri, non uerba Christi, neque uerborum sensus. Si panem, quem accepit, quemadmodum accepit,

5 sic tradidisset discipulis: nec ante conuertisset in carnem: ac porrigendo dixisset: Accipite et manducate: recte diceretur porrexisse: quod in manus acceperat: nihil enim fuisset, aliud quod porrigeretur. At quum, priusquam daret apostolis manducandum: panem conuertit in carnem: non iam accipiunt panem, quem ille susceperat, sed

10 *Comparatio elegans* corpus eius: in quod panem conuerterat. Quemadmodum, si quis, quum semen accepisset: alij daret inde natum florem: non id dedisset, quod acceperat: quamquam naturae communis ordo, alterum fecisset ex altero: ita, multo minus porrexit apostolis, id, quod in manus

15 acceperat Christus: quum panem susceptum, in suam ipse carnem *Comparatio efficax* tanto uertisset miraculo: nisi quis contendat, quoniam Aaron uirgam sumpsit in manum, et uirgam eiecit e manu: ideo cum colubro quoque, uirgae restitisse substantiam, aut colubri denuo, cum recepta uirgula. Quod

20 si cum colubro, uirga restare non potuit: quanto minus restare potest *Lutheri nugax argutia eluditur* panis, cum carne Christi, tam incomparabili substantia? Nam quod argutatur, imo nugatur Lutherus, pro suae simplicitate fidei facere: quum de uino dicat Christus: non, hoc est sanguis meus: sed, hic est sanguis meus:

25 miror, quid homini uenerit in mentem: quum istud scriberet. Quis enim non uidet, quam nihil omnino facit pro eo? imo contra, *Lutheri argumentum de articulo retortum* uideretur magis pro eo fecisse: si dixisset Christus: Hoc est sanguis meus. Habuisset enim ansam saltem Lutherus: qua, demon-

30 strandi articulum referret ad uinum. Nunc uero, quum uinum sit neutri ge[CC₄]neris: Christus ait: non hoc, sed hic est sanguis meus: et quum panis sit generis masculini: ait tandem: Hoc est corpus

---

1 *gloss* Argutula] *L*, argutula *BR*; (inquit is)] (inquit) is *L*   7 fuisset, aliud] fuisset aliud, *L*   26 pro eo? imo contra,] pro eo, imo contra? *BR*, pro eo, imo contra: *L* 27 *gloss om. L*

(*hoc*)—that is, this (*hic*) bread (he says) which He had taken and broken—is my body.'

The quibbling interpretation of Luther

"But this is the interpretation of Luther, not the words of Christ, nor the sense of His words. If He had handed to His disciples the bread which He took, just as He took it, and had not first turned it into His flesh, and had said while presenting it: 'Take and eat,' He would rightly be said to have presented to them what He had taken into His hands, for what He would be presenting to them would be nothing different. But since He changed the bread into flesh before He gave it to the apostles to eat, they now receive not the bread which He had taken up, but His body into which He had changed the bread. Just as if someone after taking up a seed were to give another

A choice comparison

person the flower sprung from that seed, he would not have given that which he had taken up, although the general order of nature would have made the one thing from the other, so, much less did Christ present to the apostles that which He had taken into His hands, since by such a great miracle He had turned the bread taken up into His very own flesh. Unless someone would argue that because Aaron took a rod

An effective comparison

into his hand and cast a rod from his hand, therefore the substance of the rod had remained together with the serpent or that of the serpent remained when the rod was taken up again. But if the rod could not remain with the serpent, how much less can bread remain with the flesh of Christ, such an incomparable substance?

"As for Luther's prattling, or rather babbling that it supports the simplicity of his faith when Christ says of the wine, not,

Luther's trifling prattling is mocked

'This (*hoc*) is my blood,' but 'This (*hic*) is my blood,' I wonder what the man had in mind when he wrote this. For who does not see that it does not support him at all? Indeed, on the contrary, it would seem rather to have supported him if Christ had said, 'This (*hoc*) is my blood.' For Luther would have had at least some excuse

Luther's argument about the article is turned back on him

for referring the demonstrative article to the wine. But as it is, although wine is of the neuter gender, yet Christ did not say, 'This (*hoc*),' but 'This (*hic*) is my blood'; and although bread is of the masculine gender, He said after all, 'This (*hoc*) is my body,' not 'This

meum, non hic: ut uterque ostendat articulus, Christum, neque
panem propinare, neque uinum, sed suum ipsius corpus et sanguinem.
NAM quod uideri uult Lutherus, pronomen, hoc, ad corpus referri,
non Christi proposito, sed occasione linguarum, nempe Latinae et
5 Graecae: ac proinde nos remittit, ad Hebraicam: an non ridiculum
est? Nam Hebraea lingua, si neutrum genus non habet: non potest
tam aperte declarare, ad utrum Christus rettulit articulum, quam
Latina uel Graeca. Nam in Hebraea lingua, si articulus fuisset
masculus, tanquam diceret: hic est corpus meum: tamen res relin-
10 queretur ambigua: quia potuisset ea locutio uideri coacta, necessitate
linguae, non habentis neutrum. Sed quum apud Latinos, panis et
corpus sint diuersi generis: is, qui transtulit e Graeca: articulum
coniunxisset cum pane: nisi apud euangelistam repperisset, demonstrationem factam de corpore. Praeterea quum Lutherus fateatur
15 idem generis discrimen esse et Graecis: facile potuisset cognoscere
euangelistas: qui scripserunt Graece: articulum fuisse posituros: qui
referretur ad panem: nisi quod conscij mentis dominicae, uoluerunt
admonere Christianos, articulo corporis, Christum non panem
communicasse discipulis, sed corpus. Quamobrem, quod Lutherus
20 interpretatur in suam partem, uerba Christi, Accipite et manducate,
hoc est corpus meum: id est, hic panis, quem acceperat: non ego, sed
ipse Christus, contra docet, sua uerba intelligi: nempe hoc, quod eis
porri[CC₄v]gebat, non esse, quod ipsis uidebatur panem, sed suum
ipsius corpus, (si recte Christi uerba recensent euangelistae) Nam
25 alioqui poterat dicere, non hoc, (quod exponeretur, id est hic) sed
aperte potius, hic panis est corpus meum: quo sermone docerentur
discipuli: id quod nunc Lutherus docet ecclesiam, nempe, in eucharistia pariter et Christi esse corpus et panem. Nunc uero, sic locutus
est, ut ostenderet manifeste, corpus dumtaxat esse, non panem.
30   *Argumentum Lutheri*   IAM quod tam magnifice transfert ad se
        ineptissimum   Lutherus: quod Christus etiam loquitur
de calice: quem nemo dicat esse transub-
stantiatum, miror hominem non pudere tam intemperantis ineptiae.

---

25 (quod exponeretur, id est hic)] (quod exponeretur) id est hic, *L*   28 panem] *L*,
sanguinem *BR*   30 *gloss* Argumentum] *L*, argumentum *BR*; transfert] *L*, trans fert *BR*

(*hic*)'; so that each article shows that Christ was setting before them neither bread nor wine but His very own body and blood.

"As for Luther's wishing it to appear that the pronoun 'this (*hoc*)' refers to the body not according to the intention of Christ but by reason of the languages, that is Greek and Latin, and so sends us back to the Hebrew, is this not ridiculous? If the Hebrew language does not have the neuter gender, it cannot so clearly declare to which article Christ referred as can Latin or Greek. For in the Hebrew language, if the article had been masculine, as though He were saying, 'This (*hic*) is my body,' the matter would still be left ambiguous because that expression could have seemed forced by the exigency of a language that has no neuter. But since 'bread' and 'body' are of different genders among the Latins, the one who translated the article from the Greek would have joined it to 'bread,' had he not discerned from the text of the evangelist that reference was made to the body. Moreover, since Luther admits that there is the same distinction of gender among the Greeks, he could easily have known that the evangelists who wrote in Greek would have set down the article which referred to the bread except that, knowing the mind of the Lord, they wished to remind Christians by the article referring to the body that Christ did not give the disciples bread in communion, but His body.

"Therefore, whereas Luther interprets to his own advantage Christ's words, 'Take and eat, this is my body,' that is, this bread which He had taken up; not I but Christ Himself teaches that His words are to be understood in a contrary sense; namely, that this which He was presenting to them was not, as it seemed to them, bread, but His very own body—if the evangelists accurately record the words of Christ. For otherwise He could have said, not 'This (*hoc*)'—which would be explained, 'that is "this (*hic*)" '—but rather, clearly, 'This (*hic*) bread is my body'; by which manner of expression He would be teaching the disciples what Luther is now teaching the church; namely, that in the eucharist the body of Christ and the bread are equally present. But now He has spoken in such a way as to show clearly that only the body is present, not the bread.

"Now as for Luther's so pompously applying to his own advantage the fact *Luther's silliest argument* that Christ speaks also about the chalice, which no one says was transubstantiated, I am amazed that the man is not ashamed of such

Quum dicit Christus, Hic calix noui testamenti in meo sanguine, quid
facit pro Luthero? Quid enim significat aliud, quam id, quod
discipulis propinabat in calice, suum esse sanguinem? An ex his
Christi uerbis ostendet nobis Lutherus, manere uini substantiam,
5 quia Christus loquitur de sanguine? aut uinum in sanguinem non
posse mutari: quia adhuc restat calix? Vtinam praeludium delegisset
sibi Lutherus ex alia materia: in qua minore periculo potuisset ludere.
Nam quum Boemos et Graecos sic excuset ab haeresi: ut haereticos
clamet, omnes esse Romanos: multo magis ostendit se Lutherus
10 haereticum: qui non solum fidem abnegat, quam tota credit ecclesia,
sed etiam, deteriora credi suadet: quam aut crediderunt Graeci: aut
unquam credidere Boemi."

QVID AIS Luthere? quid in te credis,
Catalogus mendaciorum Lutheri dum haec legit, interea rogitare lectorem?
in regem
15 an non mirari, ac detestari tuam impuden-
tiam? Dixisti regem argumenta tua re[DD₁]galiter transilire: sed
lector te uidet hic scurriliter ualde mentiri. Dixisti regem Christi
uerba truncare: sed lector te dignum censet: cui mendacissima lingua
secari debeat, et stolidum truncari caput. Dixisti regem nihil afferre,
20 nisi Oportet sic esse: lector eum uidet, tua argumenta tam uere
soluisse: ut nihil habeas, quo possis ferre subsidium.

ET TV, quo fugam tuam turpissime
Lutheri uitatio dissimules: excerpis e tam multis, unius
argumenti partem: et illam quoque, quantum potes, deprauas:
25 quam nec sic effugis. Sed nusquam tutus, huc illuc trepidus cursitas:
sicut fugientes solent. Debuit, inquis, ostendere pronomen, hoc, ad
corpus pertinere: quasi non omnes eum uideant id clarissimis argumentis fecisse, et exemplis etiam illustrasse, de semine et inde nato
flore, de uirga et inde facto serpente. Quibus, tuum illud praesidium
30 de circumstantia plane prostrauit. Et
Regis confirmationes, eius, quod tamen illa dissimulans, rursus redis cum
Lutherus negat eadem circumstantia. Accepit panem,
benedixit, fregit, ac dixit: Hoc, id est hic panis, est corpus meum. At

9–10 Lutherus haereticum] *L*, Lutherushaereticum *BR*   30 *gloss om. L*

unrestrained folly. When Christ says, 'This is the chalice of the new covenant in my blood,' what is He doing for Luther? What else does He indicate but that what He was setting before the disciples in the chalice was His own blood? Will Luther show us from these words of Christ that the substance of wine remains because Christ speaks of the blood? Or that wine cannot be changed into blood because the chalice still remains? I wish Luther had chosen for himself a prelude from some other theme, on which he could have played with less danger. For when he so thoroughly excuses the Bohemians and Greeks from heresy as to proclaim all Romans heretics, Luther shows himself a much worse heretic, who not only rejects the faith which the whole church believes but also persuades men to believe worse things than either the Greeks or the Bohemians ever believed."

What are you saying, Luther? What questions do you believe your reader will *Catalogue of Luther's lies against the king* be hurling at you the whole time he reads this? Do you not think he will wonder at and loathe your shamelessness? You said that the king regally leaped over your arguments, but the reader sees that here, like a buffoon, you lie grievously. You said that the king lops off words of Christ, but the reader judges you worthy to have your most deceitful tongue cut out and your blockhead lopped off. You said that the king presents nothing but, "It must be so," but the reader sees that the king has so truly dissolved your arguments that you have nothing with which you can defend yourself.

Moreover, in order most basely to conceal your flight, you select from so many *Luther's evasion* arguments a part of one argument, and even that, insofar as you can, you distort; not even so do you escape it, but, nowhere safe, you run fearfully here and there as men in flight usually do. He should, you say, have shown that the pronoun "this" pertains to the body, as if everyone does not see that he has done this by the clearest arguments and also illustrated it with examples about the seed and the flower born from it, about the rod and the serpent made from it. With these he has clearly destroyed that defensive argument of yours from the context. And *The king's proofs of that which Luther denies* yet, concealing those arguments, you return again with the same argument from the context: "He took bread, He blessed, He broke, and said, 'This—that is, this bread—is

interea de responsione regis, uerbum nullum: de exemplis illis magnum silentium.

Verba Lutheri

Vides hic, inquis, ut omnia illa uerba, accepit, benedixit, ac fregit, de pane dicantur. Et eundem demonstrat pronomen, hoc, Quia illud ipsum, quod accepit, benedixit, ac fregit. hoc inquam, acceptum, et benedictum, et fractum, significatur, quum dicitur, Hoc est corpus meum, non praedicatum, sed subiectum demonstrat.

O suauem interpretem

Non enim corpus suum accepit, benedixit, et fregit, sed panem: non ideo demonstrat corpus, sed panem. Haec sunt, inquit, clara uerba, quae rex nequitiosus oculit.

SED QVID rex ad ista responderit, et hoc tam aperte, [DD₁v] stultum sophisma, quam aperta ratione diluerit: hoc nequitiosus occulit Lutherus. Et tanquam omnium clausisset oculos, nequis illud posset legere: sic rursus stultissime iactat idem sophisma: rursus oculis subijciens et praedecans subiectum et praedicatum: et cathenam nobis longam faciens e glacie. Panis erat, quem accepit: ergo panis erat, quem benedixit. Panis erat, quem benedixit: ergo panis erat, quem

Collectio argumenti Lutherani

fregit. Panis erat, quem fregit: ergo panis erat, quem dedit discipulis. Sic Luthere soles uigilanti stertere naso: ut te non sentire simules: quum hanc fragilem cathenam tuam tibi rex infringeret, negans Christum dedisse, quod in manus acceperat: postquam id, quod accepit, mutauit in aliud: quemadmodum pulcherrime demonstrat exemplum illud, de flore nato ex semine. Quod exemplum, tu non es ausus attingere. Sed si teneret haec

Lutheri argumentum derogare certis scripturis

praeclara cathena tua: nec uirga Aaron ex uirga uersa fuit in serpentem: nec ex serpente rursus in uirgam: si sic sophisticari pergamus. Aaron, quod in manus sumpsit, hoc proiecit: sumpsit autem uirgam: proiecit ergo uirgam. Deinde, quod proiecit: hoc ante Pharaonem iacuit: sed non nisi uirgam proiecit: ergo non nisi uirga iacuit ante Pharaonem. Aut si simul fuisse uis, et uirgam et serpentem, licebit saltem eodem modo colligere. Quod in terra iacuit: hoc Aaron sustulit, et secum retulit:

22 negans] negas *L*

my body.' " But meanwhile, concerning the answer of the king, not a word; concerning those examples, deep silence.

You see here, you say, how all those words, "He took, blessed, and broke," are said of the bread. And the pronoun "this (*hoc*)" designates the same thing, because that very thing which He took, blessed, and broke, this I say, is signified as taken, and blessed, and broken; when the words, "This is my body," are said, it indicates not the predicate but the subject. For He did not take, bless, and break His own body. Therefore He does not indicate the body but the bread. These are clear words, he says, which the villainous king conceals.

Luther's words

O delightful interpreter

But what the king has answered to these words, and with what clear reasoning he has solved such a clearly silly sophism, this the villainous Luther conceals. And, as though he had closed the eyes of everyone so that no one could read it, he thus again most foolishly tosses out the same fallacy, again setting before our eyes and proclaiming subject and predicate and making us a long chain from ice: It was bread which He took, therefore it was bread which He blessed; it was bread which He blessed, therefore it was bread which He broke; it was bread which He broke, therefore it was bread which He gave to the disciples. Thus, Luther, you usually snore with a wakeful nose, so that you pretend you do not understand when the king broke this fragile chain of yours for you, denying that Christ gave what He had taken into His hands after He had changed what He took into something different, as that example of the flower born from the seed very beautifully proves. This example you have not dared to touch. But if this remarkable chain of yours would hold, then the rod of Aaron was neither turned from a rod into a serpent, nor from a serpent back into a rod, if we proceed to play the sophist as follows: Aaron cast down what he took into his hands; but he took up a rod; therefore he cast down a rod. Next, what he cast down lay before Pharaoh; but he cast down nothing but a rod; therefore nothing but a rod lay before Pharaoh. Or, if you wish it to have been at the same time both rod and serpent, one will at least be able to make the inference in the same manner: What lay on the ground Aaron took up and carried back

A recapitulation of the Lutheran argument

That the argument of Luther detracts from evident scriptures

sed serpens iacuit in terra: ergo serpentem e terra sustulit: et serpentem retulit domum. Quin eodem sophismate probabis nobis Euam perpetuo fuisse costam: si quis hoc sophismatis genus admittat. Quod deus de latere tulit: hoc Adae coniunxit, in [DD₂] uxorem: sed de latere eius costam tulit: ergo costam illi dedit uxorem. Quod si quis hoc sophisma tuum rideat: hic serius, ut soles, cum eodem redibis insaniens: et rem

Cynicus Lutheri mos

conaberis optinere conuitijs, exclamans: Vos asini, nunquid costam tulit deus ex Adam: et aedificauit in mulierem: et adduxit ad Adam: et ei dedit in uxorem? Nunquid igitur costa fuit, quam de Adam tulit? et quod tulit, idipsum aedificauit? et quod aedificauit, id ipsum adduxit? et quod adduxit, id ipsum coniunxit? Ergo a primo ad ultimum, costam ex Ada tulit: ergo costam Adae coniunxit. Iam si quis audeat huius sophismatis aperire mysterium: ac neget deum adduxisse costam: quam aedificauit in mulierem: sed

Hoc Luthere tuum sonat argumentum

mulierem, quam aedificauit ex costa: sicut Christum respondit rex dedisse discipulis, non panem, quem acceperat, sed corpus, quod ex pane fecerat: illum ridicule ridebit reuerendus pater: et negabit argumentum suum bene solutum esse: neque quicquam dicet esse responsum, praeter, oportet sic esse. Nec interea

Non enim opus est, id ulcus tangere

uerbum faciet ullum, de his, quibus tam aperte reuincitur.

NAM quaeso te Luthere, per stultitiam tuam: cur non es ausus resumere praeclarum illud argumentum tuum de articulo? Credo profecto, omnes articulos tuos concepisse chiragram, et podagram, ex frigore illius unius articuli: quem, quum Babylonem tuum contuli cum responso regis: ita stolide repperi tractasse te: ut nec insanus potuisset insanius: ita tractasse regem contra te: ut illud unum uulnus, quo tute causam tuam uulneraueras, mortiferum effecerit: atque totam haeresim tuam, illo uno uulnere per[DD₂v]emerit: etiam si nullum addidisset ulterius. Atque

Illic fere discit esse disertus

ideo minus miror: si dolor te non est passus, iterum tam letale uulnus, tua tibi

---

with him; but a serpent lay on the ground; therefore he took up a serpent from the ground and carried a serpent back home. Indeed, by the same sophistry you will prove to us that Eve was always a rib, if anyone allows this kind of sophism: What God took from the side of Adam He joined to Adam as wife; but He took a rib from his side; therefore He gave him a rib as wife. But if anyone should laugh at this sophism of yours, here, serious as usual, you will return raging mad with the same argument and you will try to gain your point by railing, exclaiming: "You asses, did not God take a rib from Adam and fashion it into a woman and bring it to Adam and give it to him for a wife? Was it not then a rib which He took from Adam? And did He not fashion that which He took? And did He not present to Adam the same thing that He fashioned? And did He not join to him the same thing that He presented to him? Therefore, from first to last: He took a rib from Adam; therefore He joined a rib to Adam." Now if anyone should dare to unfold the mystery of this sophism and say that God did not present a rib which He fashioned into a woman, but a woman whom He fashioned from a rib, as the king answers that Christ gave to the disciples not the bread which He had taken but the body which He had made from the bread, the reverend father will ridicule this man ridiculously and will deny that his argument has been well solved, or that any answer at all has been given except, "It must be so." Nor, meanwhile, will he utter a word about these arguments with which he is so clearly refuted.

Luther's Cynic practice

Your argument means this, Luther

There is no need to touch that wound

For I ask you, Luther, by your folly: Why have you not dared to take up again that brilliant argument of yours about the article? I believe indeed that all your joints, hand and foot, have caught the gout from the chill reception of that one article, which, when I compared your *Babylon* with the king's answer, I found that you had so stupidly handled that not even a madman could have handled it more madly, that the king had handled it against you in such a way that he rendered mortal that one wound with which you yourself had wounded your cause, and with that one wound he annihilated your whole heresy, even had he added nothing further. And so I am less surprised if pain has not allowed you to scratch open again

That fellow is almost learning to be eloquent

stultitia factum, refricare: nec illud item de non transubstantiato
calice: quod argumentum plane reperisti, nimium bene potus in calice.
Nunc ubi illorum te pudet: satis est omnia tacere, et clamare, nihil
aliud afferri contra te, quam, oportet sic esse: uerba sunt clara et
5   aperta.

Verba Lutheri   Nam hoc est, inquis, insigne sapientiae
                                   Thomisticae, quod postulatus rationem
huius articuli fidei (cum nullum articulum sciat a me admitti, nisi
apertis scripturis munitum) ipse tamen nihil aliud affert, quam oportet
10   sic esse: uerba sunt clara et aperta. Quis
Sed nec eos quidem omnes   autem tam insanus est grammaticus, qui
                                   ex hoc sermone, Hoc est corpus meum,
intelligat, aut colligat, id, quod est panis, transubstantiari in carnem,
nisi Thomistarum fex: quae etiam grammaticam nos dedocuere?

15   NON dubito Luthere (quamquam sis
Quisquis te dedocuit, tu plane   impudens) quin hic tamen sudes satis:
uideris nescire grammaticam   quum sentias apud te: quid lectores
sentiant de te, tam stolide dissimulante omnia: quae te uidere uident
omnes. Nam quod ita quaeris, Quis tam insanus est grammaticus?
20 nos hoc Luthere quaerendum relinquimus tibi: qui assidue uersaris,
cum insanis grammaticis: qui tuas haereses insanas et agrammatas,
sua picturant insana grammatica. Sed qui sic illa uerba intelligunt,
quomodo qui intelligunt, tu bis insanus appellas insanos: illi sunt,
inquam, et doctissimi quique ueterum, et sanctissimi. Quorum rex tibi
25 multos adduxit: qui panem asserunt non manere, sed in carnem
                                   uerti, tot seculis nati, non ante Thomistas
Ita nihil habet pro sancto   modo, sed et ante Thomam: quos a rege
nebulo   nominatos impudenter dissimulas: ut eos
licentius blasphemes, [DD₃] et insanus appelles insanos.

30   Quin eximius nostralis rex Henricus,
Verba Lutheri   stropha Thomistica, ausus est etiam a
me exigere, ut probem non transubstantiari, scilicet insulsissimus
Thomista, docendus etiam est elementa disputationis, qui quum

such a deadly wound inflicted on yourself by your folly; or, by the same token, that argument about the untransubstantiated cup which you clearly hit upon when you were too deep in your cups. Now, where you are ashamed of those arguments, it is enough to pass over them all in silence and to shout that nothing else has been presented 5 against you but, "It must be so; the words are clear and evident."

For this is, you say, the distinctive mark of Thomistic wisdom, that, having been *Luther's words* asked the reason for this article of faith—although he knows that no article is admitted by me unless it is supported by evident scriptures 10 —he himself nevertheless presents nothing else but, "It must be so; the words are clear and evident." But who is such a mad grammarian that from *But not even all of them* the expression, "This is my body," he would understand or infer that what is bread is transubstantiated into flesh, unless it be the dregs 15 of Thomists who have untaught us even grammar?

I have no doubt, Luther, however shameless you may be, that you are still *Whoever has untaught you, you* sweating plenty here when in your own *clearly seem to be ignorant* mind you perceive what your readers *of grammar* think of you as you so stupidly conceal all the things which everyone 20 sees that you see. As for your asking, "Who is such a mad grammarian?" we leave this question for you to ask, Luther, who are constantly involved with mad grammarians who embellish your mad and ungrammared heresies with their own mad grammar. But those 25 who understand those words as some understand them, you, twice mad, call madmen; I say they are all the most learned and most saintly of the ancients. Of these the king has brought up to you many who declare that the bread does not remain but is turned into flesh, men born *Thus the scoundrel considers* *nothing sacred* 30 so many centuries not only before the Thomists but also before Thomas, men whom you shamelessly pretend have not been mentioned by the king so that you may more boldly blaspheme them and, yourself a madman, call them madmen.

Indeed our distinguished King Henry, *Luther's words* 35 with a Thomistic trick, has even dared to demand of me that I prove that transubstantiation does not take place; clearly a very silly Thomist, he needs to be taught even the elements

affirmatiuam debeat probare, contendat ab aduersario, ut negatiuam
probet. Hos doctissimos uiros ad haere-

Ita ne uos doctus estis doctor, ticos mittamus, et ad Turcam, ut fidem
ut nesciatis, quid cui sit nostram defendant: sic, ut non sit
probandum. Disce hic
5   *Luthere tuum officium* necesse rationem fidei reddere: sed solum
dicere, proba negatiuam.

EN RVRSVS lector stropham Luthericam, hoc est stolidam
prorsus impudentiam. Debuisset reuerendus pater, principis uerba
referre: quibus ab illo dicit exigi, ut probet non transubstantiari.
10   Nam quum sciat se Lutherus, omnibus compertum esse mendacissi-
mum: potuit scire neminem ei quicquam crediturum: nisi quatenus
probaret, quod diceret. Nunc uero quum lectores regem uideant, tale
nihil exigere: sed ipsum quae debuit, ipsa luce clarius probasse: facile
ridebunt, ac reijcient hoc stolidum Lutheri commentum, cum caeteris
15   eiusdem patris uanitatibus. Verum diuino quid sibi uelit. Postquam
uidet ea soluta, quae protulit aduersus fidem publicam: nec amplius
habet quicquam, quo iam possit tam stolide dicta defendere, cupiens
a necessitate disceptationis absolui, sic interpretatur, quasi exigere ab
eo, ut reddat rationem: cur aduersus tam constantem, tam perpetuam
20   totius ecclesiae fidem, clarissimis euangelij uerbis firmatam, impiam
tueatur haeresim: hoc demum sit exigere: ut probet negatiuam. Et

Stropha Lutheri haec est eximia stropha reuerendi patris:
qua se diuersurum sperat, ac fugiturum, ne
comprehendi possit, a tar[DD₃v]dis et crassis Thomisticis.

2–3 haereticos] *L*, haerereticos *BR*   5 *gloss* Luthere] luthere *BR*

of disputation, for when he is supposed to prove the affirmative, he demands that his adversary prove the negative. Let us send these learned men to the heretics and to the Turk to defend our faith in such a way *Have you been so taught, doctor,* that it is not necessary to supply a reason *that you do not know who* for the faith but only to say, "Prove the *should prove what? Learn here,* 5 negative." *Luther, your function*

See again, reader, the Lutheric stratagem; that is, his utterly stupid shamelessness. The reverend father should have cited the words by which he says the prince demanded that he prove that transubstantia- 10 tion does not take place. For, since Luther knows that he has been discovered by everyone to be an utter liar, he could have known that no one would be ready to believe anything from him except insofar as he proved what he said. Now, indeed, when the readers see that the king demands no such thing but that he has proven clearer than light 15 what he should have proved, they will readily ridicule and reject this stupid trick of Luther's, together with other deceptions by the same father.

But I divine what he means. After he sees those arguments dissolved which he has advanced against the public faith and has 20 nothing further at all by which he can now defend such stupid statements, desiring to be freed from the necessity of a debate, he so interprets things as though to demand from him that he give a reason why he defends an impious heresy against such steadfast, such unbroken faith of the whole church, confirmed by the clearest words of 25 the gospel, as though, in fine, to demand this were to demand that he prove the negative. And this is the singular stratagem by which the reverend father *Luther's stratagem* hopes to swerve aside and flee so that he cannot be caught by the slow and lumbering Thomists. 30

Ostendit, quam stolide Lutherus conetur refellere,
solutionem principis: qua respondit ad ea loca:
quae Lutherus allegauit ex apostolo: quibus
eucharistiam probaret esse uerum
5   panem. Ca. XIII.

Verba Lutheri   SEd hactenus, philosophatus sit Thomista noster regius. Iam uidere dignum
est, quam Thomistice, theologisetur aduersus meas rationes. Cum
ego aduersus Thomisticum illum fidei articulum, posuissem fulmen
10 illud caeleste, Pauli uerbum, Corint. XII. ubi tam aperte panem
appellat hoc sacramentum ut nec regis ruditas, nec Thomistae
nequitia ullum mentiendi et ludendi effugium inuenire posset: cum
stent uerba Pauli luce clariora. Panis, quem frangimus, nonne participatio corporis domini? Non ait, Corpus, quod frangimus, non ait nihil
15 illud consecrationis reliquum, quod frangimus, aut accidentia, quae
frangimus, sed panis, quem frangimus, utique iam benedictus et
consecratus. Hic igitur panis benedictus
Quomodo Lutherus intelligat est participatio corporis domini. &c.
sacras scripturas. Aduerte
quaeso lector, quid Lutherus Simile est. I. Corint. II. Qui manducat
20 *uitio det* hunc panem. &c. Hoc bonus et suauis
Thomista, nihil neque scripturarum,
neque rationis afferens, sed ex mero suo, oportet sic esse, dicit
scripturam sanctam solere aliquando id appellare, quod fuit, uel quod
simile sit, ut Exod. VII. Deuorauit uirga Aaron, uirgas magorum, id
25 est draco, qui fuit uirga Aaron. Haec ille.

ECCE lector, ut bonus et suauis satanista noster fratralis, ait regem
nihil afferre scripturae: quo probet scripturam aliquando, aliquid
appellare, non id quod est: sed quod ante fuit. Et tamen idem bonus
et suauis Lutherus [DD₄] noster fratralis, affert, et commemorat eam
30 scripturam: quam ad id probandum attulit rex: et affert eodem ipso
in loco, in quo negat regem ullam attulisse: et sic reuerendus pater
nunquam sibi contrarius, simul dicit: rex ad istud probandum affert
scripturam: et nullam affert scripturam.
Lutheri ars disputandi An ideo non est scriptura sacra: quia est in

---

6 *gloss*] *L, om. BR*   13–14 nonne participatio corporis domini?] *L,* non participatio
corporis domini. *BR*

He shows how stupidly Luther tries to refute
the explanation with which the prince answers
those passages which Luther cites from the
apostle to prove that the eucharist is true
bread. Chapter 13.

5

But up to this point our kingly Thomist
has philosophized. Now it is worth seeing

Luther's words

how Thomistically he theologizes against my reasons. When against
that Thomistic article of faith I had cast that heavenly thunderbolt of
Paul's words in Cor. 12, where he so clearly calls this sacrament bread 10
that neither the ignorance of the king nor the wickedness of the
Thomist could find any escape through lying or raillery, since the
words of Paul stand clearer than light: "The bread which we break,
is it not the sharing of the body of the Lord?" He does not say, "the
body which we break," he does not say "the nothing left from conse- 15
cration which we break," or, "the accidents which we break," but,
"the bread which we break," surely already blessed and consecrated.
This blessed bread therefore is the sharing
of the body of the Lord, etc. Similarly,
I Cor. 2: "He who eats this bread, etc."
The good and agreeable Thomist, presenting nothing either from scripture or

How Luther understands the
sacred scriptures. Please
notice, reader, what Luther
reckons as a fault

20

from reason but on his bare assertion, "It must be so," says that the
holy scripture usually refers in this way to that which has been or to
that which is similar, as in Ex. 7: "The rod of Aaron swallowed the 25
rods of the magicians"; that is, the serpent which up till then was the
rod of Aaron. Thus his argument runs.

See, reader, how our good and agreeable friarly Satanist says that
the king presents no text of scripture to prove that scripture at times
calls a thing, not that which it is, but that which it has been previ- 30
ously. And yet our same good and agreeable friarly Luther presents
and cites that scriptural text which the king has presented to prove the
point, and he presents it in the very same passage in which he denies
that the king has presented any text, and thus the reverend father,
never inconsistent, says at one and the same time, "The king presents 35
a scriptural text to prove this point," and,
"He presents no scriptural text." Or is it

Luther's art of disputing

Exodo? Aut ideo non affert id rex: ut probet propositum: quia reuerendus pater explicare se non potest: dum ualde se uersat, ac torquet: ut probet regem per illam scripturam, non satis probare propositum? Sed hoc in loco lector, ne quid aut subducere uideamur,

5   aut affingere: sicut Lutheri uerba rettulimus: ita regis quoque uerba subiungemus.

Verba regis   "HACTENVS ista disserui, dumtaxat ut ostenderem ex ipsius Christi uerbis, et euangelistarum, ostendi non posse: quod iste se iactat ostendere, imo

10   contra liquere perspicue, in eucharistia panem non esse. QVOD in actis apostolorum ait eucharistiam appellari panem: uellem, protulisset locum: ego nullum reperio: qui non sit ambiguus: et potius uideatur de communi conuiuio dicere, quam sacramento. Apostolus tamen (fateor) panem non semel appellat, uel scripturae sequutus in

15   sermone morem: quae solet interdum uocare quippiam, non id quod est, sed quod ante fuerat: ut quum ait: Virga Aaron deuorat uirgas magorum: quae tamen tunc uirgae non erant, sed serpentes: uel contentus fortasse uocare, quod specie prae se ferebat: quum satis haberet, rudem adhuc in fide populum, lacte pascere: nec primum

20   aliud exigere, quam ut quocunque modo crederent, in sacramento esse corpus Christi: postea pau[DD$_4$v]latim, solidiore cibo pasturus: postquam adoleuissent in domino. Idem potuit, et in apostolorum actis contingere: ubi nec beatus Petrus alloquens populum, et illis Christi fidem insinuans, ausus est adhuc aperte quicquam, de eius

25   diuinitate dicere: ita abdita, et populis dubia mysteria non temere proferebant. At Christus apostolos suos, quos tam diu sua doctrina formauerat, ipso sacramenti instituendi principio, docere non dubitauit, panis uinique non amplius restare substantiam, sed manente utriusque specie, utrunque tamen, et panem et uinum, in

30   corpus et sanguinem suum esse conuersum. Quod tam aperte docuit, ut plane mirandum sit, exortum quenquam postea: qui rem tam claram, rursus uocaret in dubium. Quomodo enim potuisset apertius

---

12 ambiguus] *corr. err. L*, ambiguum *BR*   31 plane] *om. L*

not sacred scripture because it is in Exodus? Or does the king not present it to prove his point because the reverend father cannot disentangle himself while he turns and twists violently to prove that through that scriptural text the king does not satisfactorily prove his point? But in this passage, reader, lest we seem to be either with- 5
holding or forging anything, just as we have reported Luther's words, so also we subjoin the king's words.

"Up till now I have argued these points only to show from the words of Christ   *The king's words*
Himself and of the evangelists that what he boasts that he shows 10
cannot be shown; on the contrary, indeed, it is transparently clear that the bread is not in the eucharist.

"As for his saying that in the Acts of the Apostles the eucharist is called bread, I wish he had quoted the passage; I find none that is not ambiguous and that does not seem rather to speak of the common 15
meal than of the sacrament. Yet I admit that the apostle more than once calls it bread, either following the scriptural manner of speaking which usually calls a thing not that which it is but that which it had been before, as when it says, 'The rod of Aaron swallowed the rods of the magicians,' which nevertheless were then not rods but serpents; 20
or perchance content to call the eucharist that which it appeared to be, considering it sufficient to nourish with milk a people still young in the faith, and not at first to require anything else than that they believe that the body of Christ is somehow present in the sacrament, being ready afterwards to feed them gradually with more solid food 25
when they had grown up in the Lord. The same thing could have occurred in the Acts of the Apostles, where blessed Peter also, addressing the people and initiating them into the faith of Christ, did not yet dare to say anything openly about Christ's divinity; thus, they did not rashly set forth mysteries hidden and difficult for the people. But 30
Christ did not hesitate at the very moment of instituting the sacrament to teach His apostles whom He had so long formed by His teaching that the substance of bread and wine no longer remain but that while the appearance of both remain, yet both of them, the bread and the wine, have been changed into His own body and 35
blood. This He taught so plainly that it is quite astonishing that anyone has afterwards arisen to call into question again such an evident matter.

"For how could He have more clearly said that nothing of the

Contra Lutherum ex ipsis
Christi uerbis

dicere, nihil illic remanere panis: quam quum dixit: Hoc est corpus meum? Non enim dixit, In hoc est corpus meum: aut cum hoc, quod uidetis, est corpus meum: tanquam in pane, aut simul

5 cum pane, consisteret: sed hoc est (inquit) corpus meum: nimirum declarans manifeste (ut os cuiusque gannientis obstrueret) hoc totum, quod porrigebat, ipsius corpus esse. Quod ita porrectum apostolis, etiam si (quod non fecit) nomine panis appellasset: tamen quum simul admoneret audientes, idipsum, quod uocaret panem, nihil aliud

10 esse, quam suum corpus: in quod totus fuerat, ipso mutante, conuersus. Nemo potuisset dubitare: quid Christus uellet panis

Contra Lutherum ex
circumstantia

appellatione significari: eoque circumstantia ipsa (nam circumstantiam Lutherus admittit) declarat euidenter uocabulum

15 panis, quum panis mutatur in carnem, absque ulla uiolentia facta uerbo diuino, [EE₁] panis significare speciem, non substantiam: nisi

Lutheri faceta illusio

Lutherus adeo inhaereat proprietati uerborum: ut Christum credat in caelis quoque fuisse panem triticeum, aut hordiaceum: propterea quod ipse

20 dicit de se: Ego sum panis, qui de caelo descendi: aut ueris uuis onustam uitem: quia dixit ipse: Ego sum uitis uera, et pater meus agricola est: aut electos denique remunerandos in caelo uoluptate corporea: propterea, quod Christus ait: Ego dispono uobis, sicut mihi disposuit pater meus, regnum: ut edatis et bibatis super mensam

25 meam, in regno meo."

NVNC iudica lector, quam necessarium argumentum sumat Lutherus ex Paulo: quum euangelistae probent, panem in carnem uersum: Quid affert Lutherus: quo doceat, non sic a Paulo uocatum panem: quod iam non sit panis, sicut in Exodo uocatam uirgam:

30 quae tamen uirga non erat, sed serpens. SED quam male urat patrem

Meretricius mos respondendi
Lutheri

reuerendum, quod istum nodum nescit soluere: bene declarat ira reuerendi patris: per quam, sicut meretrices, ubi quid obijcitur, quod nulla ratione possunt refellere: respondere solent impuden-

35 ter, Tu mentiris, sic uenerabilis pater, in eam coniectus angustiam,

---

31 *gloss* Meretricius] *L*, meretricius *BR*　　33–34 obijcitur] *L*, oijcitur *BR*　　35 Tu mentiris, sic] *corr. err.*, Tu mentiris. Sic *BR*, Tu mentiris: Sic *L*

bread remains there than when He said, 'This is my body'? He did not say, 'In this is my body,' or 'With this which you see is *Opposition to Luther from the very words of Christ* my body,' as though it existed in or together with the bread, but He said, 'This is my body,' unquestionably declaring manifestly, in order to stop the mouth of every grumbler, that what He was presenting to them was entirely His body. Even if He had called by the name of bread what He thus presented to the apostles—which He did not do —nevertheless, since at the same time He reminded His hearers that the very thing which He was calling bread was nothing else than His own body into which the bread had been entirely converted by His own action of changing it, no one could have doubted what Christ wished us to understand by the designation, 'bread,' and for that reason the context itself—for Luther admits the argument from the context—declares *Argument against Luther from the context* clearly that the word 'bread,' when the bread is changed into flesh, signifies without any violence done to the divine word the appearance, not the substance, of bread. Unless Luther sticks so closely to the literal meaning of the words as to believe that *A witty mocking of Luther* Christ was also in heaven as wheatbread or barleybread because He says of Himself, 'I am the bread which has come down from heaven'; or that He is a vine laden with real grapes because He said 'I am the true vine and my father is the vinedresser'; or finally that the elect are to be rewarded in heaven with bodily pleasure because Christ said, 'I arrange for you as my father has arranged for me a kingdom that you may eat and drink at my table in my kingdom.' "

Now judge, reader, how cogent an argument Luther takes from Paul, when the evangelists prove that bread is changed into flesh. What does Luther present to show that what is now not bread is not termed bread by Paul in the same way as in Exodus something was called a rod which nevertheless was not a rod but a serpent? But how sorely it galls the reverend father that he does not know how to untie this knot is well manifested by the reverend father's wrath, with which, just as whores, *Luther's whorish way of answering* when something is brought up against them which they cannot refute by any reasoning, usually answer shamelessly, "You lie," so the venerable father, driven into this tight

unde nullum uidet exitum: arma sua sumit sibi: et uiam sibi ui facere
tendit per conuitia.

Verba Lutheri

Mentiris, inquit, in caput tuum rex
stolide, et sacrilege: qui fronte impudenti
5   ausus es uerbis dei infallibilibus tribuere, ut aliud sonent, quam
significent. Quantam obsecro fenestram blasphemandi, aperuerit
furor iste regis uniuersis haereticis, et fidei hostibus: si semel admissum
fuerit, scripturae authoritatem lubricis et fallacibus uerbis niti? Quid
tum, non probare, improbare, tueri, et defendere poterunt omnes
10   omnium [EE₁v] dogmatum magistri? Quanto rectius Sanctus

Cur ergo tu semper serio
mentiris

Augustinus, ne iocosum quidem mendacium, nec officiosum in sacris literis
recipere uoluit.

O sapientem et sanctum patrem Lutherum: et unicum orbis mira-
15   culum, mentiendi nescium nebulonem: qui uerecundia uere uirginea
uereatur, dei uerbis infallibilibus tribuere: ut aliud sonent, quam
significent, tam aperte praesertim contra morem et exemplum
Christi: cuius omnes omnino parabolae significant nihil aliud, quam
sonant. Et quis non uidet, quantam fenestram blasphemandi
20   aperuerit rex uniuersis haereticis, et fidei hostibus: si semel admissum
fuerit scripturae authoritatem lubricis et fallacibus uerbis niti? quid
non tum probare, improbare, tueri, et defendere, poterit malorum
omnium dogmatum magister pessimus. Vt exempli causa, si mortui

Lutheri etsi non aperta, tamen
tacita collectio

cadauer scriptura uocaret (ut saepe uocat)
25   hominem: iam Lutherus, qui negat purgatorium, sic formaret argumentum: Omnis
anima moritur cum corpore: ergo nullum est purgatorium: et (ut est
acutus) hoc pacto probaret assumptum. Qui mortuus est: adhuc
homo est: sed homo non est nisi quiddam compositum, ex anima et
30   corpore: ergo mortuus est compositus, ex anima et corpore, sed
utroque mortuo. Iam si quis illi responderet, scripturam, quum
cadauer appellat hominem, populi more loqui: nec id uocare, quod
iam est: sed quod ante fuit: Ibi statim reuerendus pater irasceretur:
et pio zelo clamaret feruidus, Mentiris stolide et sacrilege: qui fronte
35   impudenti, ausus es uerbis dei infallibilibus tribuere: ut aliud sonent,

23 pessimus.] pessimus? *L*   26 argumentum: Omnis] *corr. err.*, argumentum: omnis
BRL

spot from which he sees no way out, takes up his arms in his defense
and strives to force a way out for himself by railing.

You lie, he says, against your own head,
you stupid and sacrilegious king, who   *Luther's words*
have dared with brazen face to assign a meaning to the infallible words   5
of God so that they say something different from what they signify.
What a wide window for blaspheming, pray tell, has this raging
madness of the king opened to all the heretics and enemies of the
faith, if it is once admitted that the authority of scripture relies on
slippery and deceptive words? What then will not all teachers of all   10
doctrines be able to approve, disapprove, uphold and defend? How
much more rightly did Saint Augustine
wish to accept in sacred writings not even   *Why then do you always lie*
a jocose or obliging lie.   *seriously?*

O sage and saintly father Luther, and sole miracle of the world, a   15
knave innocent of lying, who fears with unfeigned maidenly modesty
to assign a meaning to the infallible words of God so that they say
something different from what they signify, especially so clearly
contrary to the practice and example of Christ, every single one of
whose parables signifies nothing other than it says. And who does not   20
see how wide a window for blaspheming the king has opened to all
heretics and enemies of the faith once it is admitted that the authority
of scripture relies on slippery and deceptive words? What will not the
most mischievous master of every evil doctrine then be able to
approve, disapprove, uphold and defend? For example, if the   25
scripture would—as it often does—refer to
the corpse of a dead man as a "man," then   *Luther's implicit, even if not*
Luther, who denies purgatory, would form   *explicit, line of reasoning*
his argument as follows: "Every soul dies with the body; therefore,
there is no purgatory," and—he is such a sharp one—he would   30
prove his premise in this way: "He who is dead is still a man; but
man is nothing but a certain composite of soul and body; therefore, a
dead man is composed of a soul and a body, both of them dead."
Now, if anyone should answer him that scripture, when it refers to a
corpse as a "man," is speaking in a popular manner and does not refer   35
to that which now is but to that which before was, then immediately
the reverend father would be in a rage and with devout zeal would cry
out vehemently: "You lie stupidly and sacrilegiously, who with brazen
face have dared to attribute a meaning to the infallible words of God

quam significent. Verba sonant cadauer esse hominem: ergo idem
uere significant: et sic mor[EE₂]tua est etiam anima: et sic inuicta
stat haeresis mea: quod nullum est purgatorium: et sic per hanc
fenestram, quam aperit rex, reuerendus frater Lutherus, et haeretici
5　similes, qui sunt acuti sophistae, saltu se praecipitarent ad inferos: et
ideo Augustinus, nec iocosum mendacium, nec officiosum in sacris
literis recipere uoluit. Nam is mentitur scilicet, qui in sermone utitur
ijsdem figuris: quibus utitur populus.

　　　　　　　　　　　　　　　　　Sed esto. Rex Thomisticus non dignetur
　　　　　　　Verba Lutheri
10　　　　　　　　　　　　　　　　　creatorem　suum　tanto　honore,　ut
sensum suum in uerba eius captiuet, fassus sese potius nescire,
quomodo uirga uirgam uorarit, quam temere ea deprauet. Sitque
　　　　　　　　　　　　　　　　　uerum, quod uirga dicatur draco, qui
　　　At tu mauis omnia peruertere
　　　　　　　　　　　　　　　　　fuit uirga. Qua consequentia sequetur,
　　　quam nescire uideri
15　　　　　　　　　　　　　　　　　et hic panem dici, qui panis non sit, sed
fuerit. An hoc est sine scriptura omnibus locis scripturae aptandum,
quod uno loco reperitur? Scilicet hac Thomistica sapientia fretus, sic
　　　　　　　　　　　　　　　　　argues, scriptura semel dicit uirginem
　　　Non, sed scriptura semel dicit
　　　　　　　　　　　　　　　　　esse matrem: ergo oportet multas alias
　　　uirginem esse matrem, ergo
20　　　*uirgo est mater*　　　　　　quoque esse matres: licet scriptura de his
　　　　　　　　　　　　　　　　　nihil　dicat: quemadmodum　hic　facit,
panem non esse panem oportet, quia uirga non est uirga.

QVANTVM haereat in rancidis Lutheri dentibus, istud serpentis
corium: in quam uersa est uirga Aaron, uel illud bene declarat, quod
25　tot solutionibus tam sollicite quaerens, nullam potest inuenire: quae
non sit prorsus absurda. Nam primum uult, adhuc uirgam esse, quae
sit in serpentem uersa, eadem ratione facturus, ut maneat etiam
serpens: quum denuo facta sit uirga: deinde etiam, si illic uirgam
appellet scriptura, quae uirga non sit, sed fuit: tamen id exemplum
30　frustra protulisse principem: quia ex uno loco non cogimur credere
scripturam, eodem modo loqui in omnibus. Quid non potest reuerendus frater facile sol[EE₂v]uere: si hoc est soluere, fingere se non

5 praecipitarent] praecipitant *L*

so that they say something different than they signify. The words say that a corpse is a man; therefore, they truly signify the same thing, and so the soul is also dead and so my heresy stands unconquered: that there is no purgatory"; and so through this window which the king opens, reverend friar Luther and similar heretics who are 5 shrewd sophists would leap headlong to hell; and therefore Augustine did not wish to accept in the sacred writings either a jocose or an obliging lie. For of course that man lies who in his discourse uses the same figures which the people use.

But suppose that the Thomistic king would not consider his creator worthy of *Luther's words* 10 such great honor as to render his own understanding captive to his creator's words and admit that he does not know how a rod has swallowed a rod rather than rashly pervert the rods. Suppose it is true that the serpent which has been a rod is 15 called a rod. By what consequence will it *But you prefer to pervert* follow that here also something is called *everything rather than* bread which is not but has been bread? *appear not to know* Or is this procedure which is found in one passage to be applied without scriptural authority to every passage of scripture? Of course, 20 relying on this Thomistic wisdom, you will argue thus: "Scripture says in one place that a virgin is a mother; therefore, many other virgins *No, but the scripture in one* also must be mothers, although scripture *place says a virgin is a* says nothing of them"; just as he argues *mother; therefore, a virgin* 25 here that bread must not be bread be- *is a mother* cause a rod is not a rod.

How fast this skin of the serpent into which the rod of Aaron was turned sticks to Luther's rotten teeth is plainly shown even by the fact that, though seeking so solicitously with so many solutions, he cannot 30 find any which is not completely absurd. First of all he wishes that what was turned into a serpent be still a rod; he is ready by the same reasoning to cause the serpent also to remain a serpent when it is turned into a rod again; then also, if the scripture there calls something a rod that is not but has been a rod, still the prince has presented 35 that example to no avail, because we are not compelled to believe from one passage that the scripture speaks in the same manner in all passages.

What cannot the reverend friar easily solve if to solve is to pretend

intelligere: quid debeat soluere? Nam uideri uult hoc pacto regem
dicere: Quia sic aliquando loquitur scriptura: ideo scripturam semper
ita loqui, quasi aduersus Lutherum urgentem, ex uno aut altero loco
scripturae, corpus Christi uocantis panem, necessario uere panem
5   esse: propterea quod panis ibi uocaretur: non satis regi fuerit: si alio
scripturae loco probaret, id nulla necessitate consequi: quia scripturae non sit perpetuum id appellare: quod uerissime sit: sed aliquando ex humana consuetudine id appellare, quod uidetur esse: uel
quod paulo ante fuit: sicut uirgam Aaron appellauit: quum iam
10 serpens esset non uirga: et hominem appellat interdum, quod homo
non est, sed cadauer: interdum fortasse quod est pictura uel statua.
Quum rex ergo, tantum probat illud Pauli uocantis panem, non
cogere, ut uere sit panis: sic rem tractat

Lutherum siue malicia siue   Lutherus: tanquam rex ex illo loco pro-
imperitia regis dicta male
15   *accepisse*   bare uellet, quod non sit panis: quum illud
non ex Paulo probet rex: sed ex euangelio:
simul id probans, quod Pauli uerba non probant contrarium, id quod
regis proposito abunde satis est. Et quum facile sentiat reuerendus
frater, hanc stultam sycophantiam suam omnibus esse conspicuam:
20 tamen uelut nemo posset intelligere tam acutam stropham, per duas
fere paginas, mire sibi plaudit in illa. Et tandem, uelut aculeo acu-
tissimo, regem pungit in fine.

Verba Lutheri   Rex, inquit, blaterat, uirga dicitur uirga,
et tamen non est: ergo Paulus panem
25   uocat, quod non est panis, quasi panis et uirga idem sint.

Et iam post tantam uictoriam triumphat gloriosus frater.

Quae Barathra, inquit, non inundaret Satan in ecclesiam, postquam
[EE₃] sophistae in cathedras recepti,
Quis ita disputat nisi tu? hac forma docendi et disputandi uti
30   coeperunt.

---

13 *gloss om. L*   25 quod non] *L*, quod uon *BR*; sint.] *L*, sint *BR*   27 inundaret]
mundaret *BR*, induceret *L*

that he does not understand what he ought to solve? For he will have the king seem to speak in this manner: "Because scripture at times speaks thus, therefore scripture always speaks thus," as though he were urging against Luther from one or the other passage of scripture which calls the body of Christ "bread" that it is of necessity truly bread because it was called bread in that passage. It was not enough for the king to prove from another passage that this does not necessarily follow because it is not continually characteristic of scripture to call a thing what it most truly is, but at times scripture calls a thing, according to human custom, that which the thing seems to be or that which it was shortly before, as scripture called the rod of Aaron a rod although it was at that time a serpent, not a rod; and scripture at times designates as "a man" that which is not a man but a corpse, at times perchance that which is a painting or a statue.

Although the king, then, proves only that the text of Paul calling the sacrament "bread" does not necessarily imply that it truly is bread, Luther handles the matter as though the king wished to prove from that passage that it is not bread, whereas the king does not prove that fact from Paul but *That Luther, whether by malice or by ignorance, has misinterpreted the king's words* from the gospel, at the same time proving that the words of Paul do not prove the contrary, a result which abundantly satisfies the intention of the king. And although the reverend friar easily senses that this silly skulduggery of his is obvious to everyone, nevertheless, as though no one could understand such a shrewd stratagem, he congratulates himself on it exceedingly for almost two pages. And finally, as though with the sharpest sting, he pricks the king at the end.

The king, he says, blathers: "The rod is called a rod, and yet it is not; therefore, Paul calls bread that which is not bread"; as though bread and a rod were the same thing. *Luther's words*

And then, after such a great victory, the boastful friar gloats:

What abysses, he says, Satan would let overflow into the church after the sophists, admitted into the teachers' chairs, began to use this form of teaching and disputing. *Who disputes this way, except you?*

QVAESO te lector, quis morio non rideret morionem, tanto cum
tumultu se tam ridicule commouentem: quod dicat aliquis, eodem
locutionis modo, Paulum appellasse panem, id quod ante fuit panis:
licet iam non sit panis, sed caro, quo sermonis tropo, uirgam uocauit
5   scriptura, id quod iam uirga non erat, sed draco. At istud, uelut
apprime ridiculum, ridet homo ridiculus. Ergo si dicas lector, asini
cadauer asinum sic appellari posse: quemadmodum cadauer hominis
appellatur homo: quanto cachinno ridebit te Lutherus: et negabit
admittendam similem figuram sermonis: propterea quod res ipsae
10   sint dissimili specie. Quia non sunt, in-
   Sic Luthere, argumentaberis   quiet, idem homo et asinus: sicut non sunt
   a simili?   idem, panis et uirga. Quid, si sic soluamus
argumentum: quando sic arguit mihi reuerendus pater? Non sunt
idem, homo et asinus: concedo, de aliquo asino, et aliquo homine:
15   sed respondeo, quod qui se sanum putat, quum sic argumentatur,
idem omnino sunt asinus, et ille homo. Et sic cadauer illius asini,
potest appellari asinus: sicut cadauer illius hominis, potest appellari
homo: quum prorsus idem sint ille asininus homo, et cadauerosus
asinus.

20   Sed et aliam, inquit, ostendit rex dex-
   Verba Lutheri   teritatem suam, in hac re: ut nihil nisi
Thomista credi possit. Si, inquit, Lutherus tam rigide captat uerba
scripturae, dicet et Christum esse panem triticeum in caelo, dum dicit,
Ego sum panis, qui de caelo descendi. Item naturalem uitem, ubi
25   dicit, Ego sum uitis uera. Dixi ante, nihil
   Tu rides: quia nil aliud potes   crassius et insulsius esse sub sole natum,
Thomisticis monstris. Quis enim puerorum hunc delirum regem non
rideat? Non est in ipso sensus aut uigilia, ut uideat, quid inter[EE₃v]-
sit inter sua somnia et haec uerba Christi. Ipsa enim consequentia
30   uerborum, absurditas rerum, pugnantia intelligentiarum, tum ipsius-
met interpretatio, cogunt eum de pane spirituali loqui, sicut dicit,
                                          Verba mea spiritus sunt et uita. quorum
   Adde et calicem ceruisiae   nihil est in uerbo Pauli, de pane sacra-
   pater   menti loquentis. Imo omnia urgent
35   Paulum de pane triticeo intelligi.

4 caro, quo] *corr. err.* L, caro. Quo *BR*

I ask you, reader, what idiot would not ridicule an idiot letting himself get so ridiculously worked up with such violent ranting, because someone says that Paul called "bread" that which was previously bread, although it is now not bread but flesh, in the same manner of speech and with the same figure of speech as the scripture called a rod that which was not then a rod but a serpent. But this, as something supremely ridiculous, the ridiculous fellow ridicules.

Therefore if you should say, reader, that the corpse of an ass can be called an ass just as the corpse of a man can be called a man, with what loud laughter will Luther ridicule you and deny that a similar figure of speech can be admitted because the things themselves are of dissimilar form. Because, he says, man and ass are not the same thing, just as bread *Will you argue thus from* and a rod are not the same. What if, when *similarity, Luther?* the reverend father argues with me, "Man and an ass are not the same thing," we should solve the argument thus: "I grant this about some ass and some man, but I answer that the fellow who thinks himself sane when he argues in this way is altogether the same as an ass; and thus the cadaver of that ass can be called an ass, just as the cadaver of that man can be called a man, since that asinine man and cadaverous ass are altogether the same"?

But the king, he says, shows still another *Luther's words* skill of his in this matter, so that nothing but a Thomist can be believed. "If," he says, "Luther seizes on the words of scripture so strictly, he will say also that Christ is wheat bread in heaven when He says, 'I am the bread which has come down from heaven.' Likewise a natural vine when He says, 'I am the true vine.'" I have said before that nothing is born under the sun more dense and silly than the Thomistic monsters. For what boy would not *You laugh because you can do* ridicule this raving king? He has neither *nothing else* the sense nor the alertness to see what is the difference between his own dreams and these words of Christ. For the very context of the words, the absurdity of the matters, the conflicting understandings, finally his own interpretation force the conclusion that Christ is speaking of spiritual bread, as He says, "My words are spirit and life"; of these there is no *Add a cup of beer too,* mention in the text of Paul when he *Father* speaks of the bread of the sacrament. Indeed, everything urges that Paul be understood to be speaking of wheat bread.

5

10

15

20

25

30

35

40

ECCE lector, aliam dexteritatem Lutheri: et talem, ut nihil nisi
potista credi possit: neque quicquam sub sole natum est, crassius et
insulsius potisticis monstris. Nam quum ebrius ante balbutisset uerba
scripturae, non nisi in proprio et grammatico sensu sumenda: rex
5 eius insignem stultitiam elusit: quod ex eo sequeretur, Christum esse
panem triticeum in caelo, et uitem onustam uuis: et sanctos olim
epulaturos et bibituros in regno dei. Nunc Dominus Lutherus aegre
ferens, stultitiam suam sic attactam: ridet ualde iratus: et reuerendus
pater pro sua reuerentia, ualde uerniliter scurratur: postulans, ut
10 scurrilitas sua ualeat pro solutione: quae alioqui per se tantum ualet,
quantum culex. Nam quum ait, satis apertum esse ex circumstantijs,
quo pacto Christus accipi uoluerit: quod ipse se panem uocauit, et

Dolor Lutheri   uitem. Ita rex probauit: quod Lutherus
dolet, et dissimulat, ex circumstantijs esse
15 perspicuum, quomodo Paulus accipiat panem in sacramento: quum
aperte declaret, ex illo pane factum esse Christi corpus: nisi non satis
declarat scriptura: quomodo accipiat uirgae uocabulum in Exodo:
quum eam ante narrarit ex uirga uersa in colubrum. Nam ille colu-
ber, adhuc male ebrius potista: qui uigilans dormit: et dum omnia
20 distinguit, atque (ut ipsi uidetur) acute discriminat: inguinis et
capitis, quae sint discri[EE₄]mina nescit.

Verba Lutheri   Et miror, inquit, sapientissimum hunc
Thomistam: cur non et accidentia tran-
substantiet.

25 Et paulo post nebulo rursus irridet Ambrosium: deinde quaerit.

Quae necessitas perimendae substantiae et seruandorum accidentium?

Ista quaerere solent haeretici,   NON est, cur quaeras a rege: cur non
quum haerent   transubstantiet accidentia. Quaerere debes
istud a deo: nam ille substantiam transub-
30 stantiat, non rex: qui et ideo credit deum panis mutasse substantiam,
relictis accidentibus: quia sic fieri ecclesiam suam docet idem deus,

8 stultitiam] stulticiam *L*   19 ebrius potista] ebrium potistam *BRL. See n.*   23 acci-
dentia] *L*, accidentiam *BR*   27 *gloss om. L*   31 docet idem] *corr. err. L*, docet. Idem *BR*

See another skill of Luther's, reader, and of such a kind that nothing but a potist can be believed, nor is there anything born under the sun more dense and silly than the potistic monsters. For since he had earlier stammered drunkenly that the words of scripture must not be taken except in a literal and grammatical sense, the king made 5 sport of his singular folly because the consequence of this rule would be that Christ is wheat bread in heaven, and a vine loaded with grapes, and the saints would one day eat and drink in the kingdom of God. Now the honored Luther, chagrined that his folly has been thus attacked, laughs very wrathfully, and the reverend father, in accord 10 with his reverence, plays the buffoon very waggishly, expecting his buffoonery to be strong enough to support a solution which otherwise, by itself, would have as much force as a gnat. For, whereas he says that it is sufficiently clear from the context how Christ wished His calling Himself bread and a vine to be understood, the king has thus 15 proved—a thing which Luther deplores
and conceals—that it is clear from the   *Luther's chagrin*
context how Paul understands the bread in the sacrament since he openly shows that the body of Christ has been made from that bread; unless the scripture does not sufficiently manifest how it understands 20 the word "rod" in Exodus, when it earlier narrated that the rod was changed from a rod into a snake. For that snake, still a dead-drunk potist who dreams with his eyes open and, while he distinguishes and —so he thinks—keenly discriminates everything, does not know the difference between groin and head.   25

And I am amazed, he says, at this most   *Luther's words*
wise Thomist, why he does not also
transubstantiate the accidents.

And shortly after, the rascal again mocks Ambrose, then asks:

What need is there for destroying the substance and preserving the 30
accidents?

There is no need for you to ask of the
king why he does not transubstantiate the *Heretics usually ask such questions*
accidents. You should ask this of God, for   *when they are stuck*
He, not the king, transubstantiates the substance; and the king 35
believes that God has changed the substance of bread, leaving the accidents, because the same God who has done it teaches His church

qui fecit, qui et intus docet et extra, uerbis euangelij, cum occulto
eius flatu conspirantibus, ex pane fieri corpus ipsius, hoc est panis
substantiam, uerti in substantiam corporis. Quod si uerba, quae sunt
clarissima, quicquam haberent ambigui: imo uero, si uiderentur in
5 diuersam partem potius aliquantum uergere: tamen quum Christus
se promiserit, per spiritum sanctum ecclesiam suam esse docturum:
et se cum ea futurum, usque ad consummationem seculi: Quumque
rex probarit tibi, tot ueterum testimonio,
Lutherum mentiri de fide
transubstantiationis tot recentium, hanc transubstantiationis
10 fidem, non esse, quod tu mentiris, nouam:
sed a Christo passo, totius ecclesiae perpetuam: quis non uidet, aut
tot seculis, ecclesiae suae Christum defuisse, hoc est ueritatem falsa
promisisse, aut spiritum ueritatis falsa docuisse, aut te arrogantissi-
mum esse nebulonem: qui, quomodo scriptura sit intelligenda, iubeas
15 orbem totum tuae potius stultitiae credere: quam, qui scribentibus
inspirauit, deo: nec illi sis crediturus, mutatam esse substantiam: nisi
rationem reddat tibi: quare non transubstantiet accidentia? [EE₄v]
Hoc est, deo te non habiturum fidem: nisi sic agat tecum: ut res fiat
palam, et tollatur fides. Nam Christus, ideo uideri potest accidentia
20 reliquisse: ut tectius esset corporis mysterium: ne aut meritum fidei,
tolleret euidentia rei: aut populus reformidans aedere, non perciperet
fructum sacramenti. SED et haec pulcherrima Lutheri sycophantia
est: quod quum princeps dicat, indignam esse panis substantiam:
quae cum illa misceatur substantia: quae creauit omnes: ibi Lutherus
25 in campo suo spaciatur, nugatur, scurratur, irridet: tanquam rex,
quod obiter dixit, probabile id attulisset, loco demonstrationis
necessariae. Deinde uociferatur et clamat,
Nam Lutherus non haerebit uel
cum stercoribus miscere esse ter haereticum: quod rex panem dicat
indignum, qui cum ea misceatur sub-
30 stantia: quae substantias omnes condidit. Nam hic uideri uult, tam
rudem esse principem: ut putarit corpus Christi, non esse creaturam,
sed creatorem. Et quum ubique, reuerendus frater affectet uideri
mire sapiens: hic subito uideri studet, ita stupidus: ut non senserit

---

1 occulto] *corr. err. L,* occultu *BR*

that it is so done, He who teaches both interiorly and exteriorly, with
the words of the gospel agreeing with His secret inspiration that His
own body is made from the bread; that is, the substance of the bread
is turned into the substance of the body. But if the words, which are
most clear, had any ambiguity, even indeed if they seemed rather 5
to incline somewhat to the opposite meaning, nevertheless, since
Christ promised that He would teach His church through the Holy
Spirit and that He would be with her even to the consummation of
the world, and since the king has proved to you by the testimony of
so many ancient and recent men that this 10
faith in transubstantiation is not, as you *That Luther lies about faith in transubstantiation*
pretend, new but the uninterrupted faith
of the whole church from the time of Christ's passion, who does not
see either that Christ has abandoned His church through so many
centuries—that is, that Truth has made false promises or the Spirit of 15
truth has taught false doctrine—or that you are a most arrogant
rascal who, in the matter of how scripture should be understood, order
the whole world to believe your folly rather than God who inspired
the writers of scripture, and are not ready to believe Him that the
substance has been changed unless He gives you a reason for not 20
transubstantiating the accidents? That is, you will not trust God
unless He deals with you in such a way that the matter becomes plain
and faith is taken away. For Christ can seem to have left the accidents
so that the mystery of His body might be more concealed, lest either
the manifestation of reality would take away the merit of faith, or the 25
people, fearing to eat, would not receive the fruit of the sacrament.

But this also is a very neat deception of Luther that when the prince
says that the substance of bread is unworthy to be mixed with that
substance which created all substances, then Luther struts about on
his field of battle, talks nonsense, plays the buffoon, jeers, as though 30
the king had presented that probability which he said in passing in
place of a demonstrative proof. Then he
bawls and shouts that the king is a three- *For Luther will not stick even at mixing it with shit*
fold heretic because he says that bread is
unworthy to be mingled with that substance which established all 35
substances. For here he wishes it to appear that the prince is so
ignorant as to think that the body is not a creature but the creator.
And although the reverend friar everywhere aspires to appear
wonderfully wise, here he suddenly takes pains to appear so stupid

principem ita loqui, propter diuinitatem Christi: quae per concomi-
tantiam (ut uocant) semper adest corpori: nec intellexerit homo
simplex, per communicationem idiomatum, sic homines passim loqui
de Christo: ut hominem dicant creatorem, et aeternum, et deum:
5 uicissim dicant et natum esse et mortuum.

Lutheri uerba   Praetereo hic, rhetoricissimum illum con-
                         temptum, dum duas urgentissimas simi-
litudines apposui, de ferro ignito, et deo incarnato, ubi neque igni
ferrum, neque diuinitati hominem necesse est cedere. Mihi enim,
10 etiam si non necesse sit, mea asserere: tamen satis negocij fecero
assertori, si suum figmentum aliter se posse habere demonstrauero.
Itaque possum dicere, cor[FF₁]pus Christi, sic saluo pane in sacramento esse, sicut est ignis in ferro, salua ferri substantia: et deus in
homine salua humanitate, utrobique sic mixtis substantijs, ut sua
15 cuique operatio, et natura propria maneat, et tamen unum aliquod
constituant.

FINGIS hic, regem tuas istas similitudines dissimulasse silentio:
sed qui librum principis legerit: uidebit, te dissimulare principis
responsum: quamquam similitudines tuae,
Lutheri similia dissimilia   tam dissimiles ueri sunt: ut operae
20 *esse*   precium non fuerit ullum respondisse.
Nam primum de ferro, quod affers, et igne, uide quam pulchre
coaptes. Aut ignis est, ut sensere quidam, qualitas et feruor excellens
in ferro, aut ignis congestus in poros. Si illud primum, nihil simile de
25 corpore Christi, quod non est qualitas: si secundum, ne sic quidem
quicquam quadrat similitudo tua. Nam (ut princeps prudenter
annotauit) Christus non dixit: In hoc est corpus meum, aut simul
cum hoc, sicut in ferro est ignis: sed simpliciter dixit: Hoc est corpus
meum. At nec ferrum illud ignis est, sed ignitum. Illud uero, quod
30 porrexit Christus, Christi corpus erat, si Christo credimus: si tibi
credimus, non erit Christi corpus, sed panis (ut ita dicamus) Christi-
corporeus: sicut ferrum tuum non est ignis, sed ferrum ignitum. O
caput ferreum, et frontem dignam, cui
Lutherus stigmate dignus   ferrum ignitum longas infigat literas.
35 QVOD SI uelis sic esse, corpus Christi cum pane, sicut corpus
glorificatum est, aut potest esse cum alio corpore: aut sicut anima est

14 mixtis] *L*, mixtus *BR*   15 maneat] *L*, mane at *BR*   19 *gloss om. L*   28 in ferro
est ignis] in ferro vel cum ferro est ignis *L*   30 Christo credimus] *L*, Christo credimns
BR   35 QVOD] Quam *L*

that he has not understood the prince to speak as he does because of
the divinity of Christ, which through concomitance, as they call it, is
ever present in the body; nor has the simple fellow grasped that
through the mutual sharing of properties men everywhere speak in
this way about Christ, so that they say a man is creator and eternal   5
and they say in turn that God was born and died.

I pass over here his most rhetorical con-
tempt when I applied two very cogent   *Luther's words*
analogies about fiery iron and about God incarnate, where it is not
necessary either for the iron to yield to the fire or man to the divinity.   10
For even if it is not necessary for me to defend my position, nevertheless I shall have given the defender enough trouble if I shall have
shown that his fabrication can be considered otherwise. And so I can
say that the body of Christ is in the sacrament without destroying the
bread just as fire is in iron without destroying the substance of the   15
iron, and as God is in man without destroying human nature; in each
case the substances are so mingled that each one retains its own proper
operation and nature and yet they constitute a single entity.

Here you pretend that the king has concealed those analogies of
yours by silence, but whoever reads the book of the prince will see   20
that you conceal the prince's answer;
although your analogies are so unlike the   *Luther's analogies are not*
truth that they were not worth answering   *analogous*
at all. For first of all, concerning the iron and the fire which you
brought up, see how neatly you fit them together. Either fire is, as   25
some have thought, a quality consisting of an extraordinary degree of
heat in the iron, or it is an accumulation within the pores of the iron.
If it is the first, it is not at all like the body of Christ, which is not a
quality; if the second, not even so does your analogy fit at all. For, as
the prince shrewdly noted, Christ did not say, "In this is my body,"   30
or "Together with this," as fire is in iron, but He said simply, "This is
my body." Nor is that iron fire, but fired. But that which Christ
presented was the body of Christ, if we believe Christ; if we believe
you, it will not be the body of Christ but bread—if we may say so—
Christ-bodied, just as your iron is not fire   35
but iron fired. O iron head, and forehead   *Luther worthy of a brand*
worthy to have a fired iron brand it with tall letters. But if you wish
the body of Christ to be with the bread as a glorified body is or can be
with a different body, or as the soul is with the body, nevertheless you

cum corpore: tamen in eodem luto haesitabis. Nam neque recte
loquetur, qui dicet corpus esse animam, sed animatum: neque qui sic
loquetur, hoc corpus, puta, lapis est hoc corpus glorificatum, puta,
corpus Christi, iam ianuis clausis ingredientis marmoreum parietem,
5 [FF₁v] sed in hoc lapide. aut cum hoc lapide est, hoc corpus Christi.
Sed Christus, ut tuam istam similitudinem ostenderet esse dissimilem:

Altera Lutheri parabola aeque absurda non dixit, in hoc, aut cum hoc, sed dixit
hoc est corpus meum. Iam altera simili-
tudo tua, de deo incarnato, non est ab-
10 surda modo: sed impia quoque atque sacrilega: ut ex qua sequatur,
quod deprehendit prudentissimus princeps: quod sicut deus assumpsit hominem: ita deus et homo in unitatem suppositi, assumant panem
et uinum: ut deus, qui quod semel assumpsit nunquam reliquit: nunc
tot panes, tot pocula, tam cito relicturus, assidue sumat in unitatem
15 suppositi: neque enim aliter quadrat similitudo, ut cum corpore
Christi sit panis, sicut ibi deus cum homine. Sic deus rotari sinit
haereticos, et praecipites ferri dementia: ut in stulticiam ruant, et in
insanias falsas. Et iam postquam tibi probatum uides, sensum Pauli
non probare pro te: nec illum sic uocare panem, quomodo tu con-
20 tendis, quum similes formas loquendi uideas, e scriptura sacra productas: quum euangelium uideas manifeste probare contra te: quum
euangelio nemo dubitet Pauli sensum esse conformem: quum sanctos
patres omnes, omnes fidei proceres, omnes omnino fideles a Christo
passo, tot seculis uideas, una uoce contra te testari: quum cogaris ipse
25 fateri, totius ecclesiae fidem falli non posse: denique, quum te
manifeste uideas turpissime uictum esse: iam prae furore frendens, et
ringens, et sardonium interim risum ridens, buccinas te uictorem: et
clamas te habere nunc hunc articulum praeclare confirmatum: et ut
ostendas te more tuo aliorum opera bona reddi deteriorem: plus
30 quam furiosus adiungis. [FF₂]

Verba Lutheri. Hic iam se allegat repugnantiae Antea posui, nihil referre, siue sic sentias
de transubstantiatione, siue sic. Nunc
autem decerno, impium esse et blasphemum, si quis dicat panem transubstantiari.

---

29 opera bona] *corr. err. L,* bona *om. BR*

will stick in the same mud. For he will not speak correctly who says that the body is a soul rather than ensouled, nor he who says, "This body, namely a stone, is this glorified body, namely the body of Christ now entering through a marble wall though the doors are closed," rather than, "In this stone or with this stone is this body of Christ." But Christ, in order to show that this analogy of yours is not analogous, did not say, "in this," or "with this," but He said, "This is my body."

Next, your other analogy regarding God incarnate is not only absurd but also impious and sacrilegious, so that from it *Luther's other analogy equally absurd* follows what the very wise prince detected: that just as God assumed human nature, so God and man would assume bread and wine into the unity of a supposite, so that God, who never leaves what He has once assumed, now would continuously assume into the unity of a supposite so many pieces of bread, so many cups which He would as quickly abandon, for the analogy does not otherwise fit, that bread is with the body of Christ as God is present with man. Thus God allows heretics to be rolled along, and carried headlong by madness, so that they rush into folly and into deluded madness. And now, after you see proven for you that Paul's interpretation proves nothing for you and that he does not refer to bread in the way that you argue, since you see like figures of speech cited from sacred scripture; since you see that the gospel clearly proves the opposite of your argument; since no one doubts that Paul's interpretation harmonizes with the gospel; since you see that all the holy fathers, all the leaders of the faith, absolutely all the faithful from the time of Christ's passion through so many centuries bear unanimous witness against you; since you yourself are forced to admit that the faith of the whole church cannot be deceived; finally, since you clearly see yourself most shamefully conquered; now, gnashing your teeth in fury and snarling and all the while laughing a Sardonian laugh, you trumpet yourself as victor and shout that you now consider this article excellently confirmed; and, to show that in your usual manner you are rendered worse by the good work of others, you add in an excess of raging madness:

Earlier I set down that it made no difference whether you had this opinion on transubstantiation or that. But now I *Luther's words. Here he now charges himself with inconsistency* decree that it is impious and blasphemous if anyone says that the bread is transubstantiated.

DICVNT istud, sicuti scis, non solum populus ubique christianus hodie, sed et Eusebius, Gregorius, Cyrillus, Hieronymus, Augustinus, Ambrosius, et si quis unquam fere literis, et sanctitate claruit in ecclesia Christi. Hos tu potator impius, et blasphemus, impios et
5 blasphemos audes appellare. Sed sic impius in terra blasphemas sanctos dei: quomodo apud inferos damnati, ipsum blasphemant deum. Sed ut omnes uideant, quo superbiae tuae furore detrusus sis, in hoc baratrum, deploratissimae perditionis: ut a malo te mutares in pessimum. Verba regis, quibus quum leuari potueras, tua te superbia
10 pessundedit: subiungam.

Verba regis　　　"MIROR, ex hoc dogmate, quid fructus populis spondeat Lutherus. An (quod ait ipse) ne quis propterea semet credat haereticum: quod fors ita cum Luthero sentiat? At Lutherus ipse fatetur nihil esse periculi: si quis
15 hac in re sentiat, quod tota iam sentiat ecclesia. Sed contra, tota ecclesia censet haereticum esse eum: qui sentiat cum Luthero. Non debet ergo Lutherus animare quenquam, cui bene cupit: ut secum sentiat, cuius sententiam tota condemnat ecclesia: sed debet his suadere, quos amat: ut accedant illis, quos ipse quoque iudicat in
20 nullo uersari periculo. Falsa est ergo ista Lutheri uia contra publicam fidem, non huius modo temporis, sed etiam omnium: nec liberat captiuitate credentes ei: sed educens e libertate fidei, hoc est e loco tuto (quod Lutherus ipse fatetur) captiuat, in errorem du[FF₂v]cens, in precipitium, et uias inuias, incertas, dubias, eoque plenas periculi:
25 et qui amat periculum, peribit in illo."

NVNQVID lector (amabo te) hoc non extremae dementiae est? quod quum fateatur ipse Lutherus, nos omnes, qui catholicae obsequimur ecclesiae, uia tutiori insistere (sicuti rex ex ipsius uerbis ostendit) tamen audet execrabiles ac diris deuouendos proponere: si
30 quis eius ter execrandae se non adiungat haeresi. Nam ut daremus ei, ipsum non pessime sentire, tum de religione publica, tum de salute christianorum omnium: tamen insignis stultitia merito posset appellari, incertam spem pro certo premio captare: Atque ex illa uia exilire, qua tot sancti uiri eo peruenere dubio procul: quo ipse non

---

5 appellare. Sed sic] *corr. err. L,* appellare: sed sic *BR*　　12 populis] *corr. err. L,* populus *BR*

This is said, as you know, not only by Christian people everywhere today, but also by Eusebius, Gregory, Cyril, Jerome, Augustine, Ambrose, and almost anyone who has ever been noted in the church of Christ for his learning and sanctity. These men you, impious and blasphemous tosspot, dare to call impious and blasphemous. But you on earth thus impiously blaspheme the saints of God just as the damned in hell blaspheme God Himself. But so that all may see with what raging madness of your pride you have been thrust into this abyss of hopeless perdition, so that you have changed yourself from bad to worst, I will subjoin the words of the king; although you could have been raised up by them, your pride has thrust you to the depths.

"I wonder what profit Luther promises the people from this teaching. Is it, as he *The king's words* himself says, that no one should consider himself a heretic for thus agreeing with Luther? But Luther himself admits that there is no danger if someone judges in this matter what the whole church now judges. But the whole church, on the other hand, considers as a heretic him who agrees with Luther. Luther ought not, then, to encourage anyone whose good he has at heart to agree with himself whose judgment the whole church condemns, but he ought to persuade those he loves to join those whom he himself judges to be involved in no danger.

"This way of Luther, therefore, is a false way contrary to the public faith, not only of this age but even of all ages; nor does he free from captivity those who believe in him, but leading them out of the liberty of the faith, that is from a safe place, as Luther himself admits, he takes them captive, leading them into error, into a steep place, and into trackless, uncertain, doubtful ways, and thus ways full of danger; and he who loves danger will perish in it."

Please tell me, reader, is not this the mark of extreme madness: that, although Luther himself admits that all of us who obey the catholic church pursue a safer way, as the king has shown from Luther's own words, he nevertheless dares to represent as execrable and as destined to destruction anyone who will not join up with his triply execrable heresy. For while we would grant him that he does not have the worst opinion in regard to both public religion and the salvation of all Christians, nevertheless it could justly be called signal folly to seize on an uncertain hope in place of a certain reward, and to leap out of that way by which so many holy men have undoubtedly

satis certo ausit promittere se perducturum: si uelimus sequi. Nunc
ergo, quum nemini non liqueat, nisi qui simili atque ille glaucomate
caecutit, eum in certum atque manifestum exitium tendere, et
sequentes trahere, ut in aliorum uita nomen sibi comparet: quis cui
5 anima sua chara sit, non auersetur, ac totis uiribus operam det, talem
ducem e medio tollere: ne posset aliquando per imprudentiam ab eo
seduci. Caeterum audi nunc iterum, quam magnifice tamen interim
cunctis maledicat: qui, eius gloriolae causa, sese nolunt prudentes in
barathrum inijcere.

10   Aggressurus stolida Lutheri sophismata, argutantis
missam non esse bonum opus, retegit ac refellit
primum sycophanticam illius ineptiam: qua
nugatur ita regem colligere, populus pro missa
dat sacerdotibus pecuniam: ergo missa est
15   sacrificium et opus bonum.
Ca. XIIII. [FF₃]

Quintum adest capitale, et summum, et
Verba Lutheri. At non hic demum angulare assertionis Henricianae opus,
Lutherus est Lutherus et Missam esse opus et sacrificium. Hic
haereticus hereticus
20 demum Dominus Henricus est dominus
Henricus, et Thomista est Thomista. Ac primum ex aliquo semi-
rhetore forte audiuit: sicubi aduersarij senserit robora, nimium inuicta,
oportere, rugato naso, illum rideri et contemni: ut stupidus lector,
credat antea uictum aduersarium, quam impugnetur a tanto rhetore.
25 Sic et dominus noster rex magnificis ampullis praefatur: ut sese belle
fingat tedere confutationis tam stulti et indocti Lutheri, negantis,
missam esse opus et sacrificium scilicet, Satanas uulnus sentit, ideo
prae morbo animi incertus, quid agat, mera aegritudine et impotentia me tentat irrisione, et contemptu
Quam aegre ferat contemptum irritare. Sed ille, qui dedit nobis scire
30   *elatus nebulo* cogitationes Satanae, dabit etiam nobis

19 opus et] opus bonum et *L*   29–30 *gloss* contemptum elatus] *L*, contem? ptumelatus *BR*

arrived at the place where he himself has not dared with enough certainty to promise that he would lead us if we should wish to follow him. Now therefore, since it is clear to everyone, except to one who like him is blinded by cataracts, that he is heading for certain and manifest destruction and that he is dragging along those who follow him, so that he may gain a name for himself at the cost of the life of others, what man who loves his own soul would not reject and use every effort to destroy such a leader lest he could at some time be led astray by him unawares? But now hear again how pompously meanwhile he yet curses all those who do not wish for the sake of a little glory for him to hurl themselves knowingly into the abyss.

Being about to attack Luther's stupid sophism, arguing that the mass is not a good work, he first of all reveals and refutes the fellow's deceitful folly by which he absurdly says that the king reasons thus: the people give the priests money for the mass, therefore the mass is a sacrifice and a good work. Chapter 14.

The fifth point appears as the chief and final and fundamental fortification of Henrician defense: that the mass is a work and a sacrifice. Here at last Lord *Luther's words. But here finally is not Luther Luther and the heretic a heretic?*

Henry is Lord Henry, and the Thomist is a Thomist. And first of all he probably heard from some semi-rhetorician that wherever he has sensed that the forces of the adversary are too invincible, the latter should be mocked and scorned with wrinkled nose, so that the dull-witted reader may believe that the adversary is conquered before he is attacked by such a great rhetorician. Thus also our lord king speaks beforehand with pompously swelling words so that he skillfully pretends he is weary of the confutation of such a foolish and unlearned Luther denying that the mass is a work and a sacrifice. Satan feels his wound and therefore, not knowing what to do because of the malady of his soul, tries with sheer spleen and intemperance to vex me with mockery *How vexed the conceited scoundrel is at being scorned* and scorn. But He who grants us to know the thoughts of Satan will also grant us to mock his mockery and to

irrisionem irridere, et contemptorem contemnere, suaeque insipien-
tiae fragiles ampullas cum fiducia traducere.

QVEMADMODVM in comoedia, ultimus actus debet esse
optimus: Ita Lutherus curauit: ut esset in fine stultissimus. Venit
5 enim nunc ad summam haeresim: propter quam excogitauit reliquas.
Hanc quoniam ita sibi funditus uidet euersam: ut nulla possit arte
reficere: relicta spe defentionis, totus est in suis nugis. Indigne fert,
quod ita rideatur eius tam seria et seuera sententia: quam nec
Heraclitus quidem legere potuisset absque risu: nisi quod ausus est
10 ea scribere furiosus nebulo: quae non minus impia sunt et scelerata,
quam stulta. Quae, quum qualia sint, talia iam per eruditissimum
regem comperta sunt: uere Satanas uulnus sentit: ac per os electi sui

Is grex est Lutheranorum   Lutheri rugit ac rudit: ac simul ingressus
                                porcorum gregem uoluptariorum semi-
15 rhetorum: qui inter pocula componunt libros eius: cogitationes suas
inspirat illis: non ut terrenum regem solum, sed caelestem etiam
irrideant: et postquam in profun[FF₃v]dum uenerint, homines
execrabiles: omnia sacra contemnant. Sed, qui habitat in caelis,
irridebit eos: et dominus subsannabit eos.

20   Ne nihil dicat tam insignis assertor,
          Verba Lutheri   unam affert, rationem plane potentis-
simam: qua, hactenus omnibus satisfactum est, Missam esse opus et
sacrificium. Ea est huiusmodi. Si missa non esset opus bonum, laici
certe pro ea nihil tribuerent clericis, temporalis beneficij. Obstupesce
25   lector, regia et Thomistica est haec ratio,
   Imo Lutherana et haeretica   et (ut dixi) plane potentissima. Nam
          fictio   plurimos permouit hactenus, et permouet
hodie, Hic iacet Lutherus prostratus: et nemo tam dextre eum con-
fecit, atque rex Anglorum, in hoc libro, ipsa ratione. Nam (ut nolim)
30 cogor tamen confiteri haec ita habere. Vere, inquam, missa ideo est
sacrificium, et opus bonum, quod, ut rex dicit, laici tribuunt opes
sacerdotibus pro ea.

VIS VIDERE lector, exemplar insigne, singularis sycophantiae:
Nusquam uidebis insignius, quam in hac magnifica Lutheri iactantia:

---

12 uulnus] *corr. err. L*, melius *BR*

scorn his scorn and confidently to expose to ridicule the brittle bombast of his folly.

Just as in a comedy the last act ought to be the best, so Luther has seen to it that at the end he is most foolish. For he has come now to the supreme heresy because of which he has thought out the rest. Be- 5
cause he sees this so overthrown from its foundation that he can by no trick restore it, with all hope of defense abandoned, he gives him-self wholly to trifling. He is indignant that his very serious and grave opinion is thus mocked, an opinion which not even Heraclitus could have read without laughing, except that the madly raging rascal has 10
dared to write arguments which are no less impious and wicked than they are foolish. Since the character of these arguments has now been disclosed by the most learned king, Satan truly feels his wound and through the mouth of Luther, his elect, he brays and bellows and at the same time, having entered a herd of   *This is the herd of Lutherans* 15
pigs—the sensual semi-rhetoricians who
between cups compose his books—he breathes his thoughts into them so that they mock not only an earthly king but also the heavenly one, and once the accursed men have descended into the depths they scorn everything holy. But He who dwells in the heavens will mock 20
them and the Lord will deride them.

Lest such a distinguished defender have   *Luther's words*
nothing to say, he presents one reason,
clearly the most powerful, by which up till now everyone has been satisfied that the mass is a work and a sacrifice. The reasoning goes as 25
follows: If the mass were not a good work, the laity would certainly not give the clergy any temporal favor for it. Be dumb with astonish-ment, reader; royal and Thomistic is this
reason, and, as I said, clearly most power-   *On the contrary, a Lutheran*
                                                and heretical fiction
ful. For it has prevailed on very many up   30
till now, and it will prevail today. Here Luther lies prostrate, and no one has subdued him so skillfully as the English king in this book by this very reason. For, though I do not wish it, I am nevertheless forced to confess that this is the way things are. Truly, I say, the mass is a sacrifice and a good work because, as the king says, the laity give the 35
priests riches for it.

Do you wish to see, reader, an outstanding example of matchless craftiness? You will never see a more outstanding one than in this pompous boasting of Luther, if only you read it comparing it with the

si modo eam, ad principis uerba collatam,

Vna, ex multis, sycophantia Lutheri

relegeris. Nam, quum Lutherus pro magna captiuitate posuerit: quod missa credatur esse bonum opus, oblatio, aut sacrificium: nec quicquam attulisset:
5 ex quo moueri se diceret, in tam absurdam haeresim, praeter id unum: quod iam tandem solus reperisset, missam esse testamentum.

Quaedam in Luthero a rege redarguta

Rex in illo, tria redarguit: primo gloriosam uanitatem, qua, uelut inuentum suum, iactat id Lutherus, quod nusquam
10 non praedicant gregarij fraterculi: deinde temerariam stulticiam, quod quam rem, tam multi tractant inepti, id ipsum tractat ineptius, quam quisquis illorum fuit ineptissimus. Postremo detestabilem maliciam, quod odio sacerdotum, potius quam illis relinquat fructum tempo[FF₄]ralem: studeat laicis e missa tollere fructum omnem
15 spiritalem. Itaque rex, dum hunc in modum ista tractat: his uerbis obiter attingit rabidam Lutheri maliciam.

Verba regis. Inauditi missae fructus inuenti a Luthero

"FRATERCVLI, testamentum illud inepte praedicantes, multis tamen in rebus, meliores Luthero, hoc uno tantum, Lu-
20 thero sunt impares: quod mirabiles, et hactenus inauditos missae fructus, non inuenerunt: quibus et clerus praesentis uitae fructum, et populus futurae perderent."

DEINDE rex, ut ostenderet Lutherum, non ob aliud, hoc insanum dogma statuere, quod sacerdotis missa, non prodest populo: quam
25 odio, quo prosequitur clericos, declarat, quid prouiderit et captarit Lutherus. Nempe ut laici persuasi, nihil sibi missam profuturam, nihil ipsi uicissim prodessent sacerdotibus. Nam nihil (inquit) sacerdotibus temporalis boni conferrent ob missam: e qua persuaderentur, nihil se spiritualis boni relaturos. Quod unum spectasse
30   Lutherum docet: ut clericis auferret cor-

Lutheri consilium de missa

poralem uictum, etiamsi populo simul auferret animarum uitam.

Vides lector, quantum intersit, inter bonitatem principis, et istius scurrae maliciam. Nam quum iste nomen suum dederit in clerum:

1–2 *gloss* sycophantia Lutheri] *L*, sxcophantia lutheri *BR*   30 *gloss* de missa] demissa *L*

words of the prince. For when Luther set
down as the great captivity that the mass is
believed to be a good work, oblation, or
sacrifice, and had not produced any reason by which he said he was
moved to such an absurd heresy except the single one that now at last
he alone had discovered that the mass is a testament, on that point
the king convicted him of three things: in
the first place, the boastful vanity by
which Luther vaunts as his own invention
that which the common sort of friarlings have preached everywhere;
secondly, rash folly because he handles more senselessly than all the
most senseless men a matter which so many senseless men handle;
finally, his hateful malice, because through hatred of priests, rather
than leave them temporal benefit, he strives to deprive the laity of all
the spiritual benefit of the mass. And so the king, while he treats these
points in this manner, touches in passing on the rabid malice of
Luther in the following words:

One out of many of Luther's tricks

Certain of the king's reproofs against Luther

"The friarlings who foolishly preach that
testament, though better than Luther in
many points, nevertheless in this point
only are unequal to Luther, that they have
not discovered the marvelous and till now unheard of benefits of the
mass by which the clergy would lose all benefit in the present life and
the people that of the life to come."

The king's words. Unheard of fruits of the mass discovered by Luther

Then the king, in order to show that Luther, for no other reason
than the hatred with which he pursues the clergy, establishes this mad
doctrine that the mass profits the priests not the people, declares what
Luther has foreseen and seized on; namely, that the laity, persuaded
that the mass will profit them nothing, would not themselves give the
priests any profit in return. For they would, he says, grant no temporal
good to the priests for the sake of a mass from which they were persuaded that they would gain no spiritual
good. He teaches that Luther has considered this one point so that he might take
away from the clergy their means of bodily sustenance, even though
he would at the same time be taking away from the people the life of
their souls.

Luther's intention concerning the mass

You see, reader, how much difference there is between the goodness of the prince and the malice of this buffoon. For although this

iam ecclesiam scindens, laicorum ordinem in clerum prouocat: et eos
indignatur de altari uiuere, qui altari seruiunt: tam obstinatae
maliciae, ut quum intelligat non esse causam, cur quenquam alat
altare, si nihil cuiquam prosit altare: potius quam inde uiuat
5 sacerdos dei: altare dei funditus conatur euertere. Et dummodo
corporale subsidium auferat presbiteris: animae fructum omnem
laborat eripere, omnibus omnino laicis. Hanc, [FF₄v] istius tam
execrandam maliciam, quum rex et sagacissime deprehenderit, et
aperte prodiderit, et pulcherrime redarguerit, aestuans ira Lutherus,
10 et iam manifeste furens, tanquam nemo lecturus locum esset, ex
libello principis, et stolidam Lutheri sycophantiam deprehensurus,

Lutheri figmentum

fingit calumniae figulus, ita regem colligere, Sacerdotibus laici conferunt uictum:
ergo missa est sacrificium. Et postquam istud tam belle finxit: tum
15 demum regnat in stultitia: et integras paginas implet insulsis dictis:
quae nihil attingunt aliud: quam quod ipse ridicule finxit, ex ridiculo
cerebello suo: cui nunc non possum maius imprecari dedecus: quam
ut ipsius tam bella scommata, quibus sibi uidetur belle in regem
ludere, patefacta iam calumnia, frequenter lector et accurate relegas.

20

Lutherum suis dictis satis coargui

Nullius enim uerba, queunt illum manifestius aut maiore cum opprobrio traducere: quam, quibus alios traducere se
iactat, sua.

Pulcherrime refellit, uanissimam Lutheri iactantiam:
25   qua decies gloriatur, principale fundamentum
suum regem ex professo
relinquere. Cap. XV.

AVDISTI iam lector, admirandam sycophantiam, cum non minore
stultitia coniunctam. Audi nunc aliam Lutheri magnificam gloriam:

fellow has been enrolled among the clergy, now, rending the church, he stirs up the order of the laity against the clergy and considers it improper for those men who serve the altar to live by means of the altar; a man of such stubborn malice that, although he understands that there is no reason why the altar should nourish anyone if the altar does not profit anyone, yet rather than let a priest of God live by means of the altar he tries to destroy the altar from its foundation. And if only he may take away from the priests their bodily sustenance, he labors to snatch from every single one of the laity every benefit for the soul. Since the king has most shrewdly grasped and openly exposed and most skillfully refuted such execrable malice in this fellow, Luther, blazing with wrath and now clearly raging mad as though no one would read the passage from the prince's book and detect Luther's stupid craftiness, pretends, the fashioner of slander, that the king reasons thus: "The laity bestow a living on the priests, therefore the *Luther's fabrication* mass is a sacrifice." And after he has fashioned this so prettily, then at last he reigns supreme in folly and fills whole pages with silly remarks which are concerned with nothing else but what he himself has ridiculously fashioned from his own ridiculous little brain, on which I cannot now call down any greater disgrace than that you, reader, should frequently and carefully reread his own very clever taunts, now revealed as slanders, with which he thinks he is making clever sport of the king. For no one's words can expose him to ridicule more clearly or with greater opprobrium than his own *That Luther is sufficiently* words by which he boasts that he exposes *convicted by his own* others to ridicule. *statements*

He very skillfully refutes Luther's most vain boasting by which he brags ten times over that the king professedly leaves untouched his principal foundation. Chapter 15.

You have now heard, reader, his amazing craftiness, joined with no less folly. Now hear another pompous boast by Luther which is so

quae tam gloriosa est: ut, siue sycophantia spectetur, siue stultitia, prorsus obscuret priorem.

Lutheri uerba

Non minor est amentia, quae sequitur, ubi cum multis uerbis [GG₁] me contem-
5 psisset (Hoc enim in rhetorica potissimum didicit) tandem protestatur sese relicturum intactum, id quod maxime omnium confutandum ei fuerat, nempe robur meum principale, et argumentum capitale: Vbi ex uerbis Christi probaui, missam esse testamentum, et promissionem: ideo non posse opus aut sacrificium dici. Hic infelix assertor, uictus
10 fortitudine huius roboris, misere dissimulata conscientia, non solum transit, sed protestatur etiam, sese transiturum, et alijs dimissurum. O assertorem sacramentorum. O defen-

*O te scelestum impugnatorem
sacramentorum et ecclesiae
catholicae*

sorem ecclesiae Romanae, bis Thomisticum, et omnibus indulgentiis papisticis
15 longe dignissimum. Ignosci poterat, si transisset hoc robur meum silens, at protestari sese transiturum, qui audiat, in hoc me unice et maxime fidere, et inde omnia illius profligari, hoc sic ridiculum est et stultum, ut nihil supra.

AVDISTI lector aegregias istius glorias: audi nunc uicissim uerba
20 regis: ex quibus gloriandi ansam sibi prebitam uideri uult: quae quum legeris, sat scio miraturum te, gloriosi Thrasonis infamem pudendamque sese traducentis amentiam. Principis ergo uerba sunt huiusmodi.

Verba regis

"NON CONTENDAM cum eo de
25 testamento et promissione, et tota illa diffinitione, et applicatione testamenti ad sacramentum. Non ero tam molestus ei, quam alios fortassis inueniet: si qui bonam ei partem istius fundamenti subruerint: qui et testamentum nouum dicant, promissionem esse legis euangelicae: quemadmodum uetus fuit
30 Mosaicae: et testamentum istud negent a

*Lutherus adulteratur Christi
testamentum*

Luthero satis scite tractari: neque enim
testatori nuncupandum esse nominatim,
quid relinquat haeredi: quem ex asse instituat: neque remissionem peccatorum, quam pro haereditate nuncupatam Lutherus ait, idem
35 esse quod regnum caelorum, sed [GG₁v] uiam potius ad caelum.

boastful that, whether its cunning or its folly is considered, it completely overshadows the former.

No less is the madness which follows, where when he had contemned me at *Luther's words* length—for this above all he has learned in rhetoric—he finally declares publicly that he will leave untouched that which he should above everything else have refuted, namely, my principal defense and chief argument, when from the words of Christ I proved that the mass is a testament and promise, therefore it cannot be called a work or a sacrifice. This unfortunate defender, overcome by the strength of this defense, wretchedly concealing his awareness of defeat, not only passes over it but even declares publicly that he will pass it over and leave it to others. O protector of the sacraments. O defender of the Roman *O you wicked assailant of the sacraments and of the catholic church* church, doubly Thomistic and by far the most deserving of all the papist indulgences. It could have been forgiven if he had passed over this defense of mine in silence, but to declare publicly that he will pass it by when he hears that I rely on it solely and above all, and that from it all his arguments are destroyed, this is so absurd and foolish as to be unsurpassed.

You have heard, reader, this fellow's remarkable boasts; now hear in turn the words of the king from which Luther wishes it to appear that he has been given a pretext for boasting; when you have read them I am sure that you will be amazed at the disgrace of the boastful Thraso and at his shameful madness in exposing himself. These then are the words of the prince.

"I will not argue with him about testament and promise and that entire defini- *The king's words* tion and application of the word testament to the sacrament. I will not be so troublesome to him as he will perhaps find others who may undermine a good part of this foundation for him both by saying that the new testament is the promise of the law of the gospel just as the old was of the law of Moses and by denying that this testament is very skillfully handled by Luther, since the *Luther falsifies the testament of Christ* testator need not declare specifically what he leaves to the heir whom he names as sole heir, nor is the remission of sins which Luther says was declared as the inheritance the same as the kingdom of heaven but rather the

Quas res atque alias item aliquot, quisquis urgere uolet, ac premere:
posset fortassis fundamenti Lutherani structuram, machinis aliunde
concutere. Verum istud eis permittam, qui uolent. Ego istud ei
fundamentum, quod immobile postulat esse, non mouebo: tantum
5 ostendam aedificium, quod superstruxit, facile per se corruere."
    INTELLIGIS ista Luthere? aut, si intelligas, potes sustinere: ut
perpetuo, tuo cum dedecore, tam stolide te

Nempe qui frontem iam diu iactes? Nam rex hic fundamentum tuum
perfricuerit

nullo modo concedit: sed ostendit esse
10 infirmum: et quod facile possit euerti: si quis hoc sibi desumpserit.
Interim uero se pollicetur, diruturum praeclara illa aedificia: quae
superstruxisti: quibus dirutis, frustra tibi restaret fundamentum. At
tu hic tanquam triumphator exultas: quod nactus sis tam rudem
antagonistam: ut non intelligat se, nihil agere, quicquid respondeat:
15 quandiu non expugnauit id, quod aduersarius sumit pro fundamento.
Atque hac in parte, tibi tam impense places: ut idem terque quater-
que, alio atque alio tui praeclari libelli loco, repetas: tanquam inde
traducturus admirabilem regis inscitiam, ac ruditatem: qui non
euerso fundamento, strenue se rem gessisse putet: quod dumtaxat
20 expugnauit, atque euertit aedificia. Age, fingamus interea Luthere,
fundamentum tuum esse firmissimum, missam uidelicet esse testamentum et promissionem haereditatis, ac nuncupationem haeredis.
Tenes ne memoria, quare hoc fundamentum ieceris? utrum ne, ut nullius aedificij basis esset: et sic ne fundamentum quidem [GG$_2$] esset:
25 cui nihil esset superstructum? An ideo potius iecisti: ut illam turrim
inexpugnabilem superstrueres: qua totam

Istam scilicet ob causam demolireris ecclesiam, et altare Christi

subuerteres? Nempe, missam bonum opus non esse, sacrificium non
esse, non esse oblationem. Igitur quum tu propter has turres uere
30 Babylonis propugnacula, quibus in caelum ui parabas ascendere:
struxeris illud fundamentum: an tibi uidetur imperitus bellator esse:
qui castella illa, ex quibus solis erat periculum, sic euerterit: ut neque
nocere quicquam, neque unquam refici possint: etiam si fundamentum

---

8 fundamentum] *L*, fundamtntum *BR*   14 se] *corr. err. L*, eum *BR*   20 fingamus]
L, fingamns *BR*   22–23 haeredis. Tenes ne] *corr. err. L*, haeredis: tenes ne *BR*

way to heaven. Anyone who wishes to urge and insist on these and
several other like points could probably shatter the structure of the
Lutheran foundation by engines at any point. But I will leave this to
those who wish it. I will not disturb for him this foundation, which he
declares is unshakeable; I shall only show that the structure which he   5
has built on it will easily tumble down of itself."

Do you understand these words, Luther? Or, if you understand,
will you be able to hold out boasting so
stupidly to your own shame? For the king   *That is, he who long ago laid*
here in no way grants your foundation but   *aside all sense of shame*   10
he shows that it is weak and a thing which can be easily destroyed
should anyone take this on himself. But at the same time he promises
that he will demolish those noble structures which you have built on
it, since with these demolished your foundation would remain in vain.
But at this point you exult like a conqueror because you have come   15
on an antagonist so ignorant that he does not understand that he
accomplishes nothing, no matter what he answers, so long as he has
not destroyed that which his adversary takes as a foundation. And on
this point you take such great pleasure that you repeat the same thing
three and four times in one passage after another of your brilliant   20
little book, as though by this means you would expose to ridicule the
amazing stupidity and ignorance of the king who without destroying
the foundation thinks that he has carried the encounter vigorously
because he has stormed and overturned only the superstructures.

Come, let us for the time being, Luther, pretend that your founda-   25
tion is most firm; namely that the mass is a testament and a promise
of inheritance and the naming of an heir; do you remember why you
laid this foundation? Was it that it might be the base of no building
and thus not even be a foundation since
nothing would be built on it? Or did you   *Clearly for this reason*
rather lay it so that you might build upon it that impregnable tower   30
by which you might destroy the whole and overthrow the altar of
Christ; namely, that the mass is not a good work, is not a sacrifice, is
not an oblation? Since, then, you built that foundation for the sake of
these towers, truly the bulwarks of Babylon, by which you were pre-   35
paring to scale heaven by force, does he seem to you to be an inexperienced warrior who has so completely overthrown those
strongholds which were the sole source of danger that they can
neither do any harm nor ever be rebuilt, even if he has left the

reliquerit ualidum et forte, sed tamen innoxium? An tu tam
stolidus es, quam te fingis esse: ut eum censeas nihil agere: qui talia
aedificia sic deiecerit, relicto fundamento. Ergo tam stultus es: ut
eum neges esse uictorem: qui moenia
Ita sane stultus est Lutherus
5   perruperit, atque diruerit: hostes sub-
egerit, ac diuiserit spolia: quamdiu non eruerit fundamentum moeni-
um, ac ruinae lapides auexerit? O si quis stultorum figulus hic esset
tui similis: quam multos ei liceret stultos fingere similes tui. Tu nobis
duos finxisti: quorum persona rideres stultitiam: non quam in regis
10   libello, sed in capite tuo reperisti. Huic
Tres stulti, quorum tamen
stulticiam superat Lutherus   tres stultissimos stultos liceret effingere:
quorum nemo stultior esset Luthero. Nam
si quis substernat fundamentum lapideum: deinde conetur super-
struere aedificium ex puluere: an Lutherus tam stultus est: ut hunc
15 non intelligat esse stultum? At idem nihilo stultior est, quam
Lutherus noster: qui aedificium putat dirui non posse: quandiu durat
fundamentum. QVID si quis adeo stolidus
Secundus stultus siue Lutherus
sit: ut cum fundamentum iecerit mire
profundum, et passus aliquot, si [GG₂v] uolet, latum super solidis-
20 simam rupem: post aedificet murum in palustri loco, cuius nullus
lapis per aliquot stadia tangat illud, quod iecit fundamentum? An
non et hunc plane rideret stultum, Lutherus noster: si eum glorian-
tem uideret, muri sui fortitudine: quem dicat, neque subsidere posse,
neque dirui, propter fundamenti firmitatem, tam procul a muro
25 distantis? Hunc, opinor, rideret pro stulto Lutherus: et tamen hic
stultus, nihilo stultior est Luthero nostro: qui putat absurdum esse:
quod rex aggrediatur aedificia sua diruere, relicto fundamento
ualido: cuius nullum saxum quicquam pertinet ad aedificium.
SED age, sit adhuc tertius, utroque
Tertius stultus siue Lutherus
30   stultior: qui et in arena fundamentum
ponat ex puluere: et inde procul, in lacu murum aedificet ex glacie:
hunc stultum (sat scio) rideret Lutherus: et tamen illo stulto, stultior
est Lutherus. Nam et fundamentum eius magis caducum est, quouis
puluere: et aedificium eius fragilius, quauis glacie: nec magis inter

---

3 fundamento.] fundamento? *L*   9 stultitiam] stulticiam *L*   10 *gloss om. L*
12 stultior] *corr. err. L,* stultitior *BR*   15 stultior] *L,* stultitior *BR*   19 aliquot]
aliquod *L*

foundations solid and strong, but yet harmless? Or are you as dull-witted as you pretend to be, so that you think he accomplishes nothing who has thus dashed such buildings to the ground, leaving the foundation? Are you therefore so foolish as to say that a man who has burst *Luther is clearly thus foolish* through the walls and demolished them, put down the enemy and divided the spoils, is not a victor so long as he has not torn up the foundation of the wall and carried away the stones of the ruin?

O, if there were here any fashioner-of-fools like you, how many fools like you he might fashion. You have fashioned for us two fools under whose mask you mocked the folly which you found not in the king's book but in your own head. This other fashioner-of-fools would be permitted to fashion three most foolish fools, of which no one would be *Three fools, yet Luther surpasses* more foolish than Luther. For if someone *their folly* should lay down a foundation of stone and then try to build on it a superstructure of dust, is Luther so foolish that he does not under-stand that this fellow is a fool? But the same fellow is no more foolish than our Luther, who thinks that the building cannot be demolished so long as the foundation lasts.

What if someone should be so dense that when he has laid a foundation very deep *The second fool, or Luther* and, if he will, several feet wide upon most solid rock, he after-wards builds up the wall in a swampy place where not one of its stones for a good part of a mile touches that foundation which he has laid? Would not our Luther also laugh at this utter fool if he saw him boasting about the strength of his wall, which he says can neither fall down nor be torn down because of the strength of the foundation separated by such a distance from the wall? I think Luther would mock this man for a fool, and yet this fool is no more foolish than our Luther, who thinks it absurd that the king attacks his superstructures to tear them down while leaving the strong foundation, no stone of which touches any part of the superstructure.

But come, suppose still a third person more foolish than both the others, who lays *The third fool, or Luther* on sand a foundation of dust and far from this he builds upon a lake a wall of ice; this fool, I am sure, Luther would mock; and yet Luther is more foolish than this fool. For his foundation is more likely to fall than any dust and his superstructure is more fragile than any ice, nor

se cohaerent: quam (ut est in fabulis) Ethioclis et Polynicis flammae.
Nam neque ualidam fuisse conclusionem, neque cum assumpto
cohaesisse, apertissime probauit rex: id quod Lutherus respondendo
fecit apertius.

5   AT fundamentum, ex quo se gloriatur conclusionem deducere,
quod uelut robustius, quam ut expugnari possit: iterum atque iterum
exprobrat, regem uelut ex professo relinquere: quam sit inualidum,
rex ipse monstrauit. Neque enim, tantum

Fundamentum Lutheranum a dixit, facile ab alijs posse destrui: sed
rege subrutum

10   etiam, uno fere uerbo, obiter, et aliud
agens ipse destruxit: cum dixit: Testamentum istud nouum, ita referri
posse ad nouum [GG₃] testamentum: quemadmodum testamentum
uetus, ad legem Mosaicam: quibus uerbis, quid aliud significauit
princeps: quam id ipsum, quod aperte dicit apostolus, ad Hebreos

15   XI. cum ait de Christo? Noui testamenti, mediator est: ut morte
intercedente, in redemptionem earum praeuaricationum, quae erant
sub priori testamento, repromissionem accipiant: qui uocati sunt
aeternae haereditatis. Vbi enim testamentum, mors necesse est,
intercedat testatoris. Testamentum enim in

Testamentum quibus sit mortuis confirmatum est: alioqui, nondum
20   *concessum*

ualet, dum uiuit, qui testatus est: unde nec
primum quidem sine sanguine dedicatum est. Lecto enim omni
mandato a Mose, uniuerso populo, accipiens sanguinem uitulorum et
hircorum, cum aqua et lana coccinea, et hysopo, ipsumque librum,

25   et omnem populum aspersit: dicens: Hic
Mos testandi in ueteri lege sanguis testamenti, quod mandauit ad
uos deus. Et paulo post. Contestatur autem nos, et spiritus sanctus.
Postquam enim dixit. Hoc autem testamentum, quod testabor ad
illos, post dies illos dicit dominus. Dabo leges meas in cordibus eorum:

30   et in mentibus eorum superscribam eas: et peccatorum et iniquitatum
eorum iam non recordabor amplius. Vide lector, ut mirum praestigi-
atorem putet se Lutherus: qui sic se credit omnium oculos perstringere: ut nemo possit cernere: quam absurde totum hoc testamentum
Christi, ad haeresis suae fundamentum detorqueat. Nam, quod

8 *gloss* Fundamentum Lutheranum] *L*, Fundamen–Lutheranum *BR*

is there more connection between them than there is in the legends between the flames of Eteocles and Polyneices. For the king has proved most clearly that Luther's conclusion was neither valid nor consistent with his first premise, a fact which Luther has made more clear by answering.

But as for the foundation from which he boasts that he draws the conclusion, which he again and again accuses the king of leaving untouched professedly as something too strong to be destroyed, the king himself has shown how weak it is. For he has not only said that it can easily be demolished by others, but also with almost a single word in passing and while doing something else he himself demolished it when he said, "This new testament can be referred to the new testament just as the old testament to the law of Moses"; by these words what else has the prince signified than that very thing which the apostle says clearly to the Hebrews, in chapter eleven, when he says of Christ: "He is mediator of a new covenant, that whereas a death has taken place for redemption from the transgressions committed under the former covenant, they who have been called may receive the counter-promise of eternal inheritance. For where there is a testament, the death of the testator must intervene; for a testament is valid only when men are dead, otherwise it has as yet no force so long as the testator is alive. Hence not even the first has been inaugurated without blood; for when every commandment of the law had been read by Moses to all the people, he took the blood of the calves and of the goats, with water and scarlet wool and hyssop, and sprinkled both the book itself and all the people, saying: 'This is the blood of the covenant which God has commanded for you.'" And shortly after: "Thus also the Holy Spirit testifies unto us. For afterwards he said: 'This is the covenant that I will make with them after those days, says the Lord; I will put my laws upon their hearts and upon their minds I will write them, and their sins and iniquities I will remember no more.'"

*The Lutheran foundation
undermined by the king*

By whom a testament is granted

*The manner of making a
testament in the old law*

See, reader, what a wonderful trickster Luther considers himself; he believes that he has bound up everyone's eyes so that no one can perceive how absurdly he twists this testament of Christ into the foundation of his heresy. For what the apostle clearly teaches to be

apostolus aperte docet, esse totam legem euangelicam: id iste restringit ad solam coenam dominicam: quasi sacramentum altaris, institutum in coena dumtaxat, sit Christi testamentum: quod Christus (ut
ait) moriens reliquit, distribuen[GG₃v]dum suis fidelibus. Sic solent
5 lector (ut scis) non facultates ex testamento: sed testamenta distribui.

Paulus de testamento   At Paulus aperte docet: quod, sicut lex
                            Mosaica testamentum erat uetus: sic
testamentum nouum lex est euangelica: et sicut deus ratum fecit
illud, fuso sanguine uituli, atque hirci: sic istud confirmauit fuso
10 sanguine Christi. Cuius rei, manifeste Christus admonuit discipulos:
quum diceret: Hic est sanguis noui testamenti: qui pro multis
effundetur: tanquam diceret: Hic sanguis, quem bibitis, est idem
sanguis: qui in remissionem peccatorum, paulo post effundetur in
cruce, sanguis (inquam) noui testamenti: quo confirmabitur nouum
15 testamentum meum, mea lex euangelica, sicut olim hircino sanguine
et uitulino confirmatum est testamentum uetus, lex Mosaica.
QVAESO, quam ansam apprehendit hic Lutherus: cur testamentum
Christi restringeret ad hoc sacramentum? Nam, quamquam Christi
mors operatur, et perficit redemptionem nostram: cuius hoc sacra-
20 mentum corpus est et sanguis: eadem tamen mors, ex aequo perficit
                                 sacramentalem uim, caeterorum sacra-
Christi mortem perficere omnia mentorum omnium, secundum cuiusque
sacramenta   mensuram, et deo cognitum modum.
VIDES ergo lector, quam detorte detraxerit scripturam, hunc in
25 locum Lutherus: ut inde strueret sibi fundamentum: ex quo super-
strueret arcem: unde more gigantum superos e caelo depelleret. Vides,
ut idem fundamentum, rex Angliae dissimulans, illud se tangere, ita
totum subruerit: ut ne lapidem quidem super lapidem reliquerit. Et
tamen Lutherus fundamenti sui euersionem, uicissim dissimulans,
30   nunc miris modis illudit regi: quod [GG₄]
Quam ridicule rideat regem   tam ualidum eius fundamentum non sit
Lutherus falsus ipse   ausus attingere: sed assumptum suum
habuerit pro confesso.
QUAESO te Luthere, si quis ita dicat: ego Lutherum stolidum
35 esse non dico: quanquam (ut uidetis) tam stolide sibi contraria, tam
saepe, non subito quidem dicit: sed per ocium, magno scribit studio:

---

10 Christus admonuit] *corr. err. L*, Christus id admonuit *BR*   21 *gloss om. L*
23 modum.] *L*, modum *BR*   30 *gloss om. L*

the whole law of the gospel, this fellow restricts to the Lord's supper alone, as if the sacrament of the altar instituted at the supper is the only testament of Christ which Christ in dying, as he says, left to be distributed among His faithful people. As you know, reader, this is the way that testaments, not the wealth from the testament, are 5 usually distributed. But Paul clearly teaches that as the law of Moses was the old testament, so the new testament is the law of the gospel; and as *Paul on the testament* God ratified the former by the shedding of the blood of a calf and a goat, so He confirmed the latter by shedding of the blood of Christ. 10 Christ clearly reminded the disciples of this fact when He said: "This is the blood of the new testament which shall be shed for many," as though He said: "This blood which you drink is the same blood which shall be shed on the cross a little later for the remission of sins, the blood, I say, of the new testament, by which my new testament, my 15 law of the gospel, shall be confirmed, just as once the old testament, the law of Moses, was confirmed by the blood of goats and calves."

I ask you, what pretext does Luther seize on here for restricting the testament of Christ to this sacrament? For although the death of Christ accomplishes and perfects our redemption and this sacrament 20 is His body and blood, nevertheless the same death equally perfects the sacramen- *That Christ's death perfects all* tal power of all the other sacraments, *the sacraments* according to the measure of each one and in a manner known to God. 25

You see therefore, reader, how distortedly Luther has dragged scripture into this passage so that he might construct for himself a foundation upon which he might build up a citadel whence like the giants he might drive the gods from heaven. You see how the King of England, concealing the fact that he is touching that same founda- 30 tion, has demolished it so completely that he has not left even one stone upon the other. And yet Luther, concealing in turn the destruction of his foundation, now makes marvelous sport of the king, saying that the *How ridiculously Luther, himself* latter has not dared to touch on his strong *deceitful, ridicules the king* 35 foundation but has considered his own premise acknowledged.

I ask you, Luther, if someone should say: "I do not say that Luther is stupid, although, as you see, he so often contradicts himself so stupidly, not indeed off-handedly in speaking but at leisure in

ut morionem pudeat similia somniare: Hoc tantum dico, haereticum
eum esse: et plusquam sacrilege blasphemum. Vtrum is, qui hoc
pacto loquitur, stulticiam tuam relinquit intactam: et te fatetur esse
sapientem? Mihi profecto non uidetur, non hercle magis: quam si
5   quis in mulierem ueneficij ream, quam impudicam esse constet:
                                          dicat hoc pacto: ego mulierem istam iudices
Disce hinc stolide fratercule   meretricem esse non dicam: quanquam
loqui   qui id uellet dicere, facile probare posset:
uel ex eo, quod iam quartum nullo marito peperit: Hoc tantum
10   dicam: quod satis est, in praesentem causam, illam esse ueneficam. Is
opinor, non negat: sed negando confirmat, illam esse meretricem.
Eodem modo. princeps negat se fundamentum tuum moturum:
quum illud prius uno uerbo funditus euertisset. Sed age, gratificemur
tibi: patiamur uulnus tuum dissimulare te. Ridere te sinamus, et
15   iocari foris: dum intus gemis: et pudorem tuum ploras in sinu. Fin-
                                          gamus regem fundamentum tuum prorsus
Vide Luthere, quantum tibi   concessisse, uidelicet, missam esse testa-
indulgeatur   mentum. An illo assumpto tibi concesso,
non licet illi negare: quod ex illo concludis: nempe, quod ideo non
20   possit esse sacrificium? Siccine disputatur
Haec est forma disputandi   VVittinbergae: ut si quis concedat ante-
potistarum   cedens: ideo non possit negare consequentiam? Si haec disputandi forma praescribitur: [GG₄v] ut impudentis
sit negare conclusionem: postquam concedis assumptum: uicit nos
25   plane Lutherus: et facilem sibi inuenit uiam: qua missam probet,
bonum opus non esse, non esse sacrificium. Sic enim licebit ei argu-
mentari. Lutherus est patrator et patronus malorum operum: ergo
                                          missa non est opus bonum. Lutherus est
Hic concedimus antecedens   asinus, et asinus non potest offerri in
30   sacrificium: ergo missa non est oblatio, nec sacrificium. O quot asinos,
quot porcos, inuocaret asinus et porcus Lutherus: quot stultos fingeret,
stultorum stultissimus: si quid tale reperisset in libello principis: quale
nunc in suo ingerit iterum atque iterum: tanquam semel stultum esse
parum sit. Sed operae precium est uidere, quam belle coniungat cum

---

16 *gloss* Luthere] luthere *BR, gloss om. L*; fundamentum] *L,* fundamentun *BR*   20 *gloss*
om. L   21 VVittinbergae] VVittenbergae *L*   25 sibi] *L,* si, bi *BR*   26 esse, non] *L,*
esse–non *BR*

writing, with great deliberation, so that a fool would be ashamed to dream the like; this only I say, that he is a heretic and more than sacrilegiously blasphemous." Does the man who speaks in this manner leave your folly untouched and admit that you are a wise man? I certainly do not think so; no more, by Hercules, than if someone should say against a woman accused of poisoning who is notoriously lewd: "I do not say, men of the jury, that this woman is a whore, *From this example, stupid* although whoever wishes to say that could *friarling, learn how to speak* easily prove it even from the fact that she has already borne four children outside marriage; this only I will say, which is enough for the present case, that she is a poisoner." This man, I think, does not deny but confirms by denying that the woman is a whore. In the same way the prince says that he will not disturb your foundation, although he had earlier destroyed it completely with a single word.

But come, let us humor you, let us permit you to conceal your wound. Let us allow you to laugh and joke exteriorly while interiorly you groan and bewail your shame in your bosom. Let us pretend that the king has *See, Luther, how much we* completely granted your foundation; *indulge you* namely, that the mass is a testament. Having granted you that premise, may he not deny the conclusion which you draw from it; namely, that therefore the mass cannot be a sacrifice? Is it thus that disputations are carried on at Wittenberg, so that if someone grants the antecedent he *This is the form of disputing* cannot therefore deny the consequent? If *among topers* this form of disputing is prescribed so that it is the mark of a shameless person to deny the conclusion after you grant the first premise, then Luther clearly has conquered us and has easily found himself a way to prove that the mass is not a good work, is not a sacrifice. For he will be permitted to argue as follows: "Luther is a fashioner and fosterer of wicked works; therefore the mass is not a good work. Luther is an ass, and an ass cannot be offered for a sacrifice; therefore the mass is not an *Here we grant the antecedent* oblation nor a sacrifice." O how many asses, how many pigs would ass and pig Luther invoke, how many fools would he, the most foolish of fools, fashion, if he had found in the prince's book anything such as he now keeps saying again and again in his own book; as though to be a fool once is too seldom. But it is worth seeing how

hac stultitia sycophantiam, sed tam nudam atque conspicuam, quam
auriculae sunt in asino.

Lutheri uerba. An non ita fecit,   Protestatur, inquit, rex, sese relicturum
cum reddiderit id tibi inutile?   intactum, id quod maxime omnium con-
5   futandum ei fuerat, nempe robur meum
principale, et argumentum capitale, ubi ex uerbis Christi, probaui,
missam esse testamentum et promissionem: ideo non posse opus aut
sacrificium dici.

DISPERIAM lector, ni mihi fere uocem adimat admiratio,
10 cogitanti, quam aut uere saxum sit iste nebulo, aut omnes homines
pro saxis habeat: Ait fundamentum suum fuisse, missam esse testamentum, et ideo opus aut sacrificium esse non posse: et ait regem
uictum fortitudine huius roboris, ex professo transire hoc fundamentum. Quaeso te Luthere, reuome ceruisiam istam: quae tibi caput
15 occupat. Redige (si potes) in memoriam: quod fuerit fundamentum

Nihil est turpe impuro   tuum. Si regi turpe fuit transire: an non
                                    tibi turpius est obliuisci? Fuit ne istud pars
fundamenti tui: [HH₁] quod missa bonum opus esse non potest, aut
sacrificium? Si istud erat fundamentum: quaenam erat conclusio, si
20 ista reliquit rex intacta, quomodo tu rursus respondes ad ea, quibus
rex illa dissoluit? Atque ita respondes, ut quum sudaris satis: nihil
aliud facias: quam, ut constet omnibus, nihil te reperire, quod con-
tradicas. Sed quid mortuo uerba facio? Redeo lector ad te. QVVM

Lutherum nullum probasse   nullum fundamentum probarit ex scrip-
25 *fundamentum ex scriptura*   tura: sed tantum probare conatus est:
                                    quod missa sit testamentum: quod ipsum
fundamentum ex scriptura confutatum est: ex eo fundamento, sua
collectione conclusit illas praeclaras, nihil cohaerentes conclusiones:
quod missa bonum opus et sacrificium esse non possit. Quas conclu-
30 siones, rex probauit ex illo fundamento (etiam si necessarium esset)
nullo tamen pacto consequi: et cum fundamentum illud euertisset:
in transitu, simulans id se relinquere, sic tractauit conclusiones:
tanquam fundamentum concederet: ut Lutherum tanto stultiorem
ostenderet: qui fundamentum iecisset: quod nullam partem

---

16 *gloss* Nihil] *L,* nihil *BR*   19–20 si ista] *corr. err. L,* si *om. BR*   20 intacta, quomodo]
corr. err., intacta. Quomodo *BR,* intacta, quo modo *L*   27 fundamentum] *corr. err.,*
testamentum *BRL*

prettily he joins with this folly a foxiness which, however, is as bare and conspicuous as are the ears on an ass.

The king, he says, declares publicly that he will leave untouched that which he should above all have refuted; namely, my principal defense and chief argument,

Luther's words. Did he not do this when he rendered it useless to you?   5

where I proved from the words of Christ that the mass is a testament and a promise, therefore it cannot be called a work or a sacrifice.

Damn if I am not almost speechless with amazement, reader, as I consider how this scoundrel either is truly a stone or takes all men for   10
stones; he says that his foundation was that the mass is a testament and therefore cannot be a work or a sacrifice, and he says that the king, overcome by the strength of this defense, professedly bypasses this foundation. Please, Luther, spew out that beer which has gone to your head. Call to mind, if you can, what was your foundation.   15
If it was base of the king to pass it by, is it not more base of you to forget it? Was not this a part of your foundation: that the

Nothing is base to the unclean

mass cannot be a good work or a sacrifice? If this was the foundation, what in the world was the conclusion? If the king has left these points   20
untouched, how is it that you answer in turn those arguments by which the king has destroyed them? And you answer in such a way that when you have sweated plenty you accomplish nothing else than to make clear to everyone that you have found nothing with which to contradict him.   25
But why do I mouth words to a corpse? I return, reader, to you since he has proved no foundation from scripture but has only tried to prove that the mass is a testament, which very

That Luther has proved no foundation from scripture

foundation has been refuted from scripture; from which foundation   30
he has by his syllogism concluded those remarkable, completely irrelevant conclusions: that the mass cannot be a good work and a sacrifice. The king, nevertheless, has proven that these conclusions do not in any way follow from that foundation even if it were valid; and when he had destroyed that foundation in passing, while pretending   35
to leave it alone, he handled the conclusions as though he were granting the foundation in order that he might show Luther so much the more foolish for having laid a foundation which neither upheld

Quomodo Lutherus succurrat suae stulticiae

aedificij, aut sustineret aut tangeret. Lutherus ergo, dolens ita patefactam esse fatuitatem suam: conatur, subsidium ferre per sycophantiam: sed tam apertam, ut nihil aliud sit, quam condu-

5　plicata stulticia. Dicit partem fundamenti fuisse: quod nemo non

Sorex suo proditur inditio

uidet fuisse conclusionem. Dicit id reliquisse regem: quod solum ex professo egisse regem, docet ipsius etiam Lutheri responsio. Ita belle sibi constat, homo nunquam sibi contrarius: ut dicat regem ex professo

10　praeterire tacite: quod missa non potest opus esse, aut sacrificium: Et tamen ad illa, quibus rex probat, etiam si maxi[HH₁v]me testamentum esset ac promissio: opus tamen et sacrificium nihilo minus esse, Lutherus ipse respondet: nisi forte sibi conscius est, ea, quae respondet, esse tam inepta: ut responsum suum pro responso non habeat.

15　Et sunt haud dubie lector, id quod ilico uidebis ineptissima: quod quo uideas clarius, non imitabor Lutherum: ut illius uerba (sicut ille solet in rege) narrando deprauem. Sed integra, sicut se habent, ascribam. Quae quum legeris, uidebis esse tam praua: ut nemo deprauatius narrare potuerit.

20

Verba Lutheri. Non est difficile Luthere tuas diluere rationes. Quam male urat gloriosum nebulonem se uidere uictum

Postquam uero dominus Henricus, Thomista noster, hac argentea et aurea ratione probarat missam esse opus, pergit in fortitudine sua, etiam Lutheri rationes deluere, et primo thomisticatur in hunc

25　modum. Qui lignum cedit, facit opus, ergo qui consecrat, facit opus. Quare missa etiam opus erit. Si autem est opus, non est malum, ergo bonum. Haec ille gloriosus assertor sacramentorum. Hic iacet quoque Lutherus prostratus.

AVDISTI lector, nihil illius omisimus: nunc audies uicissim uerba

30　regis: quibus et Lutheri fidem deprehendes, aliena tam syncere narrantis: ut inde gratiam comparet suis. Et illud simul intelliges: quanta rerum urgeatur inopia: qui cogitur ad nugas diuertere: et potissimam partem eorum, quibus respondendum fuit omittere:

---

5 partem] patrem *L*　　11 rex probat] rex *om. L*

nor touched any part of the superstruc-
ture. Luther, therefore, chagrined that his   *How Luther comes to the aid*
fatuity has been so exposed, tries to bring   *of his folly*
succor through cunning, but so transparently that it is nothing else
but redoubled folly. He calls a part of the foundation what everyone   5
sees to have been the conclusion. He says
that the king left alone that point which   *The shrew-mouse is betrayed by*
even Luther's own answer shows was the   *his squeak*
only point the king explicitly discussed. Thus he is prettily consistent,
a man never inconsistent with himself, when he says that the king   10
professedly passes over in silence the statement that the mass cannot
be a work or a sacrifice, and yet Luther himself answers those arguments by which the king proves that even if the mass were above all
a testament and a promise it would still be nonetheless a work and a
sacrifice; unless perhaps he is aware that his answers are so inept that   15
he does not consider his answer as an answer. And they are without a
doubt, reader, as you will see immediately, most inept; that you may
see this more clearly, I will not imitate Luther by corrupting his
words in recounting them, as he usually does to the king's, but I shall
set them down intact, just as they are. When you have read them,   20
you will see that they are so corrupt that no one could have recounted
them more corruptly.

Indeed, after Lord Henry, our Thomist,
had proved by this silver and golden   *Luther's words. It is not difficult,*
reasoning that the mass is a work, he   *Luther, to weaken your*   25
proceeds in his strength to weaken also   *reasonings. How painfully*
Luther's reasonings, and first he Thomis-   *it galls the bragging*
ticates in this manner: "He who cuts   *rascal to see himself overcome*
firewood does a work, therefore he who consecrates does a work.
Therefore the mass also will be a work. But if it is a work it is not evil,   30
therefore it is good." Thus that pompous defender of the sacraments.
Here also Luther lies prostrate.

You have heard, reader; we have omitted none of his words; now
you shall hear in turn the words of the king by which you will detect
Luther's trustworthiness in recounting so sincerely the words of   35
another in order thereby to win favor for his own words. And at the
same time you will understand with what a lack of resources he is
beset who is forced to turn aside to trifles and to omit the most

illiusque uerba antequam regis retulimus: ut cum eas uanas, ac
stolidas gloriolas efflare aliquandiu impune permiserimus: quibus se
uictorem ipse buccinat, a sperata uictoriae laude, turpius excidat:
quum regis uerba praue de industria retulisse (ut est impudens)
5 redargui palam se uiderit: quo facilius ipse superior e pugna dis-
cedere uideretur. Verba regis ita se habent. [HH₂]

Verba regis   "POST longas (inquit) ambages, diffi-
nit missam: deinde separat a missa, missae
caeremonias: excutit coenam dominicam: et uerba Christi trutinat:
10 quibus usus est: quum institueret missae sacramentum. Ibi quum
testamenti uerbum, rem uidelicet tam abstrusam reperisset: iam
(tanquam profligatis hostibus) coepit ingeminare uictoriam: et
uerbis adornat inuentum (ut iactat) suum: et tanquam mysterium,
hactenus inauditum, magno supercilio docet, quid sit testamentum.
15   Notandum esse clamat, ac memoria tenen-
Discite hic omnes ex Luthero,   dum, testamentum esse morituri promis-
quid sit testamentum   sionem: qua nuncupat haereditatem, et
instituit haeredes. Hoc igitur sacramentum (inquit) missae, nihil est
aliud, quam testamentum Christi: testamentum nihil est aliud, quam
20 promissio haereditatis aeternae, nobis Christianis: quos suos haeredes
instituit, corpus et sanguinem suum (uelut signum ratae promissionis)
adijciens. Hoc igitur decies repetit, inculcat, infigit, utpote quod
haberi uult immobile fundamentum: super quod aedificet foenum,
ligna, stipulam. Nam hoc fundamento iacto, quod missa Christi sit
25   testamentum: omnem sese iactat impie-
Concedite hanc arcem tam praeclaro tatem euersurum: quam impij (ut ait)
duci. Quot et quae sit probaturus
Lutherus ex suo fundamento   homines inuexerunt, in hoc sacramentum:
et dilucide probaturum ad communionem
recipiendam, sola fide ueniendum esse, de operibus cuiusmodi sint,
30 non admodum esse curandum, conscientia quanto magis erronea sit,
ac peccatorum uel morsu, uel titillatione moueatur, tanto sanctius

important part of those arguments which he should have answered.
And we have recounted his words before those of the king so that
when we have allowed him to breathe out for some time with
impunity those vain and stupid little boasts with which he trumpets
himself as victor, he may fall more shamefully from the hoped-for 5
glory of victory when he has seen himself clearly convicted of having
deliberately distorted the king's words—so shameless is he—in order
that he might the more easily appear to depart from the fight
victorious. The words of the king are as follows.

"After long digressions (he says), he
defines the mass; next he distinguishes the   *The king's words*   10
ceremonies of the mass from the mass itself; he examines the Lord's
supper and weighs the words which Christ used when He instituted
the sacrament of the mass. When he had discovered in them the word
'testament,'—clearly a very abstruse point—then, as though the 15
enemy were destroyed, he begins repeatedly to proclaim the victory,
and he decks out his discovery—such is his boast—with words; and
with great conceit, as though it were a mystery till now unheard of,
he teaches what a testament is. He declares
that it must be noted and held in mind   *Learn here from Luther,*
                                              everyone, what a testament is   20
that a testament is the promise of a man on
the point of death by which he publicly declares his inheritance and
appoints his heirs. This sacrament of the mass, he says, is therefore
nothing else but the testament of Christ, and the testament is nothing
else but the promise of an eternal inheritance to us Christians whom 25
He has appointed as His heirs, adding His body and blood as the sign
of the ratification of the promise. This then he repeats ten times, he
rams it down our throats, he impresses it on us as the thing which he
wishes to have considered the unshakeable foundation upon which
he will build hay, wood and stone. For, having laid this foundation, 30
that the mass is the testament of Christ, he boasts that he will destroy
all the impiety which, so he says, impious
men have introduced into this sacrament,   *Grant this stronghold to such an*
and that he will clearly prove that the   *illustrious leader. How many*
                                                and what kind of things
reception of communion must be ap-   *Luther is ready to prove*   35
proached with faith alone, that one must   *from his foundation*
not be too much concerned about works of
any kind whatsoever, that the more one's conscience is distracted and
agitated by either the bite or the titillation of sins, the more holily

accedi. Quanto serenior, purior, et errore purgatior, tanto sumi
deterius. Ad haec, missam bonum opus non esse. Missam non esse
sacrificium. Missam [HH₂v] sacerdoti tantum, non autem populo
etiam prodesse. Nihil prodesse defunctis, nihil cuiquam uiuentium.
5 Impium esse errorem, si missa canatur pro peccatis, si pro cuiusquam
necessitate, si pro mortuis. Inanem esse rem et impiam, fraternitates
et annuas defunctorum memorias. Abolendam esse, talem omnem
sacerdotum, monachorum, canonicorum, fratrum, religiosorum
denique (quos uocamus) omnium alimoniam. Haec igitur tot et tam
10 immensa bona, se reperisse gloriatur, in eo solo: quod hoc sacrosanctum sacramentum comperit, esse Christi testamentum. Iam in
sententiarios protinus (quos uocat doctores) inuehitur. Exclamat in
omnes: qui declamant apud populum: quod quum illi tam multa
scribant: hi tam multa loquantur et praedicent de eucharistiae
15 sacramento: neutri tamen attingant quicquam de testamento: sed

Hoc nimirum Luthere fatis tibi
seruatum est

impie celent populum, bonum illud in-
comparabile (quod tamen iam olim scisse
profuisset) ex missa, nihil unquam boni
laicos, neque uiuos neque defunctos, esse consecuturos. Ob cuius rei
20 ignorantiam, denunciat uniuersos hodie sacerdotes et monachos, cum
episcopis, et omnibus suis maioribus, idololatras esse, atque in statu
periculosissimo uersari."

VIDES lector, ut Lutheri omnia robora princeps bona cum fide
commemoret: ac ne dogmata quidem omittat: ne quid sibi sui roboris
25 queratur interceptum. Sed istud interim exacte pensiculandum est:
in quo periculo uersentur omnes hi: qui Lutheri dogmatibus non

Periculum eorum qui Luthero
non sunt audientes

credunt. Profecto in periculum ueniunt
(quod superos precor, ut contingat mihi)
ut excludantur ab inferis: ne ibi cum
30 vvi[HH₃]cliffo, Husso, Heluidio, Arrio, Montano, et ijs omnibus
pestilentiori Luthero, aeternum ardeant: sed in caelo beati sint
perpetuo, cum Christi sanctis, Ambrosio, Augustino, Hieronymo,
Chrysostomo, Cypriano, Basilio, atque id genus alijs, uiris beatissi-
mis: qui ea crediderunt et docuerunt de missa: quae Lutherus
35 execratur: ea sunt execrati: quae Lutherus docet credenda, non
credit. Sed paulo post ita pergit rex.

---

12 (quos uocat doctores)] (quos vocat doctores) *L,* (quos uocat) doctores *BR*

does one approach, while the more calm, pure and cleansed from sin, the worse is it received.

"Furthermore he says that the mass is not a good work; that the mass is not a sacrifice; that the mass profits only the priests but not the people also; that it does not profit the deceased nor anyone living; that it is an impious error to sing the mass for sins, for anyone's need, for the dead; that fraternities and annual commemorations of the deceased are a useless and impious practice; that all such support of the priests, monks, canons, friars, in fine all so-called religious, must be abolished. These many and measureless benefits, then, he boasts of having discovered from the sole fact of having found out that this most holy sacrament is the testament of Christ. Then he goes on to inveigh against the 'sententiaries,' as he calls doctors; he cries out against all who preach before the people because, while the former write so much and the latter speak and preach so much about the sacrament of the eucharist, yet neither touch at all on the testament but impiously conceal from the people that incomparable good, which it would yet have profited them to have known long ago, namely that the laity, whether living or dead, will never derive any good from the mass. He proclaims that because of their ignorance of this matter, all priests and monks today, together with the bishops and all their superiors, are idolators and living in a state of extreme peril."

This function has doubtless been reserved by the fates for you, Luther

You see, reader, how the prince recounts with good faith all Luther's defenses and does not even omit his teachings lest he should complain that he was deprived of any of his defense. But meanwhile this point must be carefully weighed: in what danger are all those who do not believe Luther's teachings? Certainly they come into the danger—which I pray God may happen to me—of being shut out from hell, lest they burn there forever with Wyclif, Hus, Helvidius, Arius, Montanus, and Luther—more pestilent than all the others—and, on the other hand, of being forever blessed in heaven with Christ's saints, Ambrose, Augustine, Jerome, Chrysostom, Cyprian, Basil and others like them, most blessed men, who believed and taught about the mass the things which Luther execrates; they execrated the things which Luther teaches must be believed, but does not believe. But shortly after the king proceeds thus.

The danger of those who are not Luther's listeners

"SED OPERAE praecium est uidere,

Verba regis

                   qua ex arbore tam salutares fructus colligat

Lutherus. Postquam ergo saepius inculcauit, eucharistiae sacramentum, signum esse testamenti, testamentum uero nihil esse aliud,

5   quam promissionem haereditatis: inde continuo censet consequi: ut

                       missa neque bonum opus esse possit, neque

Vnde collegerit Lutherus missam
bonum opus non esse

                    sacrificium. Quod quisquis ei concesserit:

iam illi statim admittendus erit totus ille
pestium catalogus: quo totam ecclesiae faciem confundit. At quisquis

10   negauerit illi: iam tam magno molimine nihil egerit. Nam argumenta (quibus ea docere prae se fert) pudet propemodum recensere:
ita sunt in re tantae maiestatis, nugacia prorsus et friuola. Sic enim
colligit (nam ipsius uerba recitabo) Audisti missam nihil aliud esse,
quam promissionem diuinam, seu testamentum Christi, sacramento

15   corporis et sanguinis eius commendatum. Quod si uerum est, intelligis
eam, non posse opus esse ullo modo, nec alio studio a quoquam
tractari, quam sola fide. Fides autem non est opus, sed magistra et uia

                       operum. Mirum est, quanto nixu par-

Nempe iuxta prouerbium,
Parturient montes, nascetur
20   *ridiculus mus*

           turiens, quam nihil pepererit, nisi merum

           uentum: quem, quum ipse tam ualidum

           uelit uideri: ut [HH₃v] montes possit

euertere: mihi profecto uidetur tam languidus: ut agitare non possit
arundinem. Nam si uerborum tollas inuolucra: quibus rem absurdam,
uelut simiam purpura uestit: si tollas exclamationes illas, quibus iam

25   uelut re dilucide probata, toties in totam bacchatur ecclesiam: et non
dum collata manu, tanquam ferox uictor insultat: nihil aliud restare
uidebis, quam nudum et miserum sophisma. Quid enim aliud dicit
tanto uerborum ambitu, quam missa est promissio: ergo non potest
esse opus? Quem non misereat hominis, si tam stupidus sit: ut

30   ineptiam suam non sentiat: aut quis non indignetur, si sibi conscius,
tam stupidos tamen omnes aestimet Christianos: ut tam manifestas
insanias, nequeant deprehendere. Non contendam cum eo de testamento, et promissione, et tota illa definitione, et applicatione testamenti ad sacramentum. Non ero tam molestus ei: quam alios fortassis

35   inueniet: si qui bonam ei partem istius fundamenti subruerint: qui et

---

4 esse testamenti] testamenti *om. L*   18–19 parturiens] *L*, perturiens *BR*   19 *gloss*
Parturient] *L*, Perturient *BR*   32 deprehendere.] deprehendere? *L*   34 molestus]
modestus *L*

"But it is worth seeing from what tree
Luther gathers such wholesome fruits. *The king's words*
After he has often rammed home that the sacrament of the eucharist
is the sign of the testament, but that a testament is nothing else than
a promise of inheritance, he thinks that it immediately follows there- 5
from that the mass can be neither a good
work nor a sacrifice. Whoever grants him *From what premise Luther*
this will immediately have to admit that *infers that the mass is not*
whole catalogue of plagues with which he *a good work*
disfigures the whole face of the church. But whoever denies him this 10
will have accomplished nothing despite such great effort. For one is
almost ashamed to review the arguments with which he shows himself teaching those things; in a matter of such great dignity they are
so utterly trifling and frivolous. For he syllogizes thus—I will quote
his own words—'You have heard that the mass is nothing else than 15
the divine promise or testament of Christ, enhanced by the sacrament
of His body and blood. If this is true, you understand that it cannot in
any way be a work nor be dealt with by anyone in any other spirit
than faith alone. Faith, however, is not a work but the teacher and
way of works.' It is amazing how, despite 20
the throes of such great travail, he brings *Doubtless according to the proverb:*
forth nothing but mere wind, which, *The mountains are in labor, a*
although he would have it appear powerful *ridiculous mouse is born*
enough to overturn mountains, seems to me indeed too feeble to stir a
reed. For if you remove the windings of words with which he clothes 25
the absurd matter like an ape in royal purple, if you take away those
cries with which, as though the matter were already clearly proved,
he so often raves wildly against the whole church, and with the battle
not yet joined behaves insolently like a fierce victor, you will see that
nothing else remains but a bare and wretched sophism. For what else 30
does he say in such a bombastic show of words than: The mass is a
promise, therefore it cannot be a work? Who would not feel sorry for
a man if he is so stupid that he does not sense his own folly, or who
would not be indignant if, conscious of it, he still would judge all
Christians so stupid that they cannot detect such manifest madness? 35

"I will not argue with him about testament and promise and that
entire definition and application of the word testament to the
sacrament. I will not be so troublesome to him as he will perhaps find
others who may undermine a good part of this foundation for him

testamentum nouum dicant, promissionem esse legis euangelicae
quemadmodum uetus fuit Mosaicae: et testamentum istud negent a
Luthero satis scite tractari: neque enim testatori nuncupandum esse
_nominatim, quid relinquat haeredi: quem ex asse instituat: neque
5 remissionem peccatorum, quam pro haereditate nuncupatam
Lutherus ait, idem esse quod regnum caelorum, sed uiam potius ad
caelum. Veniamus ergo nunc ad praeclaras istas Lutheri rationes:
quibus probat, missam neque bonum opus esse, neque sacrificium:
Et quanquam praestaret, prius tractare de sacrificio: tamen, quo-
10 niam ille primam quaestionem fecit de opere: [HH₄] sequemur
illum. Quum igitur ita colligit: missa est promissio: ergo non est

Quomodo probet Lutherus missam bonum opus: quia nulla promissio est
non esse bonum opus opus: dicemus missam, quam sacerdos
celebrat, non uerius esse promissionem,
15 quam fuit consecratio Christi: et simul quaeremus ab eo, an aliquod
opus tum fecerit Christus? quod si neget, mirabimur profecto, si
quum is opus faciat: qui imaginem facit ex ligno: Christus nullum
opus prorsus fecerit: quum carnem suam fecerit ex pane. Quod si
ullum opus fecerit: quin id bonum fuerit: nemo, opinor, dubitabit.
20 Nam si bonum opus fecit mulier: quae caput eius perfudit unguento:
quis potest ambigere: an bonum opus fecerit Christus: quum corpus
proprium, et in cibum exhiberet hominibus: et in sacrificium offerret
deo? Quod si negari non potest, nisi ab eo, qui in re maxime seria,
ualde uelit nugari, bonum opus fecisse Christum: nec istud etiam
25 negari potest, in missa bonum opus facere sacerdotem: quippe qui non
aliud faciat in missa: quam Christus in coena fecit et cruce. Hoc enim
declarant uerba Christi: Hoc facite in meam commemorationem.

Ostenditur missa opus esse ex Quibus uerbis, quid aliud uolebat, ut in
ipsius uerbis Christi missa representarent, ac facerent: quam
30 quod ipse faciebat in coena et cruce?
Instituebat enim, et inchoabat in coena sacramentum: quod in cruce
perfecit.''

NVNC relege quaeso lector, Lutheri nugamenta. Vide, quanta
cum fide recenseat argumenta regis: quam pulchris rationibus
35 occurrat. Quas iste nobis nugas garrit. Rex ait Christum aliquod opus

---

7 caelum.] coelum. *L*, caelum? *BR*   20 perfudit] *corr. err. L*, fudit *BR*   31 in cruce]
in *om. L*

both by saying that the new testament is the promise of the law of the gospel just as the old was of the law of Moses and by denying that this testament is very skillfully handled by Luther, since the testator need not declare specifically what he leaves to the heir whom he names as sole heir, nor is the remission of sins which Luther says was declared 5 as the inheritance the same as the kingdom of heaven but rather the way to heaven.

"Let us therefore come now to these remarkable reasons by which Luther proves that the mass is neither a good work nor a sacrifice, and although it would be preferable to treat first of sacrifice, yet, because 10 he first raised the question of work, we will follow him. When therefore he syllogizes thus, 'The mass is a promise, therefore it is not a good work because no promise is a work,' we will answer that the mass which the *How Luther proves that the mass* priest celebrates is no more truly a promise *is not a good work* 15 than was Christ's consecration, and at the same time we will ask of him whether Christ then performed a work. If he should deny this, we will indeed be surprised, if a man performs a work when he makes an image of wood, that Christ did not perform any work at all when He made His flesh from bread. But if He performed any 20 work, no one, I think, will doubt that it was a good one. For if the woman who poured ointment on His head performed a good work, who can doubt whether Christ performed a good work when He presented His own body as food to men and offered it as a sacrifice to God? But if it cannot be denied, except by him who in a matter so 25 very serious has the greatest urge to talk nonsense, that Christ performed a good work, neither can this also be denied, that in the mass the priest performs a good work, since he does nothing else in the mass than what Christ did at the supper and on the cross. For Christ's words, 'Do this in remembrance of 30 me,' declare this fact. Given these words, *The mass is shown to be a work* what else did He wish that they should *according to the words of* *Christ Himself* represent and do in the mass than what He Himself did at the supper and on the cross? For He instituted and began at the supper the sacrament which He perfected on the cross." 35

Now, reader, please reread Luther's nonsensical statements. See with how much fidelity he recounts the arguments of the king, with what fine reasonings he opposes him. What nonsense this fellow chatters to us. The king says that Christ performed a work when He

fecisse: dum suum corpus faceret ex pane, et patri offerret in cruce: nec obstitisse, quo [HH₄v] minus fuerit opus: quantumcunque fuerit testamentum. Atque ita breuiter, uno uerbo demonstrat: et quam ineptum sophisma sit, Lutheri lemma illud insolubile. Hoc sacra-
5 mentum est testamentum: ergo non potest esse opus. Deinde rex ostendit, ac probat ex euangelio, idem facere sacerdotem in missa: quod Christus in coena fecit, et cruce: in qua compleuit: quod in-ceperat in coena: praesertim quum missa potius mortis memoria sit, quam coenae, secundum illud Pauli: quod rex etiam commemorat.
10   *Pauli de missa sensus*   Haec quotiescunque feceritis: mortem domini annunciabitis. Quamobrem, quum Lutherus negare non possit: quin uere opus fuerit: quod a Christo factum est: quanquam maxime fuisset testamentum: nec aliud est, quod a sacerdote fit: quam quod factum est a Christo: nonne cogitur
15 homo prudentissimus fateri, stultissimam esse sophismatis sui sapientiam: qua uelut irrefragabile, sic argutatur? Missa est testa-mentum, et promissio: ergo non potest esse opus. Sed hic manifeste se uictum sentiens, mirabili prorsus ingenio, reperit exitum: ne quod omnes uidere uidet, ipse fateri cogeretur. Quia rex dicit eum, qui
20 consecrat, aliquid facere: ibi deprehendit homo lynceus regem dicere, missam esse bonum opus, ratione operantis, non operis operati: Quasi, qui diceret aliquid quenquam facere: is non diceret aliquid ab eodem fieri: aut quasi re non essent idem, id quod aliquis facit, et quod ab eo faciente fit: etiam si aliter consideretur quatenus tale,
25 aliter quatenus factum abs tali. Vt cautum esse oportet, cui cum homine tam acuto sit negocium. Nam, si quis dicat has scalas esse
      Quam acute scilicet Lutherus   sur[II₁]sum uersus: ilico Lutherus iurabit,
           disserat   eum negasse easdem scalas, uiam esse
                                          deorsum uersus: quia sursum et deorsum
30 sunt opposita. Sic disputant acuti dialectici. Nos homines simplices, et ideotae, putamus eandem esse uiam, et Athenis Thebas, et Thebis Athenas: et eandem missam putamus esse tam opus operatum, quam opus operantis. Caeterum bonitatem eius et fructum, qui ex illo opere

26 has scalas] *corr. err. L,* hanc uiam *BR*

made His body from bread and offered it on the cross to the Father,
and that there was no hindrance to its being a work, however much it
was a testament. And thus he also shows briefly in one word how
silly a sophism is that irrefutable premise of Luther: "This sacrament
is a testament, therefore it cannot be a work." Next the king shows   5
and proves from the gospel that the priest does the same thing in the
mass as Christ did at the supper and on the cross on which He completed what He had begun at the supper, especially since the mass is a
memorial rather of His death than of the supper, according to the
words of Paul which the king also recalls: 10
"As often as you do these things, you   *Paul's interpretation of*
proclaim the death of the Lord." There-   *the mass*
fore, since Luther cannot deny that what was done by Christ was
truly a work, even though it had been above all a testament—and
what is done by the priest is nothing else than what was done by   15
Christ—is not the most prudent man forced to admit that the wisdom
of his sophism is utterly silly with which he thus prates as if it were an
inviolable argument: The mass is a testament and a promise, therefore it cannot be a work?

But here, sensing himself to be clearly overcome, with absolutely   20
amazing genius he finds a way out, lest he be forced to admit that
he sees that which everyone sees. Because the king says that he who
consecrates does something, the keen-eyed fellow understands the
king to say there that the mass is a good work by reason of the doer,
not by reason of the work done, as if one who said that someone does   25
something would not say that something was done by that same
person, or as if in fact that which someone does and that which comes
about by his doing were not the same thing, even if it were considered
in one respect insofar as it is such and such a work and in another
respect insofar as it is done by such and such a person. How cautious   30
one needs to be to deal with such a sharp-witted fellow. For if someone should say that these stairs lead upward, Luther will immediately
swear that the man has denied that the
same stairs lead downward, because up and   *How subtly indeed Luther*
down are opposites. Thus the sharp-witted   *argues*   35
dialecticians dispute. We simple and uneducated men think that the
way from Athens to Thebes and from Thebes to Athens is the same,
and we think that the same mass is as much the work done as it is the
work of the doer. But we think that its goodness and fruit which come

peruenit ad populum: peruenire censemus ratione operis operati, non operis operantis: hoc est, quia ipsum tale est: non quia talis operatus est.

SED hic aliud etiam acumen repperit reuerendus pater: quod si
5 missa esset opus, aliquo modo sacerdotis consecrantis, iam quum omnis missa sit opus bonum: malus sacerdos consecrare non possit: uidelicet, quia malus non potest opus bonum facere. Et hoc argumentum illi uidetur tam acutum: ut

Stulta Lutheri gloriatio de
nihilo

etiam eo mire glorietur: atque ita se
10 iactet: Istud argumentum male uexabit assertorem sacramentorum. At ego potius suspicor, imo certo scio, talem argumentatorem male uexari a daemonio: qui eum ita dementat: ut non sentiat, etiam quantumuis malum hominem, posse facere opus, aut natura bonum, aut moribus, aut alij utile et meritorium,
15 etiam si damnosum sibi. Nisi forte bonum opus non est eleemosyna: aut fieri non possit a malo. Aut nisi quis cum Luthero credat, baptismum bonum opus non esse: aut malum sacerdotem non conferre baptismum alteri. Sit illud acu-

Acumen Lutheri

men Lutheri. Nos homines rusticuli credi-
20 mus, ministri maliciam dei benignitatem non claudere: Sed sicut furtiuum semen cum opere semi[II₁v]nantis furis cooperatur deus in frugem: sic in sacramentis, qualiscunque

Opus ex se bonum non deteri a
malo patratore

sacerdos sit, cum eius opere cooperatur deus, opus bonum, et gratia definita
25 perfectum. Quod insita bonitate, salutare sit illis, pro quibus fit: etiam si noceat illis, a quibus fit. Nam is, qui fecit: bonum opus male fecit: et temere tractando sacramentum, prodest alteri, noceat sibi.

QVVM regis librum legissem, et Lutheri responsum simul: et quam potui, diligentissime consyderassem: uehementer admiratus
30 sum: quid sibi Lutherus uellet in illo, tam absurdo sophismate: tandem coepi eundem locum, ex eius Babylone perpendere: ex quo fonte confusionis hic riuulus, inferni fluminis, effusus est. Et ecce, quemadmodum istic nugatur in missa: sic ibi nugacissime nugatur,

---

13 ut non sentiat] *B corr. err. L*, ut *om. R*   15 etiam si] etiamsi *L*; eleemosyna] eleemosina *B*   22 qualiscunque] *BL*, qauliscunque *R*   26 illis] *BL*, iilis *R* 27 noceat] nocet *B*, licet noceat *L*

to the people from that work come by reason of the work done, not by reason of the one doing the work; that is, because it is such and such a work, not because such and such a man has done the work.

But this other subtle point the reverend father has also discovered; that if the mass were somehow a work of the priest consecrating, then, since every mass is a good work, a wicked priest cannot consecrate; that is, because a wicked man cannot perform a good work. And this argument seems to him so keen that he even glories in it excessively and boasts *Luther's foolish boasting about* *nothing* thus: "This argument will greatly trouble the defender of the sacraments." But I rather suspect, indeed I know for certain, that such an arguer is greatly troubled by a demon who so deprives him of his wits that he does not understand that no matter how wicked a man is he can perform a work that is good either by nature or by custom or that is useful and beneficial to another, even if it is injurious to himself. Unless perchance almsgiving is not a good work or cannot be performed by a wicked man. Or unless someone believes with Luther that baptism is not a good work or that a wicked priest does not confer baptism on another person. Let that subtlety of Luther be. We poor *Luther's subtlety* rustic men believe that the wickedness of the minister does not shut out the goodness of God, but that, as God works together with the work of the thief sowing stolen seed to produce fruit, so in the sacraments, whatever kind of priest it may be, God works together with his work a good *That a work good in itself is* work and one perfected by a definite *not vitiated by a wicked* grace; the work by means of the goodness *doer* implanted in it is saving for those for whom it is performed, even if it harms those by whom it is performed. For he who performed it performed a good work badly and by rashly handling the sacrament he benefits another, harms himself.

When I had read the book of the king and at the same time the response of Luther and had examined them as carefully as I could, I very much wondered what Luther meant by such an absurd sophism; finally I began to examine carefully the same argument from his *Babylon*, from which fount of confusion this stream of the infernal river has overflowed. And sure enough, just as in the present work he talks nonsense about the mass, so he there talks most nonsensical nonsense about the notion of work; clearly so that he might enmesh

in opere: scilicet ut argutia duplici rem intricaret: et duplici stulticia
sese inuolueret. Sic enim illic asscribit.

Verba Lutheri ex babylonica
Captiuitate

5

Nullus audeat tantum insanire, ut dicat
bonum opus facere eum, qui pauper
et indigens uenit, accepturus de manu
diuitis beneficium. At missa, ut dixi, beneficium est promissionis
diuinae, per manum sacerdotum omnibus hominibus exhibitum.

EN rationem lector, missa non potest esse bonum opus: nempe
quod in missa beneficium accipimus a deo, non ei conferimus.

10   QVAESO te lector, an tu hunc putas uel reminisci uerborum
suorum, uel sua interim uerba audire, dum loquitur? Nam si nihil
esse potest bonum opus hominis: quo quis beneficium accipit a deo,
non praestat: quid illi necesse fuit, incassum tot uerba fundere: ut
probaret, in quolibet opere bono esse peccatum? Quanto fuit ei
15   facilius dicere: nullum est opus [II$_2$] bonum? Nam id aperte nunc
dicit: quum nullum esse dicat opus bonum: in quo quis accipit a deo
beneficium. Nam nec martyrium quidem, hoc pacto, bonum opus
fuerit. Siquidem nec martyr quicquam in deum confert: sed accipit
ab illo. Quod enim beneficium deo praestat martyr moriendo? An
20   non ille quoque pauper et indigens uenit accepturus de manu diuitis
dei beneficium? dum cum illo nummum exiguum aereum, grandi
permutat aureo, immo suum illi aereum reddit: ut reportet aureum.
Nam quam ab illo uitam commodato recepit miseram et momen-
taneam, eam illi reddit: ut beatam recipiat, eandemque nunquam
25   finiendam. Ergo per te Luthere, bonum

Lutheri sententia ne martyrium
quidem bonum opus esse

opus non facit martyr: dum uitam im-
pendit pro fide. At deus, quod rex obiecit
tibi, Magdalenam pronunciat bonum opus facere: cuius opus, opinor,
pro beneficio non habuit: sed mulieri magnum beneficium contulit
30   quam dignatus est ad illud officij genus admittere. Nos miseri, quum
omnia fecerimus: adhuc serui inutiles sumus: quod enim debuimus

---

2 asscribit] ascribit *B*   6 beneficium est] *BL*, benefiicium est *R*   8–9 En ... con-
ferimus] Hic uides lector, quam argute sentiat de bono opere: qui nihil habendum censet
pro bono opere: quod fiat ab homine: nisi idem fuerit beneficium, erga deum. *B. See n.*
12–13 quo ... praestat] nisi quo beneficium praestatur deo: *B*   16–19 in quo ... ab
illo.] nisi quod deum donet beneficio. Siquidem, quum omnia fecerimus, adhuc inutiles
serui sumus: quod enim debuimus facere, fecimus. Ne martyrium quidem, hoc pacto,
bonum opus erit. *B. See n.*   25 finiendam.] *B adds*, Quod igitur beneficium praestat
deo? An non omnino nullum? *See n.*   29–532/5 sed mulieri ... Et sic] Et homines
omnes aiunt eum benefacere: qui soluit debitum: etiam si distingunt omnes inter

the question in a twofold subtlety and involve himself in a twofold folly. For this is what he there sets down.

> Let no one dare be so senseless as to say that a man does a good work when he comes poor and needy to receive a benefit from the hand of a rich man. But the mass, as I have said, is the benefit of the divine promise delivered through the hand of the priests to all men.

Luther's words from the Babylonian Captivity

5

See the reasoning, reader: The mass cannot be a good work; that is, because in the mass we receive a benefit from God, we do not confer one on Him.

I ask you, reader, do you think that this fellow either remembers his own words, or listens to his own words all the while he is speaking? For if the work of a man cannot be good in which he receives a benefit from God but does not offer one, what need was there for him to pour out so many useless words to prove that in any good work whatsoever there is sin? How much easier it was to say: no work is good. For now he openly says this when he says that no work is good in which someone receives a benefit from God. For not even martyrdom, according to this reasoning, will have been a good work, since the martyr does not bestow anything on God but receives from Him. For what benefit does a martyr present to God by dying? Does he not rather also come poor and needy to receive from the hand of a rich God a benefit, when he exchanges with Him a trifling copper coin for a valuable gold one; or rather he pays back his copper in order to carry away a gold. For he returns to Him the wretched and brief life which he received from Him as a loan in order to receive a blessed life and one that is never to end. Therefore, according to you, Luther, the martyr does not perform a good work when he lays down his life on behalf of the faith. But God, as the king objected to you, declared that Magdalen was doing a good work; I do not think He considered her work a benefit, but He conferred a great benefit on the woman whom He deigned to admit to a service of that kind. We miserable men, when we have done everything, are still worthless

10

15

20

25

That in Luther's opinion not even martyrdom is a good work

30

35

---

beneficium praestitum, et solutum debitum. Solus Lutherus negat quenquam bonum opus facere: nisi qui beneficium praestat deo. Et hoc dicit is, qui dicit iustos benefaciendo peccare. Sic *B. See n.*

facere fecimus: nihil deo damus: sed in omni opere bono, a dei
beneficentia recipimus. Quod, quum omnes fateantur, solus Lutherus
asserit, ńullum esse: quod qui facit, beneficium accipit a deo non
praestat. Et istud asserit is qui dicit iustos in omni opere bono peccare.
5   Et sic homo sapiens, et nunquam sibi contrarius, asserit pariter istas
duas conclusiones. Omne bonum opus hominis habet peccatum: et
nullum est bonum opus hominis: quod possit habere peccatum.

HIC te quaeso lector, ut relegas illa Lutheri uerba magnifica:
quibus regem ait ea cogitare de missa: quae uidelicet [II₂v] ipse,
10 neque per febrem, neque per frenesim cogitare unquam potuisset.
Quantam sibi gloriam his comparauit ampullis: quando nunc omnes
aperte sentiant principem, et de missa et de bono opere loquutum
prudentissime: quum interim de utroque per suas febres, et freneses,
talia nobis excogitauit Lutherus: ut nunquam cogitare uel ipsa febris
15 tam febrilia, uel ipsa frenesis tam phrenetica potuisset.

Refellit illas ineptissimas argutias: quibus Lutherus
conatur probare, missam non esse
sacrificium. Cap. XVI.

HOC igitur egregio triumpho, triumphat malorum operum patronus,
20 aduersus opera bona: nunc uideamus, quam strenue se gerat furiosus
fraterculus, et sacrilegus sacrificulus, aduersus sacrosanctum sacrificium. Quod, quo tibi fiat lector dilucidius: principis uerba, quibus
obblaterat nebulo, praeponemus. Ea igitur hunc in modum se habent.
                                        "SED Lutherus satis sentit ipse, facile
Verba regis
25   ·   destrui, quicquid adstruxerat: si missa
possit esse sacrificium, aut oblatio: quae offeratur deo. Hanc igitur
obicem se pollicetur amoturum: quod, quo fidelius facere uideatur et

10 cogitare] cogitate *B*, co gitare *L*   13 et] *BL*, er *R*   23 obblaterat] adblaterat *B*
26 Hanc igitur] *B*, Hanc igitut *R*, Hunc igitur *L*

servants, for we have done what we were obliged to do; we give nothing
to God but in every good work we receive from the goodness of God.
Although everyone admits this, Luther alone declares that it is no
good work, because he who does it receives a benefit from God, does
not offer one. And the man who declares this says that just men sin in
every good work. And thus the wise fellow, never inconsistent with
himself, defends these two conclusions equally: every good work of
man has sin; and, there is no good work of man because it can have
sin.

Here I ask you, reader, to reread those solemn words of Luther in
which he says that the king thinks those things about the mass which
clearly he himself could never have thought either through fever or
through frenzy. How much glory he has gained for himself by these
bombastic words, since now everyone clearly senses that the prince
has spoken most wisely about the mass and about good work, whereas
at the same time concerning both these points Luther in his fevers and
frenzies has thought out for us such ideas that neither could fever itself
have thought out such feverish thoughts, nor could frenzy itself have
thought out such frenzied thoughts.

He refutes those most foolish subtleties with
which Luther tries to prove that the mass is not
a sacrifice. Chapter 16.

With this remarkable triumph, therefore, the patron of evil works
triumphs against good works; now let us see how vigorously the
frenzied friarling and sacrilegious little sacrificer conducts himself
against the sacrosanct sacrifice. So that this may become clearer to
you, reader, we shall set the words of the prince before those in which
the rascal prattles. They are then as follows.

"But Luther understands well enough
that whatever he had built up is easily   *The king's words*
destroyed if the mass can be a sacrifice or an oblation which may be
offered to God. He therefore promises to remove this obstacle; so that
he may appear to do this more honestly and effectively, he himself

efficatius: obijcit sibi ipse prius quaedam:

Quam missa non sit sacrificium   quae sibi sentit obstare. Iam et alterum
Lutheri uerba

(inquit) scandalum amouendum est: quod
multo grandius est, et speciosissimum: id est, quod missa creditur

5   passim esse sacrificium, quod offertur deo. In quam opinionem, et
uerba canonis sonare uidentur: ubi dicitur: Haec dona, haec
munera, haec sancta sacrificia. Et infra: Hanc [II₃] oblationem. Item
clarissime postulatur: ut acceptum sit sacrificium, sicut sacrificium
Abel, &c. Inde Christus hostia altaris dicitur. Accedunt his dicta

10 sanctorum patrum, tot exempla, tantusque usus per orbem constanter
obseruatus.

                  "AVDISTI lector, quas obices ipse sibi
Irridetur Lutherus

sentit obiectas. Audi nunc uicissim, quam
Herculeis uiribus aggreditur amouere: His omnibus, inquit, oportet

15 constantissime opponere uerbum et exemplum Christi. At quae sunt
igitur illa uerba Christi: quae tot olim sanctis patribus, ac toti Christi

                 ecclesiae tot ignorata seculis, uelut nouus
Lutherus nouus Esdras

Esdras, nobis Lutherus inuenit? Hoc
declarat ipse, quum dicit. Nisi enim,

Verba Lutheri

20   missam obtinuerimus esse promissionem,
seu testamentum, ut uerba clare sonant: totum euangelium, et
uniuersum solacium amittimus. Verba nunc audiuimus: restat, ut

                 uideamus exemplum. Exemplum ergo
Argumentum Lutheri ab exemplo, subiungit. Christus (inquit) in coena
ut ipse putat Christi

25   nouissima, quum institueret hoc sacramentum, et condidit testamentum: non obtulit ipsum deo patri: aut
ut opus bonum pro alijs perfecit: sed in mensa sedens, singulis idem
testamentum proposuit: et signum exhibuit. Ista sunt ergo uerba
Christi: istud est exemplum: e quibus nunc demum, Lutherus unus

30 perspicue uidet, missam non esse sacrificium, nec oblationem. Mirum
est igitur, ex tot sanctis patribus, ex tot oculis, quot in ecclesia tam
multis seculis, idem legerunt euangelium, nullum fuisse unquam tam
perspicacem, ut rem tam apertam deprehenderet: imo omnes

                 etiamnum tam caecos esse, ut ne adhuc
Respondetur argumento Lutheri

35   *de sacrificio*   quidem queant, id quod cernere se
Lutherus iactat quanquam ipso monstrante

---

1 *gloss* Quam] quod *L*; efficatius] efficacius *BL*   13 obiectas.] *B*, obiectas, *RL*
14 omnibus] *BL*, omnihus *R*

proposes to himself in advance certain ob-
stacles which he perceives to stand in his
way. Now, he says, yet another stumbling

*How the mass is not a sacrifice.
Luther's words*

block must be removed, which is much greater and very deceptive;
that is, that the mass is everywhere believed to be a sacrifice which is   5
offered to God. Even the words of the canon seem to give expression
to this opinion when they say: 'These gifts, these offerings, these holy
sacrifices.' And below: 'This oblation.' Likewise, it is most clearly
implored that the sacrifice may be received as the sacrifice of Abel,
etc. For this reason Christ is called the victim of the altar. To these   10
texts are added the words of the holy fathers, very many examples,
and the extensive custom constantly observed throughout the world.

"You have heard, reader, what objections he perceives are raised against him.

Luther is scoffed at

Now hear in turn with what Herculean powers he undertakes to   15
dispel them. To all these objections, he says, one should steadfastly
oppose the word and example of Christ. But what are those words of
Christ, unknown by so many holy fathers in times past and to the
whole church of Christ for so many ages,
which Luther like a new Esdras has found

Luther a new Esdras   20

for us? He himself declares this when he
says: 'Unless we maintain that the mass is

Luther's words

a promise or a testament, as the words clearly state, we lose the
whole gospel and all solace.' Now we have heard the words; it
remains to see an example. He therefore   25
subjoins an example. 'At the last supper,'
he says, 'when Christ instituted this sacrament and established a testament, He did

*The argument of Luther from
the example, as he himself
thinks, of Christ*

not offer it to God the Father or accomplish it as a good work for
others, but sitting at the table He presented the same testament and   30
offered a sign to each of them.' These then are the words of Christ;
this is the example; from these now at last Luther alone clearly sees
that the mass is not a sacrifice nor an oblation. It is strange then that
of so many holy fathers, of so many eyes that have read the same
gospel in the church for so many ages, there was never any so clear-   35
sighted as to perceive such an evident matter; in fact, that everyone is
even now so blind that although Luther
himself shows it to them they cannot even
yet perceive what Luther boasts that he

*An answer is given to Luther's
argument about sacrifice*

perspice[II₃v]re. An non Lutherus hallucinatur potius: et aliquid se
uidere putat: quod non uidet: et digito conatur ostendere: quod
nusquam est? Nam obsecro, qualis est ista probatio: quum docere
nititur, missam non esse sacrificium, ex eo, quod sit promissio: quasi
5   promissio et sacrificium ita sibi mutuo pugnarent, quemadmodum
frigus et calor? Quae Lutheri ratio adeo prorsus friget: ut nec
responso digna uideatur. Nam legis Mosaicae tam multa sacrificia,

Promissiones sacrificorum ueteris   quanquam essent figurae omnia futurarum
testamenti   rerum: tamen promissiones erant et ipsa.
10   Promittebant enim ea, propter quae
fiebant: non modo futura quondam illa, quorum erant figurae, sed
etiam liberationes, expiationes, purgationes, purificationes populi tunc
praesentis: pro quo more solemni quotannis offerebantur. Quae
res, quum tam aperta sit: ut nemo prorsus eam possit ignorare:
15 ridicula plane dissimulatio est ista Lutheri: quum nunc argumentetur, fieri id non posse: quod non ipse tantum, sed populus quoque
nouit tam saepe factum."

AVDISTI lector uerba regis: Audi nunc uicissim uerba nebulonis:
ut iudicare possis: quam scite scurretur fraterculus.

20   *Verba Lutheri*   Deinde, pro sacrificio missae defen-
                                           dendo, sic Thomisticatur. Esto, inquit,
Missa sit promissio, non hinc sequitur, non esse simul sacrificium,
quando in ueteri lege erant sacrificia, quae simul erant promissiones.
Respondeo. Huius Thomisticae assertionis, debuit rex uel unum
25 exemplum producere. Nunc uero pro more suo, satis esse putat, si
tantum scribat in ueteri lege sacrificia fuisse promissiones, tum mox,
Oportet sic esse. Sed tam stolido assertori (ut uideo) proponendus
esset aliquis uo[II₄]cabularius, quo disceret primum, quid significet,
tam sacrificium quam promissio. Siquidem promissio est uerbum,
30 sacrificium est res, ut etiam pueri infantes intelligant, impossibile esse,
ut promissio sacrificium, aut uerbum res sit. Me miserum, qui cum

Vere istud ais Luthere, non   talibus stulticiae monstris, tempus per-
es dignus   dere cogor, nec dignus sum, ut ingenio
                                     aut eruditione praestantes mecum cer-
35 tent. Error itaque manifestarius est, dicere in ueteri lege fuisse
sacrificia promissiones. Nisi rex assertor, lubricitate thomistica,
figurate uoluerit loqui, quod sacrificia promittebant, id est, significa-

---

8 futurarum] *BL*, futurum *R*   11 illa, quorum] *BL*, illa quorum *R*   12 purgationes]
BL, purgotiones *R*   19 scurretur] *BL*, scrurretur *R*   20 *gloss* Verba Lutheri] *om. B*
32 *gloss* ais Luthere] *B*, a̧t Luthere *R*, ait, Luthere *L*

sees. Is not Luther rather seeing things, and thinking that he sees what he does not see and trying to point out something which is nowhere? Tell me, what sort of proof is this, when he tries to teach that the mass is not a sacrifice on the grounds that it is a promise, as if a promise and a sacrifice were as mutually contradictory as cold and heat? This reasoning of Luther falls so flat that it seems unworthy of an answer. For the very many sacrifices of the Mosaic law, although they were all figures of future events, were still promises. For they promised those *The promises of the sacrifices* things for the sake of which they were *of the old testament* done, not only those future events of which they were the figures, but also deliverances, atonements, cleansings, purifications of the people then present for whom they were yearly offered by a solemn custom. Since this fact is so clear that no one at all can be ignorant of it, this dissimulation of Luther's is clearly ridiculous, since he now argues that a thing cannot be done which not only he himself but the people also know has often been done."

You have heard the words of the king, reader. Now hear in turn the words of the rascal, so that you can judge how cleverly the friarling plays the buffoon.

Next, for the sake of defending the sacri- *Luther's words* fice of the mass, he Thomisticates thus: "Granted that the mass is a promise," he says, "it does not follow from this that it is not at the same time a sacrifice, since in the old law there were sacrifices which were at the same time promises." I answer: the king should have brought up at least one example of this Thomistic assertion. But now according to his custom he thinks it enough if he writes only that in the old law sacrifices were promises, then directly, "It should be so." But as I see it, such a dull-witted defender should have been presented with some glossary from which he might learn first of all what is the meaning of sacrifice as well as promise, since a promise is a word, a sacrifice is a thing, so that even very young children understand that it is impossible for a promise to be a sacrifice or a word to be a thing. It is too bad that I, who am forced to waste my time with such *You say this truly, Luther; you* monsters of folly, am not worthy to have *are not worthy* men of outstanding genius or learning contend with me. And so it is a palpable error to say that in the old law sacrifices were promises. Unless the king defender, with Thomistic slipperiness, wished to speak figuratively, that the sacrifices promised,

bant futura in Christo. Verum, hoc non est asserere sacramenta, sed

Tu uere nugaris uerbis ludere et nugari uerbis. Siquidem, hoc
modo, promissio est signum, seu res, non
uerbum. At nos in missa potissimum, uocamus promissionem, ipsa
5 scilicet uerba Christi, sine quibus, panis et uinum essent, neque
signum, neque sacramentum, neque missa. Nam quod per sacrificia,
in fide oblata, promissiones impetrabantur, aliud est. Non enim hic,
uel de fructu, uel significatione sacrificiorum disputamus, sed de ipsa
substantia, ut sciamus, quid sit, et quid non sit sacrificium.

10 *Lutheri argutatio de missa*   NVNC expende lector, quam belle
et sacrificio   rationes principis soluerit nebulo. Nam
quum rex inter alias istius ineptias, hoc
quoque miserabile sophisma, quo sic colligit: Missa est promissio:
ergo non potest esse sacrificium: ex eo confutarit, quod etiam ueteris
15 legis sacrificia sic erant promissiones: sicut argutatur Lutherus
missam esse promissionem: recurrit nunc Lutherus: et negat sacrificia
ueteris legis, fuisse promissiones, nisi sophistice. Missam uero nihil
aliud esse omnino, nisi ueram et meram promissionem. Quid facias
lector isti stipiti: qui sic disputat: tanquam auditores omnes, plane
20 stipites essent. Solet ille uir, grauis ac seuerus, scholasticorum argutias
ridere: quum cogatur ipse saepissime ad ineptissima sophismata
confugere. Nam, quis [II₄v] nescit in sacrificijs Mosaicae legis,
manifestas fuisse promissiones dei? Cuiusmodi est illud Leuitici,
capite sexto. Pro peccato autem suo, offeret arietem immaculatum,
25 de grege: et dabit eum sacerdoti, iuxta aestimationem, mensuramque
delicti: qui rogabit pro eo coram domino: et dimittetur illi, pro
singulis, quae faciendo peccauit. Vides hic lector tam manifestam
esse promissionem: ut nusquam possit esse manifestior. At Lutherus
fortasse dicet, in talibus remissionis indulgendae per sacrificia
30 promissiones esse, non esse tamen promissiones ipsa sacrificia, sed
missam non habere promissionem adiunctam: sed ipsius missae
substantiam, nihil aliud esse, quam meram promissionem: propterea
quod missa sit testamentum: quod nihil est aliud (ut Lutherus ait)
quam promissio haereditatis. Age igitur, accedamus propius ut

---

2 *gloss* uerbis] *B*, uerbia *R*, verbia *L*; Siquidem] Si quidem *L*   13 quo] *L*, qua *BR*;
colligit] intelligit *B*   22 confugere. Nam] *BL*, confugere, Nam *R*   26 delicti] *B corr.*
err. L, dilecti *R*   31 missae] *BL*, misse *R*   34 accedamus] *om. B*

that is, signified, future events in Christ. *You indeed trifle with words*
But this is not to defend the sacraments
but to play and trifle with words, since in this sense a promise is a sign
or a thing, not a word. But in the mass especially we call a promise
those very words of Christ without which the bread and wine would 5
be neither a sign nor a sacrament nor the mass. For as for the fact that
through sacrifices offered in faith promises are fulfilled, that is
another matter. For we are not disputing here either about the fruit or
the signification of the sacrifices but about their very substance, in
order to know what is and what is not a sacrifice. 10

Now consider carefully, reader, how
prettily the rascal destroys the prince's *Luther's quibbling about mass*
reasonings. For when the king, among the *and sacrifice*
fellow's other follies, refuted also this wretched sophism according to
which he makes the inference: the mass is a promise, therefore it 15
cannot be a sacrifice, arguing that the sacrifices of the old law were
also promises just as Luther prattles that the mass is a promise; Luther
now returns and says that the sacrifices of the old law were not
promises except in a sophistical sense, but that the mass is nothing
else at all except a true and unmixed promise. What would you do 20
with this blockhead, reader, who disputes as though all his listeners
were utter blockheads? That serious and stern man is accustomed to
mock the subtleties of the scholastics, although he himself is very
often forced to take refuge in the most foolish sophisms. For who does
not know that in the sacrifices of the Mosaic law the promises of God 25
were manifest? This is the sense of that text of Leviticus, chapter six:
"For his sin he shall offer a ram without blemish out of the flock, and
shall give it to the priest, according to the estimation and measure of
the offense; and he shall pray for him before the Lord and he shall
have forgiveness for everything in the doing of which he hath 30
sinned." You see here, reader, that the promise is so manifest that it
could nowhere be more manifest. But perhaps Luther will say that in
such matters the promises of granting forgiveness exist through the
sacrifices but that the sacrifices themselves are not promises, whereas
the mass does not have a promise added, but that the substance of 35
the mass itself is nothing else but an unmixed promise because the
mass is a testament which is nothing else, so Luther says, than a
promise of inheritance.

Come, then, let us approach closer so that you may see, reader, how

uideas lector: quam misera dedecoris sui conscientia, talia deblateret
nebulo. Consideremus illud sacrificium: quod isti ipsi sacrificio, uelut

Paulus apostolus

figuram quandam praeuiam Paulus copu-
lauit apostolus: Lecto, inquit, omni
5 mandato legis a Mose, uniuerso populo, accipiens sanguinem uitulorum, et hircorum, cum aqua, et lana coccinea, et hysopo, ipsum
quoque librum et omnem populum aspersit, dicens: Hic est sanguis testamenti, quod mandauit ad nos deus. Quid dicitis nunc
domine doctor, ubi est uocabularium uestrum: quod scurramini
10 proponendum esse principi? Inspicite

*Cape tu Luthere uocabularium
tuum*

uocabularium, sacrificij ueteris. Inspicite
uocabularium, sacrificij noui. Nunquid in
utroque uocabulario, legitis idem uocabulum? Nunquid sicut
sanguis Christi uocatur in altero sanguis testamenti: sic uituli
15 sanguis, sanguis testamen[KK₁]ti uocatur in altero? An non igitur
(si quid habetis cerebri) facile uidetis consequi: ut aut testamentum
non sit promissio (et tunc perierit uobis totum fundamentum,
quod male collocastis, super testamentum: qui contendatis idem
esse prorsus adaequate, missam et testamentum) aut, si testamentum
20 sit promissio: tunc uerum esse, quod uos negatis: nempe illud sacrificium fuisse promissionem. Et sic domine doctor, ego docui uos tam
plane, quam pueros docere solent pedagogi: quod sacrificia ueteris
legis, fuerunt promissiones, non solum eodem modo, quo uos dicitis
missam esse promissionem, in lege noua, sed eodem etiam uerbo:
25 quantumuis acute disputetis, sacrificium esse rem, et promissionem
esse uerbum: et sic uidetis nunc, quam pulchre uobis procedat uester
uocabularius. Nec tamen haec eo dico: quod aut ibi contendam in
exhodo, aut hic tibi assentiam in euangelio, testamentum esse
meram promissionem: quippe qui plane uideam, id uerum esse, quod
30 rex obiter tibi tribus uerbis ostendit, merum est commentum, quod
tu affers de testamento: quod reuera et illic legem ueterem, et hic
significat nouam, iuxta illud propheticum, quod apostolus commemorat. Ecce dies ueniet, dicit dominus: et consummabo super domum
Israel, et super domum Iuda, testamentum nouum, non secundum
35 testamentum, quod feci patribus eorum, in die, qua apprehendi
manum eorum: ut aeducerem illos de terra Aegypti: quoniam ipsi

---

1 misera] *B*, misero *RL*   2 ipsi sacrificio,] ipsi, sacrificio *BR*, ipsi sacrificio *L*   9 uocabularium uestrum: quod] uocabularius uester: quem *B*   20 quod uos] *corr. err. L*, quod
et uos *BR*   22 sacrificia] *corr. err. L*, sacrificium *BR*

in the wretched consciousness of his disgrace the rascal blathers such things. Let us consider that sacrifice which the apostle Paul joined to this very sacrifice *Paul the apostle* as a kind of antecedent figure. He says: "When every commandment of the law had been read by Moses to all the people, he took the 5 blood of the calves and of the goats with the water and the scarlet wool and hyssop, and sprinkled both the book itself and all the people, saying: 'This is the blood of the covenant which God has commanded for us.' "

What do you say now, honored doctor; where is your glossary 10 which you buffoonishly say should be presented to the prince? Examine the glossary entry for the old sacrifice. Examine the glossary entry for *Take up your glossary, Luther* the new sacrifice. Do you not read in either glossary entry the same term? Is not the blood of Christ called in the one the blood of the 15 covenant just as the blood of a calf is called the blood of the covenant in the other? Do you not then readily see, if you have any brain at all, that it follows either that a testament is not a promise, and then your whole foundation will have been destroyed which you have poorly established on the notion of testament by arguing that mass and 20 testament are altogether the same in every respect; or, if the testament is a promise, then what you deny is true, namely that that sacrifice was a promise? And thus, honored doctor, I have taught you as clearly as pedagogues are accustomed to teach boys that the sacrifices of the old law were promises, not only in the same way in which 25 you say that the mass is a promise in the new law, but even by means of the same word, however keenly you argue that the sacrifice is a thing and the promise is a word; and so you see now how splendidly your glossary has profited you. And yet I do not say these things with the intention of arguing that in that passage of Exodus, or of agreeing 30 with you that here in the gospel, the testament is a mere promise, for I clearly see the truth of what the king shows you in passing with three words: it is a mere trick that you present on the notion of testament, which in fact signifies in the one passage the old law and in the other the new, according to that prophecy which the apostle recalls: 35 "Behold the day is coming, says the Lord, when I will make a new covenant with the house of Israel, and with the house of Juda, not according to the covenant that I made with their fathers on the day when I took them by the hand to lead them forth out of the land of

non permanserunt in testamento meo: et ego neglexi eos dicit dominus. Quia hoc est testamentum, quod disponam domui Israel,

Volue Luthere diligenter hoc uocabularium

post dies illos dicit dominus, dando leges meas, in men[KK₁v]tem eorum, et in

5   corda eorum superscribam eas, et ero eis in deum, et ipsi erunt mihi in populum. Et non docebit unusquisque proximum suum, et unusquisque fratrem suum, dicens: Cognosce dominum, quoniam omnes scient me a minore usque ad maiorem eorum, quia propitius ero iniquitatibus eorum, et peccatorum eorum

10   iam non memorabor. Dicendo autem nouum, ueterauit prius. Quod autem antiquatur et senescit, prope interitum est.

QVID hic dicit apostolus esse testamentum uetus? quid hic appellat nouum? an non legem ueterem, et legem nouam? idque tam aperte multis modis enuncians, ut nullum habeas tergiuersandi

15   locum, aut uanissimum commentum tuum tuendi: quod nulla, neque ratione, neque scriptura fretus, mero arbitrio tuo statuis stolide, et uelut pro imperio iubes orbem credere. Quamobrem (ut dixi) non haec eo protuli: quod in Exhodo contendam, testamenti uerbum significare promissionem: sed et ex alijs sacrificijs ostenditur pro-

20   missionem, nec obstare, nec repugnare sacrificio: quemadmodum ipse blaterasti, et ex illo probaui: quod satis est aduersus te: si testamentum foret mera promissio, sicut tu contendis: tunc aliquod saltem sacrificium fuisse promissionem in lege Mosaica, quod tu homo absurdissimus, et absurdum esse iactas et impossibile.

25
Verba Lutheri

Miratur etiam dominus Henricus, quales nam ego concionatores audierim, quod scripserim. nihil esse in concionibus de promissionibus his unquam dictum, ipse uero ad tedium usque audierit de testamento, de promissionibus, de testibus. &c. Respondeo. Et ego miror, regis esse

30   tam rude caput, et tantam amentiam, qui tam insignes conciones audierit, et adeo nihil [KK₂] didicerit, neque intellexerit uerbum dei, nostrum opus aut sacrificium esse non posse, quin contrarium sine fine blaterat.

Et iure optimo miratur

MIRATVR (opinor) dominus Henri-
35   cus, Lutheri caput tam stolide gloriosum esse: ut ex fece triuialium et rancidarum concionum, dogma ipsum

---

12 dicit apostolus] *corr. err. L*, apostolus *om. BR*   19 sed et] *corr. err. L*, et *om. BR*
21 probaui] *L*, brobaui *BR*

Egypt, for they did not abide by my covenant and I did not regard them, says the Lord. For this is the covenant that I will make with the house of Israel after those days, says the Lord: I will put my laws into their mind and upon their hearts I will write them, and I will be their God, and they shall be my people. And they shall not teach, each his neighbor and each his brother, saying: 'Know the Lord'; for all shall know me, from least to greatest among them. Because I will be merciful to their iniquities and their sins I will remember no more. Now in saying 'a new covenant,' He has made obsolete the former one. And that which is obsolete and has grown old is near its end."

Peruse this glossary carefully, Luther

What does the apostle here say the old testament is? What does he here call the new one? Is it not the old law and the new law? And he declares this so clearly in many ways that you have no room for shifting or for defending your most deceitful trick which, relying neither on reason nor on scripture, you stupidly set up by your sheer willfulness and, as it were, imperiously order the world to believe.

Therefore, as I said, I have not presented these arguments with the intention of arguing that in Exodus the word testament signifies a promise, but even from other sacrifices it is shown that the notion of promise is neither opposed to nor contrary to that of sacrifice, as you have blathered; and from that fact I have proved what is sufficiently opposed to you, that if a testament were a mere promise as you contend, then at least some sacrifice in the Mosaic law was a promise, a thing that you, a most absurd man, claim is absurd and impossible.

Lord Henry also wonders what sort of preachers I have listened to because I wrote that nothing was ever said in sermons about these promises, whereas he had heard even to the point of weariness about the testament, about promises, about witnesses, etc. I answer: And I wonder that the head of the king is so ignorant and his madness so great who has heard such distinguished sermons and has learned so little and not understood that the word of God cannot be our work or sacrifice but that he blathers the opposite endlessly.

Luther's words

Lord Henry wonders, I think, that the head of Luther is so stupidly pompous that from the dregs of commonplace and stale sermons he has drawn that very insane doctrine which, as something

And with every right he wonders

tam insanum hauserit: quod uelut nouum et inauditum prius, toti
propinaret orbi: quum hoc dumtaxat habeat noui, quod idem stultius
tractatur ab illo, quam quisquam ante tractauit. Nec pudet eum, iam
toties uictum atque reuictum turpiter, summo cum probro suo,
5   stolide nugari rursus illo despuendo sophismate.

Verba Lutheri. Vide, quam haec Si enim ulla scintilla rationis humanae
consentiant superioribus in eo uigeret, utique negare non posset
signum dei, opus dei esse erga nos. Sic
sacrificium, et promissiones dei esse uerbum dei, non opus nostrum.

10 IMO si in Luthero uigeret ulla scintilla rationis humanae, nunquam secum posset in tam paucis uersibus, tam insane pugnare.
Nunquid hic dicit manifeste nobis, tam sacrificium quam promissiones esse uerbum dei: atque usque adeo confirmat istud: ut eum
censeat, ne scintillam quidem humanae rationis habere: quisquis id
15 negare fuerit ausus? Nullam ergo scintillam rationis humanae prorsus
habet Lutherus. Nam id ipsum in eadem pagina, prorsus negauit.
Ideo enim negauit sacrificium posse promissionem esse: quia omnis
promissio uerbum sit, et omne sacrificium res: atque ob id uerbum
esse non possit: quum nulla res uerbum sit. Verum ne fingere possit,
20 me per calumniam sua uerba deprauare pro meo commodo, sua illi
uerba licet tam nuper dicta, quoniam illum oblitum esse uideo, non
grauabor commemorare denuo.

Verba Lutheri Tam stolido assertori (ut uideo) proponendus esset aliquis uo[KK₂v]cabu-
25 larius, quo disceret primum, quid significat tam sacrificium, quam
promissio. Siquidem, promissio est uerbum, sacrificium est res, ut
etiam pueri infantes intelligant impossibile esse, ut promissio sacrificium aut uerbum res sit. Me miserum, qui cum talibus stulticiae
monstris, tempus perdere cogor, nec dignus sum, ut ingenio aut
30 eruditione praestantes mecum certent.

EN hominem lector dignum, qui cum Minerua disputet: quem
miserandum sit, ita cogi tempus cum stultis perdere: quum sit ipse
tam sapiens: ut in uno uersu stolidos clamet esse: qui sacrificium
putent uerbum esse, aut esse uerbum posse: quum sit res: et post in
35 proximo fere uersu contra clamet, stolidos esse, nec ullam scintillam

---

3 tractauit] *L*, tactauit *BR*   5 sophismate.] *L*, sophismate *BR*   24–25 uocabularius]
vocabularius *L*, uocabulurius *BR*

new and before unheard of, he sets before the whole world, whereas
only this much is new about it, that it is handled more foolishly by
him than anyone has handled it before. Nor is he ashamed, though
conquered now so many times and shamefully refuted to his own
supreme disgrace, to talk stupid nonsense by spewing out again that 5
sophism.

> For if any spark of human reason thrived
> in him, he could surely not deny that the
> sign of God is a work of God towards us,
> that thus sacrifice and the promises of
> God are the word of God, not our work.

Luther's words. See how these words agree with his previous words

10

On the contrary, if any spark of human reason thrived in Luther,
he could never contradict himself so insanely in so few lines. Does he
not clearly say to us here that sacrifice as well as promises are the
word of God, and he confirms this so strongly that he considers that 15
man not to have even a spark of human reason who has dared to deny
it? Not a single spark of human reason, therefore, does Luther have.
For on the same page he completely denied that very statement. For
he denied that a sacrifice can be a promise on the grounds that every
promise is a word and every sacrifice a thing and for this reason it 20
cannot be a word because no thing is a word. But, to prevent his
being able to pretend that I distort his words through trickery to my
own advantage, since I see that he has forgotten his words, though so
recently quoted, I will not begrudge recalling them a second time.

> As I see it, such a dull-witted defender
> should have been presented with some
> glossary from which he might learn first of all what is the meaning of
> sacrifice as well as of promise, since a promise is a word, a sacrifice is a
> thing, so that even very young children understand that it is im-
> possible for a promise to be a sacrifice or a word to be a thing. It is too
> bad that I who am forced to waste my time with such monsters of folly
> am not worthy to have men of outstanding genius or learning contend
> with me.

Luther's words

25

30

Behold a man, reader, worthy of disputing with Minerva; it is
deplorable that he is thus forced to waste his time with fools since he 35
himself is so wise that in one line he cries that they are stupid who
think a sacrifice is a word or can be a word since it is a thing, and
afterwards, in almost the next line, he cries on the contrary that those

humanae rationis habere: qui negarent sacrificium esse uerbum. An
non isti sacramentorum impugnatori, foret opus non uocabulario, sed
cauterio: quo tam stolidae fronti, ad perpetuam rei memoriam, stultitiae nota inureretur.

Verba Lutheri — Deinde rex iste mendacij, qui hoc loco
scribit sese usque ad tedium audisse de
testamentis et promissionibus eiusmodi, postea de sacramento ordinis
garrit, in tota coena Christi nullam esse promissionem, non modo sibi
ipsi turpissime contra dicens, sed impudenti mendacio in coenam
domini insaniens. Sic praecipitat Papistas, furor et amentia, ut prorsus
nihil uideant, quid dicant, aut contra quid statuant.

MALE habet Lutherum: quod ei tam praeclari inuenti gloriam
fratres interciperent: non potest adhuc

*Lutherus nugas suas alijs
inuidet nugatoribus*

concoquere, quod rex eadem prius audiuit
ab alijs, eiusdem farinae fraterculis: id,
inquam, Lutherus ferre non potest. Nam, qui uolet ingenio cedere,
rarus erit: sed clamat regem esse mendacem: certe si me audiret
princeps, potius quam Lutherum habeat inimicum, totam tam stulti
inuenti laudem [KK₃] solidam reddet Luthero. Sed addit tam iratus,
ut sese loquentem non audiat, regem qui se mentitur tantum audisse
de testamentis et promissionibus, postea garrire in tota coena Christi,
nullam esse promissionem, atque ita et sibi contradicere, et in coenam
domini insanire. Primum lector, expende mirabilem reuerendi patris
prudentiam: qui ex eo quod rex ait, se plus millies audisse fraterculos
aliquot indoctos, ea praedicasse stolide: quae nunc Lutherus iactat,
sese primum sapienter inuenisse, colligit regem sibi contradicere, si
dicat utrosque nugari, et illos stultos et hunc stultiorem esse: hanc
uidelicet uocat reuerendus pater potator

*Quid Luthero sit sibi quenquam
contradicere*

repugnantiam. Deinde (salua reuerendi
patris reuerentia) reuerendus pater im-
pudenter mentitur: quum dicit regem dicere, nullam esse promissionem in coena dominica. Nam id non dicit: quippe qui fateatur

16 ingenio] ingeni *B*   17 rarus] rarius *B*

men are fools and have no spark of human reason who would deny
that the sacrifice is a word. Would not this assailant of the sacraments
have need not of a glossary but of a branding iron so that his very
stupid forehead might be branded with the mark of folly as an
everlasting reminder of the fact?   5

> Then this king of lies, who writes in this *Luther's words*
> passage that he has heard even to the
> point of weariness about testaments and promises of this sort, afterwards
> chatters in regard to the sacrament of orders that in the whole supper
> of Christ there is no promise, not only most basely contradicting him-   10
> self but with shameless lying raging madly against the supper of the
> Lord. Thus rage and madness dash the papists headlong, so that they
> see nothing at all which they may say, or against which they may
> take a stand.

It vexes Luther that his brethren have seized the glory of such a   15
noteworthy discovery; he cannot yet digest
the fact that the king has heard the same   *Luther envies other triflers his*
things before from other friarlings of the   *own trifles*
same flour; that, I say, Luther cannot endure. For he who will wish to
be inferior in genius will be rare; but he cries that the king is a liar. 20
Certainly, if the prince would hear me, rather than have Luther as
an enemy he will render to Luther the entire praise for such a foolish
discovery. But he adds, so wrathful that he does not hear himself
talking, that the king who falsely says that he has heard so much
about testaments and promises afterwards chatters that in the whole 25
supper of Christ there is no promise and thus both contradicts himself
and rages insanely against the supper of the Lord.

First of all, reader, consider carefully the marvelous shrewdness of
the reverend father, who, from the fact that the king says he has more
than a thousand times heard that several unlettered friarlings have   30
stupidly preached those things which Luther now boasts that he
himself first wisely discovered, infers that the king contradicts himself
if he says that both talk nonsense and that those former are foolish
and this latter more foolish; it is this that
the reverend father toper calls inconsist-   *What Luther means by*
ency. Then, saving the reverence of the   *self-contradiction*   35
reverend father, the reverend father shamelessly lies when he says that
the king says there is no promise in the supper of the Lord. For he

esse promissionem: sed non eius generis promissionem, quae iuuet
Lutheri causam. Neque enim ullam illic promissionem esse factam
cuiquam, propter sacramenti receptionem: quod Christus instituit in
coena: sed per sanguinis effusionem, quem Christus effudit in cruce.
5 Quod, quo uideas lector apertius: audi rursus uerba principis.

Verba regis   "SED tangemus tamen Lutherum aliquanto propius. Eucharistiam concedit
esse sacramentum: quod nisi fateretur, insaniret. At ubi repperit in
scriptura, promissam in illo sacramento gratiam? Nam ille nihil
10 recipit, nisi scripturas, et easdem claras. Legatur locus de coena
dominica: non reperiet apud ullum euangelistarum, in susceptione
sacramenti promissam gratiam. Legitur a Christo di[KK₃v]ctum.
Hic est sanguis meus noui testamenti: qui pro multis effundetur, in
remissionem peccatorum. Quibus uerbis significauit, semet in cruce
15 per passionem redempturum genus humanum. Sed quum dixit ante:
Hoc facite in meam commemorationem: nullam hoc facienti, id est
sacerdoti consecranti, aut eucharistiam recipienti, gratiam ibi
promittit, nullam peccatorum remissionem. At nec apostolus in
epistola ad Corinthios, quum interminetur male manducantibus
20 iudicium, ullam mentionem facit de gratia bene manducantium.
Quod si quid ex capite sexto Ioannis, gratiam promittat suscipienti
sacramentum carnis et sanguinis domini, ne id quidem quicquam
iuuare Lutherum potest: quippe qui totum illud caput neget, ad
eucharistiam quicquam pertinere. Videtis
Lutherus non potest tueri suam   ergo, ut istam promissionem gratiae, quam
25   *sententiam*   pro totius sacramenti fundamento, magnifice nobis in toto promisit opere, non potest in eo tueri sacramento,
quod fere solum relinquit, nisi quod necesse habet praeter scripturae
uerba, recurrat ad ecclesiae fidem."
30 NVNC uides lector, huius reuerendi patris impudentem calumniam, et non minorem stulticiam. Nam id imputat regi, quod nusquam dicit: ad id uero, quod dicit: Lutherus nihil contradicit: quum
tamen sit eiusmodi, ut totum Lutheri fundamentum subruat: illud
inquam fundamentum, quod habet pro firmissimo, nempe nihil
35 credendum esse necessario: nisi probetur euidentibus scripturis:
Princeps locum explicuit: ac fecit planum, quod dixit, nempe

8 At] *corr. err. L*, Aut *BR*   14 remissionem] *L*, remissinem *BR*   19 epistola] *L*,
epostola *BR*

does not say that; indeed, he admits there is a promise, but not a promise of the sort which helps the cause of Luther. For there was no promise made to anyone there because of the reception of the sacrament which Christ instituted at the supper, but through the shedding of the blood which Christ shed on the cross. That you may see this 5 more clearly, reader, hear again the words of the prince.

"But let us touch Luther a little more closely still. He grants that the eucharist is *The king's words* a sacrament; if he did not grant this he would be raving mad. But where has he found in scripture the grace promised in that sacrament? 10 For he accepts nothing but the scriptures and only those which are evident. Let the passage about the supper of the Lord be read; he will not find among any of the evangelists the promise of grace in the receiving of the sacrament. The words of Christ read: 'This is my blood of the new testament which shall be shed for many unto the remission 15 of sins.' By these words He signified that He would redeem the human race through His suffering on the cross. But when He said earlier, 'Do this in remembrance of me,' He there promises no grace, no remission of sins to the one who does this, that is, to the priest consecrating or to the one receiving the eucharist. But neither does the apostle in the 20 epistle to the Corinthians when he threatens judgment to those who eat unworthily make any mention of grace for those who eat worthily. But if anything from the sixth chapter of John promises grace to the one who receives the sacrament of the flesh and blood of the Lord, not even that can help Luther any, seeing that he denies that that 25 whole chapter has anything to do with the eucharist. You see therefore how, regarding this promise of grace which, as the foundation of the *Luther cannot defend his* whole sacrament, he has solemnly prom- *own opinion* ised in his whole work, he cannot defend it in that sacrament which 30 almost alone he leaves, unless he considers it necessary to have recourse to the faith of the church beyond the words of scripture."

Now you see, reader, this reverend father's shameless slander and no less folly. For he imputes to the king what the latter nowhere says, but to that which he does say Luther says nothing in return, although 35 it is nevertheless of such a kind that it demolishes Luther's whole foundation, that foundation, I say, which he considers as most firm; namely, that nothing has to be believed of necessity unless it is proved by evident scriptures. The prince has interpreted a passage and made

Lutherum non posse, ex illo loco probare e[KK₄]uidenti scriptura,
illud sacramentum habere promissionem gratiae: quum euangelium
ibi non dicat: Hic est sanguis meus noui testamenti, qui bibetur in
remissionem peccatorum: sed qui pro multis effundetur in remis-
5 sionem peccatorum. At quid respondet ad haec tam aperta Lutherus?

Lutheri responsatio   Certe nihil aliud, nisi, Tu mentiris. Nam
                               hoc illi frequens est, quum ipse mentitur.
Quamobrem, non alio opus est responso, quam ut idem ei totidem
uerbis respondeat Echo.

10   Audet etiam asserere, manifestum esse,
      Lutheri uerba   fieri a sacerdotibus, non modo id, quod
Christus in coena, sed quod et in cruce fecit. Respondeo. Quando hoc
dominus Henricus tantum dicit, et non probat, Dico ego contra,
manifestum esse, sacerdotes in missa id omittere, quod Christus in
15 coena fecit, et id facere, quod iudaei fecerunt in cruce Christo. Nec
                               dico hoc solum, sed probo quoque. Nam
Nunc domine, ego dico,   qui uerbum dei peruertit et extinguit, is
      tu mentiris   uere crucifigit filium dei, id quod faciunt
omnes, qui ex promissione opus faciunt, quum hoc uere sit ueritatem
20 dei mutare in mendacium.

   AIT regem istud dicere, et non probare: sed interim illa dissimulat
omnia, quibus id rex probauit. Tacet illud apostoli: quod testamentum mortem testatoris inuoluit. Tacet et illud eiusdem: Quotiescunque manducaueritis corpus domini, et sanguinem eius biberitis:
25 mortem domini annunciabitis: quae in cruce peracta est, non in
coena. Mors ergo pertinet ad illud sacramentum: per quam se
Christus obtulit. Item illud tacet, quod rex docuit, a spiritu sancto
ideo ecclesiam doctam infundere aquam in uinum: quia aqua cum
                               sanguine fluxit e latere Christi, morientis
Cur in missa aqua uino   in cruce. Haec omnia dissimulans, censet
30   *misceatur*   se aegregie oculos omnium festiua illa
perstrinxisse blasphemia: qua sacerdotes omnes [KK₄v] ait, iterum
crucifigere Christum: quicunque missam dicunt esse bonum opus, aut
sacrificium. At quum satis constet, id nunc facere totam ecclesiam
35 Christi: quum constet idem fecisse totam ecclesiam tot aetatibus:

---

2 promissionem] *L*, pomissionem *BR*   29 *gloss* Cur] *L*, cur *BR*

clear what he has said, namely that Luther cannot prove by evident scripture from that passage that that sacrament has the promise of grace since the gospel does not there say, "This is my blood of the new testament which shall be drunk unto the remission of sins," but, "which shall be shed for many unto the remission of sins." But what will Luther answer to such clear arguments as these? Certainly, nothing else but, "You lie." This is usual with him since he himself lies. Therefore *Luther's answer* there is no need of any other answer than that Echo answer him the same thing in as many words.

He dares also to declare that it is manifest that the priests do not only that which *Luther's words* Christ did at the supper but also that which He did on the cross. I answer: Since Lord Henry only says this and does not prove it, I say on the contrary that it is manifest that the priests in the mass leave out that which Christ did at the supper and do that which the Jews did to Christ on the cross. And I do not only say this, but I also prove it. For he who *Now, my honored sir,* *I say you lie* perverts and annuls the word of God, he truly crucifies the Son of God, a thing which everyone does who makes a work from a promise, since this is truly to change the truth of God into a lie.

He says that the king says and does not prove this, but at the same time he conceals all those arguments by which the king has proved it. He passes over in silence the statement of the apostle that a testament involves the death of the testator. He is silent also about the words of the same apostle: "As often as you eat the body of the Lord and drink His blood, you proclaim the death of the Lord," which was accomplished on the cross, not at the supper. Therefore the death through which Christ offered Himself belongs to that sacrament. He is likewise silent about what the king has shown, that the church, taught by the Holy Spirit, pours water into the wine because water with blood flowed from Christ's side as He was dying on the cross. Concealing all *Why water is mingled with the* *wine in the mass* these things, he thinks that he has singularly blinded everyone by that witty blasphemy by which he says that all priests again crucify Christ who say that the mass is a good work or a sacrifice. But since it is well enough known that the whole church of Christ now does that; since it is well known that the whole church for

quum illas ipsas missas quas celebrasse feruntur, et beatus Clemens,
et apostolus Iacobus, oblationem appellent et sacrificium: nec ullum
unquam canonem quisquam legit, tam uetustum: in quo uenerandum illud sacramentum non sit appellatum sacrificium. Quis est
5 usquam tam tepide Christianus: qui ferre possit in tot millia sanctorum, qui usi sunt illo canone: per quem sacramentum corporis et

Blasphema scurrilitas Lutheri   sanguinis dominici offertur in sacrificium,
                                    istum tam scurrili petulantia scurrantem

scurram: ut eos dicat cum Iudaeis rursus Christum crucifigere:
10 quorum plerique pro Christo, sanguinem suum non dubitarunt
effundere: pro quo Lutherus, nisi talis esset nebulo: qui grauaretur
effundere unum scyphum ceruisiae, nunquam posset in animum
inducere: ut tam stolida scurrilitate baccharetur in sanctos: et in
sanctorum blasphemijs blasphemaret deum.

15
                Verba Lutheri   Post haec urget me canone illo missae,
                                         in quo missa sacrificium nominatur,
cuius authoritate ideo me uult teneri, quod eius uerbis usus sim.
Nam ista uerba, Quotiescunque feceritis. &c. non in euangelio
reperiri dicit, sed ista, Hoc facite, In Paulo uero esse alia. Hic uide
20 infelicem Satanam, ut reptat, ut captat, ut quaeritat effugia, sed
frustra, non effugiet. Canonem ego reieci, et reijcio, quod prorsus
aperte contra euangelion, uocat sacrificia, quae sunt signa dei,
promissionibus adiecta, nobis oblata a nobis recipienda, non offerenda.
Nam quod rex dicit in euangelio non esse ista uerba, Quotiescunque
25 feceritis, quis puer non uidet, grammaticam assertori tanto deesse?
quasi uero ne[LL₁]cesse fuerit euangelistas, per omnes syllabas
concordare, et formam illam sacramenti statuere, quam nobis papistae
sic immutabilem et necessariam statuerunt, ut peccati mortalis reum
faciant, et inferno tradant, qui dictiunculam illam enim, omiserit,
30 scilicet Rhadamanti et Aeaci illi, liberrimarum conscienciarum

Hi te delyrum uel potius   carnifices, sic delyrant. Igitur testibus
furiosum reddunt   grammaticis, et communi omnium sensu,
                                  dico, idem esse, quod euangelistae de

coena dicunt, quantumuis paucis uerbis uariant, idemque esse. Hoc
35 facite, quod quotiescumque feceritis, Cauisseque credo spiritum

---

1 Clemens] *L,* clemens *BR*   29 inferno] *L,* infarno *BR*   34 Hoc] *L,* Ho c *BR*

so many ages has done the same thing; since Blessed Clement and the
apostle James referred to those very masses which they are said to
have celebrated as an oblation and a sacrifice; and since no one has
ever read any canon so ancient that in it that venerable sacrament
has not been called a sacrifice; what Christian anywhere is so luke-   5
warm that he can endure that, against so many thousands of saints
who followed that canon according to which the sacrament of the
body and blood of the Lord is offered as a sacrifice, this buffoon plays
the buffoon with such insolent buffoonery
as to say that those men together with the   *The blasphemous buffoonery*   10
Jews again crucify Christ, of whom very   *of Luther*
many did not hesitate to pour out their blood for Christ, for whose
sake Luther, if he were not such a scoundrel that he begrudges pouring out one cup of beer, could never resolve to rage with such stupid
buffoonery against the saints and in blasphemies against the saints to   15
blaspheme God.

    After these arguments he urges me with
that canon of the mass in which the mass   *Luther's words*
is called a sacrifice, by the authority of which he wishes me to be
bound because I have used its words. For those, "As often as you do,   20
etc." are not, he says, found in the gospel, but these words, "Do this,"
and different ones indeed in Paul. Here you see how the unfortunate
Satan snatches, how he seizes, how he earnestly seeks a means of
escape, but in vain; he will not escape. I have rejected the canon and
I reject it because in utterly clear opposition to the gospel it calls   25
sacrifices those things which are signs of God added to promises,
offered to us to be received, not to be offered by us. As for the king's
saying that these words, "As often as you do," are not in the gospel,
what child does not see that such a great defender fails in grammar?
As if indeed it was necessary for the evangelists to agree in every   30
syllable and to establish that form of the sacrament which the papists
have established for us so immutable and necessary that they make
guilty of mortal sin and deliver to hell one who has omitted that least
little word; like Rhadamanthus and
Aeacus those men, murderers of most free   *These render you raving or*   35
consciences, thus rave. Therefore, by the   *rather raging mad*
testimony of grammarians and of everyone's common sense, I say
that what the evangelists say about the supper is the same, however
much it may vary in a few words, and that "Do this" is the same as
"As often as you do this"; and I believe that the Holy Spirit with   40

sanctum singulari consilio, ut euangelistae eandem rem paulo aliter
scriberent, et peccarent peccatum illud irremissibile in formam
sacramenti papisticam, quo nos a futura superstitione et tyrannide
impiorum hominum tutos redderet. Neque enim minus uere con-
5   secraret, qui forma Lucae, Marci, Matthaei, Pauli uteretur, quam qui
canonis istius impij, et falsi utitur.

VERE urget te canon missae: quem tu uno loco probasti: et usus
es pro te: sed hoc nihil est contra te: qui nihil censeas esse stultius:
quam ut quisquam exigat abs te: ut uerbis

Perpetuus mos Lutheri

10   tuis debeas stare: cui perpetuus mos est:
quicquid dixeris, quum libet, rursus indictum dicere. Sed miror,
quid hic loci fuerit tibi garriendi, de euangelistarum concordia: quasi
rex eos negasset diuersis uerbis idem dicere, aut quasi quisquam
euangelistarum habeat ea uerba: quae tu ad confirmanda tua
15   sumpsisti, de tibi toties improbato canone. An ita nugando sperasti
fucum te facturum lectoribus: ne sentire possent, quam belle respondeas? Nam te festiue putas in regem ludere: cui grammaticam deesse,
quemlibet ais puerum uidere: deinde tu tantus grammaticus citatis in
testimonium grammaticis omnibus, et communi omnium sensu: dicis
20   idem esse, Hoc facite, quod hoc facite, quotiescunque feceritis. Si
tantum disputasses illo loco, sic sensisse Christum, et aliqua loquutum
alias, tali gene[LL₁v]re locutionis: ad quae propositum ei non erat,
quenquam obligare: potuisset res utcunque tolerari. Nunc uero,
quum dicis ex grammatica, et communi hominum sensu, idem esse,
25   hoc facite, quod hoc facite, quotiescunque feceritis, ego neminem
esse puerum puto tam rudem grammaticae: qui non rideat tuam
grammaticam: et tibi censeat neque communis hominum sensus,
neque peculiaris, quicquam esse, sed magis pecuinum, quam sit in
ulla pecude: per quem doceamur ex grammatica, et communi sensu
30   sic perpetuo scripturas intelligere, Hoc

Lutheri canon ad interpretandum
scripturas

facite, quotiescunque feceritis. Eleemo-
sinam date, quotiescunque dederitis.
Ieiunate, quotiescunque ieiunaueritis: et ad eundem nimirum
modum deducet: ne furtum facias, quotiescunque non feceris: deum
35   diligite, quotiescunque dilexeritis: et non mechaberis, quotiescunque

---

30 *gloss* ad interpretandum] adinterpretandum *BRL*

singular wisdom took care that the evangelists would write the same
matter a little differently and commit that unforgivable sin against
the papist form of the sacrament, so that He might render us safe from
future superstition and the tyranny of impious men. For he who would
use the form of Luke, Mark, Matthew, Paul, would consecrate no less   5
truly than he who uses the form of this impious and false canon.

Truly the canon of the mass urges you, which you have approved
in one passage and used in your own support; but this has no weight
against you who think nothing is more foolish than that someone
should demand of you that you should stand by your words, you   10
whose constant custom it is whenever you
please to declare unsaid whatever you have   *Luther's constant custom*
said. But I wonder what occasion you have had here of chattering
about the agreement of the evangelists, as if the king had denied that
they say the same thing in different words, or as if any of the evangel- 15
ists has those words which you have selected for confirming your
own position from the canon so often condemned by you. Have you,
by such trifling, hoped to trick your readers, so that they could not
understand how prettily you answer? For you think you make witty
sport against the king; you say that any boy sees that he is lacking in   20
grammar; then you, such a great grammarian, with all grammarians
and the common sense of everyone called on for a witness, say that
"Do this" is the same as "Do this as often as you do it." If only you
had argued that in that passage Christ meant such and such, and that
elsewhere He spoke certain things in such and such a manner of   25
speaking, to which it was not His intention to bind anyone, the
matter could somehow have been tolerated. But now, since you say
that according to grammar and the common sense of men "Do this"
is the same as "Do this as often as you do it," I think that no boy is so
ignorant of grammar as not to laugh at your grammar, and to judge   30
that you have nothing at all of the sense common or proper to man,
but rather a sense more brutish than is in any brute, you through
whom we are taught according to grammar and common sense thus
constantly to understand the scriptural
text, "Do this as often as you do it." Give   *Luther's canon for interpreting*   35
alms, as often as you give them. Fast, as   *scriptures*
often as you fast. And according to the same method he will doubtless
deduce: Thou shalt not steal, as often as you do not; love God, as
often as you love Him; and, thou shalt not commit adultery, as often

non mechatus fueris: et caetera simili ratione et haec est regula
reuerendi patris intelligendi scripturas, ex et grammatica, et sensu
communi, per quam possit effugere, ne quis probare possit euidentibus
scripturis, aut ullam uirtutem praeceptam esse, aut uitium ullum pro-
5 hibitum: et tunc facilius poterit sustinere, quod bona opera nihil
prosunt, nec mala nocent: sed sola fides sufficit ad salutem non ex
promissione Christi, sed ex promissione Lutheri.

Refellit illud absurdissimum Lutheri sophisma: quo
sic argutatur, Sacerdos in missa recipit
10   eucharistiam: ergo non potest
offerre. Cap. XVII. [LL₂]

Verba Lutheri   VBI uero ego scripsissem, sacrificium et
missam pugnare, cum sacrificium offer-
atur, missa uero recipiatur, hic audet audax dominus Henricus
15 Lutherum ad Bibliam prouocare, dicens, Vbi est in ueteri lege uspiam,
ullum sacrificium, quod non simul offeratur, et recipiatur? Plane hic
Lutheri iactitat summum argumentum corruere, securusque triumphat gloriosus assertor. Respondeo. Non est hoc meum summum
argumentum, sed illud, quod supra
20 *Et hoc tibi non dedit rex, si*   dominus Henricus pro Thomistica benig-
satis intelligis   nitate mihi donauit, scilicet missam esse
testamentum et promissionem, hoc inquam, capitale meum argumentum est. Tamen ut triumphatori aliquid suggeram, si dominus
Henricus, solum Bibliam semel aperuisset, et inspexisset, imo si
25 meminisset psalmi quinquagesimi, quem puer olim legit (si Christianus est) non iactasset triumphum tam Thomisticum. Siquidem illic
legisset holocaustum, quo nullum celebrius et maius sacrificium est in
lege. Hoc certe totum soli deo offerebatur, nihil ex eo recipiebatur.

HIC saltem sentiens Lutherus, infirmam esse istam aciem, quam
30 tectissime potest, dat signum receptui: et ait istud non fuisse fortissimum fundamentum suum, sed illud potius, quod missa sit testamentum: quod ait regem illi pro Thomistica ciuilitate donasse: sed

---

1 fueris: et caetera] *corr. err. L*, fueris. Caetera *BR*; haec est] *corr. err. L*, est *om. BR*
2 scripturas, ex et] *corr. err.*, ex *om. BR*, scripturas, & ex *L*   6 sed sola fides] *L*, sed sola
fides, *corr. err.*, sufficit sola fides, *BR*   15 prouocare] pronocare *B*

as you do not commit adultery; and others by a similar reasoning; and this is the rule of the reverend father for understanding scriptures according to both grammar and common sense, according to which rule he can escape anyone's being able to prove by evident scriptures that either any virtue has been commanded or any vice forbidden; and then he will more easily maintain that good works profit nothing nor do evil works cause any harm, but faith alone suffices for salvation, not according to the promise of Christ, but according to the promise of Luther.

> He refutes that most absurd sophism by which Luther quibbles thus: The priest receives the eucharist in the mass, therefore he cannot offer it. Chapter 17.

Where indeed I had written that sacrifice and mass are contrary since a sacrifice is *Luther's words* offered but the mass is received, here the daring Lord Henry dares to summon Luther to the Bible, saying: "Where is there anywhere in the old law any sacrifice which is not at the same time offered and received?" He proclaims that clearly here Luther's foremost argument is destroyed, and the boastful defender triumphs securely. I answer: My foremost argument is not this, but that which above Lord Henry, in his Thomistic goodness, has granted me; namely, that the mass is a *Even this the king did not grant you, if you understand well enough* testament and a promise; this, I say, is my chief argument. Nevertheless, if I may make a suggestion to the conqueror, if Lord Henry had only once opened the Bible and looked into it, indeed if he had remembered the fiftieth psalm which he once recited as a boy (if he is a Christian), he would not have boasted of such a Thomistic triumph, since there he would have read of the holocaust, than which there is no more solemn or greater sacrifice in the law. This certainly was offered wholly to God alone; nothing was received from it.

Here at least Luther, sensing that this line of attack is weak, gives the signal for retreat as covertly as possible and says that his strongest foundation was not this but rather the statement that the mass is a testament, which he says the king in Thomistic politeness has granted

quod omnes uident prius confutatum esse, quam donatum: post ita
donatum, ut quo magis id Luthero donauerit: eo stultiorem Lutherum
probauerit: qui stolide sibi fundamentum sumpserit: quod ei donari
sine ullo incommodo potuerit: donatum nihil ei prorsus profuerit. Et
5 tamen adhuc tam stupidus est: ut id non sentiat: sed ita nitatur illius

Lutherum ipsum iam propemodum
suis diffidere dictis

argumenti ualidissimo robore: ut iam
istud, quod idem non possit offerri, quod
recipitur, habeat propemodum pro dere-
licto: nec tamen uideo, cur alterum sit altero firmius. Nam haec duo,
10 missa est pro[LL₂v]missio: ergo non potest esse opus: et sacramentum
recipitur: ergo non offertur: sunt perquam similia sophismata, uelut
eiusdem mali corui mala oua. Verum fugiens uelitatur tamen, ne se
fugere fateatur. Nam quum sic fuisset argutatus in Babylonica,
Sacramentum altaris recipitur a sacerdote: ergo non offertur deo:
15 nam idem et recipi et offeri non potest: princeps admiratus sophisti-
cationem, quaerit, an non omnia sacrificia in lege Mosaica, et
offerebantur, et tamen recipiebantur ac manducabantur. Hic mirifice
uidetur sibi respondere Lutherus, quum profert unum sacrificium,
quod totum incendebatur: quasi satis esset ipsi, aliquod unum tale
20 reperiri: ac non potius satis esset regi aduersus Lutheri sophisma, uel
aliquod unum fuisse sacrificium: quod et offerebatur et manducabatur. Verum Lutherus, aegregie uidelicet tetigit regem: quia rex de
omnibus dixit: quum iste doceat excipiendum unum. Tanquam si rex

Quam pulchre Lutherus tangat
25 *regem scilicet*

ita quaesisset: quis tam impius est: ut
neget sacrosanctum sacramentum, a sacerdotibus oblatum, prodesse populo? Quis
tam absurdus haereticus: ut putet solam fidem sufficere, et opera
bona non exigi? Quis tam stolidus est: ut censeat populum Christianum nullis obligari legibus? et mille quaestiones huiusmodi:
30 Prosiliat ilico Lutherus, ac suo more, sic derideat principem. Quam
obliuiosus est iste rex: qui tam impium et stolidum asserit esse
neminem, ut dicat talia? Ergo ut huic assertori suggeram: si dominus
Henricus, solum semel aperuisset, et inspexisset libellos meos, non tam
fortiter asseruisset, neminem esse tam impium, neminem esse tam

8–9 derelicto] *corr. err. L*, delicto *BR*

him, but which everyone sees was refuted before it was granted; afterwards it was so granted that the more he granted it to Luther the more foolish he proved Luther, who stupidly took as his foundation that which could be granted him without any disadvantage; having been granted, it profited him absolutely nothing. And yet he is still so stupid that he does not sense this, but so relies on the very powerful strength of that argument that he now considers as almost abandoned this statement that the same thing cannot be offered as is received, yet *That Luther himself now almost distrusts his own words* I do not see why the one is stronger than the other. For these two arguments: "The mass is a promise, therefore it cannot be a work," and "The sacrament is received, therefore it is not offered," are altogether similar sophisms, like the bad eggs of the same bad raven.

But while fleeing, he still skirmishes so as not to admit that he is fleeing. For when he had thus quibbled in the *Babylon*: "The sacrament of the altar is received by the priest, therefore it is not offered to God, for the same thing cannot be both received and offered," the prince, amazed at the sophistry, asks whether or not all the sacrifices in the Mosaic law were both offered and yet received and eaten. Here Luther thinks that he gives a wonderful response when he brings forward one sacrifice which was wholly burned, as if it were enough for himself to find some one such sacrifice and not more than enough for the king against the sophism of Luther that there was even some one sacrifice which was both offered and eaten. But Luther of course has nettled the king exceedingly because the king spoke of all whereas this fellow teaches that one must be excepted. As though the king had asked *How neatly of course Luther stings the king* thus: "Who is so impious that he denies that the most holy sacrament offered by the priests profits the people? Who is such an absurd heretic as to think that only faith suffices and that good works are not required? Who is so dull-witted as to judge that the Christian people are bound by no laws?" and a thousand questions of this nature; Luther would at once leap up and in his usual manner thus jeer at the prince: "How forgetful is this king who declares that there is no one so impious and dull-witted as to say such things. Therefore, if I may make a suggestion to this defender, if Lord Henry had only once opened and examined my books, he would not so boldly declare that there is no one so impious, no one so heretical,

haereticum, neminem esse tam [LL₃] stolidum, siquidem illic,
tam impium ac stolidum haereticum facile uidisset me.

NESCIO quid hic pro se reperiat rex: ego certe nihil reperio, sed
fateri cogor hac sane parte plane uictum esse. Nec enim mihi hoc
5   desumpsi: ut si quid parum caute scriptum sit a rege, defenderem: aut
per calumniam uellicem, si quid forte ueri dicat Lutherus. Imo cupio
potius: ut uterque quicquid errarit, emen-
Candidum authoris institutum
det. Igitur, quemadmodum Luthero suas-
erim: ut tam multas, tam stultas, impie suscitatas haereses, reuocet,
10 atque recantet, ita plane regi consuluerim: ut imposterum calamo
temperet, ac scribat circumspectius: et quoties dicit, nullum sacrificium fuisse oblatum olim, quin idem manducaretur: excipiat holocaustum: Si neget quenquam quicquam creare posse de nihilo,
semper excipiat deum. Si neget ullam uirginem esse quae peperit,
15 excipiat tamen Mariam. Si neget quenquam esse tam impium aut
stolidum: ut hoc aut illud asserat immanis absurditatis haereticum
meminerit in talibus, excipere semper Lutherum.

Quin si rex meus paululum haberet
Verba Lutheri
humani sensus, uerterem triumphi quaes-
20 tionem in eum, et dicerem. Vbi est in lege ullum sacrificium,
quod recipiebatur, et non penitus totum offerebatur? An mihi sacrificium hic faciet, armos, pectuscula, et alia, quae in usum sacerdotum cedebantur? Aut offerre, rex illusor aequiuocus denuo uocabit,
quod per populum et sacerdotes ex agris afferebatur, et appli-
25 cabatur coram domino? Scilicet idem est offerre et afferre apud
dominum Henricum. Verum quid hoc
Hic uos uidemini non satis
ad me, quid nugigerulus fingat? Mihi
tenere uestra biblia
satis est in lege, quicquid offerebatur
deo, totum incendebatur. Quod autem non incendebatur, sed partim
30 sacerdoti, partim populo tribuebatur, non [LL₃v] offerebatur, sed de
oblatis seperabatur et edebatur. Verum quid ista sacra cum pro-
phanis? Igitur in calice meretricis Babylonicae nullum est sacrificium,
quod solum offertur, illa enim sunt Biblia nostri domini Henrici,
Biblia nostra referta sunt talibus sacrificijs.

35 HIC sibi uidetur acutus: et mirum se reperisse putat effugium:

---

4 sane parte plane] parte plane sane *L*   7 errarit] *corr. err. L*, erraret *BR*   10 recantet,
ita] *corr. err. L*, recantet. Ita *BR*   14 excipiat] *L*, excip iat *BR*   24 afferebatur] *corr.*
err. L, offerebatur *BR*   25 offerre et afferre] *corr. err. L*, et afferre *om. BR*

no one so dull-witted, since there he would easily have seen such an impious and dull-witted heretic, me."

I do not know what the king may find here in his defense; I certainly find nothing but am forced to admit that in this matter indeed he is clearly overcome. For I did not take it on myself to defend anything written by the king with too little caution or to belittle with misrepresentation anything true that Luther may happen to say. On the contrary, I rather desire that each should correct whatever error he has made. *The candid intention of the author* Therefore, just as I have urged Luther to revoke and retract so many, such foolish heresies impiously aroused, so I have clearly advised the king to temper his pen in the future and to write more carefully and as often as he says that there was of old no sacrifice offered without its being also eaten, he should except the holocaust; if he should deny that anyone can create anything out of nothing, he should always except God; if he should deny that there is any virgin who has given birth, he should nevertheless except Mary; if he should deny that anyone is so impious or dull-witted as to defend this or that heretical point of monstrous absurdity, let him remember in such matters always to except Luther.

On the contrary, if my king had a little human sense I would turn the triumphant *Luther's words* question on him and say: Where is there in the law any sacrifice which is received and not altogether wholly offered? Or will he mention to me here the sacrifice of the shoulders, the little breasts, and the other things which were granted for the use of the priests? Or will the equivocating king mocker again call it an offering that something was brought from the fields by people and priests and placed before the Lord? Doubtless to offer and to present is the same thing with Lord Henry. But *Here you seem not to have a very good hold on your Bible* what is it to me what the vendor of women's wares pretends? For me it is enough that in the law whatever was offered to God was wholly burned. But what was not burned, but given partly to the priest, partly to the people, was not offered but separated from the offerings and eaten. But what have these sacred things to do with the profane? Therefore in the cup of the harlot of Babylon there is no sacrifice which is only offered, for that is the Bible of our Lord Henry; our Bible is filled with such sacrifices.

Here he thinks he is sharp and he thinks that he has found a

dum distinguit inter afferre et offerre: atque id solum disputat esse
sacrificium: quod incenditur domino: caetera uero, quibus uel
sacerdos uescitur, uel hi, pro quibus offertur, negat esse sacrificium:
hic regnat, hic ridet, hic subsannat papistas: et uelut prophanos, arcet
5 ab his tam sacris distinctionibus: quibus distinguit argute inter afferre
et offerre. Sed interea miror istum reuerendum fratrem: qui miratur
esse quenquam: qui illum prouocet ad biblia, non tenere memoria

Leuitici

caput secundum Leuitici: ubi ita legimus.
Anima quum obtulerit oblationem sac-
10 rificij domino, simila erit eius oblatio. Fundetque super eum oleum,
et ponet thus: ac deferet ad filios Aaron sacerdotis. Quorum unus
tollet pugillum plenum similae et olei ac totum thus, et ponet

*Hiccine pater totum
offerebatur*

memoriale super altare, in odorem suauis-
simum domino. Quod autem reliquum
15 fuerit de sacrificio, erit Aaron et filiorum
eius, sanctum sanctorum de oblationibus domini. Quum autem
obtuleris sacrificium coctum in clybano de simila, panes scilicet
absque fermento conspersos oleo, et lagana azima oleo lita: si oblatio
tua fuerit de sartagine similae conspersae oleo, et absque fermento:
20 diuides eam minutatim, et fundes super eam oleum. Si autem de
craticula fuerit sacrificium: aeque simila oleo conspergetur: quam
offerens domino, trades in manibus sacerdotis. Qui [LL$_4$] cum

*Hic liquet non totum sacrificium
adoleri solitum*

obtulerit eam, tollet memoriale de sacrificio, et adolebit super altare, in odorem
25 suauitatis domino. Quicquid autem reli-
quum est, erit Aaron et filiorum eius, sanctum sanctorum de oblationibus domini. Omnis oblatio, quae offertur domino, absque fermento
fiet: nec quicquam fermenti ac mellis adolebitur in sacrificio domini.
Primitias tantum eorum offeretis ac munera: super altare uero non
30 imponentur in odorem suauitatis. Quicquid obtuleris sacrificij, sale
condies: nec auferes sal foederis dei tui de sacrificio tuo. In omni
oblatione offeres sal.

AN NON hic reuerende pater, manifeste dicit scriptura, id quod

---

7 tenere] *corr. err. L*, teneri *BR*   8 *gloss om. L*   19 sartagine] *L*, sartatagine *BR*

marvelous escape when he distinguishes between presenting and
offering and argues that that only is a sacrifice which is burned for
the Lord; but the other parts, with which are fed either the priest or
those for whom the offering is made, he says are no sacrifice; here he
reigns, here mocks, here he laughs loudly at the papists and keeps 5
them like profane men at a distance from these very sacred things by
means of the distinctions with which he distinguishes subtly between
presenting and offering.

But meanwhile I wonder that this reverend friar, who wonders that
there is anyone who summons him to the Bible, does not remember 10
the second chapter of Leviticus, where we
read as follows: "When anyone shall offer   *From Leviticus*
an oblation of sacrifice to the Lord, his offering shall be of fine flour,
and he shall pour oil upon it, and put frankincense, and shall bring it
to the sons of Aaron, the priest; and one of them shall take a handful 15
of the flour and oil, and all the frankincense, and shall put it as a
memorial upon the altar for a most sweet savor to the Lord. And the
remnant of the sacrifice shall be Aaron's,
and his sons', holy of holies of the offerings   *Is this wholly offered, father?*
of the Lord. But when thou offerest a sacrifice baked in the oven of 20
flour, to wit, loaves without leaven, tempered with oil, and un-
leavened wafers, anointed with oil, if thy oblation be from the frying
of flour tempered with oil, and without leaven, thou shalt divide it
into little pieces and shalt pour oil upon it. And if the sacrifice be from
the gridiron, in like manner the flour shall be tempered with oil. And 25
when thou offerest it to the Lord thou shalt deliver it to the hands of
the priest. And when he hath offered it, he shall take a memorial out
of the sacrifice and burn it upon the altar for a sweet savor to the
Lord. And whatsoever is left shall be
Aaron's and his sons', holy of holies of the   *Here it is clear that the whole*
offerings of the Lord. Every oblation that   *sacrifice was not usually burned*   30
is offered to the Lord shall be made without leaven, neither shall any
leaven or honey be burnt in the sacrifice to the Lord. You shall offer
only the firstfruits of them and gifts; but they shall not be put upon
the altar, for a savor of sweetness. Whatsoever sacrifice thou offerest, 35
thou shalt season it with salt, neither shalt thou take away the salt of
the covenant of thy God from thy sacrifice. In all thy oblations thou
shalt offer salt."

Does not the scripture here manifestly say, reverend father, that

cedet in partem sacerdotum, primum fuisse partem oblationis
sacrificij? deinde idem uocat reliquum de sacrificio: quod, quid aliud
est, quam eam partem sacrificij, quae superest? quod etiam appellat
sanctum sanctorum de oblationibus domini. An ideo uocat sanctum
5 sanctorum de oblationibus domini: quia (secundum praeclaram
rationem paternitatis uestrae) nunquam fuit oblata domino? An
paternitas uestra sic intelligit sanctum sanctorum de oblationibus
domini, id est sic separatum ab oblationibus domini: ut nunquam
fuerit pars illius oblationis, quae tota fuit oblatio domini? Paternitas
10   *Grammatica Lutheri* uestra, saepe iactat grammaticam suam:
             sed si haec sit grammatica uestra: tunc si
uultis dicere, quod non estis asinus: uos habetis necessario concedere,
quod estis de asinis: id est per grammaticam uestram seperatus ab
asinis: sed per caeterorum omnium, id est unus ex asinis: et hic
15 sensus est communior et uerior. Id ipsum etiam ostendit, quod ita
legitur in eiusdem capitis [LL$_4$v] fine. Sin autem obtuleris munus
primitiarum frugum tuarum domino, de spicis adhuc uirentibus,
torrebis eas igni: et confringes in morem farris, et sic offeres primitias
tuas domino, fundens super eas oleum et thus imponens: quia oblatio
20 domini est, de qua adolebit sacerdos, in memoriam muneris: partem
farris fracti et olei ac totum thus. In his uerbis, uidetis pater, quam
manifeste scriptura dicit, totum esse oblationem domini: quanquam
inde partem dumtaxat adolebit sacerdos. Quid illud? Reliquam
            autem partem similae, comedet Aaron
25 *Mirum qui non haec meministis* cum filijs suis, absque fermento. Ideo non
    domine Luthere   fermentabitur: quia pars eius in domini
offertur incensum. At quare non posset fermentari, postquam illa pars
separata est, et incensa: nisi quia id quoque, quod reliquum est, et
non adoletur in incensum, tamen offertur domino. Nam et ante fuit
30 praeceptum: quod omnis oblatio, quae offertur domino, absque
fermento fiet. Manifestum est ergo, hanc quoque partem, quae non
incenditur, sed manducatur a sacerdotibus, oblationem esse, quae
offertur domino. Eamque ob causam, illam quoque partem manducare iubentur, absque fermento: quam alioqui possent fermentare: si
35 sacrificium non esset, sed quod tu dicis separatum. Vis adhuc Luthere

---

30 quae offertur] *corr. err. L*, quod offertur *BR*   32 manducatur] *corr. err. L*, ducatur *BR*

that which falls to the share of the priests was the first share of the oblation of the sacrifice? Next it calls the same portion the remnant of the sacrifice; what else is this than that part of the sacrifice which is left over? It also calls this the holy of holies of the oblations of the Lord. Or does it call it the holy of holies of the offerings of the Lord because, according to the remarkable reasoning of your paternity, it was never offered to the Lord? Or does your paternity thus understand the holy of holies from the offerings of the Lord, that is, as so separated from the offerings of the Lord that there never was a part of that offering which was wholly an offering of the Lord? Your paternity often boasts of his grammar; but if this is your grammar, then if you wish to *Luther's grammar* say that you are not an ass you necessarily have to concede that you are from the asses; this means, according to your grammar, separated from the asses, but according to the grammar of everyone else it means you are one of the asses; and this is the more common and truer sense. This same fact is also shown by what is read at the end of that same chapter: "But if thou offer a gift of the firstfruits of thy corn to the Lord, of the ears yet green, thou shalt dry it at the fire and break it small like meal, and so shalt thou offer thy firstfruits to the Lord, pouring oil upon it and putting on frankincense, because it is the oblation of the Lord, whereof the priest shall burn for a memorial of the gift part of the corn, broken small, and of the oil, and all the frankincense." In these words you see, father, how manifestly the scripture says that the whole thing is an offering of the Lord although the priest will burn only a part of it. What then? But the remaining part of the flour Aaron with his sons shall eat without leaven. It shall not be leavened because a *Surprising that you do not remember these things, my honored Luther* part of it is offered as a burnt-offering of the Lord. But why could it not be leavened after that part was separated and burnt, except because that also which is left and not burnt as a burnt-offering is nevertheless offered to the Lord. For it was also commanded earlier that every offering which is offered to the Lord should be made without leaven. Therefore it is manifest that this part also which is not burned but is eaten by the priests is an offering which is offered to the Lord. For that reason they are ordered to eat that part also without leaven, which otherwise they could leaven if it were not a sacrifice but, as you say, separated.

locum apertissimum? Ista est inquit, lex hostiae pro peccato. In loco ubi offertur, holocaustum immolabitur coram domino, sanctum sanctorum est: sacerdos, qui offert eam,

Hic Luthere uideas non tenere consequentiam tuam, recipitur, ergo non offertur

comedet eam: et rursus, sicut pro peccato offertur hostia: ita pro delicto, utriusque hostiae lex erit una. Ad sacerdotem, qui eam obtulerit, pertinebit. Et iterum. Omne sacrificium similae, quod coquitur in cly[MM₁]bano: et quicquid in craticula, uel in sartagine praeparatur: eius erit sacerdotis: a quo offertur. Hic uides, etiam si
10 pars dumtaxat incenditur: tamen ita scriptura testatur: quod totum offertur: et quod a sacerdote manducandum est ab eo manducari debet: a quo offertur. Et huius rei testimonijs, tam plena est scriptura sacra: ut pene pudeat ista proponere: tanquam res egeret probatione: et tamen admiror, si deessent caetera. Quid dicet uestra
15 fraternitas ad illud sacrificium: de quo scribitur Exhodi, capite. XII. in quo agnus immaculatus masculus immolabatur totus: et totus manducabatur: et dominus doctor Lutherus, docet nos nullum sacrificium manducari solitum apud iudaeos: quia non est idem offerre et afferre. Et haec est illa sacrosancta sapientia: quam non
20 possumus capere, nos qui sumus hebetes et prophani papistae: quam suos docent perfectos acuti isti et sacrosancti potistae.

Redarguit ridiculam arrogantiam Lutheri, qui ridiculum putet, obijci aduersus se authoritatem omnium sanctorum
25 ### patrum. Caput. XVIII.

Verba Lutheri

VLtimo dicta patrum inducit pro sacrificio missario statuendo, et ridet meam stulticiam, qui solus uelim sapere prae omnibus, quod sit stultissimum .&c. Hic dico confirmari hoc nomine meam sententiam, nam hoc est,

---

3 *gloss* Luthere] *L,* luthere *BR*   5–6 pro delicto, utriusque hostiae lex erit una. Ad sacerdotem] *corr. err.,* pro delicto utriusque, hostiae lex erit, una ad sacerdotem *BR,* pro delicto, vtriusque, . . . sacerdotem *L*   11 offertur] *corr. err. L,* effertur *BR*   13 ista] *corr. err. L,* ist *BR*   26 *gloss*] *L, om. BR*

Do you still want a most clear passage, Luther? "This is," it says, "the law of the victim for sin; in the place where the holocaust is offered, it shall be immolated before the Lord. It is the holy of holies. The priest that offereth it shall eat it." And again: "As the sacrifice for sin is offered, so is also that for a trespass; the same shall be the law of both these sacrifices; it shall belong to the priest that *Here, Luther, you may see that your conclusion does not hold: It is received, therefore it is not offered* offereth it." And again: "And every sacrifice of flour that is baked in the oven, and whatsoever is dressed on the gridiron, or in the frying pan, shall be the priest's that offereth it." Here you see, even if only part is burned, nevertheless the scripture thus testifies that the whole is offered and what must be eaten by the priest should be eaten by that one by whom the offering is made. And Holy Scripture is so full of testimonies of this fact that I am almost ashamed to present these as though the matter required proof; and yet I am astonished if others would be lacking. What will your fraternity say to that sacrifice of which Exodus, chapter twelve, writes, in which a male lamb without blemish was wholly immolated and wholly eaten; and the honored doctor Luther teaches us that it was not the custom for any sacrifice to be eaten among the Jews because to offer and to present are not the same thing. And this is that sacrosanct wisdom which we cannot grasp, we who are dull and profane papists, which they teach their initiates, these shrewd and sacrosanct potists.

He convicts the ridiculous arrogance of
Luther, who thinks it ridiculous that the
authority of all the holy fathers is opposed
to himself. Chapter 18.

Finally he brings in the sayings of the fathers for the sake of establishing the *Luther's words* sacrifice of the mass, and he laughs at my folly since I alone wish to know more than everyone, which is most foolish, etc. Here I say that my opinion is confirmed by this name, for this is what I have said, that

quod dixi. Thomisticos asinos nihil habere, quod producant, nisi
multitudinem hominum, et antiquum
Quin et arrogantissimus omnium usum. Deinde ad proferentem scripturas
et gloriae auidissimus
dicere. Tu es stultissimus omnium. Tu ne
5   solus sa[MM₁v]pis? Tunc oportet sic esse. Mihi autem stultissimo
omnium hoc satis est, quod sapientissimus Henricus nullam scripturam
contra me potest producere, nec productas contra se diluere. Deinde
cogitur concedere suos patres saepius errasse, suum antiquum usum
non facere articulum fidei, in quos fidere non licet, nisi ecclesiae illi
10 multitudinis, cuius ipse defensor est cum indulgentijs.

EN iterum, quam magnifice nunc de scripturis a se productis,
tanquam aliquid produxisset ad propositum, aut quasi rex illam
unam, quam detorto collo, secum traxit inuitam, uno uerbo non
sustulisset sacrilego ac plagiario, et germano sensui restituisset: quasi
15 rex illius absurda sophismata non diluisset euidentibus scripturis: ita
nunc impudens audet dicere, scripturas
Audax mendacium et contra se productas non esse: quas ipse
manifestum Lutheri
pro se produxit non esse solutas. Sed illud
uidelicet absurdum est: quod quum uersetur in quaestione: quis nam
20 sit scripturae cuiuspiam propositae sensus, audiat aliquis dicta
sanctorum patrum omnium in idem consentientium praeferre, dicto
unius fraterculi, et sibi dissentientis haeretici. Nam illud est, quo
uideo sic uri (nec sane miror) Lutherum: quod rex ait, mirum esse ex
tot sanctis patribus, ex tot oculis, quot in ecclesia tam multis seculis,
25 idem legerunt euangelium: nullum fuisse unquam tam perspicacem:
ut rem tam apertam, quam hanc uideri uult Lutherus, potuerit
deprehendere. Neminem ergo, qui sapiat, crediturum esse Luthero:
nisi primum doceat, aut aliud euangelium legisse se, quam sancti illi
patres legerunt, aut illud idem uel legisse diligentius, uel intellexisse
30 melius: aut sibi denique maiorem esse curam fidei, quam ulli unquam
hactenus mortalium fuerit. Haec uerba regis absurda uidelicet sunt
Luthero. Ad quae [MM₂] non miror: si cupiat obsurdescere. Nam
certe, quantumuis ille sibi perfricuerit frontem: fieri tamen haud

14 ac plagiario] *L*, acplagiario *BR*

the Thomistic asses have nothing to bring forward but a multitude of
men and ancient usage; that then when someone presents the
scriptures they say: "You are the most
foolish of all men; are you alone wise?"   *Indeed, and the most arrogant*
Then, "It must be so." To me, however,   *of all men and the most*
the most foolish of all men, it is enough   *greedy for glory*   5
that the most wise Henry can bring forward no scripture against me
nor weaken the force of any brought forward against himself. Next, he
is forced to grant that his fathers have quite often erred, that his
ancient usage does not make an article of faith; against them one is   10
permitted to trust only in that church of the multitude with its
indulgences of which he himself is the defender.

   Behold again how pompously he now talks of the scriptures
brought forward by himself, as though he had brought forward anything to the point, or as if the king, with regard to that one text which   15
Luther has seized by the neck and dragged with him by force, had
not with a single word withdrawn it from a sacrilegious and tortured
meaning and restored it to its proper meaning; as if the king had not
demolished   that   fellow's   ridiculous   sophisms   with   evident
scriptures; so now the shameless fellow   20
dares to say that scriptures have not been   *The bold and manifest lie of*
brought forward against him, that those   *Luther*
which he himself has brought forward have not been resolved. But of
course it is absurd that when the point in question is what is the
meaning of any proposed scripture, someone should dare to prefer   25
the sayings of all the holy fathers agreeing on the same point to the
word of a single friarling and heretic inconsistent with himself. For I
see that it is this by which Luther is so inflamed, and I am surely not
surprised, because the king says that it is strange that of so many holy
fathers, of so many eyes as have read the same gospel in the church   30
through so many ages, not one was ever so clear-sighted that he was
able to grasp a matter as clear as Luther would have this one appear.
No one, therefore, who has any sense would believe in Luther unless
he first shows either that he has read another gospel than those holy
fathers read, or that he has read the same one more carefully or   35
understood it better, or finally that he has a greater concern for the
faith than any mortal has ever had up till now. These words of the
king are of course absurd to Luther. I am not surprised if he should
long to be deaf to them. For surely, however much he has laid aside

potest: quin ista mordax ueritas, homini mendaci male perfricet
auriculas etiam quantumuis asininas. Nam quid hic habes Luthere,
quod dicas? Producitur ab alterutro uestrum scriptura: quam
uterque agnoscit pro sacra: sed de sensu non conuenit inter uos: quid

5   hic fiet? quis iudicabit, uter uestrum
Respondebit se utpote   ueriorem afferat illius scripturae sensum.
doctum caelitus   Vter nunc petit aequius? Tu petis tibi
credi, rex uetustis patribus. Quid affers causae, cur hos recuses
iudices? Si lis difficilis est iudicatu, talibus iudicibus opus est: sin

10 facilis, non est alijs facilior, quam fuit illis. Quid illos ab hoc iudicio
reijcis: qui maxime debent recipi? Nam ex his, qui hodie uiuunt, alij
boni sunt, alij mali. Mali tibi propter uitia fauent. Boni propter
eadem tibi sunt infensi. Sic utrosque ab hoc iudicio diuersus affectus
submouet. Antiqui patres odisse te non poterant: qui tot aetatibus

15 ante defuncti sunt, quam quisquam suspicari posset, quod te merdam
talem cacodemon aliquis, aliquando foret excacaturus in terram. An
non, hoc indicium est conscientiae tuae tuo ipsius iudicio damnatis-
sime: quod recuses tales iudices? At idem prius obiecisti, sicut
appellas, papistis: quod illi postulent sibi solis credi: quum tu credi

20 postules apertissimis dei scripturis. Primum te quaeso uir prudentissime, quibus sibi solis postulant credi papistae? uidelicet solis Italis,
                        Hispanis, Germanis, Anglis, et denique
Vide lector: quod Lutherus   solis omnibus, non modo qui uiuunt hodie,
iniquum postulatum uocet   sed et quicunque boni, a Christi morte

25 uixerunt? Tam absurdi sunt: ut postulent credi solis omnibus. At tu
credi postu[MM₂v]las apertissimis dei scripturis: sed quomodo,
precor, apertum uocas: quod in tot seculis, nemo tam oculatorum
uirorum potuit cernere? Deinde quum iam controuersum sit, in
utram partem apertae sint illae scripturae, in tuam ne, an in diuer-

30 sam: quum pro tua parte neminem afferas tuae sententiae, uel
patronum uel testem: quum ecclesia contra te proferat publicum
christianorum omnium consensum: atque antiquorum patrum dictis
probet, idem etiam per tot secula omnes sensisse fideles? quis absurdum

---

5 *gloss* Respondebit] Respondit *L*   16 cacodemon] *corr. err.*, cacodaemum *BR*, cacodaemon *L*   17 indicium] *corr. err. L*, iudicium *BR*

all sense of shame, yet it cannot but happen that this biting truth should also painfully prick the ears, however asinine, of the lying fellow. For what do you have to say here, Luther? Scripture is brought forward by each of you; each of you acknowledges it as sacred; but you do not agree on its meaning; what then shall be done? Who will judge which of you presents the truer meaning of that scripture? Which now seeks more fairly? You

He will answer: himself, as one taught from heaven

seek to have yourself believed; the king seeks to have the ancient fathers believed. What reason do you present for rejecting these judges? If the suit is difficult of judgment, there is need of such judges; but if it is easy, it is no easier for others than it was for them. Why do you cast them out from this judgment who above all ought to be accepted? For of these men who live today, some are good, others evil. The evil men favor you because of your vices. The good for the same reason are hostile to you. Thus differing emotion eliminates both from this trial. The ancient fathers could not have hated you since they died so many ages before anyone could suspect that some cacodaemon would one day cack such dung as you out on the earth. Or is this not evidence of your consciousness of being condemned most completely by your own judgment, that you reject such judges?

But you earlier objected the same thing to the papists, as you call them, that they demand that only they themselves be believed whereas you demand that the most clear scriptures of God be believed. First of all I ask you, most wise man, for what men alone do the papists demand belief? It is only for the Italians, Spaniards, Germans, English, and finally for all men alone, not only who live today but also whatever good men have lived since the death of Christ. They are so ridiculous that they demand that all men alone be

See, reader, what Luther calls an unfair demand

believed. But you demand that the most evident scriptures of God be believed; but how do you call evident, I pray, what for so many ages no one of such enlightened men could discern? Moreover, since it is now a question on behalf of which side those scriptures are evident, on behalf of yours or on behalf of the opposite, since you present no one on behalf of your side as either the patron or witness of your opinion, whereas the church brings forward against you the public agreement of all Christians and proves by the sayings of the ancient fathers that all the faithful have also judged the same thing throughout

censet, nisi tu (qui omnium es absurdissimus) si malint omnes
sibi solis omnibus fidere, quam uni dum-
Hoc non putas absurdum Luthere? taxat infideli tibi? Atque haec quum tam
aperta sint: ut ea uel caecus aperte cernat: nec suum casum Lutherus
5　(quo turpissime deiectus est) aut sentire possit, aut tegere: tamen
(sicut ebrij solent) uigilans somniat delyria: et magnifice sibi decernit
triumphum.

Hic, inquit, sedeo. Hic sto. Hic maneo.
Lutheri uerba. Non est opus Hic glorior. Hic triumpho. Hic insulto
insultare, nam hae portae tibi papistis, Thomistis, Henricistis, sophistis,
10　*patent* et omnibus portis inferi. Neque curo, si
contra me stent mille Augustini, et mille Cypriani.

NVNC tibi Luthere uideris, te gessisse strenue: quasi uero magna
res sit, ad istum modum furiosum furere: et (quod deploratis haere-
15　ticis accidit miserrimum, postquam in profundum desperationis
deciderint) iam cuncta prorsus humana et diuina contemnere.
Vtinam miselle super te non urgeret os suum puteus. Tum te uideres
miser, et deplorares infelicem fortunam tuam: ac sermone uerso
clamares. Heu miser huc cecidi, huc detrudor, hic iaceo, hic derideor,
20　hic crucior, hic trucidor in profundo Baratri: hic super me clauserunt
portas suas omnes inferi: hinc in [MM₃] illa tremenda die, me
producent daemones ad iudicium: heu miserum me, quam miserandum spectaculum. Ibi tunc insultabunt mihi, quibus ego nunc
insulto, papistae, Thomistae, Henricistae, Augustini, Cypriani, et
25　omnes superi. Tunc me contemptum a Christo, quem ego prius in
ecclesia sua sanctisque contempseram, rursus reducent cacodaemones:
et portas rursus occludent inferi. Ibi iacens pauper, cum damnato
diuite, cruciatus flamma multis frustra gemitibus implorabo millies,
ut unus Augustinus, aut unus Cyprianus, quorum prius demens
30　millies, mille contempsi, uel uno digitulo in aquam tincto, linguam
mihi maledicam, et blasphemiae poenas ardore dantem, refrigeret:
atque haec ut uera Luthere futura sunt, nisi resipueris: ita deum

so many ages, who judges it ridiculous, except you who are the
most ridiculous of all men, if all men prefer to trust all themselves
alone rather than only you, a single
infidel? And although these things are so   *Do you not think this ridiculous,*
clear that even a blind man clearly dis-   *Luther?*   5
cerns them, and that Luther can neither endure nor conceal his own
overthrow, by which he is most disgracefully thrown down, nevertheless, as drunkards usually do, while waking he dreams mad dreams
and solemnly decrees a triumph for himself.

Here, he says, I sit. Here I stand. Here   10
I remain. Here I boast. Here I triumph.   *Luther's words. It is not necessary*
Here I leap with insults on the papists,   *to insult them for these gates lie*
                                                  wide open for you
the Thomists, the Henricists, the sophists,
and all the gates of hell. And I do not care if a thousand Augustines, a
thousand Cyprians, stand against me.   15

Now, Luther, you think you have acted vigorously, as if indeed it
were a great matter to rage in this raging mad manner, and, as
happens most wretchedly to abandoned heretics after they have fallen
into the depths of despair, now to contemn absolutely everything
human and divine. Would that the dungeon would not press its   20
mouth upon you, wretched little fellow. Then you would see yourself
wretched and would bewail your unhappy fortune and would cry out
with changed words: Alas, here have I fallen wretchedly, here I am
thrust down, here I lie, here I am jeered at, here I am tormented, here
I am cut down in the depths of the whirlpool, here all hell has closed   25
its gates upon me, from here on that terrible day the demons will lead
me forth to judgment; alas, wretch that I am, how miserable a spec-
tacle. There then those men will insult me whom I now insult, the
papists, Thomists, Henricists, Augustines, Cyprians, and all the
saints. Then, contemned by Christ whom I formerly had contemned   30
in His church and saints, the cacodaemons will lead me back again
and hell will shut up its gates again. Lying there a pauper together
with the condemned Dives, tortured with flame, I will implore a
thousand times with many vain groans that one Augustine, or one
Cyprian, of whom I, a thousand times mad, formerly contemned a   35
thousand, with even one little finger dipped in water might cool my
cursing tongue as it pays with burning the punishment of blasphemy;
and as these things will be true, Luther, unless you return to your

precor, ut mente reddita resipiscas miser, ac falsa facias.

Verba Lutheri   Turpissimum est tanto regi tantum librum scribere, et hoc caput meum, nempe
quod missa sit testamentum, nolle tangere. Nec est repertus, qui
5   unquam ausus sit tangere. Quotquot huc appropiant, fugiunt per
septem uias retrorsum, qui magno impetu et clamore triumphali, per
unam uiam irruerunt. Mirum est, quam uellent hic nocere, quam

Quale spectrum sit Lutherus   graue sit hoc spectrum in oculis eorum.
Sed nullus prudentius sese hic gessit, rege
10   Henrico, qui Lutherum uastaturus, protestatur sese hoc robur non
tacturum. Sed nec habeo nec ago gratias tantae beneuolentiae, imo
male ualeat ira, et furor eius, si nocere potest, et non facit.

ECCE iam decimo lector, istam ridiculam gloriam, quod neque
rex, neque quisquam ausus sit, illud insanum Lutheri caput tangere:
15   sed tam terribile et furiale spectrum sic horruerint omnes: ut quicunque per unam uiam ingressi sunt: per septem fugerint retrorsum. O
terribilem furiam. Imagi[MM₃v]natur (opinor) se nunc apud inferos
esse Cerberum: et suis se cathenis iactantem, umbras illic rictu et
latratu territare. Sed rex, quem Lutherus ait prudenter esse pro-
20   testatum, se caput illud insanum non

Lutheri cerbereum caput a rege   tacturum: ita tamen illud uno ictu con-
comminutum   tudit: ut prorsus in frusta disciderit. Tum
reliquum corpus ita concussit: ut nulla paralysis ullum corpus magis
posset soluere.

25   Furorem uero eius, quo inuehitur in me,

Verba Lutheri. Ergo quid sibi   quod docuerim, fidem sine operibus opti-
uult qui bene egerunt. &c.   mam praeparationem ad sacramentum,
et christianos non oportere legibus astringi ad percipiendum, contemno. Sunt enim uerba hominis, qui putet homines apud deum
30   legibus fieri bonos, minus sciens, quid sit fides, et opera, et quid leges
operentur malorum in conscientijs, quam insensatus iste stipes. Non
enim papistarum est haec nosse, sed (ut Petrus et Iudas dicunt)
ignorata tantum blasphemare. Conscientijs enim non legibus, sed
sola gratia consulitur, legibus, praesertim humanis, miserrime con-
35   ficiuntur.

---

16 fugerint] *corr. err. L,* fugierunt *BR*   18 rictu] *L,* rinctu *BR*   24 posset] *corr. err. L,*
possit *BR*   26 *gloss* egerunt] *L,* egernnt *BR*

senses, so I pray God that with your mind restored you may regain
your senses and make them false.

It is very mean in such a great king to
write such an important book and not to   *Luther's words*
wish to touch this my head point, namely that the mass is a testa-   5
ment. Nor has it been discovered who has ever dared to touch it.
However many draw near to this point, they flee back by seven paths
who with great force and with a triumphal shout rushed in by one
path. It is strange how they would wish to do harm here, how serious
this spectre is in their eyes. But no one has
conducted himself more shrewdly here   *What a spectre Luther is*   10
than King Henry, who, ready to destroy Luther, declares that he will
not touch this argument. But I neither have nor give thanks for such a
great kindness; rather, let his wrath and raging fury enjoy bad health
if he can do harm and does not do it.   15

Behold now for the tenth time, reader, this ridiculous boast, that
neither the king nor anyone has dared to touch that insane head point
of Luther, but that such a terrifying and raging spectre has so
frightened everyone that whoever have approached by one path,
retreated by seven. O terrifying fury! He imagines, I think, that he is   20
now Cerberus in hell and that, throwing himself about in his chains,
he affrights the shades there with his snarling and barking. But the
king, who Luther says has shrewdly declared that he will not touch
that insane head point, has nevertheless so
crushed that head with one blow that he   *The Cerberean head of Luther*
has cut it completely to pieces. Then he   *crushed by the king*   25
has so shattered the rest of the body that no paralysis could destroy a
body more.

But I contemn his madness with which he
inveighs against me, because I have   *Luther's words. What then he*
taught that faith without works is the   *means by those who have*   30
best preparation for the sacrament and   *done well, etc.*
that Christians ought not to be bound by laws to receive it. For they are
the words of a man who thinks that men become good before God
through laws, knowing less of what faith and works are and what laws   35
operate in the consciences of wicked men than this irrational block of
wood. For it is not like papists to know these things, but, as Peter and
Jude say, only to blaspheme what they do not know. For consciences
are advised not by laws but by grace alone; by laws, especially by
human ones, they are most miserably destroyed.   40

HIC in media furia Lutherus, lucido saltem gaudet interuallo, dum locum hunc salebrosum transilit per contemptum. Nam facilius est ei rationes principis contemnere, quam sua delyramenta defendere. Siquidem christianos omnes, omnibus legibus solutos esse, nec ullis
5 quenquam legibus obligari posse, et quoniam conscientijs gratia consulitur: ideo leges abrogandas esse, ne quis gratiae negligens, saltem cohibeatur a scelere: et uelut ouis errabunda pastorali baculo retrudatur in uiam. Ista certe tam

Hunc facile uincet Lutherus contemnendo

admiranda paradoxa, nunquam intellexit
10 princeps: sed nec apostolus ecclesiae papisticae Paulus, qui legem esse bonam dicit et iusticiae uinculum. Sed nec illud unquam rex (opinor) quiuit intelligere: quod optimum sit ad sacramentum ac[MM₄]cedere, bonis operibus quam maxime fieri potest uacuum. Nam sicut ecclesia confessionem prae-
15 mittit: ut recepturus quisque ueniat liber a uitijs: Ita Lutherus confessione contempta, reseruatis uitijs, cauet, ne quis ueniat segnior impeditus uirtutibus: et solam fidem praedicat sine bonis operibus sufficere. Sed haec sacrosancta mysteria, non est papistarum nosse: imo nec hominum, nec angelorum, nec ipsius etiam Christi, nisi forte
20 nunc tandem didicit a Luthero. Nam olim certe nesciuit: quum per os apostoli Iacobi dixit, Fides sine operibus

Nunquid hic Luthere exigit bona opera

mortua est: et suo ipsius ore pronunciauit, Qui bene fecerunt, ibunt in uitam aeternam: qui uero male, in ignem aeternum. Quamobrem candide lector,
25 qui iam tandem docet, tam stupenda dogmata: non est ille certe stupidus et insensatus stipes: sed homo sensus eximij planeque dignus, cuius tam sensatum caput sentiat insensatos stipites.

---

16 cauet] *corr. err.* L, caueat BR   21 *gloss* Luthere] L, luthere BR

Here in the midst of his madness Luther enjoys at least a lucid interval, when he leaps over this rugged passage by contempt. For it is easier for him to contemn the reasons of the prince than to defend his own ravings, that indeed all Christians are released from all laws, nor can anyone be bound by any laws, and because consciences are advised by grace, therefore the laws should be abrogated, lest anyone heedless of grace should at least be restrained from crime and like a wandering sheep be thrust back onto the path by the shepherd's staff. The prince has certainly never understood these amazing paradoxes; but *Luther will easily conquer this man by contemning him* neither has Paul the apostle of the papistic church, who says that the law is good and the bond of justice. But neither, I think, could the king have ever understood the statement that it is best to approach the sacrament as empty as possible of good works. For as the church sets confession before communion so that everyone may come to receive it free from vices, so Luther, contemning confession, retaining vices, warns that no one should come more sluggishly weighed down by virtues; and he preaches that faith alone without good works suffices. But it is not like the papists to know these sacrosanct mysteries; indeed, it is not like men, nor angels, nor even Christ Himself, unless perchance He has now finally learned from Luther. For at one time He certainly did not know them, since through the mouth of the apostle James He said: "Faith without works is dead," and by His own mouth He declared: "Those who have done good *Does he not here, Luther, demand good works?* shall go into life everlasting, but those who have done evil, into everlasting fire." Therefore, honest reader, he who now at last teaches such amazing doctrines, he is certainly not a stupid and irrational block of wood, but a man of unusual understanding and clearly a very rational head worthy of understanding irrational blocks of wood.

Refellit stolidam Lutheri calumniam, qua regis argumentum quoddam deprauat, ut uideatur uincere. Cap. XIX.

5

Verba Lutheri

Sed in fine huius loci, operae precium est uidere, quam anxie laboret, ut traditiones hominum necessarias statuat aduersus meam sententiam, qua statui extra scripturas nihil esse statuendum, aut si statuitur, liberum et non necessarium habendum, cum simus domini etiam

10 sabbati per Christum liberatorem. Arguit itaque rex. Primo sic. Si nihil seruandum est, nisi quod scripturis proditum est, quum scriptum non sit, sacramentum esse a Christo sumptum, sequetur, nec sacerdotes posse sa[MM₄v]cramentum sumere. Hac Thomistica hypothesi fretus, sic reducit syllogismum contra me. Sacerdotes sumunt sacra-

15 mentum necessario, et hoc non habet euangelion, ergo et alia extra

Miror, cur tibi tam odiosus sit diuus Thomas

euangelion sunt obseruanda necessario. Hoc Thomistice concluditur per regulam consequentiarum illis familiarem, quae uocatur petitio principij. Nam quod necessarium sit, sub peccato

20 mortali sumi a sacerdotibus sacramentum. Rex primum probare debuit. Ego enim liberum esse dico sumi et non sumi a sacerdotibus. Necessarium autem est per traditiones hominum et usum multorum. Quare Thomisticus rex ualde bene probat traditiones per traditiones,

Quam scurratur hic scurra

negatum per negatum, talibus enim non

25 aliis probationibus niti debet assertio sacramentorum, et tota Henricalis Ecclesia.

PROFECTO lector, Lutherus esset hoc loco non inamoenus nebulo: si regis ratio fuisset redargutioni tam commoda: quam Lutherus eam fingit in suum commodum. Nam quae iam respondet,

30 non sunt irridicula, sed omnino nihil ad rem. Nam (ut Horatius ait) nunc non erat his locus: id quod tu facile uidebis lector: quum uerba regis audieris: ad hunc enim modum se habent.

Verba regis

"NVNC ueniamus ad exemplum Christi: quo nos arbitratur Lutherus

---

He refutes the stupid misrepresentation with which Luther distorts a certain argument of the king so that he may seem to conquer it. Chapter 19.

But at the end of this passage it is worth seeing how anxiously he strives to estab- *Luther's words* 5
lish necessary traditions of men against my judgment by which I established that outside of the scriptures nothing should be established, or if it is established it should be considered free and not necessary, since we are lords even of the sabbath through Christ the liberator. 10 And so the king argues first of all thus: If nothing must be retained except what has been delivered by the scriptures, since it is not written that the sacrament was received by Christ, it will follow that neither can the priests receive. Relying on this Thomistic hypothesis, he thus raises this syllogism against me: Priests necessarily receive the sacra- 15 ment and the gospel does not have this; therefore other practices also must necessarily be observed without the gospel. This is Thomistically concluded through the rule of consequences familiar to them, which is called *I wonder why Saint Thomas is* begging the question. For the king should *so hateful to you* 20
first have proved that it is necessary under pain of mortal sin that the sacrament be received by priests. For I say that priests are free to receive and not to receive. But it is necessary through the traditions of men and the usage of many. Therefore the Thomistic king very well proves traditions through traditions, that which is 25 denied through what is denied, for on
such proofs, not on others, is the defense *Now this buffoon plays the* of the sacraments and the whole Henrical *buffoon* church supposed to rely.

Indeed, reader, in all this passage Luther would be a not un- 30 pleasant rascal, if the reasoning of the king had been as convenient to refutation as Luther fashions it to his convenience. For what he now answers is not unwitty but altogether beside the point. For, as Horace says, it was not now the place for these things; as you will easily see, reader, when you have heard the words of the king, for they are as 35 follows:

"Now let us come to the example of Christ by which Luther thinks that we are *The king's words*

uehementer opprimi: propterea quod Christus in coena sacramento non usus est pro sacrificio: nec obtulit patri. Ex quo probare conatur: quod missa, quae respondere debet exemplo Christi, quo fuit instituta, non potest esse sacrificium, nec oblatio. Si Lutherus tam rigide
5 nos reuocet ad exemplum coenae dominicae: ut nihil sacerdotes permittat facere: quod ibi Christus fecisse non legitur: sacramentum, quod consecrant, nunquam recipient.

Hic ostenditur absurditas Lutheri

Suum enim corpus Christus in euangelio non legitur re[NN₁]cepisse. Nam quod
10 doctores aliquot, eum recepisse tradunt: et quod idem canit ecclesia: nihil potest pro Luthero facere: quum illi neque doctores omnes, neque totius ecclesiae fides, ullam faciat fidem: neque credendum censeat quicquam (nam ita scribit in sacramento ordinis) nisi firmatum scripturis, et ijsdem etiam claris, cuiusmodi certe scripturas,
15 non opinor, inueniet: quod suum corpus in coena receperit Christus. Ex quo sequetur (ut dixi) nec sacerdotes debere, quod consecrant, ipsi recipere: si tam rigide nos obstringat Lutherus, ad exemplum coenae dominicae. Quod si ideo concedat recipiendum sacerdotibus: quia recaeperunt apostoli: et eos contendat id iussos facere: quod tunc
20 apostoli fecerunt, non quod Christus: hac ratione nunquam consecrabunt sacerdotes. Consecrabat enim Christus non apostoli."

VIDES hic lector, quod Lutherus argumentabatur ab exemplo Christi: sacerdotem offerre non posse corpus Christi: propterea quod Christus, cuius exemplo missa debet respondere, corpus suum in
25 coena non obtulit. Rex (ut audisti) respondit: quod si Lutherus nihil permittet, sacerdotem in missa facere: quod Christus, ex euangelio, fecisse non probatur in coena: non licebit sacerdoti, recipere corpus Christi, quod ipse consecrauit: quia in coena non legitur Christus recepisse, qui consecrauit. Quod si Luth-

Regis dilemma aduersus argumentum Lutheri

30 erus diceret ideo sacerdotes recipere: quia iussi sint id facere: quod apostoli tum fecerunt, non id quod Christus: hac ratione non consecrarent sacerdotes. Nam Christus consecrabat, non apostoli. Vbi est igitur, iste syllogismus: quem [NN₁v] Lutherus ait regem contra se colligere.

---

7 *gloss* absurditas Lutheri] ab– *BR, gloss om. L*   13 quicquam (nam ita scribit in sacramento ordinis) nisi] *corr. err. L,* quicquam. nam ita scribit in sacramento ordinis. Nisi *BR*
14 scripturas] *corr. err. L,* scripturis *BR*

violently overthrown, because at the supper Christ did not use the
sacrament as a sacrifice, nor did He offer it to the Father. From which
he tries to prove that the mass, which ought to correspond with the
example of Christ by which it was instituted, can be neither sacrifice
nor oblation. If Luther recalls us so strictly to the example of the   5
Lord's supper that he does not permit priests to do anything which
Christ is not read to have done there, then they will never receive the
sacrament which they consecrate. For we
do not read in the gospel that Christ   *The absurdity of Luther is here*
received His own body. The fact that   *shown*   10
several doctors teach that He did receive it and that the church proclaims the same teaching can give no support to Luther, since he does
not place any faith in all the doctors or in the faith of the whole
church, and he thinks that nothing at all should be believed except
what is confirmed by scriptures and those clear ones, for this is what   15
he writes on the sacrament of orders; I am sure that he will not find
in this sort of scriptures that Christ received His own body at the
supper. It will follow from this, as I said, that priests should not
receive what they themselves consecrate, if Luther binds us so strictly
to the example of the Lord's supper. But if he grants that it should be 20
received by priests on the grounds that the apostles received and
argues that they are commanded to do what the apostles then did, not
what Christ did, then according to this reasoning priests will never
consecrate. For Christ, not the apostles, consecrated."

You see here, reader, that Luther was arguing from the example of   25
Christ that the priest cannot offer the body of Christ because Christ,
to whose example the mass ought to correspond, did not offer His
body at the supper. The king, as you have heard, answered that if
Luther permits the priest to do nothing in the mass which Christ is
not proved according to the gospel to have done at the supper, the   30
priest will not be permitted to receive the body of Christ which he
himself has consecrated, because Christ who consecrated is not read
to have received at the supper. But if
Luther said that the priests receive because   *The king's dilemma against the*
they are ordered to do that which the   *argument of Luther*   35
apostles then did, not that which Christ did, then by this reasoning
the priests would not consecrate. For Christ, not the apostles, consecrated. Where then is this syllogism which Luther says that the king
sets up against him? There is absolutely none such in the king's work,

Nihil est prorsus apud regem tale: nec erat apud regem tali syllogismo locus: quum non hoc ageretur: quod Lutherus agi finxit: an
sacerdos necessario reciperet: sed quod ei recipere fas non esset, a
semet ipso consecratum corpus Christi, si Lutheri ualeret ratio: quae
5 ideo prohibebat, ne offerret sacerdos: quia non obtulit Christus: quae
Lutheri ratio etiam prohibet, ne recipiat sacerdos: quia non recepit
Christus. Vbi nunc ergo repperit illud argumentum Lutherus: quod
regem scribit facere? An non manifestum est, ipsum ex se finxisse:
nimirum ut haberet aliquid: in quod lepide posset ludere? I nunc, et
10 nega Lutherum esse lepidum, et facetum scurram. Iam et id, quod
sequitur, est altera pars eiusdem festiuae dicacitatis.

                 Verba Lutheri   Secundo, inquit sic, Christus sacramen-
                                      tum consecrauit, non apostoli, ergo non
licebit apostolis aut sacerdotibus consecrare, quia non licet aliud
15 statuere aut facere, quam scriptura habet. Quod si, miser ille Lutherus,
hic uelit effugere et dicere. Christus mandauit apostolis consecrare,
ubi dicit, Hoc facite, praeoccupat impropitius meus dominus
Henricus, dicens, Hoc esse dictum de recipiendo, non de consecrando,
Christe seruator, quam inaudita caecitas, et amentia est in istis
20 hominibus.

     Mimesis uerborum Lutheri   **CHRISTE** seruator, quantus nugator
                                     et calumniator est pater potator. Nam
neque sic potest effugere per id quod Christus iussit apostolos consecrare. Nam hoc iubendo, iussit eos tantum facere: quod ipse fecerat.
25 At hoc erat consecrare, tantum quod alijs darent. Nam Lutherus, qui
nihil recipit, nisi scripturas euidentes: probare non potest: quod
Christus suum corpus receperit: ergo [NN₂] adhuc nihil probat
Lutherus: nisi quod ex sua ratione tantum consecrabit sacerdos: non
recipiet, quod consecrabit. At apostoli, dices, prius iussi manduca-
30 bant. Verum dicis: sed non quod ipsi consecrabant: ergo nullo modo
potes exire Labyrinthum hunc: quin, si restringas sacerdotes ad
exemplum coenae dominicae: sacerdos non recipiet sacramentum:
quod ipse consecrat. Nam hoc nemo fecit in coena: sed sicut nemo
          Collectio ab exemplo   sua manu baptizatur, nemo sua manu
35   absoluitur: ita nemo sacerdos recipiet

---

4 Christi, si Lutheri] *corr. err. L*, Christi. Si Lutheri *BR*   21 *gloss* Mimesis] *L*, mimesis
BR   34 *gloss* Collectio] *L*, collectio *BR*

nor was there place for such a syllogism in the king's work, since there was being discussed not this which Luther pretended, whether the priest necessarily received, but that it was not right for him to receive the body of Christ consecrated by himself, if Luther's reasoning was valid, which forbade the priests to offer because Christ did not offer; which reasoning of Luther also forbids the priest to receive because Christ did not receive. Where then does Luther now find that argument which he writes that the king makes? Is it not clear that he himself has fashioned it himself, doubtless so that he might have something against which he could make mocking sport? Go now and deny that Luther is a witty and merry buffoon. Now that also which follows is the second part of the same witty raillery.

Secondly he says this: Christ, not the apostles, consecrated the sacrament; *Luther's words* therefore it is not permitted to the apostles or the priests to consecrate because it is not permitted to establish or do anything other than the scripture contains. But if that wretched Luther should wish to escape here and to say, "Christ commanded the apostles to consecrate when He says, 'Do this,'" my Lord Henry ungraciously seizes on this, saying that this was said about receiving, not about consecrating. Christ our Savior, what unheard of blindness and madness is in these men.

Christ our Savior, what a great trifler and pettifogger is father toper. For neither *Mimicry of Luther's words* can he thus escape through the fact that Christ ordered the apostles to consecrate. For by ordering this, He ordered them to do only what He Himself had done. But this was to consecrate only what they would give to others. For Luther, who receives nothing but evident scriptures, cannot prove that Christ received His own body; therefore Luther still does not prove anything, except that according to his reasoning the priest will consecrate only; he will not receive what he consecrates. But the apostles, you will say, ate before they were ordered to do so. True, but not what they themselves consecrated; therefore you cannot escape this labyrinth by any means; indeed, if you restrict the priests to the example of the Lord's supper, the priest will not receive the sacrament which he himself consecrates. For no one did this at the supper, but as no one is *Inference from example* baptized by his own hand, no one is absolved by his own hand, so no priest will receive the sacrament

sacramentum: quod ipse consecrauit. Et sic adhuc procedit argumentum regis, penetrans nebulam: quam nebulo conatur offundere.

IAM quod ait regem preoccupare hoc uerbum, Hoc facite, dictum esse de recipiendo, non de consecrando, uere praeoccupat istud pater
5 potator, mentiendo. Neque enim dixit istud usquam rex: quod quum ita sit: flaccet plane reuerendi patris illa faceta scurrilitas: qua sic

*Insulsi sales Domini doctoris
Martini*

interrogat ineptus regem. Domine Henrice, qua grammatica didicit dominatio uestra? quis uocabularius uobis dixit: Hoc facite,
10 id esse, quod Accipite. Et deinde respondet ipse pro rege. Respondebit, inquit, oportet sic esse: quia nomina sunt ad placitum.

PROFECTO domine Luthere, quando nihil serio disseritis: sed tantum tam stulte luditis: et cum aliorum calumnia inuentum uestrum proprium deridetis: nomen uestrum ex Luthero fiet
15

*Quin aiunt hoc esse illi patrium
nomen forte fatis inditum, ut
Hippolitum, et eiusmodi*

Luderus: quia oportet sic esse: idque non per Aristotelem, per quem nomina imponuntur ad placitum: sed secundum Cratilum Platonis, de recta nominum
ratione: aut (quem uideo magis familiarem uobis) secundum
20 Albertum, de modis significandi: qui scripsit [NN₂v] etiam uobis illum tractatulum, de secretis mulierum. Nam sicut apud illum, lapis est quasi ledens pedem: sic uos Luderus eritis, quasi ludens herus. Sed in hoc demiror stulticiae uestrae mirabilem dotem: quod nunquam fere prodit, nisi duplex. Alij fuisset satis, stolidum sic risum
25 captasse, ex eo dicto regis, rex quod nunquam dixerat. At uobis non fuit satis, nisi id dictum rideretis, quod etiam si quis diceret, ridiculus esset, non qui diceret, sed qui rideret. Nam quaeso uos domine, qua grammatica didicit dominatio uestra? quis uocabularius uobis dixit, eum non recte loqui? qui, quaerenti quid fecerit, respondeat, man-
30 ducaui, aut bibi. Imo ut plane uideas istum risum te captasse stolide, uide apostolum aperte referentem uerbum istud, Hoc facite, ad receptionem. Sic enim recitat. Accipite et manducate, hoc est corpus

---

7 *gloss* Insulsi] *L*, insulsi *BR*   18 de recta] *corr. err. L*, directa *BR*   29 eum non] *corr.
err. L*, non *om. BR*

which he himself has consecrated. And thus the argument of the king still proceeds, penetrating the cloud which the rascal tries to pour out.

Now as for his statement that the king seizes on the word, "Do this," saying that it was said about receiving, not about consecrating, truly father toper seizes on this by lying. For the king never said this; since this is so, that witty buffoonery of the reverend father clearly flags, with which he thus foolishly interrogates the king: Lord Henry, from what grammar did your lordship learn? What vocabulary or glossary said to you that "Do this" is the same as "Receive"? And then he himself answers for the king; "He will answer," he says, "it should be so," because names are arbitrary.

Honored Doctor Martin's tasteless wit

Indeed my honored Luther, since you discuss nothing seriously but only mock so foolishly and together with misrepresentation of others you deride your own discovery, your name "Luder" will be fashioned from Luther, because it should be so; and that not according to Aristotle by whom names are imposed arbitrarily, but according to Plato's *Cratilus* on the right meaning of names; or, one who I see is more familiar to you, according to Albert on the modes of signification, who also wrote for you that little treatise *On the Secrets of Women*. For just as with him a stone is as it were something wounding the foot, so you will be Luder as though a mocking-master. But in this passage I am amazed at the wonderful wealth of your folly, that it almost never makes an appearance except doubled. For another it would have been enough in this way to have sought a stupid laugh from that statement of the king which the king never said. But for you it was not enough, unless you would laugh at that statement regarding which even if someone said it, not he who said it but he who laughed at it would be ridiculous. For I ask you, my honored sir, from what grammar did your lordship learn? What glossary told you that he does not speak accurately who, on being asked what he has done, should answer, "I ate or drank"? On the contrary, so that you may clearly see that you have gained this laugh stupidly, see the apostle clearly referring this word, "Do this," to the reception of the sacrament. For thus he recounts: " 'Take and eat, this is my body which shall be delivered for you; do this in

Indeed they say that in this way a name was bestowed perhaps by the fates on some of the fathers, like Hippolytus and such

Apostoli uerba in sententiam regis

meum: quod pro uobis tradetur: hoc facite in meam commemorationem. Similiter calicem, postquam coenauit, dicens. Hic calix nouum testamentum est, in meo sanguine. Hoc facite, quoties-

5 cunque biberitis, in meam commemorationem. Quotiescunque enim .&c.

QVID apertius, quam haec uerba, Hoc facite, referri per aposto-lum ad receptionem? de quo tamen rex, quantum ego uideo, ne uerbum quidem dixit: sed dominus Luderus illudit apostolum.

10 Irascitur ei credo, quia timet, ne praeclarae diuisionis suae, quae sequitur: praeoccupare uideatur apostolus, et tollere partem alteram. Ita enim pergit pater Luderus ludere.

Lutheri uerba. Cur ergo tu fatue non intelligis clarius

Sed iam dimissis istis porcis, dicamus, Christus sumendi usum instituit, quando

15 dixit, Accipite et manducate, ut uerba ipsa [NN₃] apertissima testantur, non quidem Henricis istis et truncis, sed quibusuis pueris et fatuis. At consecrandi officium insti-tuit, dum dicit, Hoc facite. Facere enim, est hoc totum imitari, quod ipse tunc fecit.

20 HIC reuerendus pater, dimissis porcis papistis, uertit se ad asinos Lutheristas, uidelicet electos discipulos suos, dicens, Sed nunc dimissis porcis dicamus: quasi dicat, non sunt margaritae meae proijciendae ante porcos: sed uos, quos elegi, quos luto laui, quos purgaui stercore, quos haeresibus inflaui, quos sanctificaui schismate:

25 uobis inquam, datum est nosse mysteria mea. Et iam incipit eis exponere scripturam, et uitans morem Thomisticum et scholasticum, sequitur simplicitatem euangelicam, et Christi uerba partitur in duo, docens Christum duo docere, usum sumendi, et officium consecrandi. Primum ibi, Accipite et manducate. Secundum ibi, Hoc facite .&c.

30 Circa quae (secundum doctrinam reuerendi patris) notandum, quod Christus instituit omnibus, usum istius sacramenti, in memoriam sui: ut quilibet secum statueret: utrum uellet uti, an negligere: et ideo Christus dixit, Hoc facite in commemorationem meam: id est, eligite uel facere uel non facere: in cuius confirmationem, Christus, quum

---

1 *gloss* Apostoli] *L*, apostoli *BR*   8 de quo] *corr. err. L*, de *om. BR*   13-14 *gloss* Cur . . . clarius] *om. L*

remembrance of me.' Likewise the cup
after He supped, saying, 'This cup is the
new testament in my blood; do this, as
*The apostle's words for the
opinion of the king*

often as you shall drink it, in remembrance of me. For as often,
etc.'"

What is clearer than that these words, "Do this," are referred by the
apostle to the reception; about which nevertheless the king, so far as I
see, has said not even a word, but the honored Luder makes sport of
the apostle. He is angry at him, I believe, because he is afraid that
the apostle seems to seize on and take away the other part of his
remarkable division which follows; for thus Father Luder proceeds
to mock.

But now, dismissing these pigs, let us say:
Christ instituted the practice of receiving
when He said, "Take and eat," as the
words themselves most clearly testify, not
*Luther's words. Why then,
simpleton, do you not
understand more clearly?*

indeed to these Henries and blockheads, but to any boys and simpletons whatever. But He instituted the office of consecration when He
says, "Do this," for to do is wholly to imitate this which He Himself
then did.

Here the reverend father, dismissing the papist pigs, turns to
Lutherist asses, that is, his elect disciples, saying: "But now, dismissing
the pigs, let us say," as though he should say, "My pearls are not to
be thrown before pigs, but you whom I have chosen, whom I have
washed with mud, whom I have cleansed with dung, whom I have
puffed up with heresies, whom I have sanctified with schism, to you
I say it is given to know my mysteries." And then he begins to
expound the scripture to them, and, avoiding the Thomistic and
scholastic manner, he follows the simplicity of the gospel and divides
the words of Christ into two parts, teaching that Christ teaches two
things, the practice of receiving and the office of consecrating; the
first by the words, "Take and eat," the second by the words, "Do
this, etc." Concerning these things, according to the teaching of the
reverend father, it must be noted that Christ instituted for everyone
the use of this sacrament in remembrance of Himself, so that anyone
at all might determine for himself whether he wished to use or ignore
it, and therefore Christ said, "Do this in remembrance of me"; that
is, choose either to do or not to do; in confirmation of which Christ,

dixisset, Hoc facite, protinus adiecit in memoriam mei, quasi diceret,
permitto uobis liberum, utrum uelitis esse
Instituti Christi interpretatio memores, an immemores mei: sicut et
Lutherana liberum permitto mihi, utrum uelim esse
5 memor, an immemor uestri. Et hanc doctrinam ubique docuit
reuerendus pater, in Babylonica, in Assertionibus, in isto libello
contra regem, iterum atque iterum inculcans, et regi obijciens, etiam
extra proposi[NN₃v]tum, nempe nihil tale dicenti.

ERGO postquam ita dilucide docuit suos discipulos: ilico spaciatur
10 in campo suo. Nam peregrinatur animus illi, quamdiu ratione res
agitur: at quum peruentum est ad conuitia: tum demum redit
domum.

Verba Lutheri   Quid dicam, inquit, istis sacrilegis por-
tentis, qui talibus argumentis indicant,
15   quam ex impotentissima inuidia sic scripserunt, ut nihil ineptius
et insulsius fingi possit. Si enim hoc argumentum stolidi regis ualet, in
nulla re licebit Christum imitari. Finge enim Christum non instituisse,
consecrare sacramentum, quod impossibile est, tamen exemplum
consecrandi ostendit, et scribi uoluit, nisi rex noster id contendat, nos
20   neque orare, neque benefacere, neque pati oportere, quia nihil de
nostris orationibus, operibus, et passionibus, scriptum est, Vincit me
tedio plane, regis stolidissimi immensa stoliditas.

STRENVE profecto conuitiatus es, sed in caput tuum omnia. Nam
id, quod insectaris: ipse dixisti, non rex. Quaeso te, ubi dixit rex, nos
25 tam rigide obligari, ad exemplum Christi in coena? Imo tota ratio
eius militat aduersus stulticiam tuam: qua tu uolebas omnes tam
rigide obstringere ad exemplum Christi: ut quia Christus illic non
obtulit corpus suum patri: ideo nec sacerdos nunc possit offerre. Rex
contra probauit, et ostendit ex hoc stulto commento tuo, quanta
30 sequerentur absurda. Nam eo modo sequitur, ut sacerdos aut consecrare non debeat: aut non debeat manducare, quod ipse consecrarit.
Praeterea docuit, uel te fatente, licere aquam uino miscere, quod non
quadrat ad exemplum coenae dominicae. Et tu nunc scommata iactas

---

18 consecrare] consecrasse *L*   19 consecrandi] *L*, consecandi *BR*   29 et ostendit ex]
corr. err. L, ut ex *BR*   31 aut non debeat] *corr. err. L*, aut non debuit *BR*

when He had said, "Do this," immediately added, "in memory of me," as though He said: "I grant you the free choice whether *The Lutheran interpretation of the institution by Christ* you wish to be mindful or unmindful of me, just as I grant myself the free choice whether I wish to be mindful or unmindful of you." And this teaching the reverend father everywhere teaches, in the *Babylon*, in the *Assertions*, in this book against the king, again and again insisting on it and throwing it up against the king, even apart from his intention, for he says nothing of the sort.

Therefore, after he has thus clearly taught his disciples, he promptly roams about in his own arena. For his mind wanders abroad as long as a discussion demands the use of reason; but when it comes to a matter of railing, then, and then only, does it feel perfectly at home again.

> What shall I say, he says, to these sacrilegious monstrosities, who indicate by *Luther's words* such arguments how they have thus written from the most unrestrained envy so that nothing more silly and foolish can be fashioned? For if this argument of the dull-witted king is valid, then we will be permitted to imitate Christ in nothing. For suppose that Christ had not instituted the consecration of the sacrament, a thing which is impossible, nevertheless He showed the example of consecrating and wished it to be written down; unless our king argues that we ought neither to pray nor do good nor suffer because nothing has been written about our prayers, works, and sufferings. The boundless stupidity of the most stupid king quite overcomes me with weariness.

You have railed vehemently indeed, but all against your own head. For that which you rail at, you yourself, not the king, have said. I ask you, where has the king said that we are so strictly bound to the example of Christ at the supper? On the contrary, his whole reasoning wars against your folly, by which you wished to bind everyone so strictly to the example of Christ that because Christ did not there offer His body to the Father neither can the priest therefore now offer it. On the other hand, the king has proved and shown from this foolish trick of yours what great nonsense would follow. For in that manner it follows that the priest should neither consecrate nor should he eat what he himself has consecrated. Besides he has taught, even by your admission, that it is permitted to mingle water with the wine, a thing which does not square with the example of the Lord's supper.

in eum, tanquam nimis nos stringentem ad exemplum coenae dominicae: quum id solus facias ipse. Et interim omnes [NN₄] tibi portenta sumus et porci.

Lutherus in alio ridet, quod is in se admittit

Probat Luthero, certum esse non posse, quomodo
sit consecrandum corpus Christi, nisi
per fidem ecclesiae.
Cap. XX.

SED QVONIAM tibi Luthere nos papistae porci sumus: quid si quispiam ex porcis his ingrediatur asininum gregem uestrum: et tibi, tuo gregi mysteria tua rudenti, obgrunniat hoc pacto. Saluete grex asinorum, tuque adeo salue Luthere, magister et dux asinini gregis, asine maxime. Audio te iamdudum multa rudissime rudentem de missa. SED hic, te quaeso, magister asine, quoniam solus sapis in missa: quoniam ea uidisti: quae (si uera iactas) uidit ante te nemo: qui repperisti missam non esse sacrificium: et, qui sacrificium uocat, damnasti canonem: qui, cum canone falso, ut uocas, et erroneo falsitatis et erroris damnasti christianos sacerdotes omnes: quicunque fere a Christo passo missam celebrarunt: qui nihil credis dei spiritu sancto: qui Christi regit ecclesiam: qui ecclesiam facis omnino nullam: si illa non sit, cuius canon, missam appellat oblationem et sacrificium. Qui omnia uis esse libera: quae probari non possunt euidente scriptura: quam ipsam, quum libet, uel dubiam fingis esse, uel ad euidentem torques absurditatem: nec de euidentia eius, uelis cuiusquam stare iudicio, ne totius orbis qui-dem, sed solius tuo: ut scripturam euiden-tem esse, nihil aliud sit, quam euidentem [NN₄v] abs te dici: quaeso te tante missator, quid tu nobis probare potes de missa: si quis interim praetereat authoritatem ecclesiae: et tuis te petat artibus? Dic mihi, quomodo scire potes: aut quid sit

Scit enim neminem pro se sententiam laturum

---

30 sit] *corr. err. L*, scit *BR*

And now you hurl jeers at him as though he too strictly binds us to the example of the Lord's supper, whereas you yourself alone do that. And all the while we are all portents and pigs to you.

Luther mocks in another what he allows in himself

He proves to Luther that it cannot be certain how the body of Christ must be consecrated except through the faith of the church. Chapter 20.

But because to you, Luther, we papists are pigs, what if some one of these pigs should step in among your herd of asses and as you were braying your mysteries to your herd should grunt at you in this manner: Hail, herd of asses, and hail to you also, Luther, master and leader of the asinine herd, ass supreme. I have for a long time now heard you braying many things most ignorantly about the mass.

But here I ask you, master ass, since you alone understand the mass, since you have seen those things which, if your boasts are true, no one has seen before you, you who have discovered that the mass is not a sacrifice and who have condemned the canon which calls it a sacrifice, you who together with the false and erroneous canon as you call it have convicted all Christian priests of falsehood and error who, almost from the time of Christ's passion, have celebrated the mass, you who do not at all believe the Holy Spirit of God who rules the church of Christ, you who cause there to be no church at all if that one is not the church whose canon calls the mass an oblation and a sacrifice, you who wish all things to be free which cannot be proved by evident scripture, which very scripture, whenever you please, you either pretend is doubtful or twist it to an evident absurdity; nor, concerning its evidence, would you wish to stand by the judgment of anyone, not even of the whole world, but by your own alone, so that for scripture to be evident is nothing else but to be called evident by you; I ask you, great authority on the mass, what you can prove to us about the mass should someone meanwhile pass over the authority of the church and attack you with your own tricks? Tell me how you

For he knows that no one would vote for him

missa, aut quomodo celebranda, aut quibus omnino uerbis peragatur consecratio? Doces missam esse uerba Christi, cum signo uisibili: et addis. Verba illa Christi sunt ista. Coenantibus uero eis .&c. Primum quam scite istud, quod uerba Christi uocas, quae sunt euangelistae:

5 cuius generis si quid dixisset rex: qui tot stultorum genera ibi finxisti stolide, ubi nulla fuit stulticia nisi tua: quot et quales stultos lepide finxisses hic: ubi tam uera daretur occasio? Sed omissa ista stulticia tua, quaero, qua scriptura probas illa uerba euangelij, esse de substantia missae? Sed hic memini, respondebis non esse. Nihil enim

10 referre, cuius euangelistae uerbis, peragatur. Hac de re tecum non contendam: sed interim tamen memineris: ne (quod in rege facis) posthac fingas esse concessam: nam hoc ego integrum mihi seruari uolo, qui probare non dubitem, potius ex canone, quam omnibus euangelistarum libris esse consecrandum. Sed interim istud quaero,

15 qua scriptura probas esse de substantia missae: ut ullum legatur euangelium? Nam si non est: falsa esset

Perperam definiri missam a   tua finitio: qua missam esse definis prom-
Domino Martino   issionem, et euangelij uerba cum sensibili

signo adiuncto. Sin contendis esse de substantia missae: ut aliquod in

20 missa legatur euangelium: quum nihil ualere dicas, praeter euiden-tem scripturam: proba nobis per euidentem scripturam: quod hoc sit de substantia missae: ut aliquod in missa legatur euangelium. Docet nos doctor Mar[OO₁]tinus doctrinam Christi, circa missam: et rem dilucide diuidit, dicens Christum instituisse usum sumendi

25 illic, Accipite et manducate: et officium consecrandi illic, quum dicit. Hoc facite. Ergo si ad officium consecrantis pertinet, in missa legere euangelium: continetur in illis uerbis, quibus Christus tradit illud officium. At illa uerba nobis exponit clarissime doctor Martinus. Facere (inquit) est hoc totum imitari, quod ille fecit. Ergo praesidere

30 debet aliquis: qui panem accipiat, benedicat, ac frangat, donetque discipulis. At interim, nihil hic uideo scripturae: quae uel euidenter,

---

25 illic] ibi *B*; illic] ibi *B*   28 uerba] uetba *B*

can know either what the mass is or how it should be celebrated, or
by what words the consecration is accomplished. You teach that the
mass is the words of Christ with a visible sign, and you add: those words
of Christ are these, "But while they were at table, etc." First of all,
how clever it is that you call the words of Christ those which are of the   5
evangelist; if the king had said anything like that, how many and
what kind of fools would you have wittily fashioned here where such
a true opportunity would be given, you who have stupidly fashioned
so many kinds of fools there where there was no folly but your own?
But, leaving aside this folly of yours, I inquire by what scripture do   10
you prove that those words of the gospel are about the substance of the
mass? But here, I remember, you will answer that they are not. For
it does not make any difference by which evangelist's words it is
accomplished. I will not argue with you about this matter, but yet at
the same time do you recall it, so that you do not later pretend that it   15
was granted to you, as you do with the king; for I wish this
point to be retained integrally for me who do not hesitate to prove
that the consecration must take place according to the canon
rather than according to all the books of the evangelists.

But meanwhile I ask this: by what scripture do you prove that it is   20
of the substance of the mass that any gospel be read? For if it is not,
your definition would be false by which
you define the mass as a promise and as *That the mass is defined perversely*
the words of the gospel with a sensible *by the honored Martin*
sign added. But if you argue that it is of the substance of the mass   25
that some gospel be read at the mass, since you say that nothing is
valid except evident scripture, prove to us through evident scripture
that it is of the substance of the mass that some gospel be read at
the mass. Doctor Martin teaches us the doctrine of Christ about
the mass and he divides the matter clearly, saying that Christ insti-   30
tuted the practice of receiving by the words, "Take and eat," and
the office of consecrating when He says, "Do this." Therefore, if it
belongs to the office of the one consecrating to read the gospel at
mass, it is contained in those words by which Christ handed over that
office. But Doctor Martin expounds those words to us most clearly.   35
To do, he says, is to imitate wholly this which He did. Therefore
someone should preside who should take the bread, bless and break
and give it to the disciples. But meanwhile I see no scripture here
which either evidently or obscurely commands that the gospel be

uel obscure iubeat euangelium legi: quo tu Luthere uis contineri
promissionem: quae cum adiuncto sacramento constituat missam.
Nam quum dicit, Hoc facite, quod ego facio: non iussit euangelium
ullam recitari: ipse enim nullum recitabat.

5   VIDES hic Luthere missator egregie, qui ueterem missam reijcis,
reperire te nusquam posse quicquam: unde nobis istam tuam nouam
defendas. AN dices, necessaria ratione recitandum euangelium: quia
nisi per aliqua uerba illius euangelij, non fieret a sacerdote consecratio? Ego istud fateor esse uerum: quia sic me docet ecclesia: quia
10   sic Christus docet ecclesiam. At tu, qui nihili facis ecclesiam: qui
Christum blasphemas, qui docet ecclesiam: qui te protestaris nihil
habere pro certo, praeter euidentes scripturas: nunquam facies
                                 euidens ex scriptura, praesertim si quis tuo
Iam uideas Luthere tuam missam   tibi more respondet: quod per ulla euan-
consecrari non posse
15   gelij uerba fieret consecratio. Nam ut interim omittam, quod possem illud uerbum, Hoc facite, referre ad
receptionem, idque ex au[OO₁v]thoritate apostoli: posito tamen (ut
tu rem peritior apostolo tenedia bipenni diuisisti) referatur illud ad
officium consecrandi: quid habes tamen illic: quod probet consecra-
20   tionem peragi uirtute quoruncunque uerborum, illius euangelij?
An ista uidelicet, Hoc est corpus meum? Quo pacto probas istud?
Praeceptum ibi non legis: ut illa uerba dicantur, sicut in euangelio
recitantur, per modum narrantis historiam. Si uis ibi facere, quod ille
facit tum sicut iubet Christus, cum dicit, Hoc facite, debet sacerdos in
25   missa non per modum recitantis historiam, sed admonentis et
affirmantis, dicere, hoc est corpus Christi: sicut ipse non narrauit, sed
admonuit, et affirmauit, quum dixit. Hoc est corpus meum. Quid hic
dices: si contemnis ecclesiam? Quando facies hanc scripturam euidentem pro missa ut probes, necesse esse, illud euangelium in missa
30   legi? Atque haec possem defendere contra te, etiam si probasses,
Christum in illis uerbis, Hoc est corpus meum, peregisse consecrationem. Nunc uero ne in hoc quidem potes probare tu. Nam si dicas,
ilico post illa uerba fuisse corpus eius: mihi licet dicere fuisse, prius-

---

1 euangelium] *B corr. err. L*, euangelum *R*   11 nihil] *BL*, nihill *R*   13 *gloss* Luthere]
L, Luihere *R*, luthere *B*   14 ulla] *BR*, nulla *corr. err. L*   23–24 historiam. Si . . . facit
tum sicut iubet Christus,] historiam (si uis ibi facere, quod ille facit) tamen sicut iubet
Christus, *B*   25 historiam] *BL*, hostoriam *R*   29 pro missa] *B corr. err. L*, pro mis-:as
R   32 ne in hoc] in *om. L*

read, in which you, Luther, wish the promise to be contained, which together with the adjoined sacrament constitutes the mass. For when He says, "Do this that I am doing," He did not command that any gospel be recited, for He Himself was not reciting any.

You see here, Luther, outstanding authority on the mass who cast out the old mass, that you can nowhere find anything with which to defend that new mass of yours. Or will you say that by necessary reasoning the gospel must be recited because the consecration would not be brought about by the priest except through some words of that gospel? I admit that this is true, because the church teaches me so, because Christ teaches the church so. But you, who despise the church, who blaspheme Christ who teaches the church, who protest that you hold nothing as certain besides evident scriptures, you will never make it evident from scripture, especially if anyone answers you in your *Now you may see, Luther, that your mass cannot be consecrated* own manner, that the consecration would take place through any words of the gospel. For, to omit for the time being that I could refer the words, "Do this," to the reception, and that on the authority of the apostle, yet, setting this aside, as you, more expert than the apostle, have divided the matter with a Tenedian two-edged axe, let those words refer to the office of consecrating, what do you yet have there which proves that consecration is accomplished by the power of any words whatever of the gospel? Is it these words, namely, "This is my body"? How do you prove this? You do not read there a precept that those words should be said as they are recited in the gospel in the manner of one relating an account. If you wish to do there what He does, then, just as Christ commands when He says, "Do this," the priest in the mass should, not in the manner of one relating an account but as one admonishing and declaring, say, "This is the body of Christ," just as He Himself did not relate but admonished and declared when He said, "This is my body."

What will you say here, if you contemn the church? When will you make this scripture evident for the mass so as to prove that it is necessary for that gospel to be read in the mass? And I could defend these things against you even if you had proved that in those words, "This is my body," Christ accomplished the consecration. But now, not even in this can you prove anything. For if you say that immediately after those words His body was present, I may say that it was

quam frangeret: sicut apostolus dicit: Panis, quem frangimus, participatio corporis est. Nam quum ita recitant euangelistae: Accepit
panem, benedixit, ac fregit, et dedit discipulis, dicens: Hoc est corpus
meum, qua scriptura uel ratione posses refellere: si contenderem in
5 illa benedictione peregisse mutationem, et iam existens suum corpus,
fregisse et tradidisse, et id, quod res erat, dixisse: Hoc est corpus
meum: quippe quod corpus fuerit antequam illa uerba proferre
cepisset. Haec aduersus [OO_2] te facile possem defendere. Facile
possem tueri, sine ullo prorsus uerbo euangelij, posse consecrari solo
10 proposito et benedictione. Imo tolle, quod tu conaris, authoritatem
spiritus sancti, gubernantis ecclesiam: et faciam, quod ante dixi: ut
sudes satis, priusquam possis ostendere: quum duo tantum sacramenta
relinquas, Baptismum et Eucharistiam:

Quomodo uitabis hoc definitor   cur alterutrum eorum ex finitione tua,
eximie

15   sacramentum sit, potius quam illa lotio,
qua Christus lauit apostolorum pedes? Nam et illic etiam erat signum
sensibile lotionis, sicut in baptismo, et adeo necessaria promissio: ut
recusanti Petro minaretur: Nisi te lauero, non habebis partem
mecum. Deinde sicut in coena dixit, Hoc facite: ita hic quoque dixit,
20 accurate, proposito ipsius exemplo: debetis et uos alter alterius lauare
pedes. Quid posses hic dicere: si quis

Id quod solet alias, tu   tibi, qui tantum ponis duo, contenderet ex
mentiris

scriptura tibi sumendum tertium: cui com-
petat definitio tua, promissio uidelicet gratiae, cum sensibili signo:
25 qua scriptura posses istud euitare? nec hoc posses repellere, nec
missam ipsam statuere. Nam postquam mihi licet, contra uocabularia
tua, ex authoritate Pauli, uerbum illud Hoc facite, referre ad receptionem: iam tu, quum uolo, detruderis ab altera parte diuisionis tuae:
qua doces in illo uerbo, tradi consecrationis officium: et absurdum
30 esse, si quis illud referat ad receptionem. Et iam pro authoritate
consecrandi retrudam te: ut quaeras quidlibet. Quod si concedam
illa uerba referri ad officium consecrandi: nihilo tamen magis

---

14 *gloss* eximie] eximie? *L*; alterutrum] *BL*, aulterutrum *R*   25 repellere,] *BL*,
repellere. *R*   26–27 uocabularia tua] uocabularios tuos *B*   27 illud] illud, *L*
27–28 receptionem: iam] *RL*, receptionem. Iam *B*   28 detruderis] *B corr. err. L*,
deteuderis *R*

present before He broke the bread, as the apostle says: "The bread which we break is the sharing of the body." For when the evangelists thus recount: "He took the bread, blessed and broke and gave it to the disciples saying, 'This is my body,' " by what scripture or reasoning could you refute me if I argued that in that blessing He accomplished the change, and that then He broke and handed over His body which was present and said this, which was a fact, "This is my body," namely, what was His body before He began to utter those words? I could easily defend these arguments against you. I could easily defend the statement that without any word of the gospel at all the consecration could take place, merely by the presentation and blessing of the bread.

In fact, take away, as you try to do, the authority of the Holy Spirit governing the church, and I shall accomplish what I said before: that you will sweat aplenty before you can show, since you leave only two sacraments, baptism and the eucharist, why either of these is a sacrament according to your definition rather than that washing by *How will you avoid this, definer extraordinary?* which Christ washed the feet of the apostles. For even there also there was a sensible sign of washing, just as in baptism, and a promise so necessary that when Peter refused he was threatened: "Unless I wash you you shall have no part with me." Then, just as at the supper He said, "Do this," so here also He said precisely, after having presented His own example, "You also ought to wash one another's feet." What could you say here if anyone should argue *That which you are accustomed to say elsewhere: a lie* against you who lay down only two sacraments that according to scripture you should take up a third, to which your definition fits, namely, a promise of grace with a sensible sign; by what scripture could you avoid this? You could neither beat off this argument nor establish the mass itself. For after I am permitted, contrary to your glossaries, on the authority of Paul, to refer this text, "Do this," to the reception, then when I please you would be dispossessed of the other part of your division by which you teach that in that word the office of consecration is delivered and that it is absurd for anyone to refer it to the reception. And then I shall thrust you back, so that you will seek for anything whatever in defense of the authority of consecrating. But if I should grant that those words are referred to the office of consecrating, you will not any the more have

effeceris: ut probare possis euidente scriptura: quibus modis, aut
uerbis, missa peragenda sit. Neque haec [OO₂v] perinde dico, quasi
res ita sit: sed quod tu nunquam possis refellere, quin ita sit: si quis
tuo more tecum disputet. Nos uero qui

5   *Christi fidem constaturam etiam*   certum esse scimus, Christum per apostolos
    si nullum extet euangelium
    scriptum   suos ecclesiae tradidisse sacramenta sua:
certi sumus de numero, de forma, de ritu:
nec essemus incerti, etiam si nullum unquam euangelium scriptum
esset. Sic enim tradidit Paulus Corinthijs: sicut acceperat a domino.

10 Atque istud per sermonem tradiderat, ante scriptam epistolam, ex
nullis euangelistarum codicibus. Neque cuiquam dubium est, etiam
missam celebratam esse millies, antequam scripsit Mathaeus. Haec ex
prima traditione perpetuo more, seruata est. Hanc spiritus Christi
seruat, in ecclesia. In illa inquam ipsa ecclesia: quae docet, quodnam

15 uerum sit euangelium. Ab hac ecclesia, tibi discenda est missa: si recte
missam uoles dicere. Alioqui dubius et incertus circumfereris, omni
uento doctrinae: et omnia perduces in dubium: quod plane solum
paras: nec aliud moliris omnino, quam ut missam, et sacramentum,
et omnia sacra, uelut incerta tandem omnes missa faciant.

20   Ostendit pulchre, quomodo Lutherus irretitus
            confessione propria, frustra iam conatur elabi,
                uarie uersans uerbum Augustini, et
              argutans inepte inter ius iudicandi
                    dogmata, et ius condendi
25   iura. Cap. XXI.

            Lutheri uerba   Quare ad summum principium per-
                                  fidiae, eius calamum uertamus, quod est
uerbum Augustini. Euangelio non crederem, nisi [OO₃] me ecclesiae

---

5–6 *gloss* euangelium scriptum] scriptum *om. B*   12 Mathaeus] Matthaeus *BL*; Haec]
Nec *B*   15 recte] *B corr. err. L*, tecte *R*   17 et] *BL*, er *R*   23 inter ius] interius *L*

succeeded in being able to prove by evident scripture by what means
or words the mass must be accomplished. And I am not saying these
things just as if the matter were true, but because you can never disprove that it is true if someone should dispute with you in your own
manner. But we who know that it is certain *That faith in Christ would* 5
that Christ delivered His sacraments to *stand firm even if no*
the church through the apostles, we are *written gospel existed*
certain about the number, about the form,
about the rite; nor would we be uncertain even if no gospel had ever
been written. For Paul delivered it to the Corinthians just as he had 10
received it from the Lord. And he had delivered it through a discourse before the writing of the epistle, not relying on any books of the
evangelists.

Nor does anyone doubt that the mass was also celebrated a
thousand times before Matthew wrote. This was preserved according 15
to the primitive tradition by uninterrupted custom. This the Spirit
of Christ preserves in the church. In that very church, I say, which
teaches which is the true gospel. From this church you must learn
about the mass, if you wish to speak correctly about the mass.
Otherwise you will be borne about in doubt and uncertainty by 20
every wind of doctrine, and you will reduce everything to doubt; this
is clearly your only purpose, and you strive for nothing else at all than
that everyone should finally consider the mass and the sacrament and
all holy things dismissed as uncertain.

He shows excellently how Luther, ensnared by 25
his own confession, now tries in vain to escape,
variously twisting the word of Augustine and
quibbling foolishly between the right of judging
doctrines and the right of establishing laws.
Chapter 21. 30

Therefore let us turn his pen to the ulti- *Luther's words*
mate source of perfidy, which is the word
of Augustine: "I would not believe the gospel if the authority of the

authoritas commoueret, hoc uerbum sacrilegi eo torquent et de-
prauant, ut ecclesiae, hoc est meretrici Romanae (cui praeter titulum
nihil est ecclesiasticum, aut Christianum) tribuant ius, leges condendi.
Huic addit dominus Henricus, ut eiusmodi uerbi authoritate, etiam
5   me urgeat per propria uerba, ubi dixi, Apud Ecclesiam esse ius
                                           iudicandi quaelibet dogmata. Ego nulla
         Et ego nulla re tibi uideo opus   re uideo huic rudissimo capiti regis opus
              esse quam mente sana
                                           esse, quam uocabulario Gemma, uel
Breuiloquo, ut uocabula cum pueris inciperet discere, nisi id ex mera
10   Thomistarum nequitia facit, ut omnia uocabula, omnia significare
cogat, ut etiam hic ius iudicandi idem sit, quod ius statuendi uel
condendi leges. Breuiter, si Augustinus, etiam rotundis uerbis
asseruisset, ius esse alicui in Ecclesia leges condendi, quis est Augustinus? Quis nos coget illi credere? Qua authoritate eius uerbum est
15   articulus fidei? Fateor, receptum est eius uerbum, sed non satis
tutum neque firmum. Diuino edicto probandum est ius legis con-
dendae, non humano. Nunc autem Augustini uerbum non simpliciter
uitiant. Ille enim loquitur de Ecclesia per orbem diffusa, cuius est de
dogmatibus iudicare. Illi hoc tribuunt papae, quem ipsimet con-
20   fitentur membrum diaboli saepius esse, et errare. Nec solum ei
iudicandi, uerum etiam et condendi ius et copiam faciunt. Proinde
opus est, ut rudibus istis sophistis, hic declaremus, quid intersit, inter
ius iudicandi seu cognoscendi, et inter ius condendi seu imperandi.
De doctrina cognoscere et iudicare, pertinet ad omnes et singulos
25   Christianos, et ita pertinet, ut anathema sit, qui hoc ius statuit
inuictis et uariis sententiis. Matth. Attendite a falsis prophetis, qui
                                           ueniunt ad uos in uestimentis ouium.
         Aduersus doctores tales qualis   Hoc uerbum certe dicit ad populum,
            est Lutherus. Ex ecclesiae
           catholicae doctrina iudicat   aduersus doctores, et mandat eis, ut
30   *quisque docentes haeretica*   falsa dogmata eorum uitent. At quomodo
                                           uitare possunt, nisi cognoscantur? quo-
modo cognoscere, nisi ius habeant iudicandi? Nunc autem non solum
ius, sed praeceptum iudicandi statuit, ut haec sola authoritas, satis
esse queat aduersus omnium pontificum, omnium patrum, omnium
35   consiliorum, omnium scholarum sententias. [OO₃v] Quae ius
iudicandi, solis episcopis, et ministris tribuerunt, et impie ac sacrilege

---

2–3 (cui . . . Christianum)] (cui praeter titulum nihil est) ecclesiasticum, aut Christianum *B*
8 uocabulario Gemma,] uocabulario, Gemma, *B*   10 Thomistarum] *BL*, Thomestarum
R   21 et copiam] et *om. BRL*   26 Matth.] *B*, Marth. *R*, Matth. 6. *L*   27 *gloss*
Aduersus] *L*, aduersus *BR*   32 iudicandi?] *B adds* Statuit, ut haec sola authoritas, satis
esset preceptum iudicandi. *See n.*   33 praeceptum iudicandi statuit, ut] praeceptum
iudicandi. Statuit, ut *B*

church did not persuade me"; this word the sacrilegious men twist and pervert to the extent that they attribute to the church, that is, to the harlot of Rome, who except for her title has nothing either ecclesiastical or Christian, the right of establishing laws. To this Lord Henry adds that by the authority of the same kind of word he also presses me by my own words, when I said that in the church there is the right of judging any doctrine whatever. I see that this most ignorant head of the king needs nothing but a dictionary or glossary so that he might *And I see that you need nothing but a sound mind* begin to learn words with the boys, unless from sheer Thomistic wickedness he does this so that he may force all words to signify all things, so that here also the right of judging is the same as the right of establishing or founding laws.

Briefly, if Augustine had declared even in well-polished words that anyone in the church has the right of establishing laws, who is Augustine? Who will force us to believe him? By what authority is his word an article of faith? I admit his word has been accepted, but it is not sufficiently safe or firm. The right of establishing law must be proved by divine edict, not by human. But now they do not simply corrupt the word of Augustine. For he speaks of the church spread throughout the world, whose right it is to judge concerning doctrines. This they attribute to the pope whom they themselves confess to be very often a member of the devil and to be in error. And they not only give him the right and the power of judging but also even of founding law. Accordingly, it is necessary that we declare here to these ignorant sophists what is the difference between the right of judging or investigating and the right of establishing or commanding. To investigate and judge about doctrine belongs to each and every Christian, and it belongs in such a way that he is anathema who has established this right by invincible and varying opinions. Matthew: "Beware of false prophets who come to you in sheep's clothing." This word he certainly says to *Against such doctors as Luther* the people against these doctors and *is. According to the doctrine* commands them to avoid their false *of the catholic church each one judges those who* teachings. But how can they avoid them *teach heretical doctrines* unless they investigate them? How investigate unless they have the right of judging? But now he has established not only the right but the command to judge so that this authority alone can be enough against the opinions of all popes, all fathers, all councils, all schools. These opinions have attributed the right of judging to bishops and ministers alone, and have impiously and sacrilegiously snatched it away from the people, that is, from the

*O pestiferam glossam, ut
quilibet unus iudicet
aduersus uniuersos*

populo, id est Ecclesiae reginae rapu-
erunt. Stat enim Christus dicens, Attendite a falsis prophetis. Huic subscribunt
ferme omnes omnium prophetarum
5 syllabae. Quid enim agunt prophetae, nisi quod populum monent,
ne falsis prophetis credat. At quid est, hoc monere, nisi iudicandi et
cognoscendi ius, penes populum esse declarare, et confirmare,
ipsumque sui operis monefacere, et excitare, aduersus omnes omnium
suorum sacerdotum, et doctorum doctrinas. Quare hic concludimus,
10 quoties Moses, Iosue, Dauid, omnesque prophetae, in ueteri lege
populum a falsis prophetis uocant, et monent, toties clamant, man-
dant, confirmant, excitant, ius cognoscendi et iudicandi omnium
omnia dogmata. At hoc infinitis locis faciunt. Habet hic Henricus
noster, aut ullus impurus Thomista, quod istis ogganniat? Nonne

15   *Minime uero, nam tuum os
hiat adhuc*

obstruximus os loquentium iniqua?
Redeamus ad nouam legem. Christus,
Ioan .x. dicens, Oues meae uocem
meam audiunt. Vocem uero alienorum non audiunt, sed fugiunt
ab eis. Nonne hic oues facit iudices, et ius cognitionis transfert
20 ad auditores? Et Paulus, cum .I. Corint. IIII. dicit, Vnus dicat,
caeteri iudicent. Quod si, sedenti reuelatum fuerit, prior taceat.
Nonne et hic iudicium, penes auditorem esse uult? Sic quicquid
Christus, Mat. xxiiij. et ubique de falsis doctoribus, quicquid Petrus
et Paulus de falsis apostolis, magistris, et Ioannes de probandis spiriti-
25 bus praecipiunt, eo pertinet, ut iudicandi, probandi, damnandi authoritas, apud populum sit, idque iustissime.

IN HOC passu pulcherrimo, dominus doctor duo facit. Primo,
respondet ad id: quod nusquam dictum est. Secundo, respondet id,
quod stultissimum est. Circa primum notandum est: quod dominus
30 Luderus suo more conatur ludere lectorem: ut credat totam Ecclesiam christi[OO_4]anam, priusquam doceretur a domino doctore, non
recte intellexisse illud dictum beati Augustini, Non crederem
euangelio: nisi ecclesiae authoritas, me commoueret. Non enim
ecclesiam intellexisse sic, quod nisi doceretur per ecclesiam catholi-
35 cam, nescisset Augustinus, quodnam euangelium esset euangelium
uerum: sed potuisset aliquod pseudeuangelium habere pro uero: et

---

6 credat.] credat? *BL*   8 sui] suis *L*; omnium] *BL*, omium *R*   10 *B adds gloss* Horum
prophetarum (si quis alius) est Lutherus.   23 quicquid] Quicquid *B*   24 et Ioannes]
Et Ioannes *B*   25 iudicandi,] iudicandi *B*   27 facit] *BL*, facir *R*   28 respondet
id] respondet ad id *B*   33 euangelio] *BL*, euangelo *R*; authoritas] autharitas *B*
36 sed] *om. B*

Queen Church. For Christ stands firm, saying, "Beware of false prophets." To this almost all the syllables of all the prophets subscribe; for what do the *O pestilential interpretation, that any one person should judge against all men taken together* prophets do but warn the people not to believe in false prophets? But what is this warning but to declare and affirm that the right of judging and investigating is in the power of the people, and to warn them of their own work and to arouse them against all the teachings of all their own priests and doctors? Therefore we here conclude that as often as Moses, Joshua, David, and all the prophets in the old law summon the people away from false prophets and warn them, so often do they proclaim, command, confirm, and stir up the right of investigating and judging all the teachings of all men. But they do this in innumerable passages. Does our Henry, or any unclean Thomist here, have anything to snarl at these arguments?

Have we not stopped the mouth of those who speak wicked things? Let us return to the new law where Christ, in John 10, *Not in the least, for your mouth is still wide open* says, "My sheep hear my voice." In truth they do not hear the voice of strangers but they flee from them. Does He not here make the sheep judges and confer the right of investigating on His hearers? And Paul, when in I Corinthians 4, he says: "Let one speak, let the others judge. But if something is revealed to someone sitting by, let the former be silent." Does he not here mean that judgment is in the possession of the hearer? Thus whatever Christ in Matt. 24 and elsewhere commands concerning false doctors, whatever Peter and Paul command about false apostles and teachers and John about testing spirits, leads to this conclusion that the authority for judging, proving, condemning belongs to the people, and that most justly.

In this most excellent passage, the honored doctor does two things. First, he answers to that which was nowhere said. Second, he answers what is most foolish. Concerning the first, it should be noted that the honored Luder, as is usual with him, tries to make sport of the reader so that he believes that the whole Christian church before it was taught by the honored doctor did not rightly understand that saying of Saint Augustine: "I would not believe the gospel if the authority of the church did not persuade me." For, according to him, the church did not understand in this way, that, unless he were taught by the catholic church, Augustine would not have known which was the true gospel but could have considered some pseudo-gospel as the true

Quomodo Lutherus intelligat
Augustini uerba

uerum repudiare pro falso: sed illud Augustini dictum hactenus ecclesiam in-tellexisse hoc pacto: quod beatus Augus-tinus, etiam comperto, quod esset euangelium uerum, etiam si deus

5   id ore ad os fuisset ei testatus: tamen nollet credere euangelio, nisi iussus a papa. Et iste est unus error: quem dominus doctor Luderus in ecclesia deprehendit. Alius error est:

Secundus error ecclesiae a
Luthero castigatus

quod ex isto dicto Augustini, pontifices Romani sumpserunt sibi authoritatem

10   condendi ius: quum illud dictum Augustini tantum pertineat ad potestatem cognoscendi et iudicandi dogmata, et eadem iudicanda per populum: nec aliud beatus Augustinus senserit. At ecclesia, nunc tot annis sic intellexit, scilicet quasi sensisset Augustinus de potestate condendi iura: et ex illo dicto male intellecto, potestatem sibi sumpsit

15   ecclesia condendi iura. Et in hac re lector, facile uidebis doctorem Luderum dicere uerum. Nam nunquam uidebis aliquod concilium, in quo aliqua iura condita sunt: quin super illud dictum Augustini posuerit fundamentum potestatis suae: et maxime uidebis hoc in illis concilijs, in quibus iura condita sunt, ante

Irridetur Lutherus

20   Augustinum natum: et praesertim in concilio apostolorum, in quo conditi sunt apostolorum canones: et in concilio, quod [OO₄v] apostoli celebrarunt Hierosolymis: ubi statu-erunt pro tempore, de quibusdam legalibus

Tertius error a Luthero
castigatus

obseruantijs. Tertius error est: quod rex

25   Angliae male intellexit illum textum Augustini, et glossam doctoris Martini: qui confessus est, ecclesiam hoc habere a deo: ut possit discernere uerbum dei a uerbis hominum: ex qua Lutheri glossa, rex obiecit Luthero: quod ecclesia non habet hoc a deo: nisi quia deus non uult pati ecclesiam suam, in rebus

30   necessarijs errare, cum periculo. Ex quo conclusit rex, confitendum Luthero: quod ecclesia hoc etiam habeat a deo: ut uerum scripturae sensum, possit a falso discernere: quoniam alioqui frustra discerneret ueras scripturas: si non posset discernere uerum sensum, a falso. Et

---

6 error] *BL*, errot *R*   8 *gloss* castigatus] *BL*, astigatus *R*   12 populum: nec] populum.
Nec *B*   13 potestate] *BL*, potestare *R*   17 sunt] *BL*, funt *R*   19 *gloss* Irridetur]
Irrdietur *B*   25 intellexit] *BL*, in tellexit *R*   28 Lutheri] *BL*, Lurheri *R*   30 con-
fitendum] confirendum *B*   32 quoniam] quam *B*

one and rejected the true as false; but up till now the church has understood that saying of Augustine in this way, that blessed Augustine, even though it were well known which was the true *How Luther understands the words of Augustine* gospel, even if God had testified it to him mouth to mouth, neverthe- less would not want to believe the gospel unless he was commanded by the pope.

And this is one error which the honored doctor Luder has caught in the church. The other error is that according to this saying of Augustine the Roman pontiffs have arrogated to them- *The second error of the church censured by Luther* selves the authority of founding law, since that saying of Augustine pertains only to the power of investigating and judging teachings, and these must be judged by the people; nor did blessed Augustine mean anything else. But the church has understood it thus for so many years now, namely as though Augustine had meant the power of founding laws, and according to that misunderstood saying the church has taken to itself the power of founding laws. And in this matter, reader, you will see easily that doctor Luder says the truth. For you will never see any council in which any laws were founded which did not lay the foundation of its power on that saying of Augustine, and especially will you see this in those councils in which laws were *Luther is mocked* founded before the birth of Augustine, and especially in the council of the apostles in which the canons of the apostles were founded, and in the council which the apostles celebrated at Jerusalem, where they established for the time certain legal observances.

The third error is that the King of England misunderstood that text of Augus- tine and the gloss of doctor Martin, who *The third error censured by Luther* confessed that the church has from God the power to distinguish the word of God from the words of men, according to which gloss of Luther the king objects to Luther that the church does not have this from God except for the reason that God does not wish to allow His church to err dangerously in necessary matters. According to which the king concluded that Luther must admit that the church also has from God the power of distinguishing the true meaning of scripture from the false, because otherwise she would distinguish the true scriptures to no purpose if she could not distinguish the true

praeterea concedendum esse Luthero, ex suo dicto: quod ecclesia hoc
habeat a deo: ut discernat traditiones dei, a traditionibus hominum:
et falsa dogmata discernere possit, a ueris: quia in his non minore
periculo falleretur, quam in recipienda scriptura humana, loco
5　diuinae. Atque ex his consequi, ut ecclesia non possit errare in
sacramentis, et necessarijs articulis fidei: sed possit damnare Lutheri
falsa dogmata, et falsas interpretationes scripturae. Hoc argumentum
regis, uisum est patri Ludero tam absurdum: quod non uoluit
recitare: quia non ualuit refutare, sed tacite confessus omnia, dimisso
10　rege, reuertitur ad papam: et distinguit potestatem cognoscendi, a
potestate condendi: tantum rhetoricatur suo more, hoc est, more
meretricum, lenonum, portitorum, aurigarum, scurrarum: et rursus
citat uocabularia: nam illa sunt ei uice dei cuiuspiam, ex machina
propitij: quoties aliter expli[PP₁]care se non potest, et absoluere
15　suam tragoediam. Rursus ergo, uelut ex uocabulario, docet dominus

Quid intersit inter ius iudicandi　doctor: quid intersit inter ius iudicandi et
et condendi doctori Luthero　ius condendi: tamen interim fatetur
ecclesiam, sicut habet a deo ius discernendi
scripturas, sic et diiudicandi dogmata. Videamus igitur, quid lucri-
20　fecerit dominus Luderus ex hac distinctione. Differamus paulisper,
illam partem, qua quaeratur, an ullus pontifex, ulla synodus, ullus
princeps, ullus populus ullum habeat ius condendi iura. Accipiamus
interim, quod dat Luderus. Habeat ecclesia ius, discernendi scripturas et dogmata. In hoc saltem, mane Luthere. Iam reuerende
25　doctor sic arguo uobis cum fauore. Ecclesia habet ius iudicandi
dogmata per uos: sed ecclesia damnauit dogmata uestra: ergo per
uos dogmata uestra uere damnata sunt: quia in scripturis et dogmatibus, fatemini ecclesiam hoc habere a deo: ut non possit errare.
Hic non dubito, quin ut soletis, irascamini et iurgetis: sed rogo uos
30　domine doctor, respondete ad argumentum. An prouocabitis ad
uocabularium, et dicetis, ecclesiam, quae damnauit uos, esse ecclesiam papisticam: et haec ecclesia, quae habet ius iudicandi dogmata, est ecclesia catholica, per totum orbem diffusa? Ad istam

---

1 quod] *BL*, quam *R*　　　7 interpretationes] *L*, iaterpretationes *BR*　　　8 absurdum] *BL*,
abfurdum *R*　　9 refutare] *BL*, refurare *R*　　　12 lenonum] *BL*, lenorum *R*; portitorum]
potatorum *L*　　13 uocabularia] uocabularios *B*; illa] illi *B*　　18–19 discernendi scrip-
turas] *corr. err. L*, discernendi a deo scripturas *BR*　　　29 iurgetis] *corr. err. L*, iuretis *BR*
32 haec] *corr. err. L*, ex *BR*

meaning from the false. And besides, Luther must grant according to
his own statement that the church has from God the power of distinguishing the traditions of God from the traditions of men and false
teachings from true ones, because in these matters she would be
deceived with no less danger than in receiving human scripture in   5
place of divine. And according to this it follows that the church
cannot err in the sacraments and in necessary articles of faith, but can
condemn Luther's false teachings and false interpretations of scripture. This argument of the king seemed to Father Luder so nonsensical
that he did not wish to recall it because he did not have the strength   10
to refute it, but, silently admitting everything, dismissing the king, he
returns to the pope and distinguishes the power of investigating from
the power of founding; only he rhetoricates in his own manner, that
is, in the manner of harlots, panders, porters, charioteers, buffoons,
and he again cites the glossaries, for they take the place for him of any   15
kindly *deus ex machina* whenever he cannot extricate himself otherwise
and bring his tragedy to a close. Again therefore, as though from a
glossary, the honored doctor teaches what
is the difference between the right of   *What to Doctor Luther is the*
                                            difference between the right of
judging and the right of founding; never-   *judging and of founding*   20
theless, at the same time he admits that the
church, as she has from God the right of distinguishing the scriptures,
so also has the right of judging teachings. Let us see therefore what
gain the honored Luder makes from this distinction. Let us put off
for a little while that part in which he asks whether any pontiff, any   25
synod, any prince, any people has any right of founding laws. Let us
accept for the time being what Luder grants. Let the church have the
right of distinguishing scriptures and teachings. In this at least abide,
Luther. Now, reverend doctor, I argue thus with you, with your
permission. The church has the right of judging doctrines, according   30
to you; but the church has condemned your doctrines; therefore,
according to you your doctrines are truly condemned because you
admit that in scriptures and in doctrines the church has from God the
power not to err. Here I do not doubt but that, as is usual with you,
you will be in a rage and rail, but I ask you, honored doctor, answer   35
the argument. Or will you summon us to a glossary and say that the
church which condemned you is the papistic church and that this
church which has the right of judging doctrines is the catholic church
spread throughout the whole world? To this answer, the right of the

responsionem, tacito interea iure pontificis, ego sic argumentum red-
integro: quod in nullo actu multitudinis, requiritur, quod omnes ad
unum consentiant: sed ista ecclesia, quam uos appellatis papisticam,
quae damnat ubique uestra dogmata, est multo maxima pars orbis
5 christiani: ergo adhuc per uos dogmata uestra mala sunt: quia
damnata sunt per ecclesiam catholicam, [PP₁v] quae in talibus male
iudicare non potest. Praeterea ad eandem ecclesiam pertinet iudicare:
quae sint falsa dogmata: ad quam iudicare pertinet: quae sint uerae
scripturae. Sed eadem ecclesia, quae docet et iudicat: quae sunt
10   uerae scripturae: illa inquam eadem
Lutherus damnatur ab his, ecclesia docet et iudicat, falsa esse dogmata
penes quos fatetur esse uestra. Ergo omni modo dogmata uestra
iudicandi authoritatem damnata sunt.

QVID rursus dicitis domine doctor: quod effugium praestat uobis
15 uester uocabularius? Mirabile certe. Nam inuenit ius iudicandi
dogmata, non pertinere ad pontificem: non ad sacerdotes: non ad
synodum, et concilia: sed per hanc authoritatem Christi: Attendite a
falsis prophetis, probat authoritatem tributam populo, aduersus
omnes sanctos pontifices, omnia concilia, et omnes sanctos patres:
20 quasi aliam fidem docuerint sancti patres: aliam crediderit fidelis
populus. Docet nos igitur dominus doctor, idem esse attendite a falsis
        prophetis: quod attendite a sanctis patri-
Igitur sedulo cauet ipse, ne sit bus: et didicit ex uocabularijs, idem signi-
sanctus pater ficare falsum prophetam, et sanctum
25 patrem. Igitur, postquam uno atque altero loco, ex scriptura sacra
sic allegato, probauit dilucide: quibus oportuit iudicibus iudicium
dogmatum non ad clerum pertinere, sed ad populum. Tandem sic
gloriosus uictor insultat. Habet hic Henricus noster, aut ullus impurus
Thomista, quod istis obganniat? Nonne obstruximus os loquentium
30 iniqua? Non certe domine, non dum obstruxistis os omnium loquentium iniqua: quia adhuc os uestrum non obstruxistis: quod
loquitur iniquissima. [PP₂]

SED agite domine doctor, nolo uobiscum contendere, tantum
quaero, quid profecistis, quum a clero prouocastis ad populum? certe
35 ex fumo fugistis in flammam. Nam sicut nullus est clerus in aliqua
ecclesia, per totum orbem diffusa: qui non damnat dogmata uestra

---

10 *gloss* Lutherus] *L*, Lutherus. *BR*   18 tributam populo] *corr. err. L*, tributam a populo
BR   33 nolo] *corr. err. L*, uolo *BR*

pontiff being meanwhile passed over in silence, I thus renew the argument that in no action of a multitude is unanimous consent required, but this church which you call papistic, which everywhere condemns your doctrines, is by far the greatest part of the Christian world; therefore, still according to you, your teachings are evil because they have been condemned by the catholic church which in such matters cannot judge wrongly. Besides, to judge which are false doctrines belongs to that same church to which it belongs to judge which are the true scriptures. But the same church which teaches and judges which are the true scriptures, that same church, I say, teaches and judges that *Luther is condemned by those* your doctrines are false. Therefore, in every *who he admits possess the* way your doctrines are condemned. *authority of judging*

What do you say in return, honored doctor? What escape does your glossary provide you? A marvelous one, indeed. For he has found that the right of judging doctrines does not belong to the pontiff, not to the priests, not to synod and councils; but according to this authority of Christ, "Beware of false prophets," he proves that authority is granted to the people against all the holy pontiffs, all the councils, and all the holy fathers, as if the holy fathers taught one faith, the faithful people believed another. The honored doctor teaches us therefore that "beware of false prophets" is the same as "beware of holy fathers," and he has learned from glossaries that false prophet means the same *Therefore he carefully avoids* as holy father. Therefore, after several *being a holy father* passages cited from sacred scripture in this way, he has clearly proved, by the proper judges, that the judgment of doctrines should have belonged not to the clergy but to the people. Finally the boastful conqueror taunts thus: Has our Henry or any unclean Thomist anything to snarl here at these arguments? Have we not stopped the mouth of those who speak wicked things? Certainly not, my honored sir, not until you have stopped the mouth of all those who speak wicked things; because you have not yet stopped your own mouth, which speaks the most wicked things.

But come, honored doctor, I do not wish to argue with you; I only inquire: What have you accomplished when you have appealed from the clergy to the people? Certainly you have escaped from the smoke into the flame. For as there is no cleric in any church spread through the whole world who does not condemn your doctrines on orders and

de ordine, et missa: sic nullus est usquam populus, neque Christianus,
neque quem uos longe pluris aestimatis turchicus: qui non damnat
dogmata uestra de iure condendi iura. Quamobrem, quum omnis
undique populus, ad quem (per uos) pertinet ius iudicandi dogmata,
5 iudicat hoc uestrum dogma: quod nullus habet ius condendi ius, non
solum esse impium, sed etiam stolidum: adhuc non effugitis, quin hoc
dogma recte sit damnatum, et uere sit impium, et uere stolidum. Tunc
reduco sic syllogismum contra uos domine doctor. Illi, quos uos
dicitis habere ius iudicandi dogmata:
10 *Lutherum impie sentire etiam* iudicant omnes unanimiter, illud dogma
sua confessione uestrum, quo docetis, nulli ius esse condendi ius, impium esse dogma et stultum: ergo per confessionem
alterius partis, quod ecclesia potestatem habet iudicandi dogmata,
probata est altera quoque pars illa, quam negastis, quod eadem
15 ecclesia ius habet condendi iura: quia quae potestatem habet
iudicandi dogmata, iudicat falsum esse et stolidum dogma: quod uos
docetis, illam ius non habere condendi iura. Nam si ullum ius est ulli,
certe ius est ecclesiae super ecclesiam: sicut cuique potestas est super
se ipsum. At uestra negat prudentia, non solum ecclesiam Romanam
20 habere ius condendi iura, sed etiam illam ecclesiam, quam conceditis
habere ius iudicandi dogma, id est ecclesiam (ut dicitis) toto [PP₂v]
orbe diffusam. Et sic uidetis prudentissime pater, uos tam perite
distinguere: ut uestrae distinctionis, altera pars alteram perimat.

Ostendit Lutheri sententiam, omnium absurdissimam:
25   qua docetur unusquisque sibi ipsi credere,
            contra authoritatem caeterorum
                omnium. Cap. XXII.

Lutheri uerba   Nam unusquisque suo periculo recte aut
                    false credit, ideoque cuique pro se curan-
30   dum est, ut recte credat, ut etiam communis sensus, et salutis necessitas, urgeat necessario iudicium doctrinae penes auditorem esse.

---

2 turchicus] Turcicus *L*   5 condendi ius,] *corr. err. L*, condendi, ius *BR*   14 probata]
corr. err. L, Probata *BR*   25 unusquisque] *corr. err. L*, unumquemque *BR*

the mass, so nowhere is there any people, neither Christian nor Turk
—whom you esteem far more—who does not condemn your doctrines
on the right of establishing laws. Therefore, since all people everywhere, to whom, according to you, belongs the right of judging
doctrines, judge this doctrine of yours that no one has the right of
founding a law to be not only impious but also stupid, you still do not
escape without your doctrine's being rightly condemned as both truly
impious and truly stupid. Then I thus form the syllogism against you,
honored doctor. Those who you say have the right of judging
doctrines all judge unanimously that that
doctrine of yours by which you teach that   *That even by his own confession*
no one has the right of founding law is an   *Luther judges impiously*
impious and foolish doctrine; therefore, according to the confession
of the one part, that the church has the power of judging doctrines,
there is proved also that other part which you have denied, that the
same church has the right of founding laws, because she who has the
power of judging doctrines judges as false and stupid the doctrine
which you teach, that she does not have the right of founding laws.
For if anyone has any right, certainly the church has a right over the
church, just as each one has power over himself. But your wisdom
denies not only that the Roman church has the right of founding laws
but also that church which you grant has the right of judging doctrine,
that is, the church as you say spread throughout the whole world.
And so you see, most wise father, that you distinguish so expertly that
the one part of your distinction utterly destroys the other part.

He shows that Luther's opinion, by which
each one is taught to believe for himself
against the authority of everyone else, is the
most absurd of all. Chapter 22.

For each one believes rightly or falsely at
his own risk, and therefore each one must   *Luther's words*
look out for himself that he believes rightly, so that even common
sense and the necessity of salvation urge necessarily that the judgment
of doctrine is in the power of the hearer. Otherwise it is said to no

Alioqui frustra dicitur, Omnia probate, quod bonum est tenete. Et
iterum, Spiritualis omnia iudicat, et a nemine iudicatur. At quilibet
christianus est spiritualis, a spiritu

At quilibet christianus te
iudicat haereticum

Christi. Omnia uestra (inquit) siue
Apollo, siue Paulus, siue Cephas, id est
de omnium dictis et factis iudicandi ius habetis.

NVNC audis lector, admirabilem sapientiam. Fortassis addubi-
tasti prius, an reuerendus pater esset semifatuus: nunc non dubitabis
amplius: quin sit plusquam sesquifuriosus. Authoritatem iudicandi
dogmata, primum sustulit pontifici: uideri potuisset transferre ad
concilium. Transtulit a concilijs, putasses ad cleri totius multitudinem. Transtulit prorsus a clero, transferre uidebatur ad populum.
Nunc transfert a populo, et defert ad quemlibet. Hunc tu sanum
putas? Atqui nunc (sentio) sapit certe maxime. Res est altioris
consilij, quam putabam. Nam Catelina,

Callidum Lutheri consilium

si potuisset uti prouocatione tali, saluus
esset. Si damnatus a patribus, prouocaret ad populum, damnatus a
[PP₃] populo prouocaret, ad quemlibet, nec ualuisset omnium iusta
damnatio, quandiu in populo reperiretur similis illi quispiam, qui
damnatum absolueret. Atqui hac prouocatione se protegit Luderus.
Olim pontifici permisit iudicanda, quae scripsit de indulgentijs: et
statim praetimens sibi, sicut fugit impius nemine persequente, primum ex dimidio coepit appellare, tollens ei potestatem de iure diuino.
Paulo post prouocauit in totum, testatus eius pontificis potestatem
iure prorsus nullo fulciri: sed tamen prouocauit ad concilium, ibi
saltem fassus, esse iudicandi ius: et tamen cautus adiecit, non simpliciter proximum: sed proximum, quod in spiritu sancto foret con-
gregandum. Idque eo fecit consilio (sicut

Deprehensam a rege Lutheri
calliditatem

bene deprehendit princeps) ut in quocunque concilio damnaretur: ibi negaret esse
spiritum: homo (ut rex lepide scribit) nimium spiritalis: qui nusquam fatetur esse spiritum sanctum: nisi in sinu suo. Verum adhuc

---

1 tenete] *L*, te nete *BR*   4 uestra (inquit)] uestra sunt (inquit) *L*   31 scribit] *corr.*
err. L, scribet *BR*; nimium] *corr. err.*, nimirum *BRL*

point: "Test all things; hold fast that which is good." And again:
"The spiritual man judges all things, and he himself is judged by no
man." But any Christian whatever is
spiritual from the Spirit of Christ. "All   *But any Christian whatever*
things are yours," he says, "whether   *judges you a heretic*   5
Apollo or Paul or Cephas"; that is, you have the right of judging
about the words and deeds of everyone.

Now you hear, reader, admirable wisdom. Perhaps you were
inclined to doubt before whether the reverend father was semi-
foolish; now you will no longer doubt that he is more than sesqui-   10
furious. First of all he took away from the pontiff the authority of
judging doctrines; he could have seemed to transfer it to the council.
He transferred it from the councils, you might have thought, to the
multitude of the whole clergy. He transferred it altogether from the
clergy; he seemed to transfer it to the people. Now he transfers it from   15
the people and delivers it to anyone whatever. Do you think this man
is sane? And yet now I perceive he is certainly most wise. The matter
is of a deeper design than I thought. For
Catiline, if he could have used such an   *Luther's shrewd design*
appeal, would have been saved; if, when condemned by the senators,   20
he appealed to the people, when condemned by the people he
appealed to anyone whatever, and the just condemnation of everyone
would not have had force so long as anyone at all like him would be
found among the people who would free him from condemnation.
But by this appeal Luder protects himself.   25

Once he allowed that what he wrote about indulgences should be
judged by the pope; and immediately, fearing for himself, just as an
impious fellow flees though no one is pursuing him, he began to
appeal half of the concession by taking away from the pope the power
of divine law. Shortly after, he appealed the whole concession, having   30
testified that the power of that pontiff was supported by no law at all;
but yet he appealed to a council, having admitted that there at least
was the right of judging; and yet, cautious, he added, not simply the
next council but the next one which must be gathered together in the
Holy Spirit. And he did this with the   35
intention, as the prince well grasped, that   *Luther's shrewdness caught by*
in whatever council he were to be con-   *the king*
demned he would deny that the Spirit was there; a man, as the king
wittily writes, exceedingly spiritual since he admits that the Holy

fatebatur, aliquod saltem concilium esse: quod per spiritum sanctum
iudicaret dogmata. Sed nunc omnia rursus damnat concilia, etiam
Nicenum. Quod, homo nunquam sibi contrarius, et simul damnat et
fatetur optimum. Igitur a concilio prouocat ad populum. Ibi multis
5 uerbis disputauit residere, quam, tam saepe aliunde alio transtulit,
potestatem iudicandi dogmata. At quum populum quoque, uel
maxime sentiat eius damnare dogmata, nec unius cuiusquam nationis

Hoc demum pacto habeat
Lutherus ius iudicandi

populum, sed omnem omnium gentium toto orbe diffusum, eo rem deducit denique:
10   ut iudicandi potestatem relinquat apud
quemlibet unum. Sperat enim nihil dici tam absurdum posse: ut non
[PP₃v] unum saltem aliquem, alicunde reperiat assensorem. Illum
igitur si quem forte tam stolidum possit inuenire: ne totius orbis
consensu uacillet, armat impudentia, et furore praemunit. Tollit
15 omnem scrupulum, iubet unumquenque sibi fidere. Nam alioqui
(inquit) frustra diceretur, omnia probate: quod bonum est tenete. Et
ideo uidelicet, quid bonum sit, quid malum, in dogmatibus aduersus
uniuersos: unusquisque sibi credat ipsi. Quid ni? Nam spiritualis
(inquit) iudicat omnia, et a nemine iudicatur. At quilibet (inquit)
20 Christianus est spiritualis, a spiritu Christi. Nam omnia uestra sunt
(inquit) siue Apollo, siue Paulus, siue Cephas, id est de omnium
dictis, et factis iudicandi ius habetis.

VISVS sum mihi profecto, Luderi stulticiam bene tangere: quum
ista apostoli, Omnia uestra sunt, ostendissem afferri, ab isto stolidis-
25 sime: quum ex eius argumento sequeretur, nos iudices esse, non
solum papae, sed etiam Petri et Pauli. At nunc uideo, nihil tam
absurdum fingi posse: quod non possis efficere: ut ille pro absurdo
non habeat: sed et absurdiora proferat, et dicat esse meram sapientiam. Nam ante fecerat iudices Petri et Pauli totum populum: Nunc
30 uero iudicem Petri facit et Pauli, e populo singulum quemque. Sic
igitur arguit nunc doctor Luderus. Omnia uestra sunt, siue Paulus,
siue Cephas, et sic de singulis, id est de omnium dictis habetis ius

---

1 quod] *L*, qui *BR*   11 Sperat] *corr. err. L*, Speret *BR*   24–25 stolidissime] *corr. err.*
L, stolidissimo *BR*

Spirit is nowhere but in his own bosom. But still he was admitting that there is at least some council which might judge doctrines through the Holy Spirit. But now again he condemns all councils, even the Nicene. This council the man, never inconsistent with himself, at the same time condemns and admits to be the best. Therefore he appeals   5 from the council to the people. There, he argues in many words, resides the power of judging doctrines which he has so often transferred from one place to another. But since he senses that the people also, indeed above all, condemn his doctrines, and not the people of any one nation, but all the people of all the nations spread through   10 the whole world, he finally reduces the matter to the point where he leaves the *By this means let Luther at last have the right of judging* power of judging to anyone whatever. For he hopes that nothing can be said so absurd that he will not find at least one person somewhere agreeing. Him therefore, if he can by   15 chance discover anyone so dull-witted, lest he should waver because of the agreement of the whole world, he arms with impudence and fortifies with raging madness. He takes away every scruple, he orders each person to trust in himself. For otherwise, he says, it would be said to no point: "Test all things, hold fast to what is good." And   20 therefore of course let each one believe himself against all men together concerning what is good, what evil, in doctrines. Why not? "For the spiritual man," he says, "judges all things and is judged by no man. But any Christian whatever," he says, "is a spiritual man from the Spirit of Christ. 'For all things are yours,' he says, 'whether   25 Apollo, or Paul, or Cephas'; that is, you have the right of judging about the words and deeds of everyone."

I thought indeed that I handled well the folly of Luder when I had shown that this fellow brought up most stupidly those words of the apostle, "All things are yours," since according to his argument   30 it would follow that we are judges not only of the pope but even of Peter and Paul. But now I see that nothing can be fashioned so absurd that you cannot cause him not to consider it as absurd, but he will bring forward even more absurd arguments and say they are sheer wisdom. For before he had made the whole people judges of Peter   35 and Paul, but now he constitutes as judge of Peter and Paul each single person from among the people. Thus then doctor Luder now argues, "All things are yours, whether Paul or Cephas," and this about individuals, that is, you have the right of judging about the

iudicandi. Et hoc dicitur non uniuersis, sed singulis: sicut et illud, spiritualis omnia iudicat, et a nemine iudicatur. At quilibet christianus est spiritualis, ergo quilibet Christianus habet ius iudicandi: hoc est sentiendi, quic[PP₄]quid uidetur sibi, de doctrina Petri, et Pauli,

5 et Marci, et Matthaei, et Ioannis, et Lucae, et apostolorum, et christianorum omnium. Nam ista ratio, non magis facit: nec Lutherus eam magis obijcit aduersus doctores, scholas, et concilia, quam aduersus Petrum et Paulum: quorum in hoc nomina citat: ut et eorum quoque doctrinam, iudicio cuiusque subijciat: tanquam

10 idem sentiente Paulo, quum scripsit, Omnia uestra sunt, siue Apollo, siue Paulus, siue Cephas. Et ista Lutheri ratio, qua nihil est absurdius, tam ualida tamen uidetur Luthero: ut inde sibi sumpserit authoritatem doctor Luderus iudicandi: quod epistola Iacobi apostoli, nihil habeat dignum apostolico spiritu. Sed ad quem finem affert hanc

15 rationem doctor Luderus? nempe ut quoniam unusquisque (ut ait) suo periculo recte aut false credit, atque ob id cuique pro se curandum est: ut recte credat: ideo non curet quisquam pontificem, aut concilia, aut ecclesiam, aut sanctos patres, aut populum, aut Petrum, aut Paulum, sed de uniuersis audacter iudicet quilibet: et quia suo

20 periculo credit: ideo sine periculo sibi credat aduersus orbem totum, iuxta consilium illud sapientis. Fili ne innitaris prudentiae tuae, et ne sapiens uideri uelis in oculis tuis.

VIDES hic lector, istius absurdissimi uiri manifestas insanias. Vides

Quanto se hic secus gessit
25 *quam Lutherus*

ipsius uerba, tibi bona fide numerata: nihil a nobis, aut recitando curtatum, aut interpretatione detortum. Satis scio, si nos eius uerba summatim essemus complexi, subituram fuisse nonnullis suspitionem: quasi quae is recte scripsisset, essent deprauata narrando: et ipsius telis in eum pugnatum esset: qui nihil syncere recen-

30 set. [PP₄v] At ego quum scirem nemini futurum credibile, quenquam tam absurda cogitasse (ne stulticiam hominis cuiquam linquerem dubiam) statui eius ipsius uerba recitare, et sua manu illi notam furoris inurere. Quamobrem quo minus adhuc dubites illum nihil

---

2–3 christianus . . . habet] *corr. err. L*, christianus, habet *BR*   4 uidetur] *corr. err. L*, iubetur *BR*   11 qua] *corr. err. L*, quia *BR*   24 numerata] *corr. err.*, *L* nunerata *BR*

words of everyone. And this is said, not to all men as a whole, but to individuals, just as also that text: "The spiritual man judges all things and he is judged by no man." But any Christian whatever is a spiritual man, therefore any Christian whatever has the right of judging; that is, of thinking what he pleases about the doctrine of Peter and of Paul and of Mark and of Matthew and of John and of Luke and of the apostles and of all Christians. For this reasoning does not operate more, nor does Luther raise it as an objection more, against the doctors, schools, and councils than against Peter and Paul, whose names he cites in this passage, so that he subjects their doctrine also to the judgment of each person, as though Paul were of the same mind when he wrote, "All things are yours, whether Apollo, or Paul, or Cephas." And this reasoning of Luther, than which nothing is more absurd, nevertheless seems so valid to Luther that from it doctor Luder has taken to himself the authority of judging that the epistle of James the apostle has nothing worthy of the apostolic spirit.

But to what end does doctor Luder present this reasoning? Namely, that because each one, so he says, believes truly or falsely at his own risk, and for this reason each must look out for himself that he believes rightly, therefore no one should bother about the pontiff, or the councils, or the church, or the holy fathers, or the people, or Peter, or Paul, but anyone whatever should judge boldly about all men taken together, and because he believes at his own risk, therefore he may believe himself without risk against the whole world, according to that advice of the wise man: "Son, do not rely upon your own prudence, and do not wish to appear wise in your own eyes."

You see here, reader, the manifest ravings of this most absurd man. You see his very words, recounted to you in good faith, with nothing either shortened *How differently he conducts* by us in the relating or twisted in interpre- *himself here than Luther does* tation. I know well enough that if we had comprised his words in a summary, a suspicion would have entered the minds of some, as though what he had written correctly had been corrupted in the telling, and as though the fight had been carried on with his own weapons against him who relates nothing honestly. But since I knew that no one would believe that anyone had thought out such absurd arguments, lest I should leave the folly of the man doubtful to anyone, I have determined to recite his very words and with his own hand to brand him with the mark of raging madness. Therefore, so that you

cogitare sapientius, sed uere uelle quenque suo stare iudicio: audi,
quid dicat paulo post.

Verba Lutheri

At hic dicent, si singulorum est ius
iudicandi et probandi, quis erit modus,
5   si iudices dissenserint et unusquisque, secundum suum caput iudi-
carit? quare necesse est unum esse, cuius iudicio stent caeteri contenti, ut salua sit unitas ecclesiae. Respondeo. Hoc cauillum nullos
rectius decet, quam Thomistas. Quaero

*Quod non sit, acceptum
referimus tibi*

enim et ego, quis hodie modus est, ubi
10   omnes iudicio unius papae stant? ubi
hic est unitas salua? An hoc est unitatem esse saluam, externo papae
nomine uniri? Vbi manet unitas cordium? Quis est certus in conscientia sua, papam recte iudicare? At nisi certitudo sit, nulla est
unitas. Ideo sub papa est quidem pompa externae unitatis, sed intus
15   non nisi confusissima Babylon, ut nec lapis super lapidem sit, nec cor
cum corde sentiat. Vt uideas, quam feliciter medeatur rebus spiritualibus, humana temeritas suis statutis. Alia igitur uia unitas ecclesiae
quaerenda est.

VIDES quam solicite hoc agat Luderus: ut nemo timeat fidere sibi
20   ipsi. Nam et pro cauillo habet: quod omnia sic essent incerta: et tot
diuersitates in fide, quot capita forent in populo. Et uelut simili
cauillo deridet: si quis in fidei rebus pontifici malit acquiescere, quam
fluctuare, et omni uento doctrinae circumferri, aut soli prorsus inniti
sibi. Et loquitur tanquam pontifex aliam

*Id uidelicet pontifici impingens,
quod ipse facit*

25   doceat fidem, quam eam, quae populo
Christiano publica est: imo negat esse
ullam fidem, in qua consentiunt Christiani: qui parent pontifici. Sed
sic mentitur esse alij aliam: ut nec cor cum corde sentiat: [QQ₁] et
hanc uanitatis iniquitatem, cor eius congregauit sibi: ut dum per-
30   suadeat omnibus nihil usquam esse certi: sed unumquenque suo
periculo credere, perducere posset unumquenque metu suo periculi:
ut nihili faciens authoritatem totius ecclesiae, nihili faciens sanctos
patres, et doctores, et ueteres omnes interpretes, interpretetur e suo

---

1 sapientius] *corr. err. L,* sapientis *BR*   8 *gloss* Quod] *L,* quod *BR*   31 suo] sui *BL*

may have still less doubt that he thinks nothing wiser but that he truly wishes each person to stand by his own judgment, hear what he says shortly after.

But here they will say, if it is the right of individuals to judge and prove, what *Luther's words* will be the limit if the judges have disagreed and each one has judged according to his own head? Therefore it is necessary that there be one by whose judgment the others stand content, so that the unity of the church may be safe. I answer: this quibble becomes no one better than the Thomists. For I also ask, what is the limit today when all stand by the *That there is none, we place* judgment of one pope? Where is unity *to your credit* safe here? Is this what it means for unity to be safe, to be united under the external name of the pope? Where does unity of hearts abide? Who is certain in his conscience that the pope judges rightly? But unless there is certainty, there is no unity. Therefore under the pope there is a certain pomp of external unity but interiorly nothing but the most confused Babylon, so that neither is there stone upon a stone, nor does heart agree with heart. So that you see how happily human rashness amends spiritual matters with its own decrees. By another way, then, must the unity of the church be sought.

You see how anxiously Luder discusses this matter, so that no one may fear to trust himself. For he also considers as a quibble the argument that everything would thus be uncertain, and that there would be as many varieties in faith as there would be heads among the people. And with a like quibble, as it were, he jeers if anyone prefers in matters of faith to yield to the pontiff rather than to be driven to and fro and be carried about by every wind of doctrine, or to rely entirely on himself alone. And he speaks as though the pontiff teaches a different faith *Forcing on the pontiff, of course, that which he himself does* than that which is common to the Christian people; indeed, he denies that there is any faith on which Christians who obey the pontiff agree. But he thus lies that one has one belief, another a different one, so that heart does not agree with heart; and this wickedness of deceit his heart has gathered to itself so that, while he persuades everyone that nothing is anywhere certain but that each one believes at his own risk, he can win each one over through his own fear of danger, so that, despising the authority of the whole church, despising the holy fathers and the doctors and all the ancient

quisque sensu scripturam sacram: et sibi, quam libeat, fidem formet
nouam. Nam quum Petri quoque, et Pauli iudicem fecit quenque

Ratio iudicij ferendi de ueteribus   Lutherus: conscendat quisque tribunal in
ex sententia Lutheri   corde suo: et utrumque iudicet, Hic bene
5   dicit Paulus, hic male. Hic probe Petrus
docet, hic docet perperam. Hic recte consulunt ecclesiae, sicubi
suadent credere: hic Thomistice, sicubi iubent bene facere. Iacobus
uero, quum sit apostolus, nihil habet omnino spiritus apostolici:
quem non pudet scribere, Fides sine operibus mortua est. Vnus
10 dumtaxat est, cuius nemo iudex est: qui quicquid dicit, certum est: is
doctor Luderus est, qui certus est, sua dogmata se habere de caelo: de
cuius aduentu, propheta praedixit, dicens, Tertius e caelo cecidit
Cato. Et item alius. Iam noua progenies, caelo demittitur alto. Et
idem propheta prophetauit, quo demittendus sit, quum ait, Facilis
15 discensus Auerni. Nam ille textus, de doctore Ludero loquitur ad
literam.

Verba Lutheri   Alia igitur uia, ecclesiae unitas quaer-
                  enda est. Haec est, quam Christus ponit
Ioan. VI. Erunt omnes docibiles dei, Omnis qui audiuit a patre
20 meo, uenit ad me, ille inquam internus spiritus solus, unanimes
habitare facit in domo. Hic docet, idem sapere, idem iudicare,
                  idem cognoscere, idem probare, idem
Et hic docet omnes, quod tu   docere, idem confiteri, idem sequi. Vbi
impie erres   ille non fuerit, impos[QQ₁v]sibile est,
25 ut unitas sit. Et si qua fuerit, externa et ficta est. Quare et deo
nihil curae est, ut impij homines unum uel non unum sint, qui
unitate spiritus inanes sunt. Suis filijs ad externam unitatem sufficit,
unum baptisma, et unus panis, tanquam communes caracteres et
symbola, per quae fidei suae, et spiritus unitatem profitentur et
30 exercent. Papistica ecclesia suam unitatem in unitate externi sui idoli
papae locat, internae autem, confusionis erroribus dispersa in omnes
uoluntates Satanae.

NVNC in mentem mihi lector uenit illud euangelium: quo daemones ex ore furiosi, Christum inuiti, tortique confessi sunt: Iesu

---

1 scripturam sacram] *BL,* scripiuram saeram *R*   7 bene facere] benefacere *L*
17 ecclesiae] ec clesiae *B,* Ecclesiae *L*   22 *gloss* Et] *L,* et *BR*   23 *gloss* erres] rres *B*
33 uenit] *B,* uenir *R,* venit *L*

interpreters, each one will interpret sacred scripture according to his own understanding and form for himself whatever faith he chooses. For since Luther has made each person the judge of Peter and also of Paul, each person may mount the tribunal in his own heart and judge both men: Here *The method of passing judgment* 5 Paul speaks well, here badly. Here Peter *on the ancients, according to* *Luther's judgment* teaches rightly, here he teaches wrongly. Here they advise the church rightly, wherever they persuade one to believe; here Thomistically, wherever they command to do good. But James, although he is an apostle, has nothing at all of the apostolic 10 spirit, since he is not ashamed to write: "Faith without works is dead." There is only one of whom no one is judge; who, whatever he says, it is certain; that is doctor Luder, who is certain that he has his doctrines from heaven, whose coming the prophet foretold, saying: "A third Cato has fallen from heaven." And likewise another: "Now 15 a new offspring is sent down from high heaven." And the same prophet prophesied to what place he must be sent down, when he said: "Smooth is the descent to Avernus." For that text speaks of doctor Luder to the letter.

By another way, then, must the unity of *Luther's words* 20 the church be sought. This is the way which Christ lays down in John 6: "They shall all be taught of God. Everyone who has heard from my Father comes to me." That interior Spirit alone, I say, makes those who dwell in a house to be of one mind. He teaches men to understand the 25 same thing, to judge the same, to investi- *And here He teaches everyone* *that you impiously err* gate the same, to prove the same, to teach the same, to confess the same, to follow the same thing. Where He is not present, it is impossible that there be unity. And if there is any, it is external and fictitious. Therefore also it is no concern of God's that 30 impious men should be one or not one who are empty of the unity of the Spirit. For His sons there suffices for external unity one baptism, and one bread, as common characters and signs through which they profess and exercise the unity of their faith and spirit. The papistic church places its unity in the unity of its external idol, the pope, but is 35 scattered by the errors of internal confusion unto all the whims of Satan.

Now there comes into my mind, reader, that gospel text in which the demons, reluctant and tortured, confessed Christ from the mouth

Christe fili Dauid, quid ante tempus uenisti torquere nos? Nam hic
plane daemoni, qui Lutherum possidet, ueritas extorsit inuito
responsum id, quo totam Lutheri sectam funditus euertit. Etenim hoc
ipsum est Luthere, quod tibi toties ad

5   *Lutherum concedere id iam, quod*   aures inclamauimus: et noluisti audire
     maxime ei aduersum sit

sanctum dei spiritum, ecclesiae suae intus
inspirare ueritatem. Illum internum spiritum, omnes reddere docibiles dei, illum solum facere: ut habitent unanimes in domo, Illum
docere, ut idem sapiant, idem iudicent, idem cognoscant, idem
10   probent, idem confiteantur, idem sequantur, idem doceant. Illum
internum spiritum solum esse, qui faciat, ut habitent unanimes in
domo: ut qui extra domum sunt, non sint

     Hi sunt Lutherani   unanimes: sed per haereses et sectas dissi-

deant. Haec ecclesia Catholica, quam tu appellas papisticam: quam
15   tu sic dissentire mentiris: ut cor cum corde non sentiat: ita per hunc
internum dei spiritum consentit, in articulis fidei: ut unanimiter
infidelitatis tuae dogmata condemnet. Tota ecclesia, per totum
orbem diffusa, matrimonium habet pro sacramento: ordinem habet
pro [QQ$_2$] sacramento: poenitentiam habet pro sacramento: et quid
20   opus est commemorare singula? Haec unanimiter et nunc sentit
ecclesia: et per tot sensit secula. Quod si tu ac tuus grex aliud cre-
ditis: nihilo minus ecclesia unanimis est in domo. Nam purgauit, ac
depurauit, quum te purulentam uomicam lancinauit, atque eiecit e
corpore. Fateris nunc, ubi dei spiritus est, ibi consensum esse. Illum
25   intus docere, quae uera sint. Profer ergo ecclesiam, quae consentit
tecum: dic, quibus in terris, ecclesia sit uere malignantium: ubi
populus, aut tam impius usquam sit, aut stolidus, ut contra spiritum
dei, qui per tot secula docuit christianos omnes, idem contra te
credere, nunc tandem credat homini

     Catalogus haeresum Lutheri
30   furioso tibi, ordinem non esse sacramen-

tum: qui spretis apostoli minis suscipiat eucharistiam, quam maxime
potest peccatorum titillatione turbata conscientia, solam fidem
sufficere, bonis operibus non opus esse, apostolum, qui neget illud,

---

3 funditus] *BL*, fnnditus *R*   14–15 quam tu sic] *BL*, qnam tu sic *R*

of the madman: "Jesus Christ, son of David, why have you come to torment us before the time?" For here, clearly, truth has wrenched from the reluctant demon which possesses Luther that response by which it overthrows the whole of Luther's sect from its foundation. For this is the very thing, Luther, which we have so often dinned into your ears and you did not wish to hear, that the Holy *That Luther now concedes that which is most opposed to him* Spirit of God interiorly inspires His church with truth, that that interior Spirit renders all taught of God, that He alone makes those who dwell in a house to be of one mind, that He teaches so that they understand the same thing, judge the same, investigate the same, prove the same, confess the same, follow the same, teach the same, that that interior Spirit is the only one who makes men who dwell in a house to be of one mind, so that those who are outside the house are not of one *These are the Lutherans* mind but are divided by heresies and sects. This catholic church, which you call papistic, which you falsely say is so at variance that heart does not agree with heart, so agrees through this interior Spirit of God in articles of faith that it unanimously condemns the teachings of your faithlessness. The whole church, spread throughout the whole world, holds matrimony as a sacrament; it holds orders as a sacrament; it holds penance as a sacrament; and what need is there to recall individual details? These things the church both thinks unanimously now and has thought through so many ages. But if you and your herd believe something different, the church is nonetheless of one mind in its house. For it cleansed and purified itself when it cut you off, a festering boil, and cast you from its body.

Now you admit that where the Spirit of God is, there is agreement, that He teaches interiorly what is true. Bring forward, then, the church which agrees with you; tell me in what lands the church truly consists of wicked men; where are the people anywhere either so impious or dull-witted that, in opposition to the Spirit of God, who has taught all Christians through so many ages to believe the same thing against you, they now at length believe you, a raving madman, that orders *Catalogue of Luther's heresies* is not a sacrament, the people who, scorning the threats of the apostle, receive the eucharist with a conscience agitated as much as possible by the tickling of sins, who believe that faith alone suffices, that there is no need of good works, that the apostle who denies this understands

nihil sapere spiritus apostolici, Christianum quenquam legibus
obligari non posse, et mille absurdissimas impietates eiusmodi. Potes
ne ullam ecclesiam nominare: cui tam stulta persuaseris: quae sibi
fas esse censeat recalcitrare magistratibus: et utile credat esse, uiuere
5   sine legibus? Sat scio nullum populum potes. Ergo quum dei
spiritum fatearis esse, qui populum faciat unanimem in domo: Et
eadem de rebus necessarijs sentientem, uelis nolis, tibi fatendum est,
illam ecclesiam esse catholicam et dei domum: in qua per tot secula
censerunt omnes unanimiter, aduersus insensatam sententiam tuam:
10   et tibi dei spiritum prorsus deesse: qui detrusus e domo toti dissentis
ecclesiae, in qua [QQ₂v] contra te totus per orbem populus, tot
seculis operante deo consentit. Tecum consentit nullus. Quid dico
populus? imo demiror, si tecum sentiat
Hoc non est infrequens Luthero,   quisquam unus homo. Nam hoc certo scio,
ut a se dissentiat
15   tecum non consentis ipse. Nam primum
confessus es, ecclesiam hoc habere a deo: ut falli non possit, in discernendis dei uerbis, a uerbis hominum. Deinde adactus rationibus
regis, fassus es ecclesiam idem ius habere, in diiudicandis dogmatibus.
Quid ergo sibi uult, quod postea dicis, unumquemque suo periculo
20   credere? quasi deus optimus, quenquam perplexum redderet: nec
aperiret exitum. Quaeso te, si uerum est, quod ante dixisti, quo suo
periculo credit: qui toti credit ecclesiae, de quopiam articulo fidei
consentienti? quum ecclesiam fatearis, hoc habere a deo: ut in
diiudicandis dogmatibus, falli non possit: quippe quae per te quoque
25   ne consentire quidem posset in articulum fidei, nisi intus illo docente
spiritu: qui facit habitare unanimes in domo.
ECCE Luthere, quibus ambagibus insanienti tibi, tandem inuito
ueritas extorta est: qua fateris ignarus eas, in quibus ecclesia tota tot
consensit seculis: quas tot libellis hactenus insectatus es, tanquam
30   traditiones hominum: nunc, inquam, subito fateris ignarus esse
traditiones dei: sine cuius occulto flatu, tam late fusus dei populus, in
unum conspirare non posset: quum ille solus sit: qui quod fateris,

3 quae] *L*, qui *BR*   13 populus?] *L*, populus *BR*   24 dogmatibus] *L*, dogmatis *BR*

nothing of the apostolic spirit, that no Christian can be bound by laws, and a thousand most absurd impieties of this same sort. Can you name any church which you have persuaded of such foolish things; which thinks that it has the right to resist magistrates, and believes that it is useful to live without laws? I know well enough that you cannot name any people. Therefore, since you admit that it is the Spirit of God who makes people who dwell in a house to be of one mind and in agreement on necessary matters, you must admit willy-nilly that that church is the catholic church and the house of God in which through so many ages all men have judged unanimously against your irrational opinion, and that the Spirit of God is wholly absent from you who, thrust from the house, disagree with the whole church, in which the whole people throughout the world by the working of God has for so many ages agreed against you. With you none agrees. Why do I say people? Indeed, I wonder if any one man agrees with you. For this I know for cer-tain, that you do not agree with yourself. *This is not infrequent with Luther, that he disagrees with himself* For first of all you confessed that the church has this power from God, that she cannot be deceived in distinguishing the words of God from the words of men. Then, forced by the reasonings of the king, you admitted that the church has the same right in judging doctrines. What then does it mean, what you afterwards say, that each one believes at his own risk? As if God, all good, would render anyone confused and not open a way out. I ask you, if what you said before is true, with what risk to himself does he believe who believes the whole church when it agrees on any article of faith, since you admit that the church has from God the power not to be deceived in judging doctrines? In fact, also according to you, she could not even agree on an article of faith except by the interior teaching of that Spirit who makes those who dwell in a house to be of one mind.

Behold, Luther, as you madly rave with these roundabout argu-ments the truth is finally wrested from you against your will, by which truth you admit unwittingly that those traditions on which the whole church has agreed for so many ages, which in so many books up till now you have railed at as the traditions of men, now, I say, you suddenly admit unwittingly that they are the traditions of God, without whose secret inspiration the people of God, so widely scattered, could not harmoniously agree, since it is He alone who, as

habitare faciat unanimes in domo. Et inde, quam haec exciderint,
ignaro. Nam protinus perinde ac si nihil horum prorsus audisses
unquam, quae iam ipse dixisti: dicis ilico talia: ut istis, quae dixisti
modo, non aliter pugnent, [QQ₃] ac pugnant cum luce tenebrae.

5   *Lutheri uerba*   Tu nunc uide, cuius spiritus fuerint
                                        sacrilega illa, et abominanda concilia,
quae aduersus tanta totius scripturae fulmina, apertissimasque sententias ausa sunt, sibi pontificibus arrogare ius iudicandi, et cognos-
                                        cendi, insuper et imperandi, et condendi.
10   *At mihi nemo uidetur plura*   Absque dubio Satanae istae fuerunt
        arrogare, quam tu   cogitationes, quibus in orbem inundauit
operationes erroris, et abominationem in loco sancto statuit securis-
sima tyrannide, postquam populo erepta est authoritas iudicandi, qua
pauere cogerentur falsi doctores, et patefacta uia per stolidam populi
15   superstitiosamque obedientiam et patientiam uniuersis erroribus et
abominationibus irruendi.

NON tibi uidentur lector, per istud os impium, inferae spirare
furiae? Nam quaeso te Luthere per istos, qui te exagitant infernos
        Imo potius ex omni sylua   daemones, quum tui similes pestes, caco-
20 *congerenda ligna, ad cremandum*   daemon aliquis immittat in dominicum
            Lutherum   gregem, dum res excutitur, censes totum
christianum populum ex toto orbe, uelut ad comitia Consulum
conuocandum simul in campum Martium, et uiritim exquirenda
suffragia? Quae arrogantia est, si de gregis periculo potissimum
25 tractent pastores? Quibusnam id negocium potius cupiat delegatum
populus, quam episcopis: ad quos maxime spectat, esse de populi
salute sollicitos? Si, quod tu saepe iactas, deum adesse concedis in
medio eorum: ubicunque sunt duo, uel tres congregati in ipsius
nomine: ibi negabis esse: ubi in eius nomine, maximis de causis sint
30 congregati tam multi? Recordare rursus, eorum quae dixisti proxime,
deum esse, qui in ecclesia sua consensum operatur. Ex omni parte
ecclesiae late per orbem diffusae, congregati sunt ad concilium. et

17 per istud os impium] *L*, per istud impium *BR*   22 comitia] *L*, commitio *BR*
29 maximis] *L*, maxime *BR*

you admit, makes those who dwell in a house to be of one mind. And how this admission thence escaped you, I do not know. For immediately thereafter, as if you had never heard anything at all of these things which you yourself just now said, you immediately say such things that they contradict what you have just said no differently than 5 darkness contradicts light.

Now see of what spirit were those sacrilegious and abominable councils, which against such great thunderbolts of the entire scripture and the most clear judgments have dared to arrogate 10 to themselves, the pontiffs, the right of judging and of investigating, in addition to commanding and founding. Without a doubt these were the thoughts of Satan, by which he has flooded the world with the operations of error and set up the abomination in the holy place 15 with the most secure tyranny after the authority of judging was snatched from the people, by which false doctors were forced to tremble, and the way was laid open through the stupid and superstitious obedience and patience of the people for rushing in with universal errors and abominations. 20

Luther's words

But it seems to me that no one arrogates more than you

Does it not seem to you, reader, that through this impious mouth infernal furies breathe? For I ask you, Luther, through those demons of hell who torment you, when some cacodaemon sends plagues like you into the flock of the Lord, do you think that while the matter is being examined the whole Christian people from the whole 25 world should be called together at one time, as to an assembly of consuls to the Campus Martius, and their votes sought man by man? What sort of arrogation is it if the pastors before all others treat of the danger of the flock? To whom should the 30 people rather wish that business delegated than to the bishops, to whom it especially belongs to be anxious about the safety of the people? If, as you often declare, God is present in their midst wherever two or three are gathered together in His name, will you deny that He is there where so many are gathered in His name for most 35 important reasons? Recall again those things which you said a little while ago: that it is God who works agreement in His church. From every part of the church scattered widely throughout the world men gathered together for a council, and, as shortly after even you do

Nay rather, from every forest, wood should be gathered to burn Luther to ashes

quod paulo post nec ipse negas, uiri optimi plerique ac san[QQ₃v]ctis-
simi consenserunt inter se, redierunt quisque domum. concensit in
eadem fere totum per orbem fusus populus. At per quem consentit
populus christianus? an non fassus es id per illum fieri intus docentem
5   deum, qui habitare facit unanimes in domo? Ergo quod ante fassus
es esse dei, debaccharis fuisse cogitationes Satanae: quibus patefieret
uia per stolidam populi superstitiosamque obedientiam uniuersis
abominationibus irruendi.

VIDES nunc lector Lutheri constantiam: uides mala, quae nasci
10 repperit ex optimorum patrum in dei nomine congregato concilio.
Sed quomodo malis istis occurramus, hoc ante docuit: quum dixit,
Vnumquenque suo periculo recte aut falso credere. Igitur si statuatur:
ut quisque credat, quicquid uelit: iam uera inuenta est uia: qua
nullus error possit irrepere.

15   *Verba Lutheri*   Et ut hic mei Henrici et sophistarum
                             recorder, qui a longitudine temporum
et multitudine hominum pendent cum sua fide. Primum negare
non potest, huius rapti iuris tyrannidem ultra mille annos durasse.
Nam in ipso concilio Niceno omnium optimo, iam tum incipiebant
20 leges condere, et ius istud sibi uendicare. Atque ab eo tempore
hactenus inualuit, ut nihil receptius sit, nec firmius aliquid multitudine hominum et diuturnitate probari possit, quam hoc ius. adeo, ut
nemo id non putet hodie sanum, rectum, ac diuinum esse. At hic uides
sacrilegium et impietatem esse aduersus euidentissimas et inuictas
25 scripturas dei. Quare si tantus error et tale sacrilegium, tanta longitudine temporis, tanta multitudine hominum, uel consentiente, uel
seducta, uel probante regnauit aduersus ueritatem dei, semel uolo hic
omnibus sophistis et papistis capitale eorum argumentum de longitudine et multitudine ad puluerem usque contritum, et os obstructum,
30 ut uideant, cur deus nolit nos ul[QQ₄]li creaturae quantumuis longae
et multae et magnae credi, sed soli suo infallibili uerbo.

VEL istud quis non sentiat, insanum esse, qui scripsit, nisi is sit
insanus, qui legit? Nam et Nicenum concilium fatetur optimum: et

---

1 ipse] *L*, ipsi *BR*   2 consenserunt inter se,] *L*, consenserunt, inter se *BR*

not deny, very many of the best and most holy men agreed among themselves, each one returned home; the people spread throughout almost the whole world agreed on the same things. But through whom do the Christian people agree? Have you not admitted that this happens through that God teaching interiorly who makes those who 5 dwell in a house to be of one mind? Therefore what you earlier admitted to be of God you now rave to have been the thoughts of Satan, by which the way was laid open through the stupid and superstitious obedience of the people for rushing in with universal abominations. 10

You see now, reader, Luther's consistency; you see the evil things which he has discovered to arise from the council of the best fathers gathered in the name of God. But how we should resist these evils he has taught before this when he said that each one believes truly or falsely at his own risk. Therefore if it is decreed that each one should 15 believe whatever he wishes, now is found the true way by which no error can creep in.

And, that I may here recall my Henry and the sophists, who depend with their *Luther's words* faith on length of time and a multitude of men, first of all, he cannot 20 deny that the tyranny of this usurped right has lasted more than a thousand years. For in the council of Nicea itself, the best of all, they began already then to establish laws and to claim this right for themselves. And from that time even to this it has grown strong so that nothing is more accepted nor can anything be proved more firmly 25 by multitude of men and length of time than this right, so much so that no one today does not think it sound, right, and divine. But here you see that there is sacrilege and impiety against the most evident and invincible scriptures of God. Therefore, if such a great error and such a sacrilege has reigned against the truth of God because of such a 30 great length of time, such a great multitude of men either agreeing, or led astray, or approving, I wish here that once for all the chief arguments of all the sophists and papists concerning length of time and multitude were crushed even to dust and their mouth stopped so that they might see why God does not want us to believe any creature, 35 however long-lasting and numerous and great, but only His own infallible word.

Who does not sense that the man who wrote this is a madman, unless he is a madman who reads it? For he even admits that the

tamen illud ait initium fuisse omnium malorum, et incepisse iam
ipsos optimos et sanctissimos uiros sacrilegium et impietatem, aduersus euidentissimas et inuictas scripturas dei: quod facere non potuissent, nisi aut stultissimi aut pessimi. Nam si euidentissimae scripturae
5 fuerunt: caecissimi fuerunt, si non uiderunt: si uiderunt: impij: qui
contempserunt. Et tantum sacrilegium et impietatem improperat
homo sacrilegus et impius tanto numero uirorum talium: quos ipse
quoque fatetur optimos: ut semel ostendat se, tam sanctis patribus
impietatis poenas dare, et manifesto furore plecti: qui tam stolide,
10 pugnantia cogitur ore sacrilego delyrare: quam nemo posset, non
agitatus furijs. Vt illud omittam, quod ibi quoque mentitur, quum ait,
In concilio Niceno primum coepisse condi leges: quum satis constet
apostolos, et concilio communiter, et seorsum singulos condidisse
leges, sicut et rex obiecit, ad quae nihil omnino Lutherus respondet.

15   *Verba Lutheri*   Habemus itaque absque omni contro-
                                    uersia, ius de doctrina cognoscendi, et
iudicandi, seu probandi esse penes nos, non penes concilia, pontifices,
patres, doctores. At hinc non sequitur esse simul penes nos ius con-
                                    dendi leges. Nam hoc solius dei est.
20   *Vide, si non omnia pro suo*   Nostrum est legem et uerbum eius
         dicat commodo   cognoscere, probare, iudicare, et secer-
nere ab omnibus alijs legibus, sed nequaquam condere aut mandare.
Neque enim sequitur ex uerbo Christi, Attendite a falsis prophetis,
ergo uestrum est prophetare, imo ut Petrus ait, Nunquam uoluntate
25 humana est allata prophe[QQ₄v]tia et nulla interpretatio scripturae,
fit ex proprijs, sed inspiratione spiritus sancti, locuti sunt sancti dei
homines. Ita non sequitur. Oues meae uocem meam audiunt, ergo
                                    oues uocem meam condent uel facient,
     Ecce quam spectantia ad   imo contrarium sequitur. Vocem meam
       negocium proferat
30   ego condo, oues autem conditam
agnoscunt, probant, et sequuntur.

HIC uideo, magnum ius esse non penes concilia, pontifices, patres,
doctores, sed penes uos, quos quaeso uos? Ego putabam Martinum

---

2–3 aduersus] *BL*, aduerfus *R*   5 fuerunt:] *corr. err.*, sunt: *BR*, sunt, *L*   6 contemp-
serunt] *L*, contempserint *BR*   8–9 ut semel ostendat se, tam sanctis . . . dare, et] vt semel
se, tam sanctis . . . dare ostendat, et *L*   14 respondet] *BL*, refpondet *R*   28 *gloss*
spectantia] spectatia *L*

Nicene council was the best; and yet he says that it was the beginning of all evils, and that those most good and holy men then began a sacrilege and impiety against the most evident and invincible scriptures of God, which they could not have done unless they were either most foolish or most wicked. For if the scriptures were most evident, they were most blind if they did not see them; if they saw them, they were impious who contemned them. And the sacrilegious and impious man reproaches with so great a sacrilege and impiety so great a number of such men whom he himself also admits were the best, that once for all he shows that he pays the penalty of impiety to such holy fathers and that he is entangled in manifest madness who is driven to rant such stupidly conflicting things with his sacrilegious mouth, as no one could who is not tormented by furies. Thus I shall omit that which he also falsely says there when he asserts that in the Nicene council laws first began to be founded, since it is sufficiently well known that the apostles both commonly in council and separately established individual laws, as the king also has objected, to which Luther answers nothing at all.

And so we hold without any question that the right of investigating about *Luther's words* doctrine and of judging or of approving is in our power, not in the power of councils, pontiffs, fathers, doctors. But it does not follow from this that the right of founding laws is likewise in our power. For this belongs to God alone. It is our right to investigate His law and word, to *See if he does not say everything to his own advantage* approve, judge, and distinguish it from all other laws, but not at all to found or command. For neither does it follow from the word of Christ, "Beware of false prophets," that therefore it is your right to prophesy; on the contrary, as Peter says: "Not by the will of man was prophecy brought at any time, and no interpretation of scripture is made privately, but holy men of God spoke by the inspiration of the Holy Spirit." Thus, it does not follow: My sheep hear my voice; therefore, the sheep sound or cause my voice; rather, *See what excellent arguments he presents for his cause* the contrary follows: I sound my own voice, but the sheep recognize it when sounded, they approve and follow it.

Here I see that the great right is not in the power of councils, pontiffs, fathers, doctors, but in your power; which you, please? I

Luderum esse reuerendum patrem, esse doctorem, nunc uos negatis
utrumque. Esse quidem dicitis illud ius cognoscendi, non penes
patres, neque doctores, sed penes uos. Quos ergo uos? non uos patres,
sed fratres: uos, non doctores, sed indoctos. Bene dicitis profecto
5 domine. Tunc ego uideo per uos: quod patres et doctores habuerunt
doctrinam penes se: sed uos qui estis indoctus frater habetis penes uos,
non doctrinam, sed ius iudicandi doctrinam sine doctrina. Nam
doctrinam non cognoscitis, sed habetis ius cognoscendi.

SED nullus habet (ut dicitis) ius condendi leges. Nam hoc solius
10 dei est: et sic non solum reges, et populi condentes leges, sed et
apostoli, qui fecerunt idem, eodem spiritu, more Luciferi sibi
usurparunt potestatem dei. Sed tamen mitior est in Babylonica
reuerendus frater. Nam ibi dicit. neminem posse ponere unam
syllabam super christianum quenquam, sine ipsius consensu, sed cum
15 eius assensu posse. Atque ita per illam regulam reuerendi fratris potest
saltem condi lex: quae tantisper ualeat, donec aliquis alius ueniat in
regionem, qui nunquam consensit in legem: id quod ubique fere fiet
intra biduum. Nunc uero nulla condi [RR₁] potest omnino: ut plane
se doceat in re tam seria Luderus inepte ludere. Igitur postquam tam
20 mirabili sapientia, se gessit Luderus in hac materia, magnifice statim
concludit.

Verba Lutheri

Igitur uos estis lupus et satanae
minister et falsus propheta

25

Quare uidemus hic, omnes pontifices,
omnia concilia, omnes scholas, qui aliud
in ecclesia sonant, quam uerbum dei
solius, esse lupos, Satanae ministros, et
falsos prophetas. Simul intelligimus
insignem Henrici nostri, et omnium Thomistarum stoliditatem, qui
os suum impudens in caelum ponunt, et dicere audent, in hoc
sacrilego libello. Etiam si sacramentum ordinis non esset in scripturis
30 institutum, tamen penes ecclesiam esse ius instituendi eius. Et quam
stulte uerbum Augustini, quod de euangelio per ecclesiam toto orbe
cognito et probato loquitur, aptarit ad ius traditionum, arbitrio
impiorum hominum statuendarum. Iste est modus intelligendi dicta
patrum, et scripturae. Hi sunt, qui scribunt assertiones sacrament-
35 orum. Horum multitudo et diuturnitas est potestas faciendi articulos

---

1 Luderum esse] *BL*, Luderum esst *R*, Luderum esset *corr. err.*   4 fratres: uos,] *corr.*
err., frattes: uos, *R*, fratres uos, *B*, fratres: vos *L*; indoctos] *BL*, indictos *R*; Bene dicitis]
BL, Benedicitis *R*   9 SED]*BL*, EED *R*   15 posse] *om. B*; fratris] *L*, fratris, *B*, fratres
R   20 gessit] *corr. err. L*, gesset *BR*; materia, magnifice statim] *corr. err. L*, materia magnifice, statim *BR*   28 audent] andent *B*

was thinking that Martin Luder is a reverend father, is a doctor; now you deny both. You say indeed that that right of investigating is not in the power of the fathers, nor the doctors, but in your power. Which you, then? Not you fathers, but you friars; not you doctors, but you untaught. You say well, indeed, my honored sir. Then I see that, according to you, fathers and doctors had doctrine in their possession; but you, who are an untaught friar, have in your possession not doctrine but the right of judging doctrine without doctrine. For you do not investigate doctrine but you have the right of investigating it.

But no one, so you say, has the right of founding laws. For this belongs to God alone, and so not only kings and peoples founding laws but also apostles who have done the same thing in the same spirit have, like Lucifer, usurped for themselves the power of God. But yet in the *Babylon* the reverend friar was milder. For there he says that no one can lay one syllable upon any Christian without his own consent, but that with his assent one can do so. And thus according to that rule of the reverend friar a law can at least be established which has force for so long a time until someone else comes into the region who never agreed to the law; a thing which will happen almost everywhere within two days. But now none at all can be established; so that Luder clearly shows that in such a serious matter he makes foolish sport. Therefore, after Luder has conducted himself in this matter with such wonderful wisdom, he immediately concludes pompously.

Wherefore we see here that all pontiffs, all councils, all schools which express in the church something other than the word of God alone, are wolves, ministers of Satan, and false prophets. At the same time we understand the extraordinary stupidity of our Henry and of all Thomists who set their shameless mouth against heaven and dare to say in this sacrilegious book that even if the sacrament of orders had not been instituted in the scriptures, nevertheless the right of instituting it is in the power of the church. And how foolishly he adapted the word of Augustine, which he speaks about the gospel recognized and proved by the church in the whole world, to the right of establishing traditions by the free choice of impious men. This is the manner of understanding the statements of the fathers and of scripture. These are the men who write defenses of the sacraments. The multitude of these men and length of time is

Luther's words

Therefore you are a wolf and a minister of Satan and a false prophet

fidei, tam stupidi et hebetes, ut inter cognoscere et imperare nihil discernant.

IAM decies declarauimus uerbum dei, tam illud esse, quod deus absque scripto suae dicit ecclesiae: quam quod scriptura comprehen-
5 sum est. Sed quando manifestum est, Luderum loqui tantum de uerbo dei scripto: manifestum est, quod mentitur plane minister iste Satanae: qui clamat omnes ministros esse Satanae, quicunque sonant aliud in ecclesia: quam uerbum dei scriptum, in scriptura sacra. Nam hac ratione minister iste Satanae ministrum Satanae pronunciat
10 apostolum, qui dixit: Seruate, quae praecepi uobis, siue per ser-
monem, siue per epistolam, qui multa et
Quoties hoc dictum tibi uis docuit et instituit, non ex uerbo dei
Luthere? scripto, sed ex non scripta traditione dei.
Nam et illud ipsum de eucharistiae sacramento, Paulus non ex uerbo
15 dei scripto, sed ex non scripta dei traditione [RR₁v] tradidit Corinthijs. Quin et euangelistam pronunciat, ista ratione ministrum esse
Satanae: qui non solum docuit uerbum dei non scriptum, sed etiam
scripsit ipse, omnia dei uerba, neque scripta esse, neque scribi posse.
Quamobrem quum euangelista scribat, nec omnia scripta esse, nec
20 scribi posse: tibi nunc Ludere scriptura quaerenda est: quae probet,
quicquid ex dictis, factis, institutis Christi, non potuere scriptores
comprehendere, uelut erychthonium quempiam deformem ac
monstrosum partum, aeternis esse tenebris damnatum, et eum esse
ministrum Satanae: qui eorum omnium quicquam sonet in ecclesia:
25 quae scripta quidem non sunt: quae tamen fecit, quae tamen docuit
Iesus, et a patre missus spiritus. Tu nunc Luthere, qui nihil admittis,
nisi scripturas: profer scripturas, quibus
Is proferet suam doctrinam uetitum probes talia quenquam scribere.
AT si quis (inquis) talia scribat, quae pro dei uerbis asserat, atque
30 affirmet: ille Satanae minister est.

INTERIM extorsimus isti ministro Satanae, non esse protinus ministrum Satanae, qui praeter dei solius uerbum scriptum, hoc est praeter solum scripturae uerbum, aliud sonet in ecclesia.

---

11 *gloss* Quoties] *L*, quoties *BR*   14 Paulus] *corr. err. L*, populus *BR*   20 nunc] nec *L*
23 eum esse] esse *om. L*   25 scripta] scriptura *L*

the power of making articles of faith, men so stupid and dim-witted
that they make no distinction between investigating and commanding.

We have already declared ten times that the word of God is as
much that which God speaks to His church without writing as that
which is comprised in writing. But since it is clear that Luder speaks
only of the written word of God, it is clear that this minister of Satan
plainly lies who declares that all are ministers of Satan who say
anything else in the church than the word of God written in sacred
scripture. For by this reasoning this minister of Satan declares the
apostle a minister of Satan, who said:
"Keep the teachings that you have learned   *How many times do you want
whether by word or by letter," who both   this said to you, Luther?*
taught and instituted many things not according to the written word
of God, but according to the unwritten tradition of God. For even that
very teaching about the sacrament of the eucharist Paul delivered to
the Corinthians not according to the written word of God but according to the unwritten tradition of God. Indeed, Luther also declares the
evangelist according to this reasoning to be a minister of Satan, who
not only taught the unwritten word of God but also himself wrote that
all the words of God were neither written nor could be written.
Therefore, when the evangelist writes that neither have all things
been written nor can they be written, you must now seek, Luther, a
scriptural text which proves that whatever of the words, deeds,
institutions of Christ the writers could not include has been condemned to everlasting darkness like some deformed Erichthonius and
monstrous birth, and that he is a minister of Satan who expresses
anything at all of those things in the church, which indeed were not
written but which nevertheless Jesus did, which nevertheless He
taught, together with the Spirit sent by the Father. Now, Luther, you
who admit nothing but the scriptures,
bring forward the scriptures by which you   *He will bring forward his
prove that anyone is forbidden to write   own doctrine*
such things. But, you say, if anyone writes such things which he
asserts and affirms as the words of God, that man is a minister of
Satan.

Meanwhile we have wrested from this minister of Satan that he is
not wholly a minister of Satan who, apart from the written word of
God alone, that is, apart from the word of scripture alone, expresses
another word in the church.

AT VT non sit (inquiet) minister Satanae, qui loquitur aliud dei
uerbum, praeter id quod in scriptura sacra scriptum est: tamen est
minister Satanae, qui non solum sit locutus, aut scripserit, sed et
asseruerit.

5   AT HIC quoque mentitur iste minister Satanae. Nam si fas est
scribere Christi uerbum, quod dictum est: certe fas est et affirmare,
quod uerum est. Tandem huc paulatim detrudetur iste minister
Satanae, ut descedens ab eo, [RR₂] quod dixerat prius: nunc eum
dumtaxat asserat esse ministrum satanae,

Quam in omnem partem se
10   *uertit iste Proteus*   quicunque alios cogat ad credendum
ullum dei uerbum, quod non habetur in
scriptura canonica. Respondeat ergo nobis iste minister Satanae: Si
quicquam ex illis, quae quidem scripta non sunt: quae tamen fecit,
docuit, tradidit Iesus: quid si ex his (inquam) aliquid aliquis referat
15 Luthero, et relatum iubeat credere: sed referat is, de quo certus sit,
eum, qui referat, errare quicquam, aut falli in ea re discernenda non
posse? utrum peccaret ille, qui iuberet credere, an Lutherus, si
recuset credere? non dubito, quin hic fateretur se teneri: ut credat
reuelationi tam certae. At Luderus ipse fatetur, ecclesiam falli non
20   posse in iudicando uerbo dei: ergo eccle-

Quoties uincitur Lutherus sua
       confessione   siae narranti quicquam eorum, quae fecit,
quae docuit, quae tradidit Iesus, credere
tenetur Luderus. Ipse Satan apud inferos, non tenetur sua cathena
fortius, quam hac cathena stringitur eiusdem Satanae minister
25 Luderus. Nam si dicat se, quum fateretur ecclesiam habere a deo: ut
possit dei uerba discernere a uerbis hominum, hoc censisse dumtaxat
de uerbo scripto, non etiam de eo dicto: quod esset quidem, aut
factum aut dictum, a deo: sed tamen non scriptum in scriptura
canonica. Iam ante detrusus est ab illo praesidio, postquam
30   rationibus regis adactus, fatetur ecclesiam

Quomodo Lutherus a rege coactus
      sententiam mutarit   habere hoc quoque: ut possit diiudicare
non solum scripturam, sed etiam quaelibet
dogmata. Neque enim idem censet scripturas esse, quod dogmata,
praesertim homo tam frequens apud uocabularios. Quod si id fassus
35 non esset: tamen quantumuis impudens fuerit: necessario fatebitur,

17 Lutherus] Luderus *L*   27 dicto] dictum *BRL*

But, he will say, although he is not a minister of Satan who speaks another word of God besides that which is written in sacred scripture, nevertheless he is a minister of Satan who has not only spoken or written but also defended this word.

But here also this minister of Satan lies. For if it is lawful to write   5
the word of Christ which was spoken, certainly it is lawful to declare that it is true. This minister of Satan will finally be thrust down gradually to this point, that, departing from what he had said formerly, he now declares that only that man is a minister of Satan who forces others to believe any word of   10
God which is not contained in the canoni-   *How this Proteus turns himself*
cal scripture. Let this minister of Satan   *in every direction*
then answer us: If anything at all of those things which indeed have not been written, but which Jesus did, taught, and delivered; what if, I say, someone reported something of these things to Luther and   15
ordered him to believe what was reported, but, as concerns him who reports, Luther is certain that he who does the reporting cannot make any error or be deceived in discerning that matter? Would that man sin who ordered him to believe, or would Luther if he should refuse to believe? I have no doubt but that he would admit here that he is   20
bound to believe a revelation so certain. But Luder himself admits that the church cannot be deceived in
judging the word of God; therefore, when   *How often Luther is overcome by*
the church relates anything at all of those   *his own confession*
things which Jesus did, which He taught, which He delivered, Luder   25
is bound to believe. Satan himself in hell is not bound more strongly by his chain than the minister of that same Satan, Luder, is straitened by this chain. For if he should say that when he admitted that the church has the power from God of distinguishing the words of God from the words of men, he meant this to be said only of the written   30
word, not also of that word which was indeed either done or said by God but yet not written in the canonical scripture, already before-
hand he has been thrust down from that
defense, when, on being forced by the   *How Luther, forced by the king,*
                                          changed his opinion
reasonings of the king, he admits that the   35
church also has the power of judging not only scripture but also any doctrines whatever. He particularly, a man so versed in glossaries, does not judge that the scriptures are the same as doctrines. But if he had not admitted that, still, however shameless he has been, he will

nisi nobis probet, quod deus [RR₂v] qui potuit ecclesiam docere, quis
uerum scriberet: non posset eam docere, quis uerum diceret: aut deo

Solue Luthere hoc dilemma   demum id fuisse curae, ne falleretur
                                 ecclesia mendacibus chartis, uoluisse uero,
5 ut falleretur mendacibus linguis.

NVNC ergo uides lector, quod iste minister Satanae, qui scribit
omnes esse ministros Satanae: quicunque in ecclesia loquuntur aliud,
quam solum uerbum dei, solus exemplo magistri sui Satanae, solus
(inquam) torquet, inuertit, et blasphemat uerbum dei.

10   Refellit apertissimam Lutheri sycophantiam, qua
            regem mentitur dicere ecclesiam habere
                  ius instituendi sacramenti
                    ordinis. Cap. XXIII.

                                           Simul intelligimus insignem Henrici
            Verba Lutheri. Quanto   nostri et omnium Thomistarum stolidi-
15   *impudentior tu qui quod deus*
            instituit maledictis insectaris   tatem, qui os suum impudens in caelum
                                           ponunt, et dicere audent in hoc sacrilego
libello, etiam si sacramentum ordinis non esset in scripturis institutum,
tamen penes ecclesiam esse ius instituendi eius, et quam stulte uerbum
20 Augustini, quod de euangelio per ecclesiam toto orbe cognito et
probato loquitur, aptarit ad ius traditionum arbitrio impiorum
hominum statuendarum. Iste est modus intelligendi dicta patrum et
scripturas. Hi sunt qui scribunt assertiones sacramentorum. Horum
                                           multitudo et diuturnitas est potestas
            Tu ita discernis: ut omnia   faciendi articulos fidei tam stupidi et
25   *imperes, cognoscas nihil*
                                           hebetes, ut inter cognoscere et imperare
                                           nihil discernant.

DE VERBO Augustini quam recte scribat Lutherus, opinor esse
dictum satis. Nunc de eo dicendum, quod rex scripsit penes ecclesiam
30 esse ius instituendi sacramenti. [RR₃] Legi lector atque relegi totum
regis librum: ut uiderem, quomodo, quibus uerbis istud diceret: quod

26 cognoscere] *L*, cognosce re *BR*   29 eo] *L*, deo *BR*

necessarily admit it, unless he proves to us that God, who was able to
teach the church who wrote the truth, could not teach her who spoke
the truth; or finally that God took care
that the church should not be deceived by   *Solve this dilemma, Luther*
deceitful writings but wanted her to be deceived by deceitful tongues. 5

Now then you see, reader, that this minister of Satan, who writes
that all are ministers of Satan who speak anything else in the church
than the word of God alone, alone by the example of his master
Satan, alone, I say, tortures, perverts and blasphemes the word of
God.   10

He refutes Luther's most evident deceitfulness by which he falsely maintains that the king says the church has the right of instituting the sacrament of orders. Chapter 23.

At the same time we understand the ex-   15
traordinary stupidity of our Henry and   *Luther's words. How much more*
of all Thomists who set their shameless   *shameless are you who revile*
mouth against heaven and dare to say in   *with abusive language what*
this sacrilegious book that even if the   *God has instituted?*
sacrament of orders had not been instituted in the scriptures, neverthe- 20
less the right of instituting it is in the power of the church. And how
foolishly he adapted the word of Augustine, which he speaks about the
gospel recognized and proved by the church in the whole world, to
the right of establishing traditions by the free choice of impious men.
This is the manner of understanding the statements of the fathers and 25
scriptures. These are the men who write defenses of the sacraments.
The multitude of these men and length of time is the power of
making articles of faith, men so stupid
and dim-witted that they make no dis-   *You make such a distinction so*
tinction between investigating and com-   *that you may command all*
manding.   *things, investigate nothing*   30

I think enough has been said about how accurately Luther writes
of the word of Augustine. Now we must speak about the fact that the
king has written that the right of instituting a sacrament is in the
power of the church. I have read and reread, reader, the whole book   35
of the king to see how, in what words he said this, that the church

ecclesia posset instituere sacramentum ordinis, etiam si institutum
non esset a deo: certe non inuenio id aperte

Quod nihil solidi habet Lutherus   dictum per asseuerationem, sed tantum
leuissima quaeque sectatur

repetendo, quae probauerat, dicit obiter
5   quiddam, non tamen prorsus idem, quod ei Lutherus imputat, sed ex
quo reor eum arripuisse ansam: qua illud, ut solet, colligat. Nam
uerba regis ista sunt.

"NVNC QVONIAM probauimus ex

Verba regis   ipsius Lutheri fundamento, sacramenta,
10   quae credit ecclesia, non aliunde quam a deo potuisse constitui,
etiam si nihil inde prorsus in scriptura legeretur: uideamus tamen, an
scriptura tam nullam omnino mentionem faciat huius sacramenti."

EN LECTOR candide, quibus uerbis rex in sacramento ordinis
dicit ecclesiam potuisse instituere sacramentum ordinis, etiam si non
15   fuisset institutum a deo. Sic intelligit uerba regis Luderi sapientia, sic
recenset Luderi synceritas. Sic orbis iudicium reuerendi patris uir-
gineus reuereretur pudor. Hic est cuius uerbo, contra sanctos patres, et
uerbum dei stare debeat mundus: et quia dicit ipse se certum esse
dogmata sua se habere de caelo: ideo scilicet certi sunt omnes, quod
20   frater mendacissimus non potest mentiri.

Taxat lepide Lutheri gloriosum triumphum de missa. Cap. XXIIII.

Lutheri uerba   Reuertamur ad propositum. Missam
itaque extorsimus, et triumphamus ad-
25   uersus assertorem sacramentorum, non esse opus [RR₃v] neque
sacrificium, sed uerbum et signum gratiae diuinae, quibus erga nos
utitur pro fide in eum erigenda et firmanda. Videmusque, quam sit
infatuatus Satan, ut quo diutius et magis,

Quanta est Lutheri calliditas,   in nos furat et scribat, eo insulsius et
qui iam satanam magistrum
30   *suum deprehendat stulticiae*   ineptius delyret. Nam iste liber regis, ut
omnium, qui contra me scripti sunt, fere

2 *gloss* Quod] *L,* quod *BR*

could institute the sacrament of orders even if it had not been instituted by God; I certainly do not find it said openly by way of emphatic
assertion, but only in repeating what he
had proved, he does say in passing some-   *Because he has nothing solid,*
thing, yet not precisely the same thing as   *Luther pursues all the most*
Luther imputes to him, but something from   *trivial points*   5
which I think he has seized on a pretext with which, as is usual, he
makes an inference. For these are the words of the king.

"Now since we have proved from
Luther's own foundation that the sacra-   *The king's words*   10
ments which the church believes could not have been established
otherwise than by God, even if nothing at all were read about them
in scripture, let us nevertheless see whether scripture makes no
mention at all of this sacrament."

Behold, honest reader, with what words the king says of the sacra- 15
ment of orders that the church could have instituted the sacrament of
orders, even if it had not been instituted by God. Thus the wisdom of
Luder understands the words of the king; thus the honesty of Luder
quotes. Thus the virginal modesty of the reverend father stands in awe
of the judgment of the world. This is the man by whose word the   20
world is supposed to stand firm against the holy fathers and the word
of God; and because he himself says that he is certain that he has his
doctrines from heaven, therefore of course all are certain that the most
lying friar cannot lie.

He wittily twits Luther's boastful triumph   25
on the mass. Chapter 24.

Let us return to the point at issue. And
so we have wrenched away the mass by   *Luther's words*
force and we triumphantly proclaim against the defender of the sacraments that it is not a work nor a sacrifice but a word and a sign of   30
divine grace which He employs toward us to arouse and strengthen
faith in Him. And we see how Satan has been made a fool of, so that the
longer and the more he rages and writes
against us so much more bunglingly and   *How great is Luther's shrewdness,*
foolishly does he rave. For this book of   *who now grasps that Satan is*
the king, as it is almost the best Latin of   *his master of folly*   35

est latinissimus, ita est certe omnium ineptissimus et stolidissimus, ut pene nostris Lupsensibus scriptoribus, eum tribuerim, qui sic solent argutari, quando argutantur optime.

QVAM MIRABILIS rerum nouator est Dominus Martinus, post-
5 quam fecit nobis nouam religionem, et nouam fidem: nunc nouo more triumphat ante uictoriam. Solebat aegre triumphum impetrare,

Noua ratio triumphandi Luthero usurpata

qui saepe uicisset. Sed is decies iam trium-phat, quia ter decies uictus est. Verum idcirco minus est istud mirandum, quia
10 ueteres ab alijs impetrabant. Luderus uero triumphum suum sibi decernit ipse. Sed quid ni facile triumphet, de tam fatuo libello, quam fuit libellus ille principis: qui ut omnium, qui contra Luderum scripti sunt fere fuit latinissimus: ita fuit omnium, si credimus Luthero, stultissimus. Quid ni? Nam et ideo id, quod ipse fatetur, illis
15 maxime placuit, qui maxime cupiunt scilicet, quicquid aduersus illum scribitur, maxime esse stolidum: et ideo etiam Dominus Luderus tam uehementer irascitur: quia illum librum facile potest

Hinc uidelicet lachrymae hinc ille fraterculi furor

per ludum iocumque refellere: utpote cuius stulticia Lutheri sapientiam depre-
20 hendit, et impietates eius ostendit, et publice traduxit stolidae solertiae consilia: quibus sibi uisus est callide uiam ingressus, qua Christi sacramenta omnia, omnem fidem religionemque subuerteret.

Verba Lutheri

Triumphata uero missa, puto nos totum
25 papam triumphare. Nam super missam ceu rupem nititur totus papatus cum suis [RR₄] monasterijs, episcopatibus, collegijs, altaribus, ministeriis, et doctrinis, atque adeo cum toto uentre suo. Quae omnia ruere necesse est ruente missa eorum sacrilega et abominanda. Sic Christus per me coepit abomina-
30 tiones in loco sancto stantes reuelare, et destruere eum, cuius aduentus

Is tu es Luthere omnibus modis

fuit per operationem Satanae in pro-digiis, et signis mendacibus. O miserum illum defensorem ecclesiae papisticae. O miseram ecclesiam, quae frustra indulgentias suas pro tanto libello profudit. Nisi quod digna

---

2 Lupsensibus] Lypsensibus *L*   18 *gloss om. L*   30 destruere] *L*, destuere *BR*

all those which have been written against me, so it is certainly the most foolish and stupid of all, so that I almost attributed it to our Leipzig writers, who are thus accustomed to quibble when they quibble at their best.

What a wonderful innovator is the honored Martin; after he has made us a new religion and a new faith, now by a new custom he proclaims his triumph before the victory. It used to be the custom that one who had conquered often obtained his triumph with difficulty. But this man has already triumphed ten times because he has been *A new reason for triumphing* conquered three times ten times. But this *seized on by Luther* is less to be wondered at since the ancients obtained their triumph from others. But Luder himself decrees his triumph for himself. But why should he not easily triumph over such a foolish book as was that book of the prince, which, as it was almost the best Latin of all those which have been written against Luder, so it was of all of them, if we believe Luther, the most foolish? Why not? And therefore, as he himself admits, it was especially pleasing to those who especially desire of course that whatever is written against him be especially stupid; and therefore also the honored Luder is in such a violent rage, because he can easily refute that book by jeering and joking, seeing that its folly has caught on to Luther's wisdom and showed his impieties and *Hence of course the tears,* publicly exposed to ridicule the designs of *hence that raging madness* his stupid sagacity by which he thought he *of the friarling* had shrewdly entered the path by which he might destroy all the sacraments of Christ, all faith and religion.

Having indeed triumphed over the mass, I *Luther's words* think we triumph over the pope entirely. For on the mass as on a rock does the whole papacy rely with its monasteries, episcopacies, colleges, altars, ministries, and doctrines and indeed with its whole belly. All these necessarily fall into ruin with the ruin of their sacrilegious and abominable mass. Thus through me has Christ begun to reveal the abominations standing in the holy place and to destroy him whose coming occurred *You are he, Luther, in every* through the operation of Satan in prod- *way* igies and deceitful signs. O that wretched defender of the papistic church. O wretched church, which vainly lavished its indulgences for the sake of such an important book; unless

merces reddita est tam defensori quam libello. Quales enim sunt indulgentiae, talis est ecclesia, talis defensor, talis et libellus.

TANQVAM diceret, postquam nunc in caelum conscendi, sub-uectus alis anseris: possum iam quolibet radiis prodeambulare solari-

5　bus, et ex alto tanquam formicas despicere papas omnes, et omnes episcopos, collegia, monasteria, sacerdotes, equites, duces, principes,

Lutheri fastuosa gloriatio　omnia subieci pedibus meis, postquam ad aquilonem posui solium meum, et factus

sum similis altissimo. Sic Satan abominationem statuit in loco sancto,

10　dum abominandum fraterculum suscitat in ecclesia dei, dum sacrilegum ac detestabilem nebulonem furiosis inflat furijs: qui sacramentorum ignauus hostis, tumore uano pugnet aduersus eum: cuius aduentus fuit cum humilitate: qui post ueniet cum potentia: quum spiritu oris sui in puluerem difflabit istum, superbiae et

15　diffidentiae filium: qui iam gloriatur stolidus in malicia, et sibi

Tantum non hoc dicit Lutherus　uidetur potens in iniquitate: dum secum dicit insipiens in corde suo, non est deus.

O miserum aduersarium sacramentorum, quem tunc sacramentorum gratia destituet. O miserum illusorem caracterum, quem tunc

20　baptismi caracter et caracter ordinis, uelut inusta stigmata traducent transfugam, tradentque [RR₄v] supplicio. O miserum irrisorem ecclesiae catholicae, quae tunc uicissim miser in tuo ridebit interitu. Tunc illusor indulgentiae, heu quibus suspirijs optabis indulgentiam: quum negata uenia recipies meritam iniquitatis mercedem in aeternis

25　ignibus: qui diabolo et angelis eius tui similibus praeparati sunt.

---

7 *gloss* fastuosa] fatuosa *L*　　16 *gloss* Tantum] *L*, tantum *BR*

a fitting reward was paid to the defender as to the book. For such as are indulgences, such is the church, such the defender, such also the book.

As though he said, "Now that I have mounted into heaven, borne aloft on the wings of a goose, I can now stroll wherever I please on the rays of the sun, and from a height look down on all popes as though they were ants, and on all bishops, colleges, monasteries, priests, knights, dukes, princes; I have subjected all things beneath my feet after I placed my *Luther's proud boasting* throne toward the north, and have become like to the most high." Thus Satan has set up the abomination in the holy place when he raises up the abominable friarling in the church of God, when he puffs up the sacrilegious and loathsome scoundrel with raging furies, who as a cowardly enemy of the sacraments fights with empty bombast against Him whose coming was in humility, who will afterwards come with power, when with the breath of His mouth He will scatter into dust this son of pride and faithlessness who now stupidly boasts in malice and thinks him- *Only this Luther does not say* self powerful in wickedness when together with him the fool says in his heart, there is no God.

O wretched adversary of the sacraments, whom at that time the grace of the sacraments will leave desolate. O wretched mocker of the sacramental characters whom at that time the baptismal character and the character of orders, branded like marks of disgrace, will degrade as a deserter and deliver to punishment. O wretched mocker of the catholic church, which at that time will in its turn laugh at you, wretch, in your ruin. Then, mocker of forgiveness, alas with what sighs you will long for forgiveness when, with forgiveness refused, you will receive the deserved reward of iniquity in the everlasting fires which have been prepared for the devil and his angels like you.

Refutantur Lutheri nugamenta aduersus
sacramentum ordinis. Cap. XXV.

Verba Lutheri   Haec mihi pro defensione primi sacra-
                                         menti, satis sint. In quo asserendo max-
5   ime laborauit assertor dominus Henricus, ut qui non ignorauit in
       hoc esse sitam summam salutis papistici regni. Caetera cogor differre
       obrutus multis alijs occupationibus, tum maxime transferenda Biblia,
       Certe prosperas quantum uales   necessaria scilicet opera. Ne satanae
                                         studia ipse prosperem nimio.

10   HACTENVS satis laboratum sit Domino Ludero, pro impugna-
       tione primi sacramenti. Iam lassatus in uia iniquitatis, caetera cogitur
       differre, totus obrutus in transferenda Biblia, necessaria scilicet
       Quomodo Lutherus uertat biblia opera: ut Satanae studia prosperet nimio,
                                         dum scripturam sacram sic uertat: ut
15   inuertat sensum: ac faciat fucum illiteratae plebeculae: quae ad
       haeretici uersionem examinet haereses: ad quas probandas plumbea
       illa regula iam inflexa sit de industria.

Verba Lutheri   Satanas per hos insulsos libellos me im-
                                         pedire cogitat, sed nihil efficiet. Neque
20   magni operis fuerit stolidos Thomistas, in reliquis sex sacramentis
       confutare.

       SATANAS excogitauit suo militi causam, quam praetendat fugae.
       Nam ad se eum uocat, alio missurus milita[SS₁]tum: ubi magis ei
       necessariam nauet operam: si quid praestare possit in euertendo
25   *Vt nihil sceleris intentatum*   biblio. Nam quod in sacramentis tentauit
       relinquit Lutherus   apud mentis compotes, uidet conatum
                                         frustra. Interea soluens obsidionem, mina-
       tur eo rediturum se: postquam euerterit biblion: neque magni operis
       fore, reliqua sex expugnare sacramenta, uictori tanto: qui in eo,

---

25 *gloss om. L*   29 tanto] *corr. err. L,* tonto *BR*

Luther's trifling remarks against the sacrament of orders are refuted. Chapter 25.

Let this suffice for me in answer to the
defense of the first sacrament. In defend-
Luther's words

ing it Lord Henry the defender especially labored as one who was not 5
unaware that in this is placed the ultimate safety of the papistic
dominion. I am forced to put off the others, overwhelmed by many
other concerns, but especially by the
translating of the Bible, clearly a neces-
You certainly prosper them as much as you can

sary work, lest I myself prosper the efforts 10
of Satan too much.

The honored Luder may well have labored enough up till now for
his attack on the first sacrament. Now, wearied in the way of iniquity,
he is forced to put off other things, being wholly overwhelmed in translating the Bible, clearly a necessary work so that he may prosper the 15
efforts of Satan exceedingly, while he so
translates sacred scripture as to mistrans-
How Luther translates the Bible

late its meaning and tricks the uneducated
common folk, who from a translation by a heretic ponder heresies, to
prove which that leaden rule has been deliberately bent. 20

Satan thinks through these senseless
books to hinder me, but he will accom-
Luther's words

plish nothing; nor will it have been any great effort to refute the dull-
witted Thomists on the remaining six sacraments.

Satan has figured out a case for his soldier, which he brings forward 25
as an excuse for flight. For he summons him to himself, planning to
send him to fight elsewhere where he may carry out vigorously a
work more necessary for him, if he can accomplish anything in mis-
translating the Bible. For what he tried on
the sacraments among men of sense, he
That Luther leaves no crime untried

sees to have been attempted in vain. 30
Raising the siege for the time being, he threatens that he will return
to it after he has mistranslated the Bible, and that it will be no great
effort for such a mighty conqueror to take the remaining six sacraments by storm, who in that one which he first assaulted labored in 35

quod primum oppugnauit, operam luserit: et reiectus cum dedecore, uictus turpissime, fusus fugatusque discesserit.

Verba Lutheri   Nihil proferunt responsione dignum per tota sex sacramenta, praeter illud unum, quod de sacramento ordinis adducit Paulum, scilicet ad Titon, iubentem, ut per ecclesias ordinet presbyteros. Hoc loco enim uult institutum ordinis sacramentum.

NVNC doctor Luderus non habet ocium ludendi: currit enim celeriter amissis copijs, et insequentes timens, trepidus, uelut canis, e nilo bibit et fugit. Reliqua praeterit *Hoc erat facilius quam confutare ea* omnia, uelut contemptim: quae tu quum ex ipso regis libello legeris: uidebis facile, cur praetereat. Interim arripit illud apostoli ad Titum. Nam regem sentire dicit, quod ibi sacramentum ordinis fuit institutum.

HIC tuam lector imploro fidem, aduersus istius nebulonis stolidissimam perfidiam. Quoties quam aperte dicit, et inculcat rex, imo quoties quam aperte probat, nullum sacramentum aut institutum esse, aut institui posse nisi a deo: quam euidenter id ipsum iterum atque iterum nominatim repetit in sacra- *Num consyderat Lutherus, quae loquitur?* mento ordinis? et nunc ait iste nebulo stolidissimus regem dicere, sacramentum ordinis institutum esse ab apostolo. At in sacramento unctionis extremae, quum iste scurra blasphemus aduersus apostolum Iacobum, di[SS₁v]ceret se non crediturum apostolo de sacramento unctionis extremae: quippe qui non haberet ius instituendi sacramenti, hoc est promittendi gratiam cum signo uisibili. Rex ita respondet, apostolum tradidisse populo, quod ipse acceperat a Christo. Sicut et apostolus Paulus tradidit Corinthijs, quod acceperat *Vides lector hic quam nihil pro sano dicat Lutherus* a Christo. Neutrum dicit instituisse. Quod si rex dixisset, id quod iste mentitur ab eo dictum: nempe quod sacramentum ordinis institutum fuit a Paulo: quare non hic rursus idem elatrauit in Paulum: quod illic rabidus

---

1–2 et reiectus . . . discesserit] *corr. err.*, et reiectus, cum dedecore uictus, turpissime fusus, fugatusque decesserit *BR*, & reiectus cum dedecore victus turpissime fusus fugatusque decesserit *L*   28 *gloss* Vides] *L*, uides *BR*

vain and, beaten back with disgrace, most shamefully conquered,
routed and put to flight, left the battle.

They present nothing worthy of an
answer throughout the whole six sacra-
ments besides that one text which he cites on the sacrament of orders,   5
namely, where Paul orders Titus to ordain presbyters throughout the
churches. For by this passage he would have the sacrament of orders
instituted.

Luther's words

Now doctor Luder has no leisure for mockery, for he runs swiftly,
having lost his supplies, and fearing his pursuers, alarmed, like a dog   10
he drinks from the Nile and flees. He
passes by all the rest as though in contempt; when you have read them from the
book of the king itself you will easily see why he passes over them.
Meanwhile he seizes on that text of the apostle to Titus. For he says   15
that the king understands that the sacrament of orders was instituted
in that text.

*This was easier than to
refute them*

Here, reader, I invoke your honesty against the most stupid dishonesty of this scoundrel. How often the king says so clearly and
insists, indeed, how often he proves so clearly that no sacrament   20
either has been instituted or can be instituted except by God; how
evidently he has repeated this very thing again and again explicitly
in discussing the sacrament of orders. And
now this most stupid scoundrel says that
the king says that the sacrament of orders   25
was instituted by the apostle. But on the sacrament of extreme unction,
when this blasphemous buffoon said against the apostle James that he
would not believe the apostle on the sacrament of extreme unction since
he did not have the right to institute a sacrament, that is, to promise
grace with a visible sign, the king answers in this way, that the apostle   30
delivered to the people what he himself had received from Christ, just
as the apostle Paul delivered to the
Corinthians what he had received from
Christ. He says that neither of them insti-
tuted a sacrament. But if the king had said what this fellow falsely   35
claims was said by him, namely, that the sacrament of orders was
instituted by Paul, why did the fellow not bark again here the same
thing against Paul as he there barked madly against James, that he

*Does not Luther reflect on what
he speaks?*

*You see here, reader, how Luther
says nothing rationally*

elatrauit in Iacobum, se non crediturum Paulo, de sacramento
ordinis, etiam si esset apostolus? Nam nullum apostolum habere
potestatem condendi sacramentum, id est promittendi gratiam cum
signo uisibili. Cur hic dissimulat istud nebulo, si rex illud scripsit:
5   quum illic se cohibere non potuit a blasphemia: ubi scripsit aduersus
alios, quorum nescio, an id quisquam scripserit? Quomodo potuit rex
sentire, sacramentum ordinis institutum ab apostolo: quum toties
aperte dicat, apostolos institutos esse sacerdotes a Christo? et tamen
hoc eum dicere dicit pater Luderus: qui toties mentitur se nunquam
10   *Lutheri tergiuersatio*   mentiri. Nunc uides lector solers strato-
gema fugientis Luderi: quo fumum offun-
dat, qui fugam tegat.

          Verba Lutheri   Sed non uidet larua Thomistica, quid
uel ego dicam, uel ipsemet respondeat.
15   Ego ordinem negaui sacramentum esse, id est promissionem et
signum gratiae adiectum, quale est baptismus et panis, non negaui,
imo asserui esse uocationem et institutionem ministri et concionatoris,
siue hoc fiat authoritate unius apostoli, uel pontificis sola, uel populi
eligentis et consentientis simul nihil refert. Quamquam rectius fiat
20   populo eligente et consentiente, quomodo apostoli Actuum .iiij.
septem diacones insti[SS₂]tuerunt. Nam ut Paulus Titon iubet
presbiteros ordinare, non tamen sequitur, solum Titon sua authoritate
id fecisse, sed exemplo apostolorum, per suffragia populi eos instituisse,
alioqui pugnabunt uerba Pauli cum exemplo apostolorum. Quae
25   uero de impositione manuum ad ordinis sacramentum trahit, uident
                                  pueri nihil ad ordinis sacramentum
   Imo tuus hic mos est, torquere   pertinere, sed more suo papistico, sic e
        scripturam quo lubet   scripturis facit quodcunque uisum fuerit.
Impositio manuum tunc erat donatio uisibilis spiritus sancti.

30   VERE non uides larua Ludere, quid uel dicas ipse, uel respondeat
princeps. Neque enim rex probauit tibi sacramentum ordinis, esse
tantum uocationem et institutionem ministri, et concionatoris: sed
tam uere sacramentum esse quam baptismus est, aut eucharistia,
idque secundum tuam ipsius finitionem, hoc est uere conferre
35   *Quis apertius Luthere?*   gratiam, cum signo sensibili. Sed neque tu
Ludere dixisti simpliciter promissionem

---

35 *gloss* Luthere] *L,* luthere *BR*

would not believe Paul on the sacrament of orders even if he was an
apostle? For no apostle has the power to establish a sacrament, that
is, to promise grace with a visible sign. Why does the scoundrel dissimulate this here if the king wrote that, when there he could not
restrain himself from blasphemy where he wrote against others, of   5
whom I do not know whether anyone wrote that? How could the king
think that the sacrament of orders was instituted by the apostle when
so often he says clearly that the apostles were instituted priests by
Christ? And yet father Luder says that he says this, he who so often
lies that he never lies. Now you see, reader,   10
Luder's shrewd stratagem as he flees, by   *Luther's vacillation*
which he spreads out smoke to conceal his flight.

But the Thomistic spectre does not see
either what I am saying or what he himself   *Luther's words*
should answer. I denied that orders is a sacrament, that is, a promise 15
and sign of grace added, such as are baptism and the bread; I did not
deny, on the contrary, I stated emphatically that it is a calling and
instituting of a minister and preacher, whether this is done by the
authority of one apostle or by that of the pope alone, or by that of the
people choosing and agreeing together makes no difference. Although   20
it would be done more correctly by the choice and agreement of the
people, as the apostles, Acts 4, instituted seven deacons. For although
Paul orders Titus to ordain presbyters, it does not nevertheless follow
that Titus alone did this on his own authority, but by the example of
the apostles he instituted them through the formal approbation of the   25
people; otherwise, the words of Paul will conflict with the example of
the apostles. Indeed, children see that what he drags in about the
imposition of hands for the sacrament of orders does not belong to the
sacrament of orders, but in his own
papistic way he treats as according to the   *On the contrary, this is your*
scriptures whatever has seemed best. The   *custom, to twist the scripture*   30
imposition of the hands was at that time   *as you please*
the visible conferring of the Holy Spirit.

Truly you do not see, spectre Luder, either what you yourself are
saying or what the prince answers. For the king did not prove to you   35
that the sacrament of orders is only a calling and an instituting of a
minister and preacher, but that it is as truly a sacrament as baptism
is or the eucharist, and that according to your own definition; that is,
that it truly confers grace with a sensible
sign. But neither did you, Luder, say   *Who is clearer, Luther?*
                                                                        40

gratiae, cum adiecto signo sensibili sacramentum esse, sicut nunc
te uideri uis dixisse. Imo negasti plane promissionem ullam gratiae
factam a Christo, cum adiecto uisibili signo, sacramentum esse: nisi
eadem promissio cum suo signo comprehensa legatur euidente
5   scriptura. Hac in re tibi restitit rex. Hac in re te mentitum probauit
euidente scriptura. Nam et omnia pro-

Hic Luthere disce, quid regi   bauit a Christo instituta, uerbo et facto,
tecum non conueniat

prorsus absque scriptura: nec omnia, quae
fecit Christus, esse comprehensa scripturis: id uero probauit rex
10 euidentissimis scripturis. At nec ecclesiam in talibus errare posse
falliue, quatinus ad sacramenta spectat. id non euidentibus tantum
scripturis probauit, sed euidentibus etiam rationibus, et ex tua
confessione iacto fundamento, te pertraxit illuc: ut tibi necesse fuerit,
etiam fateri caetera. [SS₂v] quaecunque tam obstinate negaueras. Et
15 tamen ex abundanti probauit tibi in sacramento ordinis, gratiam
illam cum signo uisibili, patere quoque ex scripturis ipsis, ex quibus
diuersa tibi loca protulit, apertiora quoque ex eodem apostolo: quam
sit ille locus ad Titum: cuiusmodi sunt unus aut alter ad Timotheum.
Atque ita hac in re rursus patet tua nescio impudentior an stultior
20 sycophantia, et stolidissimum effugium tuum, quo fingis, quod
impositio manuum tunc fuit donatio

Commentum Lutheri de impositione   uisibilis spiritus sancti, non collatio gratiae:
manuum

quasi non multis manum imposuerint
laicis: dum eos ordinauerunt in clericos: quibus iam ante donatus
25 fuerat in signo sensibili spiritus sanctus: aut quasi spiritus sanctus, adueniens in sensibili signo, christianis nullam secum gratiam
conferat.

SED et istud aeque stolidum est effugium: quum apostoli uerba,
quibus perspicuum est, ordinem fuisse collatum per episcopos, sic
30 declinas: ut id fatearis quidem, caeterum non probari ex eo, quod
episcopus ordinauit, ordinasse solum sine suffragijs populi: ne uerba
Pauli pugnarent cum exemplo apostolorum, instituentium diaconos:
scilicet quia quum tales in clerum essent

Diluitur Lutheri interpretatio   electuri: quibus dispensatio crederetur
de exemplo apostolorum
35   rerum temporalium, noluerunt uti suo

---

11 falliue] fallive *L*, falli ue *BR*; quatinus] *corr. err. L*, quantumuis *BR*   16 uisibili,
patere] *corr. err.*, uisibili. Patere *BR*, visibili patere *L*   23 manum] *L*, manuum *BR*
33 *gloss* Lutheri] *L*, lutheri *BR*

simply that a promise of grace with a sensible sign added is a sacrament, as you now wish to appear to have said. On the contrary, you clearly denied that any promise of grace made by Christ with a visible sign added is a sacrament unless the same promise with its sign is read included in evident scripture. In this matter the king resisted you. In 5 this matter he proved by evident scripture that you lied. For he proved that all were instituted by Christ through word and deed altogether apart from scripture, and that not all the things which Christ did are included in scriptures; indeed the king proved 10 this by most evident scriptures. But that the church cannot in such matters err or be deceived so far as pertains to the sacraments, this he proved not only by evident scriptures but also by evident reasonings and, the foundation having been laid from your own confession, he dragged you along forcibly to the point where it was necessary for you 15 to admit also the other things that you had so stubbornly denied. And yet he proved to you abundantly concerning the sacrament of orders that that grace with a visible sign is evident also from the scriptures themselves, from which he presented to you various passages, also from the same apostle, clearer than is that passage to Titus; of the 20 same sort are several to Timothy. And thus in this matter there is again evident your trickery—I know not whether it is more shameless or more foolish—and your most stupid escape by which you pretend that the imposition of the hands was at that time 25 the visible conferring of the Holy Spirit, not the bestowing of a grace; as if they did not impose the hand on many laymen when they ordained them as clerics, to whom the Holy Spirit had already before been given in a sensible sign; or as if the Holy Spirit, approaching in a sensible sign, bestows on Christians no grace together with Himself. 30

But this also is an equally stupid escape when you so avoid the words of the apostle, by which it is clear that orders were conferred by bishops, that you admit this indeed, but say that it is not proved from the fact that the bishop ordained that he ordained alone without the approbation of the people, lest the words of Paul conflict with the 35 example of the apostles in instituting deacons; clearly because, when they were about to elect such men to the clergy to whom the dispensation of temporal goods

Here learn, Luther, why the king does not agree with you

Luther's fabrication on the imposition of hands

Luther's interpretation on the example of the apostles is destroyed

iure: ut absque populo deputarent ipsorum loco, uictum cuique
diuisuros diaconos: quia magis extra suspitionem fore uidebant
populo: quos ipse diuisores praetulisset: ideo scilicet pugnaret cum
hoc exemplo Paulus, si uolebat Titum ut in praeficiendo presbytero
5 spiritalium rerum ministro: conferret sacramentum ordinis sine
suffragijs populi, in eo [SS₃] loco, ubi cuiusque merita nota essent
ipsi, qui consecraturus erat episcopo. Nam interdum, ubi id minus
erat notum: permittebant episcopi populo: ut nominaret, quem
censeret optimum: quae res magis erat

Vides Luthere, quam nihil
10 *proderit commentum tuum*

commendatio quaedam uirtutis, et probatae uitae testimonium, quam ius elec-
tionis. Sed hic dicis, nihil tua referre: siue ordinetur sacerdos
authoritate unius apostoli uel pontificis sola, siue populi eligentis et
consentientis simul. Ecce, quomodo turpiter retro fugis. Nunquid in
15 Babylonica scripsisti manifeste, nullo modo episcopum sine populo,
posse sua sola authoritate facere sacerdotes: nec opus esse ordinationibus aut consecrationibus, usque adeo, ut haec tua tibi uerba rex
obiecerit?

Verba Lutheri. Ex Babylone

Si sacerdotes cogerentur admittere om-
20 nes aequaliter sacerdotes esse, quotquot
baptizati sumus, sicut reuera sumus, illisque solum ministerium, nostro
tamen consensu, datum, permissum nullum eis super nos ius imperij,
nisi quantum nos sponte nostra admitteremus.

HIS uerbis aperte negas pontificem solum, posse facere sacerdotem,
25 nisi consensu uestro. Nam te quoque eximis prorsus ordini sacer-
dotali: atque adnumeras laicis: idque in paucis uerbis facis aperte
septies: ut plane facias perspicuum te tibi

Neque enim est nisi Satanae,
cuius sacra colit

sacerdotem non esse amplius. Nempe quia
te ordinauit episcopus absque consensu
30 laicorum: et adhibuit consecrationem. quam tu uelut superstitiosam
execraris. Nam et ita scribis paulo post.

---

3 pugnaret] pugnare *L*   10 *gloss* proderit] *corr. err. L*, proferit *BR*

was to be entrusted, they did not wish to employ without the people
their own right to set up in their own place deacons to distribute
provisions to each one, because they saw that those men would be
more free from suspicion among the people whom the people themselves had put in charge as distributors; therefore, of course, Paul   5
would conflict with this example if he wished Titus, in putting a pres-
byter in charge as minister of spiritual goods, to confer the sacrament
of orders without the formal approbation of the people in that place
where the merits of each one were known to the very bishop who was
to consecrate. For at times when the matter was less well known the   10
bishops permitted the people to name the one whom they judged
best; which practice was more a kind of
commendation of virtue and a testimony   *You see, Luther, how your trick*
of an approved life than the right of   *has profited nothing*
election. But here you say that it makes no difference to you whether   15
the priest is ordained by the sole authority of a single apostle or
pontiff or by that of the people choosing and agreeing together.
Behold how shamefully you beat a retreat. Did you not write clearly
in the *Babylon* that the bishop could in no way make priests on his
authority alone without the people, and that there was no need of   20
ordinations and consecrations, so much so that the king raised these
words of yours as an objection to you?

> If priests were forced to admit that as
> many of us as are baptized are all equally   *Luther's words from the*
> priests, as in fact we are, and that the   *Babylon*   25
> ministry alone is given to them, yet by our consent, and that no right of
> command over us is granted them except insofar as we allowed it of
> our own free choice. . . .

By these words you clearly say that the pontiff alone cannot make
a priest except by your consent. For you completely remove yourself   30
also from the sacerdotal order and number yourself among the laity,
and this you do clearly seven times in a few words, so that you make
it perfectly clear that in your own mind
you are no longer a priest. No doubt   *Nor is he, except of Satan,*
because the bishop ordained you without   *whose worship he celebrates*
                                                                          35
the consent of the laity and employed consecration which you
execrate as superstitious. For even so you write shortly after.

Lutheri uerba   Negari non potest, ecclesias olim a senior-
                        ibus fuisse rectas absque istis ordination-
ibus et consecrationibus, propter aetatem et longum rerum usum,
in hoc electis. [SS₃v]

5   ECCE, quam aperte scripsisti dudum, episcopum sine populo non
posse sacerdotem facere, et ordinationibus aut consecrationibus opus
non esse. At nunc manifeste uictus, utrumque fateris falsum. Sed
tamen addis, nihil tua referre: quasi dicas, Tam impudens nebulo
sum, ut mea nihil referat, quam aperte conuincar insaniae. Nam et
10 istud quoque, quod et in Babylonica scripsisti, et nunc repetis,
                              ordinem esse tantum officium concion-
Quoties Luthere uis tibi solui
                              andi, Rex et ratione tibi sustulit, et
euidentibus plane scripturis: e quibus unum locum aut alterum uisum
est commemorare: ut uideat lector, quam belle Luderus ludat in re
15 tam sancta et seria. Sic enim scribit princeps.
                        "ORDINEM Lutherus negat sacra-
Verba regis
                        mentum esse: et ritum tantum esse dicit
eligendi concionatoris. Nam qui non concionantur: nihil minus ait
esse, quam sacerdotes: nec aliter sacerdotes esse, quam homo pictus
20 est homo: contra Paulum apostolum, qui ad Timotheum scribens ait,
Qui bene praesunt presbiteri, duplici honore digni sunt, maxime qui
laborant in uerbo et doctrina. Apostolus hic manifeste docet, quamquam ij praecipue duplici honore digni sunt, qui quum presbiteri
sint, laborant in uerbo et doctrina. tamen et qui hoc non faciunt, non
25 solum esse presbiteros, sed et bene praeesse posse, et duplicem quoque
honorem promereri. Alioqui non dixisset, maxime qui laborant in
uerbo et doctrina: sed solum ij, qui laborant in uerbo et doctrina.
Praeterea ne possit dicere Luderus, id quod dicit, officium sacerdotis
                              erga populum, nihil esse nisi praedicare.
Lutherana missae definitio
30   Nam missas, inquit, canere, nihil est aliud
quam commu[SS₄]nicare se ipsum: hoc inquam (ut appareat) quam
falsum sit rursus audiamus apostolum. Omnis, inquit, pontifex, ex
hominibus assumptus, pro hominibus constituitur in his, que sunt ad
deum: ut offerat dona et sacrificia pro peccatis. An non apostolus

11 *gloss* Luthere] *L*, luthere *BR*   15 sancta] *L*, sanncta *BR*   30 canere] cauere *L*
31 inquam] *L*, imquam *BR*

It cannot be denied that the churches *Luther's words* were once governed by elders chosen for this function because of their age and long experience in affairs, without these ordinations and consecrations.

Behold how clearly you wrote formerly that the bishop cannot make a priest without the people and that there is no need of ordinations or consecrations. But now, clearly vanquished, you admit that both are false. But yet you add that it makes no difference to you, as if you should say: I am such a shameless scoundrel that it makes no difference to me how clearly I am convicted of madness. For even this also which you wrote in the *Babylon* and now repeat, that orders is only the *How often, Luther, do you want this solved for you?* office of preaching, the king has taken away from you both by reason and by clearly evident scriptures, from which it seemed good to recall one or another passage so that the reader may see how prettily Luder mocks in a matter so holy and serious. For thus the prince writes.

"Luther denies that orders is a sacrament, and he says that it is only a rite for *The king's words* electing a preacher. He says that those who do not preach are by no means priests, nor are they priests in any other way than as a painted man is a man; contrary to the apostle Paul who, writing to Timothy, says: 'Let the presbyters who rule well be held worthy of double honor, especially those who labor in the word and in teaching.' The apostle here manifestly teaches that, although those men are especially worthy of a double honor who, since they are presbyters, labor in the word and in teaching, yet those also who do not perform this function are not only presbyters but can also rule well and deserve a double honor. Otherwise he would not have said, 'especially those who labor in the word and teaching,' but only, 'those who labor in the word and teaching.'

"Moreover, so that Luder cannot say, as he does, that the office of the priest toward the people is nothing but to preach—for to chant masses, he says, is nothing else than to give oneself communion—that it may appear *Lutheran definition of the mass* how false this is, I say, let us again hear the apostle. 'Every high priest,' he says, 'taken from among men is appointed for men in the things pertaining to God that he may offer gifts and sacrifices for sins.' Does not the apostle clearly declare that

aperte declarat etiam pontificis officium istud, ut pro hominibus offerat sacrificium deo? Quod quum scribat, quamquam hebraeis, tamen christianis, quos nolit iudaizare, datum est loqui de pontifice legis utriusque: atque ideo, bis Lutherum suo premere testimonio.

5   *Missam et sacrificium et*   Nam et missam docet esse sacrificium: et
       oblationem esse   offerri pro populo, quum ecclesia nullum offerat aliud, et docet offerendi officium, praecipuam partem esse muneris pontificij. Et certe nisi falsum esset, quod dicit Lutherus, facile uidetis consequi: ut quum nemo nisi

10 sacerdos possit consecrare corpus domini, si e tot sacerdotum millibus, qui concionari nesciunt, nullus uere sacerdos est, sed tantum uocatur equiuoce, quemadmodum homo
  Ex opinione Lutheri plerosque   pictus uocatur homo, totus christianus
  omnes christianos esse idololatras   orbis clerum populumque ferme non habet

15 alium, quam idolatras, panem pro Christo colentes, et genua sua curuantes ante Baal."

CVR haec omisit Luderus? quibus tam aperte probat rex, ad sacerdotis officium praecipue pertinere: ut in missa pro populo sacrificet: quum contendat iste nec in missa fieri sacrificium, nec

20 sacerdotium quicquam esse, nec pontificium, nisi dumtaxat ritum eligendi concionatoris: nec istud pudet effrontem blaterare: quum clare uideat, solos ab initio usque sacerdotes consecrasse, concionatos uero nonnunquam, qui non fuerint sacerdotes: id quod in Actis [SS₄v] apostolorum constat, fecisse beatum Stephanum non sacer-

25   dotem, sed diaconum: ut manifestum sit,
  Proprium officium sacerdotis   maxime proprium sacerdotis officium, in eo situm esse, ut pro populo consecret. Sed adijciam ex libello regis locum alium.

            "SI LAICVS quisque aequalem habet
    Verba regis
30   potestatem cum sacerdote, in quocunque sacramento: et ordo sacerdotij nihil est: cur ita scribit apostolus
            Timotheo? Noli negligere gratiam, quae
  Paulus de sacerdotio   in te est: quae data est tibi per prophetiam, cum impositione manuum presbiterij. Et alibi ad eundem? Admoneo

it is also the office of the high priest to offer sacrifice to God for men? Since he writes this to those who, though Hebrews, are nonetheless Christians, whom he does not wish to live in the Jewish manner, it is granted that he is speaking of the high priest of both laws, and therefore that he twice urges Luther with his testimony. For he also teaches 5 that the mass is a sacrifice and that it is offered for the people, since the church *That the mass is both a sacrifice* offers none other, and he shows that the *and an oblation* duty of offering it is the chief part of the high priest's function. And certainly, if what Luther says were not false, you easily see that it 10 follows that, since no one but a priest can consecrate the body of the Lord, if of the many thousands of priests who do not know how to preach not one is truly a priest but is only equivocally so called, as a painted man is called a man, then the whole Christian world has as clergy and *According to Luther's opinion* 15 people hardly anything other than idola- *almost all Christians are* ters worshipping bread for Christ and *idolaters* bending their knees before Baal."

Why did Luder omit these words? By them the king so clearly proves that to offer sacrifice in the mass for the people belongs espe- 20 cially to the office of priest, whereas this fellow argues that no sacrifice takes place in the mass and that the priesthood is nothing, nor is the high priesthood, except only a rite for electing a preacher; and the shameless fellow is not ashamed to blather this although he clearly sees that only priests have consecrated continuously from the begin- 25 ning, although occasionally some preached who were not priests, a fact which is evident in the Acts of the Apostles; that blessed Stephen acted not as a priest but as a deacon, so that it is manifest that the office especially proper to a priest resides in this, that he consecrate for the people. *The function proper to the* 30 But I will add another passage from the *priest* king's book.

"If each layman has equal power with the priest in any sacrament whatever, and *The king's words* if the order of the priesthood is nothing, why does the apostle write 35 thus to Timothy: 'Do not neglect the grace that is in you which was granted to *Paul on the priesthood* you through prophecy with the laying on of hands of the presbyterate'? And elsewhere to the same person: 'I admonish you to stir up

te, ut resuscites gratiam dei, quae in te est, per impositionem manuum
mearum. Iterum. Nemini, inquit, cito manus imposueris, neque
communices peccatis alienis. Denique hunc in modum apostolus
scribit ad Titum. Huius rei gratia, reliqui

Apostolus Paulus de sacerdotio

5   te Cretae: ut ea, quae desunt, corrigas: et
constituas per ciuitates presbiteros, sicut et ego disposui tibi. Habes
nunc lector semel sub oculis apostoli pauca loca, et non multa uerba:
quibus inter se collatis, facile potes deprehendere falsa fictaque esse
omnia, quibus tam inordinate Lutherus debacchatur in ordinem.

10   Nam quos dicit populi consensu fieri, Paulus ostendit fieri ab episcopo, quem in hoc ait se reliquisse Cretae: ut oppidatim presbiteros
constitueret: nec tamen temere, sed sicut ipse praesens disposuerat.
Vides impositis manibus, fieri sacerdotem.

Quomodo fierent sacerdotes olim

Et ne dubitari possit, simul conferri
15   gratiam, uides, illam manuum impositione collatam. Resuscita,
inquit, gratiam, quae data est tibi per impositionem manuum
mearum. Et illud quoque. Noli negligere gratiam, quae in te est,
quae data est tibi per prophetiam, cum impositione ma[TT₁]nuum
presbiterij. In ijs te exerce. Miror igitur non pudere Lutherum, quum

20   negat sacramentum ordinis, haud ignarus in manibus omnium uersari
uerba Pauli? quae doceant, non nisi a sacerdote fieri sacerdotem, nec
sine consecratione fieri: in qua et signum adhibeatur corporeum, et
tantum spiritalis infundatur gratiae: ut is, qui consecratur, non solum
accipiat ipse spiritum sanctum: sed etiam

Sacerdotium nec nouam rem
esse nec ignotam ecclesiae

25   potestatem conferendi alijs. Nouum uero,
qui potest esse, de quo scribit apostolus?
Quomodo ignoratum ecclesiae, quod in omnibus Christi legitur, et
nunquam non legebatur ecclesijs? Quibus ex rebus, manifestum est
tam multis, quae tanta cum confidentia, pro compertissimis Lutherus

30   eblaterauit in ordinem, ne unam quidem syllabam fuisse ueram, per
maliciam ficta falsaque omnia."
VEL EX his particulis uides lector, quam scite tractet Luderus
sacramentum ordinis: qui quaecunque non ualet soluere, tacito

---

4 *gloss* Paulus] *L*, paulus *BR*   15 gratiam, uides,] gratiam, vides *L*, gratiam uides, *BR*;
impositione] *corr. err. L*, impositionem *BR*

the grace of God which is in you by the laying on of my hands'?
Again, 'Do not lay hands hastily upon anyone, and do not be a
partner in other men's sins.' Finally the
apostle writes in this way to Titus: 'For this   *The apostle Paul on the*
reason I left you in Crete that you should   *priesthood*   5
set right anything that is defective and should appoint presbyters in
every city, as I myself directed you to do.' You now have before your
eyes, reader, once and for all a few passages of the apostle, and not a lot
of verbiage; by comparing them with each other, you can easily grasp
that all the arguments with which Luther so intemperately rants   10
against orders are false and fictitious. For those who he says become
priests by the consent of the people, Paul shows are made so by the
bishop, whom he says he left at Crete for the purpose of appointing
presbyters in every town, and yet not hastily but as he himself, when
present, had directed. You see that a   15
priest is made by the imposition of hands.   *How men became priests*
And lest it can be doubted that grace is   *long ago*
conferred at the same time, you see that it is conferred by the imposition of hands. 'Stir up the grace,' he says, 'which is given to you
by the laying on of my hands.' And this also: 'Do not neglect the   20
grace that is in you which was granted you through prophecy with
the laying on of the hands of the presbyterate. Give yourself wholly to
these things.' I wonder therefore that Luther is not ashamed when he
denies the sacrament of orders while aware of the fact that everyone
reads the words of Paul which teach that a priest is not made except   25
by a priest, nor does he become one without consecration, in which
both the corporal sign is applied and so much spiritual grace is
poured into him that he who is consecrated receives not only the
Holy Spirit himself but also the power of
conferring Him on others. How indeed can   *That the priesthood is not a*
it be a new thing of which the apostle   *new thing nor unknown*   30
writes? How can that be unknown to the   *to the church*
church which is read and has always been read in all the churches of
Christ? It is clear that of these things, so numerous, which Luther has
blathered against orders with such confidence as being most evident,   35
not even one syllable was true, but all was fabricated and false
through his malice."
     Even from these details, reader, you see how skillfully Luder
handles the sacrament of orders, who passes over in silence whatever

praeterit omnia. Sed tum uidelicet, tractabit accuratius: postquam
redierit ab euerso biblio. Cupio mediusfidius idem ut tractet denuo.

Lutherum ea quae tractat in peius emendare

Nam sic tractauit hactenus: ut mihi spem
indubiam prebeat: quo rem tractarit
saepius, eo fore, ut multo tractet insanius.

Refellit ea, quae Lutherus
iterum timide tangit, et stolide,
de matrimonio. Cap. XXVI.

Verba Lutheri

Et quid dicam? ne nomen sacramenti
quidem intelligere uoluit, quod euidenter
ostendit, quum locum Pauli Ephe. V. tractat de matrimonio, quem
Paulus de Christo et ecclesia ponit, dicens. Sacramentum hoc magnum est, ego uero dico in Chri[TT₁v]sto et ecclesia.

Luderus Luderum agit

IMO Luderus ludere maluit quam intelligere: quae rex in illum scripsit locum:
nisi quod uerius puto, maluit suo more dissimulare stolide, tanquam
ipso rem praetereunte silentio, nemo locum posset e regis libello
legere. Quem locum lector quum legeris: ibi demum senties eam
rem, sic esse tractatam a rege, ut non sit mirum, nihil reperisse
Luderum, quod hic respondeat. Atque ideo praeterijsse, quasi nihil
esset dictum.

Verba Lutheri

Neque enim scriptura patitur, ut matrimonium sacramentum dicatur, quum
sacramentum usu totius scripturae significet, rem secretam et absconditam, quam sola fide consequi possis. Matrimonium autem adeo non
est res abscondita, aut fide percepta, ut nisi palam ob oculos fiat, matrimonium esse non possit, cum sit copula maris et foeminae externa, et
publica professione et conuersatione confirmata. Sed nihil mirum,
Thomistas asinos sic delyrare, apud quos nihil, neque sani neque
recti deus esse uoluit.

he has not the power to solve. But then of course he will handle it more exactly after he has returned from the mistranslation of the Bible. I most certainly hope that he will treat the same thing a second time. For he has so handled it up till now that he offers me the undoubted hope that the *That Luther changes for the* oftener he has handled the matter, so *worse whatever he handles* much the more madly will he handle it.

He refutes the arguments which Luther again touches on timidly and stupidly concerning matrimony. Chapter 26.

And what should I say? He did not even *Luther's words* wish to understand the name "sacrament," as he clearly shows when he handles in relation to matrimony the passage of Paul in Ephesians 5, which Paul set down in relation to Christ and the church, saying: "This is a great mystery, I mean in reference to Christ and to the church."

On the contrary, Luder preferred to jeer at rather than to understand what the *Luder acts the mocker* king wrote on that passage, unless, as I think is more true, he preferred in his usual manner to conceal it stupidly, as though by his passing over the matter in silence, no one could read the passage from the king's book. When you have read this passage, reader, there at least you will perceive that that matter has been so handled by the king that it is no wonder that Luder has discovered nothing to answer here, and that he therefore has passed it over as if nothing had been said.

For scripture does not allow matrimony to be called a sacrament, since by the *Luther's words* practice of the whole scripture a sacrament signifies a thing secret and hidden which can be attained by faith alone. But matrimony is so far from being a thing hidden or perceived by faith that if it is not contracted openly before our eyes, it cannot be matrimony, since it is the external bond of man and wife confirmed both by public profession and association. But no wonder that the Thomist asses so rant, among whom God has wished nothing to be either sane or right.

QVID hic dicam lector? Ego me plane fateor hic insanire maxime,
si non hic Luderus insaniat. Sacramentum,

Sacramentum quid sit Luthero   inquit, significat rem secretam et absconditam: sed matrimonium non est res abscondita: ergo matrimonium
5   non est sacramentum. Domine doctor, per uestram fidem, imo per
infidelitatem uestram, per quam regulam tenet ista consequentia:
quum in praemissis mutatur copula a significare ad esse, nisi uocabu-
larij uestri uobis dicunt, quod haec duo uerba, Sum et Significo, idem
significant. Alioqui si ualet illud argumentum, similiter ualet et hoc.
10   Omnis homo sedet, sed Luderus non currit: Ergo Luderus non est
homo. Domine doctor, quo peregrinatur animus uester: [TT₂] quum
sic desipitis? an haereticos deus percellit insania? Sacramentum
significat rem secretam et abditam, esto. Matrimonium non est res
secreta nec abdita: quid tum postea? Nec sacramentum dicis esse rem
15   abditam, sed significare rem abditam. Dic igitur eodem modo,
                                     Matrimonium non significare rem secre-
Expugnatur Lutheri ratio de   tam, nec abditam: et ex eo conclude, non
matrimonio   esse sacramentum: sed tunc mentiris in
minore. Nam sicut baptismus corporis, significat ablutionem animae:
20   sic matrimonium significat coniugium, inter Christum et ecclesiam:
quae res est, opinor, abdita et secreta: licet sacramentum, id est eius
                                     signum, sit sensibile: sicut ablutio animae
Matrimonium esse sacramentum   est res abdita et secreta: licet eius sacra-
uel Lutheri definitione   mentum, id est signum sacrum, signum sit
25   sensibile. Dicite, quaeso domine doctor, nunquid hoc saltem loco uos
fatemini tam stolide plane scribere: ut nullus asinus potuerit stolidius
rudere?

                                     Quanquam ego hoc uulgato usui dedi,
Verba Lutheri   ut sacramenta uocent, quae potius signa
30   uisibilia sunt. Tantum negaui, in scripturis sacramenta uocari.

                                     DEVS bone, quantus stupor est in isto
Stupida Lutheri obliuio   stipite: qui in hac una breui periodo, bis
insanit? primum, ait ista, quae uocantur sacramenta, potius esse
signa uisibilia. At quum iam in proximo prius uersu dixisset: sacra-

---

13 Matrimonium] *L*, Natrimonium *BR*   34 At quum] *corr. err.*, At *om. BR*, At cum *L*

What shall I say here, reader? I fully admit that here above all I am a raving madman, if Luder is not here a raving madman. The word sacrament, he says, signifies a thing secret and hidden, but matrimony is not a thing hidden, therefore matrimony is not a sacrament.

What Luther thinks a sacrament is

5

Honored doctor, by your faith, or rather by your faithlessness, according to what rule does this conclusion hold, since in the premises the copula is changed from "to signify" to "to be," unless your glossarians tell you that these two expressions, "I am" and "I signify" signify the same thing? Otherwise, if that argument is valid, the following is also likewise valid: Every man sits, but Luder is not running, therefore Luder is not a man. Honored doctor, where is your mind wandering when you are so silly? Or does God strike heretics with insanity? A sacrament signifies a thing secret and hidden; granted. Matrimony is not a thing secret or hidden; what then follows? You do not say that a sacrament is a thing hidden but that it signifies a thing hidden. Say then in the same way that matrimony does not signify a thing secret or hidden and conclude from that that it is not a sacrament; but then you lie in the minor premise. For as baptism of the body signifies washing of the soul, so matrimony signifies the union between Christ and the church, which is a thing, I think, hidden and secret, although the sacrament, that is its sign, is sensible; just as the washing of the soul is a thing hidden and secret although its sacrament, that is the sacred sign, is a sensible sign. Tell me I pray, honored doctor, do you not admit that at least in this passage you plainly write so stupidly that no ass could have brayed more stupidly?

10

Luther's reasoning on matrimony is refuted

15

20

25

That matrimony is a sacrament even by Luther's definition

30

Although I have yielded this to popular usage, that they may call sacraments what are rather visible signs, I only denied that they are called sacraments in the scriptures.

Luther's words

Good God, what dullness is in this dolt, who in this one brief sentence twice acts the madman. First of all he says that these things which are called sacraments are rather visible signs. But since he had already said, in the line

Luther's stupid forgetfulness

35

mentum significat rem archanam, et absconditam, quaero, de quo
sacramento dixit illud? De baptismo ne dixit, et eucharistia? Sic
opinor. Nam illa sola fatetur esse sacramenta. At de re significata,
non loquitur, utpote de ablutione animae. Nam illa non significat
5 rem abditam: sed est ipsa res ab[TT₂v]dita. Sacramentum igitur, de
quo loquitur, quod significat rem abditam, est in baptismo ablutio
corporis, in eucharistia species panis et uini. Quaeso te nunc Ludere,
an non et illa sunt signa uisibilia? tam hercle sunt, quam matrimonium. Quid ergo tibi uis insanissime: quum uelut per somnium stertis,
10 ea quae tu negas esse sacramenta, potius esse signa uisibilia: quum
nihilo potius sint signa uisibilia, quam ea ipsa, quae tu concedis esse
sacramenta? Non dubito, quin, Luderus quum legerit haec, doli-
turum sit homini, quod semisomnis scripserit tam delyra somnia:
sudabit satis: et omnem uertet lapidem: si qua reperire possit aliquid,
15 quo tantam saltem palliet uecordiam. Gestio profecto uidere, quem
pannum purpurae tanto praetexat ulceri. An (ut est impudens)
simulat se tantum definire sacramenti uocabulum: quum dicit, sacramentum usu scripturae significare rem abditam, et sic locutum esse,
tanquam diceret, homo semper significat quiddam rationale. Et ita
20 sacramentum usu scripturae semper significat rem absconditam, sed
matrimonium non est res abscondita: matrimonium igitur non est
illud, quod usu scripturae uocatur sacramentum. Si fingat Luderus

Qualiter Lutherus se tuetur istud, ita se tuebitur, quomodo si quis sic
declinet ictum, callidus: ut capite repellat
25 a brachio. Quid enim finget isto commento stolidius? Nam ut uerum
est, nullum esse sacramentum, quod non aliquo sensibili signo
designet rem secretam: ita uerum est, nullum illorum signorum
significare perpetuo rem secretam, sed eorum uocabula communiter
significare, dumtaxat illas ipsas res: quae sunt aliquando signa
30 rerum sacrarum. Nam et [TT₃] ablutio quatenus sacramentum significat rem abditam, nempe lotionem animae: tamen communiter
id non significat: nec eius uocabulum communiter designat sacramentum. Quid est enim communiter ablutio, aut baptismus? aliud
ne quam quaelibet lauatio corporis? Quamobrem si se putet hac
35 stropha Luderus elapsurum: plane labetur in latrinam. Nam si sic

---

1 absconditam, quaero,] *corr. err. L,* absconditam. Quaero, *BR*   23 *gloss* Lutherus]
L, lutherus *BR*   24 ictum] *corr. err. L,* istum *BR*

just before that, that the word sacrament signifies a thing hidden and
concealed, I ask, of what sacrament did he say that? Did he say it of
baptism and the eucharist? I think so. For he admits those alone as
sacraments. But of the thing signified he does not speak, namely the
washing of the soul. For that does not signify the thing hidden but is   5
itself the thing hidden. Therefore the sacrament of which he speaks,
which signifies the thing hidden, is in baptism the washing of the body,
in the eucharist the species of bread and wine. I ask you now, Luder,
whether or not these also are visible signs? They are as much so, by
God, as matrimony. What therefore do you mean, you utter madman,   10
when you snore as in a dream that those things which you say are not
sacraments are rather visible signs, whereas they are no more visible
signs than those very things which you grant are sacraments? I have
no doubt that when Luder has read these things, the man will be
chagrined that he has written half sleeping such raving dreams; he will   15
sweat plenty and will turn every stone to see if in any way he can find
anything to mitigate at least such great madness. I am eager indeed to
see with what cloth of purple he will cover such a great sore. Or,
shameless as he is, does he pretend that he is only defining the word
sacrament when he says that sacrament by the practice of scripture   20
signifies a thing hidden, and that he spoke as though he were
saying that the word man always signifies a certain rational being?
And thus the word sacrament by the practice of scripture always
signifies a thing hidden, but matrimony is not a thing hidden; therefore, matrimony is not that which by the practice of scripture is called   25
a sacrament. If Luder should pretend this,
he will be defending himself in the same   *How Luther defends himself*
way as though someone should ward off a blow so shrewdly that he
beats it off from his arm with his head. For what will he fashion more
dull-witted than this trick? For as it is true that there is no sacrament   30
which does not by some sensible sign indicate a secret thing, so it is
true that none of those signs always signifies a secret thing, but the
words for them generally signify only those very things which are at
times the signs of sacred things. For even washing as a sacrament
signifies a thing hidden, namely the washing of the soul; yet, generally   35
it does not signify that, nor does its word generally indicate a sacrament. For what is a washing or a baptism generally other than a
certain bathing of the body? Therefore if he should think that by
this trick he will escape, he will plainly slip into a latrine. For if the

nobis argutetur dominus doctor, Sacramentum scripturarum omnium usu, significat rem secretam, atque abditam: sed matrimonium
non est res secreta nec abdita: ergo matrimonium non potest esse
sacramentum: opponam domino doctori argumentum isti similli-
mum, hoc pacto. Sacramentum usu scrip-

5 *Refellitur Lutheri argumentum* turarum omnium significat rem secretam
de sacramentis atque abditam: Sed ablutio uel baptismus
non est res abdita: et species panis et uini non est res abdita. Imo
quia dominus doctor irridet speciem, neque panis neque uinum
10 sunt res abditae: ergo neque baptismus, neque species panis et
uini, neque panis et uinum, possunt esse sacramenta. Inueniat mihi
dominus doctor, solutionem huius argumenti mei: et simul inueniet
solutionem sui. Defendat se dominus doctor, qui hactenus uerbo
saltem confessus est, illa duo esse sacramenta. Certe nisi uolet illa
15 duo tollere, quod plane conabitur aliquando: Imo re ipsa iam diu
fecit: fateri cogetur istam rationem suam nihil habere rationis.
Quin fateri cogetur, ex ipsius assumpto,

Ex Lutheri assumpto matrimonium matrimonium uerum sacramentum appel-
uerius esse sacramentum landum esse, potius quam baptismum
quam baptisma ipsum. Nam ablutio neque rem abditam
20 significat: nisi quatenus sacramentum est: neque semper sacramentum fuit, neque nunc semper est. Matrimonium autem ab initio
[TT₃v] fuit sacrum signum rei sacratissimae.

NEC minus insanum est istud, quod ais te nihil aliud quam negasse,
25 quod matrimonium, et caetera sacramenta, quae damnas, sacramenta uocentur in scripturis. Siccine

Lutherus quam belle se Ludere ludis tandem? nihil ne negas
castiget amplius? paulo ante negasti: quod sint
sacramenta: nunc nihil negas, nisi quod uocentur sacramenta in
30 scripturis. Soluta est igitur ista lis, et tota causa cessisti: nisi quis
contendat illa sacramenta omnia, uocabulo sacramenti uocari in
scriptura sacra. Sed quaeso te, quis unquam tibi mouit illam litem?
Quis id contendit unquam? Olim negasti ueteres ecclesiae patres,
ordinem uocasse sacramentum. Rex te uetustissimorum testimonio

---

7 Sed] sed *L*; ablutio] *corr. err. L*, oblutio *BR*

honored doctor thus quibbles with us that the word sacrament by the practice of all the scriptures signifies a thing secret and hidden, but matrimony is not a thing secret or hidden, therefore matrimony cannot be a sacrament, I will oppose to the honored doctor an argument very similar to this, as follows:
The word sacrament by the practice of all *Luther's argument on sacraments* the scriptures signifies a thing secret and *is refuted*
hidden, but washing or baptism is not a thing hidden and the species of bread and wine are not a thing hidden—rather, since the honored doctor jeers at the notion of species, neither bread nor wine are things hidden—therefore neither baptism, nor the species of bread and wine, nor bread and wine, can be sacraments. Let the honored doctor find me a solution to this argument of mine, and at the same time he will find a solution for his own. Let the honored doctor defend himself, who till now has confessed at least by word that those two are sacraments. Certainly, unless he wishes to take those two away, which he clearly will try some day—indeed, as a matter of fact he has already done it long ago—he will be forced to admit that this reasoning of his has nothing of reasoning in it. Indeed,
he will be forced to admit, according to his *According to Luther's premise* own premise, that matrimony must be *matrimony is more truly a* called a true sacrament rather than bap- *sacrament than baptism*
tism itself. For neither does washing signify a thing hidden, except insofar as it is a sacrament, nor has it always been a sacrament, nor is it now always a sacrament. But matrimony from the beginning was a sacred sign of a most sacred reality.

Not any less insane is your statement that you have denied nothing else but that matrimony and the other sacraments which you condemn are called sacraments in scriptures.
Is it thus, Luder, that you finally make *How prettily Luther corrects* sport? Do you deny nothing further? A *himself*
little while ago you denied that they are sacraments; now you deny nothing except that they are called sacraments in the scriptures. This quarrel is settled then, and you have yielded the whole case, unless someone should argue that all those sacraments are called by the name sacrament in sacred scripture. But I ask you, who ever started this quarrel with you? Who ever argued thus? Once you denied that the ancient fathers of the church called orders a sacrament. The king proved by the testimony of most ancient men that you lied. Now you

probauit esse mentitum. Nunc uelut rem magnam profers, quod
saltem scriptura ea non uocat sacramenta. Hui quam ualidum iecisti
telum. Profer obsecro scripturam sacram, quae baptismum uocet
sacramenti uocabulo. Profer, quae sic uocet eucharistiam. Inuenies
5 opinor, in scriptura nullum sacramentum, uocabulo sacramenti
nominatum, praeter istud unum, quod stolide nunc oppugnas, matrimonium. Audistin unquam quenquam lector, in re tam sancta et
seria, tam impudenter stolideque nugantem?

Scite et iocunde tractat ea,
10 quae Lutherus uelut summam
rerum scurriliter aggessit in
fine. Cap. Vltimum.

Verba Lutheri   Summa rerum haec est. Totus liber
Henrici nititur hominum uerbis et usu
15 seculorum, nullis dei uerbis neque usu spiritus, ut i[TT₄]psemet fateri
cogitur. Contra, summa mearum rerum est, uerba hominum et usum
seculorum, ut tollerari et teneri possint, sicubi non pugnant scripturis
sanctis, tamen articulos fidei, et necessariam obseruantiam non facere.
Si itaque rex Henricus coniunctis omnium Thomistarum, papistarum,
20 daemonum, et hominum uiribus et studijs poterit ostendere necessariam humanorum uerborum obseruan-
Ita reuera es, si uelles   tiam, uictus est Lutherus suo ipsius
agnoscere   iudicio et confessione. Nam tum demum
articulos fidei habebo, quicquid uel Thomistae iusserint. Si non
25 poterit, uictor est Lutherus. Quid enim aliud uolunt? Neque enim si
mille millies libros scripserint contra me, aliud a me postulare
poterunt.

SVMMA rerum haec est. Totus Luderi liber nihil est aliud, quam
mera farrago uerborum scurrilium, cum
Summa libri Lutherani   deprauatione uerborum dei, contemptu
30 sanctorum omnium, et blasphemia spiritus sancti, sicut ipsemet fateri
cogitur. Contra, Summa rerum principis
Summa libri regis   est Assertio sacramentorum: quae luce

---

2 ea non uocat] *corr. err. L,* non *om. BR*   12 Vltimum.] XXVII. *L*   13 *gloss*] *L, om.*
BR   16 summa mearum] summma earum *L*   29 scurrilium, cum] *corr. err. L,*
scurrilium. Cum *BR*

propose as a great issue that scripture at least does not call them sacraments. Oh, what a powerful weapon you have hurled! Set forth, I pray, the sacred scripture which calls baptism by the name sacrament. Set forth one which calls the eucharist by this name. You will find, I think, no sacrament named by the term sacrament in scripture   5 except this one which you now stupidly attack, matrimony. Have you ever heard anyone, reader, in a matter so sacred and serious, so insolently and stupidly talking nonsense?

He treats cleverly and delightfully those
points which Luther buffoonishly brought   10
together as the sum of the matter at the
end of his work. Last chapter.

The sum of the matter is this: The whole
of Henry's book relies upon the words of   *Luther's words*
men and the usage of the ages, not on the words of God or on the   15
usage of the Spirit, as he himself is forced to admit. On the other hand, the sum of my arguments is this, that the words of men and the usage of the ages, although they can be maintained and preserved wherever they do not contradict the sacred scriptures, still do not constitute articles of faith or make for a necessary observance. And so,   20
if King Henry, by the conjoined forces and efforts of all Thomists, papists, demons and men, can show the necessary observance of human words, then Luther is conquered
by his own judgment and confession. For   *So you are indeed, if you*
then I will finally hold as articles of faith   *would be willing to*
whatever even the Thomists will com-   *acknowledge it*   25
mand. If he cannot do this, Luther is the victor. For what else do they want? Not even if they have written a million books against me, will they be able to ask anything else from me.

The sum of the matter is this: The whole book of Luther is nothing   30
else but a sheer conglomeration of buffoon-
ish words, with distortion of the words of   *The sum of the Lutheran book*
God, contempt of all the saints, and blasphemy against the Holy Spirit, as he himself is forced to admit. On the other hand, the sum of the prince's arguments is the defense of
the sacraments, which he has proved more   *The sum of the king's book*   35

clarius, probauit esse non traditiones hominum, sed traditiones dei:
atque id probauit ratione, scripturis, et ipsius confessione Lutheri. Si
itaque Lutherus, coniunctis omnibus suis combibonibus coniunctis
scurris et nebulonibus, coniunctis laruis et cacodemonibus, blas-
5   phemiarum suarum inspiratoribus: si poterit, inquam, ostendere,
quod impiorum nebulonum scurrilitas, plus ualere debet, quam
traditiones dei, uictor est Lutherus. Si non poterit, uictus est Lutherus,
ipsius confessione Lutheri. Quid enim aliud uult? Nam qui contra
illum scribunt, etiam si millies mille libros scribant, nihil aliud ab illo
10   postulaturi sunt: quam ut audiat, quid ei
        Quam iniquus semper fuerit   dictum sit: et meminerit, quid ipse dixerit:
              Lutherus
                                          quorum hactenus ab eo neutrum [TT₄v]
quisquam impetrare potuit.

                                          Neque enim ego quaero, quid Ambrosius,
          Verba Lutheri
15   Augustinus, concilia, et usus seculorum
dicant. Non (inquam) disputo, quid a quoquam dictum, uel non
dictum, scriptum uel non scriptum sit, sed an hoc dictum et scriptum
necessarium sit seruatu, an sit articulus fidei, an liget conscientiam.

NEMO est (opinor) qui ideo tibi uel Ambrosium opponat, uel
20   Augustinum, uel sanctorum quenquam, uel concilia, uel synodos:
quia nesciat, quam arroganter et stolide contemnas omnes prae te,
sed quia munire populum salutari student antidoto, contra furiale
uenenum tuum. Nam quum uideant contra tuam sententiam, stare
pro sacramentis ecclesiae, non unum aliquem ueterum, sed uniuersos:
25   dubitare non possunt, illam fuisse publicam fidem ecclesiae catholicae,
quaecunque unquam fuit in terris ecclesia, uere catholica. Quam tua
confessione probauit rex in sacramentis falli atque errare non posse.
Praeterea, quum tu fatearis ibi adesse Christum: ubicunque sint duo
                                          uel tres congregati in nomine eius: facile
        Quam distorte coniungit   sentit populus, nihil tibi mentis esse: quum
30   *Lutherus omnia*
                                          illinc disputas abfuisse Christum: ubi
congregati sunt in nomine Christi ducenti uel trecenti, ijdemque ex
eruditissimis, atque undecunque sanctissimis. Quamobrem satis
intelligit populus, ecclesiam catholicam, etiam si non facit articulos

15 *gloss*] *L, om. BR*   24 non unum aliquem] *corr. err. L,* unum *om. BR*

clearly than light to be, not the traditions of men, but the traditions of God, and he has proved this by reason, by the scriptures, and by the confession of Luther himself. And so, if Luther with all his pot-fellows combined, with all his buffoons and rascals combined, with all his spectres and cacodaemons (the inspirers of his blasphemies) com- 5 bined, if he can, I say, show that the buffoonery of impious scoundrels has more validity than the traditions of God, then Luther is the victor. If he cannot, then Luther is conquered by the confession of Luther himself. For what else does he want? If those who write against him should write even a million books they will be demanding 10 nothing else from him than that he listen to what is said to him and remember what he himself has said. Up till now no one has been able to gain either of these aims from him.

How wicked Luther has always been

For neither do I ask what Ambrose, Augustine, the councils and the usage of the ages say. As I say, I do not dispute about what has or has not been said by anyone, what has or has not been written, but I question whether this saying and writing must necessarily be obeyed, whether it is an article of faith, whether it binds the conscience. 20

Luther's words 15

I think there is no one who has opposed to you either Ambrose or Augustine or any of the saints whatever, or the councils, or the synods because he is unaware of how arrogantly and stupidly you scorn everyone but yourself; rather they do this because they are eager to defend the people with a saving antidote to your raging poison. For 25 when they see that in opposition to your opinion, not just any one ancient writer, but all of them uphold the sacraments of the church, they cannot doubt that that was the common faith of the catholic church, wherever in the world there was a church truly catholic. By your confession the king proved that this church cannot be deceived 30 and err concerning the sacraments. Besides, since you admit that Christ is present wherever two or three persons are gathered together in His name, the people easily see that you are not in your right mind when you argue that Christ was not present there 35 where there were gathered together in the name of Christ two hundred or three hundred persons, and these some of the most learned and holy men from all over the world. So the people under-stand well enough that the catholic church, even if it does not make

How distortedly Luther joins everything

fidei, probare tamen et docere ueros articulos fidei: sicut probat et
docet, quodnam sit euangelium: etiam si non faciat euangelium.
Non igitur dicit quisquam, uerba totius

Sacramenta ecclesiae tradita per uerbum dei

ecclesiae esse aequalia uerbo dei, sed
5   ecclesiam docere, quod sacramenta sibi
tradita sunt per uerbum dei: in quo discernendo, tu quoque [VV₁]
Ludere fassus es, eam falli non posse. Atque ita semper tua confessione constringeris, praesertim quum tibi probatum sit, non hodie
tantum hoc sentire ecclesiam: quam tu uocas papisticam: quae
10   tamen reuera est ecclesia catholica, sed idem sensisse semper: quaecunque unquam in terris fuit ecclesia uere catholica. Quae res patet et
conciliorum decretis et sanctissimorum consensu patrum, locis ac
temporibus tam diuersis, idem tamen constanter sentientium: ut
quum illis uniuersis unus dissentias, nihil aliud facias, quam stultitiam
15   tuam impiam atque impudentem traducas.

Verba Lutheri. Verum ais,
scripturis enim te impugnat,
quas tu oppugnas

Nec fuit opus mihi, Henrico rege magistro, qui me haec doceret, qui adeo
pulchre ea nouerim, ut etiam impugnarim, ut miranda sit stultitia Satanae,
20   quae his me impugnet, quae ipse impugno, et perpetuo principium
petit.

IMO opus est tibi, Henrico rege magistro: qui te ista dedoceat:
quae rex te tuus docuit Satanas: qui uere rex est super omnes filios
superbiae: qui te sic infatuat, ut perpetuo temet inscius impugnes
25   ipse: nec unquam tibi constes: sed aliud stans aliud sedens sentias.
Nam quod ais, eos qui tibi sanctos patres opponunt: et concilia
perpetuo principium petere: tu perpetuo surdus es: quia tibi non
libet audire. Nam si ulla unquam ecclesia uere christiana fuit: illa
certe fuit: cuius fidem testantur scripta sanctorum patrum, eam
30   fuisse, quam tu nunc impugnas. Quamobrem quum tute fatearis
ecclesiam in diiudicando dei uerbo falli non posse, et tamen dicis
eandem, quae tam diu iudicauit sacramenta per dei uerbum initio
tradita falsam esse: perspicuum etiam pueris est, et te mentiri
falsissime, et tecum [VV₁v] pugnare turpissime.

---

3 *gloss* Sacramenta] *L*, sacramenta *BR*   12 conciliorum decretis] *corr. err. L*, decretis
om. BR; sanctissimorum] *L*, santissimorum *BR*   13 tamen] *BRL*, tam *corr. err.*
30 Quamobrem] *L*, Qamobrem *BR*

articles of faith, still does prove and teach true articles of faith, just as it proves and teaches which is the gospel, even if it does not make the gospel. Therefore, no one is saying that the words of the whole church are equal to the words of God, but that the church teaches that the sacraments have been handed on to her through the word of God; in discerning which, Luder, you also have admitted that she cannot err. And thus, you are always straitened by your own confession, especially since it has been proved to you that not only today is the church of this mind—the church which you call papistic, which nevertheless is in fact the catholic church—but that it has always thought thus, whichever church anywhere in the world has been truly catholic. This fact is clear both from the decrees of the councils and from the agreement of most holy fathers from very diverse places and times still consistently holding the same judgment, so that, when you, a single individual, disagree with all these men together, you do nothing else but betray your impious and shameless folly.

The sacraments handed down to the church by the word of God

Nor did I need King Henry as a master to teach me these things, since I know them well enough even to have attacked them, so that I must wonder at the folly of Satan, which attacks me with the arguments which I myself attack and which constantly begs the question.

Luther's words. You speak truly for he attacks you with the scriptures which you assail

On the contrary, you do need King Henry as master to unteach you the arguments that your own king, Satan, has taught you, he who is truly king over all the sons of pride, who has so infatuated you that without realizing it you are constantly contradicting yourself; nor are you at all consistent, but you judge one thing standing, another sitting. As for your statement that those who oppose to you the holy fathers and the councils constantly beg the question, you are constantly deaf because you do not choose to listen. For if any church was ever truly Christian, it was certainly that one whose faith the writings of the holy fathers testify to have been the faith which you are now attacking. Therefore, since you yourself admit that the church cannot be deceived in distinguishing the word of God, but yet you say that this same church is false which has for so long judged that the sacraments were handed on by the word of God from the beginning, it is clear even to boys both that you lie most falsely and that you are contradicting yourself most shamefully.

PRAETEREA quum de scripturae
Quid regi cum Luthero conueniat sensu surgit quaestio, quum tibi cum rege
quid non conuenit, quae sit scriptura: sed in eo
dissentit abs te, quod ait te male interpretari scripturam: nec eam id
5 significare, quod tu contendis: hic uero uidetur tibi ridicule princi-
Quomodo rex petat principium pium petere: si pro sua sententia suffraga-
torem alleget uetustissimum quenque, ac
sanctissimum, ex antiquis patribus: qui nec illius gratiam potuerunt
aucupari, nec odisse te: propterea quod tot seculis ante mortui sunt:
10 quam te teterrimam pestem, in terras Orcus euomeret. Qui sic
principium petit, quam ridicule ridetur abs te? non hercle minus
ridicule, quam si quis demonstraturus conclusionem Gaeometricam,
primum abs te petat: ut concedas dimidium, minus esse suo toto,
deinde, quum tu aut tam stolidus sis, ut id non sentias: aut tam
15 impudens, ut prudens neges: ille te tuae relinquens stultitiae, nihilo
minus pergit illud sibi postulatum sumere: atque ex eo deducat
Lutheri in disputando mos reliquum. Iam si tu recurras denuo, ac
mille nugeris ineptijs, illum nihil demon-
strasse, sed uitiosissime principium petere: et ex eo rem deducere,
20 quod tu initio negaueris, atque ibi sardonio risu, rictum caninum
distendas, et iactes eum probare negatum per negatum, quid aliud
faceres, quam quod facis nunc: ut te, tam stolido risu, pro stolido
puncto ridendum proponas.

Verba Lutheri. Imo ille pro dei De libertate, et captiuitate quaero, pro
25 *sermone tu pro licentia scelerum* libertate ego pugno. Rex pro captiuitate
pugnat. Ego rationem libertatis signaui.
Rex rationes captiuitatis omittit, et solum blaterat, quae sit captiuitas.
Debitores facit, et culpam non assignat. Valeat itaque ineptus, et
miserabilis defensor captiuitatis Babylonicae, [VV₂] et suae papisticae
30 ecclesiae.

VT SEMPER audit aegre Luderus, quicquid ei non est commodum. Nam quoties eum docuit princeps, ab ecclesiae parte libertatem esse, et omnia tuta. Contra uero, ab ipsius parte captiuitatem

---

2 cum] *corr. err. L,* quum *BR*   4 abs te, quod ait te] *corr. err. L,* abs te. Ait te *BR*
10 teterrimam] *L,* teterrimum *BR*   13–14 suo toto, deinde] *corr. err. L,* suo toto.
Deinde *BR*   16 deducat] *corr. err. L,* deducit *BR*   20 negaueris, atque] *corr. err. L,*
negaueris. Atque *BR*   21 per negatum, quid aliud] *corr. err. L,* per negatum. Quid
aliud *BR*   22–23 pro stolido puncto ridendum proponas] pro stolido ridendum
puncta propronas *corr. err.,* pro stolido ridendum proponas *BRL*   24 *gloss* Imo] *L,*
imo *BR*   28 et culpam] *L,* ei culpam *BR*

Besides, when the question arises as to the meaning of a scriptural text, when the king agrees with you on the identity of the *On what the king agrees with Luther, on what not* scriptural text but disagrees with you in that he says you misinterpret the text and that it does not signify what you contend, it seems to you 5 a ridiculous begging of the question if, in support of his own opinion, he cites all the *How the king begs the question* most ancient and most sacred supporters from among the ancient fathers, who could neither have sought his favor nor hated you, since they died so many centuries before Orcus 10 vomited you as a most horrible plague onto the earth. How ridiculously you ridicule one who begs the question in this way! It is indeed no less ridiculous than the following: Someone wishing to demonstrate a geometrical conclusion first asks you to concede that the half is less than its whole; then, since you are either so stupid as 15 not to grasp this principle, or so shameless that you would knowingly deny it, leaving you to your folly, he proceeds anyway to employ this postulate and from it he deduces his conclusion. Now if you should return again *Luther's manner in disputing* and trifle with a thousand absurdities, saying that he has demon- 20 strated nothing but is most perversely begging the question and deducing the matter from that premise which you initially denied, and there with a Sardonian smile you should distend your dog jowl and boast that he proves what is denied through what is denied, what would you be doing different from what you are now doing, when 25 with your stupid raillery you propose what must be laughed at as a stupid argument?

I ask about liberty and slavery; I fight for liberty; the king fights for slavery. I have *Luther's words. On the contrary he is for the word of God,* indicated the reason for liberty; the king *you for the license of* 30 omits the reasons for slavery and only *crimes* blathers about what slavery is. He makes us guilty and does not assign any fault. And so away with this absurd and wretched defender of the Babylonian captivity and of his own papistic church. 35

As always, Luder hears badly whatever is not advantageous to him. For how often the prince has taught him that liberty and all safety stem from the side of the church, but that on the other hand

et periculum summum, atque istud probauit, etiam iacto fundamento
ab ipsius Luderi confessione. Sed si quis illud illi rursus inclamet ad
aures, non magis audierit ebrius Lutherus, quam Fusius ebrius olim,
Dum Ilionem obdormit catienis mille ducentis, Mater te appello
5 clamantibus. Verum dormiat ille, uel (quod solet) altum stertat
uigilans. Tibi tamen lector, locum recensebo rursus ex libello
principis: quem quum audieris, dubitare non poteris ex utra parte
stet captiuitatis periculum.

Verba regis

10   "AT LVTHERVS ipse fatetur, nihil
esse periculi, si quis hac in re sentiat, quod
tota iam sentit ecclesia. At contra, tota ecclesia censet haereticum esse
eum: qui sentiat cum Luthero. Non debet ergo Lutherus animare
quenquam, cui bene cupit: ut secum sentiat. Cuius sententiam tota
condemnat ecclesia. Sed debet his suadere,

Hoc Luthere, si sapis, suade ijs,
quos charos habes

15 quos amat: ut accedant illis, quos ipse quoque iudicat in nullo uersari periculo. Falsa
est ergo ista Lutheri uia, contra publicam fidem, non huiusmodi temporis, sed etiam aetatum omnium. Nec liberat captiuitate credentes
ei: sed educens e libertate fidei, hoc est loco sancto (quod Lutherus
20 ipse fatetur) captiuat in errorem, ducens in praecipitium, et uias
inuias, incertas, dubias eoque plenas periculi: et qui amat periculum
perit in illo." [VV₂v]

Verba Lutheri

In fine si quem offenderit mea in regem
asperitas, hoc sibi responsum habeat.
25 Cum insensatis monstris, me hoc libro agere, qui omnia mea optima
et modesta scripta, tum humillimam meam submissionem contempserunt, et magis ex mea modestia in-

At praeter te nemo uidet istam
tuam modestiam

duruerunt. Deinde a uirulentia, et
mendacijs abstinui, quibus liber regis
30 refertissimus est. Nec magnum est, si ego regem terrae contemno et
mordeo, quando ipse nihil ueritus est, regem caeli in suis sermoni-

Hoc tu Luthere facis

bus blasphemare, et uirulentissimis mendacijs prophanare.

12 Luthero]*L*, Luhero *BR*   14 his suadere] his his suadere *L*

captivity and the greatest danger come from Luther's own side, and
he has proved this, laying the foundation of his argument on the
admission of Luder himself. But if anyone should once more shout
that into his ears, the drunken Luther would no more hear it than
did the drunken Fusius once when he slept through the role of 5
Ilione, although twelve hundred Catienuses shouted: "Mother, I am
calling you." But let the fellow sleep, or as he is used to doing, let him
snore while awake. Nevertheless, for your sake, reader, I will again
review the passage from the prince's book; when you hear it, you will
not be able to doubt on which side stands the danger of captivity. 10

"But Luther himself admits that there is *The king's words*
no danger in anyone's agreeing with the
opinion of the whole church in this matter. On the other hand,
though, the whole church judges that he who agrees with Luther is a
heretic. Therefore Luther ought not to encourage anyone whose 15
welfare he has at heart to agree with himself, whose opinion the whole
church condemns. Rather he ought to per-
suade those whom he loves to join those *If you are wise, Luther, persuade*
whom he himself also judges to be involved *those whom you hold dear of*
in no danger. Therefore, this way of Luther *this* 20
is false, opposed to the common faith not only of this time but even of
all ages. Nor does he free from captivity those who believe in him, but
leading them from the liberty of the faith, that is, from a holy place
(as Luther himself admits), he imprisons them in error, leading them
into a steep place and along trackless, uncertain and doubtful ways, 25
and to that extent ways full of danger. And he who loves danger
perishes in it."

To conclude, if my harshness toward the *Luther's words*
king has offended anyone, let him have
this as his answer. In this book I was dealing with senseless monsters 30
who despised all of my excellent and restrained writings, as well as my
abject submission, and who grew more
hardened as a result of my moderation. *But besides you no one sees this*
Moreover, I have refrained from the *moderation of yours*
bitter invective and the lies with which the book of the king is replete. 35
Nor is it such a great matter if I scorn and bite a king of earth when
he has not been afraid to blaspheme the
king of heaven by his words and to *This you do, Luther*
profane Him with the most noxious lies.

EX TOT mendacijs, ex tot blasphemijs, unum saltem proferre
Luderus exempli loco debuerat, maxime ne quis uere illud imputet ei :
quod ille falso prius imputauit principi. Quem mentitur, nullum
Lutheranae repugnantiae locum indicasse: quum indicarit plus
5 decem. Caeterum illa proferat Luderus, quum uacabit. Sed interim
Luderi mendacissimas in deum blasphemias, effecit princeps, ne quis
omnino nesciat : nisi qui non legerit, aut sit talis omnino, qui aquam
non reperiat in pelago. Nam et aperte (id

Talis erat Lutheri semper quod rex ostendit) omnes blasphemat
lenitas
10   sanctos : quicunque scripturam sacram,
scriptis illustrarunt suis. Blasphemat apostolum Iacobum. Blasphemat apostolum Paulum. Christi blasphemat ecclesiam. Blasphemat
sacramenta Christi : quae tanquam hominum inuenta contemnit.
Blasphemat ipsum Christum : cuius sacramentum primum et caeter-
15 orum ianuam, non aliud fere facit, quam securam in facinus omne
licentiam. Blasphemat spiritum sanctum : cuius doctrinam totam
uelut mendacem, quoad potest, priuat fide, quamcunque docuit
sine scriptura. Totam denique blasphemat

Haec Lutheri in deum pietas trinitatem, in cuius inflexibilem uolunta-
20 tem, re[VV₃]fert ineuitabilem scelerum omnium necessitatem.
IAM illud, quam ridiculum, quod excusat se, ne uideatur scilicet
nimis inclementer mordere principem. Ego profecto non dubito,
regem illi facile morsus omnes condonaturum. Quippe qui uerum
uideat illud esse Senecae. Raro mordet canis, qui latrat. Latratibus
25   profecto Lutherus aequiperat Cerberum :

Lutherus latrator magis morsu uix culicem. Verum quid ni latret
quam mordax
strenue, uir uidelicet optimus et modestissi-
mus : quando cum insensatis (ut ait) agit monstris : quae non sentiant
eius omnia scripta esse ipsius unius preconio optima, et modestissima,
30 id est haeresibus et blasphemijs tam inflata : quam nullum unquam
utrem quisquam inflauit uento. Quae monstra induruerunt, etiam ex
illius humillima submissione : qua sic se

Qualis sit Lutheri submissio submisit fraterculus uicario Christi : quomodo iudaei se submiserunt Christo : quum datis alapis flexerunt

---

6 Luderi] *L*, luderi *BR*   18 *gloss* Haec] *L*, haec *BR*

From so many lies, from so many blasphemies, Luder ought to have presented at least one as an example, especially to prevent anyone's truly charging him with what he falsely charged the prince. He lies when he says that the king indicated no contradictory passage in Luther's writings, whereas the king has indicated more than ten such. But let Luther produce those examples when he has the leisure for it. But meanwhile the prince has seen to it that no one at all can be unaware of Luther's most lying blasphemies against God, unless it be someone who has not read him, or who is altogether the kind of person that does not see water in a flood. As the king has shown, Luther openly blasphemes all the saints who shed light on the scriptures with their writings. He blasphemes the apostle James. He blasphemes the apostle Paul. He blasphemes the church of Christ. He blasphemes the sacraments of Christ, which he contemns as the inventions of men. He blasphemes Christ Himself, whose first sacrament and the doorway to the rest he makes almost nothing other than a secure license for every evil deed. He blasphemes the Holy Spirit; whatever of the Holy Spirit's doctrine has been taught without scripture he deprives of faith as far as he can as though it were wholly false. Finally he blasphemes the whole Trinity, to whose unbending will he attributes the inevitable necessity of all evil deeds.

Such was ever Luther's mildness

This is Luther's piety toward God

Now for the ridiculous excuse which he makes for himself— namely, lest he seem to be biting the king too mercilessly—I really have no doubt but that the king will easily overlook all his bites, as one who sees the truth of Seneca's remark: The barking dog rarely bites. In his barking Luther is truly equal to Cerberus, but in his bite hardly to a gnat. But why not let him bark fiercely, this truly good and most moderate man, when, as he says, he is dealing with senseless monsters who do not understand that all his writings are, by his own praise alone, excellent and most restrained; that is to say, more inflated with heresies and blasphemies than anyone ever inflated a bag with wind. These monsters have been hardened even by the fellow's most humble submission, with which he submitted as a friarlet to the vicar of Christ just as the Jews submitted themselves to Christ when, slapping Him in the face, they bent

Luther more a barker than a biter

The nature of Luther's submission

genua, clamantes per ludibrium, Aue rex Iudaeorum. Verum a
mendatijs et uirulentia, prorsus abstinuisse se testatur, ipse, cui nihil
est aliud in calamo, quam calumniae, mendacia, sycophantiae: cui
nihil est aliud in animo, quam uirus, tumor, inuidia. Qui nihil in

5 *Depictus ex suis uirtutibus*   capite concipit praeter stultitias, furores,
   Lutherus   amentias. Qui nihil habet in ore, praeter
                                         latrinas, merdas, stercora. Quibus foedius
et spurcius, quam ullus unquam scurra scurratur: quorum nemo
repertus est unquam, praeter istum, tam stolidus plagepatida: ut sibi
10 stercus in os conijceret: quod alij spueret in sinum. Quamobrem
quum sit huiusmodi, nihil miror si nunc indignus habeatur: quocum
quisquam disputet. Certe quandoquidem totum se deuouit inferis, et
obdurauit in schismate: nec [VV₃v] unquam decreuit haereses

                                         recantare: statuere tamen secum debet
15 *Hoc etiam eius laudi, cuius*   aliquam saltem, ut habeat ciuilis honesta-
   appetens est, foret non inutile   tis rationem: quo sibi potius uendicet
authoritatem dogmatistae, quam uilis in haeretico scurrae. Quod si
quando uolet, si disceptabit serio, si mendacia sua recantet, ac syco-
phantias, si abegerit stultitias, furores, et hactenus nimium familiares
20 furias, si merdas suas resorbeat, et sua relingat stercora: quibus tam
fede linguam suam, calamumque conspurcat, Non deerunt, qui de re
graui grauiter, quod decet, disserant. Verum si ad istum, quo cepit,
modum scurrari pergat, et furere, si grassari calumnia, nugari
stultitia, insanire dementia, scurrilitate ludere: nec aliud in ore
25 gestare, quam sentinas, cloacas, latrinas, merdas, stercora, faciant
quod uolent alij, nos ex tempore capiemus consilium, uelimus ne sic
bacchantem ex eius tractare uirtutibus et coloribus suis depingere: an
furiosum fraterculum et latrinarium nebulonem, cum suis furijs et
furoribus, cum suis merdis et stercoribus, cacantem cacatumque
30 relinquere. [XX₁]

---

15 *gloss* foret] *L,* fotet *BR*   30 relinquere.] *Signature VV₄ is a blank leaf; More's peroration*
begins on XX₁

their knees to Him, shouting in mockery: "Hail, king of the Jews."
But he testifies that he has absolutely refrained from lies and invective,
the very person in whose pen there is nothing but calumnies, lies and
deceptions; in whose spirit there is nothing but venom, bombast and
ill will; who conceives nothing in his mind   5
but folly, madness, and insanity; who has   *Luther painted according to his*
nothing in his mouth but privies, filth and   *virtues*
dung, with which he plays the buffoon more foully and impurely than
any buffoon, of whom none has ever been found besides this one such
a stupid butt of men's scorn that he would cast into his mouth the   10
dung which other men would spit out into a basin. Therefore, since
he is this sort of person, I am not at all surprised if he is now considered unworthy for anyone to dispute with him. Surely, since he has
devoted himself totally to hell, and has persisted in schism, and has
determined never to retract his heresies, he   15
still ought to resolve on showing some   *This also would not be useless*
regard at least for public dignity, by which   *for his praise, of which*
he might claim for himself the authority of   *he is desirous*
a teacher of dogma rather than that of a worthless heretical buffoon.
If he will ever be willing to do this, if he will carry on his disputation   20
in a serious manner, if he will retract his lies and deceptions, if he will
leave off the folly and rage and the till now too familiar mad ravings,
if he will swallow down his filth and lick up the dung with which he
has so foully defiled his tongue and his pen, there will not be lacking
those who, as is fitting, will discuss serious matters in a serious way.   25
But if he proceeds to play the buffoon in the manner in which he has
begun, and to rave madly, if he proceeds to rage with calumny, to
mouth trifling nonsense, to act like a raging madman, to make sport
with buffoonery, and to carry nothing in his mouth but bilge-water,
sewers, privies, filth and dung, then let others do what they will; we   30
will take timely counsel, whether we wish to deal with the fellow thus
ranting according to his virtues and to paint with his colors, or to
leave this mad friarlet and privy-minded rascal with his ragings and
ravings, with his filth and dung, shitting and beshitted.

PERORATIO OPERIS, IN QVA MVL-
ta pie, ingeniose, et docte, nec minus
amoene tractantur.

NIHIL uereor optime lector, quin aequitas tua facile condonet mihi:
5   quod hoc in libro toties ea leges, quae tuus opinor auersetur pudor.
Mihi profecto nihil potuit accidisse molestius, quam eo necessitatis
adigi: ut quicquam honestis auribus ingererem: quod uerbis in-
honestis offenderet. Sed nullum uitandi

Cum cretensi cretissandum, ut est   fuit effugium, nisi decreuissem (quod
in prouerbio

10   perquam obnixe contenderam) Lutheri
scurrilem librum prorsus non attingere. Alioqui si respondendum
omnino fuit, homini ad intendendas calumnias excubanti, nec omitti
quicquam decuit, quod ille scripsisset: nec mutari uerba licuit, quum
rerum nihil subesset: nec honeste recitari ualuit, quod inhoneste
15   scriptum esset. Postremo, qui fieri potest, ut qui scurriles eius syco-
phantias refellere suscipiam: nebulonis impuri uerbis impurissimis
pure puteque respondeam? Nam is eo modo rem tractat: ut plane se
declaret meditari secum, immortalitatis quoddam genus absurdissimum, eaque iam coepisse perfrui, et totus esse, uersari, uiuere in
20   huiusmodi sensu et titillatione gloriolae, quod futurum praesumat

Fama Luthero futura   post aliquot adhuc aetatum miryadas: ut
recordentur et loquantur homines, fuisse
olim aliquando apud seculum prius nebulonem quendam, cui nomen
Luthero fuerit: qui quum cacodaemones impietate uicisset, ut dignis
25   emblemmatis ornaret suam sectam, picas garrulitate, lenones im-
probitate, prostibula [XX₁v] obscoenitate, scurras omnes scurrilitate
superarit. Qui id studuerit, curarit, effecerit, ut uelut philosophorum
sectae ex ipsis habent uocabula: et Gnato meditatus sit parasiti
itidem, ut Gnatonici uocentur: sic absurdissimum genus haereti-
30   corum impietatis, scelerum, spurciciaeque colluuies, appellentur

Lutherum haereticos omnes   Lutherani. Nam quaeso te lector, quod
antiquos aequiparare   unquam genus haereticorum tam absurdum fuit, ut comparetur isti? Quod unum

The peroration of the work, in which many points are handled piously, cleverly and learnedly, as well as pleasantly.

I have no fear, good reader, but that your sense of fairness will make allowance for me that in this book you so often read such things as I think your sense of modesty shuns. Indeed, nothing more irksome could have happened to me than to be forced to such a point of necessity that I should inflict on decent ears anything that would offend by indecent words. But there was no way of avoiding it unless I had deter- *With a Cretan one must act the Cretan, as the proverb says* mined, as I had tried to do with all my strength, not to touch the buffoonish book of Luther at all. Otherwise, if a response absolutely had to be made to a man on the lookout for spreading calumnies, nothing that he had written should have been omitted, nor was it allowable that words be changed when there was no substance to them, nor was it effective to recount decently what had been written indecently. Finally, how can it be that I who undertake to refute his buffoonish tricks should answer purely and cleanly the most impure words of an impure rascal? For he handles the matter in such a way that he clearly declares that he contemplates within himself a certain most absurd kind of immortality and has already begun to enjoy it and wholly to be in, to be engaged in, to live in, this kind of sense and tickling of paltry glory which he presumes will come after yet some myriads of ages, so that men will recall and say that once long *Luther's future fame* ago there was in a former age a certain rascal by the name of Luther who, when he had got the better of cacodaemons in impiety, in order to adorn his sect with fitting emblems, surpassed magpies in chatter, pimps in wickedness, prostitutes in obscenity, all buffoons in buffoonery. This he zealously strove for, took pains about, accomplished so that as the sects of philosophers have names after the philosophers themselves, and Gnatho contemplated that parasites likewise should be called Gnathonites, so the most absurd race of heretics, the dregs of impiety, of crimes, and filth, should be called Lutherans. For I ask you, reader, what race *That Luther equals all the ancient heretics* of heretics was ever so absurd as to be compared to this one? It renews every one

nihil non renouat earum haeresum, quas suis quamque temporibus
Christianus orbis olim damnauit, oppressit, extinxit: quarum
omnium cineres iste fax inferni denuo semel accendit. Qui quum ipso
facto praetendat pietatem, ut doctissimorum uirorum libellos
5 praeteream, qui hanc personam, fucumque ab ore improbo reuulsere,
si rem ipsam spectes, arborem lector facile ex eius fructu cognosces.
Nam si memoria tecum reuolueris ab ipsis Christianismi cunabulis,
ueteres ecclesiae proceres, uidebis lector ut quicquam ab illis sanctis-
sime cultum est, ita ab Lutheranis istis maxime haberi contemptui.
10 Quid olim tanta ueneratione celebratum est quam sacrosanctum

Lutheri in missam contumelia sacrificium missae? Quid ab istis porcis ita
fedatum est, et conculcatum, et paulomi-

nus abolitum? Nam quod unum adhuc in quoque templo sacrum
seruant, (quod ipsum suis impietatibus polluunt atque prophanant)
15 quum neque sacrificium esse contendant, neque populo quicquam
prodesse praedicent: an non uiam sibi struunt, qua propediem etiam

Lutheri de precibus opinio ipsum unum, quod reliquerunt, sacrum
eliminent? Iam preces quanti faciant,

uides: qui non solum eiecerunt horarias, sed illas etiam uniuersas,
20 quas iam inde ab initio in defunctorum subsidium [XX$_2$] perpetuo
decantauit ecclesia. Qua in re, quis non abominetur immanitatem
tantam? Nam si (quod illi falso contendunt) maxime foret ambiguum,
utrum preces uiuorum defunctis conducerent: tamen quae inuidia
fuerit pios affectus exercere, et periclitari preces: in quibus, ut dubius
25 esses, an fortasse prodesses, ita certus esses, quod nocere non posses.
Quid olim religiosius habitum est ieiunio? Quid exactius obseruatum

Isti homines malunt in peiorem quadragesima? Nunc isti tandem homines
partem peccare spiritu perfecti, ne diem a die diiudicare
uideantur, omnem diem dedicant baccha-

30 nalibus. Quis nescit olim, quo in precio fuerit continentia? quam
saeuere mandata fides coniugalis, quam probata ueteribus uiduarum
castitas, quam assidue, quam accurate laudata uirginitas? Atque
haec omnia authore ipso Christo. Nunc Antichristus iste pudicitiam
fere prorsus omnem sustulit. Sacerdotes, monachi, deo dicatae

---

8 proceres, uidebis lector] proceres, videbis lector *L*, proceres uidebis lector, *BR*

of those heresies which the Christian world once condemned, overwhelmed, quenched, each one in its own time; the ashes of all of these this firebrand of hell once more enkindles. Since by this very deed he makes a pretext of piety, to pass over the books of most learned men who have ripped this mask and disguise from his wicked face, if you consider the matter itself, reader, you will easily recognize the tree from its fruit. For if you turn over in your memory the ancient leaders of the church from the very beginnings of Christianity, you will see, reader, how whatever was honored most holily by them is thus held in the utmost contempt by these Lutherans. What was once celebrated with so much veneration as the most holy sacrifice of the mass? What has been so defiled by these pigs and trodden underfoot and all but abolished? *Luther's abuse of the mass* This one thing, indeed, they still preserve sacred in every temple, but this very thing they pollute and profane by their impieties, since they both contend that it is not a sacrifice and preach that it does not profit the people anything; are they not constructing for themselves a way by which they will very soon cast out even that one sacred thing which they have left? Now how much they value prayers you see, since they not only throw *Luther's opinion on prayers* out the canonical hours but also those universal prayers which even from the beginning the church has continually chanted for the support of the deceased. On this point who will not detest such great cruelty? For if, as they falsely argue, it were especially doubtful whether the prayers of the living were profitable to the dead, nevertheless what ill will would it have been to exercise devout affections and to make a trial of prayers by which, though you might be doubtful perhaps whether you were of service, yet you would be certain that you could do no harm? What was once held to be more religious than fasting? What was more exactly observed than Lent? Yet now these men, finally perfected by the spirit, lest they seem to distinguish day from day, *These men prefer to sin in a worse manner* dedicate every day to bacchanalian orgies. Who does not know how continence was once prized? How strictly conjugal fidelity was commanded, how esteemed by the ancients the chastity of widows, how zealously, how rightly virginity was praised? And all these things by the authority of Christ Himself. Now this Antichrist has taken away almost completely all sense of modesty. Priests, monks, virgins dedicated to God, now by the favor of the

uirgines, auspice diabolo, in ecclesia malignantium, legitimorum
nomine coniugum, magna cum pompa daemonum, nepharias
celebrant nuptias et foedus fidemque, quam uel homini pactam,
nemo nisi malus uiolat, uiolare non metuunt pactam deo: securi
5 uidelicet nuptias indulgente Luthero, qui numerosas simul uxores
etiam (quam solam uocat digamiam ueram) incipit ostentare.
Propediem haud dubie confirmaturus, ubi uirorum cuneis satis se
munierit aduersus mulierum turmas. Interim uero, quo gratificetur
et illis, quam multis, quam faciles aperit exitus in Babylonica, quibus
10 liceat a maritis abscedere, si qui soluendo non fuerint in coniugali
debito: nisi maritus ipse tam aequus sit, ut conducat alicunde
uicarium, qui sua uice fi[XX₂v]deliter soluat uxori. Atque haec, quae
non impia modo sunt, sed tam inepta quoque: ut uideri possint a me
deprauata per iocum, uidebis lector in Babylonica, sic ab illo con-
15 firmata serio: ut satis mirari non possis, usquam inuenire quemquam,
quem non impense pudeat appellari discipulum, tam absurdi prorsus,
insanique magistri. Sed magnus in malum stimulus est spes libertatis
et licentiae: quae quum altera manu protenditur, altera intentatur
metus. (Nam neque quicquam est Lutheranis uiolentius.) Quid miri
20 est, si ijsdem artibus promouet se secta Lutheri: quibus inualuit,

Lutherani similes Turcarum factioni. Contumeliae Lutheranorum in diuos ipsos

atque inualescit indies: non absimilis isti
sectae Turcarum? si non et Turcas ipsos
istorum uincit impietas. Nam hoc plane
constat, nusquam tanta cum contumelia
25 uexatas esse sanctorum imagines: quanta uexantur indies sceleratissi-
mis digitis istorum nebulonum: qui non uerentur eas non modo e
sanctissimis sedibus diuellere, diuulsas abijcere, abiectas proterere,
sed et protritis quoque et conculcatis, per omne ludibrij et contumeliae genus insultare. Atque haec Lutherus aspicit laetus in diuorum
30 effigies patrari (quorum honores et cultus omnes tollendos esse censet
e medio, ceu nocentissima scandala) quum interim circumferri atque
adorari gaudeat uenerabilem scilicet imaginem suam. Sed quoniam

Pietas Lutheri

diuis omnibus impietatem suam conscius
uidet inuisam: eorum uicissim omnium

19 metus. . . . Quid] metus, nam neque quicquam est Lutheranis violentius, quid *L*
22 sectae] secta *BRL*

devil, in the church of the wicked, under the title of lawful spouses, with great pomp of demons celebrate nefarious nuptials, and the contract and fidelity which even when ratified by man none except the wicked violate, they do not fear to violate, though it is ratified by God; they are secure of course with Luther condoning their nuptials, who begins to promise also numerous wives at once, which alone he calls the true second marriage. Very soon no doubt he will confirm this promise when he will have sufficiently fortified himself with troops of men against squadrons of women. But meanwhile, so that he may oblige those also, to how many persons, how easily he opens exits in the *Babylon*, by which it is permitted to leave one's spouse if any have not been able to pay their conjugal debt, unless the husband himself is so fair that he brings in a substitute from elsewhere who will in his place faithfully pay the debt to the wife. And these things, which are not only impious but also so silly that they can seem to be distorted by me for the sake of a joke, you will see, reader, in the *Babylon* so seriously confirmed by him that you cannot wonder enough that he ever finds anyone who is not thoroughly ashamed to be called the disciple of so utterly absurd and insane a master.

But a great stimulus to evil is the hope of liberty and license; while it is extended in the one hand, fear is stretched out in the other. For neither is anything more violent than the Lutherans. What wonder is it if Luther's sect advances itself by these same arts, by which it has grown strong and continues to grow strong from day to day, not unlike that sect of the *The Lutherans are like the* Turks—that is, if the impiety of these men *faction of the Turks. The insults of the Lutherans* does not surpass even the Turks them- *against the saints themselves* selves? For this is plainly evident, that never have the images of the saints been mistreated with such insult as they are mistreated from day to day by the most criminal fingers of these scoundrels, who do not fear not only to tear them away from their most holy shrines, to cast them aside when torn away, to trample them down when cast aside, but also to abuse them trampled down and trodden underfoot by every kind of mockery and insult.

And these things Luther gleefully beholds perpetrated against the images of the saints, all of whose honors and veneration he judges should be abolished as most harmful scandals, while in the meantime he rejoices that his own truly venerable image is carried about and worshipped. But because he sees, conscious *Luther's piety* of his guilt, that his impiety is hateful to all

uenerationi atque honoribus inuidet. Deiparam uirginem uenerantur
et Turcae: cuius nec nomen fere ferunt Lutherani. Nam qui ferre
queant honores Mariae: quando Christi quoque crucifixi sanctissimam imaginem, sceleratissimi scurrae conspergunt [XX₃] obscoenis-
5 simis exurendorum corporum suorum excrementis? Hi sunt istius
sectae spiritales fructus. Huc tandem creuit Lutherana pietas. Cuius
haereseos sceleribus uniuersis una patrocinatur impietas: qua se
uideri uolunt, et disputant necessario tales esse: tanquam in quodlibet
facinus impellat homines, certa et destinata uoluntas dei. Dubitas
10 dubitas inclyta Germania, qui talia serunt spiritalia, qualia sint
aliquando messuri carnalia? Quin nunc, ut audio, male se proferunt
cardui: et incipit deus ostendere, quo pacto probet istam sectam:
quum sacerdotes, qui ducunt uxores, non alijs coniungi sinit, quam

Puritas et sanctitas
15 *Lutheranorum*

scortis publicis. Et quos legitimo coniugio
uetuit copulari quondam, nisi purissimis
uirginibus: horum nunc incestas et scel-
eratas nuptias non patitur coalescere, nisi cum spurcissimis prosti-
bulis. Quid quod passim sponsos tales misera primum traductos
infamia, dein morbis, inopia, et egestate perditos, paulopost ad
20 latrocinia dilabentes, publico demum punit supplicio? Atque utinam
intra fecem istam sistat ultio: sed illa (nisi propere eatur obuiam)
uagabitur aliquanto longius. Nam ut desciscentem Clerum non
illibenter aspiciunt plerique principum, nimirum hiantes in deficien-
tium possessiones, quas uelut ex derelicto sperant inuasuros sese, et
25 Romano pontifici gaudent obedientiam subtrahi, dum spem con-
cipiunt fore, ut ipsi omnia disponant, diuidant, et dissipent inter se
domi: ita non est, quod dubitent: quin eo respiciat populus, ut
principum uicissim iugum excutiant, et possessionibus exuat suis:
quod quum aliquando patrarit ebrius sanguine principum et [XX₃v]
30 nobilium cruore luxurians, ne plebei quidem magistratus patiens ex
Lutheri dogmate calcatis legibus, anarchos et exlex, sine freno, sine
mente lasciuiens, in sese demum conuertet manus: et uelut terrigenae

20 dilabentes] *L*, dilabantes *BR*

the saints, he hates in turn the veneration and honors of all of them.
Even the Turks venerate the virgin mother of God, whose name the
Lutherans hardly endure. For how can they endure the honors of
Mary when these most criminal buffoons bespatter the most holy
image of Christ crucified with the most foul excrement of their   5
bodies destined to be burned? These are the spiritual fruits of that
sect. To this point at last has grown Luther's piety. A single impiety
protects all the crimes of this heresy: according to it, they want
themselves to seem to be, and they argue that they are, necessarily
such as they are—on the grounds that the certain and destined will of   10
God drives men into every kind of crime. Do you doubt, do you doubt,
illustrious Germany, that those who sow such spiritual goods as these
are, will one day reap carnal goods? Indeed now, as I hear, the thistles
are reproducing their bad fruit, and God is beginning to show how He
approves this sect, when He does not allow the priests who take wives   15
to be joined to any other than public
strumpets. And in the case of those whom   *The purity and sanctity of*
He once forbade to be joined in legitimate   *the Lutherans*
wedlock, except to most pure virgins, He does not now allow their
incestuous and criminal nuptials to take place except with the most   20
foul prostitutes. What about the fact that everywhere such spouses,
exposed at first with wretched infamy, then ruined by illness, poverty
and destitution, shortly afterwards slipping into robbery, He finally
punishes with public penalty? And would that the vengeance be
confined within these dregs, but unless it is speedily resisted, it will   25
spread somewhat farther. For just as very many of the princes look
not without pleasure on a degenerating clergy, undoubtedly because
they pant for the possessions of those who defect and hope to seize
them on the grounds of abandonment, and just as those princes
rejoice that obedience is withdrawn from the Roman pontiff with the   30
hope that they will be able to dispose and divide and squander it all
for themselves at home, so too there is no reason for them to doubt
but that the people look to the time when they may shake off in turn
the yoke of the princes and strip them of their possessions; once they
have accomplished this, drunk with the blood of princes and revelling   35
in the gore of nobles, enduring not even common rule, with the laws
trampled underfoot according to Luther's doctrine, rulerless and
lawless, without restraint, wanton beyond reason, they will finally turn
their hands against themselves and like those earthborn brethren, will

illi fratres, mutuo se confodiet. Christum precor, uanus ut uates fiam: fiam autem, si resipiscent homines, et nascentibus malis occurrent. Alioqui uereor, ne fiam, quod nolim, uerus. Sed ista uiderit Germania. Ego ad Lutheri librum redeo: qui quum talis sit, qualem
5 uides, id est mera farrago uerborum scurrilium, uenia lector meum dignaberis, sicubi non satis tersum uideris, quem illius sordes infecerint. Quod si longior interdum uidear, aequitas tua consideret: quum et illius recensenda uerba fuerint, et adiungenda, quae scripsit princeps: necnon aliquid adijciendum de meo: quo palam fieret
10 Lutheri calumnia, non potuisse contingere: quin res aliquantum cresceret: ut illud interim taceam, quod iudiciorum omnium consuetudine plures clypsedras impetrat, qui respondet. Quod si minus rei seriae scituque dignae reperire te, quam pro libelli quantitate censeas: ne id quidem iure potes imputare mihi: cui nec extra librum
15 eius euagari licuit: nec aliud illinc afferre, quam quod ibi fuit. Et tamen interiecta mihi quaedam spero: quae sic Lutheri fundamenta subruant: ut simul necesse sit impia uiri dogmata, stolide superstructa, corruere: illud certe non dubito, nihil e regis libro uellicatum esse Luthero: in quo non aperte reuicerim impudentem Lutheri syco-
20 phantiam. Denique ut non talem confiteor esse libellum meum, qualis orbi legendus edi postulet: ita nec talem esse confido, [XX₄] quem iure debeat ille contemnere, quisquis Lutheri nugas dignatur legere. Nam si quis eius nenias fuerit aspernatus: illi nec opus est, nec opto, tempus hoc in libro conterat. Imo nihil mihi magis in uotis est, quam
25 ut illam aliquando diem uideam: qua et has nugas meas, et illius omnes insanas haereses, mortales omnes abijciant: ut obruto pessimarum rerum studio, sepultis iurgiorum stimulis, et contentionum obliterata memoria, illucescat animis serenum fidei lumen: redeat syncera pietas, et uere christiana concordia: quam aliquando precor,
30 ut reddat, ac restituat terrae: qui in terram uenit, pacem daturus e caelo. FINIS. [YY₁]

---

1 ut uates] ut *om. L* 31 FINIS] *Signature XX₄v is blank in B and R*

mutually run each other through. I pray Christ I may become a false prophet; I shall if men will come to their senses and resist the rising evils. Otherwise, I fear that I will become what I do not wish, a true prophet. But let Germany see to these things.

I return to Luther's book; since it is such as you see, that is, a mere conglomeration of buffoonish words, you will, reader, consider my book worthy of pardon wherever you see what that fellow's filth has infected to be not sufficiently clean. But if at times I seem too long-winded, let your fairness consider that since his words had to be recorded, and those added which the prince wrote, as well as something added of my own so that the misrepresentation of Luther might become evident, it could not but happen that the work should grow somewhat, not to mention meanwhile the fact that by the custom of all the courts the respondent obtains a longer time to speak. But if you think that you find less of serious matter and matter worthy of approval than is proportionate to the size of the book, not even that can you rightly impute to me, to whom it was not permitted to stray beyond the limits of that man's book, nor to present anything else from it than what was there. And yet I hope that some things have been thrown in by me which so undermine Luther's foundations that together with them the man's impious doctrines stupidly built upon them will necessarily fall into ruin; this I certainly do not doubt, that nothing from the book of the king was carped at by Luther in which I did not clearly refute Luther's shameless deceitfulness. Finally, as I confess my book not to be the kind that demands publication as something that must be read, so I trust it is not the kind which a person ought rightly to contemn who deigns to read Luther's trifles. For if anyone has spurned his chatter, there is no need, nor do I desire, that he waste his time on this book. Indeed, my most earnest prayer is that I may sometime see the day in which all mortals will cast aside both these trifles of mine and all the insane heresies of that fellow, so that, with the pursuit of the worst things consigned to oblivion, with the incitements to railing buried, and the memory of contentions wiped out, the serene light of faith may shine into souls, sincere piety and truly Christian harmony may return; and I pray that He who came into the world to bring peace from heaven, may one day bring back and restore that harmony to the world. The end.

IOANNIS VITALLI LONDINENSIS CARMEN IN LVTHERVM.

MISSVS ab extremis liber iste Luthere Britannis,
  Venit in exitium tela secunda tuum.
5 Maximus, Henricus rex, et fortissimus heros,
  Corporis insignis, ingenijque bonis,
Et uerae fidei defensor acerrimus idem,
  Concussit uires ante Luthere tuas.
Fusus et afflictus (frustra tamen) usque repugnas:
10 Et uictor dici, dein male sane petis.
Non aliter quam qui, superatus ab hoste palaestra,
  Victoris collo pendet ab ipse sui.
Ac se deiectum minime, contendit ab illo:
  Succumbat quamuis iam resupinus humi.
15 Destruit hanc technam Rosseus tibi, neu modo quisquam
  Tam stolida falli possit ab arte facit.
Hic ita consilium tibi detegit ordine totum,
  Imo adeo insani propositum cerebri:
Vt uideant quam sis stolide sceleratus, et omnes
20 In stolidum iactent talia uerba caput:
Ecce triumphali Luther hic sublimis ab axe,
  Fertur, io, festis spargite stercoribus.
Dignus honos homini, qui foede uincitur: et se
  Victorem bucca buccinat ipse sua.

1–2 IOANNIS ... LVTHERVM] LODOVICI VERAMVNDI, FRANCISCI
LVCELLI E SORORE NEPOTIS, ADOLESCENTIS HVMANISSIMI CARMEN
IN LVTHERVM *B. The three commendatory poems are placed after the introductory letters of Rosseus
and Carcellius in L.*   3–4 MISSVS ... tuum] IN caput, ecce liber uenit iste Luthere,
nephandum Missus ab Hispanis, altera tela tuum. *B*   5 Henricus rex] Anglorum rex *B*
6 ingenijque] ingenij que *B*   10 male sane] malesane *B*   15–24 Destruit ... sua.]

  Senserat hanc fraudem cautus Barauellus, et ipse,
    Ne possis alijs imposuisse, facit.
  Quin ita consilium quoque detegit ordine totum,
    Propositum prodit sic tibi mente nephas:
  Vt quoniam uictus toties tamen ipse negare,
    Et noua uictori bella parari tuo
  Ausus es, imo tuam toto certamine laudem
    Asseris, et nulla uiuere lege putas.
  Te uideant omnes, quam sis absurdus et excors:
    Deuoueantque scelus foemina uirque tuum. *B*

POEM ON LUTHER
BY JOHN VITALIS OF LONDON

This book sent by the remote Britons, Luther, has come, a second shaft for your destruction. Henry, king most great and hero most brave, remarkably favored in body and mind, and himself a most 5 fierce defender of the true faith, shattered your powers before, Luther. Routed and ruined you still fight back, but in vain, and then insanely seek to be called victor, no differently than a wrestler overcome by his opponent who hangs from the neck of his conqueror and argues that he is not beaten by him at all, although he sinks down now 10 supine on the ground. This trick Ross has destroyed for you, and he acts so that no one can now be deceived by such a stupid stratagem. Here he exposes your whole plan point by point, or rather the design of a brain so insane that all may see how stupidly wicked you are and hurl at your stupid head these words: Lo, Luther is borne aloft 15 here by his triumphal car. Hurrah! Shower him with festal shit, honor worthy of the man who is shamefully overcome and trumpets himself as victor with his own mouth.

NICOLAI PACHETI AD LVTHERVM CARMEN ADMONITORIVM. [YY₁v]

ACCIPE, quo tutus mihi iam uideare, Luthere,
  Accipe, quo solo uiuere posse modo:
5   Vndique si potis es patrios occludere fines,
  Intret ut ad mystas ne liber iste tuos.
Nam tua traducit sic dogmata falsa libellus,
  Sic aperitque tuos iste Luthere dolos.
Vt semel in tota fuerit si plebe receptus,
10   Haec in noticiam prodierintque tuis,
Non ullus precibus tibi sit locus inde relictus,
  Quo minus a populo dilaniere tuo.

1 PACHETI] PANORMI *B*

AN ADMONITORY POEM TO LUTHER
BY NICOLAS PACHETUS

Take the means that will make you now appear safe to me, Luther;
take the means that alone can let you live—if you can, shut the bounds
of your fatherland from all sides, so that this book may not penetrate   5
to the priests of your mystic rites. For this book so exposes your false
doctrines and so reveals your deceits, Luther, that if it is once
received among the whole people, and these things come to the notice
of your followers, not a place will be left to your prayers thereafter to
keep you from being rent to pieces by your own people.   10

LAVRENTII NEVVLI EPITA-
PHIVM IN LVTHERVM OM-
NIBVS BONIS IAM
MORTVVM.

5   QVI stetit in caelum quondam caelique parentem,
     Iecit et in sanctos qui maledicta patres,
  Qui leges hominum contempsit, et omnia iura,
     Et nullo uoluit uiuere consilio,
  Sed quantum libuit, tantum licuisse putauit,
10   Ac nil pro sancto, nil habuitque pio,
  Contegit haec cinerem factum breuis urna Lutherum,
     Tartara pro meritis incolit umbra suis. [YY₂]

---

1 LAVRENTII NEVVLI] *L*, LAVREMTII NEVVLI *R*, RODERII CIDI *B*

AN EPITAPH
BY LAWRENCE NEWLIUS
ON LUTHER ALREADY DEAD
TO EVERYTHING GOOD

Him who once stood against heaven and the father of heaven, who 5
hurled curses even at the holy fathers, who scorned the laws of men
and all laws and wished to live by no counsel, but thought himself
free to do as much as he pleased, and held nothing sacred, nothing
pious, him this small urn conceals, turned to ashes, Luther. He dwells
in Tartarean shade for his sins. 10

NE MIRERIS OPTIME LECTOR, tot schedas unius literae nota
inscriptas eodem in loco, id eo accidit quod iam opere excuso, superuenit aliud exemplar, ab ipso authore denuo castigatum: in quo ipse
multa adiecerat, multa mutauerat. Eoque factum est: ut multae sint
5 schedae dissectae: prout author quid mutarat. Porro, ubi quid
addiderat coacti sumus, omnia literis insignire, ex eo loco: in quem
inserenda erant (uti in H. et A. fecimus) quum rationem commodi-
orem nullam reperiebamus. Praeterea quoniam chartarum frontes,
non sunt numeris annotatae lector, quo, si quid inquirendum est,
10 inuenire possis facilius: iam quod est proximum, literis ijs, quibus
chartarum calces signatae sunt, pro numerorum notis utere. Verum
illud quoque te scire uelim, ubi in litera H. multae sint chartae sine
notis, omnes paginas, quarum calces notam literae non habent, sub
nota proxime praecedente censeri. Ideoque, in his castigationibus,
15 leges interdum septimam paginam et octauam. Itaque ex earum
literarum ordine, errata quae inter excudendum acciderunt, sic
corrigito. [YY$_5$v]

ATQVE HAEC quidem omnia sunt: quibus sensum perturbari
posse existimauimus. Leuiora autem illa, utpote, orthographia
20 deprauata, et huiusmodi: quae facile abs te lector candide, et ani-
maduerti et emendari possint, tibi reliquimus: quorum etiam ipsorum
plaeramque partem castigauimus. Hic igitur, uiri eruditissimi
Guilielmi Rossei, operis doctissimi festiuissimique, finis esto. Quod, tu
lector, si quidem mecum sentis, dispeream nisi legisse uoles, propter
25 et amenitatem et acumen disserendi: quibus, non minus erudiri, quam
delectari poteris. [(ZZ$_1$)]

1–17 NE . . . corrigito.] *om. BL*   17 corrigito.] *The list of errata, running from sig.* YY_2 *to*
sig. YY_5v, *follows in R. It is omitted in B and L.*   18 quidem] quedim *R*   18–26 *ATQVE*
. . . poteris.] om. BL   26 poteris.] *Sig.* YY_6 *is blank in R. The Index, beginning on sig.* ZZ_1
(the ZZ *signature is unsigned throughout), runs to* ZZ_4. ZZ_4v *is blank. L omits the Index entirely.*

So that you may not be surprised, most excellent reader, that so many sheets have been inscribed with the mark of a single letter in the same passage, this happened for this reason, that, after the work had already been printed, another copy arrived, emended again by the author himself: in this he himself had added many things, had 5 changed many things. And for that reason it happened that many sheets were cut in pieces in order to conform to the author's changes. Moreover, where he had added something, we were forced to mark all the things which he had added with the letters from that passage into which they had been inserted (as we did in H and A) since we 10 did not find any more convenient method. Besides, since the tops of the leaves have not been marked with numbers, so that you the reader, if you need to look for something, can more easily discover it —this indeed is the next best thing—use in place of the marks of the numbers those letters by which the bottoms of the leaves have been 15 designated. But I should like you also to know this, that, where within the H signature there are many leaves without marks, all the pages, the bottoms of which do not have a signature, are classified under the mark immediately preceding. And for that reason, in connection with these emendations, you will read at times the seventh page and the 20 eighth. Therefore, in this way correct the errata which happened during the printing in accordance with the order of these letters.

And, indeed, these are all things by which we thought that the meaning could be obscured. Those less important matters, however, namely corrupted orthography and things of this sort, which can 25 easily be both noticed and corrected by you, fair reader, we have left for you; even of these very things, we have corrected the major part. Let this, then, be the end of the most learned and most witty work of the most learned William Ross. If, indeed, you, the reader, agree with me, may I perish if you shall not wish to have read this work, 30 because of both its charm and its shrewdness of treatment; by these you will be able to be no less instructed than delighted.

INDEX EORVM, QVAE IN HOC
OPERE CONTINENTVR.

INDEX OF THOSE THINGS
WHICH ARE CONTAINED IN THIS WORK.

traditionibus dei. G.3. fa.1. et deinceps per totum caput nonum, et
rursus. RR. primo fa.1. et deinceps per totam faciem primam. RR.2.
Lutherus ostenditur tergiuersari stolide, dum conatur controuersum
facere, quae sit ecclesia catholica. H.1. fa.2. et deinceps per totum
5 caput decimum.

Quam inepte stolideque Lutherus adducat atque applicet scripturas.
I.2. fa.1. et deinceps per totum cap. 12. Idem rursus K.3. fa.1. et per
totum caput quartum decimum, in quo uidebis, et ridebis eum plus
quater decies insanientem.

10 Lepide refellitur insulsum Lutheri lemma impugnantis diuturnitatem
fidei catholicae per collationem diuturnae superstitionis Iudaicae,
Turcarum, et gentilium. I.3. fa.2. et deinceps per totum caput. 13.
Lutherus credendum negat non solum antiquis patribus, sed etiam
Eliae, Hieremiae, Ioanni Baptistae, et caeteris prophetis omnibus.
15 K.4. fa.1. per totum.

Paulo apostolo derogat fidem Lutherus, et contemnit Iacobum
apostolum. O.2. et .3. et fa.1.4. [(ZZ₂)]

Qualia sint, quae Lutherus e medio censet esse tollenda, ceu nocentissima scandala. M. primo fa.2.

20 Quam stolide Lutherus tergiuersetur de operibus et fide, impudenter
fingens regem falso illi imputare, quod solam fidem dicat sufficere,
sine bonis operibus. M.3. fa.1. et deinceps per totum caput. 16. et
caput. 17.

Refellit Lutheri stultitiam improbam, qui leges omnes censeat abro-
25 gandas. N. primo fa.2. et deinceps per totum caput. 18.

Ostenditur, Lutherus id unum agere, ut demoliatur scripturas ipsas,
pro quibus simulat se pugnare. O. primo. fa.1. et deinceps per totum
caput decimum nonum.

Quantum periculi fuerit, spretis antiquis interpretibus, unumquem-
30 que sibi de scripturae sensu fidere. O.4. fac.1. in fine, et deinceps
usque finem. P.1.

Probat Lutherum ubique petere principium. P.2. fa.1. et deinceps
usque ad finem libri primi, totus hic locus tractatur iucunde.

De indulgentijs per totum quaternionem. R.

35 Aristotelem quam stolida Lutherus taxet argutia, disputans, non aliud
esse bonum uirum, et aliud bonum principem. R.3. fa.1. per totum
caput secundum.

20 Quam] Quod *BR*   36 R.3.] R.1. *BR*

P. 108, and thence throughout the ninth chapter, and again, Pp. 632–38.

He shows that Luther stupidly boggles, when he tries to make the identity of the church a matter of dispute. P. 116 and thence throughout the tenth chapter.   5

How ineptly and stupidly Luther cites and applies the scriptures. P. 214 and thence throughout chapter 12. The same thing again. P. 234 and throughout the fourteenth chapter, in which you will see, and laugh at, him acting like a madman more than fourteen times.

He wittily refutes Luther's silly premise attacking the long duration of   10
the catholic faith by comparison with the long enduring superstition of the Jews, Turks, and heathen. P. 220 and thence throughout chapter 13.

Luther denies not only that the ancient fathers, but also that Elijah, Jeremiah, John the Baptist, and all other prophets, must be believed.   15
P. 236 and following.

Luther disparages confidence in the apostle Paul, and despises the apostle James. Pp. 284–92.

What sort of things they are which Luther thinks must be taken out of circulation as the most harmful scandals. P. 254.   20

How stupidly Luther wavers on the matter of works and faith, shamelessly pretending that the king falsely attributes to him the statement that faith alone suffices, without good works. P. 258 and thence throughout chapters 16 and 17.

He refutes the wicked folly of Luther, who is of the opinion that all   25
laws should be repealed. P. 270 and thence throughout chapter 18.

He shows that Luther does only one thing: destroy the very scriptures for which he pretends to fight. P. 282 and thence throughout the nineteenth chapter.

How much danger there will be, if the ancient interpreters are   30
scorned, in each one believing for himself about the meaning of scripture. Pp. 292–98.

He proves that Luther begs the initial premise everywhere. P. 298 and thence up to the end of the first book; this whole subject is treated delightfully.   35

About indulgences. Pp. 324–32.

How stupidly Luther censures Aristotle for subtlety and argues that a good man and a good prince are not two different things. P. 334 throughout the second chapter.

26 FF. prim.] EE. prim. fa. 2. *BR*

About the papacy. P. 340 and thence throughout the fourth chapter.
Concerning the communion of the laity under both kinds. Pp.
352–438.
How beautifully Luther tempers his opinion, obviously because there
must be freedom to communicate any time and any place, and to   5
celebrate without having fasted. Pp. 420–26.
How confusedly Luther treats this, that the water is mingled with the
wine in the mass. Pp. 426–38.
Luther urges that no one mix in water, because he says that this has
an evil significance, the same place.   10
The rascal treats Blessed Ambrose scurrilously. P. 440 and thence
throughout the eleventh chapter.
He treats whether bread remains with the body of Christ. Pp.
448–94.
The subject of dispute between the prince and Luther, whether   15
scripture sometimes calls something not that which it is, but that
which it seems to be, or that which it once was, is treated. Pp.
470–84, where you will see not merely one stupid deception of
Luther.
He answers Luther's query, why God in the eucharist does not   20
transubstantiate the accidents. P. 484.
He answers that deception of Luther, by which he casts heresy against
the king, when he pretends that the king says that the body of Christ
is not a creature but the creator. P. 486.
He refutes the analogies of Luther, by which he tries to prove that   25
the bread remains along with the body of Christ just as fire remains
with iron, or divinity with humanity. P. 488.
How impiously Luther, fleeing the good work of others, becomes
worse, and how impiously he blasphemes all the holy fathers and calls
them impious and blasphemous. Pp. 490–94, from which it plainly   30
appears that either all the ancients were unlearned or this one is
most unlearned; all the ancients were stupid or this one is most
stupid; all the ancients were criminal, or this one is most criminal.
From the confession of Luther himself that the doctrine of Luther
confers no good. P. 492.   35
He answers that most stupid boast which Luther makes more than
ten times, that the king professedly leaves untouched his principal
foundation, namely that the mass is a testament. Pp. 500–14. There

usque finem. GG.4. ibi uidebis lector Lutheri fundamentum ex imo prorsus erutum atque subuersum.

Rursus de eodem. KK.1.

Expenditur, an missa sit bonum opus. HH.1. fa.2. et deinceps usque
5 ad finem. II.

Detegitur Lutheri ineptia nugantis in opere operantis et opere operato. HH.4. fa.2.

Respondetur ad id, quod Lutherus argutatur, quod si missa bonum opus esset tunc malus sacerdos missam consecrare non posset. II.1.
10 et.2.

Confutatur stolidum illud dogma Lutheri, quod missa non potest esse sacrificium. II.2. fa.2. et deinceps usque ad finem. OO.2.

Refellitur illud despuendum Lutheri sophisma, Missa est promissio: ergo non potest esse sacrificium. II.3. fa.2. et deinceps usque ad
15 finem. KK.2.

Refellitur impudens Lutheri calumnia, qua regem mentitur dicere, nullam esse promissionem in tota coena Christi. KK.2. fa.2. ultra finem. KK.3.

Nebulo blasphemat scurriliter omnes sanctos patres. KK.4.

20 Operae precium est uidere quanto cum fastu quam stolide interpretetur haec euangelij uerba, Hoc facite in meam commemorationem. KK.4. fa.2. et deinceps per totam. 1. pag. LL. [(ZZ$_3$v)]

Stolidissime sibi repugnat Lutherus. KK.2.

Refellitur illud Lutheri sophisma stolidum, quo sic argutatur, sacer-
25 dos in missa recipit eucharistiam, ergo non potest offerre. LL.2. et deinceps usque ad. MM.

Redarguitur atque retunditur ridicula arrogantia, qua ridiculum putat obijci aduersus se authoritatem omnium sanctorum patrum. MM.1.2. et .3. per totum. Idem rursus. VV.1. per totam paginam.

30 Refutatur Lutheri sycophantia et argumentatio tam stolida, ut mirari possis, quo peregrinatus fuerit animus eius MM.4. et deinceps usque finem. NN.3.

Probatur Luthero certum esse non posse ex scripturis, quo modo sit celebranda missa, aut quo pacto sit omnino consecrandum corpus
35 Christi, nisi per fidem publicam et ecclesiae Christianae consuetudinem. NN.4. fa.1. et deinceps usque ad finem. OO.2.

Ostenditur pulchre, quomodo Lutherus irretitus propria confessione frustra conetur elabi, uarie uersans uerbum illud Augustini, Non

32 NN.3.] HH.3. *BR*   36 NN.4.] HH.4. *BR*

you the reader will see Luther's foundation absolutely and utterly
overthrown and toppled.
On the same thing again. P. 540.
He considers whether the mass is a good work. Pp. 516–28.
He exposes the ineptitude of Luther, talking nonsense in the matter   5
of the work of the doer and the work done. P. 526.
He answers Luther's argument, that if the mass were a good work
then a wicked priest could not consecrate the mass. Pp. 528–32.
He disproves that stupid doctrine of Luther, that the mass cannot be
a sacrifice. Pp. 532–98.   10
He refutes that abhorrent sophism of Luther: the mass is a promise,
therefore it cannot be a sacrifice. Pp. 536–46.
He refutes the shameless slander of Luther, his lie that the king says
that there is no promise in the whole supper of Christ. Pp. 546–50.
The rascal blasphemes scurrilously all the holy fathers. P. 550.   15
It is worthwhile to see with how much arrogance and how stupidly he
interprets these words of the evangelist, Do this in remembrance of
me. Pp. 552–56.
Most stupidly Luther contradicts himself. P. 544.
He refutes that stupid sophism of Luther by which he quibbles thus: 20
the priest receives the eucharist in the mass, therefore he cannot offer
it. Pp. 556–66.
He convicts and confutes the ridiculous arrogance with which
Luther thinks it ridiculous that the authority of all the holy fathers is
opposed to himself. Pp. 566–76. The same thing again. Pp. 674–76.   25
He refutes Luther's deception and argumentation, which are so
stupid that you can wonder whither his mind had roamed. Pp.
578–90.
He proves to Luther that it cannot be certain from the scriptures in
what way the mass must be celebrated or how the body of Christ must   30
be consecrated at all, except through the public faith and the custom
of the Christian church. Pp. 590–98.
He shows excellently how Luther, ensnared by his own confession,
tries in vain to escape, variously twisting that word of Augustine, I

crederem euangelio, nisi authoritas Ecclesiae me commoueret.
OO.2. fa.2. et deinceps usque finem RR.2. Et ibi uidebis quam inepte
argutetur inter ius condendi iura et ius iudicandi dogmata.

Ostenditur Lutheri dogma stultissimum, quo docetur quisque, ut sibi
5 credat contra authoritatem caeterorum omnium PP.2. fa.2. et deinceps usque ad. QQ.

Daemon qui Lutherum possidet, contra semet ipsum ueritatem
fatetur inuitus. QQ.1. fa.1. et deinceps usque finem. QQ.2.

Refellitur Lutheri scurrilis blasphemia aduersus synodus [(ZZ$_4$)] et
10 generalia concilia QQ.3. fa.1. et deinceps usque. RR.

Lutherus non argumentatur, sed argumentitur. RR.2. fa.2.

Refelluntur, quae Lutherus eblaterat in sacramentum ordinis. RR.4.
fa.2. et deinceps usque. TT.

Refelluntur, quae Lutherus argutatur de sacramento matrimonij.
15 TT.1. fa.1. et deinceps usque finem. TT.3. ibi Lutherum uidebis
elanguescere, uacillare, titubare, concidere.

Scite et iucunde tractat ea, quae Lutherus uelut rerum summam
scurriliter aggessit in finem. TT.3. fa.2. et deinceps usque ad finem.
VV.3.

20 Respondetur ad ea, quibus Lutherus nugatur aduersus Ambrosium
Catharinum de ecclesia. H. per totum.

Lutherus omnem prorsus ecclesiam tollit in terris. H.10. et deinceps.
Idem. H.13. et deinceps.

Stolidissima Lutheri secum repugnantia. H.14. fa.2. et deinceps.
25 Alia non minus stolida. H.15. fa.2.

Quam absurde sibi de scripturae sensu credit Lutherus magis, quam
sanctis ecclesie patribus. H.16. fa.2.

Pulchre per literas demonstratur, signa per quae Lutherus ecclesiam
scribit reddi certo cognitam, illud non posse praestare: atque ita
30 Lutherum tota causa cadere: quum fateatur ecclesiam certam esse
oportere. H.17. fa.2. et deinceps.

---

7 Lutherum] Lurherum *BR*   11 Lutherus] Luthetus *BR*   20–31 Respondetur . . . et
deinceps.] *om. B*

would not believe the gospel if the authority of the church did not persuade me. Pp. 598–638. And there you will see how foolishly he quibbles between the right of establishing laws and the right of judging doctrines.

He shows that Luther's doctrine is most stupid, by which each one is taught to believe for himself against the authority of everyone else. Pp. 610–20.

The demon which possesses Luther confesses reluctantly that the truth itself is against him. Pp. 620–26.

He refutes the scurrilous blasphemy of Luther against synods and general councils. Pp. 626–34.

Luther does not argue, but he lies. P. 638.

He refutes those things which Luther babbles against the sacrament of orders. Pp. 646–62.

He refutes those things which Luther prattles about the sacrament of matrimony. Pp. 662–70. There you will see Luther grow faint, stagger, totter, fall prostrate.

He treats cleverly and delightfully those points which Luther scurrilously brought together as the sum of the matter at the end of his work. Pp. 670–82.

He answers Luther's nonsense against Ambrose Catharinus on the question of the church. Pp. 116–210.

Luther utterly destroys the whole church on earth. P. 156.

The same thing. P. 172.

The most stupid self-contradiction of Luther. P. 178.

Other things no less stupid. P. 180.

How absurdly Luther believes for himself about the meaning of scripture rather than the holy fathers of the church. P. 182.

He shows excellently by passages that the signs through which Luther writes that the church is rendered well known for certain cannot furnish this; and in this way Luther loses his whole case, since he confesses that the church should be known for certain. P. 186.